iLife '04

THE MISSING MANUAL

*The book that
should have been
in the box*

D1522872

iLife '04

THE MISSING MANUAL

David Pogue

POGUE PRESS™
O'REILLY®

Beijing • Cambridge • Farnham • Köln • Paris • Sebastopol • Taipei • Tokyo

iLife '04: The Missing Manual

by David Pogue

Published by O'Reilly Media, Inc., 1005 Gravenstein Highway North, Sebastopol, CA 95472.

O'Reilly Media books maybe purchased for educational, business, or sales promotional use. Online editions are also available for most titles: *safari.oreilly. com*. For more information, contract our corporate/institutional sales department: (800) 998-9938 or *corporate@oreilly.com*.

September 2004: First Printing

RepKover™ This book uses RepKover™, a durable and flexible lay-flat binding.

ISBN: 0-596-00694-2

Table of Contents

Part Four: iDVD

Part Five: GarageBand

Part Six: Troubleshooting

The Missing Credits

About the Authors

David Pogue is the weekly computer columnist for the *New York Times*, technology correspondent for *CBS News Sunday Morning*, and the creator of the Missing Manual series. He's the author or co-author of 35 books, including thirteen in this series and six in the "For Dummies" line (including *Macs, Magic, Opera,* and *Classical Music*). In his other life, David is a former Broadway show conductor, a magician, and a pianist. News and photos await at *www.davidpogue.com*.

He welcomes feedback about Missing Manual titles by email: *david@pogueman. com*.

J. D. Biersdorfer (iTunes chapters) writes the weekly computer Q & A column for the Circuits section of *The New York Times.* She also writes an occasional Circuits feature story and has penned articles for *The New York Times Book Review,* the *AIGIA Journal of Graphic Design,* and *Rolling Stone.* After living all over the country as a former Air Force brat and theater technician, she planted herself in New York City in 1989. In her limited spare time, she plays the banjo and watches far too much CNN Headline News. Email: *jdbiersdorfer@mac.com*.

Erica Sadun (iDVD chapters) holds a PhD in Computer Science from the Georgia Institute of Technology. She has written, co-written and contributed to almost two dozen books about technology, particularly in the areas of programming, digital video, and digital photography. An unrepentant geek, Erica has never met a gadget she didn't need. Her checkered past includes run-ins with NeXT, Newton, and a vast myriad of both successful and unsuccessful technologies. When not writing, she and her geek husband parent three adorable geeks-in-training, who regard their parents with unrestrained bemusement. Email: *erica@mindspring.com*.

Derrick Story (contributor to the iPhoto chapters) is the managing editor of O'Reilly Network (*www.oreillynet.com*) and Mac DevCenter (*www.macdevcenter.com*), which he created in December, 2000 for O'Reilly Media. His other books include *Digital Photography Pocket Guide, 2nd Edition; Digital Video Pocket Guide;* and *Digital Photography Hacks.* Derrick continues to hone his shooting skills through his photo business, Story Photography (*www.storyphoto.com*), which specializes in digital imaging and special events. His photographs are featured in this book.

About the Creative Team

Nan Barber (copy editor) co-authored *Office X for the Macintosh: The Missing Manual* and *Office 2001 for Macintosh: The Missing Manual.* She's the principal copy editor for the Missing Manual series, having edited the Missing Manual titles on Mac OS X, Mac OS 9, AppleWorks 6, iMovie, Dreamweaver, Windows XP, and iPhoto. Email: *nanbarber@mac.com.*

Rose Cassano (cover illustration) has worked as an independent designer and illustrator for 20 years. Assignments have spanned everything from the nonprofit sector to corporate clientele. She lives in beautiful southern Oregon, grateful for the miracles of modern technology that make living and working there a reality. Email: *cassano@cdsnet.net.* Web: *www.rosecassano.com.*

Dennis Cohen (technical reviewer) has served as the technical reviewer for many bestselling Mac books, including several editions of *Macworld Mac Secrets* and most Missing Manual titles. He is the author or co-author of *FileMaker Pro 7 Bible, Mac Digital Photography, iLife Bible,* and numerous other books. Email: *drcohen@mac.com.*

Karl Petersen (iMovie troubleshooting section) lives with his wife, Joan, and a collie on Bainbridge Island, WA, a 30-minute ferry ride from Seattle. (It's the ferry Michael Douglas runs onto in *Disclosure.*) A break between jobs (including a stint in the Peace Corps and a career in insurance) gave Karl the chance to explore the first Macs, and he never looked back. He also writes software.

Joseph Schorr (co-author, iPhoto chapters), a former *Macworld* contributing editor, began collaborating with David Pogue in 1982—on musical comedies at Yale. Years later, they co-authored six editions of *Macworld Mac Secrets.* Now that Joe is a product manager at Apple, he's not technically supposed to work on books like this. Still, many chapters of this book are based on his original prose.

Phil Simpson (design and layout) works out of his office in Stamford, Connecticut, where he has had his graphic design business since 1982. He is experienced in many facets of graphic design, including corporate identity, publication design, and corporate and medical communications. Email: *pmsimpson@earthlink.net.*

Acknowledgments

The Missing Manual series is a joint venture between Pogue Press (the dream team introduced on these pages) and O'Reilly Media (a dream publishing partner).

This book was a special project, a "best of" compilation from the four individual Missing Manual titles (on iTunes, iPhoto, iMovie & iDVD, and GarageBand). The contributors to this book, therefore, were those who contributed to the individual volumes.

From Apple, I had insanely valuable assistance from Fred Johnson, Paul Towner, Xander Soren, and Gary Drenan.

Caroline Savello was the InDesign guru who masterfully melded four books into one. I'm also grateful to Kate Briggs, John Cacciatore, Stephanie English, Danny Marcus and Sada Preisch for their copy editing and proofreading smarts; Adam Goldstein, Boy Genius, for production assistance; Tim Franklin for his writeup on QuickTime Web pages; Glenn Reid for tech-editing two iMovie editions (not to mention writing the software!); and to David Rogelberg.

Finally, thanks to Kelly and Tia, my favorite iMovie stars, and my wife, Jennifer, who made this book—and everything else—possible.

The Missing Manual Series

Missing Manuals are witty, superbly written guides to computer products that don't come with printed manuals (which is just about all of them). Each book features a handcrafted index; cross-references to specific page numbers (not just "see Chapter 14"); and RepKover, a detached-spine binding that lets the book lie perfectly flat without the assistance of weights or cinder blocks.

Recent and upcoming titles include:

- *Mac OS X: The Missing Manual* (Panther and Tiger editions) by David Pogue

- *FileMaker Pro 7: The Missing Manual* by Geoff Coffey

- *iPhoto 4: The Missing Manual* by David Pogue

- *GarageBand: The Missing Manual* by David Pogue

- *iPod & iTunes: The Missing Manual, 2nd Edition* by J.D. Biersdorfer

- *iMovie 4 & iDVD: The Missing Manual* by David Pogue

- *Google: The Missing Manual* by Sarah Milstein and Rael Dornfest

- *Switching to the Mac: The Missing Manual* by David Pogue

- *Mac OS X Power Hound, Panther Edition* by Rob Griffiths

- *Dreamweaver MX 2004: The Missing Manual* by David Sawyer McFarland

- *Mac OS 9: The Missing Manual* by David Pogue

- *Office 2004 for Macintosh: The Missing Manual* by Nan Barber, Tonya Engst, and David Reynolds

- *AppleWorks 6: The Missing Manual* by Jim Elferdink and David Reynolds

- *Windows XP Home Edition: The Missing Manual* by David Pogue

- *Windows XP Pro: The Missing Manual* by David Pogue, Craig Zacker, and Linda Zacker

THE MISSING CREDITS

Introduction

At its best, Apple has always focused on one particular mission: identifying powerful but complex technologies and distilling them into far simpler packages. You shouldn't have to be a professional working for a media conglomerate, says Apple, to harness cutting-edge technology for your own creative expression and entertainment.

That's the philosophy behind the iLife '04 software suite. Each of the five programs in this $50 package is a streamlined, attractive, easy-to-use version of software that was once hopelessly complex (or hopelessly expensive).

Each of the five programs is designed to serve as the digital hub for a different kind of artistic expression:

- **iTunes,** for managing, playing, buying, and sharing digital music.
- **iPhoto,** for downloading photos from your digital camera, and organizing, sharing, and printing them.
- **iMovie,** for editing footage from a digital camcorder, adding effects, sound, and credits, and then presenting the result.
- **GarageBand,** for composing and recording terrific-sounding songs of your own.
- **iDVD,** for burning DVDs containing the movies, music, and photos from iTunes, iPhoto, iMovie, and GarageBand. Professional DVDs in every way—except you get to make them yourself!

Technically speaking, you can perform all of the same tasks using other software brands and other kinds of computers. But not as easily, not as consistently, not as pleasurably, and certainly not for a grand total of $50 (or free with a new Mac).

iLife Integration

Leaning the five programs of iLife isn't really as difficult as learning, say, five Windows programs, because Apple has designed these programs to work alike—and to work together.

Now, as Figure I-1 illustrates, the integration of the five iLife programs isn't quite as fluid as popular mythology would have it. You can't move information from any program into any other; you can move it only in directions that make sense.

Figure I-1:
You can't move photos into GarageBand or movies into iPhoto. But as the black arrows show, you can move iTunes music into any other iLife program, or material from any other iLife program into iDVD. (That's right: There's no arrow from GarageBand into iDVD, but you can get your GarageBand pieces there via iTunes.)

The real payoff of adopting Apple's version of all five programs is that you save so much time learning them. Over and over again, Apple reuses the same elements: a color picker, a spell-checker, and so on. Learn once, use often.

Here are some of the most important iLife software conventions. You'll see these controls and windows in many different circumstances, no matter which program you're using at the time.

The iTunes Selection Panel

Three of the iLife programs—iMovie, iDVD, and iPhoto—come with a window into your iTunes music collection. (To see it in iMovie, click the Audio button. In iPhoto, click the Slideshow button. In iDVD, open the Customize panel, click the Media button, and choose iTunes from the pop-up menu.) Having direct access to your music files saves you a lot of hunting around on your hard drive when you want to use this or that song as the background music for a DVD, movie, or slideshow.

You can see the basic mini-iTunes window in Figure I-2.

Figure I-2:
In general, the mini-iTunes window found in iMovie, iPhoto, and iDVD works a lot like the list of songs in the real iTunes. For example you can double-click a song to listen to it (or click once and then click the triangular Play button). Click the same button—now shaped like a square Stop button—when you've heard enough.

Note that above the list, the pop-up menu lists all of your iTunes playlists (subsets of songs), for your browsing convenience.

Other tips:

• Rather than scroll through a huge list, you can locate the tracks you want by using the capsule-shaped Search box near the bottom of the window. Click in the Search field, and then type a word (or part of a word) to filter your list. iPhoto searches the Artist, Song, and Album fields of the iTunes Library and displays only the matching entries. To clear the search and view your whole list again, click the X in the Search field.

- Click one of the three headers—Artist, Song, or Time—to sort the iTunes music list alphabetically by that criterion.

- You can also change the arrangement of the three columns by grabbing the headers and dragging them into a different order.

- Better yet, if you place your cursor carefully on the vertical dividing line between the column headings, you'll find that you can drag it sideways to change the relative sizes of the columns. That's especially handy when all you can see of the Artist is, for example, Elect...estra.

Check Your Spelling

You can use Mac OS X's built-in spelling checker to proofread your prose in all kinds of useful places. You can check iPhoto's text boxes (for the coffee-table books that you order), iMovie's titles and credits, and iDVD's onscreen text boxes.

As in a word processor, you can ask the Mac to check your spelling several ways:

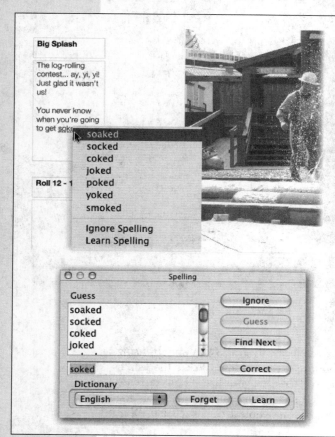

Figure I-3:

Top: Control-click any word that's underlined with a red, dashed line. If the resulting shortcut menu contains the correct spelling, choose it. Otherwise, choose Ignore or Add (to teach Mac OS X that word for future spell checks).

Bottom: If you prefer a more word processor–like spelling check, you can summon this box.

The first "misspelled" word already appears. If the correct version appears in the list, double-click it (or single-click it and then click Correct). If not, type the correct word into the box below the list and then click Correct.

On the other hand, if the word in your text box is fine as it is, click either Ignore ("I want this word spelled this way; stop underlining it and move on") or Add ("Not only is this name or word spelled correctly, but I may use it again. Add it to your dictionary so you'll never flag it again").

- **Check a single word or selection.** Highlight a word, or several, and then choose Edit→Spelling→Check Spelling (⌘-semicolon). If the word is misspelled in iPhoto's opinion, a red, dashed line appears under the word. Proceed as shown in Figure I-3.

- **Check a whole text block.** Click inside a title or comment box and then choose Edit→Spelling→Spelling (⌘-colon). The standard Mac OS X Spelling dialog box appears, also shown and described in Figure I-3.

- **Check as you type.** The trouble with the spelling commands described here is that they operate on only a single, tiny text block at a time. To check your entire photo book, you must click inside each title or caption and invoke the spelling command again. There's no way to have iPhoto sweep through your entire book at once.

Your eyes might widen in excitement, therefore, when you spot the Edit→ Spelling→Check Spelling As You Type command. You'd expect it to make the Mac flag words it doesn't recognize *as you type them.* Sure enough, when this option is turned on, whenever you type a word not in the Mac's dictionary, a colorful dashed underline appears. To correct a misspelling, Control-click it. A shortcut menu appears. Proceed as shown in Figure I-3.

But don't get too excited: This option turns itself *off* every time you click into a new text box. Using the mouse (there's no keyboard shortcut), you have to turn it on again for every title and caption. The regular Check Spelling command looks positively effortless by comparison.

The Color Picker

Here and there—in iMovie's Title generator and iPhoto's Web-page design dialog box, for example—Mac OS X offers you the opportunity to choose a *color* for the text, background, and so on.

The dialog box that appears (Figure I-4) offers a miniature color lab that lets you dial in any color in the Mac's rainbow. There are actually several color labs, arrayed across the top, each designed to make color-choosing easier in certain circumstances:

- **Color Wheel.** Drag the scroll bar vertically to adjust the brightness, and then drag your cursor around the ball to pick the shade.

- **Color Sliders.** From the pop-up menu, choose the color-mixing method you prefer. *CMYK* stands for cyan, magenta, yellow, and black. People in the printing industry will feel immediately at home, because these four colors are the component inks for color printing. (These people may also be able to explain why *K* stands for *black.*)

- **RGB** is how a TV or computer monitor thinks of colors: as proportions of red, green, and blue. And *HSB* stands for Hue, Saturation, and Brightness—a favorite color-specifying scheme in scientific circles.

In each case, just drag the sliders to mix up the color you want, or type in the percentages of each component.

- **Color Palettes** presents canned sets of color swatches. They're primarily for programmers who want quick access to the standard colors in Mac OS X. (The Web Safe Colors list is useful for Web designers, so they can tell whether a color will display properly on other computers.)

Figure I-4:
You can store frequently used (or frequently admired) colors in the mini-palette squares at the bottom of the Colors box. To do that, drag the big rectangular color swatch (next to the magnifying glass) directly down into one of the little squares, where it will stay fresh for weeks.

If you don't have space for all the colors you want, drag down the small circular dot at the bottom of the window to make room for more.

- **Image Palettes** offers the visible rainbow arrayed yet another way: in cloudy, color-arranged streaks. (Cool tip: If you drag a graphics file directly into the dialog box, it will appear in the spectrum's place. That's a handy trick if you're trying to identify the color of a certain spot of an image, for example. And don't miss the pop-up button at the bottom of the dialog box, which offers a few other stunts).

- **Crayons.** Now *this* is a good user interface. You can click each crayon to see its color name: "Mocha," "Fern," "Cayenne," and so on. (Some interior decorator in Cupertino had a field day naming these crayons.)

In any of these color pickers, you can also "sample" a color that's outside the dialog box—a color you found on a Web page, for example. Just click the magnifying-glass icon and then move your cursor around the screen. You'll see the sliders and numbers change inside the dialog box automatically when you click.

Preferences

Just about every Mac program has a Preferences command tucked into its application menu (the menu named after the program, like iPhoto or iMovie). What's nice about the iLife suite, though, is that its keystroke is the same in every program: ⌘-comma.

It's also nice that the resulting dialog box is a separate window that you can leave open as you work (you don't have to close it after making a selection). When you're finally finished with the Preferences dialog box, just click its upper-left, red Close button (or press ⌘-W).

About This Book

The iLife programs may be simple, but they're not simplistic. They offer a wide range of powerful, flexible features that let you create music, movies, pictures, and DVDs worthy of professional work. Unfortunately, many of the best techniques aren't covered in the only "manual" you get with iLife—its sparse electronic help screens.

This book is designed to serve as the iLife manual, as the book that should have been in the box. It explores each program in depth, offers shortcuts and workarounds, and unearths features that the online help doesn't even mention.

FREQUENTLY ASKED QUESTION

The Sum of All Books?

I see that you've also written individual Missing Manual books on iTunes, iMovie & iDVD, GarageBand, and iPhoto. If I have this book, do I need those too?

Probably not.

iLife '04: The Missing Manual is adapted from those four other books, but it's not exactly the same. It's been slimmed down somewhat from the component source book. Otherwise, it would be over 1,400 pages long, which would put it over that 20-pound weight limit that bookstores are so picky about.

So what do you get in the individual books that's missing from this one? Here are some examples: *iMovie 4 & iDVD: The Missing Manual* includes three chapters about good camcorder and film technique. *iPhoto 4: The Missing Manual* has several chapters about how to use your digital camera for best results. *GarageBand: The Missing Manual* offers a crash course in music, plus two chapters on shareware plug-ins and add-ons for GarageBand. And *iPod & iTunes: The Missing Manual* includes lots more detail on the iPod, including a good deal of information for Windows PC owners.

If you find yourself spending most of your time in one particular program, it may be worth checking the relevant book out of the library to soak in the extra detail that's not in this all-in-one book.

Otherwise, though, everything you need is right here: The tips, the tricks, the shortcuts, the behind-the-scenes details on how iLife programs store your projects on the hard drive, and 500 illustrations. This book offers such complete coverage of the i-programs, in fact, it could have been called *iBook*—but that one was taken.

About the Outline

iLife '04: The Missing Manual is divided into six parts. The first five correspond to the iLife programs: iTunes, iPhoto, iMovie, iDVD, and GarageBand. At the end of the book, you'll find troubleshooting chapters that correspond to those programs.

About→These→Arrows

Throughout this book, and throughout the Missing Manual series, you'll find sentences like this one: "Open your Home→Library→Preferences folder." That's shorthand for a much longer instruction that directs you to open three nested folders in sequence, like this: "In the Finder, choose Go→Home. In your Home folder, you'll find a folder called Library. Open that. Inside the Library window is a folder called Preferences. Double-click to open it, too."

Similarly, this kind of arrow shorthand helps to simplify the business of choosing commands in menus, as shown in Figure I-5.

Figure I-5:
In this book, arrow notations help to simplify folder and menu instructions. For example, "Choose ⌘→Dock→Position on Left" is a more compact way of saying, "From the ⌘ menu, choose Dock; from the submenu that then appears, choose Position on Left," as shown here.

About MissingManuals.com

At *www.missingmanuals.com*, you'll find news, articles, and updates to the books in this series.

But if you click the name of this book and then the Errata link, you'll find a unique resource: a list of corrections and updates that have been made in successive printings of this book. You can mark important corrections right into your own copy of the book, if you like.

In fact, the same page offers an invitation for you to submit such corrections and updates yourself. In an effort to keep the book as up-to-date and accurate as possible, each time we print more copies of this book, we'll make any confirmed corrections you've suggested. Thanks in advance for reporting any glitches you find!

In the meantime, we'd love to hear your suggestions for new books in the Missing Manual line. There's a place for that on the Web site, too, as well as a place to sign up for free email notification of new titles in the series.

The Very Basics

You'll find very little jargon or nerd terminology in this book. You will, however, encounter a few terms and concepts that you'll see frequently in your Macintosh life. They include:

- **Clicking.** This book offers three kinds of instructions that require you to use the mouse or trackpad attached to your Mac. To *click* means to point the arrow cursor at something onscreen and then—without moving the cursor at all—press and release the clicker button on the mouse (or laptop trackpad). To *double-click,* of course, means to click twice in rapid succession, again without moving the cursor at all. And to *drag* means to move the cursor while keeping the button pressed.

  When you're told to ⌘-*click* something, you click while pressing the ⌘ key (next to the Space bar). Such related procedures as *Shift-clicking, Option-clicking,* and *Control-clicking* work the same way—just click while pressing the corresponding key on the bottom row of your keyboard. (The Option key is called the Alt key on some non-U.S. keyboards, by the way.)

- **Menus.** The *menus* are the words in the lightly striped bar at the top of your screen. You can either click one of these words to open a pull-down menu of commands

---

UP TO SPEED

The Requirements

Officially, Apple lists the requirements to run the iLife programs like this. First, you need a Mac with a G3, G4, or G5 processor inside. It should have at least 256 megabytes of memory and 4.3 gigabytes of free hard-drive space (if you plan to install all five programs). And it has to be running Mac OS X version 10.2.6 or later, complete with QuickTime 6.5 or later.

You also need a monitor that can display at least 1024 by 768 pixels. And you can't easily install GarageBand or iDVD unless your Mac has a DVD-playing drive.

Some of the programs, however, are more demanding. You can't use GarageBand's built-in instrument sounds, for example, unless your Mac has a G4 or G5 processor. iDVD won't even run unless you have a 733-megahertz G4 chip or something faster.

In the real world, however, savvy Mac fans consider some of those requirements the Computer Jokes of the Day. Thes Apple specs aren't just the minimums—they're the bare, desperate, stranded-on-a-desert-island minimums.

For example, 256 megabytes isn't nearly enough to get any meaningful work done with GarageBand or iDVD. And running iPhoto on a G3 Mac might be theoretically possible, but it's crushingly slow.

Bottom line: A much more practical minimum for running the iLife programs is a Mac with 512 megabytes of memory (or more—much more), with at least a G4 processor, running Mac OS X 10.3 and QuickTime 6.5.1 or later.

After that, the only requirement is a creative gene in your body.

(and then click again on a command), or click and *hold* the button as you drag down the menu to the desired command (and release the button to activate the command). Either method works fine.

Note: Apple has officially changed what it calls the little menu that pops up when you Control-click something on the screen. It's still a contextual menu, in that the menu choices depend on the context of what you click—but it's now called a *shortcut menu.* That term not only matches what it's called in Windows, but it's slightly more descriptive about its function. Shortcut menu is the term you'll find in this book.

• **Keyboard shortcuts.** Every time you take your hand off the keyboard to move the mouse, you lose time and potentially disrupt your creative flow. That's why many experienced Mac fans use keystroke combinations instead of menu commands wherever possible. ⌘-P opens the Print dialog box, for example, and ⌘-M minimizes the current window to the Dock.

When you see a shortcut like ⌘-Q (which closes the current program), it's telling you to hold down the ⌘ key, and, while it's down, type the letter Q, and then release both keys.

If you've mastered this much information, you have all the technical background you need to enjoy *iLife '04: The Missing Manual.*

Part One: iTunes 4

1

Getting Music Into iTunes

As the MP3 music craze of the late 1990s swept across the globe, software programs for playing the new music files on the computer began to pop up around the Internet. If you're old enough, you may even remember using Mac programs like SoundApp, SoundJam MP, and MacAmp.

When iTunes debuted in January 2001, Apple reported that 275,000 people downloaded it in the first week. The iTunes software proved to be a versatile, robust all-around music management program made exclusively for Macintosh. And it was *free*.

Even in that first version of iTunes, you could import songs from a CD and convert them into MP3 files; play MP3s, audio CDs, and streaming Internet radio; create custom playlists; burn audio CDs without having to spring for extra CD burning software; zone out to groovy animated laser-light displays in the iTunes window while songs played; and transfer music to a few pre-iPod, Mac-friendly portable MP3 players.

Today, iTunes is much more. In fact, it's the hub of the digital hub; it's the only iLife program that communicates directly with all four of the *other* iLife programs. Among many other feats, it lets you download perfectly legal music files from well-known artists using the Music Store feature and zip them over to your iPod in no time, all from within iTunes and without buying a single CD.

The version that came with your copy of iLife '04 is probably outdated at this point; Apple releases another version of iTunes every few months. But unlike the other iLife programs, iTunes is free. Each time Apple unleashes a new version, you'll be notified by Mac OS X's Software Update feature, which pops up on the screen and offers to update your copy via the Internet. Accept its invitation without fail.

A Quick Tour

This chapter is all about *filling* your copy of iTunes with music. Chapter 2 is all about *playing* that music (but here's the gist of it: Double-click a song to hear it).

Before you go about stocking up on tunes, though, it's worth taking a moment to get your bearings. The round-ended display at the center top of the iTunes window—the status area—tells you what song is playing, who's playing it, which album it came from, and how much playing time remains. To the left are volume and song navigation controls; to the right is a search box for hunting down or looking up specific singers or songs. Figure 1-1 presents a guided tour of the controls and functions on the iTunes screen.

Figure 1-1:
The iTunes window shows all of your playlists, the various places to find music in the Source list, and all of the songs in the chosen source. Here, for example, you can see the entire contents of the iTunes library.

In version 4.5 and later, the circled gray arrows take you online to the iTunes Music Store. Or Option-click these little arrows to jump into iTunes's Browser for the song or album you clicked (page 47).

The Source panel at the left of the iTunes window displays all of the audio sources you can tap into at the moment. If you have a CD in the computer's drive, for example, it shows up in the Source list, as does your iPod when it's connected.

Clicking a name in the Source column makes the main song-list area change accordingly, like this:

- Click the icon of a CD you've inserted; the disc's track list appears.

- Click a playlist (page 51); the contents of that music mix appear in the window.

- Click the Radio icon for a list of Internet radio stations, or the Party Shuffle icon to—well, see page 36.

Tip: You can show or hide the Radio and Party Shuffle icons in the Source list by visiting the General pane of iTunes's Preferences dialog box.

- Click the Music Store icon; you jump to Apple's online music emporium where you can browse, preview, and buy songs (Chapter 4).

As shown in Figure 1-1, the iTunes window is brimming with tools for managing your music, all of which are described in detail in the following chapters. But first you'll need some music to work with. The next section explores one of the most popular uses for iTunes—ripping digital audio files from compact discs.

Window Fun

Don't be misled by the brushed-aluminum look of the iTunes window. In fact, you can push and pull the various parts of the window like taffy.

- You can resize the panes within the iTunes window. Look for a shallow dot between panes; it denotes strips that you can drag to resize adjacent panes.

- The main song list is separated into columns, which you can sort and rearrange. Click a column title (like Artist or Album) to sort the list alphabetically by that criterion. Click the black triangle next to the column title to reverse the sorting.

- Change the order of the columns by dragging them. For example, if you want to have Album right next to the Song Name, drag the word Album horizontally until it's next to Song Name.

UP TO SPEED

Box Full of Buttons

The round button up in the top-right corner of iTunes changes depending on what you're doing. Here's what each one means and when you see it.

The Browse button appears when you click the Library icon to look through your collection or shop in the iTunes Music Store.

This version of the Burn CD button shows up when a playlist is selected in the Sources area or you have a separate playlist window open onscreen.

If you have taken iTunes up on its offer to burn a CD by clicking on the previous button, this icon appears as the disc-burning process begins.

The Import button indicates you've inserted a CD into your computer and are ready to rip some songs into your iTunes library.

When the iTunes Visualizations are turned on, clicking the Options button lets you adjust the frame rate and other visual settings.

To check for new radio stations and other live streams available in the iTunes Radio area, click the Refresh button.

- To adjust the width of a column, drag the vertical divider line on its right side.

- To resize all the columns so that they precisely fit the information in them, Control-click any column title and choose, from the contextual menu, Auto Size All Columns. Double-clicking on the vertical column lines automatically resizes them to fit the text as well.

- To add more columns (or less), Control-click any column title. From the pop-up list of column categories (Bit Rate, Date Added, and so on), choose the name of the column you want to add or remove. Column names with checkmarks are the ones that are currently visible.

Tip: Want to track your own listening habits? Turn on the Play Count in iTunes Options. Now you can see just how many times you have played "I Want You Back" by the Jackson 5 since you ripped that CD of old Motown gems to your hard drive. Checking out the Top 25 Most Played playlist in the Source window can also let you know where your ears have been lately.

If you intend to make a *lot* of adjustments to your list of columns, though, it's much faster to make the changes all at once. Choose Edit→View Options to produce the dialog box shown in Figure 1-2, where you can turn columns on and off en masse.

Figure 1-2:
The View Options box from the iTunes Edit menu lets you see as many—or as few—categories for sorting your music as you can stand.

Even in this tiny, unassuming dialog box, a trick or two awaits. If you Option-click any checkbox that's turned on, you turn all of them off. And vice versa.

If you want to turn all of them off except Album and Artist, for example, you'll save time by Option-clicking a turned-on box to turn them all off—and then turning the two you want back on.

Minimizing the window

Lovely as the iTunes window may be, it can take up a heck of a lot of screen real estate. When you're just playing music while you work on other things, you can shrink iTunes down to a svelte display panel that takes up a fraction of the size of the full window.

In fact, iTunes can run in three size modes: small, medium, or large (Figure 1-3). Here's how you pull this off:

- **Large.** This is what you get the first time you open iTunes.

- **Medium.** You can switch between large and medium by clicking the green zoom button at the top- or middle-left corner (or choosing Window→Zoom).

Figure 1-3:
And what size music would you like today? You can choose large, medium, or small. Only the large version has the space to serve as command central for MP3s, Internet radio, visual effects, and the kitchen sink.

GEM IN THE ROUGH

Arbitrary Groupings

Speaking of the iTunes information columns: The column called Grouping lets you override the usual sorting criteria and keep together a bunch of songs of your own choosing. (If you don't see the Grouping column, Control-click *any* column heading and choose Grouping, so that a checkmark appears next to its name.)

Many classical albums, for example, contain different symphonies, concertos, and other musical forms, all on one disc. How can you make sure that all of Mozart's *Concerto for Piano No. 5 in D Major (K 175)* stays together, and doesn't get mixed in with concertos 6 and 8 from the same CD?

Easy. Select all the "songs" that belong together (by ⌘-clicking them). Then choose File→Get Info. iTunes asks if you're sure you want to edit the file information for all of the selected pieces at once; yes, you do.

In the Get Info box, type *Piano Concerto 5* (or whatever group name you want). Now, when you click OK, you return to the main iTunes list.

To sort your list by grouping name, so that grouped pieces appear consecutively in the list, just click the word Grouping at the top of the column.

• **Small.** If your desktop isn't big enough for even the small iTunes window in Figure 1-3 at lower left, try taking it down a notch. To create the mini bar shown at lower right in Figure 1-3, start with the medium-size window. Then drag the resize handle (the diagonal lines in the lower-right corner) leftward. To expand it, just reverse the process.

Music from CDs

Ripping a CD means "converting its recordings into digital files on the computer." (Too bad recording industry executives didn't know that when they accused Apple's "Rip, Mix, Burn" ad campaign of promoting piracy. They evidently—and incorrectly—thought that "rip" meant "rip off.")

With the proper iTunes settings, ripping a CD track and preparing it for use with the iPod is fantastically easy. Here's how to go about it.

Phase 1: Choose an Audio File Format

Before you get rolling with ripping, decide which format you want to use for your music files: MP3, AAC, AIFF, WAV, or Apple Lossless (Figure 1-4). This may be more choice than you really wanted, but learning the pros and cons of each format is worth the effort, especially if you're about to commit a huge stack of CDs to digital format. You don't want to have to convert them all a second time.

Figure 1-4:
To choose the CD-ripping and file-converting format you prefer, choose iTunes→ Preferences, click the Importing tab, and choose the format you want.

"Create files names with track number" arranges the songs you import in the same order in iTunes as they were on the CD–even if you don't choose to rip every song on the album.

The Apple Lossless option works only on dock-connecting 2003 iPods and later, including the iPod Mini. Owners of the pre-dock iPods that came out in 2001 and 2002 are out of luck.

MP3

Suppose you copy a song from a Sheryl Crow CD directly onto your computer, where it takes up 47.3 MB of hard disk space. Sure, you could now play that song without the CD in your CD drive, but you'd also be out 47.3 megs of precious hard drive real estate.

Now say you put that Sheryl Crow CD in your computer and use your favorite encoding program to convert that song to an MP3 file. The resulting MP3 file still sounds really good, but only takes up about 4.8 MB of space on your hard drive—about 10 percent of the original. Better yet, you can burn a lot of MP3 files onto a blank CD of your own—up to 11 hours of music on one disc, which is enough to get you from Philadelphia to Columbus on Interstate 70 with tunes to spare.

MP3 files are so small because the compression algorithms use perceptual noise shaping, a method that mimics the ability of the human ear to hear certain sounds. Just as people can't hear dog whistles, most recorded music contains frequencies that are too high for humans to hear; MP3 compression discards these sounds. Sounds that are blotted out by louder sounds are also cast aside. All of this space-saving by the compression format helps to make a smaller file without overly diminishing the overall sound quality of the music.

New portable MP3 player models come out all the time, but many people consider the iPod's arrival in 2001 to be a defining moment in the history of MP3 hardware.

Tip: MP3 is short for MPEG Audio, Layer 3. And MPEG stands for Moving Pictures Experts Group, the association of engineers that also defined the specifications for the DVD video format, among others.

AAC

The Advanced Audio Coding format may be relatively new (it became official in 1997), but it has a fine pedigree. Scientists at Dolby, Sony, Nokia, AT&T, and those busy folks at Fraunhofer collaborated to come up with a method of squeezing multimedia files of the highest possible quality into the smallest possible space—at least small enough to fit through a modem line. During listening tests, many people couldn't distinguish between a compressed high-quality AAC file and an original recording.

What's so great about AAC on the iPod? For starters, the format can do the Big Sound/Small File Size trick even better than MP3. Because of its tighter compression technique, a song encoded in the AAC format sounds better (to most ears, anyway) and takes up less space on the computer than if it were encoded with the same quality settings as an MP3 file. Encoding your files in the AAC format is how Apple says you can stuff 10,000 songs onto a 40 GB iPod.

The AAC format can also be copy-protected (unlike MP3), which is why Apple uses it on the iTunes Music Store. (The record companies would never have permitted Apple to distribute their property without copy protection.)

Note: You can think of AAC as the Apple equivalent of WMA, the copy-protected Microsoft format used by all online music stores except Apple's. For better or worse, the iPod doesn't recognize copy-protected WMA files; it can download $1-a-song music only from Apple's iTunes Music Store.

Since the iPod can play several different audio formats, you can have a mix of MP3 and AAC files on the device if you want to encode your future CD purchases with the newer format. If you want to read more technical specifications on AAC before deciding, Apple has a page on the format at *www.apple.com/mpeg4/aac.*

Note: AAC is the audio component of MPEG-4, a new video format that's designed to get high-quality video compressed enough to travel over computer networks (even pokey old modem lines) and still look good onscreen.

WAV

The iPod was designed to handle AAC and MP3 formats the most efficiently, but it's not limited to them.

WAV, for example, is a standard Windows sound format, going all the way back to Windows 95. (Macs can play WAV files, too.) Windows fans download WAV recordings for everything from TV-show snippets to start-up sounds and other system alert noises. A WAV song usually sounds better than the same song in MP3—but takes up more room on the iPod.

AIFF

The AIFF standard (Audio Interchange File Format) can create sound files that sound spectacular—in fact, these are the audio files on commercial music CDs—but they hog hard drive space. For example, if you stick Prince's Purple Rain CD into your computer, double-click the disc icon, and drag the song file for "Let's Go Crazy" onto your desktop, you'll soon have a 46.9 MB AIFF file on your hard drive. Although the sound fidelity is tops, the files are usually ten times bigger in size than MP3s.

Apple originally developed the AIFF standard, but AIFF files play on other operating systems, too.

Note: If you insist on putting gargantuan files like AIFFs on your iPod, you'll have to worry about running out of battery power as well as disk space.

A modern iPod comes with a 32 MB memory chip. Yes, it serves as skip protection, because it stores 25 minutes' worth of MP3 or AAC music. But it also serves as a battery-life enhancer, because the hard drive stops spinning whenever the music plays from the memory buffer.

If you have big song files on the iPod, the memory buffer holds less music. When it runs out of music data, the iPod has no choice but to read from the hard drive, which runs your battery down much faster.

Audible

You can listen to more than just music on your iPod; you can also listen to the spoken word. Not books on tape, exactly, but more like books on MP3—courtesy of *www.audible.com*.

There, you can find over 18,000 spoken recordings to download. These are downloadable versions of the same professionally produced audio books you see in stores: the latest bestsellers in popular genres, children's books, and even old science fiction faves like Neal Stephenson's Snow Crash. Details on page 72.

Apple Lossless Encoder

As you probably know, a program like iTunes creates MP3 and AAC files by throwing away some of the audio data (mostly stuff you can't hear). Geeks call these *lossy* formats. But for true audiophiles with impeccable taste and bionic ears, lossy formats make music sound thin, tinny and screeching.

Of course, WAV and AIFF are *lossless*—no audio data is lost—but these files take up a huge amount of hard-drive space, to the tune of 40 to 50 MB per pop song.

In iTunes 4.5 and later, you can use the Apple Lossless Encoder instead. It offers great-sounding files that take up about half the space of an uncompressed CD track. (It requires not only iTunes 4.5 or later, but also QuickTime 6.5.1. and iPod Update 2004-04-28 or later.)

Tip: Before you stack up the CDs next to the computer for an afternoon of ripping, you may want to test your format preferences by ripping test songs in various formats. Let your ears tell you which format and bit rate sounds best to you.

Phase 2: Choose a Bit Rate

That's a lot of sound-file formats to choose from, so here's some simple advice: most people use either the familiar old MP3 format or the spunky new AAC option. AIFF and WAV formats may offer better sound quality than MP3 and AAC, but result in larger file sizes, which takes up more space on your hard drive and your iPod, if you have one. AAC usually creates files that are 30 to 40 percent smaller than an MP3 recorded at the same *bit rate*.

Now, bit rate may sound like one of those unbelievably geeky computer terms (which it is), but it plays a big role in how your music sounds when you snag a song from a CD and convert it to MP3 or AAC format. When it comes to sound quality, all digital audio files are not created equal.

The bit rate has to do with the number of *bits* (*binary digits*—tiny bits of computer data) used by one second of audio. The higher the number of bits listed, the greater the amount of data contained in the file, and the better the sound quality.

Tip: Eight bits make a byte. So why are audio files measured in kilobits (thousands of bits), and not the more familiar kilobytes?

Force of habit. Geeks measure size and storage capacity in bytes, but network speeds and data-transfer speeds have always been measured in bits. When you encode an MP3 file, the transfer and compression of the audio data into the new format is measured in kilobits.

Files encoded with lower bit rate settings—like 64 kilobits per second—don't include as much audio information from the original sound file. They sound thin and tinny compared to a file encoded at, say, 160 kbps.

Just as you can't compare megahertz ratings across different chip families (like Pentium III vs. Pentium 4), you can't compare bit rates between AAC and MP3 files. A 128 kbps AAC file generally sounds much better than a 128 kbps MP3 file. In fact, tests by the group that developed the AAC standard found that a 96 kbps AAC file generally sounds better than a 128 kbps MP3 file. (Your ears may differ.) As a bonus, the AAC version takes up much less space on your hard disk and iPod. You probably don't want to encode AAC files lower than 128 kbps, though, as the sound quality will begin to suffer noticeably.

For both formats, the higher the bit rate, the larger the file size. For example, an MP3 file encoded at 160 kbps sounds a heck of a lot better than one recorded at 96—but takes up over twice as much disk space (1.5 MB vs. 700 KB).

Figure 1-5:
The iTunes Preferences dialog box is where you give iTunes permission to go to the Internet to bring back CD information. You can also set the size of the program's display font for the Source and Song lists to either "Small" or "Large," and opt to show the Genre column in your iTunes browser window.

Got a lot of CDs to rip but no time to burn? From the "On CD Insert" pop-up menu, choose "Import Songs and Eject" to make iTunes automatically snag the track names, rip the tunes, and hand the CD back to you.

For MP3s, most people find that 128 kbps is a good compromise of file size and sound quality. At that rate, MP3 files take up roughly one megabyte of space per minute of music. The 128 kbps rate is considered high quality for the AAC format—which is why iTunes comes factory set to 128 kbps. (Songs for sale in the iTunes music store are 128 kbps AAC files, too.)

You're not stuck with the 128 kbps rate for your own home-ripped tracks. If you're a classical music fan and want to hear every nuance of a symphony, go for 160 or even 192 kbps. On the other hand, if you're listening to garage rock while strolling city streets, 96 kbps may sound fine, while giving you plenty of room on your iPod.

To make this kind of change, choose iTunes→Preferences and click the Importing icon (Figure 1-5).

Note: The iPod can also play files encoded in the MP3 VBR format, in which sophisticated software has adjusted the song's bit rate continuously along its length. (VBR stands for Variable Bit Rate.) The song winds up using more data during sonically complex parts of a song (higher bit rates) and lower settings during simpler parts. By constantly adjusting the bit rate, a MP3 VBR file conserves space more efficiently than a song encoded at a high bit rate all the way through.

To set up iTunes for MP3 VBR, go to Preferences, select Importing→MP3 Encoder. From the Setting pop-up menu, choose Custom to find the option for VBR encoding.

Phase 3: Download Song Names and Track Information

When you first insert a music CD, you may be disappointed to discover that to the computer, the album is named "Audio CD," and the songs on it are called "Track 1," "Track 2," and so on. It turns out that most audio CDs don't include any digital information about themselves. So if you don't do anything to solve the problem, after you've ripped, say, seven CDs into iTunes, you'll find that you have seven songs called Track 1, seven songs called Track 2, and so on—not the easiest way to organize your music.

There are two ways to remedy the problem: You can type the information in manually, or let iTunes go on the Internet to find out for itself.

The manual method

After you load up a CD, you can type in all of the song information for each track. To do so, click the track's name once to highlight its row, and then a second time to open up the renaming box. Edit away.

Tip: You can edit the information in the Artist, Album, or Genre columns the same way.

You should consider this purely theoretical information, however; you'd be nuts to go about naming your CDs and tracks this way. Read on.

The online way

If you have an Internet connection, choose iTunes→Preferences (or press ⌘-comma). The Preferences dialog box opens. Make sure that the settings in the bottom half of the dialog box match Figure 1-5. This setup allows the computer to zip out to the Internet to get the specific song information for the CD you've just inserted.

Behind the scenes, it's consulting a massive, comprehensive CD Database (CDDB), maintained by a company called Gracenote (*www.gracenote.com*). After iTunes sends information from the disc to the Gracenote CDDB servers, the database identifies the album and sends back the song titles and other data for iTunes to display.

(Firewall software may interfere with downloading CD track information. If you suspect that problem, ask your administrator to confirm that your computer's Internet settings are correct.)

If you don't have a high-speed connection, you may not want the computer dialing up every time you insert a CD. In that case, turn off "Connect to the Internet when needed." Instead, you may prefer to ask for the CD information when you're already connected to the Internet. Just choose Advanced→Get CD Track Names.

Phase 4: Convert the Song to a Digital Audio File

Once the songs on the CD have been identified, the song and artist names, time, and other information pops up in the main part of the window, as shown in Figure 1-6. Each song has a checkmark next to its name, indicating that iTunes will convert and copy it onto the computer when you click the Import button.

If you don't want the entire album—who wants anything from Don McLean's *American Pie* album besides the title track?—you can turn off the songs you *don't* want. Once you've picked your songs, click Import in the upper-right corner of the screen.

Tip: You can ⌘-click any box to deselect all checkboxes at once. To do the reverse, ⌘-click a box next to a list of unchecked songs to turn them all on again. This is a great technique when you want only one or two songs in the list; turn *all* checkboxes off, then turn those *two* back on again.

Another way to select a single song is to click it in the iTunes window and then choose Advanced→Convert Selection to MP3 (or whatever format you have chosen for importing). You can also use this menu item to convert songs that are *already* in your library to different audio formats.

As the import process starts, iTunes moves down the list of checked songs (Figure 1-6), ripping each one to a file in your Home→Music→iTunes→iTunes Music folder. Feel free to switch into other programs, answer email, surf the Web, and do other work while the ripping is under way.

Once the importing is finished, each imported song bears a green checkmark, and iTunes signals its success with a little melodious flourish. And now you have some brand new files in your iTunes music library.

Phase 4: Add Cover Artwork

Songs you download from the iTunes Music Store (Chapter 4) often include artwork, usually a picture of the album cover. iTunes displays the pictures in the lower-left corner of its main window.

But you shouldn't have to be a slave to the artistic tastes of some faceless, monolithic record company; you can install any art you like for any song. If Pachelbel's *Canon in D* makes you think of puppies, you can have baby dachshund photos appear in the iTunes window every time you play that song.

The only stipulation is that the graphic you choose must be in a format that QuickTime can understand: JPEG format, GIF, PNG, TIFF, or Photoshop, for example. Just keep in mind that the bigger the image size, the bigger the overall file size of the audio file and the more hard drive space you fill up.

Figure 1-6:
When you click Import, iTunes converts the selected songs from the CD to MP3, AAC, AIFF, Apple Lossless, or WAV files on your hard drive (depending on what you've selected in Preferences). The status bar at top shows the song being imported, the amount of time left, and the speed of the conversion. Songs in progress sport a wavy line in an orange circle.

Adding an image to an individual song: drag-and-drop method

To add an image file to a song you're listening to in iTunes, click the Show/Hide Song artwork button at the bottom of the iTunes window. The artwork pane appears. As shown in Figure 1-7, faint gray words appear in the pane, telling you exactly where to drag the image file. Just drag any graphics file right off of the desktop (or any other Finder folder) and into this space to install it there.

Tip: If you find an image on the Web that you love, right-click (or Control-click) it and choose Download Image to Disk to save it to your hard drive (the wording depends on your browser). Most browsers nowadays let you drag images off the Web page onto your desktop, too. Either way, you can drag the resulting graphic into the iTunes artwork pane.

Figure 1-7:
To copy a picture into the iTunes artwork pane, just drag it into the designated spot in the corner of the window (after you've selected the song you want to illustrate), as shown here before and after. You can also double-click any image that appears in this panel to view it in a separate window.

And speaking of CD cover art: In iTunes 4.5 and later, you can print out a perfectly sized CD jewel-case insert, complete with song list, by choosing File→Print, selecting a format, and clicking the Print button.

Figure 1-8:
Click a song and press ⌘-I, or choose File→Get Info, and click the Artwork tab. Click the Add button to select a digital photo from your hard drive. You can use almost any kind of photo or image file with your music. If you like the result, click OK.

Adding an image to an individual song: dialog box method

Instead of dragging a graphic off your desktop, you may prefer to use the Get Info dialog box, where at least you can inspect the image before accepting it. Figure 1-8 shows the way.

Tip: You can even install *multiple* graphics for an individual song. Just drag multiple images into the artwork pane; thereafter, you can click through them with the arrows at the top of the Selected Song bar. If you use the Get Info dialog box shown in Figure 1-8, you can click Add, and then ⌘-click the multiple graphics files to achieve the same result.

If you decide you want to get rid of any artwork or change what's attached to your songs, click the track and press ⌘-I. Click the Artwork tab, then click the art in the window. Click the Delete button to remove the image.

Artwork Made Easy

If you have a scanner, the original CD, and a large amount of free time, you can scan in album cover artwork yourself.

Alas, life is too short already. If that scenario doesn't appeal to you, there are plenty of places around the Web to download pictures of album covers that have been previously scanned and are just hanging out for you to copy.

Amazon.com and AllMusic.com have comprehensive selections, as do most sites that sell CDs. That's still a lot of manual effort, though: looking up an album, Control-clicking or right-clicking its artwork, choosing Copy from the contextual menu, and finally pasting into iTunes.

Fortunately, a great little free Mac OS X program called Clutter can spare you even that effort. (You can download it from *http://sprote.com/clutter.*) After you launch Clutter while playing a song in iTunes, it recognizes the song and automatically downloads an image of the album cover from Amazon.com.

The program has a pretty good track record, so to speak, for finding pop and rock album covers, but more esoteric fare may come up blank.

The album cover art appears both in Clutter's Now Playing window and the Dock. You can also drag the image onto your desktop to create a sea of tiny, floating album-cover windows, as shown here. When you click a cover, iTunes jumps to that album and starts playing it.

Clutter stores the album images it uses on your hard drive, where you can snatch a copy for use in your iTunes artwork window. To find the images, go to Home→Library→Images→com.sprote.clutter→CDs and open the folder name of the artist you're looking for. Drag the JPEG file into the iTunes artwork pane to add the image to your song file.

Adding an image to an entire album

To select the same art for *all* the songs on an album (or by the same artist), saving yourself a little time, open the iTunes browser (page 47) by clicking the eyeball icon at the top right of the screen. Click the name of an artist or album in the browser, and then press ⌘-I to open the Multiple Song Information box. (You'll see a worrisome alert box from iTunes, asking if you're sure about editing multiple items. Click Yes.)

In the Multiple Song Information dialog box (Figure 1-9), turn on the Artwork checkbox, and then double-click in the white area. In the window that opens, navigate to and select the image file you want to use for all the songs on the album, and then click OK. (Of course, you can also drag a graphic into this white box, right off your desktop.) You'll see a progress bar as iTunes applies the artwork and any other group settings you've chosen for the files.

Click OK, confirm your decision one last time, and then enjoy the new album art.

Tip: You can apply the same image over and over again into all the songs in the same *playlist.* Visit *http://malcolmadams.com/itunes* and download a copy of the "Selected Artwork to All in Playlist" AppleScript. The next time you have an image that you want to associate with all the songs on a particular playlist, just fire up that script.

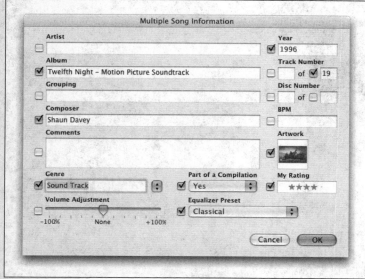

Figure 1-9:
The Multiple Song Information box can save a lot of time because it allows you to change information all at once for all the songs listed in the Artist, Album, or Genre categories. For example, you can assign the Equalizer's "Classical" preset to all your files in the Classical genre, add a picture of a yellow submarine to all of your Beatles tracks, or adjust the title of all the songs at once on a mislabeled album.

Importing Other Music Files into iTunes

Not all sound files come directly from the compact discs in your personal collection. As long as a file is in a format that iTunes can comprehend (MP3, AAC, AIFF, WAV, WMA, Apple Lossless, or Audible), you can add it to the iTunes music library by any of several methods.

Note: The AAC format includes a copy-protection feature that MP3 doesn't have. Songs you buy from the iTunes Music Store and music encoded from your own CDs with iTunes work, but you may have trouble playing or moving other copy-protected AAC files (like those bought from, for example, LiquidAudio.com).

- If menus are your thing, choose File→Add File to Library. In the resulting dialog box (Figure 1-10), locate and click the file you wish to add, or ⌘-click several files to highlight them all at once. Click Choose to bring it, or them, into iTunes.

Figure 1-10:
Select the file you'd like to add to your expanding iTunes library with the File→Add File to Library command. If the files you want to add are not in iTunes-friendly formats, you can find scores of shareware on the Web that can convert different audio formats. Some of these sites include MP3 machine (www.mp3 ma-chine.com), the Hit Squad (www.hitsquad.com), and MP3-Converter (www.mp3-converter.com).

FREQUENTLY ASKED QUESTION

A Trip to the Library

Where exactly does iTunes store its music library on my computer's hard drive? Can I move the music library if my hard drive starts to get full?

The music library is the program's personal database. It stores all of the songs you've imported into the program, as well as all of the playlists you created from those songs. This database file sits in your Home→Music→iTunes Music folder.

If you rudely drag the iTunes Music folder to a different place without telling iTunes, it will think the songs are gone. The next time you start the program, you'll find it empty. (While iTunes remains empty but calm, *you* may have heart

palpitations as you picture your music collection vanishing in a puff of bytes.)

To move the iTunes Music folder to a new drive, just let the program know where you're putting it. Move the folder to the desired location, then choose iTunes→Preferences and click the Advanced icon or tab. In the area labeled iTunes Music Folder Location, click the Change button, and navigate to the place where you moved the iTunes Music folder. Finally, click OK.

Exhale.

- You can drag a file or folder full of sound files onto the iTunes icon on the Dock to add the music to the library.

- You can also drag the files or folders straight into the iTunes window.

Now, when you read about iPhoto later in this book, you'll discover that dragging graphics into the iPhoto window from your hard drive creates a copy of them, which iPhoto stashes safely into its own private collection, deep within your Home folder.

Ordinarily, iTunes does the same with music files: When you drag one into its window, the program duplicates it, placing the copy into its own iTunes Music folder. That way, if you wind up moving or discarding the original during a frenzied cleanup binge, you won't return to iTunes to discover the song missing.

The copying business does, however, use up your hard-disk space faster, since every music file is getting doubled. Fortunately, you can override this behavior. Just choose iTunes→Preferences, click the Advanced tab, and turn off "Copy files to iTunes Music folder when adding to library."

From now on, iTunes will merely note the original locations of any music files you introduce, rather than making copies. If you move or delete those files, iTunes will no longer be able to track or play them.

Note: Don't have an iPod but still find yourself craving your iTunes tracks when you have to drag yourself away from the Mac? Thanks to a tidy deal between Apple and Motorola, you'll soon be able to download iTunes songs (including tracks you've purchased from the Music Store) to certain Motorola wireless phones by way of a Bluetooth or USB connection. The mobile-phone version of iTunes won't be available until the first half of 2005, but keep it in mind when you need to pick out that new cellphone.

Getting Music Out of iTunes

T he first chapter of this section is all about getting music into iTunes, whether from a CD or by dragging audio files onto your hard drive. Now comes the payoff: the chance to hear and even see your songs playing, to burn them onto a CD, or to share them with friends and family over a network.

Playing Music

To turn your computer into a jukebox, click the triangular Play button in the upper-left corner of the iTunes window, or press the Space bar. The computer immediately begins to play the songs whose names have checkmarks in the main list. (You can also double-click a song's name to make it start playing.)

The central display at the top of the window shows not only the name of the song and album, but also where you are in the song, as represented by the diamond in the horizontal strip. Drag this diamond, or click elsewhere in the strip, to jump around in the song.

Or just click the tiny triangle at the left side of this display to see a pulsing VU meter, indicating the current music's sound levels at various frequencies.

Tip: You can also control CD playback from the Mac's Dock. Just Control-click the iTunes icon (or click and hold on it) to produce a pop-up menu offering playback commands like Pause, Next Song, and Previous Song, along with a display that identifies the song currently being played.

As music plays, you can control and manipulate the music and the visuals of your Mac in all kinds of interesting ways. As a result, some people don't move from their machines for months at a time.

Visuals

Visuals is the iTunes term for an onscreen laser-light show that pulses and dances in perfect sync to the music you're listening to. The effect is hypnotic and wild. (For real party fun, invite some people who grew up in the 1960s to your house to watch.)

To summon this psychedelic display, click the flower-power icon in the lower-right corner of the window (see Figure 2-1). The show begins immediately—although it's much more fun if you choose Visualizer→Full Screen so that the movie takes over your whole monitor. True, you won't get a lot of work done, but when it comes to stress relief, visuals are a lot cheaper than a hot tub.

Figure 2-1:
No matter what you're listening to, the animated full-color patterns produced by the iTunes Visualizations feature can make it a more interesting experience. (This feature works really well with the original cast album from "Hair" or anything by Jimi Hendrix.)

Once the screen is alive with visuals, you can turn it into your personal biofeedback screen by experimenting with these keys:

Key	Function
?	Displays a cheat sheet of secret keystrokes. (Press it repeatedly to see the other shortcut keys.)
F	Displays, in the upper-left corner of your screen, how many frames per second iTunes' animation is managing—a quick, easy way to test the power of your graphics circuitry.

T	Turns *frame rate capping* on or off—a feature that limits the frame rate to 30 frames per second, to avoid sapping your Mac's horsepower when you're working in other programs (not really much of an issue in Mac OS X, of course).
I	Shows/hides information about the current song.
C	Shows/hides the current Visuals configuration (the name of the current waveform, style, and color scheme) in the upper-right corner of the screen.
M	Turns slide show mode on or off. In slide show mode, the visuals keep changing color and waveform as they play. (Otherwise, the visuals stick with one style and color.)
B	Turns on an Apple logo in the center of the Visuals screen.
R	Chooses a new waveform/style/color at random.
Q or W	Cycles through the various waveform styles stored in iTunes.
A or S	Cycles though *variations* on the currently selected waveform.
Z or X	Cycles through color schemes.
Number keys	Cycles through the ten different preset, preprogrammed waveform/color/style configurations.
D	Restores the default waveform settings.

Tip: These are the secret keystrokes for the *built-in* visuals. The Web is crawling with add-on modules that have secret keystrokes of their own.

Keyboard Control

You can control iTunes' music playback using its menus, of course, but the keyboard can be far more efficient. Here are a few of the control keystrokes worth noting:

Function	Keystroke
Play, Pause	Space bar
Next song/previous song	Right arrow, left arrow
Next source/previous source	Down arrow, up arrow
Louder	⌘-up arrow
Quieter	⌘-down arrow
Mute	⌘-M
Fast-forward, rewind	Option-⌘-right arrow, -left arrow
Eject	⌘-E
Turn Visuals on	⌘-T
Turn Visuals off	⌘-T or mouse click
Full-screen visuals	⌘-F
Exit full-screen visuals	⌘-T, ⌘-F, or mouse click

Shuffle, Repeat

iTunes has all the shiny controls you'd expect to find on a decent CD player, and more. In the Controls menu, for example, you'll find playback controls like these:

- The **Shuffle** command tells iTunes to get randomly funky with the order of the songs currently listed in your iTunes window at the time—an album listing, a single playlist, or all the songs in the library. A checkmark next to the Shuffle command means that the setting is already turned on; select Shuffle again to toggle it off. *Shortcut:* Click the Shuffle button, second from left at the bottom of the iTunes window.

- The **Repeat Off, All,** and **One** choices on the Controls menu make iTunes automatically play current playlists or albums over and over (Repeat All) or just once (Repeat One). **Repeat Off** disables the repeat function altogether. (You can choose only choose one of these commands at a time, and the checkmark shows you which setting is active.)

The Graphic Equalizer

If you click the Graphic Equalizer button (third from bottom right in Figure 2-1), you get a handsome floating control console that lets you adjust the strength of each musical frequency independently (Figure 2-2). (Or just press ⌘-2 to get the console onscreen.)

Tip: You can also make an Equalizer pop-up tab appear as one of the iTunes columns. Choose Edit→View Options and turn on the Equalizer checkbox.

To apply Equalizer settings to a specific selected song, press ⌘-I or choose File→Get Info, and click the Options tab, shown at bottom in Figure 2-2.

You can drag the Preamp slider (at the left side of the Equalizer) up or down to help compensate for songs that sound too loud or soft. To design your own custom preset pattern with the Preamp and the other ten sliders, click the pop-up tab at the top of the Equalizer and select Make Preset.

FREQUENTLY ASKED QUESTION

Auto-Playing Music CDs

In Mac OS 9, you could set the QuickTime Settings control panel to play music CDs automatically when they're inserted into the Mac. Can Mac OS X do that?

Sure!

First, make sure that iTunes is slated to open automatically when you insert a music CD. You do that on the CDs & DVDs panel of System Preferences (use the "When you insert a music CD" pop-up menu).

Then all you have to do is make sure iTunes knows to begin playing automatically once it launches. Choose iTunes→ Preferences, click the General icon, and from the On CD Insert pop-up menu, choose Begin Playing, and click OK.

Preventing Ear-Blast Syndrome

No longer must you strain to hear delicate Chopin piano compositions on one track, only to suffer from melted eardrums when the hyperkinetic Rachmaninoff cut kicks in right after it. The Sound Check feature attempts to bring the disparate volumes onto line, making the softer songs louder and gently lowering the level of the more bombastic numbers in the iTunes library. Audiophiles may nitpick about the Sound Check function, but it can be quite useful, especially for times, like bicycling uphill, when constantly grabbing at the iPod's volume controls on the remote or scroll wheel are inconvenient.

The first step using Sound Check is to turn it on. In iTunes, open the Preferences box (⌘-comma). Click the Effects icon or tab and turn on the box for Sound Check.

If you have an iPod, also connect your iPod and select it from the iTunes Source list when it pops up. Then click the iPod Preferences button at the lower right side of the iTunes window.

Figure 2-2:
Top: Drag the sliders (bass on the left, treble on the right) to accommodate the strengths and weaknesses of your speakers or headphones (and listening tastes). Or save yourself the trouble by using the pop-up menu above the sliders to choose a canned set of slider positions for Classical, Dance, Jazz, Latin, and so on. In iTunes 3 and later, these settings even transfer to the iPod.

Bottom: You can also apply preset or customized equalizer settings to individual songs under the Options tab in the song's Get Info box (shown here in Windows).

In the resulting dialog box, click the Effects icon and turn on the Sound Check dialog box. You also need to turn on Sound Check on the iPod itself: From the iPod's main screen, choose Settings→Sound Check and click the Select button.

Internet Radio

Not satisfied with being a mere virtual jukebox, iTunes also serves as an international, multicultural radio without the shortwave static. You can find everything from mystical Celtic melodies to American pop to programming from Japan, Italy, Germany, and other spots around the globe.

Computers with high-speed Internet connections have a smoother streaming experience, but the vast and eclectic mix of musical offerings is well worth checking out even if you have a dial-up modem. Just click the Radio icon in the Source list to see a list of stations, as shown in Figure 2-3.

UP TO SPEED

Party Shuffle On, Dude

The standard iTunes Shuffle feature can be inspiring or embarrassing, depending on which songs the program happens to play. Especially when your guests discover the Milli Vanilli tracks buried in the depths of your collection.

Party Shuffle (iTunes 4.5 or later) lets you control which songs iTunes selects when it's shuffling at your next wing-ding. It also shows you what's already been played and what's coming up in the mix, so you'll know what to expect.

To use it, click the Party Shuffle icon on the iTunes Source list. (If you don't see it, visit the Preferences dialog box, click General, and turn on Party Shuffle.) Until you turn it off, iTunes will display a message each time that describes what Party Shuffle does.

Now you see an extra panel at the bottom of the iTunes window, as shown here. Using the pop-up menu, select a music source for the mix—either an existing playlist or your whole Library. If you don't like the song list that iTunes proposes, click the Refresh button at the top of the iTunes window to generate a new list of songs from the same source.

Next, use the pop-up menus in the Display area to specify how many songs you want to see coming up in the mix, and how many recently played ones you want to see. iTunes can show you anywhere from 0 to 100 songs, either coming or going, and it can play tracks more often according to their play counts and ratings.

As in any iTunes playlist, you can manually add songs, delete them from the playlist, or rearrange the playing order. Party Shuffle may grab the same track multiple times, especially if you turn on "Play higher ranked songs more often," so watch for unwanted dupes.

(The shortcut menu that appears when you Control-click a song lets you add it again into the Party Shuffle mix—or, if you're seized with a sudden inspiration for your mix, designate it to play next.)

Once you're satisfied, click the Play button and let the music play on. With plenty of upcoming tracks displayed, you can feel free to mingle with guests without having to worry about your less-favorite songs crashing the party mix out of the blue.

If you find your radio streams are constantly stuttering and stopping, try this: Choose iTunes→Preferences. In the Preferences dialog box, click the Advanced icon or tab. From the Streaming Buffer Size pop-up menu, choose Large. Click OK.

Having the buffer set to Large may increase the waiting time before the music starts flowing through your computer from the Internet, but it allows iTunes to hoard more music at once to help make up for interruptions caused by network traffic.

Tip: It's possible to save music streams to your computer's hard drive, although the practice dances dangerously close to copyright infringement. Programs like Streamripper X (from *http://streamripperx.sourceforge. net*) let you save radio streams as MP3 files.

Figure 2-3:
The Radio list displays the categories and subcategories that can take you around the world in 80 stations with iTunes. Click the Refresh button to update the station list.

Burning a CD or DVD

If want to record a certain playlist on a CD for posterity—or for the Mr. Shower CD player in the bathroom—iTunes gives you the power to burn. In fact, it can burn any of three kinds of discs:

- **Standard audio CDs.** This is the best part. If your computer has a CD burner, it can serve as your own private record label. (Apple has a list of external CD recorders that work with iTunes at *www.apple.com/support/itunes.*) iTunes can record selected sets of songs, no matter what the original sources, onto a blank CD. When it's all over, you can play the burned CD on any standard CD player, just like the ones from Tower Records—but this time, you hear only the songs you like, in the order you like, with all of the annoying ones eliminated.

Tip: Use CD-R discs. CD-RW discs are not only more expensive, but may not work in standard CD players. (Not all players recognize CD-R discs either, but the odds are better.)

- **MP3 CDs.** A standard audio compact disc contains high-quality, enormous song files in the AIFF format. An *MP3* compact disc, however, is a data CD that contains music files in the MP3 format.

  Because MP3 songs are much smaller than the AIFF files, many more of them fit in the standard 650 or 700 MB of space on a recordable CD. Instead of 74 or 80 minutes of music, a CD-R full of MP3 files can store *10 to 12 hours* of tunes.

  Just about any computer can play an MP3 CD. But if you want to take the disc on the road or even out to the living room, you'll need a CD player designed to read both standard CDs and discs containing MP3 files. Many modern players can play both CDs and MP3 CDs, and the prices are not much higher than that of a standard CD player. Some DVD players and home-audio sound systems can also play MP3 CDs.

Note: You can't easily convert copy-protected AAC files into MP3 files, so you can't burn an MP3 CD from a playlist that contains purchased music. If you're determined to do that, certain workarounds are available. You could use certain frowned-upon utility programs from the Web. Or you could burn the AAC files onto a CD and then rip *that* into iTunes, exactly as described earlier in this chapter. At that point, the songs are MP3 files.

- **Backup DVDs.** If your Mac has an Apple SuperDrive that can play and record both CDs and DVDs, you have another option. iTunes can also back up 4.7 gigabytes of your music collection at a time by copying it to a blank DVD. (The disc won't play in any kind of player, of course; it's just a glorified backup disk for restoration when something goes wrong with your hard drive.)

You pick the type of disc you want to make in the Preferences dialog box (Figure 2-4). Then proceed as follows:

1. **Select the playlist you want to burn. Check to make sure you have all the songs you can fit, in the order you want them in.**

   Consult the readout at the bottom of the window, which lets you know how much playing time is represented by the songs in the playlist.

Note: Although earlier versions of iTunes would stop burning a long playlist once it got to the last full song it could fit on a disc, iTunes 4.2 and later versions ask you to insert another disc if it runs out of room on the first one and then picks up where it left off.

2. **When you're ready to roll, click the Burn Disc button at the top-right corner of the iTunes window.**

   The icon changes into a yellow-and-black graphic that resembles the symbol used for fallout shelters in the 1950s.

3. Insert a blank CD into your computer's drive when prompted. Click the Burn Disc button again after the program acknowledges the disc.

iTunes prepares to record the CD, which may take a few minutes. In addition to prepping the disc for recording, iTunes has to convert the music files to the standard format used by audio CDs.

Once iTunes has taken care of business, it lets you know that it's now burning the CD. Again, depending on the speed of your computer and CD burner, as well as the size of your playlist, the recording process could take several minutes.

When the disc is done, iTunes pipes up with a musical flourish. Eject the CD (by pressing the Eject key at the upper right of your keyboard, for example) and label the top of the newly minted music storehouse with a magic marker (or your favorite method).

Figure 2-4:
Choose iTunes→ Preferences, and then click Burning. Here, you select the recorder you wish to use, as well as what kind of CD to make: a standard disc that will play in just about any CD player, an MP3 CD that will play in the computer's CD drive (and some newer home decks), or a backup just for safekeeping.

CD Covers and Printed Playlists

In versions of iTunes before 4.5, you had to do a lot of gymnastics just to make a nice-looking song list to tuck into the CD jewel case of a freshly burned disc. Not to make you relive any bad memories, or anything, but you had to export the playlist as a text file, import it into a word-processing program, format the type, and then, six hours later....*Print*. Nowadays, you just choose File→Print, select a formatting option, and click the Print button.

The iTunes Print box is now full of choices:

- You can print out a perfectly sized insert for a CD jewel case, complete with song list on one side and a miniature mosaic of all your album artwork on the other, as you can see in Figure 2-5. For a simpler CD insert, there's also a text-only option on a plain background. (If you opt for the CD jewel case, your resulting printout even comes with handy crop marks you can use to guide your X-Acto blade when trimming it down to size.)

- If you want something simpler, select Song Listing from the pop-up menu for a plain vanilla list of tracks on the playlist.

- The Album Listing option prints out a comprehensive list of all the original albums that you used when cherry-picking the songs for the playlist.

The Theme menu in the Print dialog box offers even more formatting fun, like adding User Ratings to a Song Listing sheet.

Tip: Want to use one of your own personal photos for the cover of your CD case? Just add artwork to a track (described on page 25) and then choose Edit→Print →Theme: Single Cover to place your own picture on the front.

Figure 2-5:
With a playlist selected, go to File→ Print to call up the iTunes print box. Pick and click the Print format you desire, select a theme (single picture or a mosiac, plain old text, etc.), and click the Print button for hard-copy proof of your CD-mixing prowess.

Playing Songs Across a Network

If you've taken the trouble to set up a home network so your family can share a printer, an Internet connection, and so on, more treats await. With iTunes 4, you share songs and playlists with up to five networked computers—Macs, PCs, or a mix of both. You could, for example, tap into your roommate's jazz collection without getting up from your desk, and she can sample the zydeco and tejano tunes from your World Beat playlists. The music you decide to share is streamed over the network to the other computer.

Note: In iTunes 4.0, you could even listen to music on Macs *elsewhere on the Internet,* as long as you knew their IP addresses (network addresses). It didn't take long for people to figure out how to exploit this feature and share music all over the Internet in sneaky ways that Apple had never intended.

In response to hysterical phone calls from the record companies, Apple removed this feature (and the Advanced→Connect to Shared Music command) in version 4.0.1. Now you can connect only to other machines on your own office network.

To share music across a network, the machines involved must meet a few requirements:

- The Macs on the network need to be using at least iTunes 4.0.1 and Mac OS X 10.2.4 or later. The Windows computers need iTunes 4.1 or later.

- The computers must be on the same *subnet* of the network. (If you don't know what that means, read on.)

- The iTunes Sharing preferences for each computer involved need to be configured properly.

Preparing to Share

The *Subnet Mask* (that is, the chunk of the network you're on) is identified by four numbers separated by periods, like this: 255.255.255.0. (Nobody ever said networking was user-friendly.)

To check your Mac's subnet number, open System Preferences and click the Network icon. In Mac OS X 10.3, double-click Built-In Ethernet, AirPort, or whatever line appears at the top of the summary list. You'll see your network info displayed, including the subnet mask.

Sharing Your Own Music

To "publish" your tunes to the network, choose iTunes→Preferences and click the Sharing icon. Turn on "Share my music" (see Figure 2-6 at top). You can choose to share your entire collection, or just selected playlists.

Tip: Using iTunes 4.5 and later, you can even share your tunes with another account holder who's logged into the *same* Mac simultaneously, using Mac OS X's *fast user switching* feature. You just have to make sure iTunes is open in both accounts.

Sharing music can get a little wacky if the first account is already playing a song when you start playing a second one; you get both songs playing at once, with no way to turn off the first person's music from the second person's account. It's one way to get Elvis to duet with Usher, but probably not the most listenable.

Whatever you type in the Shared Name box in the Sharing preferences will show up in your friend's iTunes Source list. You can also require a password as a key to your own music library—a handy feature if you feel that your colleagues mooch off you quite enough in other areas of life.

You can share AAC, MP3, AIFF, WAV, Apple Lossless files, and radio station links with your network buddies, but not Audible or QuickTime files. And sharing means "streaming" here. You can listen to shared music, but you can't burn someone else's music files to a CD, copy them to an iPod, or add them to your own library.

Finally, remember that songs bought from the iTunes Music Store can play on a maximum of five machines. If you want to listen to such a song across the network, one that hasn't been authorized on your computer, you must first enter the Apple account name and user password that was used to purchase the song.

Figure 2-6:
Top: The iTunes 4 Sharing Preferences box lets you share as much of your music collection as you would like with other people on the same network. It also allows you to seek out music on other connected computers yourself. To share your music, you must first turn on the sharing feature and indicate what you want to put out there for others to sample.

Bottom: Once you've decided to share, your subnet pals can sample your collection right from their iTunes Source lists.

Listening to Someone Else's Tunes

Once they've been shared, other people's iTunes libraries generally appear right in your Source list, labeled with whatever name your benevolent buddies have chosen for the shared collection. (See Figure 2-6, bottom.)

Double-click the desired song to fire it up and play through your computer's speakers. (Type the password first, if your pal has set one up.)

Tip: Want to know if a certain song is shared? Select the title and press ⌘-I, or choose File→Get Info. If the word "Remote" appears next to Kind in the Summary area, you're looking at a shared file.

If the other person's tunes aren't showing up, choose iTunes→Preferences and click the Sharing icon. In the preferences box (Figure 2-6), turn on "Look for shared music."

Turning Off Music Sharing

If you want a little privacy for your music collection, go back to the iTunes Preferences box (Figure 2-6) and click the Sharing icon. Turn off "Share my music" and click OK to disable the feature until the next time you're feeling generous. Your playlists are no longer visible to other people on the network.

AirPort Express and AirTunes

The AirPort Express, which resembles a PowerBook AC adapter after a few months of gym workouts, is a handy-dandy 802.11g Wi-Fi base station for a wireless network, just like its big brother, the AirPort Extreme.

"So," you say, "Why do I care about wireless networking in a book about my iLife '04 programs? I just want to learn how to use iTunes."

This is why: AirPort Express was made with iTunes in mind. Thanks to a built-in feature called AirTunes, you can wirelessly stream your iTunes music from your Mac, through the air, and out from your home stereo speakers (which are plugged into the AirPort Express)—all without tripping over a long and pesky cable connecting your Mac upstairs to your home audio system downstairs. All you need are these:

- An AirPort Express mobile base station, which Apple will gladly sell you for $130 at *www.apple.com/airportexpress*. It includes the AirTunes software.

- A Mac with an AirPort card and Mac OS X 10.3 or later. (If you have a wireless network in place, you already have one of these. By the way, both Macs and PCs can pump music out to an AirPort Express.)

- Version 4.6 or later of iTunes.

- A cable that connects your home sound system (or powered speakers) to the Line Out port on the bottom of the AirPort Express. It can be either a digital fiber-optic cable or analog Y-shaped cable (that is, the stereo miniplug-to-dual-RCA connectors common on audio equipment).

Once you buy the pocket base station, some set-up software gently guides you through the chores like naming the base station and getting iTunes ready for its broadcast debut. Make sure to plug the AirPort Express into an electrical outlet close to your stereo system and use the proper cable to connect the two.

After the setup process is finished, a new little pop-up menu appears at the bottom of your iTunes window (Figure 2-7), displaying the name you just bequeathed to AirPort Express. Choose that and then click the iTunes Play to start broadcasting.

Tip: The AirPort Express also has a port to connect a USB-enabled printer, which lets all of the computers on your wireless network share the same printer.

	Time	Artist	Date Added
e			
n Wine	3:22	Fountains Of Wayne	5/13/04 6:26 PM
uture In Sales	3:06	Fountains Of Wayne	5/13/04 6:26 PM
Mom	3:18	Fountains Of Wayne	5/13/04 6:26 PM
sack	3:00	Fountains Of Wayne	5/13/04 6:26 PM
er Place	4:06	Fountains Of Wayne	5/13/04 6:26 PM

Stereo in PlayStation Room

Figure 2-7:
Use the pop-up menu in the lower corner of the iTunes window (top) to choose where you want your music to be heard. If you have more than one AirPort Express base station (bottom)—in Apple's dreams!—then you can use this pop-up menu to specify which stereo you want to pump out the music.

When your remote speakers are turned off, by the way, don't forget to choose Computer from this pop-up menu. Otherwise, you'll hear nothing at all from iTunes.

Managing Your Music

At its heart, iTunes is nothing more than a glorified database. Its job is to search, sort, and display information, quickly and efficiently. Here, for example, are some powerful managerial tasks it stands ready to handle.

Deleting Songs

If you want to delete a song or songs—like when you outgrow your Britney Spears phase and want to reclaim some hard drive space by dumping those tracks from the *Oops...I Did It Again* album—click the title in the Albums pane, select the songs you want to delete from the song list, and press Delete.

Tip: Selecting songs works just like selecting files in the Finder. For example, you can select a consecutive batch by clicking the first song's name, then Shift-clicking the last. Or you can add individual songs to the selection (or remove them from the selection) by ⌘-clicking their names.

When iTunes asks if you're sure you want to delete the music, click Yes. You'll usually be asked twice about deleting a song, the first time for deleting it from a list, the second time about deleting the music file from your iTunes music library altogether. If you want your hard drive space back, click Yes to both.

Searching for Songs

You can call up a list of all the songs that have a specific word in their title, album name, or artist attribution, just by typing a few letters into the Search box at the top of the window. With each letter you type, iTunes shortens the list of songs that are visible, confining it to tracks that match what you've typed.

For example, in Figure 3-1, typing *train* brings up a list of songs by different performers that all have the word "train" somewhere in the song's information—maybe the title of the song, maybe the band name. This sort of thing could be useful for creating themed playlists, like a mix for a Memorial Day barbecue made from songs that all have the word "sun" or "summer" in the title.

Figure 3-1:
The Search box in the iTunes window can quickly find all the songs in the library that match the keyword you enter. To erase the Search box so that you see all of your songs again, click the little circled X button at the right side of the box.

Figure 3-2:
When you click an Artist name in the left column, you get a list of all attributed albums on the right side. To see the songs you've imported from each listed album, click the album name. The songs on it appear in the main list area of the iTunes window, beneath the Browser panes.

The Browser

The Browse button is the eyeball in the upper-right corner of the window. (It appears only when the Library icon is selected in the source list at the left side of the screen.) It produces a handy, supplementary view of your music database, this time organized like a Finder column view (shown in Figure 3-2).

Tip: Can't get back that full list of albums on the right Album pane after you've clicked on a name in the Artist list in the left pane? Go to the top of the Artist list and click All. The complete album list reappears.

It's worth noting, by the way, that this two-panel Browser can become a *three*-panel browser, much to the delight of people who enjoy the phrase "drill down." Figure 3-3 has details.

Figure 3-3:
The Genre pane in iTunes preferences can add another whole layer of categorizing for your music collection. If you don't see the Genre pane when you start iTunes for the first time, you need to turn it on in Preferences. Press ⌘-comma, or choose iTunes →Preferences→General, and then turn on "Show genre when browsing."

Ratings

Although there's no way to give a song two thumbs up within iTunes, you can label each song in your collection with a star rating (one to five). Not only can you, too, now feel like a *Rolling Stone* record critic, but you can also use your personal rating system to spontaneously produce playlists of the hits, nothing but the hits.

To add a rating to a song in the Song list window, first make sure the My Rating field is turned on in the iTunes Options box (⌘-J). Then proceed as shown in Figure 3-4.

Once you've assigned ratings, you can sort your list by star rating (click the My Rating column title), create playlists of only your personal favorites, and so on.

Tip: One the newer iPods, you can even rate songs on the go; your ratings will transfer back to iTunes. To rate a song on the iPod, start playing it and tap the Select button twice from the Now Playing screen. Use the scroll wheel to spin across the ghostly gray dots onscreen and transform them into the number of stars you feel the song deserves.

Figure 3-4:
Click inside the My Rating column. The horizontal position of your click determines how many stars you're giving. You can also add a rating by selecting a song title, pressing ⌘-I to open its Get Info box, and then clicking the Options tab.

Song Information

You have a couple different ways to change song titles in iTunes—to fix a typo or other incorrect information, for example.

In the song list, click the text you want to change, wait a moment, then click again to make the renaming rectangle appear. Type to edit the text, exactly as when you change a file name on the desktop.

Another way to change the song's title, artist name, or other information is to click the song in the iTunes window and press ⌘-I to bring up the Get Info box. (Choose File→Get Info if you forget the keyboard shortcut.) Click the Info tab (Figure 3-5) and type in the new track information. This is the way to go if you have several pieces of information to change.

Remember, too, that you can change the information for a whole batch of selected songs at once. See page 28 for details on the Multiple Song Info dialog box.

Tip: Once you've got a song's Get Info box up on the screen, you can use the Previous and Next buttons to navigate to the other tracks grouped with it in the iTunes song list window. This way, if you want to rapidly edit all the track information on the same playlist, on the same album, in the same genre, or by the same artist, you don't have to keep closing and opening each song's Get Info box.

Converting Between File Formats

iTunes isn't just a cupboard for music; it's also a food processor. You can convert any song or sound file into almost any other format: MP3 to AIFF, AAC to WAV, MP3 to AAC, and so on.

Tip: If you're going from a compressed format like MP3 to a full-bodied, uncompressed format like AIFF, you shouldn't hear much difference in the resulting file. Quality could take a hit, however, if you convert a file from one compressed format to another, like MP3 to AAC. If you're a stickler for sound but still want the space-saving benefit of the AAC format, it's best just to set the iTunes preferences to encode in AAC format and re-rip the song from the original CD.

To get the conversion underway, choose iTunes→Preferences and click the Importing button. From the Import Using pop-up menu, pick the format you want to convert to, then click OK.

Figure 3-5:
Lower right: The Get Info box for each is where you can add, correct, and customize information for each song.

Upper left: Click the Summary tab for the lowdown on the song's bit rate, file format, and other fascinating technical details.

Now, in your iTunes library, select the song file you want to convert, and then choose Advanced→Convert Selection to AAC (or MP3 or AIFF or whatever you just picked as your import preference).

If you have a whole folder or disk full of potential converts, hold down the Option key as you choose Advanced→Convert to AAC (or your chosen encoding format). A window pops up, which you can use to navigate to the folder or disk holding the files you want to convert. The only files that don't get converted are protected ones: Audible.com tracks and AAC songs purchased from the iTunes Music Store.

The song or songs in the original format, as well as the freshly converted tracks are now in your library.

Joining Tracks

If you want a seamless chunk of music without the typical two-second gap of silence between CD tracks, you can use the Join Tracks feature to stitch together a sonic sampler in one big file. This feature is great for live albums or other CDs that run one song into the next.

To rip multiple songs as one track, pop in the CD you want to use, download the song information, make sure the list is sorted by track number, and then Shift-click to select the tracks you want to join during the ripping process. You can only join tracks that are in sequential order on the CD.

Once you've got the tracks selected, go to Advanced→Join CD Tracks. iTunes displays a bracket around the selected tracks, and indents the names of the tacked-on ones. If you change your mind and want to separate one of the tracks from the group, select it and go to Advanced→Unjoin CD Tracks. (You can Shift-click to peel off multiple tracks from the group, too.)

Click the Import button to rip the selected songs to one big track.

Tip: Suppose you're trying to join up some tracks, but iTunes is having none of it—it's dimming the Join Tracks command in the menu. The solution: Make sure that the tracks on the CD are sorted according to ascending Track Number. (If not, click the top of the very first column on the left of the iTunes window. The top of the column should be colored blue and the triangle pointing upward.) Then try Join Tracks again.

Start and Stop Times for Songs

Most of the time, there's musical interest in every juicy moment of the songs that you download, buy, or rip from CDs. Every now and then, though, some self-indulgent musician releases a song with a bunch of onstage chitchat before the music starts. Or maybe you've got a live album with endless jamming at the end, as a song plays out.

Fortunately, you don't have to sit there and listen to the filler each time you play the file. You can adjust the start and stop times of a song, so that you'll hear only the juicy middle part.

As you play the song you want to adjust, observe the iTunes status display window; watch for the point in the timeline where you get bored (Figure 3-6, top). Say, for example, that the last two minutes of that live concert jam is just the musicians riffing around and goofing off. Note where *you* want the song to end.

Then select the track you want to adjust. Choose File→Get Info to call up the information box for the song, and proceed as shown in Figure 3-6 at bottom.

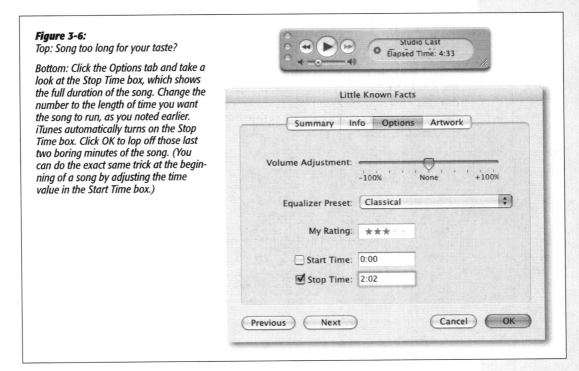

Figure 3-6:
Top: Song too long for your taste?

Bottom: Click the Options tab and take a look at the Stop Time box, which shows the full duration of the song. Change the number to the length of time you want the song to run, as you noted earlier. iTunes automatically turns on the Stop Time box. Click OK to lop off those last two boring minutes of the song. (You can do the exact same trick at the beginning of a song by adjusting the time value in the Start Time box.)

The shortened version plays in iTunes and on the iPod, but the additional recorded material isn't really lost. If you ever change your mind, you can go back to the song's Options box, turn off the Stop Time box, and return the song to its full length.

Playlists

A *playlist* is a list of songs that you've decided should go together. It can be made up of pretty much any group of songs arranged in any order. For example, if you're having a party, you can make a playlist from the current Top 40 and dance music in your music library. If you're in a 1960s Brit Girl Pop mood, you can make a playlist that alternates the hits of Dusty Springfield, Lulu, and Petula Clark. Some people may question your taste if you, say, alternate tracks from *La Bohème* with Queen's *A Night at the Opera*, but hey—it's *your* playlist.

Making a New Playlist

To create a playlist, press ⌘-N, or, if you're being paid by the hour, choose File→New Playlist or click the + button below the Source area of the iTunes window.

All freshly minted playlists start out with the impersonal name Untitled Playlist. Fortunately, its renaming rectangle is open and highlighted; just type a better name. As you add them, your playlists alphabetize themselves in the Source window.

Once you've created and named this spanking new playlist, you're ready to add your songs. You can do this in two different ways.

If this is your first playlist, opening the playlist into its own window might make it easier for you to see what's going on. To do so, double-click the new playlist's icon in the Source list, which opens a window next to your main iTunes window. From here, drag the song titles you want over to the new playlist window. Figure 3-7 demonstrates the process. (You can also open the iTunes Music Store into its own window with the double-click trick.)

Figure 3-7:
Making a playlist is as easy as dragging song titles from your library window to your new playlist window. The other way to add songs to a playlist is to drag them over from the Songs window and just drop them on the new playlist's icon in the Source list. (If you have a lot of playlists, though, you risk accidentally dropping songs on the wrong icon.)

Don't worry about clogging up your hard drive. When you drag a song title onto a playlist, you don't *copy* the song; you're just giving iTunes instructions about where to find the files. In essence, you're creating an *alias* or *shortcut* of the original. You can have the same song on several different playlists.

Note: Anytime you see an exclamation mark next to a title in the iTunes song list, iTunes is alerting you that it can no longer find that song in its library. The song may have been moved or deleted by accident.

If you think you know where you moved it, double-click the song title and navigate to where you think the song is living. Once you find it, select the song file and click Choose.

Modifying a Playlist

If you change your mind about the order of the tunes you've selected for a playlist, just drag the song titles up or down within the playlist window to reorder them.

You can also drag more songs into a playlist, or delete the titles from the list if you find your playlist needs pruning. (Click the song in the playlist window and hit Delete or Backspace to get rid of it. When iTunes asks you to confirm your decision, click Yes.) Remember, deleting a song from a playlist doesn't delete it from your music library—it just removes the title from your *playlist*. (Only pressing Delete when the *Library* icon is selected gets rid of the song for good.)

Tip: If you want to mix up the songs on a playlist but don't feel like thinking about it, iTunes can do it for you. Click the Shuffle button at the bottom of the iTunes window. You'll hear your playlist songs in a random order.

Deleting a Playlist

The party's over and you want to delete that playlist to make room for a playlist for next week's bash. To delete a playlist, click it in the Source list and press Delete. (Again, this just zaps the playlist itself, not all the stored songs you had in it. Those are still in your iTunes Music folder.)

Tip: Want to change the name of your iPod? Once you've connected the iPod to the computer, click the iPod's name to select it and then click again to highlight the text. Type whatever name you'd like to call your iPod, and then click somewhere else. If you're using your iPod as a FireWire disk, you can also click it on the desktop and type a new name for it, just as you can with any file or folder.

Smart Playlists

Just as you can have iTunes vary your song order for you, you can also have the program compose playlists all by itself. Once you give it some guidelines, a *Smart Playlist* can go shopping through your music library and come up with its own mix for you. The Smart Playlist even keeps tabs on the music that comes and goes from your library and adjusts itself on the fly.

You might tell one Smart Playlist to assemble 45 minutes' worth of songs that you've rated higher than four stars but rarely listen to, and another to play your most-often-played songs from the Eighties. Later, you can listen to these playlists with a turn of the iPod's control dial, uninterrupted and commercial-free.

To start a Smart Playlist in iTunes, press Option-⌘-N or choose File→New Smart Playlist. A Smart Playlist box opens: It has a purple gear-shaped icon next to the name in the Source list, while a regular playlist has a blue icon with a music note icon in it.

Tip: When you press Option, the + button for Add New Playlist at the bottom of the iTunes window turns into a gear icon. Click the gear button to get a new Smart Playlist to appear in the Source list, all ready for you to set up.

Now you can give the program detailed instructions about what you want to hear. You can select the artists you want to hear and have iTunes leave off the ones you're not in the mood for, pluck songs that only fall within a certain genre or year, and so on. You can make a Smart Playlist using information from any field in the song's tag, like a collection of every tune in your library that's track 17 on an album.

Click the little + sign at the end of each line to keep adding criteria, or click the – sign to remove one. See Figure 3-8 for an example.

Figure 3-8:
This Smart Playlist seeks out all Bob Dylan songs in your collection, either written or performed by Bob, on albums released before 1980, but not including any songs from the Dylan At Budokan album. This playlist would even include versions of his songs performed with other musicians, too.

Then, provided the "Live updating" checkbox is turned on, iTunes will always keep this playlist updated as your collection changes, as you change your ratings, as your Play Count changes, and so on.

A Smart Playlist is a dialogue between you and iTunes: You tell it what you want in as much detail as you want, and the program responds back with what it thinks you want to hear. Once you lay out the boundaries, iTunes pores through the current contents of your music library and generates the playlist.

Tip: If you find Smart Playlists are becoming an obsession, take a browser ride over to *www.smartplaylists. com*. There, you will find many like-minded individuals exchanging tips, tricks, and tales about Smart Playlists, iTunes, and what they'd like Apple to add to the *next* version of the program.

The iTunes Music Store

The recent explosion in Internet song swapping presented the recording industry with a paradoxical challenge: to stop music lovers from freely trading files over the Internet, while trying to make money themselves by selling copy-protected music online. The early attempts, backed by the major record companies, featured a monthly fee, a puny song catalog, and no ability to burn the bought music to CDs or save it onto music players. What a deal!

Needless to say, people stayed away in droves. The free (and free-form) world of KaZaA, LimeWire, and similar file-trading services were much more attractive.

Then Apple took a whack at it. In April 2003, the iTunes Music Store debuted, an online component of iTunes that scored the hat trick that other companies had yet to achieve: digital audio downloads that were easy, cheap, and—drum roll, please—legal. Here's a look inside the store, and how to shop it.

Welcome to the Music Store

The iTunes Music Store has the backing (and the song catalogs) of five big music companies, plus an increasing number of independent ones. Its inventory contains over a million songs from major-label artists like Bob Dylan, U2, Missy Elliott, Jewel, Sting, and hundreds of other musicians in a range of popular styles like Rock, Pop, R & B, Jazz, Folk, Rap, Latin, Classical, and more—and the collection grows by thousands of songs a week. You can also browse, sample, or buy any of 5,000 audiobooks from Audible.com.

Tip: To see what songs have been added recently, click the Just Added link at the left side of the main Music Store page.

Farther down the page, you can also see and hear what famous people are listening to in the store's Celebrity Playlist section. It never hurts to know what Wynton Marsalis and Kevin Bacon are listening to these days.

You can browse the virtual CD racks from the comfort of your own computer, listen to the first 30 seconds free from any track in the store, and download desired songs for 99 cents each with a click of the mouse. There are no monthly fees. And your digitally protected downloads don't go *poof!* into the ether if you decide to cancel your subscription, as they do with certain rival services. All your downloaded songs go right into iTunes, where they are just a sync away from your iPod's traveling music collection.

You can play the downloaded songs on up to five different iTunes 4–equipped Macs or PCs (in any combination), burn them onto an unlimited number of CDs, and download them to as many iPods as you like. Thousands of people use the Music Store every day, in fact, without even realizing that the songs are copy protected.

Apple's success with the iTunes Music Store—over 100 million downloads by mid-2004—caught its rivals' attention. These days, Apple's imitators in the dollar-a-song biz include Napster 2.0, MusicMatch, Sony, and even Wal-Mart. (Remember, though, that music from these services come in Microsoft's Windows Media Audio format, which won't work on the iPod. Except Sony's music service, which uses its own proprietary file format—but that doesn't play on the iPod, either.)

Figure 4-1:
The Browse button and Search box in the iTunes window perform their song-locating duties on the Store's inventory. Each listing in the Choose Genre pop-up menu has its own set of pages.

Below it, you can see a lot of the latest Music Store bells and whistles: movie trailers, radio charts, etc.

In the summer of 2004, Real Networks announced that the songs on its own Rhapsody music-download service were now iPod-playable, meaning that the company somehow reverse-engineered Apple's song file format. Apple wasted no time in announcing that (a) it was furious, and (b) it would simply change the iPod's software so that songs from non-Apple music stores would once again stop working.

A Store Tour

With iTunes running, click the Music Store icon in the iTunes Source list on the left pane of the program's window (Figure 4-1). If you use a dial-up modem, fire it up as you would to check email or surf the Web. If you have a cable modem or DSL, a message about connecting to the store appears in the status display at the top of the iTunes window.

Note: As you can imagine, the whole Music Store business works *much* better over high-speed Internet connections.

Setting Up an Account

After you click the Music Store icon in the iTunes Source list and connect to the store, you land on the home page, which works like a Web page.

If you're in the mood to buy, you might as well take care of setting up your Apple Account now. To do so, click the Account: Sign In button on the right side of the iTunes window. A Sign In box appears.

If you've ever bought or registered a product on Apple's Web site, signed up for the AppleCare tech-support plan, have a .Mac membership, ordered an iPhoto photo book, or used another Apple service, you probably have an Apple ID already. All you have to do is remember your user name (usually your email address) and password.

FREQUENTLY ASKED QUESTION

Changing the Information in Your Apple Account

I moved and need to change my billing address for the iTunes Music Store. How do I do that?

You can change your billing address, switch the credit card you have on file for your music purchases, or edit other information in your Apple Account without calling Apple. Just start up iTunes, click the Music Store icon on the Source list, and sign in to your account by clicking the Sign In button.

Once you've signed in, you'll see your account name (email address) next to the Account button. Click it. In the box that pops up, type in your password again and click View Account, then click the Edit Credit Card button. You're ready

to change your billing address or credit-card information. In the main account area, you can also set up an allowance or buy iTunes Music Store gift certificates.

If you want to change your user name, password, or secret identity-proving question, click the Edit Account Info button. (Click Done when you're done.)

Note, by the way, that any changes you make to your Apple Account through iTunes affect other programs or services you might also use with your account, like ordering picture prints with iPhoto.

If you've never had an Apple ID, click Create Account. The iTunes Music Store Welcome screen lists the three steps you need to follow to set up your Apple account:

1. **Agree to the terms for using the store and buying music.**

2. **Create an Apple Account.**

3. **Supply a credit card number and billing address.**

As your first step to creating an Apple Account, you must agree to the long scrolling legal agreement on the first screen. The 23-part statement informs you of your rights and responsibilities as an iTunes Music Store customer. (It boils down to this: *Thou shalt not download an album, burn it to CD, and then sell bootleg copies of it down at your local convenience store.*)

Click the Agree button to move on to Step 2. On the next screen, you're asked to create a user name, password, and secret question and answer. If you later have to email Apple because you've forgotten your password—hey, it could happen—this is the question you'll have to answer to prove that you're you. Apple also requests that you type in your birthday to help verify your identity.

On the third and final screen, provide a valid credit card number with a billing address. After you click Done, a screen congratulates you on your account-setup prowess.

Click Done. From now on, you can log into the Music Store by clicking the Account Sign In button in the upper-right corner of the iTunes window.

Figure 4-2:
If you connect with a dial-up modem, you may want to turn on "Buy using a Shopping Cart," so that you won't have to wait for each song to download before proceeding with your next purchase. You might want to turn on "Load complete preview before playing," which prevents gaps and stops in listening to the sound clips because of slow connection speeds or network traffic. Click OK when you're done.

The Shopping Cart

Thanks to Apple's 1-Click option, iTunes can instantly download a selected track as soon as you click the Buy Song button. That's a quick and painless experience for people with high-speed Internet connections.

If you have a dial-up modem, though, you may not want to sit there and wait for each song to download. Each song may take several minutes, which can severely impede your shopping rhythm.

To solve this problem, iTunes offers a Shopping Cart option. When you use it, all the songs you buy pile up until the end of the session; then iTunes downloads them all at once when you click the Shopping Cart icon in your iTunes Source list (and then click Buy Now). This way, you can go off and do something productive (or unproductive) while the stack of tracks takes its time squeezing through the dial-up connection.

If this idea appeals to you, choose iTunes→Preferences. In the Preferences dialog box, click the Store icon, and proceed as shown in Figure 4-2.

Searching and Shopping

You don't have to log in to browse the store—only when you want to buy music or audiobooks. And music is everywhere you turn in the iTunes Music Store. Click any album cover or text link to zoom right to it. The upper left corner area of the Music Store home page offers a pop-up menu to jump straight to the Genres you want.

You can also use the Power Search tool, shown at top in Figure 4-3, to zero in on a specific song, artist, album, genre, or composer—or just peruse the text-based lists, as shown in Figure 4-3 at bottom.

When you find a performer you're interested in, click the name to see a list of songs or albums on hand for purchase. If you click an album name, all of the songs available from it appear below in the Details window. Double-click a track to hear a 30-second snippet of it to see how it suits you, or to make sure that's really the song you were thinking of, before buying it.

You navigate the iTunes Music Store aisles just like a Web browser. Most song and artist names are hyperlinked—that is, you can click their names, or album cover images, to see what tracks are included.

Click the Back button in the Store window to go back to the page you were just on, or click the button with the small house on it to return to the Music Store home page.

Tip: When browsing the store, you may see a small, gray, circular icon bearing a white arrow in some columns of the Details window. That's the "More Info this way!" button. Click it to jump to a page bearing details about the subject, like a discography page next to a singer's name in the Artist column, or to the main page of artists for the genre listed.

The main iTunes Music Store page also displays links to new releases, exclusive songs that can be purchased only from the Music Store, Apple staff favorites, songs scheduled to become available in the near future, sneak peeks at unreleased tunes, and the Billboard Top 100 charts going back to 1946.

Figure 4-3:
Top: Click the Power Search link on the Music Store's home page to do some serious sleuthing for specific songs.

Bottom: One click leads to another when browsing the iTunes Music Store. Click Browse, then pick a Genre and then click an Artist on the next list to see the albums available by that musician or group. Once you have settled on a genre, the store unfurls a list of all the artists in that category.

Adjusting the Columns

Just as you can modify the look and information displayed for your own music library in iTunes, you can customize your columns in the iTunes Music Store. See Figure 4-4 for an example of how to modify which columns of detail information to display.

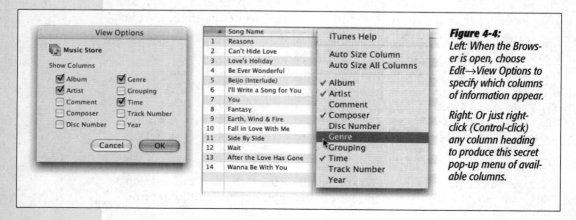

Figure 4-4:
Left: When the Browser is open, choose Edit→View Options to specify which columns of information appear.

Right: Or just right-click (Control-click) any column heading to produce this secret pop-up menu of available columns.

Remember, too, that you can drag column headings (like Time, Artist, or Price) horizontally to rearrange them, or drag the divider lines between them to adjust the column widths.

Buying a Song or Album

Making a purchase is as easy as clicking the Buy Song button next to a song (Figure 4-5).

Figure 4-5:
When you download an album, or even just one song from an album, you get music files in the AAC format. A color picture of the album cover is attached to the song file, which you can display in the artwork pane of the iTunes program window when you're playing that song.

The songs for sale in the iTunes Music Store cost 99 cents each. Most albums cost $10 to $14, which is quite a bit cheaper than the $17 or so you'd pay to buy the same album on CD. Plus, you don't have to worry about finding a parking space at the mall.

Tip: Many musicians in the Featured Artists area also have a free video that you can watch right in iTunes. Depending on your connection speed, it may take a few minutes for the video to download. Unfortunately, iTunes stops playing other songs, so that it can concentrate on snagging the clip. You're forced to download in silence.

The solution: Double-click it in the Source list to open it in a separate window. Now the iTunes tunes can keep spinning away in the background, giving you something to listen to as the video download proceeds.

Once you click that Buy Song button, the iTunes Music Store comes to your service. Now you see an "Are you sure?" alert box. Click the glowing Buy button to confirm your purchase decision, or Cancel if you suddenly remember that your credit card is a bit close to the edge this month. (You can also turn on "Don't warn me about buying songs" if you feel that there's quite enough nagging in your life already.)

Tip: Don't see a song or album in the iTunes Music Store that you really want to buy? Click the Requests & Feedback link on the Music Store's home page and send your plea to Apple. There's no guarantee they'll add it, but it can't hurt to make your wishes known.

Publishing Your Own Playlists (iMixes)

An *iMix* is a playlist that you publish on the Music Store, so everyone on earth can see your masterwork. You can name it, write your own liner notes explaining your mixing inspiration, and put it out there for everyone to see (Figure 4-6).

Figure 4-6:
Here's a typical iMix in the iTunes Music Store, posted by someone who listens to the same songs over and over again. If you like someone's mixing skills, you can give the collection a 5-star rating, tell your friends about it, or even buy all the songs on the list.

Start by signing into your Music Store account. Then, in the iTunes Source list, select the playlist you want to publish. (If it contains any songs that Apple doesn't sell, they'll get knocked off the list—which may ruin your carefully constructed mix.)

When you click the playlist, a gray arrow appears next to its title. Click the arrow to begin the publishing process (or choose File→Publish Playlist to Music Store). In the warning box, click Publish (and turn on "Do not show this message again" if you're sick of naggy little alerts in your face).

On the next screen, name your iMix and add your thoughts on making it.

Finally, in the iMix window, click Publish. Now other people can see your playlist, rate it, be inspired by it, or—and let's face it, here's the main thing—buy the songs for themselves.

To tell all your pals about your brand new iMix, click the Tell a Friend button on your new iMix page. iTunes sends a virtual birth announcement by email, complete with album-cover art.

Tip: Want to e-mail a friend a direct link to your brand new iMix, or anybody else's? Control-click the playlist's icon on the iMix page and, from the shortcut menu, choose "Copy iTunes Music Store URL." Next, create a new message in your e-mail program and paste in the link you just copied.

GEM IN THE ROUGH

Charting History

Quick! What was the Number One song during your senior year in high school? What tunes were topping the music charts during your college years? If you've ever paid attention to any sort of a Top Ten list, odds are you were looking at a Billboard chart.

Billboard, something of an industry bible among music professionals, is a weekly magazine that's been tabulating and reporting lists of the popular songs and albums for over 50 years. These days, the company now uses high-tech methods to chart

the hits in several music categories. SoundScan, for example, is a computerized system that tracks retail music sales. The tabulators also keep a close ear on what songs are spilling out of radio stations around the country. All these numbers get crunched together into a formula that's part of the Billboard chart recipe.

In addition to all the other ways to find and buy your favorite

songs, the iTunes Music Store lets you riffle through the Billboard top 100 charts going all the way back to 1946. (Missing entries in the song list—like the top three songs for 1968—reflect songs that iTunes doesn't have for sale, usually because the record companies or the bands haven't given permission for online sale yet.)

To see the charts, click the Charts link at the left side of the main page. Glancing at an old Billboard chart can serve as a sonic snapshot of a particular musical era: You see the songs listed, and you're instantly transformed back to the time when you heard them first (if, that is, you were even *alive* then).

Check out charts from the early Sixties, and you learn just how hip the girl-group sound was. Go back a few years further, and you discover the hip-shaking Reign of Elvis. Jump forward several decades, and you see hip hop transforming the cultural airwaves.

Apple will send you an e-mail message congratulating you on your successful iMixing along with a link for your iMix. The Store keeps iMixes on its site for a year.

Gift Certificates

Gift certificates make perfect presents for People Who Have Everything, especially when purchased by People Who Are Lousy Shoppers. These redeemable email coupons are also an excellent way to save face in potentially unpleasant situations (*"Honey, you may think I forgot our anniversary again, but…check your email!"*).

With iTunes Music Store gift certificates, available both from the iTunes store or from Apple's Web site, you can send your friends and family $10 to $200 worth of credit to go hog-wild in Apple's music emporium.

To buy one, click Gift Certificates on the main page of the iTunes Music Store. After you choose delivery by either email or U.S. Mail, the process is like buying anything on the Web: You fill in your address, gift amount, personalized message, and so on.

If you already have an Apple ID, you can log in and request to have your credit card billed; if not, sign up for one. Once you complete all the pixel paperwork, your gift certificate will be on its way.

Tip: Before sending off a gift certificate, discreetly check whether your recipient's computer meets the iTunes 4 requirements. People on Windows 98, Windows Me, and older operating systems may be in for an even bigger pang of disappointment than if you gave them a box of cheap tube socks.

Spending

Whether they come in the mailbox by the front door or the one on the computer, iTunes Music Store gift certificates are meant to be spent. Here's how they work:

Figure 4-7:
Receiving and redeeming an iTunes Music Store gift certificate is as easy as opening your email and clicking Redeem Now to add the gift credits to your account. You can also send paper gift certificates through the U.S. mail.

- If you're lucky enough to be the recipient of an iTunes email gift certificate (Figure 4-7), redemption is just a click away. The Redeem Now button at the bottom of the message takes you straight to the Music Store, where the certificate's confirmation number pops up automatically. Click Redeem in the Music Store window to credit your account and start shopping.

- If the gift arrived by postal mail, start up iTunes and click Music Store in the Source list. On the main Music Store page, click the link for Gift Certificates. On the next screen, click Redeem Now. Type in the confirmation number printed on the lower edge of the gift certificate and click Redeem.

If you already have an iTunes Music Store account, log in and start shopping. If you've never set your mouse pointer inside the store before, you'll need to create an Apple Account. You have to provide your name and address, but you don't have to surrender a credit card number. If you choose None, you can use your gift certificate as the sole payment method—and end your shopping experience once you've burned through it.

iTunes Allowance Accounts

Allowance accounts are a lot like iTunes store gift certificates. You, the parent (or other financial authority), decide how many dollars' worth of music or audiobooks you want to give to a family member or friend (from $10 to $200, in increments of $10). Unlike gift certificates, however, allowance accounts automatically replenish themselves on the first day of each month—an excellent way to keep your music-loving kids out of your wallet while teaching the little nippers how to budget their money throughout the month.

Both you and the recipient need to have Apple IDs. To set up a monthly allowance, click the Allowance link on the main page of the iTunes Music Store and fill out the form on the next screen. After you select the amount of credit you want to deposit each month, fill in your recipient's Apple ID and password. (There's also an option to create a new account for the monthly allowance.)

Once the giftee logs into the designated Apple Account, the spending can begin—no credit card required. Once the allowance amount has been spent, that's it for music until the following month. (Of course, if the recipient *does* have a credit card on file, he can always put the difference on the card.) If you need to cancel an allowance account, go to your Account Info page (page 70) to take care of the matter.

Tip: Can't remember how much money you have left on your gift certificate or in your allowance account? Look at your iTunes window the next time you're logged into the store. Your balance appears right next to your account name.

The Interrupted Download

If your computer crashes or you get knocked offline while you're downloading your song purchases, iTunes is designed to pick up where it left off after you restart the program and reconnect to the Internet. If for some reason it doesn't go back to downloading, choose Advanced→Check for Purchased Music to log back into the Music Store to resume your downloading business.

Signing Out

If other people have access to your computer when you're not around, consider wrapping up your shopping session by clicking your name (next to the Account button on the Music Store window) and then Sign Out. Unless you're one of those exceedingly benevolent types, you probably don't want anyone else to come along and charge up your credit card with a music-buying marathon.

Locating Your New Tracks

You can find your new tracks by clicking Purchased Music in the iTunes Source list (Figure 4-8). As the dialog box says, you can work with the Purchased Music playlist as though it were any other playlist. That is, even if you delete a track from it, the song itself still remains in the iTunes music library. And behind the scenes, the corresponding music file stays in your Home→Music→iTunes→iTunes Music folder.

Figure 4-8:
When you click the Purchased Music playlist after buying music, iTunes offers an explanation of how the playlist works (top) and fills out your list with the newly bought songs (bottom). From here, you can play the songs, drag them into other playlists, transfer them to your iPod, or burn them to a CD to play on the stereo.

What to Do with Music You've Bought

As you know, the iTunes Music store gives you a lot more freedom to use your downloaded songs than other music services. There are a *few* restrictions, though.

Play It on Five Computers

You can play Music Store–bought songs only on an *authorized* computer. Authorization is Apple's copy protection scheme.

Between work, home, and the family network, not everyone spends time on just one computer these days. So Apple lets you play your Music Store songs on up to five computers at once: Macs, PCs, or any combination. You just need to type in your Apple user name and password on each computer. Each must make an Internet connection to relay the information back to Music Store headquarters.

Authorizing Computers

You authorized your first machine when you signed up for an Apple Account for the iTunes store.

To authorize a song to play on another computer, follow these steps:

1. **Find the song you want to transfer.**

   This step, of course, involves *finding* the song on your hard drive.

   Method 1: Open your Home→Music→iTunes→iTunes Music folder. Music Store files are easily recognizable by their .m4p file name extensions.

   Method 2: Just drag the song you want out of the iTunes window and onto your desktop.

2. **Copy the song to the second computer.**

   Copy the song file onto a CD or USB flash drive; email it to yourself; transfer it across the network; or whatever method you prefer for schlepping files from machine to machine.

   Deposit the songs in the Home→Music→iTunes→iTunes Music folder on the Computer #2.

3. **Bring the copied song into iTunes on the second computer.**

   To do that, you can either choose File→Add to Library (and then select and open them), or just drag their icons right into the iTunes window.

4. **In your iTunes list, select a transferred song and click the Play button.**

   iTunes asks for your Apple Account user name and password.

5. **Type your Apple ID and password, and click OK.**

This second computer is now authorized to play that song—and any other songs you bought using the same Apple Account.

Note: Although you may feel like AAC stands for Always Authorizing Computers, remember that this whole authorizing business is necessary only to play songs you've *bought.* To play songs you've ripped into AAC format from CDs, for example, or to play everyday MP3 files, you don't have to authorize anything.

Deauthorizing Computers

You won't be able to play the purchased music on a sixth computer if you try to authorize it. When you connect to the authorization system over the Internet, it will see five other computers already on its list, and deny your request.

That's a drag, but copy protection is copy protection—and it's much better than rival music services, which permit you to play downloaded music only on *three* machines (just like iTunes did before 2004).

In any case, you have to deauthorize one of the other computers if you want to play the music on Number 6. To deauthorize a computer, choose Advance→Deauthorize Computer, and then type in your Apple Account user name and password. The updated information zips back to Apple over the Internet.

Tip: Thinking of putting that older computer up for sale? Before you wipe the drive clean and send it on its way, be sure to deauthorize it, so your new machine will be able to play your songs from the iTunes Music Store. Erasing a hard drive, by itself, does not deauthorize a computer.

Copy It to Your iPod

Not only can you download your purchased songs to your iPod, but you can download it to *unlimited numbers* of iPods. Apple placed no copy restrictions on iPod joy.

Tip: If your iPod is a pre-2003 model, you must first update its software to version 1.3 or later. Otherwise, the iPod won't recognize files in the AAC format.

When you buy a song, it lands in the iTunes playlist called Purchased Music. But you can easily drag it into other playlists you've concocted within iTunes. The songs, artists, and albums appear just like any other tracks in iTunes.

Burn It to a CD

You can also burn purchased tracks to blank CDs, so you can listen to them in the car or on the big component rack in the living room. Here, Apple has put in only one tiny, almost irrelevant form of copy protection: If you've made store-bought songs part of a certain playlist, you can't burn more than seven CD copies of it in a row without making at least one change to the song list.

And if you find *that* limitation restrictive, you must be so dedicated a music pirate that you wear an eye patch and a parrot on your shoulder.

Share it Across the Network

You can also share purchased music tracks with other people on your same office network—by playing them live, not by copying the actual files. Details on page 40.

Back It Up

If your hard drive croaks and takes your entire music library with it, you have two alternatives. (a) Buy all of your Music Store songs all over again. (b) Calmly reach for the backup CD or DVD you had the foresight to make before disaster struck.

Backing up your music library

To back up your entire music collection, you want to copy the *iTunes* folder in your Home→Music folder.

Backing up this folder, huge though it may be, backs up not just your songs, but all the other work you've done in iTunes (creating and naming your playlists, organizing your columns, and so on).

You can use any standard backup method for this:

- Copy the folder to another computer via network cable.

- Burn it onto a blank CD (if the folder fits) or a DVD (if you have a DVD-burning computer).

- Use a program like Dantz Retrospect to back it up onto Zip disks, multiple CDs, or whatever you've got.

When your hard drive croaks, restore your backed-up iTunes folder by dragging it back into your Music folder. You're saved.

Backing up playlists

iTunes 4 also has a built-in backup feature. Note, however, that it can back up only one playlist at a time. This backup procedure isn't the same thing as burning an *audio* CD. Here, you're burning a *data* disc. That's important if you want to preserve the original file formats in your iTunes music library and avoid turning your high-quality AIFF files, for example, into squished-down MP3 files. To make this important change to your Burning desires, see Figure 4-9.

Figure 4-9:
Choose iTunes→ Preferences, click Burning, and click the button for data CD or DVD. Selecting the Data format for your disc will copy your files in their original MP3, AAC, or Audible formats without converting them to standard audio CD files, which would happen if you created an audio CD.

After you've chosen the Data format for your backup disc, make a playlist that includes all the files you want to copy to the CD or DVD. Keep an eye on the total size at the bottom of the window to be sure it will fit on one disc: about 650 megabytes for a CD, 4.7 gigabytes for a DVD. (If not, you'll have to file your songs away into multiple playlists—one per backup disc—to spread out your collection over multiple discs.)

Burn it to disc by clicking the Burn Disc button on the iTunes window. Insert a blank disc when the machine asks for one, and then click the Burn Disc button again to start copying.

If your hard drive ever dies, copy this data disc's files back onto the computer and re-import them into iTunes to rebuild your library from the backup disc.

Backing up non-music data

If you've got a .Mac account (Apple's $100-a-year suite of online services), you can use the handy Backup program to save copies of your personal files to a remote Web site, recordable disc, or external hard drive—including your list of iTunes playlists.

Music Store Billing

The iTunes Music store keeps track of what you buy and when you buy it. If you think your credit card was wrongly charged for something, or if you suspect that one of the kids knows your password and is sneaking in some forbidden downloads before

---

GEM IN THE ROUGH

Back Up Only What Needs Backing Up

They say that backing up is hard to do—but mainly, it's hard to remember what you've already backed up and what still needs attention.

Here, however, is a sneaky trick that makes iTunes help you make backups of all the songs you've bought or ripped since the last time you backed up your iTunes Music folder. This means you won't have to burn the whole darn library to a stack of CDs or DVDs each time, and can just fill a disc with the new stuff you've added.

After you've backed up your music files to disc for the first or latest time, open iTunes and choose File→New Smart Playlist.

In the Smart Playlist set-up box, change the pop-up menus to say *Date Added—is after—[today's date]*. Make sure Live Updating is turned on, and that there's no limit set for the amount of songs on the playlist. When you click OK, give your new playlist a name, like Smart Backup.

The next time you're ready to burn a data backup disc, back up only your Smart Backup playlist to get the only latest library additions.

Then, once you've burned it to CD, choose File→Edit Smart Playlist change the Date Added to today's date, so that iTunes starts keeping track of the new stuff for your next backup.

you get home from work, you can contact the store or check your account's purchase history page to see what's been downloaded in your name.

The Customer Service Page

If you have general questions about using the iTunes Music Store, have a problem with your bill, or want to submit a specific query or comment, the online Customer Service center awaits. To get there, connect to the Internet and then choose Help→ Music Store Customer Service.

Click the link that best describes what you want to learn or complain about. For billing or credit-card issues, click Purchase Information.

Note: The iTunes Music Store sends out invoices by email, but they don't come right after you buy a song. You usually get an invoice that groups together all the songs you purchased within a 12-hour period, or for every $20 worth of tunes that you buy.

Your Purchase History

To have a look at just how addicted you've grown to buying songs, open iTunes, click the Music Store icon in the Source List, and sign into the store. When you see your user name appear next to the Account button in the iTunes Music Store window, click it. In the box that pops up, click the View Account button.

When you get to the Account Information screen, click Purchase History. In the list that comes up, you see all of the songs you've bought (Figure 4-10).

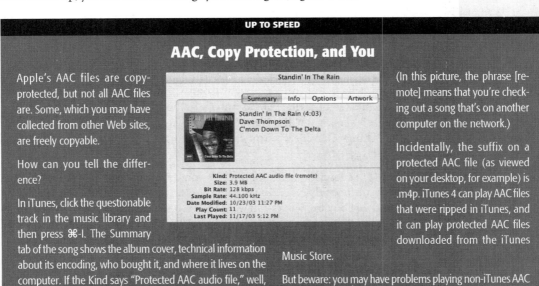

UP TO SPEED

AAC, Copy Protection, and You

Apple's AAC files are copy-protected, but not all AAC files are. Some, which you may have collected from other Web sites, are freely copyable.

How can you tell the difference?

In iTunes, click the questionable track in the music library and then press ⌘-I. The Summary tab of the song shows the album cover, technical information about its encoding, who bought it, and where it lives on the computer. If the Kind says "Protected AAC audio file," well, you've got your answer.

(In this picture, the phrase [remote] means that you're checking out a song that's on another computer on the network.)

Incidentally, the suffix on a protected AAC file (as viewed on your desktop, for example) is .m4p. iTunes 4 can play AAC files that were ripped in iTunes, and it can play protected AAC files downloaded from the iTunes Music Store.

But beware: you may have problems playing non-iTunes AAC tracks from another online music service or Web site.

If you see songs on the list that you didn't buy, and you're sure that other people who use your computer didn't buy them, contact Apple. Because the account is linked to a credit card, you'll want to take care of the situation right away.

Tip: Every wonder how something would play in Peoria? Now you can see for yourself *what's* playing in Peoria, thanks to the Radio Charts feature of the iTunes Music Store. Just click the Radio Charts link on the Store's main page to see what's at the top of the pops on 1,000 stations around the country.

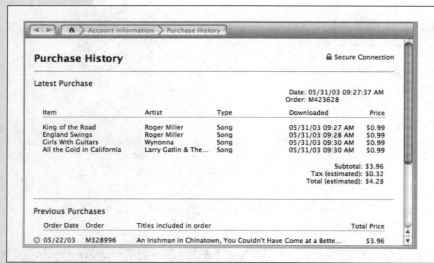

Figure 4-10:
The Purchase History area records all of the songs and albums downloaded and charged to an Apple Account, which can be useful for bracing yourself for the coming credit card bill. The list starts with the most recent ones.

"Books on Tape" from Audible

Audible.com, which you can shop right from within the iTunes Music Store, is a virtual store filled with digital "books on tape"—not just books, but also everything from vocalized versions of the New York Times to programs like National Public Radio's All Things Considered. You can hear free samples of most files on the site before you buy.

If you choose to subscribe, $15 a month gets you one recorded book a month, plus a daily, weekly, or monthly magazine or radio show. You can also skip the subscription business and just buy the books you want for a flat fee. Prices vary, but the audio file usually costs less than the hard copy and fits in your pocket better. "The Da Vinci Code," a popular mystery novel selling for $25 in book stores, was $20 on Audible.com.

Formats within formats

Audible.com files that come from its Web site (and not from the iTunes Music Store) use the .aa file name extension. You can't convert .aa files to MP3, but you can burn them to an audio CD to play on the stereo, and you can copy them to your iPod.

Most recordings from Audible.com come in a variety of sound resolutions, from low-fi, AM radio–like sound to a really good MP3 quality. The Audible resolutions that work on the iPod are called Formats 2, 3, and 4 (from worst to best quality). Better audio quality, of course, means a bigger file to download.

For example, the 18-hour audio book for Snow Crash is split into two files. The first half is a 34 MB download in Format 2, a 63 MB download in Format 3, or a 127 MB download in Format 4. The various formats cost the same, but unless you have a broadband connection, you'll probably want to stick with the smaller file size.

Tip: If you decide you don't like the way a format sounds, you can download your selection again in a different format by logging back into your account on the Audible.com page–a benefit you don't get at the iTunes Music Store.

To make sure that iTunes is set to handle Audible files, choose iTunes→Preferences, click the General icon, and next to "Use iTunes for Internet Music Playback," click the Set button. When you download a book file from Audible.com, it shows up right in iTunes.

Before you listen to it, iTunes asks you to type in the name and password you set up with Audible.com, as shown in Figure 4-11 at top. Thereafter, you can listen to it at your desk (Figure 4-11, bottom) or transfer it to your iPod like any other track.

Figure 4-11:
Top: You can play your purchased Audible file on up to three computers, burn it to a CD, or transfer it to an iPod. (Sound like a familiar set of rules, iTunes shoppers?)

Bottom: iTunes plays your audio book just like any other track in your library. Longer books are split into multiple parts for easier downloading from the Audible.com site.

You play them just like regular audio files; the iPod even remembers where in the audio book you stopped listening, so you can pick up where you left off the next time. Better yet, these little electronic bookmarks are synchronized between iTunes and the iPod; if you're listening to a chapter of a book on your iPod while walking home from work, you can connect the iPod to your Mac to transfer the bookmark. Then you can continue listening at your desk, in iTunes, without missing a sentence.

Tip: It's fun to wander around in the iTunes Music Store as your own music plays, but it's extremely easy to drift away from your playlist-in-progress. If you want to go directly back to the song that's currently playing, just click the curled arrow on the right side of the oval iTunes display window.

This handy icon is called the Snapback arrow, and it serves as a one-click shortcut to the File→Show Current Song menu dance (or the keyboard shortcut ⌘-L). It only works when there's a song actually playing, but you can use it in your own collection or when while traipsing around song previews in the Music Store.

The iPod Connection

I tunes is a lot of things to a lot of people. But for hundreds of thousands of people, iTunes is primarily the loading dock for an iPod. Once connected to the Mac, the iPod is ready to accept whatever you want to give it.

This chapter is dedicated to that concept of iPod as Satellite to Your Computer. All you need is the FireWire or USB 2.0 cable for the connection that gets songs and files off the mother ship and onto the ultraportable, ready-to-go iPod.

Your Very First Sync

Connecting the iPod is simple: Just plug its FireWire cable (or its dock) to the FireWire jack on your Mac. iTunes opens automatically and begins copying your entire music library to the player (see Figure 5-1). Or, if you have Mac OS X 10.3.4 or later and a recent iPod model (or iPod Mini), you can use a USB 2.0 cable instead.

Tip: If you *don't* want iTunes to appear automatically every time the iPod is connected, you can turn off this option in the iPod Preferences dialog box (Figure 5-2).

Variations on the Auto-Transfer Theme

The beauty of the iTunes/iPod system is that whatever music you add to your Mac gets added to the iPod automatically, effortlessly. You've always got your entire music collection with you. Just plugging in the iPod inspires iTunes to open up and sync.

It's conceivable, however, that you won't always want complete and automatic syncing to take place whenever you connect the 'Pod. Maybe you use the iPod primarily as an external hard drive, so you don't especially care to have iTunes jumping up like a West Highland terrier every time you plug in the iPod. Maybe you want to synchronize only *some* of your music, not all of it.

Fortunately, you're in complete control of the situation.

Figure 5-1:
The Source list (left side) displays an icon for the iPod whenever it's connected, as well as your music library, list of playlists, songs from the iTunes Music Store, and Internet radio stations. The bottom of the window shows the amount of space left on the iPod, the number of songs, and consecutive days the iPod can play music without repeating songs.

Stop Auto-Opening iTunes

If you like, you can command your jukebox software to open only when *you* want it to, rather than every time the iPod is plugged in.

When the iPod plugged in, click its icon in the Source list. Then click the iPod-shaped icon in the bottom right part of the iTunes window (identified in Figure 5-2). The

Figure 5-2:
Left: Click the circled button to call up the iPod Preferences dialog box. (The second button provides access to equalizer settings; the third controls screen displays. The last button dismounts the iPod from the computer.)

Right: In the iPod Preferences box, you can choose to have the iPod update everything automatically or just certain playlists. "Manually manage songs and playlists" lets you move just the songs you want to the iPod.

iPod's Preferences box appears, where you can turn off the "Open iTunes when at-tached" checkbox.

Transfer Only Some Songs

The auto-sync option pretty much removes any thought process required to move music to the iPod. But if you'd rather take control of the process, or you just want to transfer *some* songs or playlists, you can change the synchronization settings.

With the main iTunes window open, click the name of your iPod in the Source list on the left side of the window. Look at the bottom of the iPod window for the four small buttons along the right side (Figure 5-2). Click the first button, which has a small graphic of an iPod on it, to open the iPod Preferences dialog box.

Once the Options dialog box is open, click the third tab, labeled Synchronization.

The dialog box before you lets you control how the autosyncing of your music library goes:

Complete automatic synchronization

"Automatically update all songs and playlists" means that your computer's music collection and your iPod's will be kept identical, no matter what songs you add or remove from the computer.

If you have a PalmPilot or PocketPC, you may be thinking to yourself: "*Ah, sweet synchronization! I won't have to worry about losing any data, because everything is updated all the time no matter where I input them!*"

There is a difference, however: Unlike a palmtop, the iPod's synchronization with the computer is a one-way street. If a song isn't in iTunes, it won't be on your iPod. Delete a song from iTunes, and it disappears from the iPod the next time you sync up.

This, of course, is the iPod's system for preventing music piracy. If song copying were a two-way street, people could wander around with their iPods, collecting songs from any computers they came across, and then copy the whole mass back up to their home computers.

On the bright side, the autosync system means that you never worry about which songs are where. With the autosync option, what is in the computer's music library is on the iPod, and that's that.

Sync up selected playlists only

Choosing to only sync up only certain playlists can save you some time, because you avoid copying the entire music library each time. This tactic is helpful when, say, you have a workout playlist that you fuss with and freshen up each week. You can choose to update only that playlist instead of waiting around for the whole iPod to sync. (This feature is also handy if you're a multi-iPod household. Each iPodder can maintain a separate playlist.)

Once you turn on "Automatically update selected playlists only," you're shown a list of the playlists you've created. Turn on the ones you want synced.

Manually manage songs and playlists

There may be times when you don't want any automatic synchronization at all. Maybe, for example, you've deleted some audio files from your hard drive that you still want to keep on your iPod. If you leave automatic syncing turned on, iTunes will erase any songs from the iPod that it doesn't have itself.

Turning on "Manually manage songs and playlists" means that no music will be auto-copied to the iPod. You'll have to do all the copying yourself.

Note: When you turn on this option, iTunes says, "Disabling automatic update requires manually unmounting the iPod before each disconnect." It's telling you that from now on, when you're finished working with the iPod, you'll have to click the Eject button in the lower-right corner of the iTunes window. This action safely releases the iPod from the computer connection.

From now on, you'll have to drag songs onto the iPod manually (Figure 5-3). After you close the iPod Preferences box, click the small triangle next to your iPod in the Source list. It reveals all the songs and playlists on the iPod, which work just like any other iTunes playlists.

Figure 5-3:
You can add songs to the iPod playlists by dragging them out of your main iTunes Library list, delete them by clicking their names and then pressing the Delete key, click the New Playlist button (the + icon) to create a fresh playlist, drag playlists onto playlists to merge them, and so on.

To delete songs off the iPod, click its icon in your iTunes Source list. Then, in the main song-list window, click the songs you don't want anymore, and then press Delete. The songs will vanish, both from the iPod's list in iTunes and from the iPod itself.

Tip: The Only Update Checked Songs option in the iPod Preferences box (Figure 5-9) can be useful in this situation. It ensures that iTunes will update the iPod only with songs whose title checkmarks you've turned on. If you have songs that aren't part of your iTunes music library, make sure they're unchecked—and therefore unerased—during an automatic synchronization.

The Unspeakable Act: iPod to Mac Copying

The iPod was designed to be the destination of a one-way trip for your tunes: music slides down the cable *to* the iPod, but songs on the player never make the trip back to the Mac.

This design was perfectly intentional on the part of its creators. As noted earlier, Apple's position appears on a sticker on every iPod: "Don't steal music." If the iPod let you copy music both ways, people might be tempted to turn the device into a pocket music-sharing service, capable of copying free copyrighted songs from computer to computer.

The truth is, though, that not everyone who wants to upload songs from the iPod to a computer is stealing music. You may have perfectly legitimate reasons for wanting to be able to do so.

For example, say your computer's hard drive self-destructs, vaporizing the 945 MP3 files that you've made from your paid-for CD collection. You legally own those copies. Shouldn't you have the right to retrieve them from your own iPod?

Most people would answer "yes." Some might even thump their fists on the table for emphasis.

And then they would clear their throats and ask, "Well, how can I do it, should I ever need to copy files off my iPod?"

Note: Once again, the following methods are printed here not to encourage you to steal music, but instead to help you back up and manage the songs that you already own.

The Hidden World of the iPod

Turning the iPod into a FireWire hard drive lets you copy everyday computer files back and forth from your Mac. But when it comes to your *music* files, you won't even

---

TROUBLESHOOTING MOMENT

"Do Not Disconnect"

The universal symbol for NO!, pictured as a circle with a slash through it ($\emptyset$), is a common sight when the iPod is connected to the Macintosh. It appears whenever the two drives are busy exchanging music and data (and probably a little hard-disk humor on the side). If you're using the iPod as an external hard disk, or you've turned off the iPod's automatic synchronization feature, you'll see a lot of this Dr. $\emptyset$.

Breaking the connection while all this is going on can result in lost files and possibly a scrambled song. So if you need to unplug the iPod and get going for work, be sure to *unmount*

it properly (remove its icon from the screen) first.

To do that, click the Eject button in the iTunes window; by dragging the desktop icon of the iPod into the Mac's Trash; or by Control-clicking the iPod icon on your screen and choosing Eject from the contextual menu.

When you've ejected the iPod correctly, its screen flashes a large happy check mark (older iPods) or pulls up the standard main menu, ready for action (2003 and later models).

---

be able to *find* them. The iPod and its music management programs use a special database for storing and organizing the music files—and it's invisible.

The name of the super-secret invisible iPod music folder is called iPod_Control, and there are software utilities that can make it visible. (You can download them from the "Missing CD" page of *www.missingmanuals.com.*) For example:

iPod Viewer

For beginners, the nicely designed iPod Viewer program (Figure 5-4) makes the whole copying-to-the-Mac procedure very simple. iPod Viewer 2.0 is designed for Mac OS X 10.2 (Jaguar) and later.

Once you install iPod Viewer, open the program with your iPod attached to the Mac; click your Poddy little pal in the list. The program's preferences let you arrange your songs in the order you want. Then, when you click the Import From iPod button at the top of the iPod Viewer window (Figure 5-4), the program pulls in the list of everything on the iPod.

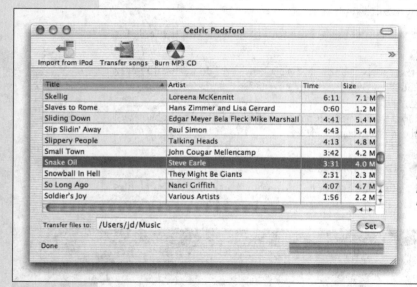

Figure 5-4:
The free iPod Viewer program lets you select all or just some of the songs you want to copy over to the Mac. The program also gives you the option of deciding what folder to put the imported songs into. Just click the Transfer Songs button at the top of the window to start copying. You can also make a CD of the imported files by clicking the Burn MP3 CD button.

OmniWeb

Yes, OmniWeb is a Web browser. But in addition to surfing the Net with it, you can also surf the hidden contents of your iPod and copy songs back to your computer. The OmniWeb browser sells for $30, but you can download a trial copy from the "Missing CD" page at *www.missingmanuals.com.* (Although paying for a Web browser may seem like a bizarre idea, OmniWeb has some wonderful features like spell-checking, ad-blocking, and automatic bookmark-updating.)

To use OmniWeb to browse the iPod, drag the iPod icon off your desktop and into the browser window.

A list of all the files on the iPod appears, including the elusive iPod_Control folder. Double-click iPod_Control, and then the folder within it titled Music, shown in Figure 5-5. You see a list of folders, all starting with F. Within these folders lie your songs. Double-click the songs you want to copy to the Mac; OmniWeb does the rest.

Figure 5-5:
After you drag the desktop iPod icon onto the OmniWeb browser window, the program clearly displays the secret iPod_Control folder. Inside iPod_Control is the Music folder and the iPod's secret stash of songs.

Name	Size	Last Change
.DS_Store	6.0 kB	May 29, 2003 10:53 PM
Device	folder	Dec 27, 2003 03:03 PM
iPodPrefs	38 bytes	Dec 29, 2003 03:29 PM
iTunes	folder	Dec 29, 2003 03:29 PM
Music	folder	Dec 23, 2003 12:54 PM

iPod.iTunes

Built for speed, iPod.iTunes keeps the Mac and iPod constantly in sync with each other, and only copies songs *not* found in the iTunes library. In case of a disastrous hard drive crash on the Mac side, iPod.iTunes can fully restore music files and playlists in the iPod, and can even fix those accidents where you mistakenly delete music from iTunes.

The program also makes it possible to *clone* an iPod, making an exact duplicate of its contents, and can synchronize music and playlists together or separately. Once installed, iPod.iTunes walks you through its synchronization procedure in great detail.

TinkerTool

You know how in those Invisible Man movies, people could only see him if he had a hat or a coat or a mask on, or spilled something on his invisible self? It was all about revealing the hidden aspects.

You can do the same thing with your invisible iPod files with the aid of some helpful freeware by way of Germany. TinkerTool, available on the "Missing CD" page at *www.missingmanuals.com,* is a system utility for Mac OS X that can make hidden files visible.

Once you have installed TinkerTool on your Mac, you'll see an icon for it in System Preferences. Click TinkerTool; in the box that pops up, turn on "Show hidden and system files," and then click the Relaunch Finder button. Figure 5-6 shows the way.

When the Finder restarts, you see all the formerly secret invisible system files right there on your screen, as though someone had spilled paint on the Invisible Man. You see a lot of .DS_Stores all over the place, but step over them and connect your iPod to the Mac.

Double-click the iPod's icon to see all the files that live on it, including the iPod_Control folder that holds all of your music files (Figure 5-6, bottom). You can click through the folders from iPod_Control→Music→F00 (all the iPod's music folders are named F-something) and drag the files you wish to copy to your Mac's own hard drive.

Figure 5-6:
Top: Turn on the box in the Finder options to show hidden and system files in the Tinker-Tool Finder preferences box, and you'll see a lot more on your iPod after you relaunch the Finder.

Bottom: With the hidden files out in the open courtesy of TinkerTool, you can browse the iPod's contents like any other hard drive.

Part Two: iPhoto

2

Camera Meets Mac

In case you haven't heard, the digital camera market is exploding. In 2004, sales of digital cameras—*24 million* of them—finally overtook the sale of film cameras. It's taken a few decades; the underlying technology used in most digital cameras was invented in 1969. But film is finally on the decline.

And why not? The appeal of digital photography is huge. When you shoot digitally, you never have to pay a cent for film or photo processing. You get instant results, viewing your photos just moments after shooting them. As a digital photographer, you can even be your own darkroom technician—without the darkroom. You can retouch and enhance photos, make enlargements, and print out greeting cards using your home computer. Sharing your pictures with others is far easier, too, since you can burn them to CD, email them to friends, or post them on the Web. As one fan puts it: "There are no 'negatives' in digital photography."

On the other hand, while digital photography is full of promise, it's also been full of headaches. During the early years of digital cameras, just making the camera-to-computer connection was a nightmare. You had to mess with serial or USB cables; install device drivers; and use proprietary software to transfer, open, and convert camera images into a standard file format. If you handled all these tasks perfectly—and sacrificed a young male goat during the spring equinox—you ended up with good digital pictures.

iPhoto Arrives

Apple's answer to all these problems is iPhoto, a simple and uncluttered program designed to organize, edit, and distribute digital photos without the nightmarish hassles. Like Apple's other iPrograms (iMovie, iTunes, iDVD, and so on), its design subscribes to its own little 80/20 rule: 80 percent of us really don't need more than about 20 percent of the features you'd find in a full-blown, $650 digital-asset management program.

iPhoto approaches digital photo management as a four-step process, with each step corresponding to one of the following major areas of the program:

- **Import.** Working with iPhoto begins with feeding your digital pictures into the program. This is the part of iPhoto covered in this chapter.

- **Organize.** This step is about sorting and categorizing your chaotic jumble of pictures so that you can easily find them and arrange them into logical groups. Chapter 7 covers all of iPhoto's organization tools.

- **Edit.** iPhoto provides the basic tools you need for rotating, retouching, resizing, cropping, or brightening your pictures. Editing is the focus of Chapter 8.

- **Book.** iPhoto comes with a built-in page-layout program dedicated to a single purpose: helping you design a linen-covered, acid-free, hardback book of your photos. See Chapter 10.

Note: Although much of this book is focused on using digital cameras, remember this: You *don't* have to shoot digital photos to use iPhoto. You can just as easily use it to organize and publish pictures you've shot with a traditional film camera and digitized using a scanner (or had Kodak convert them to a Photo CD). Importing scanned photos is covered later in this chapter on page 92.

Figure 6-1:
Top: If you're upgrading from an earlier version of iPhoto, this warning is the first thing you see when you launch iPhoto 4. Once you click the Upgrade button, there's no going back—your photo library will no longer be readable with iPhoto 1 or 2.

Bottom: If you upgrade from iPhoto 4.0 to a later version (like 4.0.1), Apple has yet another speed boost to offer you. To take advantage of it, though, you must let iPhoto study your photos and build new, faster-displaying thumbnail representations of them—a process that can take a very long time if you have a lot of pictures.

The Photo Library needs to be upgraded to work with this version of iPhoto.

Your Photo Library will not be readable by previous versions of iPhoto after the upgrade. The upgrade process may take several minutes depending on the number of photos in the library.

[Quit]   [Upgrade]

Your thumbnails need to be upgraded.

In this version of iPhoto, the small preview images, or "thumbnails," have been improved. Upgrading the thumbnails will take a while, depending on the number of photos in your library. Do you want to upgrade your thumbnails now?

[Later]   [Upgrade]

Getting Your Pictures into iPhoto

Double-click the iPhoto icon to launch the program. After you dismiss the "Welcome to iPhoto" dialog box (which contains a quick recap of the program's benefits), iPhoto checks to see if you have an older version, and if so, offers to convert its photo library (Figure 6-1).

Finally, you arrive at the program's main window, the basic elements of which are shown in Figure 6-2.

Figure 6-2:
Here's what iPhoto looks like when you first open it. The large photo-viewing area is where thumbnails of your imported photos will appear. The pane at the bottom of the window changes depending on which of iPhoto's four modes you're in—Import, Organize, Edit, or Book.

Source list

Photo viewing area

Drag to adjust panel sizes

Mode buttons

Zoom in/Zoom out

If you've been taking digital photos for some time, you probably have a lot of photo files already crammed into folders on your hard drive or on Zip disks or CDs. If you shoot pictures with a traditional film camera and use a scanner to digitize them, you've probably got piles of JPEG or TIFF images stashed away on disk already, waiting to be cataloged using iPhoto.

This section explains how to transfer files from each of these sources into iPhoto itself.

Connecting with a USB Camera

Every modern digital camera can connect to a Mac using the USB port. If your Mac has more than one USB jack, you can use any of them for your digital camera.

Plugging a USB-compatible camera into your Mac is the easiest way to transfer pictures from your camera into iPhoto. The whole process practically happens by itself.

1. **With your camera turned off, plug it into one of your Mac's USB jacks.**

   To make this camera-to-Mac USB connection, you need what is usually called an *A-to-B* USB cable; your camera probably came with one. The "A" end—the part you plug into your camera—has a small, flat-bottomed plug whose shape varies by manufacturer. The Mac end of the cable has a larger, flatter, rectangular, standard USB plug. Make sure both ends of the cable are plugged in firmly.

   iPhoto doesn't have to be running when you make this connection. The program opens itself and springs into action as soon as you switch on the camera (unless you've changed the factory settings in Image Capture, a little program that sits in your Applications folder).

Note: If this is the first time you've ever run iPhoto, it asks if you *always* want it to run when you plug in the camera. If you value your time, say yes.

---

2. **Turn on the camera.**

   If iPhoto is running, it immediately detects that there are new photos available for download and gets ready to import them. If iPhoto isn't running, your Mac is smart enough to detect the presence of the connected camera and launch iPhoto.

Note: There's no danger in plugging in your camera while it's turned on; it's just that the Mac doesn't recognize certain camera models until their power comes on. If, for some reason, iPhoto doesn't "see" your camera after you connect it and turn it on, try turning the camera off, then on again, while it's plugged in.

   You can tell whether iPhoto is ready to do its job by checking the information area at the bottom panel, as shown in Figure 6-3. You should see the name of your camera, along with a status line indicating how many pictures iPhoto has detected on it. (The number may be somewhat larger than you expect if you forgot to erase your last batch of photos.)

3. **Turn on the "Erase camera contents after transfer" checkbox, if you like.**

   Think about this one for a moment. It's the one big decision you have to make when importing your photos. If you turn on "Erase camera contents after transfer," iPhoto will automatically delete all photos from your camera's memory card once they're safely on the Mac.

   The advantage of using this option is that your camera's memory card is instantly and effortlessly wiped clean, making it ready for you to fill with more pictures.

   Of course, iPhoto isn't supposed to delete your pictures until *after* it has successfully copied them all to the Photo Library. However, it's not beyond the realm of possibility that a hard disk could fail during an iPhoto import, or that a file could get corrupted when copied, thereby becoming unopenable. If you want to play it safe, leave the "Erase camera contents after transfer" option turned off.

Then, after you've confirmed that all of your photos have been copied into the iPhoto Library folder, you can use the camera's own command to erase its memory card.

4. Click the Import button.

If you chose the auto-erase feature, you'll see a final "Confirm Move" dialog box, affording you one last chance to back out of that decision. Click Delete Originals if you're sure you want the camera erased after the transfer, or Keep Originals if you want iPhoto to import *copies* of them, leaving the originals on the camera.

In any case, iPhoto swings into action, copying each photo from your camera to your hard drive.

The program also creates a *thumbnail* of each picture—a tiny, low-resolution version that appears, like a slide on a slide sorter, in the iPhoto window.

Tip: If you're *not* in the habit of using the "Erase camera contents" option, you may occasionally see the "Import duplicates?" message shown at the top in Figure 6-3. iPhoto notices the arrival of duplicates and offers you the option of downloading them again, resulting in duplicates on your Mac, or ignoring them and importing only the *new* photos from your camera. The latter option can save you a lot of time.

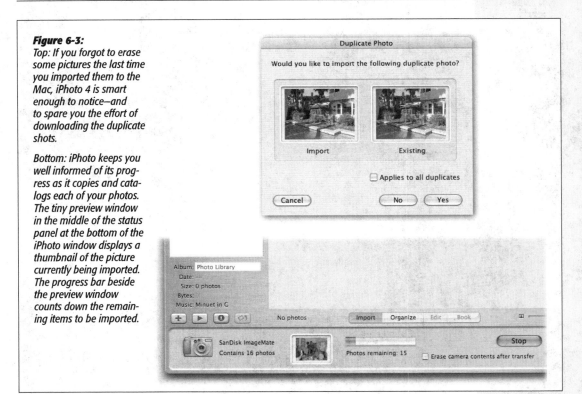

Figure 6-3:
Top: If you forgot to erase some pictures the last time you imported them to the Mac, iPhoto 4 is smart enough to notice—and to spare you the effort of downloading the duplicate shots.

Bottom: iPhoto keeps you well informed of its progress as it copies and catalogs each of your photos. The tiny preview window in the middle of the status panel at the bottom of the iPhoto window displays a thumbnail of the picture currently being imported. The progress bar beside the preview window counts down the remaining items to be imported.

When the process is over, your freshly imported photos will be on display in the main iPhoto window, awaiting your organizational talents.

If your camera is fairly old, you may now have to "eject" the camera's memory card, as described in the box below. If you fail to do this, then unplugging the camera will produce a nasty onscreen scolding that says, "In the future, please put away the device before removing the device."

5. **Turn off the camera, and then unplug it from the USB cable.**

You're ready to start having fun with your new pictures.

USB Card Readers

A USB *memory card reader* offers another great way to transfer photos from the camera to iPhoto. Most of these card readers, which look like tiny disk drives, are under $20; some can read more than one kind of memory card.

UP TO SPEED

The Memory Card's Back Door

When you connect an older digital camera to the Mac, its memory card shows up as a disk icon at the upper-right corner of your desktop, as shown here.

Newer cameras don't show up this way—but you can get the same effect by inserting your memory card into a card reader attached to your Mac.

Inside the disk window, you'll generally find several folders, each cryptically named by the camera's software. One of them contains your photos; another may contain movies.

Opening this "disk" icon is one way to *selectively* delete or copy photos from the card. (If you do that, though, eject and reconnect the camera before importing into iPhoto, to avoid thoroughly confusing the software.)

Finding the folder that contains the memory card's photos also offers you the chance to copy photos *from* your hard drive *to* your camera—just drag them to the "disk" icon in the Finder.

Finally, more Mac fans are getting into the fun of capturing digital movies with their digital still cameras—but wondering how they're supposed to transfer these movies to the Mac. (iPhoto doesn't muddy up its hands with that job; it handles only still photos.)

Now you know the answer: just open the memory card "disk," find the folder that contains the movie files (they usually bear the file name suffix .AVI or .MOV), and drag them onto your Mac.

The downside of having your card icon show up is that you have to eject it manually after importing your photos into iPhoto. You can drag it to the Trash, Control-click it and choose Eject, click its Eject icon in the Sidebar (Mac OS X 10.3 or later), or use any other disk-ejecting tactic.

P.S. If your camera *doesn't* show up as an icon, you can always open the Image Capture program in your Applications folder. It's capable of selectively deleting or importing photos and can also import your digital movies.

Instead of connecting the camera to a cable, card-reader owners transfer their photos by removing the camera's memory card and inserting it into the reader, which they leave connected to the Mac all the time. iPhoto recognizes the reader as though it's a camera and offers to import (and erase) the photos, just as described on the preceding pages.

This method offers several advantages over the USB-cable method. First, it eliminates the considerable battery drain involved in pumping the photos straight off the camera. Second, it's less hassle to pull a memory card out of your camera and slip it into your card reader (which is always plugged in) than it is to constantly plug and unplug camera cables. Finally, this method lets you use almost *any* digital camera with iPhoto, even those too old to include a USB cable connector.

Tip: iPhoto doesn't recognize most *camcorders,* even though most models can take still pictures. Many camcorders store their stills on a memory card just as digital cameras do, so a memory card reader is exactly what you need to get those pictures into iPhoto.

Connecting with a USB-compatible memory card reader is almost identical to connecting a camera. Here's how:

1. **Pop a memory card out of your camera and insert it into the reader.**

   Of course, the card reader should already be plugged into the Mac's USB jack.

   As when you connect a camera, iPhoto acknowledges the presence of the memory card reader in its status panel and reports the number of images it finds. As described on page 88, you can turn on the "Erase camera contents after transfer" checkbox if you want iPhoto to automatically clear the memory card after copying the files to your Mac.

2. **Click Import.**

   iPhoto swings into action, copying the photos off the card.

3. **Switch to the Finder. Eject the memory card's icon from the desktop as you would a CD (drag it to the Trash, for example), and then remove the card from the reader.**

   Put it back into the camera, so it's ready for more action.

Importing Photos from Non-USB Cameras

If your camera doesn't have a USB connection *and* you don't have a memory card reader, you're still not out of luck.

First, copy the photos from your camera/memory card onto your hard drive (or other disk) using whatever software or hardware came with your camera. Then bring them into iPhoto using one of these two methods:

- Drag the files directly into the main iPhoto window, which automatically starts the import process. You can also drop an entire *folder* of images into iPhoto to import the contents of the whole folder, as shown in Figure 6-4.

Tip: Take the time to name your folders intelligently before dragging them into iPhoto, because the program retains their names. If you drag a folder directly into the main photo area, you get a new *film roll* named for the folder (page 102); if you drag the folder into the album list at the left side of the screen, you get a new *album* named for the folder. And if there are folders *inside* folders, they, too, become new film rolls and albums. Details on all this are in Chapter 7.

• Choose File→Import (or press Shift-⌘-I) in iPhoto and select a file or folder in the Open dialog box (Figure 6-5).

Tip: If your camera or memory card appears on the Mac desktop like any other removable disk, you can also drag its photo icons, folder icons, or even the "disk" icon itself directly into iPhoto.

Figure 6-4:
When you drop a folder into iPhoto, the program automatically scans all the folders inside it, looking for pictures to catalog. It creates a new film roll for each folder it finds. iPhoto ignores irrelevant files and stores only the pictures that are in a format it can read.

Importing Existing Graphics Files

If you've already got digital photos—or any other kinds of graphics files—stored somewhere on your computer, the easiest way to import them into iPhoto is simply to drag their icons into the main iPhoto window (as described previously), or by using the File→Import command (Figure 6-5).

You can also select and import files from CD-ROMs, DVDs, Jaz or Zip disks, or other disks on the network. If your photos are on a Kodak Photo CD, you can insert the CD (with iPhoto already running) and then click the Import button on the Import pane, just as if you were importing photos from a connected camera. As always, iPhoto makes fresh copies of the files you import, storing them in one centralized photo repository (the iPhoto Library folder) on your hard drive. The program also creates thumbnail versions of each image for display in the main iPhoto window.

Through this process and all other importing processes, remember this: iPhoto *never moves* a file, whether from a memory card or disk. It only copies it.

Figure 6-5:
When the Import dialog box appears, navigate to and select any graphics files you want to bring into iPhoto. You can ⌘-click individual graphics to select more than one simultaneously, as shown here. You can also click one, then Shift-click another one, to highlight both files and everything in the list in between.

The File Format Factor

iPhoto can't import digital pictures unless it understands their file format, but that rarely poses a problem. Just about every digital camera on earth saves photos as either JPEG or TIFF files—and iPhoto handles both of these image formats beautifully.

Beware, though, that some of the better digital cameras include an option for saving images in a nonstandard file format that's unique to the camera manufacturer. Kodak, Olympus, and Nikon cameras, for example, can all save images in what's called RAW format, which iPhoto can't read. If you're planning on bringing digital photos straight into iPhoto for editing and organizing, make sure your camera settings have been configured to save photos as JPEGs or TIFFs. Otherwise, you'll have to convert the RAW files into JPEG or TIFF files using the camera maker's software.

Of course, iPhoto also lets you load pictures that have been saved in a number of other file formats, too—including a few unusual ones. They include GIF, PNG, FlashPix, BMP, PICT, Photoshop, MacPaint, SGI, Targa, and even PDF (Acrobat) files, just in case you want to keep your brochures and tax returns in iPhoto.

If you try to import a file that iPhoto doesn't understand, you see the message shown in Figure 6-6.

The Post-Dump Slideshow

Once you've imported a batch of pictures into iPhoto, what's the first thing you want to do? If you're like most people, this is the first opportunity you have to see, at full size, the masterpieces you and your camera came up with.

In iPhoto 4, a glorious new feature awaits you: a slideshow with the tools you need to perform an initial screen of the new pictures—like deleting the baddies, rotating the sideways ones, and identifying the best ones with star ratings.

To begin the slideshow, click the Last Roll icon in the Source list at the left side of the screen to identify which pictures you want to look over.

Figure 6-6:
Here's iPhoto's way of telling you that you just tried to feed it a file that it can't digest: an EPS file, an Adobe Illustrator drawing, QuickTime movie, or PowerPoint file, for example.

Of course, you can always open up an EPS or PostScript file in your Preview program, and then export it into a more iPhoto-friendly format from there.

UP TO SPEED

JPEG and TIFF

Most digital cameras capture photos in a graphics-file format called JPEG. That's the world's most popular file format for photos, because even though it's compressed to take up a *lot* less disk space, the visual quality is still very high.

Some cameras offer you the chance to leave your photos *uncompressed* on the camera, in what's called TIFF format. These files are huge—you'll be lucky if you can fit *one* TIFF file on the memory card that came with the camera—but retain 100 percent of the picture's original quality. (You'd be hard-pressed to detect the quality loss in a JPEG file, but technically speaking, there is some.)

iPhoto recognizes both kinds of files when you import them. (For that matter, iPhoto can also import graphics files in BMP, GIF, MacPaint, PICT, PNG, Photoshop, SGI, Targa, and FlashPix formats, as described later in this chapter.)

Note, however, that the instant you *edit* a TIFF-format photo (Chapter 6), iPhoto converts it into JPEG.

That's fine if you plan to order prints or a hardback book (Chapter 10) from iPhoto, since JPEG files are required for those purposes. But if you took that once-in-a-lifetime, priceless shot as a TIFF file, don't do any editing (even rotating) in iPhoto if you hope to maintain its perfect, pristine quality.

Note: On a freshly installed copy of iPhoto, this icon is labeled Last Roll. If you've fiddled with the iPhoto preference settings, it may say, for example, "Last 2 Rolls" or "Last 3 Rolls," and your slideshow will include more than the most recent batch of photos. If that's not what you want to see, just click the actual photo that you want to begin the slideshow (in the main viewing area).

Now click the Play triangle underneath the Source list. iPhoto fades out of view, and a big, brilliant, full-screen slideshow of the new photos begins, accompanied by music.

You can read more about slideshows in general in Chapter 9. What's useful here, though, is the new iPhoto 4 control bar shown in Figure 6-7. You make it appear by wiggling your mouse as the show begins.

Figure 6-7:
As the slideshow progresses, you can pause the show, go backward, rotate a photo, delete a bad shot, or apply your star rating to a picture, all courtesy of this new control bar.

If you'd rather have it visible during all slideshows of this album or roll, click the Slideshow button at the bottom of the screen—in regular iPhoto, not during a slideshow—and turn on "Display slideshow controls."

Back, Pause, Next   Rotate   Ratings   Delete This Photo

As you can see by the figure, this is the perfect opportunity to throw away lousy shots, fix the rotation, and linger on certain photos for more study—all without interrupting the slideshow. You can even apply a rating by clicking the appropriate star in the band of five; later, you can use these ratings to sort your pictures or create *smart albums*. See Chapter 7 for full detail on rating stars and smart albums.

Here's the full list of things you can do when the onscreen control bar is visible:

- Click the Play/Pause button to start and halt the slideshow. The space bar toggles these controls—and the control bar doesn't have to be visible when you press it.

- Click the left and right arrows to browse back and forth through your photos. The left and right arrow keys on your keyboard do the same thing.

- Press the up or down arrow keys on your keyboard to make the slides appear faster or slower.

- Click the rotation icons to flip photos clockwise or counterclockwise, 90 degrees at a time.

- Click one of the five dots to apply a rating in stars, from one at the left to five all the way at the right. Or use the number keys at the top of the keyboard or on the numeric keypad: press 3 to give a picture three stars, for example.

- Click the Trash can icon to delete a photo from the album you're viewing (but not from the Photo Library). Or simply hit Delete (or Del) on your keyboard.

Tip: There are keyboard shortcuts for all of these functions, too, that don't even require the control bar to be on the screen. See page 165.

Click the mouse anywhere off the control bar to end the slideshow.

This onscreen control bar is a welcome addition in iPhoto 4. In the days of iPhoto 2 and earlier, you had to end the slideshow every time you wanted to delete or rotate a photo, then start the show all over again.

Where iPhoto Keeps Your Files

Whenever you import pictures into iPhoto, the program makes *copies* of your photos, always leaving your original files untouched.

- When you import from a camera, iPhoto leaves the photos right where they are on its memory card (unless you use the "Erase" option).

- When you import from the hard drive, iPhoto leaves the originals in whichever folders they're in. As a result, transferring photos from your hard drive into iPhoto *more than doubles* the amount of disk space they take up. In other words, importing 1 GB of photos requires an additional 1 GB of disk space, because you'll end up with two copies of each file—the original, and iPhoto's copy of the photo. In addition, iPhoto creates a separate thumbnail version of each picture, consuming about another 10 K to 20 K per photo.

FREQUENTLY ASKED QUESTION

Moving the iPhoto Library

Do I have to keep my photos in the iPhoto Library folder? What if I want them stored somewhere else?

No problemo! iPhoto has come a long way since the days when it could keep track of photos only if they were in its own folder structure within the iPhoto Library folder.

Just quit iPhoto. Then move the *whole* iPhoto Library folder (currently in your Home→Pictures folder) to another location—even onto another hard drive.

Then open iPhoto again. It will proclaim that it can't find your iPhoto Library folder. Click the Find Library button to show the program where you put the folder. Done deal!

---

iPhoto stores its copies of your pictures in a special folder called iPhoto Library, which you can find in your Home→Pictures folder. (To find your Home folder, begin in the Finder and choose Go→Home.) If the short name you use to log into Mac OS X is *mozart*, the full path to your iPhoto Library folder from the main hard drive window would be Macintosh HD→Users→mozart→Pictures→iPhoto Library.

Tip: You should back up this iPhoto Library folder regularly—using the Burn command to save it onto a CD or DVD, for example. After all, it contains all the photos you import into iPhoto—essentially, your entire photography collection. Chapter 12 offers much more on this file management topic.

What all those numbers mean

Within the iPhoto Library folder, you'll find a set of mysteriously numbered files and folders. At first glance, this setup may look bizarre, but there's a method to iPhoto's madness. It turns out that iPhoto meticulously arranges your photos within these numbered folders according to the *creation dates* of the originals, as explained in Figure 6-8.

Figure 6-8:
Behold the mysteries of the iPhoto Library. Once you know the secret, this seemingly cryptic folder structure actually makes sense, with all the photos in the library organized by their creation date.

At the top level are the year folders—2004, 2003, and so on. Within those folders are subfolders for each month (01 for January, 02 for February, and so on), and nested within those are subfolders labeled for each day of each month. So a photo that was originally taken on August 21, 2003, is stored in iPhoto Library→ 2003→08→21.

Other folders in the iPhoto Library

In addition to the numbered folders, you'll find several other items nested in the iPhoto Library folder, like AlbumData.xml, Data folder, Library.cache, and so on. These are support folders that iPhoto uses for its album feature, for storing iPhoto's thumbnails of your pictures, and so on.

Folders inside the year/month/date folders

A few mysterious icons appear inside each year/month/date photo folder, too, right alongside your JPEG photo files. They include:

- **Thumbs folder.** Here, iPhoto stores the small thumbnail versions of the pictures in your Photo Library—the "slides" that actually appear in the iPhoto window.

  These images are numbered according to the importing sequence, as described in the previous Note.

- **Originals folder.** Some photo folders may contain an Originals folder. It doesn't appear until you use one of iPhoto's editing tools (Chapter 8) to touch up a photo. The Originals folder is the key to one of iPhoto's most remarkable features: the Revert to Original command.

  Before it applies any potentially destructive operations to your photos—like cropping, red-eye removal, brightening, black-and-white conversion—iPhoto *duplicates* the files and stuffs pristine, unedited copies of them in the Originals folder. If you later decide to scrap your changes to a photo using the Revert to Original command—even months or years later—iPhoto moves the unedited file back into its original location, returning your photo to its originally imported state.

Note: Don't confuse the files in the Originals folders with your *true* originals–the files on your hard drive, camera, or memory card that you first imported into iPhoto. As mentioned earlier, iPhoto *never* touches those originals; they stay exactly where they were when you imported them.

Look, don't touch

While it's enlightening to wander through the iPhoto Library folder to see how iPhoto keeps itself organized, don't rename or move any of the folders or files in it. Making such changes will confuse iPhoto to the point where it will either be unable to display some of your photos or will just crash.

The Digital Shoebox

I f you've imported your photos into iPhoto using any of the methods described in the previous chapter, you should now see a neatly arranged grid of thumbnails in iPhoto's main photo viewing area. You're looking at what iPhoto refers to as your *Photo Library*—your entire photo collection, including every last picture you've ever imported. This is the digital equivalent of that old shoebox you've had stuffed in the closet for the last ten years, brimming with snapshots waiting to be sorted and sifted, often never to be seen again.

You're not really organized yet, but at least all your photos are in one place. Your journey out of chaos has begun. From here, you can sort your photos, give them titles, group them into smaller sub-collections (called *albums*) and tag them with keywords so you'll be able to find them quickly. This chapter helps you tackle each of those organizing tasks as painlessly as possible.

The Source List

Even before you start naming your photos, assigning them keywords, or organizing them into albums, iPhoto imposes an order of its own on your digital shoebox.

The key to understanding it is the *Source list* at the left side of the iPhoto window. This list will grow as you import more pictures and organize them—but right off the bat, you'll find icons like Photo Library, Last 12 Months, and Last Roll.

Photo Library

The very first icon in the Source list is called Photo Library. This is a very reassuring little icon, because no matter how confused you may get in working with subsets of photos later in your iPhoto life, clicking Photo Library takes you back to your entire picture collection. It makes *all* of your photos appear in the viewing area.

Photo Library by Year

In previous versions of iPhoto, the Photo Library was nice enough, although it got a bit unwieldy if you had 2,000 pictures in it (the rough maximum of iPhoto 2). But now that iPhoto can easily handle 25,000 photos, Apple realized that people needed some way to break down this tidal wave of pixels.

Enter the year icons, shown in Figure 7-1. When you click the Photo Library "flippy triangle," iPhoto's Source list now shows small yellow calendar icons, one for each year going back to 2001 (and a catch-all for earlier images).

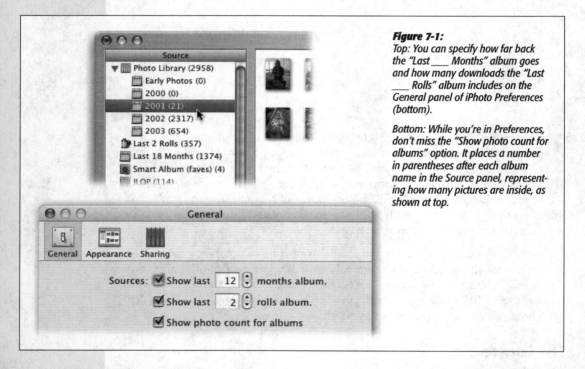

Figure 7-1:
Top: You can specify how far back the "Last ___ Months" album goes and how many downloads the "Last ___ Rolls" album includes on the General panel of iPhoto Preferences (bottom).

Bottom: While you're in Preferences, don't miss the "Show photo count for albums" option. It places a number in parentheses after each album name in the Source panel, representing how many pictures are inside, as shown at top.

When you import your entire digital photo collection (or upgrade from an earlier version of iPhoto), the program files each photo by the date you took it. You can click Photo Library to see all your photos amassed in one window, or click, say, the 2003 icon to see just the ones you took in that year.

The year icons are also very helpful when you're trying to put together an iPhoto slideshow or pinpoint one certain photo. After all, you usually can remember what year you took a vacation or when someone's birthday was. The year icons help you narrow down your search without having to scroll through your entire Photo Library.

Photo Library by Month

iPhoto 4 also adds to the Source list the Last 12 Months icon. It's the same idea as the calendar-year icons, except that it puts the most recent photos at your fingertips. The idea, of course, is that most of the time, the freshest photos are the most interesting to you.

Actually, it doesn't even have to say "Last 12 Months." You can specify how many months' worth of photos appear in this heap—anywhere from one month to a year and a half—by choosing iPhoto→Preferences (see Figure 7-1) and going to the General panel. This feature is the ideal way to find the pictures from this past Christmas, photos from your kid's most recent birthday, or wedding pictures from your most recent marriage.

Last Roll

Each time you import a new set of photos into iPhoto—whether from your hard drive, a camera, or a memory card—that batch of imported photos constitutes one *film roll.*

Of course, there's no real film in digital photography, and your pictures aren't on a "roll" of anything. But if you think about it, the metaphor makes sense. Just as in traditional photography, where each batch of photos you shoot is captured on a discrete roll of film, in iPhoto, each separate batch of photos you download into the program gets classified as its own film roll.

Most of the time, you'll probably work with the photos that you just downloaded from your camera. Conveniently, iPhoto always keeps track of your most recently added film roll, so you can view its contents without a lot of scrolling.

That's the purpose of the roll-of-film icon called Last Roll in the Source list. With one click, iPhoto displays only your most recent photos, hiding all the others. This feature can save you a lot of time, especially as your Photo Library grows.

In fact, iPhoto 4 lets you specify how *many* film rolls you want listed here; choose iPhoto→Preferences and click the General icon (see Figure 7-1). Simply change the number where it says "Show last __ rolls album." (In the unlikely event that you don't find this icon useful, you can also hide it entirely by turning off the corresponding checkbox.) For example, if you've just gotten back from a three-day Disney World trip, you probably want to see your last *three* imports all at once. In that case, you'd change the last rolls setting to *3.*

Other Icons in the Source List

Library, year icons, and Last Roll icons aren't the only items you'll find in the Source list. Later in this chapter, you'll find out how to create your own arbitrary subsets of pictures called albums. Later in this book, you'll find out how to swipe photos from other people's collections via iPhoto sharing. And later in life, you may discover the geeky joy of dumping photos onto CDs or DVDs—and then loading them back into iPhoto whenever you darned well feel like it. CD and DVD icons can show up in the Source list, too.

As you go, though, remember this key point: Photos in your iPhoto Library, Last Roll, and Last Month icons are the *real* photos. Delete a picture from one of these three collections, and it's gone forever. (That's not true of albums, which store only aliases—phantom duplicates—of the real photos.)

More on Film Rolls

iPhoto starts out sorting your Photo Library by film roll, meaning that the most recently imported batch of photos appears at the bottom of the window. Your main iPhoto window may look like a broad, featureless expanse of pictures, but they're actually in a clear order. Here are a few ways you can change this sort order:

- To change the sort order to reflect the *creation* date of the photos (rather than the date they were imported), choose View→Arrange Photos→by Date.

- To view photos sorted alphabetically by their *names*, choose View→Arrange Photos→by Title. (Titles are described on page 113.)

- In a new iPhoto 4 twist, you can sort your pictures by rating, so that your masterpieces are at the top of the window, with the losers way down below. Choose View→Arrange Photos→by Rating. (See page 118 for the full story on ratings.)

- Whether you choose to sort photos by film roll or date, you can *reverse* the sort order so that the most recent items appear at the *top* of the iPhoto window instead of the bottom—an idea that can save you a lot of scrolling through thumbnails. Choose iPhoto→Preferences, go to the Appearance panel, turn on "Place most recent photos at the top," and close the Preferences window. (If you choose this preference in conjunction with the By Title viewing option mentioned in the previous paragraph, your photos appear in *reverse* alphabetical order.)

Tip: If you drag a *folder* of photos into iPhoto, the name of the folder becomes the name of the film roll, so it pays to bring photos into iPhoto from intelligently named folders. In fact, if you import a series of nested folders containing photos, each individual folder of images gets grouped together as its own separately named film roll. By contrast, if you drag a group of individual files into iPhoto, the group gets a generic label like "Roll 45."

Your Own Personal Sorting Order

I don't want my photos sorted by creation date or *import date—I want to put them in my* own *order. I tried using View→Arrange Photos→Manually, but the command is dimmed out! Did Apple accidentally forget to turn this on?*

No, the command works—but only in an *album*, not in the main Photo Library. If you create a new photo album (as explained later in this chapter) and fill it with photos, you can then drag them into any order you want.

Displaying film rolls

If you choose View→Arrange Photos→by Film Roll, iPhoto returns to sorting your photos by film roll, even if you had previously chosen to sort the photos by rating, title, or date. (The Film Roll option in the View menu is dimmed when you're looking at an album or the Last 12 Months collection.)

Tip: To hide or show the film roll dividers, just choose View→Film Rolls. Better yet, use the keyboard shortcut Shift-⌘-F. (The presence or absence of the dividers doesn't affect the sorting order.) You can see these film-roll dividers in Figure 7-2.

Figure 7-2:
This tidy arrangement is the fastest way to use iPhoto. Display the photos grouped by film roll, and then hide the photo batches you're not working with. Click the triangle beside each header to expand or collapse the film roll, just like a folder in the Finder's list view. Note that the header for each roll lists the date that you imported this batch, along with a count of the pictures in the roll. If you dragged a folder of files into iPhoto—or if you named the roll once the pictures were imported—the film-roll header also lists the name of the enclosing folder.

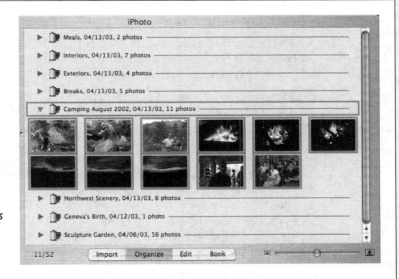

You'll probably find this arrangement so convenient that you'll leave it on permanently. As your Photo Library grows, these groupings become excellent visual and mnemonic aids to help you locate a certain photo—sometimes even months or years after the fact.

Furthermore, as your Photo Library becomes ever more massive, you may need to rely on these film-roll groupings just for your sanity: By collapsing the flippy triangles next to the groups you're not looking at right now (Figure 7-2), you speed up iPhoto considerably. Otherwise, iPhoto may grind almost to a halt as it tries to scroll through ever more photos. (About 25,000 pictures is its realistic limit for everyday Macs.)

Tip: Click anywhere on the film row divider line—on the film roll's name, for example—to simultaneously select all the photos in a film roll.

Even if you opt not to display the film roll divider lines in the photo viewing area, you can still *sort* the pictures in your Photo Library by film roll. Just choose View→ Arrange Photos→by Film Roll. You won't be able to see where one film roll ends and the next begins, but the photos will be in the right order.

Creating film rolls manually

Film rolls are such a convenient way of organizing your pictures that in iPhoto 4, Apple has given you a radical new feature: You can create film rolls manually, out of any pictures you choose.

This feature violates the sanctity of the original film roll concept—that each importing batch is one film roll, and that *albums* are what you use for arbitrary groupings. Still, in this case, usefulness trumps concept—and that's a good thing.

You just select any bunch of pictures in your Photo Library (using any of the techniques described on page 106), and then choose File→New Film Roll From Selection. iPhoto creates and highlights the new roll, like any normal film roll (see Figure 7-2 for an example). iPhoto gives the newborn roll a generic name like "Roll 54" or whatever number it's up to, but you can always rename it, as described on page 103.

Tip: You can *merge* film rolls using this technique, too. Just select photos in two or more existing film rolls before choosing File→New Film Roll From Selection. iPhoto responds by removing the pictures from their existing film rolls, and moving them into a new, unified one. (If you selected all the photos in a couple of film rolls, the original film rolls disappear entirely.) The power and utility of this tactic will become more and more attractive the more you work with big photo collections.

And speaking of cool film-roll tips: You can move any photo into another film roll just by dragging it onto the film roll's row heading!

Renaming and dating film rolls

iPhoto ordinarily labels each film roll with either a roll number (if you imported individual files from a camera or disk) or a folder name (if you imported a folder of photos). In either case, you can easily change the name of the film roll to something more descriptive.

To edit the name of a roll, click the little roll-of-film icon in the film roll divider line. Now the Title text box at the lower-left edge of the window identifies the roll's current name. Just type a new name into this box—ideally, something that helps you remember the batch of photos at a glance.

Using this same technique, you can also change the *date* that appears in the film roll header. This date usually identifies when you imported the photos, but for most purposes, that date is relatively irrelevant. What you probably care more about is the day or month that the photos were actually *taken.*

Once again, start by clicking the roll-of-film icon in the film roll divider. This time, type a new date in the Date text box on the Info pane. You can type the date in a variety of formats—*4 September 2004, September 4, 2004,* and *4/9/04* all work—but you must use a complete date, including day, month, and year. If you don't, iPhoto will take a guess, filling in the missing information for you—and sometimes getting it wrong.

Tip: Another great way to redate a bunch of pictures at once is to use iPhoto 4's new batch processing feature, described on page 113.

Working with Your Photos

All right: You've gotten the hang of the Source list, the Photo Library, and film rolls. Enough learning about iPhoto; it's time to start *using* iPhoto.

Scrolling Through Your Photos

Browsing, selecting, and opening photos is straightforward. Here's everything you need to know:

- Use the vertical scroll bar to navigate through your thumbnails.

Tip: If your photos scroll by too fast for you to find the ones you want, try using iPhoto's Slow Scroll mode. Hold down the Option key while dragging the scroll box in the scroll bar. You get a much slower, smoother scroll, making it easier to navigate to a specific row of thumbnails.

- Scrolling can take awhile if you have a lot of images in your Photo Library, especially if you haven't collapsed the film rolls you're not using, as described earlier. But you can use this standard Mac OS X trick for faster navigation: Instead of dragging the scroll box or clicking the scroll bar arrows, *Option-click* the portion of the scroll bar that corresponds to the location you want in your Photo Library. If you want to jump to the bottom of the Photo Library, Option-click near the bottom of the scroll bar. To find photos in the middle of your collection, Option-click the middle portion of the scroll bar, and so on.

Note: By turning on "Scroll to here" in the General panel of your System Preferences, you can make this the standard behavior for Mac OS X scroll bars–that is, you won't need the Option key.

- Press your Page Up and Page Down keys to scroll one screenful at a time.

- Press Home to jump to the very top of the photo collection, or End to leap to the bottom.

- To create the most expansive photo viewing area possible, you can temporarily hide the Source list at the left side of the window. To do so, drag the divider bar (between the Source list and the main photo viewing area) all the way to the left edge of the window. You've just hidden the Source list.

To reveal that panel again, grab the left edge of the iPhoto window and drag it to the right.

Tip: You can speed up iPhoto's scrolling by turning off the Drop Shadow option in the Appearance section of iPhoto's Preferences window.

Size Control

You can make the thumbnails in iPhoto grow or shrink using the Size Control slider (on the right side of the iPhoto window, just under the photo viewing area). Drag the slider all the way to the left, and you get micro-thumbnails so small that you can fit 200 or more of them in the iPhoto window. If you drag it all the way to the right, you end up with such large thumbnails that you can see only one picture at a time.

Tip: You don't have to *drag* the Size Control slider; just click anywhere along the controller bar to make the slider jump to a new setting. Using this technique, you can instantly change the size of thumbnails from large to small, for example, by clicking once at the left end of the controller.

By the way, you might notice that this Size Control slider performs different functions, depending on what mode iPhoto is in. In Organize mode, it controls the size of thumbnails; in Edit mode, it zooms in and out of an individual image; and in Book mode (Chapter 10), it magnifies or shrinks a single page.

Tip: You may want to adopt a conservative dragging approach when using the size slider, because iPhoto may respond slowly in enlarging or shrinking the photos. Drag in small movements so the program can keep pace with you.

Selecting Photos

To highlight a single picture in preparation for printing, opening, duplicating, or deleting, click the icon once with the mouse.

That much may seem obvious. But many first-time Mac users have no idea how to manipulate *more* than one icon at a time—an essential survival skill.

To highlight multiple photos in preparation for deleting, moving, duplicating, printing, and so on, use one of these techniques:

- **To highlight all the photos.** Select all the pictures in the set you're viewing by pressing ⌘-A (the equivalent of the Edit→Select All command).

- **To highlight several photos by dragging.** You can drag diagonally to highlight a group of nearby photos, as shown in Figure 7-3. You don't even have to enclose the thumbnails completely; your cursor can touch any part of any icon to highlight it. In fact, if you keep dragging past the edge of the window, iPhoto scrolls the window automatically.

Tip: If you include a particular thumbnail in your dragged group by mistake, ⌘-click it to remove it from the selected cluster.

- **To highlight consecutive photos.** Click the first thumbnail you want to highlight, and then Shift-click the last one. All the files in between are automatically selected, along with the two photos you clicked (Figure 7-4, top). This trick mirrors the way Shift-clicking works in a word processor, the Finder, and many other kinds of programs.

Figure 7-3:
You can highlight several photos simultaneously by dragging a box around them. To do so, start from somewhere outside of the target photos and drag diagonally across them, creating a whitish enclosure rectangle as you go. Any photos touched by this rectangle are selected when you release the mouse.

- **To highlight random photos.** If you want to highlight only, for example, the first, third, and seventh photos in a window, start by clicking photo icon No. 1. Then ⌘-click each of the others. Each thumbnail sprouts a colored border to indicate that you've selected it (Figure 7-4, bottom).

If you're highlighting a long string of photos and then click one by mistake, you don't have to start over. Instead, just ⌘-click it again, and the dark highlighting disappears. (If you do want to start over from the beginning, just deselect all selected photos by clicking any empty part of the window.)

The ⌘ key trick is especially handy if you want to select *almost* all the photos in a window. Press ⌘-A to select everything in the folder, then ⌘-click any unwanted photos to deselect them.

Tip: You can also combine the ⌘-clicking business with the Shift-clicking trick. For instance, you could click the first photo, then Shift-click the tenth, to highlight the first ten—and then ⌘-click photos 2, 5, and 9 to *remove* them from the selection.

Once you've highlighted multiple photos, you can manipulate them all at once. For example, you can drag them en masse out of the window and onto your desktop—a quick way to export them. (Actually, drag them onto a *folder* in the Finder to avoid spraying their icons all over your desktop.) Or you can drag them into an album at the left side of the iPhoto window. Just drag any *one* of the highlighted photos; all other highlighted thumbnails go along for the ride.

In addition, when multiple photos are selected, the commands in the File and Edit menus—such as Duplicate, Print, and Revert To Original—apply to all of them simultaneously.

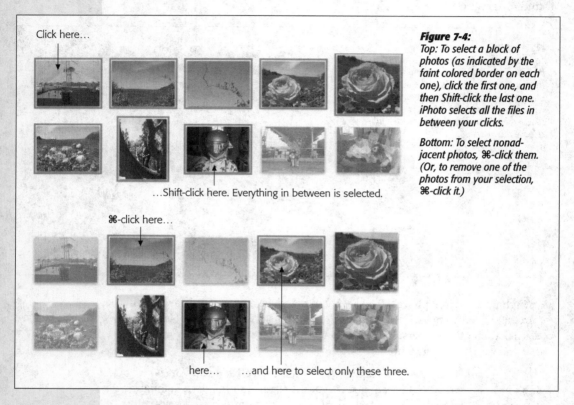

Click here…

…Shift-click here. Everything in between is selected.

⌘-click here…

here… …and here to select only these three.

Figure 7-4:
Top: To select a block of photos (as indicated by the faint colored border on each one), click the first one, and then Shift-click the last one. iPhoto selects all the files in between your clicks.

Bottom: To select nonadjacent photos, ⌘-click them. (Or, to remove one of the photos from your selection, ⌘-click it.)

Opening Photos

iPhoto wouldn't be a terribly useful program if it let you view only postage-stamp versions of your photos (unless, of course, your photos happen to *be* pictures of postage stamps). Fortunately, iPhoto lets you open photos at full size, zoom in on details, and even conduct some basic editing to make them look better. (Editing photos is covered blow-by-blow in the next chapter.)

The easiest way to open a photo is simply to double-click a thumbnail. Unless you've changed iPhoto's settings, the photo opens in the main iPhoto window, scaled to fit into the viewing area.

This is the way most people start out opening pictures using iPhoto, and there's nothing technically wrong with this method. But it does have several drawbacks:

- You can have only one picture open at a time this way.

- Pictures opened by double-clicking are always scaled to fit within the iPhoto window, even if that means scaling them *upward,* over 100 percent of their actual size. As a result, smaller pictures wind up pixellated and distorted as they're stretched to fill the whole window.

  Worse, at this point, there's no way to zoom *out.* You can zoom in further, but you can't reduce the magnification.

- You have no way of knowing if your photo *has* been scaled to fit in the window, since iPhoto doesn't display the magnification level it's using. You can't tell if you're looking at a small photo displayed at 100 percent, or a gigantic photo that's been scaled down to 26 percent.

- Double-clicking a thumbnail catapults you directly into iPhoto's *Edit mode,* hiding all your other thumbnails and transforming the lower panel in the iPhoto window into the Edit pane, with its various cropping, red-eye removal, and color changing tools. That's great if you're ready to start editing photos. But if you opened the picture simply because you wanted to see it at full size, you now have to click the Organize button (just under the photo viewing area), or double-click the big picture, to return to Organize mode so you can view and sort photos.

The better way to open photos

You can avoid all of these problems by using iPhoto's much smarter, but less obvious, method of opening photos: Open each picture *in its own window.*

There are two ways to do this:

- Go to iPhoto→Preferences and change the photo-opening setting. On the General panel, select the "Opens in separate window" button. Then close the window.

Tip: Pressing Option *reverses* whichever choice you make here. That is, if you've chosen "Opens in Edit view" in the Preferences window, then *Option*-double-clicking a thumbnail opens the photo into a separate window instead. Conversely, if you've chosen "Opens in separate window," Option-double-clicking a thumbnail overrides your choice and opens it into the main iPhoto viewing area.

(Option-double-clicking has no effect if you've selected the third Preferences option, "Opens in other," which is described in Chapter 8.)

- Control-click the photo. Choose "Edit in separate window" from the shortcut menu.

When a photo opens in its own window, all kinds of control and flexibility await you. First, you can scale it up *or* down simply by making the window larger or smaller (by dragging its lower-right corner). You can close an open photo from the keyboard by pressing ⌘-W. And best of all, you can open multiple pictures and look at them side by side, as shown in Figure 7-5.

Figure 7-5:
When you open photos in their own windows, you can you look at several at the same time—a critical feature when comparing similar shots. And you can keep your other thumbnails in view, allowing you to easily open additional photos without closing the open ones. Note that the title bar tells you which magnification level iPhoto's using to display each photo.

Another way to zoom

As mentioned earlier, one way to change the magnification level of a photo opened in its own window is to change the size of the window itself. Enlarge the window to zoom in; shrink it to zoom out.

But you can make a window only so big by dragging its corner before you run out of screen, or so tiny before it just can't be shrunk any further. Therefore, to take advantage of iPhoto's full zoom range (5 to 400 percent), you need to use the Zoom *buttons.*

Zoom buttons? Where? They're on iPhoto's *Edit toolbar,* which may be hidden. If you don't see it, make sure you've opened a photo in its own window, and then click the capsule-shaped button in the upper-right corner of the window. You'll find the Zoom buttons on the left side of the toolbar, as shown in Figure 7-6. (There's much more about using and customizing the Edit toolbar in Chapter 8.)

These buttons let you use iPhoto's full zooming power, regardless of the size of your monitor or the size of your photos.

Tip: Once you've zoomed in, you can ⌘-drag inside the photo area to scroll in any direction. That's more direct than fussing with two independent scroll bars.

Zoom where you want to zoom

Normally, when you use any of iPhoto's zooming tools—either the Zoom slider in the main iPhoto window or the Zoom buttons in a separate window—iPhoto zooms in toward the *center* of the photo. If you want to view a portion of the photo that's not near the center, you have to scroll to it after zooming.

Figure 7-6:
Once you've revealed the Edit Toolbar, you can increase or reduce the magnification of photos by using the Zoom buttons on the left. The increments of magnification become progressively smaller with each button-click as you zoom out, and progressively larger as you zoom in.

One interesting phenomenon: Using the Zoom buttons disables iPhoto's zoom-by-changing-the-window-size feature (until you close the photo window and reopen it).

Figure 7-7:
To zoom into a specific portion of a photo, first define your target by dragging out a rectangle with the mouse (top left). Then, when you use any of the standard zooming tools, iPhoto puts your target in the center (lower right), so you can home in on exactly the details you want to see by scrolling.

Here's a way to tell iPhoto exactly which part of a picture you want to blow up, so that you don't have to do any scrolling at all: drag diagonally across the part of the picture you want to enlarge, as shown in Figure 7-7. As you drag out your rectangular target area, the parts of the photo outside the target temporarily dim.

With your target defined, you're ready to zoom. Drag the Zoom slider in the main iPhoto window or click the Zoom button in the Edit toolbar. As iPhoto zooms in on the photo, it automatically steers toward your target rectangle, positioning that part of the photo toward the center of the window.

Tip: If you've equipped your Mac with a mouse that has a scroll wheel on the top, you can scroll images up and down while zoomed in on them by turning that wheel. To scroll the zoomed area *horizontally,* press Shift while turning.

Titles, Dates, and Comments

Just below the Source list, at the left side of the iPhoto window, you'll find a display of basic information about all the photos in your collection. The information displayed in this Info pane changes depending on what you've selected in the photo viewing area (see Figure 7-8).

Tip: If you don't see the photo information described here, you may have the Info pane hidden. Click the 🔵 button in the main iPhoto window to reveal the info. Click it twice to reveal the Comments field described on page 116.

- When a single photo is selected, iPhoto displays that picture's creation date, dimensions (in pixels), and file size. Beneath that you'll see the name of the Music track that will play when the currently selected Photo Library or album presents a slideshow (see Chapter 9).

- When multiple photos are selected, you see the *range* of their creation dates, plus how many are selected and how much disk space those photos occupy.

- When no photos are selected, the Info area displays the total number of pictures in your Photo Library, the grand total file size of your library, and a range of creation dates taking in *all* your photos. This last statistic is really pretty cool, in that it amounts to a running stopwatch that measures the span of your interest in digital photography (as of the iPhoto era, anyway).

Tip: The file size info can be extremely useful when creating backups, copying photos to another disk, or burning CDs. One glance at the Info panel—with no photos selected—tells you exactly how much disk space you'll need to fit your entire collection.

For each photo in your collection, iPhoto displays two other important chunks of information, both of which you can directly edit right in the Info pane: the Title and Comments.

Photo Titles

Every photo that you import into iPhoto receives a title, a unique name that's used
to identify the picture within iPhoto. When importing files from your hard drive,
iPhoto assigns titles based on those files' names. But if you're loading photos directly
from your digital camera, the names of your files are probably useless numeric tags
like CRS000321.JPG, CRS000322.JPG, and so on.

By all means, change these titles to something more meaningful. Just select a thumbnail, click in the Title field (just under that Source list), and type in a new title, as
shown in Figure 7-8.

Figure 7-8:
*You can make a photo's title as long as you
want—but it's smart to keep it short (about ten
characters or so). This way, you can see all or
most of the title in the Title field (or under the
thumbnails, if you turn on the Title checkbox, as
explained later in this chapter).*

Creating meaningful titles isn't just useful for keeping track of photos within iPhoto.
Later, when you publish your digital albums online or in print (Chapter 10), iPhoto
will use these names as titles on your Web and book pages.

Changing titles en masse

The trouble with naming your photos is that hardly anybody takes the time. Are you
really going to sit there and make up individual names for 25,000 photos?

Mercifully, iPhoto 4 now lets you change the names of your photos all at once, thanks
to a new "batch processing" command. No, each photo won't have a unique, descriptive name, but at least they can have titles like *Spring Vacation 2* and *Spring Vacation
3* instead of *IMG_1345* and *IMG_1346*.

To use it, choose Photos→Batch Change, or Control-click some selected photos and
choose Batch Change from the shortcut menu. The Batch Change sheet drops down
from the top of the window (see Figure 7-9).

Tip: Don't be fooled by the command name Batch Change. Photo 4 still can't *edit* a batch of photos. You can't, for example, scale them all down to 640 x 480 pixels, or apply the Enhance filter to all of them at once.

Figure 7-9:
iPhoto 4's new batch processing feature lets you specify Titles, Dates, and Comments for any number of photos you select.

Top: When you assign a date and time to a batch of pictures, turn on "Add ____ minute between each photo" to give each a unique time stamp, which could come in handy later when you're sorting them. Besides, you didn't take them all at the exact same moment, did you?

Bottom: When you title a batch of pictures, turn on "Append a number to each photo" to number them in sequence as well.

Your options, in the Batch Change pop-up menus, are:

- **Empty.** Set the titles to "empty" if you want to un-name the selected photos, so that they're all blank. You might appreciate this option when, for example, you're working on a photo book (Chapter 10) and you've opted for titles to appear with each photo, but you really want only a few pictures to show up with names under them.

- **Text.** This option gives you an empty text box into which you can type, for example, *Ski Trip*. When you click OK, iPhoto names all of the selected pictures to match.

  If you turn on "Append a number to each photo," iPhoto adds digits after whatever base name you choose—for example, *Ski Trip 1, Ski Trip 2,* and so on.

- **Roll Info.** Choose this command to name all the selected photos after the roll's name—"Grand Canyon 2004," for example. iPhoto automatically adds the photo number after this base name.

- **Filename.** If you've been fooling around with naming your photos, and now decide that you want their original, camera-blessed file names to return (IMG_1345 and so on), use this command.

- **Date/Time.** Here's another approach: Name each photo for the exact time it was taken. The dialog box gives you a wide variety of formatting options: long date, short date, time of day, and so on.

Tip: Once you've gone to the trouble of naming your photos, remember that you can make these names appear right beneath the thumbnails for convenient reference. Choose View→Titles to make it so.

Photo Dates

When you select a single photo, you can actually *change* its creation date by editing the Info pane's Date field. You can switch the date from the day the digital file was created to the day the photo was actually taken, for example.

In fact, you can also use the Batch Change command to rewrite history, resetting the dates of a group of photos all at once, as shown in Figure 7-9.

(We trust you won't use this feature for nefarious ends, such as "proving" to the jury that you were actually in Disney World on the day of the office robbery.)

Comments

Sometimes you need more than a one- or two-word title to describe the contents of a photo, an album, or a film roll. If you want to add a lengthier description, you can type it in the Comments field in the Photo Info pane, as shown in Figure 7-10. (If you don't see the Comments field, click the ⓘ button—twice, if necessary—to bring it into view.) Even if you don't write full-blown captions for your pictures, you can use the Comments field to store little details such as the names, places, dates, and events associated with your photos.

The best thing about adding comments is that they're searchable. After you've entered all this free-form data, you can use it to quickly locate a photo using iPhoto's search command.

Tip: If you speak a non-English language, iPhoto 4 just made your life easier. As you're typing comments, you can choose Edit→Special Characters. Mac OS X's Character Palette opens, where you can add international letters like É, ø, and ß. Of course, it's also great for classic phrases like "I ♥ my cat."

Adding comments to photos, albums, or film rolls

To add a comment to a photo, select it, and then click in the Comments field. Keep the following in mind as you squirrel away all those bits and scraps of photo information:

- You don't have to *type* to enter data into the Comments field. You can paste information by using the standard Paste command, or even drag selected text from another program (like Microsoft Word) right into the Comments box.

- If you feel the need to be verbose, go for it; the Comments box holds thousands of words. Careful, though: The field has no scroll bars, so there's a limit to how much of what you paste or type you'll actually be able to see.

Note: You can't even scroll the Comments box by pressing the arrow keys until the insertion point bumps the top or bottom edge of the box, forcing it to scroll. Even dragging with the mouse all the way to the top or bottom of the box doesn't work. If you've got a lot to say, your best bet is to make the box taller and the Source list wider, as described next.

- You can resize the Comments box by making the Info pane larger, as shown in Figure 7-10. Grab the divider bar above the Title field and drag upward to heighten the Info panel (and the Source list correspondingly shorter). You can also drag the bar between the Source list and the photo viewing area to the right, to widen the Info pane.

Figure 7-10:
Got a picture that's worth a thousand words? The Comments field can handle it. But you'll have to make iPhoto's Info pane pretty large to see all 1,000 words. By dragging the bars dividing the Info pane, Source list, and photo viewing area, you can adjust the amount of space each takes up in the iPhoto window. In this example, the Info pane dominates the view, with the Album pane and viewing area squished to the edges.

- If no photos, or several photos, are selected, the notes you type into the Comments box get attached to the current *album,* rather than to the pictures.

- You can add the same comment to a group of photos using iPhoto 4's Batch Change command. For example, ⌘-click all the pictures of your soccer team, choose Edit→ Batch Change, choose Comments from the first pop-up menu, and type a list of your teammates' names in the Comments field. Years later, you'll have a quick reminder of everyone's name.

You can just as easily add comments for an album (click it in the Source list, making sure that no individual photos are selected) or a film roll whose name you've highlighted.

Comments as captions

While the Comments field is useful for storing little scraps of background information about your photos, you can also use it to store the *captions* that you want to appear with your photos when you publish them. In fact, some of the book layouts included with iPhoto's book-creation tools (Chapter 10) automatically use the text in the Comments field to generate a caption for each photo.

(On the other hand, you don't *have* to use the Comments box text as your captions. You can always add different captions when you're editing the book.)

The Photo Info Window

The small Info pane in the main iPhoto window displays only the most basic information about your photos: title, date, and size. For more detailed information, use the Show Info command. It opens the Photo Info window, where iPhoto displays a surprisingly broad dossier of details about your photo: the make and model of the digital camera used to take it, for example, and even exposure details like the f-stop, shutter speed, and flash settings (Figure 7-11).

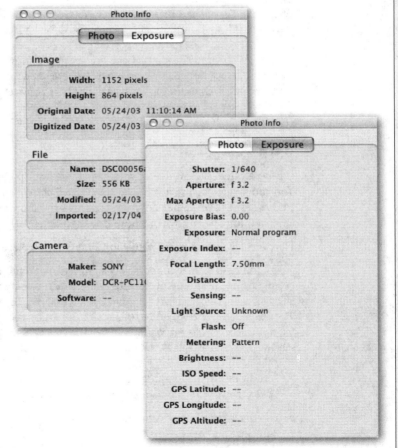

Figure 7-11:
The Photo Info window reports details about your photos by reading the EXIF tags that your camera secretly embeds in your files.

Left: iPhoto uses the Original Date (or lacking that, Modified date) information to sort your photos in the Photo Library and place them in the year albums.

Right: On the Exposure panel, you can tell at a glance that this photo was shot without a flash, at a shutter speed of 1/640, and with an f-stop setting of 3.2. Tracking this information can be useful in determining which settings on your camera produce the best-quality digital photos in a certain set of conditions.

To open the Photo Info window, select a thumbnail and then choose File→Show Photo Info (or press ⌘-I). (If more than one photo is selected, you'll get only a bunch of dashes in the info window.)

The Photo Info window contains two tabs: Photo and Exposure. The Photo panel contains information about the image file itself—when it was originally created, when it was first imported, and when it was last modified. If the image was shot with a digital camera (as opposed to being scanned or imported from disk), the make and model of the camera appear at the bottom of the window (see Figure 7-11).

Tip: Reading the details on the Exposure panel can be eye-opening. For example, if you put your camera into its automatic mode and take a few pictures, this is a great way to find out—and learn from—the shutter and lighting settings the camera used.

How on earth does iPhoto know so much about how your photos were taken? Most digital cameras embed a wealth of image, camera, lens, and exposure information in the photo files they create, using a standard data format called *EXIF* (Exchangeable Image Format). iPhoto automatically scans photos for EXIF data as it imports them.

Note: Some cameras do a better job than others at embedding EXIF data in photo files. iPhoto can extract this information only if it has been properly stored by the camera when the digital photo is created. Of course, most (if not all) of this information is missing altogether if your photos didn't come from a digital camera (if they were scanned in, for example).

Rate Your Photos

iPhoto 4 offers a great new way to categorize your pictures—by how great they are. You can assign each picture a rating of 1 to 5 stars, then use the ratings to sort your Photo Library, or gather only the cream of the crop into a slideshow (Chapter 9), smart album (page 126), or photo book (Chapter 10).

Here are the ways you can rate your digital masterpieces:

- In Edit or Organize mode, select a photo (or several) and choose Photo→My Rating; from the submenu, choose one through five stars.

Tip: If the top of the screen is just too far away, you can also Control-click any one of the selected thumbnails (or, in Edit mode, anywhere on the photo) and choose the My Rating command from the shortcut menu. Its submenu is exactly the same as what you'd find in the Photo→My Rating command.

- In Edit or Organize mode, select a photo (or several) and press ⌘-1 for one star, ⌘-2 for two stars, and so on. Press ⌘-0 to strip away any existing ratings.

- During a slideshow, twitch the mouse to bring up the onscreen control bar. In the bar, click the row of dots to turn them into rating stars (click the third dot to give the current photo three stars, for example). Or just press the number keys on the keyboard to bestow that number of stars as the slides go by.

- To remove a rating, select the photo and choose Photo→My Ratings→None. You're saying, in effect, "This photo has not yet been rated." *Keyboard shortcut: ⌘-0.*

Tip: Once you've applied your star ratings, you can view the actual little stars right under the corresponding thumbnails by choosing View→My Ratings (or pressing Shift-⌘-R).

Deleting Photos

As every photographer knows—make that every *good* photographer—not every photo is a keeper. At some point, you'll probably want to delete some of your photos.

The iPhoto Trash

iPhoto has a private Trash can that works just like the Finder's Trash. (You can see it nestled at the bottom of the Source list as shown in Figure 7-12.) When you want to purge a photo from your Photo Library, you drag it to the Trash. Instead of deleting the photo immediately, iPhoto lets it sit there in the Trash "album," awaiting permanent disposal via the Empty Trash command. This feature gives you one more layer of protection against deleting some precious picture accidentally.

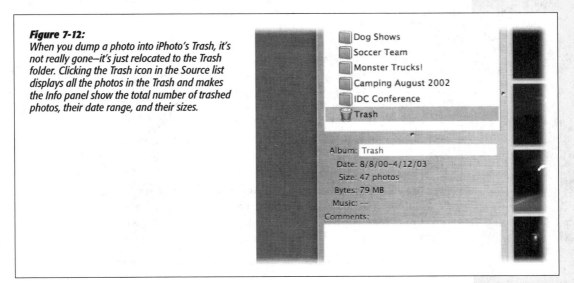

Figure 7-12:
When you dump a photo into iPhoto's Trash, it's not really gone—it's just relocated to the Trash folder. Clicking the Trash icon in the Source list displays all the photos in the Trash and makes the Info panel show the total number of trashed photos, their date range, and their sizes.

You can relegate items to the Trash by selecting one or more thumbnails in the Photo Library and doing one of the following:

- Drag the thumbnails into the Trash.

- Control-click a photo and choose Move to Trash from the shortcut menu.

- Press ⌘-Delete or choose Photos→Move to Trash.

To view the photos that you have piling up in the Trash, awaiting their journey to the great Fotomat in the sky, click the Trash icon, as shown in Figure 7-12. If you decide you don't really want to get rid of any of these trashed photos, it's easy to resurrect them: Just drag the thumbnails out of the Trash and onto the Photo Library icon in the Source list, or else choose Photos→Restore to Photo Library. You've just rescued them from photo-reject limbo and put them back into your main photo collection.

Tip: You can also move photos from the Trash back into your Photo Library by selecting them—yes, in the Trash "album"—and then pressing ⌘-Delete. Think of it as the un-Trash command.)

To *permanently* delete the photos in the Trash, choose File→Empty Trash, or Control-click the Trash icon to access the Empty Trash command via a shortcut menu. iPhoto displays an alert message, warning you that emptying the Trash removes these photos permanently and irreversibly. (Of course, if you imported the photos from files on disk or haven't deleted them from your camera, you can still recover the original files and reimport them.)

Note: As you might expect, dragging photos into the Trash doesn't reduce the total size of your Photo Library by a single byte, because iPhoto is still storing a copy of each photo in its Trash folder. Only when you *empty* the Trash does the iPhoto Library folder actually shrink in size.

Whatever pictures you throw out by emptying the trash also disappear from any albums you've created. (Deleting a photo from an *album* is different, as described in the box on page 121. More on albums later in this chapter.)

Tip: If you'd rather delete a photo instantly and permanently, without all of this Trash foolishness, drag it clear out of the iPhoto window and onto the Trash icon in your *Dock.*

Albums

No matter how nicely you title, sort, and arrange photos in your digital shoebox, it's still a *shoebox* at this point, with all your photos piled together in one vast collection. To really get organized and present your photos to others, you need to arrange your photos into *albums.*

In iPhoto terminology, an album is a subset of pictures from your Photo Library. It's a collection of photos that you group for easy access and viewing. Represented by a little album-book icon in the Source list at the left side of the screen, an album can consist of any photos that you select, or it can be a *smart album* that iPhoto assembles by matching certain criteria that you set up—all pictures that you took in 2003, for example, or all photos that you've rated four stars or higher. (If you've used smart playlists in iTunes, you'll recognize the concept.)

While your Photo Library as a whole might contain thousands of photos from a hodgepodge of unrelated family events, trips, and time periods, a photo album has a focus: Steve & Sarah's Wedding, Herb's Knee Surgery, and so on.

As you probably know, mounting snapshots in a *real* photo album is a pain—that's why so many of us still have stacks of Kodak prints stuffed in envelopes and shoeboxes. But with iPhoto, you don't need mounting corners, double-sided tape, or scissors to create an album. In the digital world, there's absolutely no excuse for leaving your photos in hopeless disarray.

Technically, you're not required to group your digital photos in albums with iPhoto, but consider the following advantages of doing so:

- It makes finding photos much faster. By opening only the relevant photo album, you can avoid scrolling through thousands of thumbnails in the Photo Library to find a picture you want—a factor that takes on added importance as your photo collection expands.

Note: The Search feature in iPhoto 2 that let you search your Photo Library by titles and comments has been removed from iPhoto 4. As you'll see in the next section, the smart album feature now does the same thing.

- Only in a photo album can you drag your photos into a different order. To change the order of photos displayed in a slideshow or an iPhoto hardbound book, for example, you need to start with a photo album (see Chapters 9 and 10).

Creating an Album by Clicking

Set up a new photo album in iPhoto using any of the following methods:

- Choose File→New Album.

- Press ⌘-N.

- Control-click in a blank area of the Source list and choose New Album from the shortcut menu.

- Click the + button in the iPhoto window, below the Source list.

A dialog box appears, prompting you to name the new album. Type in a descriptive name (*Summer in Aruba, Yellowstone 2004, Edna in Paris,* or whatever), click OK, and watch as a new photo album icon appears in the Source list (Figure 7-13). Now you can add photos to your newly spawned album simply by dragging in thumbnails from your Photo Library.

Figure 7-13:
There's no limit to the number of albums you can add, so make as many as you need to logically organize all the photos in your Photo Library. New albums are always added to the end of the list, but you can change the order in which they appear by simply dragging them up or down in the list.

Creating an Album by Dragging

You can also drag a thumbnail (or a batch of them) from the photo viewing area directly into an empty portion of the Source list. In a flash—well, in about three seconds—iPhoto creates a new album for you, named Album-1 (or whatever number it's up to). The photos you dragged are automatically dumped inside.

Similarly, you can drag a bunch of graphics files *from the Finder* (the desktop behind iPhoto) directly into the Source list. In one step, iPhoto imports the photos, creates a new photo album, names it after the folder you dragged in, and puts the newly imported photos into that album.

Tip: Remember that you can drag photos directly from the Finder onto a photo album icon in the Source list, forcing iPhoto to file them there in the process of importing.

Creating an Album by Selecting

This quick album-creation technique takes advantage of a new command in iPhoto 4: File→New Album From Selection. Scroll through your Photo Library and select any pictures you like using the methods described on page 106; they don't have to be from the same film roll, or even the same year. When you're done, choose New Album From Selection, type a name for the new album, and click OK.

Adding More Photos

To add photos to an existing album, just drag them onto its icon. Figure 7-14 illustrates how you can select multiple photos (using any of the selection techniques described on page 106) and drop them into an album in one batch.

Figure 7-14:
When you drag multiple photos in iPhoto, a little red numeric badge appears next to the pointer telling you exactly how many items you've got selected. In this example, 21 pictures are being dragged en masse into a photo album.

The single most important thing to understand about adding photos to an album is this: Putting photos in an album doesn't really *move* or *copy* them. It makes no difference where the thumbnails start out—whether it's the Photo Library or another album. You're just creating *references,* or pointers, back to the photos in your master Photo Library. This feature works a lot like Macintosh aliases; in fact, behind the scenes, iPhoto actually does create aliases of the photos you're dragging. (It stashes them in the appropriate album folders within the iPhoto Library folder.)

What this means is that you don't have to commit a picture to just one album when organizing. One photo can appear in as many different albums as you want. So, if you've got a great shot of Grandma in Hawaii and you can't decide whether to drop the photo into the Hawaiian Vacation album or the Grandma & Grandpa album, the answer is easy: Put it in both. iPhoto just creates two references to the same original photo in your Photo Library.

Tip: To rename an existing photo album, double-click its name or icon in the Source list. A renaming rectangle appears around the album's name, with text highlighted and ready to be edited.

Viewing an Album

To view the contents of an album, click its name or icon in the Source list. All the photos included in the selected album appear in the photo viewing area; the other photos in your Photo Library are hidden.

You can even browse more than one album at a time by highlighting their icons simultaneously:

- To view the contents of several adjacent albums in the list, click the first one, then Shift-click the last.

- To view the contents of albums that aren't consecutive in the list, ⌘-click them.

Tip: Viewing multiple albums at once can be extremely useful when it's time to share your photos. For example, you can make prints or burn an iPhoto CD archive (as explained in Chapters 10 and 14) with the contents of more than one album at a time.

Remember, adding photos to albums doesn't remove them from the Photo Library itself, your master collection. So if you lose track of which album contains a particular photo, just click the Photo Library icon at the top of the Source list to return to the overview of your *entire* photo collection.

Tip: You can put your albums in any order. Just drag them up or down in the Source list.

Moving Photos Between Albums

There are two ways to transfer photos from one photo album to another.

- To *move* a photo between albums, select it and then choose Edit→Cut (or press ⌘-X), removing the photo from the album. Click the destination photo album's name or icon, and then choose Edit→Paste (or press ⌘-V). The photo is now a part of the second album.

- To *copy* a photo into another album, drag it onto the icon of the destination album in the Source list. That photo is now a part of both albums.

Removing Photos from an Album

If you change your mind about how you've got your photos organized and want to remove a photo from an album, open the album and select the photo. (Be sure that you're viewing the contents of a photo *album* in the photo viewing area and not the main Photo Library, the Last 12 Months collection, or the Last Roll collection. Deleting a photo from those sources really does delete it for good.)

Then do one of the following:

- Choose Edit→Cut, or press ⌘-X.

- Choose Edit→Clear.

- Press the Delete key.

- Press the Del (forward-delete) key.
- Control-click the photo, and then, from the shortcut menu, choose Remove from Album.

The thumbnail disappears from the album, but of course it's not really gone from iPhoto. It's still in your Photo Library.

Duplicating a Photo

You can't drag the same photo into an album twice. When you try, the thumbnail simply leaps stubbornly back into its original location, as though to say, "Nyah, nyah, you can't drag the same photo into an album twice."

It's often useful to have two copies of a picture, though. As you'll discover in Chapter 10, a photo whose dimensions are appropriate for a slideshow or desktop picture (that is, a 4:3 proportion) are inappropriate for ordering prints (4 x 6, 8 x 10, or whatever). To use the same photo for both purposes, you really need to crop them independently.

In this case, the old adding-to-album trick isn't going to help you. This time, you truly must duplicate the file, consuming more hard drive space behind the scenes. To do that, highlight the photo and choose File→Duplicate (⌘-D). iPhoto switches briefly into Import mode, copies the file, and then returns to your previous mode. The copy appears next to the original, bearing the same name plus the word "copy."

Note: If you duplicate a photo in an album, you'll see the duplicate both there and in the Photo Library, but not in any other albums. If you duplicate it only in the Photo Library, that's the only place you'll see the duplicate.

Putting Photos in Order

If you plan to turn your photo album into an onscreen slideshow, a series of Web pages, or a printed book, you'll have to tinker with the order of the pictures, arranging them in the most logical and compelling sequence. Photos in the main Photo Library or in a smart album (page 126) are locked into a strict sort order—either by creation date, rating, or film roll—but once they're dragged into a photo album, you can shuffle them manually into a new sequence.

To custom-sort photos in an album, simply drag and drop, as shown in Figure 7-15.

Figure 7-15:
Arrange photos in any order you want by dragging them to a new location within a photo album. In this example, two selected photos from the top-left corner are being dragged to a new location in the next row. The 2 indicates the number of photos being moved; the black vertical bar indicates where iPhoto will insert them when you release the mouse.

Duplicating an Album

It stands to reason that if you have several favorite photos, you might want to use them in more than one of iPhoto's presentations (in a slideshow and a book, for example). That's why it's often convenient to *duplicate* an album: so that you can create two different sequences for the photos inside.

Just highlight an album and then choose File→Duplicate. iPhoto does the duplicating in a flash—after all, it's just duplicating a bunch of tiny aliases. Now you're free to rearrange the order of the photos inside, to add or delete photos, and so on, completely independently of the original album.

Tip: For quick duplicating, you can also Control-click an album in the list and choose Duplicate from the shortcut menu. Duplicating a smart album creates an identical album, which you can then edit as described on the preceding pages.

Merging Albums

Suppose you have three photo albums that contain photos from different trips to the beach, called Spring Break at Beach, Summer Beach Party, and October Coast Trip. You'd like to merge them into a single album called Beach Trips 2003. No problem.

Select all three albums in the Source list (⌘-click each, for example). The photos from all three albums now appear in the photo viewing area. Now create a new, fourth album, using any of the usual methods; select all of the visible thumbnails; and drag them into the new album.

You've now got one big album containing the photos from all three of the original albums. You can delete the three source albums, if you like, or keep all four around. Remember, albums contain only references to your photos—not the photos themselves—so you're not wasting space by keeping the extra albums around. The only penalty you pay is that you have a longer list of albums to scroll through.

Deleting an Album

To delete an album, select its icon in the Source list, and then choose Edit→Clear or press the Delete (or Del) key. You can also Control-click an album and choose Delete Album from the shortcut menu. iPhoto asks you to confirm your intention.

Deleting an album doesn't delete any photos—just the references to those photos. Even if you delete *all* your photo albums, your Photo Library remains intact.

Smart Albums

Albums, as you now know, are the primary organizational tool in iPhoto. Since the dawn of iPhoto, you've had to create them yourself, one at a time—by clicking the +

button beneath the Source list, for example, and then filling up the album by dragging photo thumbnails.

iPhoto 4, though, can create albums *for* you, thanks to *smart albums.* These are self-updating folders that always display pictures according to certain criteria that you set up—all pictures that you took in 2003, for example, or all photos that you've rated four stars or higher. (If you've ever used smart playlists in iTunes, you'll recognize the idea immediately.)

To create a smart album, choose File→New Smart Album (Option-⌘-N), or Option-click the + button below the Source list. Either way, the Smart Album sheet slides down from the top of the window (Figure 7-16).

Figure 7-16:
The Smart Album dialog box is really just a powerful search command, because iPhoto is really just a powerful database. You can set up certain criteria, like this hunt for photos taken during a certain time period.

The controls here are designed to set up a search of your Photo Library. Figure 7-16 illustrates how you'd find pictures that you took in the last two months of 2003—but only those that have four- or five-star ratings and mention your friend Casey in the title or comments.

Click the + button to add a new criterion row to be even more specific about which photos you want iPhoto to include in the smart album. Use the first pop-up menu to choose a type of photo feature (keyword or date, for example) and the second pop-up menu to tell iPhoto whether you want to match it ("is"), eliminate it ("is not"), and so on. The third part of the criterion row is another pop-up menu or a search field where you finally tell iPhoto what to look for.

- You can limit the smart album's reach by limiting it to a certain **Album,** or, by choosing "is not" from the second pop-up menu, *eliminate* an album from consideration. All your albums are listed in the third pop-up menu.

- **Any Text** searches your Photo Library for words or letters that appear in the title, comments, or keywords (page 129) that you've assigned to your photos.

Tip: If you can't remember how you spelled a word or whether you put it in the Comments or Title field, choose "Any Text," choose "contains" from the second pop-up menu, and in the search field type just the first few letters of the word ("am" for Amsterdam, for example). You're bound to find some windmills.

- **Comments, Filename, Keyword,** and **Title** work the same way, except they search *only* that part of the photo's information. Search for "Keyword" "is" "Family" (choose "Family" from the third pop-up menu) to find only those pictures that you specifically assigned the keyword "Family," for example, and not just any old photos where you typed the word "family" somewhere in the comments.

- **Date** is one of the most powerful search criteria. By choosing "is in the range" from the second pop-up menu, you can use it to create an album containing, for example, only the pictures you took on December 24 and 25 of last year, or for that five-day stretch two summers ago when your best friends were in town. Or if you've been on an extended picture-snapping spree, you can choose "is in the last" from the second pop-up menu and choose a limited number of days, weeks, or months from the third pop-up menu.

- The **My Rating** option on the first pop-up menu really puts the fun into smart albums. Suppose you've been dutifully giving your pictures star ratings from 1 to 5, as described on page 118.

  Here's the payoff. You can use this smart album feature to collect, say, only those with five stars to create a quick slideshow of just the highlights. Or choose "is greater than" two stars for a more inclusive slideshow that leaves out only the real duds.

- **Roll** lets you make iPhoto look only in, for example, the last five film rolls that you took (choose "is in the last" from the second pop-up menu and type *5* in the box). Or, if you're creating an album of old shots, you can eliminate the last few rolls from consideration by choosing "is not in the last."

- Click the – button next to a criterion to take it out of the running. For example, if you decide that date shouldn't be a factor, delete any criterion row that tells iPhoto to look for certain dates.

When you click OK, your smart album is ready to show off. When you click its name in the Source list (it has a little gear icon), the main window shows you the thumbnails of the photos that match your criteria. The best part is that iPhoto will keep this album updated whenever your collection changes—as you change your ratings, as you take new photos, and so on.

Tip: To change the parameters for a smart album, click its icon in the list and then choose Photos→Show Info (⌘-I). The Smart Album sheet reappears.

Keywords

Keywords are descriptive words—like *family, vacation,* or *kids*—that you can use to label and categorize your photos, regardless of which photo album they're in.

The beauty of keywords in iPhoto is that they're searchable. Want to comb through all the photos in your library to find every close-up taken of your children during summer vacation? Instead of browsing through multiple photo albums, just perform an iPhoto search for photos containing the keywords *kids, vacation, close-up,* and *summer.* You'll have the results in seconds.

Keywords are also an integral part of iPhoto 4's new smart albums feature, as described on the previous pages.

Note: The Keywords feature, which was such an important part of iPhoto 2, has been stripped down a bit in iPhoto 4. The Keywords window shown in Figure 7-17 used to let you search for words found in your titles and captions as well as keywords. Since that function has been taken over by smart albums, the Keywords window is now all keywords, all the time.

Figure 7-17:
The second photo here has been assigned four keywords. You can tell which ones—Nature, Sports, Outdoor, and Urban—because when you select the photo, the corresponding keywords appear highlighted in gray in the Keywords list.

To remove all these keywords after assigning them to a photo, click Re-move. To get rid of a specific keyword, click that word in the list first, and then click Remove.

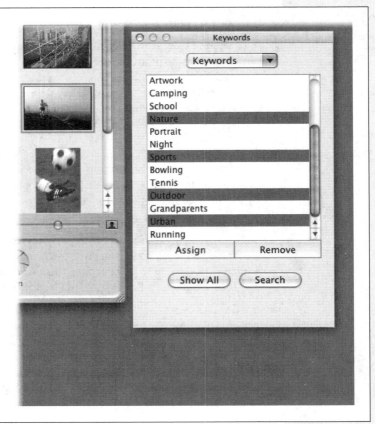

Editing Keywords

To start working with iPhoto's Keywords feature, choose Photos→Show Keywords (or press ⌘-K) to open the Keywords window (Figure 7-17). This is where you edit your keyword list, assign keywords to specific photos, and search for photos using keywords. (You can edit and assign keywords in any of iPhoto's four modes, but it makes the most sense to do it in Organize mode, where you can see thumbnails of all your photos.)

Apple gives you five sample entries in the Keywords list to get you rolling: Favorite, Family, Vacation, Kids, and Birthday. But these are intended only as a starting point. You can add as many new keywords as you want—or delete any of Apple's—to create a meaningful, customized list:

- To add a new keyword, choose New from the Keywords pop-up menu at the top of the window. A new entry called "untitled" appears in the Keywords list, ready to be edited. Just type in your new keyword name.

- To delete a keyword, select it in the list and then choose Delete from the Keywords pop-up menu. As you might expect, you can delete multiple keywords by Shift-clicking or (for noncontiguous selections) ⌘-clicking any number of keywords in the list before choosing the Delete command.

- To rename a keyword, select it in the list, choose Rename from the Keywords pop-up menu, and edit the name.

Note: Be careful about renaming keywords after you've started using them; the results can be messy. If you've already applied the keyword *Fishing* to a batch of photos, but later decide to replace the word *Fishing* with *Romantic* in your keyword list, all the Fishing photos automatically inherit the keyword Romantic. Depending on you and your interests, this may not be what you intended.

It may take some time to develop a really good master set of keywords. The idea is to assign labels that are general enough to apply across your entire photo collection, but specific enough to be meaningful when conducting searches.

Here's a general rule of thumb: Use *albums* to group pictures of specific events—a wedding, family vacation, or beach party, for example. (In iPhoto 4, you can use *film rolls* for the same purpose, if you prefer; see page 102.) Use *keywords* to focus on general characteristics that are likely to appear through your entire photo collection—words like Mom, Dad, Casey, Robin, Family, Friends, Travel, and Vacation.

Suppose your photo collection includes a bunch of photos that you shot during a once-in-a-lifetime trip to Rome last summer. You might be tempted to assign *Rome* as a keyword. Don't…because you probably won't use *Rome* on anything other than that one set of photos. It would be smarter to create a photo album or film roll called *Trip to Rome* to hold all those Rome pictures. Use your keywords to tag the same pictures with descriptors like Travel or Family. It also might be useful to apply keywords that describe attributes of the photos themselves, such as Close-up, Landscape, Portrait, and Scenic—or even the names of the people *in* the photos, like Harold, Chris, and Uncle Bert.

Assigning Keywords

To use keywords to perform searches, you must first assign them to your photos. Here's how the process works:

1. **Choose Photos→Show Keywords, or press ⌘-K.**

   The Keywords window appears.

2. **Select a photo, or several, in the photo viewing area.**

   You can assign keywords when viewing thumbnails in the main Photo Library, or in a specific photo album. Use any of the selection techniques described on page 106.

3. **Click the entries in the Keywords list that you would like to assign to the selected photo(s).**

   You can click as many of the keywords as you want, thereby assigning multiple keywords, as shown in Figure 7-17. Shift-click to select several consecutive keywords in the list, or ⌘-click to select multiple, nonadjacent entries.

4. **Click Assign.**

   iPhoto assigns the keywords to the selected photos.

Tip: Instead of clicking Assign, you can simply Option-double-click a keyword to assign it to the selected photos.

You can see which keywords you've applied to each photo by looking at the Keywords window. When you select a photo, its assigned keywords show up highlighted in the Keywords list, as shown in Figure 7-17.

Better yet, if you have iPhoto set up to show keywords in the main photo viewing area (choose View→Keywords or press Shift-⌘-K), you'll immediately see the assigned keywords underneath each photo, as shown in Figure 7-18.

If you want to remove any of these keywords after assigning them, use the Remove button in the Keywords window, as explained in Figure 7-17. But don't confuse *removing* keywords with *deleting* keywords. Removing a keyword strikes it from a specific photo; deleting it (using the pop-up menu in the Keywords window) removes the word permanently from the keywords list—and, of course, from all photos to which you've assigned it.

The Checkmark "Keyword"

You may have noticed that one entry in the keyword list is not a word, but a symbol—a small checkmark. You can't edit this particular entry; it's always just a checkmark.

The checkmark works just like the other keyword entries. But instead of assigning a particular keyword to photos, it flags them with a small checkmark symbol, as shown in Figure 7-19. You'll find this marker extremely useful for temporary organizational tasks.

Figure 7-18:
You might find it easier to keep track of which keywords you've assigned by displaying them right in the photo viewing area. Choose View→Keywords, or press Shift-⌘-K, to make them appear.

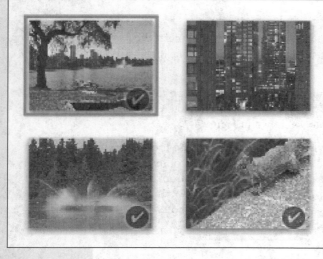

Figure 7-19:
The idea behind the checkmark button is to provide an easy, uncomplicated way of earmarking a series of photos while sifting through your collection.

For example, you might want to cull only the most appropriate images from a photo album for use in a printed book or slideshow. As you browse through the images, use the checkmark button to flag each shot you want. Later, you can use the Search function (described next) to round up all of the images you checkmarked, so that you can drag them all into a new album en masse.

You remove checkmarks from photos just as you remove keywords: With the Keywords window open, select a checkmarked photo, click the checkmark in the Keywords list, then click Remove. (If you click Remove without first clicking the checkmark, iPhoto will remove not just the checkmark, but any other keywords you had assigned to the photo.)

Tip: Just after moving your checkmarked photos to an album, remember to remove the checkmark from all of them while they're still selected. That way, you won't get confused the next time you want to use the checkmark button for flagging a batch of photos.

Searching by Keyword

Whether you tag photos with the checkmark symbol or a series of keywords, the big payoff for your diligence arrives when you need to get your hands on a specific set of photos, because iPhoto lets you *search* for them.

To perform a keyword search, open the Keywords window (⌘-K). Then double-click a keyword in the Keywords list. (Or, if you're charging by the hour, click the word and then click Search.)

iPhoto immediately rounds up all photos labeled with that keyword, displays them in the photo viewing area, and hides all others.

Here are the important points to remember when using iPhoto's keyword searches:

- To search for photos that match multiple keywords, select all keywords you want—by Shift-clicking (to select a range of consecutive keywords) or ⌘-clicking (for noncontiguous entries) in the Keywords list—and *then* click Search.

Note: When you use multiple keywords, iPhoto finds only the photos that match *all* of those criteria. In other words, if you select *Friends*, *Candid*, and *Vacation* in a keyword search, iPhoto displays only those photos that contain *all three* keywords.

If you want to find photos tagged with the word Friends *or* Candid *or* Vacation, you have to perform those searches individually, using a single keyword each time.

- You can confine your search to a single album by selecting it before searching. Similarly, clicking the Photo Library in the list before searching (or Last Roll, or Last 12 Months) means that you want to search that photo collection. (You cannot, however, select multiple albums and search only in those.)

- Remember, double-clicking a keyword performs a search; Option-double-clicking *assigns* the word to the selected photo(s).

- Click Show All to restore the view to the whole album or whole Photo Library you had visible before you performed the search.

Customizing the Shoebox

iPhoto starts out looking just the way you see it in Figure 7-4, with each of your pictures displayed as a small thumbnail against a plain white background. This view makes it easy to browse through photos and work with iPhoto's various tools. But hey, this is *your* digital shoebox. With a little tweaking and fine-tuning, you can completely customize the way iPhoto displays your photos.

Start with a visit to iPhoto→Preferences and click the Appearance button.

Figure 7-20:
Here's the same Photo Library with two very different customized views.

Top: In the first example, the thumbnails are set to a very small size, with drop shadows, against a white background. The Source list, Information panel, and Comments are displayed.

Bottom: The second view features large thumbnails, with borders, against a dark gray background. The Source list is hidden, but the titles for each photo are displayed.

Changing the View

The controls in the Appearance panel of the Preferences window lets you change the overall look of your Photo Library (see Figure 7-20). Here are your options:

- **Add or remove a border or shadow.** The factory setting, Drop Shadow, puts a soft black shadow behind each thumbnail in the photo viewing pane, a subtle touch that gives your Photo Library an elegant 3-D look.

  As pretty as this effect is, however, there's one great reason to turn it *off*: It slows iPhoto down slightly, as the program has to continually redraw or resize those fancy shadows behind each thumbnail whenever you scroll or zoom. Switch to either the Border or No Border setting and you'll be rewarded with faster scrolling and smoother zooming whenever you change the size of thumbnails (as described in the next section). The Border setting puts a thin white frame around each picture. You won't see this border unless you change the background color, as explained in the next paragraph.

- **Change the background color.** Right under the No Border radio button, a slider lets you adjust the background color of the photo viewing pane. Actually, the term "color" is a bit of an overstatement, since your palette of color choices includes white, black, or any shade of gray in between.

FREQUENTLY ASKED QUESTION

Return of the Find Command

Hey—where's the Find command?

It's not there any more. You're supposed to use the smart album feature to find photos according to certain criteria.

Still, the Find command of iPhoto 2 had charms of its own—and you can recreate it for nostalgia's sake.

Create a new smart album and name it Find. Set up the criteria as shown here: the first row says "Any Text "contains," and the next couple say "Keyword contains." Click OK.

At the moment, your new smart album doesn't contain any pictures, of course. But when you want to find certain photos, click the Find album and press ⌘-I, which reopens the smart album sheet. Type the phrase you're looking for into the text box (to search among comments or titles), or specify the keyword you want, and then press the Return or Enter key. Presto: the matching pictures appear in the smart album.

The next time you open this homemade Find dialog box, the same search term will still be in the text box; just type over it, if necessary, to perform a new search.

- **Adjust the Alignment.** Turn on the "Align photos to grid" checkbox if you want the thumbnails in your Photo Library to snap into evenly spaced rows and columns, even if your collection includes thumbnails of varying sizes and orientations, as shown in Figure 7-21.

Figure 7-21:
The "Align to grid" option is insignificant if all your photos are the same size and orientation. But with a variety of horizontal and vertical images, as shown here, photos stay in strict rows and columns (right) despite their size and shape differences. The window on the left shows an "unaligned" version of the same thumbnails.

- **Change the date order.** Turning on "Place most recent photos at the top" puts them at the top of the main iPhoto window. It's sort of like seeing your most recent email messages at the top of your inbox. If you turn this checkbox off, you'll have to scroll all the way down to see your most recent pictures.

- **Choose text size.** The pop-up menu at the bottom of the Appearance panel lets you choose Small or Large for the album names in the Source list, depending on your eyesight. As for keywords and the other text in the iPhoto window, you're stuck with one size—tiny.

Showing/Hiding Keywords, Titles, and Film Roll Info

If you want to display thumbnails along with the titles and keywords you assign your pictures using iPhoto, you can switch these view options on or off by choosing View→ Titles (Shift-⌘-T) and View→Keywords (Shift-⌘-K). Titles and keywords appear under each thumbnail (see Figure 7-18).

As with most of iPhoto, your formatting options are limited. You can't control the font, style, color, or size of this text. Your only choice is to either display the title and keywords or to keep them hidden.

Editing Your Shots

Y ou can't color-correct photos, paint in additional elements, mask out unwanted backgrounds, or apply any special effects filters in iPhoto, as you can with editing programs like Photoshop and GraphicConverter. Nonetheless, iPhoto is designed to handle seven basic photo fix-up tasks:

- **Enhance.** With one click, this tool endeavors to make photos look more vibrant by tweaking the brightness and contrast settings and adjusting the saturation to compensate for washed-out or oversaturated colors.

- **Cropping.** The cropping tool lets you cut away the outer portions of a photo to improve its composition or to make it the right size for a printout or Web page.

- **Retouch.** This little brush lets you paint out minor imperfections like blemishes, freckles, and scratches.

- **Brightness/Contrast.** These sliders can tone down bright, overexposed images or lighten up those that look too dark and shadowy. While the Enhance button takes an all-or-nothing approach to fixing a photo, the Brightness and Contrast controls let you make tiny adjustments to the settings.

- **Red-Eye.** This little filter gets rid of one very common photo glitch—those shining red dots that sometimes appear in a person's eyes as the result of flash photography.

- **Black & White.** Turns your color photos into moody, black-and-white art shots.

- **Sepia.** Makes new photos look faded and brownish, for that old-time daguerreotype look. It's the only new editing tool in iPhoto 4.

For anything beyond these simple touch-up tasks, you need to open your photos in a more powerful editing program—which you can easily do from within iPhoto, as explained later in this chapter.

Using the Editing Tools

All iPhoto editing is done in a special editing mode, which you can open up by any of the following methods:

- With a photo selected, click the Edit button in the middle of the main iPhoto window. iPhoto's editing tools appear in the lower pane.

- Double-click a thumbnail. If you have iPhoto set to open photos right in the main window (which is the factory setting), iPhoto jumps into Edit mode and enlarges the selected photo to fill the window. The tools appear, once again, at the bottom.

- If you've instructed iPhoto to open a photo in a separate window when you double-click its thumbnail, the Edit tools appear in a top-mounted toolbar, as shown in Figure 8-1. (If the toolbar isn't visible, click the capsule-shaped button in the upper-right corner of the window to make it appear, or choose Window→ Show Toolbar.)

Figure 8-1:
iPhoto's editing tools appear in the toolbar when you open a photo in its own window. A >> symbol at the right end of the toolbar (as shown here) means that the window is too narrow to display all the tools. Just drag the window wider to show all tools, or click the double-arrow to access the tools via a pop-up menu.

- Control-click a thumbnail or a photo in its own window; from the shortcut menu, choose "Edit" (to edit right in iPhoto's main window) or "Edit in separate window." (If have a two-button mouse for your Mac, you can right-click instead.)

One-Click Fixups: The Enhance Button

The Enhance button provides a simple way to improve the appearance of less-than-perfect digital photos. You click one button to make colors brighter, skin tones warmer, and details sharper. See Figure 9-2 for an example.

But if you want to know *exactly* what the Enhance button does, good luck. Apple guards that information as though it's a top-secret meatloaf recipe. iPhoto's online help makes only a nebulous statement about it "improving colors," but provides no explanation as to *how* they're improved.

What's clear is that the Enhance button analyzes the relative brightness of all the pixels in your photo and attempts to "balance" the image by dialing the brightness or contrast up or down and intensifying dull or grayish-looking color. In addition to this overall adjustment of brightness, contrast, and color, the program makes a particular effort to identify and bring out the subject of the photo. Usually, this approach at least makes pictures look somewhat richer and more vivid.

Using the Enhance Button

If you're editing a photo in iPhoto's main window, you'll find the Enhance button on the lower pane of the window, along with iPhoto's other editing tools. To enhance a photo, just click the Enhance button. There's nothing to select first, and no controls to adjust. (It's something like Photoshop's Auto Levels command in that regard.)

Tip: You can also Control-click a photo to choose Enhance from the shortcut menu.

If you've opted to open a photo in a separate window for editing, you won't see the Enhance button in the toolbar. To bring it out of hiding, add the button to the Editing toolbar, as explained on page 149. (Or just invoke the command using the Tip above.)

Tip: After using the Enhance button, you can hold down the Control key to see your unenhanced "before" photo. Release the key to see the "after" image.

By pressing and releasing the Control key, you can toggle between the two versions of the photo to assess the results of the enhancement.

Figure 8-2:
The Enhance command works particularly well on photos that are slightly dark and that lack good contrast, like the original photo on the left. Using iPhoto's Brightness and Contrast sliders alone helped a little, as shown in the middle photo, but the Enhance button produced the best results, as shown at the far right.

As you use the Enhance button, remember that iPhoto's image-correcting algorithms are simply best guesses at what your photo is supposed to look like. It has no way of knowing whether you've shot an overexposed, washed-out picture of a vividly colored sailboat, or a perfectly exposed picture of a pale-colored sailboat on an overcast day.

Consequently, you may find that Enhance has no real effect on some photos, and only minimally improves others. Remember, too, that you can't enhance just one part of a photo. When you click the Enhance button, iPhoto runs its enhancement routine on the whole picture. If you want to selectively adjust specific portions of a picture, you need a true photo editing program like GraphicConverter or Photoshop Elements.

Tip: If using the Enhance command does improve your photo, but just not enough, you can click it repeatedly to amplify its effect—as many times as you want, really. It's just that applying Enhance more than three times or so risks turning your photo into digital mush.

If you go too far, remember that you can press ⌘-Z (or choose Edit→Undo) to backtrack. In fact, you can take back as many steps as you like, all the way back to the original photo.

In some cases, you'll have to do more than click the Enhance button to coax the best possible results from your digital photos. You may have to do further tweaking with the Brightness and Contrast sliders as explained later in this chapter.

Cropping

iPhoto's cropping tool is a digital paper cutter. It neatly shaves off unnecessary portions of a photo, leaving behind only the part of the picture you really want.

You'd be surprised at how many photographs can benefit from selective cropping. For example:

- **Eliminate parts of a photo you just don't want.** This is a great way to chop your brother's ex-girlfriend out of an otherwise perfect family portrait, for example (provided she was standing at the end of the lineup).

- **Improve a photo's composition.** Trimming a photo allows you to adjust where your subject matter appears within the frame of the picture. If you inspect the professionally shot photos in magazines or books, for example, you'll discover that many pros get more impact from a picture by cropping tightly around the subject, especially in portraits.

- **Get rid of wasted space.** Huge expanses of background sky that add nothing to a photo can be eliminated, keeping the focus on your subject.

- **Fit a photo to specific proportions.** If you're going to place your photos in a book layout or turn them into standard size prints (Chapter 10), you may need to adjust their proportions. That's because there's a substantial discrepancy between the *aspect ratio* (length-to-width proportions) of your digital camera's photos and those of film cameras—a difference that will come back to haunt you if you order prints. The following discussion covers all the details.

How to Crop a Photo

Here are the steps for cropping a photo:

1. **Open the photo for editing.**

   You can use any of the methods mentioned earlier in this chapter.

2. **Make a selection from the Constrain pop-up menu, if you like (shown in the toolbar in Figure 8-3).**

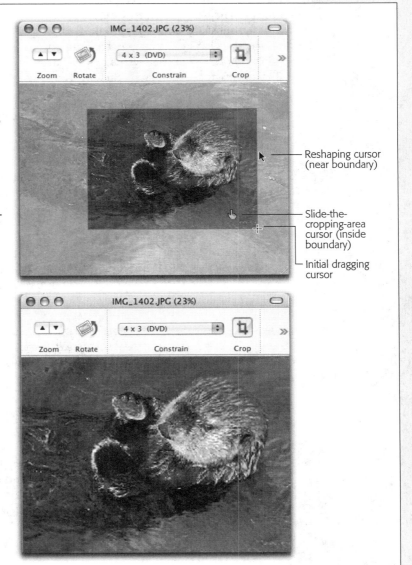

Figure 8-3:
When you crop a picture, you drag out (draw) a rectangle in any direction using the cross-hair pointer to define the part of the photo you want to keep. (To deselect this area—when you want to start over, for example—click anywhere in the foggy area.)

Top: The three different cursor shapes you may see, depending on where you move the pointer: The + crosshair for the initial drag, the arrow when you're near a boundary (for re-shaping), or the pointing-hand for sliding the entire rectangle around the photo.

Bottom: Once you've drawn the rectangle and clicked Crop, the excess margin falls to the digital cutting room floor, thus enlarging your subject.

Reshaping cursor (near boundary)

Slide-the-cropping-area cursor (inside boundary)

Initial dragging cursor

The Constrain pop-up menu controls the behavior of the cropping tool. When the menu is set to None, you can draw a cropping rectangle of any size and proportions, in essence going freehand.

When you choose one of the other options in the pop-up menu, however, iPhoto constrains the rectangle you draw to preset proportions. It prevents you from coloring outside the lines, so to speak.

This feature is especially important if you plan to order prints of your photos (Chapter 10). When you attempt to do so, you'll notice that you can order prints only in standard photo sizes: 4 x 6, 5 x 7, 8 x 10, and so on. As noted on page 169, however, most digital cameras produce photos whose proportions are 4 to 3 (width to height). That's great for onscreen slideshows, DVDs, and iPhoto coffee-table books, because your Mac screen, television, and iPhoto book layouts use 4-to-3 dimensions, too—but that doesn't divide evenly into standard print photograph sizes.

That's why the Constrain pop-up menu offers you canned choices like 4 x 6, 5 x 7, and so on. Limiting your cropping to one of these preset sizes guarantees that your cropped photos will fit perfectly into Kodak prints. (If you don't constrain your cropping this way, Kodak will decide how to crop them to fit instead of you.)

Note: Even though the Constrain menu ensures the right *proportions*, it doesn't in any way guarantee that the total *size* of the final photos is adequate. See the box "When Cropping Problems Crop Up" on page 144 for more about properly sizing your photos.

Other crop-to-fit options in the Constrain menu let you crop photos for use as a desktop picture ("1024 x 768 [Display]," or whatever your actual monitor's dimensions are), as a 4 x 6-inch print, to fit into one of the Book layouts available in iPhoto's Book mode, and so on.

Tip: Opening a photo into its own separate editing window (by Control-clicking its thumbnail and choosing "Edit in separate window") triggers a bonus feature: two boxes in the toolbar labeled Custom. Into these text boxes, you can type any proportions you want: 4 x 7, 15 x 32, or whatever your eccentric design needs happen to call for.

As soon as you make a selection from this pop-up menu, iPhoto 4 draws a preliminary cropping rectangle—of the proper dimensions—on the screen, turning everything outside it dim and foggy.

In general, this rectangle always appears in landscape (horizontal) orientation. To make it vertical, open the pop-up menu a second time and choose Constrain as Landscape. (The exception is the constrain choice called "4 x 3 (DVD)," which starts you out with a horizontal rectangle as a time-saving convenience.)

Tip: Actually, there's a quicker way to rotate the selection from horizontal to vertical (or vice versa): Option-drag across the photo to draw a new selection rectangle, as described in the next step. The selection rectangle crisply turns 90 degrees.

Now, the cropping area that iPhoto suggests with its foggy-margin rectangle may, as far as you're concerned, be just right. In that case, skip to step 5.

More often, though, you'll probably want to give the cropping job the benefit of your years of training and artistic sensibility by *redrawing* the cropping area:

3. **Click anywhere in the foggy area to get rid of the rectangle. Then position the mouse pointer (which appears as a crosshair) at one corner of your photo. Drag diagonally across the portion of the picture that you want to *keep*.**

As you drag a rectangle across your photo, the portions *outside* the selection—the part of the photo that iPhoto will eventually trim away—get dimmed out once again (Figure 8-3).

Tip: Even if you've turned on one of the Constrain options in step 2, you can override the constraining by pressing ⌘ after you begin dragging.

Don't worry about getting your selection perfect, since iPhoto doesn't actually trim the photo until you click the Crop button.

4. **Adjust the cropping, if necessary.**

If the shape and size of your selection area is OK, but you want to adjust which part of the image is selected, you can move the selection area without redrawing it. Position your mouse over the selection so that the pointer turns into a hand icon. Then drag the existing rectangle where you want it.

You can even change the *shape* of the selection rectangle after you've released the mouse button, thanks to an invisible quarter-inch "handle" that surrounds the cropping area. Move your cursor close to any edge or corner so that it changes from the + shape to an arrow. Now you can drag the edge or corner to reshape the rectangle (see Figure 8-3).

If you get cold feet, you can cancel the operation by clicking once anywhere outside the cropping rectangle (to remain in Edit mode) or by double-clicking anywhere on the photo (to return to Organize mode). Or, if the photo is open in its own window, just close the window.

Note: Despite its elaborate control over the *relative* dimensions of your cropping rectangle, iPhoto offers no indication at all over its *actual* size in pixels. If you want to crop a photo to precise pixel dimensions, you'll have to do the job in another program, like GraphicConverter or Photoshop Elements. (See page 151 for instructions on flipping into a different program for editing.)

5. **When the cropping rectangle is set just the way you want, click the Crop button.**

   Alternatively, Control-click the photo and choose Crop from the shortcut menu. (That method is handy if the Crop button on the toolbar isn't visible.)

   If throwing away all those cropped-out pixels makes you nervous, relax. When you click Crop, iPhoto, behind the scenes, makes a duplicate of the original photo before doing the deed—a handy safety net for the day you decide to revert back to the uncropped version, months or years later.

   If you realize immediately that you've made a cropping mistake, you can choose Edit→Undo Crop Photo to restore your original.

   If you have regrets *weeks* later, on the other hand, you can always select the photo and choose File→Revert to Original. iPhoto reinstates the original photo from its backup, discarding every change you've ever made.

Note: When you crop a photo, you're cropping the photo in *all albums* in which it appears (Chapter 7). If you want a photo to appear cropped in one album but not in another, you must first duplicate it (highlight it and then choose File→Duplicate), then edit each version separately.

Painting Out Freckles, Scratches, and Hairs

iPhoto's Retouch brush lets you paint away scratches, spots, hairs, or any other small flaws in your photos with a few quick strokes. (See Figure 8-4.)

The operative word here is *small*. The Retouch brush can't wipe out a big blob of spaghetti sauce on your son's white shirt or completely erase somebody's mustache.

UP TO SPEED

When Cropping Problems Crop Up

Remember that cropping always *shrinks* your photos. Take away too many pixels, and your photo may end up too small (that is, with too low a resolution to print or display properly).

Here's an example: You start with a 1600 x 1200 pixel photo. Ordinarily, that's large enough to be printed as a high-quality, standard 8 x 10 portrait.

Then you go in and crop the shot. Now the composition is perfect, but your photo only measures 800 x 640 pixels. You've tossed out nearly a million and a half pixels.

The photo no longer has a high enough *resolution* (pixels per inch) to produce a high-quality 8 x 10. The printer is forced to

blow up the photo to fill the specified paper size, producing visible, jaggy-edged pixels in the printout. The 800 x 640 pixel version of your photo would make a great 4 x 5 print (if that were even a standard size print)—but pushing the print's size up further noticeably degrades the quality.

Therein lies a great advantage of using a high-resolution digital camera (5 or 6 megapixels, for example). Because each shot starts out with such a high resolution, you can afford to shave away a few hundred thousand pixels and still have enough left over for good-sized, high-resolution prints.

Moral of the story: Know your photo's size and intended use—and don't crop out more photo than you can spare.

It's for tiny fixups that don't involve repainting whole sections of a photo. (For that kind of photo overhaul, you need a real photo editing program like the ones described at the end of this chapter.)

The Retouch brush works its magic by blending together the colors in the tiny area that you're fixing. It doesn't cover the imperfections you're trying to remove, but *blurs* them out by softly blending them into a small radius of surrounding pixels.

Tip: The Retouch brush is particularly useful if your photo library contains traditional photographs that you've scanned in. You can use it to wipe away the dust specks and scratches that often appear on film negatives and prints or that are introduced when you scan the photos.

Figure 8-4:
The key to using the Retouch brush is to target small areas and use restraint so that you don't overblur the area you're working on. Notice how the Retouch brush was used on the original photo (top) to subtly soften wrinkles around the eye and remove imperfections in the upper left corner (bottom).

Using the Retouch Brush

The Retouch brush appears in the lower pane of the main iPhoto window as soon as you enter Edit mode. If you've opted to open a photo in a separate window for editing, use the Customize Toolbar command to add the Retouch brush to the Editing toolbar, as shown in Figure 8-7.

Alternatively, when in Editing mode, you can select the Retouch brush by Control-clicking a photo and choosing Retouch from the shortcut menu.

Once you've selected the Retouch brush, your pointer turns into a small crosshair with a hole in the middle. Using the center of the crosshair, target the imperfection and "paint" over it, using a series of short strokes to blend it with the surrounding portion of the picture. Don't overdo it: If you apply too much retouching, the area you're working on starts to look noticeably blurry and unnatural, as if someone smeared Vaseline on it.

Fortunately, you can use the Edit→Undo command (⌘-Z) to take back as many of your brush strokes as necessary.

Note: On high-resolution photos, it can take a moment or two for iPhoto to process each individual stroke of the Retouch brush. If you don't see any results, wait a second for iPhoto to catch up with you.

Brightness/Contrast

No software can rescue a photo that was taken with very poor lighting, but a little time spent with the Brightness and Contrast sliders can make many photos look much more vivid, with deeper, more saturated colors. If the Enhance command (described earlier in this chapter) doesn't produce quite the results you were hoping for, you may be able to further improve the quality of your photo by adjusting these controls.

The Sliders

These controls are easy to use. Just drag each slider to the left or right to decrease or increase the overall brightness and contrast of a photo (see Figure 8-5). The results appear almost instantly, so you can experiment freely.

The brightness and contrast controls can also salvage shots that were either too light or too dark when they were taken. Again, you can't add details that simply aren't there, but brightening a dark shadowy image, or deepening the contrast on a washed-out image, can coax out elements that were barely visible in the original photo.

Tip: When your adjustments are subtle, it's sometimes hard to tell how much you've really improved a photo without comparing the results directly to the original, unedited one. Remember that pressing the Control key temporarily restores the photo to its pre-edited condition. By pressing and releasing Control, you can toggle back and forth as much as you want, comparing the two versions before deciding to keep the changes permanently.

Figure 8-5:
These sliders allow you to make incremental adjustments in brightness and contrast, but they can be sluggish on large photos.

You can save some time by clicking anywhere along a slider bar to make the controller jump directly to that point. Click the sun or circle icon at the ends of the sliders to crank the brightness or contrast all the way up or down.

As long as you remain in Edit mode, you can back out of your changes no matter how many of them you've made. For example, if you've adjusted the Brightness and Contrast sliders, you can remove those changes using the Edit→Undo Brightness/Contrast command (⌘-Z).

In fact, you can remove these changes even after you've performed other editing functions, like cropping or rotating. The only catch is you must back out of the changes one at a time. In other words, if you change the contrast on a photo, then crop it, and then rotate it, you'll have to use the Undo command three times—first to unrotate, then to uncrop, and finally, to undo the contrast setting.

But once you leave Edit mode—either by closing the photo's window or by double-clicking it, thereby returning to Organize mode—you lose the ability to undo your edits. At that point, the only way to restore your photo is to choose the File→Revert to Original, which removes all the edits you've made to the photo since importing it.

Red-Eye

Red-eye is light reflected back from your subject's eyes. The bright light of your camera's flash passes through the pupil of each eye, illuminating the blood-red retinal tissue at the back of the eye, which is reflected back into the camera lens. Red-eye problems worsen when you shoot pictures in a dim room, because your subject's pupils are dilated wider, allowing even more light from the flash to illuminate the retina. (See the top picture in Figure 8-6 for an example.)

If it's too late to avoid red-eye to begin with (by using an external flash, for example), and people's eyes are already glowing evilly, iPhoto's Red-Eye tool lets you alleviate red-eye problems by digitally removing the offending red pixels. Here's how:

1. **Open your photo in Edit mode.**

   Change the zoom setting, if necessary, so that you have a close-up view of the eye that has the red-eye problem.

2. **Use the crosshair pointer to select the face (by dragging a box across it).**

   The more face you select, the better the tool does, since it distinguishes red from almost-red by comparing the eyes with the facial tones. So grab a generous number of pixels, including the eyes.

3. **Click the Red-Eye button.**

   (The Red-Eye button is dimmed until you've actually selected a portion of the photo. If you're editing in a separate window, as shown in Figure 8-6, you may have to use the >> menu at the right end of the toolbar to find the Red-Eye command.)

   iPhoto neutralizes the red pixels, painting the pupils solid black.

   Of course, this means that everybody winds up looking like they have *black* eyes instead of red ones—but at least they look a little less like the walking undead.

B & W, Sepia

The B & W (Black and White) and Sepia tools don't correct anything. They simply drain the color from your photos. B & W converts them into moody grayscale images (a great technique if you're going for that Ansel Adams look); Sepia repaints them entirely in shades of antique brown (as though they were 1865 daguerreotypes).

Open a photo in Edit mode, and then click the Black & White or Sepia button. That's all there is to it. If you change your mind, you can use File→Undo to restore the color immediately, or choose File→Revert to Original at any point to return to your original file.

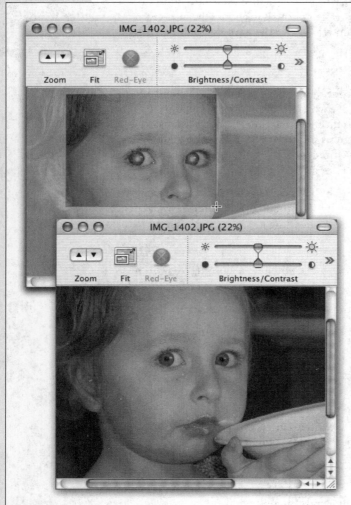

Figure 8-6:
Top: Anything even slightly red in your photo gets blackened out by iPhoto's Red-Eye tool. Select a good chunk of the face, omitting anything else that's visibly red (lips, clothing, furniture, and so on).

Bottom: Truth be told, the Red-Eye tool doesn't know an eyeball from a pinkie toe. It just turns any red pixels black, regardless of what body part they're associated with. Friends and family members look more attractive—and less like Star Trek characters—after you touch up their phosphorescent red eyes with iPhoto.

Tip: If you don't see the B & W or Sepia buttons, you can always Control-click the photo and choose the corresponding command from the shortcut menu.

Rotate

Unless your digital camera has a built-in orientation sensor, iPhoto imports all photos in landscape orientation (wider than they are tall). The program has no way of knowing if you turned the camera 90 degrees when you took your pictures. Once you've imported the photos, just select the sideways ones and rotate them into position (if indeed you didn't do so during your first slideshow, as described on page 95).

You don't have to be in Edit mode to rotate photos. Remember, you can select thumbnail images when you're in Organize mode and then use one of the following methods to turn them right-side up:

- Choose Edit→Rotate→Counter Clockwise (or Clockwise).

- Click the Rotate button in the main iPhoto window, just under the Info pane (it's the rightmost of the four buttons on the pane). (Option-click this button to reverse the direction of the rotation.)

- Press ⌘-R to rotate selected photos counter-clockwise, or Shift-⌘-R to rotate them clockwise.

- Control-click a photo and choose Rotate→Clockwise (or Counter Clockwise) from the shortcut menu.

Tip: After importing a batch of photos, you can save a lot of time and mousing if you select *all* the thumbnails that need rotating first (by ⌘-clicking each, for example). Then use one of the rotation commands above to fix all the selected photos in one fell swoop.

Incidentally, clicking Rotate (or pressing ⌘-R) generally rotates photos counter-clockwise, and Option-clicking (Shift-⌘-R) generally rotates them clockwise. But you can swap these directions by choosing iPhoto→Preferences and changing the Rotate setting on the General tab of the Preferences dialog box.

Note: When you rotate an image saved in GIF format in iPhoto, the resulting rotated picture is saved as a JPEG file. The original GIF is stored unchanged in an Originals folder in the iPhoto Library folder (see Chapter 6).

Customizing the Toolbar

Like the toolbar in all Mac OS X Finder windows, the Editing toolbar—the one that appears when you open a photo in its own window—can be customized to contain the particular editing tools you use the most.

With at least one photo open in its own window, start by choosing Window→Customize Edit Toolbar. (Alternatively, you can click the Customize button on the toolbar, or Control-click a toolbar button and choose Customize Toolbar from the shortcut menu.) The toolbar's customization panel fills the window (Figure 8-7). You now have a dozen more icons at your disposal, ready to be installed on the toolbar.

Figure 8-7:
The ability to edit the toolbar can be very handy. Suppose, for example, that you tend to use the same Constrain settings (like 4 x 3) for most of your cropping. Just drag the proposed tool candidates upward into place, and then click Done.

And now, a tip: If you find that the toolbar takes up too much space, Control-click anywhere on it and choose Text Only from the shortcut menu.

To put a new item on the toolbar, just drag it into position. To remove an existing tool, drag it off the toolbar. It vanishes in a puff of smoke, Mac OS X–style. Here are some of the changes you might consider making:

- Several tools—including the Enhance button and the Retouch brush—don't come factory-installed in the Editing toolbar. It's up to you to add them.

- iPhoto offers buttons for each of the constrained cropping options described earlier. If there's one cropping size that you find yourself using frequently, put it in the toolbar.

- Get rid of the tools you never use, to keep the toolbar free from clutter. If you never crop to a custom size, for example, you can drag the Custom constraining fields out of the way. (You can always restore tools later.)

- Even if you don't add or remove any buttons, you can drag the ones that are already there into a new order, putting them exactly where you want them. (You can do this at any time, even when the customization panel isn't open, by ⌘-dragging the buttons on the toolbar.)

- Drop separator lines between the various tools to group them visually on the toolbar according to your preference.

Tip: You can restore the toolbar to its original condition by dragging the default set of tools at the bottom on the customization panel to the toolbar.

No need to worry about adding too many items to this toolbar. If you keep piling on the icons, it sprouts a fly-out menu on the right side, listing every button, as shown in Figure 8-1.

When you're finished dragging extra buttons to the toolbar, click Done to close the Customize panel and activate your new icons.

Tip: While your mind is on fiddling with the toolbar, remember that you can control the size of its icons and their labels, just as in many other Apple programs. The trick is to ⌘-click the white, capsule-shaped Toolbar button in the upper-right corner of the window. With each click, you cycle through to the next smaller configuration of the toolbar. You can keep going until the icons themselves disappear, and only button labels in tiny type remain.

Beyond iPhoto

If you're serious about digital photographs, iPhoto's tools by themselves aren't going to cut it. You'll have to spring for a more full-featured image-editing program, such as Adobe Photoshop, Photoshop Elements, Canvas, GraphicConverter, or a similar program.

Photoshop is by far the most popular tool for the job, but at about $600, it's also one of the most expensive. Unless you intend to perform sophisticated image-editing and compositing (sandwiching together parts of different photos into one image), save yourself some money and buy Photoshop Elements. It's a trimmed-down version of Photoshop with all the basic image-editing stuff and just enough of the high-end features. It costs less than $100, and a free trial version is available online. (Your digital camera may even have come with Photoshop Elements right in the box.)

Before you go software shopping, though, check out your own hard drive. If you bought your Mac recently, you may already have the image-editing software you need. Apple includes GraphicConverter—a simple but powerful editing program with Photoshop-like tools—on some Mac models.

In any case, these programs offer tools that iPhoto lacks: sharpness controls, saturation adjustment, color correction, and so on.

Opening Photos in Other Programs

To open a photo in a "real" editing program, first open that program so that its icon appears in the Dock. Then drag a thumbnail from iPhoto's window directly onto the program icon. (Of course, you can also drag a picture from iPhoto's window onto the application's *desktop* icon, or an alias of it.) In fact, you can even drag several thumbnails at once to open all of them simultaneously.

If you've already been working in, say, Photoshop, you might be tempted to use its File→Open command to open an iPhoto photo directly. But the drag-and-drop method is far more efficient; if you use File→Open, you'll have to navigate through the oddly numbered folders of the labyrinthine iPhoto Library folder (page 96) to locate the picture you want.

Tip: When you edit a photo in another program, you're essentially going behind iPhoto's back; the program doesn't have a chance to make a safety copy of the original. Therefore, you're sacrificing your ability to use the Revert to Original command to restore your photo to its original state in case of disaster .

The sneaky workaround: Just make one tiny change to the photo *in iPhoto* before you drag its thumbnail onto another program's icon. Rotate it all the way around, for example—anything to force iPhoto to create a backup. Thereafter—whether you edit the photo in another program or not—you can restore the photo to its original condition at any time.

Setting up an external editing program

The drag-and-drop approach is great if you *occasionally* want to open a photo in another program. But if you find yourself routinely editing your photos in another program, there's a much easier method: Just set up iPhoto to open your photos in that program automatically when you double-click. You set up this arrangement as follows.

FREQUENTLY ASKED QUESTION

In iPhoto, Less Is More

I just finished editing a batch of photos, cropping each picture to a much smaller size. But now my iPhoto Library folder is taking up more *space on my hard drive! How can making the photos smaller* increase *the size of my photo collection? Shouldn't throwing away all those pixels have the opposite effect—shrinking things down?*

Your cropped photos do, in fact, take up much less space than they did. Remember, though, that iPhoto doesn't let you monkey with your photos without first stashing away a copy of each original photo, in case you ever want to use the Revert to Original command to restore a photo to its original condition.

So each time you crop a picture (or do any other editing) for the first time, you're actually creating a new, full-size file on your hard drive, as iPhoto stores both the original *and* the edited versions of the photo. Therefore, the more photos you edit in iPhoto, the more hard drive space your photo collection will take up.

Incidentally, it's worth noting that iPhoto may be a bit overzealous when it comes to making backups of your originals. The simple act of rotating a photo, for example, creates a backup (which, considering how easy it is to re-rotate it, you might not consider strictly necessary). If you've set up iPhoto to open a double-clicked photo in another program like Photoshop, iPhoto creates a backup copy *even if you don't end up changing it* in that external program.

If this library-that-ate-Cleveland effect bothers you, you might investigate the free program iPhoto Diet (available from the "Missing CD" page of *www.missingmanuals.com,* for example). One of its options offers to delete the backups of photos that have simply been rotated. Another deletes perfect duplicates that iPhoto created when you opened those photos in another program without editing them.

There's even an option to delete *all* backups—a drastic option for people who believe that their photos will never be better than they are right now.

1. **Choose iPhoto→Preferences.**

   The Preferences window opens.

2. **Click the General button, if necessary. For the "Double-click photo" preference settings, select the "Opens photo in" radio button, then click Select Application.**

   A standard Open dialog box appears so you can navigate to your favorite photo editing program.

3. **Choose the program you want to use for editing, then click Open.**

   When you're done, close the Preferences window.

Now, whenever you double-click a thumbnail, iPhoto launches the designated editing program and uses it to open your photo.

One big advantage of this method is that it lets iPhoto track your editing activity—yes, even in other programs. iPhoto can therefore update its thumbnail versions of your photos to reflect the changes. It can also preserve the original version of the photos you edit externally, so that you can later use the Revert to Original command if disaster should strike any time later, as explained later in this chapter.

Freedom of choice

It's nice to be able to edit photos in external programs, but it's a lot of trouble to switch that feature on and off; a trip to iPhoto→Preferences is involved every time. If you're like many photo fans, what you want is to use iPhoto's convenient editing features *most* of the time, ducking out to other programs only when you need more industrial-strength features.

Fortunately, iPhoto offers a couple of tricks that let you switch to an external editor only on demand:

- Clicking the Edit button below the photo-viewing area *always* opens a selected photo for editing right in iPhoto, regardless of your Preferences setting.

- Better yet: If you Control-click a thumbnail, the shortcut menu offers you three choices: "Edit" (in the main iPhoto window), "Edit in separate window," or "Edit in external editor." (The last option is available only if you've selected an editing program as described earlier.) No matter what your settings in Preferences may be, this route always gives you the choice of all three editing modes.

Reverting to the Original

iPhoto includes built-in protection against overzealous editing—a feature that can save you much grief. If you end up cropping a photo too much, or cranking up the brightness of a picture until it seems washed out, or accidentally turning someone's lips black with the Red-Eye tool, you can undo all your edits at once with the Revert to Original command. Revert to Original strips away *every change you've ever made* since the picture arrived from the camera. It leaves you with your original, unedited photo.

The secret of the Revert to Original command: Whenever you use any editing tools, iPhoto—without prompting and without informing you—instantly makes a duplicate of your original file. With an original version safely tucked away, iPhoto lets you go wild on the copy. You can remain secure in the knowledge that in a pinch, iPhoto can always restore an image to the state it was in when you first imported it.

Note: The unedited originals are stored in an Originals folder inside the photo folder for each date, deep in your Home→Pictures→iPhoto Library folder. (The Originals folder doesn't exist until you edit at least one photo.)

To restore an original photo, undoing all cropping, rotation, brightness adjustments, and so on, select a thumbnail of an edited photo or open the photo in Edit mode. Then choose File→Revert to Original. iPhoto swaps in the original version of the photo—and you're back where you started.

As noted earlier, iPhoto does its automatic backup trick whenever you edit your pictures (a) within iPhoto or (b) using a program that you've set up to open when you double-click a picture. It does not make a backup when you drag a thumbnail onto the icon of another program. In that event, the Revert to Original command will be dimmed when you select the edited photo.

Bottom line: If you want the warmth and security of Revert to Original at your disposal, don't edit your pictures behind iPhoto's back. Follow the guidelines in the previous two paragraphs so that iPhoto is always aware of when and how you're editing your pictures.

The iPhoto Slideshow

iPhoto's slideshow feature offers one of the world's best ways to show off your digital photos. Slideshows are easy to set up, they're free, and they make your photos look fantastic. This chapter details not only how to put together an iPhoto slideshow, but how to give presentations that make you and your photos look their absolute best.

About Slideshows

When you run an iPhoto slideshow, your Mac presents the pictures in full-screen mode—no windows, no menus, no borders—with your images filling every inch of the monitor. Professional transitions take you from one picture to the next, producing a smooth, cinematic effect. If you want, you can even add a musical soundtrack to accompany the presentation. The total effect is incredibly polished, yet creating a slideshow requires very little setup.

The One-Click Slideshow

If you haven't already tried iPhoto's slideshow feature, give it a whirl right now. It requires only a single click.

With either a photo album or your entire Photo Library displayed in the iPhoto window, click the Play button under the Info pane (see Figure 9-1). A moment later, your Mac's screen fades to black, and then the show begins. Each photo is displayed full screen for two seconds, and then softly fades out as the next one dissolves into view. The default musical soundtrack—J. S. Bach's Minuet in G—plays in the background. (You'll always find the currently selected soundtrack listed in the Info panel at the left side of the iPhoto window.)

As noted in Chapter 6, this is a great feature for reviewing photos you've just dumped into the Mac from the camera. In fact, that delicious moment when you first see the pictures at full-screen size—after having viewed them only on the camera's two-inch screen—is just what Apple's engineers had in mind when they designed the Play button.

Remember to wiggle your mouse during the slideshow when you want to summon iPhoto 4's new onscreen control bar (page 95).

When you've had enough, click the mouse or press almost any key to end the show and return to the iPhoto window. (Otherwise, iPhoto will run the show in a continuous loop forever.)

Figure 9-1:
The quickest way to kick off a slideshow in iPhoto is to click the Play button in the main iPhoto window, shown by the cursor here. There's no keyboard shortcut, but you can hit any key except the arrow keys and the Space bar to stop a show once it's running.

Setting Up the Show

Of course, this canned slideshow is just a starting point. To put together a presentation that will dazzle friends and family, you're invited to select the most impressive photos, choose the perfect background music, and even control how fast or slow the show moves along. Best of all, you can save different slideshow settings for *each album,* as described later in this chapter.

Choose Your Photos

When putting together a slideshow, your first task is choosing the photos you want to include.

As a starting point, here's how iPhoto determines which photos *it* includes:

• If no photos are selected, iPhoto shows all the pictures currently in the photo viewing area, starting with the first photo in the album or Photo Library.

Most people, most of the time, want to turn one album into a slideshow. That's easy—just click the album before starting the slideshow. It can be any album you've created, a smart album, the Last Roll album, or one of iPhoto's built-in monthly and yearly albums. As long as no individual pictures are selected, iPhoto will reveal all the pictures in the currently open album.

Note: You can run a slideshow from a photo album, or from your entire Photo Library—but not from *multiple* albums. You can select more than one album simultaneously (by ⌘-clicking them), but when you click Play, iPhoto uses only the first album for the slideshow.

- If only one photo is *visible* (but not selected) in the photo viewing area, then the slideshow consists of that one picture. The music still plays—you just end up with a one-picture show.

- If one photo is *selected,* iPhoto uses that picture as its starting point for the show, ignoring any that come before it. Of course, if you've got the slideshow set to loop continuously, iPhoto will eventually circle back to display the first photo in the window.

- If you've selected more than one picture, iPhoto includes *only* those pictures in its slideshow.

Not all pictures are good pictures

Choosing photos for your slideshow involves more than just picking the photos you like the best. You also have to make sure you've selected pictures that are the right size.

Why is the size so important? Because iPhoto always displays slideshow photos at full-screen dimensions—and on most of today's monitors, that means at least 1024 x 768 pixels. If your photos are smaller than that, iPhoto stretches them to fill the screen, often with disastrous results. If you include a tiny 320 x 240 pixel snapshot in a slideshow, for example, the resulting image, blown up to more than ten times its normal size, turns into a chunky, jaggy-edged mess (Figure 9-2).

UP TO SPEED

How Big Is My Monitor?

To know if your photos are large enough to be displayed distortion-free on your monitor, you have to know how many pixels it takes to fill your screen.

And to know that, you need to know your screen's *resolution.* Choose →System Preferences, and open the Displays panel.

In the Resolutions list, you'll find all the resolutions that your monitor can handle, with the current resolution highlighted. If the selection says, for example, 1024 x 768, you know that photos must be at least 1024 pixels by 768 pixels to fill your screen without iPhoto having to stretch them to fit.

Note: Although iPhoto blows up images to fill the screen, it always does so proportionately, maintaining each photo's vertical-to-horizontal aspect ratio. As a result, photos often appear with vertical bars at the left and right edges when viewed on long rectangular screens like the Apple Cinema Display, the 17-inch iMac or PowerBook, and so on. To eliminate this effect, see page 161.

Figure 9-2:
Here's an example of what happens when a 240 x 180 pixel photo ends up in a slideshow. Projected at full-screen dimensions, a portrait that looks great at its normal size becomes jaggy-edged and fuzzy—unflattering to both the subject and the photographer. If you plan to use your photos in a slideshow, make sure your digital camera is set to capture pictures that are at least 1024 x 768 pixels.

WORKAROUND WORKSHOP

Small Photos, Big Show

You can't control the size of your pictures as they appear during a slideshow, as they always fill the screen. To ensure that the results look good, you need to make sure all your photos are sized to fill the screen *properly,* as mentioned earlier in this chapter.

But what if you're *stuck* with photos that are simply not big enough? Suppose you're charged with putting together a slideshow for the family reunion, and the only pictures you have of Uncle Rodney happen to be scanned photos that are only 640 x 480 pixels?

You can't cut Rodney out of the slideshow, but at the same time, you know Aunt Lois won't take kindly to having her husband appear onscreen hideously distorted. ("Why does Rod look so jagged?" you can imagine her saying. "What did you do to him?") Here's one simple way to have smaller photos displayed perfectly in a slideshow and keep everyone happy:

Using a program like GraphicConverter or Photoshop Elements, create a new document that's exactly the right size for your screen. If your monitor's set to 1024 x 768 pixels, create a document that's 1024 x 768 pixels. Fill the background of the blank document so that it's black, to match the black between slides. (Actually, you can use whatever background you like.)

Now open the small photo that you want to include in your slideshow. Paste a copy of it into the center of your blank document. Save the results and then import the image file into iPhoto.

You now have a new picture, perfectly sized for your slideshow. Your small photo will appear onscreen at the proper size, with a black border around it. No, the photo won't fill the screen, but at least it will appear just as clear and distortion-free as the larger photos.

Determining the size of your photos

If you're not sure whether your photos are big enough to be slideshow material, iPhoto provides two easy ways to check their sizes:

- Click a thumbnail in the photo viewing area, and then look at the Size field in the Info pane. You'll see something like "1600 x 1200." That's the width and height of the image, measured in pixels.

- Select a thumbnail and choose Photos→Show Info, or press ⌘-I to open the Show Info window. The width and height of the photo are the first two items listed in the Image section of the Photo pane.

Putting photos in the right order

iPhoto shows your pictures in the same order you see them in the photo viewing area. In other words, to rearrange your slides, drag the thumbnails around within their album. Remember that you can't drag pictures around in the Photo Library, a smart album, the Last 12 Months collection, or the Last Roll folder—only within a photo album.

Note: If iPhoto appears to be shamelessly disregarding the order of your photos when running a slideshow, it's probably because you've got the "Present slides in random order" option turned on in the Slideshow dialog box, as described in the following section.

Slideshow Settings

With your photos selected, you're ready to configure the settings for your slideshow. In Organize mode, click the Slideshow icon at the bottom of the iPhoto dialog box to explore your options. The Slideshow dialog box has two panels—Settings and Music—as shown in Figure 9-3. In iPhoto 4, you have more ways than ever to customize your slideshow:

Transitions

In previous versions of iPhoto, you were stuck with one type of transition—the crossfade or *dissolve,* in which one slide gradually fades away as the next "fades in" to take its place. In iPhoto 4, you have a choice of five transition effects:

- **None.** An abrupt switch—a simple cut—to the following image.

- **Cube.** Imagine that your photos are pasted to the sides of a box that rotates to reveal the next one. If you've ever used the Fast User Switching feature in Mac OS 10.3, you've got the idea.

- **Dissolve.** This classic crossfade should be familiar to users of previous versions of iPhoto or the screen saver feature in Mac OS X.

- **Mosaic Flip.** The screen is divided into a bunch of squares, each of which rotate in turn to reveal part of the new image, like puzzle pieces turning over.

- **Wipe.** The new image sweeps across the screen, pushing the old one off the other side.

If you choose a transition other than Dissolve or None, a pop-up menu and slider below the pop-up menu offer you the chance to choose a direction and speed for the effect.

- **Direction.** Determines the direction the new image enters from. Choose Right to Left, Top to Bottom, or vice versa. (Most people find Left to Right the most comfortable way to experience a transition, but a slow top-to-bottom wipe is pleasant, too.)

- **Speed.** Move the slider to the right for a speedy transition, or to the left for a leisurely one. Take into account your Timing setting, described below. The less time your photo is onscreen, the better off you are with a fast transition speed, so that your audience has time to see the picture before the next transition starts. However, moving it *all* the way to the right produces a joltingly fast change.

Tip: For a smooth, but unobtrusive transition, choose Dissolve, with the Speed slider moved almost all the way to the right. It's less abrupt than None, but it puts all the emphasis on the pictures, not the transition.

Figure 9-3:
The Slideshow dialog box is where you set slideshow timing for each show. You can go as fast as one second per slide, or bump the number up to 60 seconds each for a very leisurely presentation. (You can type a number larger than 60 in the "Play each slide..." field, but iPhoto will ignore you. It refuses to spend any more than one minute on each shot, no matter how good a photographer you are.)

Using the pop-up menus and Speed slider at the top of this dialog box, you can choose from five transition effects and decide how quickly you want them to go by.

Slide timing

If left to its own devices, iPhoto advances through your pictures at the rate of one photo every two seconds. If that seems too brisk or too slow, you can change the rate.

In the Slideshow dialog box, use the "Play each slide for __ seconds" controls to specify a different interval, as shown in Figure 9-3.

Tip: You can also speed up or slow down a show that's already under way, just by pressing the up or down arrow keys. Behind the scenes, iPhoto adjusts the number of seconds in the Slideshow dialog box accordingly.

The timing you choose here doesn't affect the timing or speed of the *transitions,* as in iPhoto 4. You set the transition speed independently using the slider, as described above.

Note: You can't set different timings for different pictures. It's one-timing-fits-all—within each show, anyway. You *can* set a different timing for each album.

Present slides in random order

An iPhoto slideshow normally displays your pictures in the order they appear in the photo viewing area. If you'd like to add a dash of surprise and spontaneity to the proceedings, turn on the "Present slides in random order" checkbox. iPhoto will shuffle the pictures into whatever order it pleases.

Repeat slideshow

When iPhoto is done running through all your photos in a slideshow, it ordinarily circles back and starts playing the whole sequence from the beginning again. If you want your photos to play just once through, turn off the "Repeat slideshow" checkbox.

Scale photos to fill screen

If any photos in your slideshow don't match your screen's proportions, you may want to turn on "Scale photos to fill screen." For example, if your slideshow contains photos in portrait orientation—that is, pictures taken with the camera rotated—iPhoto fills up the unused screen space on each side with vertical black bars.

Turning on "Scale photos" makes iTunes enlarge the picture so much that it completely fills the screen. This solution, however, comes at a cost: Now the top and bottom of the picture are lost beyond the edges of the monitor.

When the middle of the picture is the most important part, this option works fine. If the black bars bother you, the only other alternative is to crop the odd-sized pictures in the slideshow album so that they match your monitor's shape. (See "Cropping" on page 140.)

Display titles

Every photo in your collection can have a name—a title. If you turn on this option, iPhoto superimposes each photo's title during the slideshow, in a small white-on-black box in the upper-right corner of the screen.

Needless to say, the cryptic file names created by your digital camera (IMG00034. JPG) usually don't add much to your slideshow. But if you've taken the time to give your photos helpful, explanatory names ("My dog age 3 mos"), then by all means turn on the "Display titles" checkbox.

Display slideshow controls

As discussed on page 95, you can always summon iPhoto's new onscreen control bar by twitching the mouse during a slideshow; then, if a few seconds go by without any mouse activity, the bar politely fades away again.

If you turn on "Display slideshow controls," however, then the control bar appears automatically every time this slideshow begins—no mouse wiggling required—and remains onscreen all the time.

Display my ratings

You can differentiate your stunning award-winners from the photographic dogs by adding ratings to each, on a one-to-five-star scale. If you turn on this option, iPhoto superimposes a small ratings bar on the bottom of each slideshow picture. (You can't change the rating using this mini-bar; it's for display purposes only. Of course, a quick mouse wiggle summons the full-blown control bar, complete with its own star-rating panel that you *can* change.)

Note: The control bar and the star-rating panel occupy the same space near the bottom of the slideshow "canvas," so they can't both be on the screen at the same time. That's why the "Display my ratings" checkbox is grayed out when "Display slideshow controls" is turned on.

---

iTunes: The Soundtrack Store

Perhaps more than any other single element, *music* transforms a slideshow, turning your ordinary photos into a cinematic event. When you pair the right music with the right pictures, you do more than just show off your photos; you create a mood that can stir the emotions of your audience. So if you really want your friends and family to be transfixed by your photos, add a soundtrack.

That's especially easy if, like many Mac OS X fans, you've assembled a collection of your favorite music in iTunes. In iPhoto 4, for the first time, you have the choice of an individual song from your iTunes Library or an entire *playlist*. Gone are the days of listening to the same tune repeating over and over again during a lengthy slideshow—a sure way to go quietly insane (unless, of course, you really like that song…a *lot*).

The possibilities of this new feature are endless, especially combined with iPhoto's new smart albums feature. You can create a smart album that contains, say, only photos of your kids taken in December, and give it a soundtrack composed of holiday tunes, created effortlessly using a smart playlist in iTunes. Instant holiday slideshow!

Your first iPhoto slideshow is born with a ready-to-use soundtrack—J. S. Bach's Minuet in G. In fact, Apple sends iPhoto to you equipped with *two* Bach classics—the Minuet in G and *Jesu, Joy of Man's Desiring*.

Not to knock Bach, but it's fortunate that you're not limited to two of his greatest hits. To switch to a soundtrack of your own choosing, click the Music button at the top of the Slideshow dialog box (Figure 9-4). If you use iTunes, every track in your iTunes Library automatically appears here. You can search and sort through your songs and playlists, just as though you were in iTunes itself.

To get started, click the Music button near the top of the Slideshow dialog box. As shown in Figure 9-4, a pop-up menu reads Sample Music; the two Bach pieces mentioned above appear in a list below. If you have songs of your own in iTunes, choose iTunes Music Library from this pop-up menu to access them (this option is grayed out if you don't have any music files in iTunes).

Figure 9-4:
The Music tab of the Slideshow dialog box lets you choose a playlist (or your entire iTunes Library). By clicking the column headings, you can sort the list by Song, Artist (as shown here), or Time.

If you have a long slideshow (600 photos, say), use the pop-up menu to choose an iTunes playlist rather than an individual song. iTunes will repeat the song (or playlist) for as long as your slideshow lasts.

Your iTunes playlists appear on this menu, too. In other words, you can use this pop-up menu either to select an entire playlist to use as your soundtrack, or to call up a playlist for the purpose of listing the songs in it, thereby narrowing your search for the one song you seek.

Page 3 offers the details on using this box, but here are some iPhoto-specific tips:

- To use an entire playlist as a soundtrack for your slideshow, select it from the pop-up menu. At slideshow time, iPhoto will begin the slideshow with the first tune in the playlist, and continue through all the songs in the list before starting over.

- To use an individual song as a soundtrack, click its name in the list. That song will loop continuously for the duration of the slideshow.

Once you've settled on (and clicked) an appropriate musical soundtrack for the currently selected album, click Save Settings (to memorize that choice without starting the slideshow) or Play (to begin the slideshow right now). From now on, that song or playlist will play whenever you run a slideshow from that album. (It also becomes the *proposed* soundtrack for any new slideshows you create.)

Alternatively, if you decide you don't want any music to play, turn off the "Play music during slideshow" checkbox on the Music panel of the Slideshow dialog box.

Note: You can't select multiple songs from the song list in the Slideshow dialog box. The Shift-click and ⌘-click keystrokes that work in so many Mac dialog boxes are useless here. If you have in mind a group of several songs that would make a perfect backdrop for your slideshow, the solution is to create a new playlist in iTunes, taking care to drag into it the desired songs from your Music Library, in the order that you want them to play. Switch back to iPhoto, and choose that playlist from the pop-up menu in the Slideshow dialog box (see Figure 9-4).

Nicely enough, you can even use songs you've bought from Apple's iTunes Music Store. (If you get "not authorized" messages when you try, see page 585 for troubleshooting tips.)

FREQUENTLY ASKED QUESTION

Slideshow Smackdown: iPhoto vs. iMovie

I've read that iMovie makes a great slideshow program, too. Supposedly I can import my photos, add music, and play it all back full-screen with cool cross-dissolves, just like you're saying here. Which program should I use?

The short answer: iPhoto for convenience, iMovie for control.

In iMovie, you can indeed import photos. You can add them to the timeline at the bottom of the window in any order. What's more, you have individual control over their timing (1 second for the first slide, 3 seconds for the second, or whatever) and the crossfades between them (dissolve between slides 1 and 2, a left-to-right "wipe" between slides 2 and 3, and so on). You can even add what Apple calls the Ken Burns Effect: slow, elegant pans and zooms for certain photos, much like the Mac OS X screen saver.

The music options are much greater in iMovie, too. Not only can you import music straight from a music CD (without having to use iTunes as an intermediary), but you can actually record a narration into a microphone as the slideshow

plays. And, of course, you have a full range of title and credit-making features at your disposal, too.

When the show looks good, you can export it to a QuickTime movie just as described in Chapter 18—or, for the absolute finest in picture quality, to Apple's iDVD software for burning onto a real DVD. (A Mac with a DVD burner, called an Apple SuperDrive, is required.)

But iPhoto has charms of its own. Creating a slideshow is *much* less work in iPhoto, for one thing. If you want a slideshow to loop endlessly—playing on a laptop at somebody's wedding, for example, or at a trade show—iPhoto is also a much better bet. (iMovie can't loop.)

Remember, too, that iPhoto is beautifully integrated with your various albums. Whereas building an iMovie project is a serious, sit-down-and-work proposition that results in *one* polished slideshow, your Photo Library has as many different slideshows as you have albums—all ready to go at any time.

Different Shows, Different Albums

You can save different slideshow settings for each album in your Photo Library, something you couldn't do in the program's earliest incarnations.

To save settings for a specific photo album, first choose the album from the Source list, then click the Slideshow icon in the lower pane of the iPhoto window to open the Slideshow dialog box (you have to be in Organize mode to see the button). Pick the speed, order, repeat, and music settings you want, then click Save Settings. The settings you saved will automatically kick in each time you launch a slideshow from that album.

You'll never have to remember which song you've chosen for a given album, either. When you click the album's name, the name of the saved iTunes track appears right in the Info panel of the main iPhoto window, as shown in Figure 9-1.

Running the Show

Once you've picked your photos, set your options, and selected a music track, your show is ready to run. Click the Play button (the triangular button beneath the Source list) in the main iPhoto window. The slideshow begins instantly.

Control Over the Show

iPhoto slideshows run themselves, advancing from photo to photo according to the timing you set in the Slideshow dialog box. However, you can control a slideshow after it starts running in a number of ways. Some of these functions are also represented by icons on the control bar (see page 95), but it's nice to know that you can also trigger them from the keyboard, with or without the control bar:

- **Pause it.** Press the Space bar at any point to pause a slideshow. The music keeps playing, but the photos stop advancing. If the control bar isn't onscreen, a glowing Pause indicator briefly appears in the lower portion of the picture. When you're ready to move to the next slide and resume the auto-advancing of pictures, press Space again. A small Play indicator appears onscreen momentarily to confirm that iPhoto has understood your command.

- **Manual advance.** Press the right or left arrow keys to advance to the next or previous photo, overriding the preset timing. In fact, once you hit either arrow key, the slideshow shifts into manual mode and stops advancing the photos altogether. A small translucent bar with arrows and a Play button appears onscreen to indicate that iPhoto is listening to your key presses.

At this point, you can continue to use the arrow keys to move through all the photos—or stay on one photo for the rest of your life, for all iPhoto cares. As with the pause command, the music track keeps on playing. (To stop the music, you must end the slideshow.)

In short, this is a terrific setup for a slideshow that you're narrating in person.

- **Back to auto-advance.** To put a slideshow back into autoplay mode after you've used one of the arrow keys, press the Space bar. The photos advance automatically once again. Or, just wait a moment. As the onscreen arrows or control bar fade away, auto-advancing will resume.

- **Speed it up or slow it down.** Press the up or down arrow keys to speed up or slow down the slideshow on the fly. You'll discover that iPhoto can't create a stroboscopic, three-frames-per-second effect; one picture per second is about its maximum speed. (Give the poor thing a break—it's got a *lot* of data to scoop off the hard drive and throw onto your screen.)

Note: The changes you make manually are temporary. The next time you run a slideshow, you'll start again with the timing set in the Slideshow dialog box.

- **Rate the photos.** Even if you haven't summoned the control bar, you can rate photos as they flash by just by tapping the corresponding number keys on your keyboard: 1, 2, 3, 4, or 5 for the corresponding number of stars, or 0 to remove the rating.

- **Rotate the photos.** If a photo appears sideways, press ⌘-R to rotate it counter-clockwise, or Option-⌘-R to rotate it clockwise. (Or vice versa, if you've fooled around with iPhoto's Preferences dialog box.)

- **Delete the duds.** When a forgettable photo appears, press the Delete or Del key on your keyboard to move it to the iPhoto Trash, without even interrupting the show. (Unless you have very understanding family and friends, you may want to do this *before* you show the pictures to others for the first time.)

Slideshows and iDVD

If you have a Mac equipped with a DVD-burning SuperDrive, you have yet another slideshow option: Instead of running a presentation directly from iPhoto, you can send your slideshow—music and all—from iPhoto to iDVD. Using iDVD, you can transform the pictures from your album into an interactive slideshow that can be presented using any DVD player. (Just picture the family clicking through your photos on the big-screen TV in the den!)

Learn how to do the iPhoto-to-iDVD conversion in Chapter 20.

Prints and Books

Using iPhoto to print your pictures is pretty easy. But making *great* prints—the kind that rival traditional film-based photos in their color and image quality—involves more than simply hitting the Print command.

One key factor, of course, is the printer itself. You need a good color inkjet printer that can produce photo-quality printouts. Fortunately, getting such a printer these days is pretty easy and inexpensive. Even some of the cheapo inkjet printers from Epson, HP, and Canon can produce amazingly good color images—and they cost less than $100. (Of course, you make it up to the printer company on the back end when you buy more ink cartridges. Depending on how many prints you make, what you spend on these expensive cartridges can easily double or triple the cost of the printer in a year.)

Even with the best printer, however, you can end up with disappointing results if you fail to consider at least three other important factors when trying to coax the best possible printouts from your digital photos. These factors include the resolution of your images, the settings on your printer, and your choice of paper.

Resolution and Shape

Resolution is the number of individual pixels squeezed into each inch of your digital photo. The basic rule is simple: The higher your photo's resolution, or *dpi* (dots per inch), the sharper, clearer, and more detailed the printout will be. If the resolution is too low, you end up with a printout that looks blurry or speckled.

Low-resolution photos are responsible for more wasted printer ink and crumpled photo paper than any other printing snafu, so it pays to understand how to calculate a photo's dpi when you want to print it.

Calculating resolution

To calculate a photo's resolution, divide the horizontal or vertical size of the photo (measured in pixels) by the horizontal or vertical size of the print you want to make (usually measured in inches).

Suppose a photo measures 1524 x 1016 pixels. (How do you know? See Figure 10-1.) If you want a 4 x 6 printout, you'll be printing at a resolution of 254 dpi (1524 pixels divided by 6 inches = 254 dpi), which will look fantastic on paper. Photos printed on an inkjet printer look their best when printed at a resolution of 220 dpi or higher.

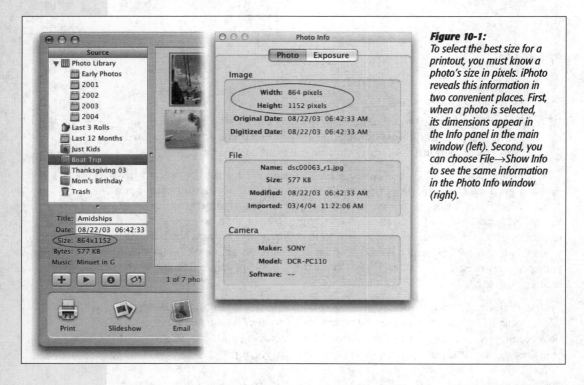

Figure 10-1:
To select the best size for a printout, you must know a photo's size in pixels. iPhoto reveals this information in two convenient places. First, when a photo is selected, its dimensions appear in the Info panel in the main window (left). Second, you can choose File→Show Info to see the same information in the Photo Info window (right).

But if you try to print that same photo at 8 x 10, you'll get into trouble. By stretching those pixels across a larger print area, you're now printing at just 152 dpi—and you'll see a noticeable drop in image quality.

While it's important to print photos at a resolution of 250 to 300 dpi on an inkjet printer, there's really no benefit to printing at higher resolutions—600 dpi, 800 dpi, or more. It doesn't hurt anything to print at a higher resolution, but you probably won't notice any difference in the final printed photos—at least not on inkjet printers. Some inkjets can spray ink at finer resolutions—720 dpi, 1440 dpi, and so on—and using these highest settings produces very smooth, very fine printouts. But bumping the resolution of your *photos* higher than 300 dpi doesn't have any perceptible effect on their quality.

Aspect ratio

You also have to think about your pictures' *aspect ratio*—their proportions. Most digital cameras produce photos with 4-to-3 proportions, which don't fit neatly onto standard print paper (4 x 6 and so on). You can read more about this problem on page 169. (Just to make sure you're completely confused, print paper is measured *height by width*, whereas digital photos are measured *width by height*.)

If you're printing photos on letter-size paper, the printed images won't have standard Kodak dimensions. (They'll be, for example, 4 x 5.3.) You may not particularly care. But if you're printing onto, say, precut 4 x 6 photo paper (which you choose in the File→Page Setup dialog box), you can avoid ugly white bands at the sides by first cropping your photos to standard print sizes.

Tweaking the Printer Settings

Just about every inkjet printer on earth comes with software that adjusts various print quality settings. Usually, you can find the controls for these settings right in the Print dialog box that appears when you choose File→Print. To reveal these printer-specific controls in iPhoto, click the Advanced Options button in the Print dialog box, and then choose an additional command from the pop-up menu (Figure 10-2).

Figure 10-2:
Click Advanced Options in the standard iPhoto Print dialog box to open this important box. Here, choose Print Settings, Quality & Media, or a similar command from the pop-up menu (depending on your printer type) to see the controls for paper type, print quality, and so on.

Before you print, verify that you've got these settings right. On most printers, for example, you can choose from several different quality levels when printing, like Draft, Normal, Best, or Photo. There might also be a menu that lets you select the kind of paper you're going to use—plain, inkjet, glossy photo, and so on.

Choose the wrong settings, and you'll be wasting a lot of paper. Even a top-of-the-line Epson photo printer churns out awful photo prints if you feed it plain paper when it's expecting high-quality glossy stock. You'll end up with a smudgy, soggy mess. So each time you print, make sure your printer is configured for the quality, resolution, and paper settings that you intend.

Paper Matters

When it comes to inkjet printing, paper is critical. Regular typing paper—the stuff you'd feed through a laser printer or copier—may be cheap, but it's too thin and absorbent to handle the amount of ink that gets sprayed on when you print a full-color digital photo. If you try to print large photos on plain paper, you'll end up with flat colors, slightly fuzzy images, and paper that's rippled and buckling from all the ink. For really good prints, you need really good paper.

Most printers accommodate at least five different grades of paper: plain, High Resolution (a slightly heavier inkjet paper—not glossy, but with a silky-smooth white finish on one side), Glossy Photo (a stiff, glossy paper resembling the paper that developed photos are printed on), Photo Matte (a stiff, non-glossy stock), glossy *film*, made of polyethylene rather than paper (which feels even more like traditional photographic paper), and so on.

These better photo papers cost much more than plain paper, of course. Glossy photo paper, for example, might run $30 for a box of 50 sheets, which means you'll be spending about 60 cents per 8 x 10 print—not including ink.

Still, by using good photo paper, you'll get much sharper printouts, more vivid colors, and results that look and feel like actual photographic prints. Besides, at sizes over 4 x 6 or so, making your own printouts is still less expensive than getting prints from the drugstore, even when you factor in printer cartridges and photo paper.

Tip: To save money and avoid wasting your high-quality photo paper, use plain inkjet paper for test prints. When you're sure you've got the composition, color balance, and resolution of your photo just right, load up your expensive glossy photo paper for the final printouts.

Printing from iPhoto

When you choose File→Print (⌘-P) in iPhoto, you're presented with iPhoto's own private version of the Print command, with six photo-specific printing options at your disposal: Standard Prints, Full Page, Greeting Cards, Contact Sheet, N-Up, and Sampler.

Each of these six printing styles is discussed in detail below.

Standard-Sized Prints

Use this method to print out photos that conform to standard photo sizes, like 5 x 7 or 8 x 10. This is especially useful if you intend to mount your printed photos in store-bought picture frames, which are designed to handle photos in these standard dimensions.

1. **Select the thumbnail(s) of the photo(s) you want to print.**

   Alternatively, you can open the photo in Edit mode before you print it; the Print command is accessible in all of iPhoto's modes. You can also select more than one photo—a good idea if you want to get the most out of your expensive inkjet paper (see step 5). Just highlight the ones you want, using the techniques described on page 106.

2. **Choose File→Print, or press ⌘-P.**

   The iPhoto Print dialog box appears.

3. **From the Style pop-up menu, choose Standard Prints.**

   This is the factory setting, but if you've been printing other formats, you may have to switch it back.

4. **Using the Size buttons, choose the print size you want.**

   You have three standard photo sizes to choose from—4 x 6, 5 x 7, and 8 x 10. Remember, though, that choosing a larger size stretches the pixels of your photo across a larger area, reducing the photo's resolution and potentially degrading its print quality. For best results, don't choose 8 x 10 unless the picture you're printing is at least 1200 x 1800 pixels. (A yellow triangle warns you if the resolution is too low; see Figure 10-4.)

   The Preview panel displays how your photo will be positioned on the paper, as shown in Figure 10-3.

Figure 10-3:
See that warning icon on the top right corner of the preview? That's iPhoto's warning that the selected print size is too large, given the resolution of your photo. If you ignore the warning, your printout will likely have jagged edges or fuzzy detail.

5. **Select the number of photos you want printed on each page.**

   When the "One photo per page" checkbox is turned off, iPhoto fits as many photos as it can on each page, based on the paper size (which you select using the File→ Page Setup command) and the photo size that you've chosen. Conversely, when the checkbox is turned on, you get one photo at the center of each page.

When printing to letter-size paper, iPhoto can fit two 4 x 6 or 5 x 7 pictures on each page. (If you're printing one photo per sheet—if you're using 4 x 6 paper, for example—use the Full Page option described below, not "One photo per page.")

6. **Choose the number of copies you want to make.**

You can either type the number into the Copies field or click the arrows to increase or decrease the number.

7. **Click the Print button (or press Enter).**

Your printer scurries into action, printing your photos as you've requested.

Tip: Printing photos using these standard sizes works best if your digital photos are trimmed so that they fit perfectly into one of the three preset dimensions—4 x 6, 5 x 7, or 8 x 10. Use iPhoto's Constrained Cropping tool, explained on page 142, to trim your photos to precisely these sizes.

Greeting Cards

When you choose Greeting Card from the Style pop-up menu of the Print dialog box, iPhoto automatically rotates and positions your photo (Figure 10-4). You could conceivably print out cards on standard letter-size paper and then fold it into halves or quarters, but this option is actually designed for printing on special inkjet greeting-card paper. This kind of glossy paper stock, made by Epson and others, comes prescored and perforated for tidy edge-to-edge printing and crisp folding.

Figure 10-4:
iPhoto's Greeting Card printing doesn't create any actual greeting card content—no titles, holiday-themed icons, fancy borders, or pithy verses here. All you get is a printout of your photo on an otherwise blank sheet of paper, ready to be folded into a greeting card–shaped configuration.

You have two choices: Single-fold, which prints your photo onto a half sheet of paper, or Double-fold, which fits your photo into a quarter-page printing area. The Preview panel on the left side of the Print dialog box illustrates how each of these options will appear in the final printout.

Printing Full Page Photos

iPhoto's Full Page printing option reduces or enlarges each photo so that it completely fills a single page.

With Full Page printing, it takes 10 pages to print 10 photos, of course—but when you make Standard Prints or Contact Sheets, iPhoto can fit more than one photo on each page.

Tip: iPhoto's print dialog box tells you how many photos you've selected and how many pages it will take to print them all. However, this information is easy to miss because it appears in dim, grayed-out text near the center of the dialog box, under the Margins slider.

Contact Sheets

The Contact Sheet option prints out a *grid* of photos, tiling as many as 112 different pictures onto a single letter-size page (8 columns, 14 rows, in this example).

Photographers use contact sheets as a quick reference tool when organizing photos—a poor man's iPhoto, if you think about it. But this printing option is also handy in some other practical ways:

- By printing several pictures side by side on the same page, you can easily make quality comparisons among them without using two sheets of paper.

- Use contact sheet printing to make test prints, saving ink and paper. Sometimes a 2 x 3 print is all you need to determine if a picture is too dark or if its colors are wildly off when rendered by an inkjet printer. Don't make expensive full-page prints until you're sure you've adjusted your photo so that it will print out correctly.

- You can easily print multiple copies of a *single* picture if you want to produce lots of wallet-sized (or smaller) copies. (You can also do this using the N-Up option described on page 174.)

Contact Sheet printing options

To make Contact Sheet prints, choose Contact Sheet from the Style pop-up menu in the Print dialog box. Your printing options vary:

- If no photos are selected, the Contact Sheet option will print *all* the photos in the current album (or Photo Library, if that's what's selected). Use the Across slider (Figure 10-5) to change the size of the grid and, therefore, the number of photos that will appear on each printed page. iPhoto will print as many pages as needed to include all the photos in your current view.

- If several photos are selected, iPhoto will print a contact sheet containing only the selected photos.

- When only *one* photo is selected, iPhoto clones that one photo across the whole grid, printing one sheet of duplicate images at whatever size you specify using the slider control.

N-Up

With the N-Up option, you can tell iPhoto exactly how many photos you want printed on each page. The five preset grid configurations let you tile 2, 4, 6, 9, or 16 pictures on each sheet of paper. iPhoto automatically rotates photos as needed to make them fit perfectly into the grid size you choose.

N-Up printing may sound an awful lot like the Contact Sheet option just described, but it's slightly different. When printing Contact Sheets, you specify how many *columns* you want in your photo grid and, based on your choice, iPhoto crams as many photos on the page as it can—even if they end up the size of postage stamps. With N-Up Printing, you control the total number of pictures printed on each page, with a maximum of 16 photos in a 4 x 4 grid.

Tip: If you need your photos to be printed at a specific size—to fit in a 5 x 7 picture frame, for example—use the Standard Prints option instead of N-Up. With Standard Prints, you can specify the exact *size* of the photos; with N-Up, you can't.

Figure 10-5:
To fit even more pictures on a contact sheet, turn on the Save Paper checkbox, which appears only when you're printing more than one photo. It not only squishes the pictures closer together on the page, but also automatically rotates vertical photos so that they fit into an evenly spaced grid, again reducing white space. With more photos squeezed onto each page (bottom), you end up using less paper than you would otherwise (top).

N-Up printing options

As with printing contact sheets, your N-Up printing options depend on what you've got selected in the iPhoto window when you choose the Print command and choose N-Up from the Style menu.

- If no photos are selected, iPhoto will print *all* the photos in the current album (or the Photo Library, if that's what's selected). Use the "Photos per page" pop-up menu to set the number of photos that will appear on each printed page, as shown in Figure 10-6. iPhoto will print as many pages as needed to include all the photos in your current view.

- If you select several photos, iPhoto will print a grid containing only those.

- When only *one* photo is selected, iPhoto prints one sheet of duplicate images at whatever grid size you specify.

Figure 10-6:
Need a sheet of wallet-sized photos to send to relatives? The easiest way to make them is via the N-Up printing option. Just turn on the "One photo per page" checkbox so that you have two, three, or four rows of duplicate pictures. You can print up to 16 copies of a photo on each sheet.

Sampler Pages

While the Contact Sheet and N-Up options produce a straight grid of evenly-sized photos on each printed page, the Sampler option lets you print a grouping of photos at *different sizes* on a single page—just like the portrait galleries you might get from a professional photographer. For example, you can print a sheet that contains a combination of one large photo and five smaller photos, as shown in Figure 10-7.

Once you choose Sampler from the Style menu in the Print dialog box, you can choose from two different Sampler templates from the Template pop-up menu. Sampler 1 puts three pictures on each page—one large photo on the top, with two smaller ones beneath it. Sampler 2 produces the six-photo layout shown in Figure 10-7.

The Sampler option offers the same "One photo per page" checkbox available with N-Up printing (explained in Figure 10-7). Turn it on to fill each page with multiple copies of a single photo, just like the school photos brought home by fourth-graders worldwide each year.

Positioning photos in Sampler templates

You can pick exactly which of the photos from your collection are included in Sampler printouts by selecting them in the iPhoto window *before* choosing the Print command. If you have no photos selected, iPhoto will build Sampler pages using *all* the photos currently visible in the iPhoto window. If you have just one photo selected, iPhoto will fill the Sampler page with duplicates of the single photo. The order of the photos in your Photo Library determines how they're positioned in the printout, as explained in Figure 10-7.

Figure 10-7
The thing to keep in mind when setting up Sampler pages is that the first photo in your current selection is always the one that iPhoto picks as the "large" photo in the layout. If you want a specific photo to end up in the jumbo photo slot, make sure it's either the first one in the album or first among those you select. If you decide to rearrange the photos on the soon-to-be-printed page, close the Print dialog box, drag the thumbnails into a different order in the main iPhoto window, and then choose Print again.

The Preview Button

A mini-preview of your printout-to-be is always visible on the left side of the Print dialog box. But this postage stamp preview is far too small to show much detail. Worse, it shows you only the *first page* of a multipage job.

FREQUENTLY ASKED QUESTION

Changing Page Sizes

iPhoto's Print command lets me choose the size of the photos I want to print, but not the size of the paper I'm printing them on. Can't I pick a different paper size?

Yes, but remember that you change this kind of setting in the Page Setup dialog box, not the Print dialog box. Choose File→Page Setup, and then select the paper size you want using the Paper Size pop-up menu.

For a better preview, click Preview. iPhoto processes the print job, just as if you had hit Print—a "Print" progress bar appears at this point, indicating that the job is "on its way" to the printer. Instead of transmitting the job to your printer hardware, however, iPhoto creates a temporary PDF (Acrobat) file. It opens in Preview, the free graphics-viewing program that comes with Mac OS X.

Tip: Depending on the size of your print job, building a preview can take awhile. iPhoto must process all the image data involved, just as if it were really printing.

You end up with a full-size, full-resolution electronic version of your printout. Using the commands in Preview's Display menu, you can zoom in or out to view details, scroll across pages, and move from page to page (to preview every page of a contact sheet, for example). You're seeing exactly how iPhoto is going to render your printout when it actually hits the printer, using the print options you selected.

If you like what you see in the PDF preview, you have the following two choices:

- Close the Preview window, return to iPhoto, and choose File→Print again (the Print dialog box will have closed itself automatically). Now, confident that you're going to get the results you expect, click the Print button and send the printout to your printer.

- If you want to *keep* the preview—in order to distribute an electronic version of a contact sheet, for example—you can save it, using the Save As command The result is a PDF file, which anyone with a Mac, Windows PC, or Unix machine can open using the free Acrobat Reader program that comes on every computer.

Save As PDF

The Save As PDF button, a standard part of all Mac OS X Print dialog boxes, lets you save a printout-in-waiting as a PDF file instead of printing it on paper. Any type of iPhoto printout—greeting card, contact sheet, sampler, and so on—can be converted to PDF. After opening the Print dialog box, set up your print options the way you want, click the Save As PDF button, name the PDF in the Save to File dialog box, and click Save. (Saving the file can take awhile if you're converting several pages of photos into the PDF.)

Tip: You can also save a print job as a PDF file *after* you've previewed the results, just by using the Save As command in Preview.

Ordering Prints Online

Even if you don't have a high-quality color printer, traditional prints of your digital photos are only a few clicks away—if you have an Internet connection and you're willing to spend a little money, that is.

Thanks to a deal between Apple and Kodak, you can order prints of your digital photos directly from within iPhoto. After you select the size and quantity of the pictures you

want printed, one click is all it takes to have iPhoto transmit your photos to Kodak
Print Services and bill your credit card for the order. The rates range from 39 cents
for a single 4 x 6 print to about $23 for a jumbo 20 x 30 poster. Your finished photos,
printed on high-quality glossy photographic paper, are sent to you within two days.

Tip: If you plan to order prints, first crop your photos to the proper dimensions (4 x 6, for example), using
the Crop tool as described in Chapter 6. Most digital cameras produce photos whose shape doesn't quite
match standard photo-paper dimensions. If you send photos to Kodak uncropped, you're leaving it up to
Kodak to decide which parts of your photo will be lopped off to fit. (More than one Mac fan has opened the
envelope to find loved ones missing the tops of their skulls.)

By cropping the pictures to photo-paper shape before you place the order, *you* decide which parts get eliminated. (You can always restore the photos to their original uncropped versions using the Revert to Original
command described on page 153.)

To order prints, select the photos you want to print, click the Organize button below the
main iPhoto window, and then click the Order Prints icon on the bottom panel.

Now the Mac must go online to check in with the Kodak processing center. If you
have a dial-up connection, your Mac dials out automatically. (If the Mac can't make
an Internet connection at all, the Order Prints window, shown in Figure 10-8, doesn't
open.)

Figure 10-8:
*The Order Prints window lets
you order six different types of
prints from your photos—from
a set of four wallet-sized prints
to mammoth 20" x 30" posters.
Use the scroll bar on the right
to scroll through all the photos
you've selected to specify how
many copies of each photo you
want to order. If you need to
change your shipping, contact,
or credit card information,
click the Edit 1-Click Settings
button to modify your Apple
ID profile.*

If you don't already have an Apple account (page 57), click Set Up Account and get yourself registered with Apple.

Finally, select the sizes and quantities you want. For example, if you want 4 x 6 or 5 x 7 prints of every photo you've selected, use the text boxes at the top of the dialog box to specify how many copies you want of each.

For more control over sizes and quantities of individual photos, ignore those boxes. Instead, fill in the numbers individually for each photo, scrolling down through the dialog box as necessary. The total cost of your order is updated as you make selections.

Tip: If you want *mostly* prints of one size—5 x 7's, for example—type the quantity into the "5 x 7 prints, quantity" box at the top of the window, so that iPhoto fills in that number for every photo. Now you're free to *change* the quantity for the few photos that you *don't* want to order at 5 x 7.

As you order, pay heed to the alert icons (little yellow triangles) that may appear on certain lines of the order form (visible, in spades, in Figure 10-11). These are iPhoto's standard warnings, declaring that certain photos don't have a high enough resolution to be printed at the specified sizes. A 1600 x 1200 pixel photo makes a great 5 x 7, but a terrible 16 x 20 enlargement. Unless you're the kind of person who thrives on disappointment, *never* order prints in a size that's been flagged with a low-resolution alert.

Tip: You'll see the same warning icon when you print your own photos and order photo books (Chapter 10). As always, you have few attractive choices: order a smaller print, don't order a print at all, or order the print and accept the lower quality that results.

Finally, click the "Buy Now" button to order the prints. Your photos are transferred, your credit card is billed, and you go sit by the mailbox.

A dialog box appears, showing the reference number for your order and a message saying that you'll be receiving a confirmation via email.

At first glance, you might not consider ordering prints online the most economical method. A batch of 24 standard 4 x 6 snapshots costs about $9, plus shipping, which is more than you'd pay for processing a roll of film at the local drugstore.

Still, this service is economical in other ways. For example, you get to print only the prints that you actually want, rather than developing a roll of 36 prints only to find that only two of them are any good. It's far more convenient than the drugstore method, and it's a handy way to send top-notch photo prints directly to friends and relatives who don't have computers. Furthermore, it's ideal for creating high-quality enlargements that would be impossible to print on the typical inkjet printer.

Publishing a Photo Book

After a certain point, gift-giving becomes exhausting. What the heck do you get your dad after you've already given him birthday and holiday presents for 15 or 35 years?

If you have iPhoto, you've got an ironclad, perennial answer. The program's Book feature lets you design and order (via the Internet) a gorgeous, linen-covered, 9 x 11-inch hardbound book, printed at a real bindery and shipped back to you in a slipcover. Your photos are printed on the glossy, acid-free, single-sided pages, complete with captions, if you like.

After a certain point, gift-giving becomes exhausting. What the heck do you get your dad after you've already given him birthday and holiday presents for 15 or 35 years?

A ten-page book costs $30 (extra pages are $3 each). That's about the least you could hope to pay for a handsome, emotionally powerful gift *guaranteed* never to wind up in an attic, at a garage sale, or on eBay. In short, it's a home-run gift every time.

But the iPhoto book is not *only* a gift. You should also consider ordering them for yourself—one each for your vacation, wedding, child, or whatever. These books are amazing keepsakes to leave out on your coffee table—the same idea as most families' photo albums, but infinitely classier and longer lasting (and not much more expensive).

Phase 1: Pick the Pix

The hardest part of the whole book-creation process is winnowing down your photos to the ones you want to include. Many a shutterbug eagerly sits down to create his very first photo book—and winds up with one that's 49 pages long (that is, $147).

As a general rule, each page of your photo book can hold a maximum of six pictures. (iPhoto also offers canned book designs called Catalog and Yearbook, which hold up to 32 tiny pictures per page in a grid. At that size, however, your pictures don't exactly sing. Instead, the whole thing more closely resembles, well, a catalog or yearbook.)

The best-looking books generally have varying numbers of pictures per page—one, four, three, two, whatever. In general, the number of pictures you'll fit in a ten-page book may be far lower than 40—25, for example.

The first step is to create an album filled with the pictures you really want in the book. In Organize mode, you can drag pictures in, which can be an excruciating experience, especially if you and a collaborator are trying to work together.

As you work, constantly keep in mind the photo *sequence*. Drag them around in the album to determine a preliminary order. You'll have plenty of opportunity to fine-tune each page of the book (and rearrange the pictures on it) later in the process. When you're still in Organize mode, the only critical task is to place the two most sensational or important photos first and last (for the cover and the last page of the book).

Phase 2: Choose a Theme

Once you've corralled the book's pictures into an album of their own, click the album, and then click the Book button below the main picture area (Figure 10-9). (If you forget to click an album before clicking Book, iPhoto will scold you.)

Now you see something like Figure 10-9: a large preview page at top, and a scrolling bank of thumbnails below, representing the book's pages. iPhoto has just turned into a page-layout program.

Tip: Light blue lines surround each photo and text box. These *guides,* as they're called, won't appear in the printed book. They're there just for convenience, to help you visualize how the finished layout will look. Still, if they bother you, turn off the Show Guides checkbox in the lower-left corner of the window.

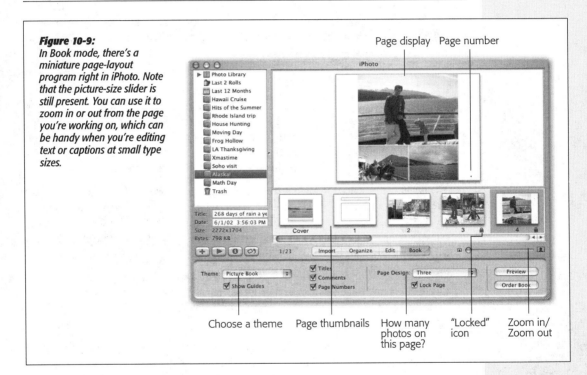

Figure 10-9:
In Book mode, there's a miniature page-layout program right in iPhoto. Note that the picture-size slider is still present. You can use it to zoom in or out from the page you're working on, which can be handy when you're editing text or captions at small type sizes.

Before you dive in, take a moment to get your bearings. Note that the thumbnails are numbered—an early-warning system that shows you how many pages long your book will be (read: how expensive). If you're like most people, your initial layout will be much too long. Not to worry; you'll fix that in a moment.

In book-design mode, you can't add photos to your album, take any photos out, or reassign them to different pages. You can perform tasks like these as you work on your book—but you must click the Organize button to do so.

What you can do, however, is design your book pages, and that process begins when you choose a *theme* for the book—a canned design. Use the Theme pop-up menu at the lower-left corner of the iPhoto screen for this purpose (Figure 10-9). Before you begin fiddling with individual pages, try each of the themes in turn, studying the thumbnails and page previews to get a feeling for the effect.

Caution: Choose carefully. You can switch to a different theme for this album later, but you'll lose *all the custom text and photo groupings* you've performed so far.

You won't lose your captions, because those are the Comments stored with every photo in your collection. "Custom text" refers to the text you type into Introduction pages and onto every page of the Story Book design. (If you have, in fact, typed any custom text, iPhoto warns you about this loss when you try to switch layout themes.)

If you want to experiment with a different theme once you've spent some time with one, *duplicate the album first.* (With the album highlighted in the list, choose File→Duplicate.) Now you can change the theme on the duplicate without destroying the work you've done on the original.

Your choices are:

- **Catalog.** This design looks exactly like a mail order catalog: a picture on the left, and a name and description on the right—eight times per page (or one, or four). It's neatly aligned and somewhat conservative. For example, there's a page design called Introduction, where you can pour a lot of text, such as your shipping policies, a letter from the founder, what this season's catalog offers, and so on.

  It's also good for more than just designing catalogs, however. It would be an ideal "face book" (with mini biographies) for, say, a dating agency or personnel director. It's also a candidate for a regular photo album, in the event you're the kind of person who wants it to look square and gridlike, like a *real* photo album book from Office Max.

- **Classic.** It's easy to deduce the philosophy behind this conservative, clean design: maximum photos, minimum text. Photos are as large as possible on the page (up to six per page), and each offers only enough room for a title and a very short caption.

- **Collage.** This design is a wacky, energetic layout in which *no* photos are square with the page. Everything falls at a tilt, as though tossed onto a coffee table helter-skelter. If there's more than one photo per page, they may even *overlap.*

- **Picture Book.** This design is as stark as it gets: maximum photos, period. There's no text, and only minimum margins. Thus, on one-photo-per-page pages, the photo stretches gloriously from one edge of the page to the other—a *full bleed,* as publishers say.

  This dramatic design can be emotionally compelling in the extreme. The absence of text and minimization of white space seems to make the photos speak—if not shout—for themselves.

Tip: Keeping in mind that the book is published *horizontally,* in landscape mode, will help you maximize page coverage. For example, on pages with only one photo, a horizontal shot looks best. It will fill the page, edge to edge. On pages with two photos, two side-by-side vertical (portrait-mode) shots look best. They'll appear side by side, filling the page top to bottom.

- **Portfolio.** Modeled after a photographer's portfolio, this design has elements of both Catalog and Picture Book. Like Catalog, it provides text boxes that accommodate a title and description for each photo. But as with Picture Book, the photos are otherwise displayed at maximum size, with very little white space between them.

   The whole effect is a tad industrial-looking, so you probably wouldn't want to use it as a "memory book" for some trip or event. It's useful in situations where Catalog would be right, except that it's more interesting to look at, thanks to the varied photo sizes.

- **Story Book.** This layout is the big brother to Collage. Once again, you get a zany layout of crooked, overlapping photos. The difference: In this design, text boxes appear on each page for captions, which are always parallel to the page edges and therefore anchor the design. Like Collage, this theme works best when fun, craziness, or lightheartedness is your desired effect.

- **Year Book.** This theme lets you fit up to 32 photos on each page—just as in a high school yearbook. Of course, if you choose greater quantities, the photos themselves get smaller—but iPhoto always leaves you enough room for a title ("Chris Jones") and a little description ("Swim team '02; voted Most Likely to Enter the Priesthood").

Tip: Make an effort to choose a quantity of photos that neatly fills the final page, or at least a row of it. Otherwise, the final page can look a bit half-finished.

Try choosing each of these themes in turn from the Themes pop-up menu. The thumbnails of your pages give you immediate feedback about the suitability of each design for your book project.

Phase 3: Design the Pages

Once you've selected an album and a theme, the most time-consuming phase begins: designing the individual pages.

iPhoto thinks of the pictures in your book as a *continuous stream* that flows from left to right, in precisely the same order as in the album you've selected. You can drag your page thumbnails around with the mouse to rearrange them—but behind the scenes, you're simultaneously rearranging the photos in the album. Similarly, if you drag photos around in the Organize window for your album, you'll wind up rearranging the pages of your book. Figure 10-10 should drive this point home.

Tip: You'll soon discover that designing a book is a much happier experience if you work on your pages strictly from *left to right*. Doing so reduces the likelihood that your photos will sproing out of order unexpectedly, as described on page 186.

To begin work on a page, click its thumbnail. Now you have three decisions to make: how many photos should appear on the page, what text should appear, and what the text should look like.

Tip: Even in Book mode, you can still rotate photos, rename them, change their dates, or delete them, just as you would thumbnails in Organize mode (see Chapter 7).

Before:

Book mode

Organize mode

After:

Book mode

Organize mode

Figure 10-10:
Top: There's a rigid correspondence between the order of the photos in your book and the order they appear in the album (in Organize mode).

Bottom: If you drag a page into a new position in Book mode, you'll find the photos' new order reflected in Organize mode. See how the two circled photos have moved in the lower shot of Organize mode?

(Note: If your book is derived from a smart album, all bets are off. Rearranging pages in Book mode, in that case, do not affect the order in the smart album.)

The Cover

Start with the Cover page—the first thumbnail in the row. When it's selected, the cover photo appears in the main picture area. This is the picture that will be pasted (and centered) on the linen cover of the actual book. (The cloth cover of your book will be one of several handsome dark colors, *not* white as it appears here.)

You can't do much with the cover except to change the title or subtitle; see "Edit the Titles and Captions," on page 189. You'll choose the cover color in a later step.

Tip: The picture you see here is the *first picture* in the album. If it's not the photo you want on the cover, click the Organize button and drag a different photo to the beginning of your album.

Pictures per Page

Click the thumbnail for page 2. If you did some preliminary arranging work in your album, your photos should already be in roughly the right *order* for the book pages—but not necessarily the right *groupings*.

You control how many pictures appear on a page—and, to an extent, their layout—by choosing a number from the Page Design pop-up menu. (iPhoto saves your work automatically.) Your choices are:

- **Cover.** The first thumbnail in your book *must* have the Cover design.

  On the other hand, subsequent pages can *also* have the Cover layout. You can use this quirk to your advantage. For example, in a book that documents your trip to three countries, a "cover" layout can introduce each country's batch of photos.

- **Introduction.** In most themes, this special page design has no photos at all. It's just a big set of text boxes that you can type (or paste) into. Here's where you can let the audience know about the trip, the company, or the family; tell the story behind the book; praise the book's lucky recipient; scare off intellectual-property thieves with impressive-sounding copyright notices; and so on.

Tip: An Introduction page (one of the choices in the Page Design pop-up menu) doesn't have to be the first page of the book (after the cover). You can turn *any* page into an Introduction page. Such pages make great section dividers.

They're especially useful in designs that use the Picture Book theme that otherwise have no text at all. An Introduction page can set the scene and explain the following (uncaptioned) pages of pictures.

- **One, Two, Three, Four…** These commands let you specify how many photos appear on the selected page. iPhoto automatically arranges them according to its own internal sense of symmetry. Use these options to create a pleasing overall layout for the book and give it variety. Follow a page with one big photo with a page of four smaller ones, for example.

- **One with Text.** Unique to the Collage theme, this choice on the Page Design pop-up menu places one picture on the left side of a page with a long, narrow text box to the right. It's like a vertical alternative to the Introduction page.

- **End.** The Page Design pop-up menu for the Story Book theme offers a bonus page design called End. Use it for the last page of the book.

The End page is designed to hold three pictures, and you'd be well advised to fiddle with your album until the last page does, in fact, have three photos on it. Otherwise, you'll wind up with a strange, half-filled look on the End page. For example, if there's only one photo on it, that picture will sit halfway off the left margin, as though sailing off to the left ("Later, dude!"), and the rest of the page will be blank.

Tip: Normally, your selection from this pop-up menu affects only the page you're working on. But if you want all the pages to look the same, hold down Option as you pick a design. iPhoto applies that design to all pages in the book. (This business involves laying out all of your pages again, even those that you've locked.)

Each time you change the number of photos on a page, something happens that you may find disconcerting: Pictures on the *following* pages slide onto earlier or later pages. Figure 10-11 illustrates this phenomenon.

Page 3 starts with two photos... ...but you're asking for three.

Now it has three, having sucked in a new photo from page 4.

Figure 10-11:
Top: Suppose iPhoto proposes putting two photos on page 3. (Note the all-black photo on page 4.)

Bottom: When you choose Three from the Page Design menu, you're telling iPhoto that you want three photos on page 3. The program responds by sucking in the next photo (on the following page) to fill its quota. Yes, there are now three pictures on page 3, as you requested—but the all-black square photo has now left page 4, causing all photos after it to slide leftward, rippling all the way through your book.

This syndrome can drive you wiggy if it winds up disrupting a page that you've already tweaked to perfection—a problem you'll almost certainly encounter if you don't work on your pages from left to right.

The solution is simple. Once a page has the right photos on it (and the right *number* of photos), lock it by turning on the Lock Page checkbox at the lower edge of the window. (A tiny padlock icon appears on the page's thumbnail.)

From now on, even if you change the number of shots on an earlier page, the page you locked will remain undisturbed.

Even this trick, though, requires some caution. Keep in mind the following gotchas:

- Once you've locked a page, the Page Design pop-up menu no longer functions for that page. You have to unlock a page before you can change the number of pictures on it.

- If you do unlock a page, watch out…you're taking the muzzle off a spring-loaded design. Because iPhoto is maintaining a picture group that, in its head, is out of sequence (relative to Organize mode), unlocking a page may cause its pictures to explode into other locations. As a result, you'll witness a ripple effect that's likely to scramble *all* unlocked pages in your book.

- If you use the Theme pop-up menu to change themes, all bets are off. Changing themes blasts *all* layout work into oblivion, locked or not.

Photo and Page Sequence

As you work, continue to consider the overall effect of your layout. You can't drag pictures from one page to another, but—thanks to a new iPhoto 4 feature—you can drag them around *within each page*. Just click the photo you want to move, wait for a thin yellow border to appear, and then drag until it's *over* the photo (or photo spot) where you want it to go. When the existing picture sprouts a pink border, let go of the mouse button; the two pictures swap places (Figure 10-12).

You still can't drag a photo from one page to the next. You can, however, rearrange entire *pages*. Just drag the page thumbnails left or right in their track. If you return to Organize mode, you'll see that the photos have shifted there, too, to reflect their new order in the book; again, see Figure 10-10.

Cover = Page in the Album

I want to use my cover photo as one of the pages in the book, just like they do in real coffee-table photo books. How do I do it?

In Organize mode, click the photo and then choose File→ Duplicate (⌘-D).

Now you have two copies of the photo. Drag one to the front of the line in the album (to use as the cover). Drag the other into the mass of other photos, so that you can now use it in one of the interior page layouts.

In fact, if using a combination of dragging pictures on pages and dragging whole pages around turns into an exercise in frustration for you, you can always switch into Organize mode, drag the photos into the exact order you want, then switch back into Book mode for the finishing touches.

And give thanks: Before iPhoto 4, Organize mode was the *only* way to rearrange pictures in a book. Now you have a choice.

Note: The exception to all this: Dragging pictures in Organize mode doesn't work in smart albums.

Before

After

Figure 10-12:
In some ways, you are at the mercy of iPhoto's design templates. You can't dictate how the photos overlap their neighbors (in Story Book), or how much space separates pictures in Picture Book, shown here.

And yet—ring them bells! Fire them flares! In iPhoto 4, you can, at last, drag to swap photos on a single page.

If the photos have the same shape, they simply swap positions, which sometimes means that you can swap a quarter-page photo with the half-page picture next to it.

If they have different proportions, swapping photos sometimes means that you can flip the tall one from one side of the page to the other, as shown here.

Sometimes chronological order is the natural sequence, especially for books that will be mementos of special events like trips, parties, and weddings. But there's nothing to stop you from cheating a bit—rearranging certain scenes—for greater impact and variety.

As you drag your pictures into order, consider these effects:

- Intersperse group shots with solo portraits, scenery with people shots, vertical ones with horizontals.

- On multiple-photo pages, exploit the direction your subjects face. On a three-picture page, for example, you could arrange the people in the photos so that they're all looking roughly toward the center of the page, for a feeling of inclusion.

- Group similar shots together on a page.

Page Limits

The book can have anywhere from 10 to 50 pages. If you create fewer pages, you'll be warned during the book-ordering process that you're about to pay for a ten-page book with blank pages at the end. If you create more than 50 pages, you won't be allowed to place the order at all.

There's nothing to stop you from creating multiple books, however. ("Our Trip to New Jersey, Vol. XI," anyone?)

Hiding Page Numbers

Each built-in theme includes page numbers stamped on the lower-right corner of each page. You never have to worry about a page number winding up superimposed on one of your pictures, though. A picture *always* takes priority, covering up the page number.

Even so, you may feel that page numbers intrude on the mood your book creates. If so, just eliminate them by turning off the Page Numbers checkbox at the lower-left corner of the window.

Tip: As you work, you may discover photos here and there that need a little editing—cropping, brightening, and so on (Chapter 8). No problem: Just double-click a picture in the book-page display window to open it in either Edit mode or an external photo-editing program. Close the editing window, or click the Book button again, when you're finished.

Phase 4: Edit the Titles and Captions

In every theme, iPhoto offers you text boxes that you can fill with titles, explanations, and captions. Most layouts have space for this kind of text on every page. Only the Picture Book design is text-free (except for the cover and introduction page).

In any case, taking the time to perfect this text is extremely important. A misspelling or typo you make here may haunt you (and amuse the book's recipient) forever.

In general, iPhoto offers the following four kinds of text boxes:

- **The book title.** This box appears on the book's cover and, if you've added one, Introduction page. When you first create a book, iPhoto proposes the *album's* name as the book name, but you're welcome to change it.

  A second text box, all set with slightly smaller-type formatting, appears below the title. Use it for a subtitle: the date, "A Trip Down Memory Lane," "Happy Birthday Aunt Enid," "A Little Something for the Insurance Company," or whatever.

- **The introduction.** Applying the Introduction page design to a page gives you a huge text block that you can fill with any introductory text you think the book needs.

UP TO SPEED

The Heartbreak of the Yellow Exclamation Point

As you work on your book design, you may encounter the dreaded yellow-triangle-exclamation point like the one shown here. It appears everywhere you want to be: on the corresponding page thumbnail, on the page display, on the page preview (which appears when you click Preview), and so on.

If you actually try to order the book without eliminating the yellow triangles, you even get a warning in the form of a dialog box: "Low Quality Warning: One or more photos in your book may print at too low a quality based on the design you have chosen. Do you want to continue?"

All of this boils down to one heartbreaking problem: At least one of your photos doesn't have enough resolution (enough pixels) to reproduce well in the finished book. If you ignore the warning and continue with the ordering process, you're likely to be disappointed by the blotchy, grainy result in the finished book.

You may remember from Chapter 1 that the resolution of your digital camera is relatively irrelevant if you'll only be showing your pictures onscreen. It's when you try to *print* them that you need all the megapixels you can get—like

now.

The easiest solution is to shrink the photo on its page. And the easiest way to do *that* is to increase the *number* of pictures on that page. (Some layouts put both large and small photos on the same page. In that case, you may have to click Organize and drag photos around so that your low-res, problem-child picture lands in one of the smaller slots.)

Decreasing a picture's size also squeezes its pixels closer together, improving the dots-per-inch shortage that iPhoto is warning you about.

If even that dramatic step doesn't eliminate the yellow warning emblems, try to remember if you ever cropped this photo. If so, your last chance is to click Organize, click the photo, and then choose File→Revert To Original. Doing so will undo any *cropping* you did to the photo, which may have thrown away a lot of pixels that you suddenly find yourself needing. (If Revert To Original is dimmed, then you never performed any cropping, and this last resort is worthless.)

Finally, if nothing has worked so far, your only options are to eliminate the photo from your book or to order the book anyway.

Tip: An Introduction page doesn't have to be the first page of the book (after the cover). You can turn *any* page into an all-text Introduction page. Such pages make great section dividers.

They're especially useful in Picture Book designs that otherwise have no text at all. Whatever you type or paste into the Introduction page can set the scene and explain the following (uncaptioned) pages of pictures.

- **Photo titles.** In most layouts, iPhoto displays the name of each photo. If you haven't already named each picture, you'll get only the internal iPhoto name of each picture—"IMG_0030.JPG," for example. You can edit this name either in the text box on your page preview, or in the Title text box at the left side of the iPhoto window (Figure 10-13).

Figure 10-13:
iPhoto offers two different places to enter text. Using the boxes at the left side of the screen is usually faster, since you don't have to wait for iPhoto to zoom in to the text box. A yellow, nonprinting warning sign appears if the text box is too small to display all of the comment text (or the full photo name).

"Real" title and comment boxes   On-page title and comment boxes   Text overflow warning

- **Comments.** The larger text box that appears for each photo (in some layouts) is for a caption. It automatically displays any comments you've typed into the Comments box for a photo at the left side of the iPhoto screen. Or, to be precise, it displays the first chunk of that text.

Note, by the way, that some of the layouts don't show nearly as much text as the "real" Title or Comments box does. In these cases, iPhoto has no choice but to chop off the excess, showing only the first sentence or two. A yellow, triangular exclamation point appears next to any text box that has overflow of this kind—your cue to edit down the text to fit the text box on the layout (Figure 10-13).

Note: On the other hand, iPhoto may give you "false positives," showing a yellow triangle (and text visually wrapping on the screen) when, in fact, the text will look just fine when it's printed. (This problem is especially apparent with small text and a reduced-size display of the page.) To find out what you'll *really* get, make a final proofreading pass using one of the techniques described on page 195.

Editing Text

You're welcome to edit the photo titles or comments in either place: right here in the layout, or back in the Info box for the individual photos. In general, the editing process is straightforward:

- Click inside a text box to activate the insertion-point cursor, so you can begin typing. iPhoto zooms in on the page and scrolls it, if necessary, so that the type is large enough to see and edit. When you click outside a text box—on another part of the page, for example—the page shrinks again to fit the window.

- You can select text and then use the Edit menu's Cut, Copy, and Paste commands to transfer text from box to box.

- You can also move selected text *within* a text box by dragging it and dropping it. The trick is to *hold down* the mouse button for a moment before dragging. Add the Option key to make a *copy* of the selected text instead of moving it.

- Double-click a word, or triple-click a paragraph, to neatly highlight it.

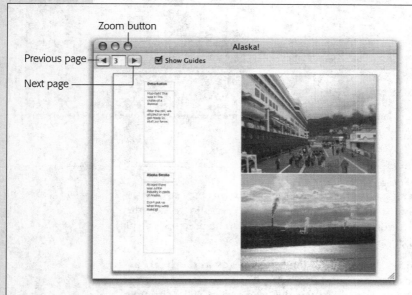

Zoom button

Previous page

Next page

Figure 10-34:
In Preview mode, you can flip through your book one page at a time by clicking the arrows at the top. (You can also jump to a certain page by typing a number into the box and then pressing the Return key.)

For best results, click the Zoom button to make the window as large as possible on your screen. You can turn off the light blue box boundaries, if you like, by turning off "Show Guides."

- Press Control-right arrow or Control-left arrow to make the insertion point jump to the beginning or end of the line.

- To make typographically proper quotation marks ("curly like this" instead of "this"), press Option-[and Shift-Option-[, respectively. And to make a true long dash—like this, instead of two hyphens—press Shift-Option-hyphen.

But here's the biggest tip of all: *Edit your text in Preview mode.* (Click the Preview button at the lower-right corner of the window, or just double-click one of the book's page thumbnails; see Figure 10-14.)

In Preview mode, each page appears in its own window, which you can make as large as you like. iPhoto therefore doesn't have to zoom and unzoom as you click each text box, which makes the editing go faster. And because you can see the whole page (instead of only the portion that fits within the photo viewing area), you have a better sense of your text block's look and proportions relative to the picture.

Tip: Can't seem to get the size, placement, or variety of type that you want? Then the heck with iPhoto and its straitjacketed text boxes—you can use whatever type you want.

All you have to do is jump into a graphics program, like Photoshop Elements, AppleWorks, or GraphicConverter. Create a JPEG graphic document that's 1350 x 1800 pixels, with a resolution of 150 dots per inch (dpi). Now fill it with text, using the graphic software's text tools. You have complete freedom of fonts and placement.

Finally, bring this graphic into iPhoto. Use it as a single "photo" on the page where you want the text to appear. It's crude and crazy, but it works!

Hiding Text

As noted earlier, the Picture Book theme is especially dramatic because it *lacks* text. The pictures spill across the pages, strong and big.

Bear in mind, though, that you can turn off the text for *any* of the layout themes. Just turn off the corresponding checkbox (Titles or Comments) in the lower-left corner of the iPhoto window. (You can also leave *individual* boxes empty, of course.)

Note: You can't *add* titles or comment boxes to a theme that doesn't have them, however. The pages in the Picture Book theme don't have any text on them, and no amount of turning the Titles and Comments checkboxes on or off can change that.

Formatting Text

To a certain extent, you can change the fonts, sizes, and styles of type in your book. To begin, choose Edit→Font→Show Fonts (or press ⌘-T). As shown in Figure 10-15, Mac OS X's standard Font panel appears. Now click inside the kind of text box you want to change, and then click any font you like.

All right, "any" may be stretching it. The truth is:

- You can't change the *size* of the type—only the font and style.

- In general, whatever changes you make apply to *every* title or comment box in the entire book. There's no way to make one caption look different from other captions, or to format only part of a sentence (so that you can italicize a single word, for example).

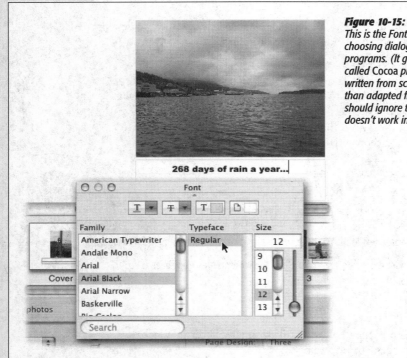

Figure 10-15:
This is the Font panel, a standard type-choosing dialog box in certain Mac OS X programs. (It generally appears only in so-called Cocoa programs—those that have been written from scratch for Mac OS X rather than adapted from a Mac OS 9 version.) You should ignore the Sizes column, because it doesn't work in iPhoto.

- There are two exceptions to the previous point. If you select some words and then Control-click them, a shortcut menu appears. Choosing Italic or Bold from its Font submenu affects all text in all boxes—but choosing *Underline* affects only the selected words. (It looks pretty crude, but that's a different conversation.)

The Font submenu even offers a Show Colors command. It opens a color palette; using it, you can apply different colors, too, to individual text selections. Yes, the bright, multicolored result might look a little bit like it was designed by Barney the Dinosaur, but the Color option is worth keeping in mind when you're preparing books about, for example, someone's fourth birthday party.

- Most people have good luck using almost any font in the Font panel. You should know, though, that Apple *officially* recommends only these fonts: Helvetica, Helvetica Neue, Century Gothic, Papyrus, GillSans, MarkerFelt, Baskerville, and Brushscript, without any variations of them (bold, italic, and so on).

Check Your Spelling

Ordinarily, you might scoff at the overkill—what difference does a typo make in a photo-organizing program, for goodness' sake? But your tune will change the very day you get your $30 (or $150) hardbound photo book in the mail, proudly titled, "Our Trip to the Grand Canyin."

For details on spell checking in iLife, see page 4.

Unfortunately, even a spelling checker won't find missing words, inadvertently repeated words, or awkward writing. For those situations, what you really want is for iPhoto to *read your captions aloud* to you.

No problem: Just highlight some text by dragging through it, and then Control-click the highlighted area. A shortcut menu appears, containing the Speech command.

Phase 5: Preview the Masterpiece

Ordering a professionally bound book is, needless to say, quite a commitment. Before blowing $30 or more on a one-shot deal, you'd be wise to proofread and inspect it from every possible angle.

Preview It Onscreen

One easy way to inspect your book is to click the Preview button in the lower-right corner of the screen—or just double-click the thumbnail for any page. iPhoto fills your screen with an electronic version of the selected page for your inspection, as shown in Figure 10-14.

Print It

As any proofreader can tell you, though, looking over a book on paper is a sure way to discover errors that somehow elude detection onscreen. That's why it's a good idea to print out your own, low-tech edition of your book at home before beaming it away to Apple's bindery.

While you're in Book mode, choose File→Print. After the standard Mac OS X Print dialog box appears, fire up your printer and click Print when ready. The result may not be linen-bound and printed on acid-free paper, but it's a tantalizing preview of the real thing—and a great way to give the book one final look.

Turn It into a PDF File

Sooner or later, almost everyone with a personal computer encounters PDF (Portable Document Format) files. Many a software manual, Read Me file, and downloadable "white paper" comes in this format, because it's universal (Mac, Windows, Unix), it has very high resolution, and you can search for text inside it.

If you suspect other people might want to have a look at your photo book before it goes to be printed—or if they'd just like to have a copy of their own—a PDF file makes a convenient package.

Here's how to create a PDF file:

1. With your book design on the screen in front of you, choose File→Print.

   The print dialog box appears.

2. Click the Save as PDF button.

   The Save sheet appears.

3. Type a name for the file, choose a folder location for it, and click Save.

   Your PDF file is ready to distribute. (Fortunately, the recipients will be able to correct the rotation within Adobe Acrobat using its View→Rotate Counterclockwise command.)

Phase 6: Send the Book to the Bindery

When you think your book is ready for birth, click the Organize button. In the row of icons at the bottom of the screen, click Order Book.

After several minutes of converting your screen design into an Internet-transmittable file, iPhoto offers you a screen like the one shown in Figure 10-16. (If your book is *shorter* than ten pages, iPhoto first warns you that you're about to pay for a bunch of blank pages. Ten pages is the *minimum* for a book.)

At this stage, your tasks are largely administrative.

Figure 10-16:
Bottom left: Choose a color, a quantity, and a recipient.

Top right: You won't be allowed to choose a quantity or recipient, though, until you've first signed up for an Apple account, which you'll enjoy using over and over again to order books and stuff from the Apple online stores.

To sign up for an account, click the Set Up Account button (not shown here, but it would appear in place of Buy Now if this were your first time). To correct or update your account info later, click the Account Info at the bottom of the first dialog box (lower left).

- **Choose a cover color.** Use the Cover Color pop-up menu to choose Black, Burgundy (red), Light Gray, or Navy (blue). The books in the illustration, including the handy magnified swatch, change color to show you what you're getting. (If you're ordering more than one book, they must all have the same color.)

- **Inspect the charges.** If you've gone beyond ten pages, you'll see that you're about to be charged $3 per additional page.

- **Indicate the quantity.** You can order additional copies of the same book. Indeed, after you've spent so much time on a gift book for someone else, you may well be tempted to order yourself a copy.

As you'll soon discover, you can't make any additional progress until you've signed up for an Apple account and turned on "1-Click Ordering." (See page 142.)

From the Ship To pop-up menu, choose the lucky recipient of this book. Then, from the Ship Via pop-up menu, indicate how you want the finished book shipped.

POWER USERS' CLINIC

The Secret, Really Really Final PDF

Looking over your final book as a PDF file in Preview is a pretty darned effective way to give it a final look-over.

Incredibly enough, though, even this PDF doesn't show you *exactly* what you're about to submit to Apple. It doesn't show you exactly the final type layout, for example, which is why some people wind up with chopped-off text boxes even though they looked fine in Preview. Nor does it show whether any photo files are corrupted, resulting in blank pages.

When a book doesn't print out quite right, Apple is generally very forgiving, and will invite you to resubmit the book's file to try again. But sometimes, you don't have the time to wait for a second attempt—for example, when it's December 21 and you really need that book for Christmas.

In such cases, you'll be glad that you know how to inspect the actual, secret PDF book file that iPhoto sends to Apple. Here's how to find it (these directions are for Mac OS X 10.3, but the 10.2 procedure is similar):

Assemble your book, and click the Order Book button. Just af-

ter the "Assembling Book" progress window disappears, you arrive at the Order Book screen shown in Figure 10-10.

Switch back to the Finder. Choose Find→File. Set the first row of pop-up menus to read, "Name" "contains" iPhoto.

Click the + button to create a new row. Set its pop-up menus to read, "Visibility " "invisible items," as shown here.

Click Search.

On the Search Results screen, you'll find a folder named iPhoto. Double-click it to find a secret file named something like Book-107690896.pdf. When you open this PDF, you'll find it filled with wacky crop marks and other oddities, but it shows exactly, precisely what you'll get when that handsome volume arrives at your house in hardback form. This is your last chance to look it over for imperfections.

This is the actual file that you'll send to Apple's printing plant.

If it looks good, close the document, return to iPhoto, specify how many copies you want, and click Buy Now.

("Standard" shipping takes about four days and costs $8. "Express" means overnight or second-day shipping and costs $15.)

Note: You can order books if you live in Europe, Japan, or North America, but Apple offers shipping only to people in the same region (Europe, Japan, or North America).

Finally, indicate how many copies of this book you want, using the Quantity control, and click Buy Now. After a few minutes, you'll see a confirmation message.

When the book arrives, you'll certainly be impressed by the linen-covered cover and the heavy, glossy pages. The photos are printed on Indigo digital presses (fancy digital four-color offset machines), but aren't what you'd call Kodak quality—or even photo-inkjet-on-glossy-paper quality.

But the book itself is classy, it's handsome…and it smells good!

Photos Online—
And On Your Network

Even if you don't have a high-quality color printer, traditional prints of your digital photos are only a few clicks away. Sending photos via email, sharing them across the network, using them as a screen saver, or posting them on a Web page couldn't be more convenient, for both you and your audience. And compared with making printouts, sending them electronically is faster, less expensive, and much better for the rain forest.

Emailing Photos

The most important thing to know about emailing photos is this: *full-size photos are usually too big to email.*

First, a little math: A typical 4-megapixel shot might consume a megabyte of disk space. So sending along three shots would constitute a 3-megabyte package.

Why is that bad? Let us count the ways:

- It will take you 12 minutes to send (using a standard dial-up modem).

- It will take your recipients 12 minutes to download. During that time, the recipients must sit there, not even knowing what they're downloading. And when you're done hogging their time and account fees, they might not consider what you sent worth the wait.

- Even if they do open the pictures you sent, the average high-resolution shot is much too big for the screen. It does you no good to email somebody a 4-megapixel photo (2272 x 1704 pixels) when his monitor's maximum resolution is only 1024 x 768. If you're lucky, his graphics software will intelligently shrink the image to fit his screen; otherwise, he'll see only a gigantic nose filling his screen. But you'll still have to contend with his irritation at having waited 12 minutes for so much superfluous resolution.

- The typical Internet account has a limited mailbox size. If the mail collection exceeds 5 MB or so, that mailbox is automatically shut down until it's emptied. Your massive 3-megabyte photo package might be what pushes your hapless recipient's mailbox over its limit. She might miss out on important messages that get bounced as a result.

For years, this business of emailing photos has baffled beginners and enraged experts—and for many people who haven't yet discovered iPhoto, the confusion continues.

It's all different when you use iPhoto. Instead of unquestioningly attaching a multi-megabyte graphic to an email message and sending the whole bloated thing off, its first instinct is to offer you the opportunity to send a scaled-down, reasonably sized version of your photo instead (see Figure 11-1). If you take advantage of this feature, your modem-using friends will savor the thrill of seeing your digital shots without enduring the agony of a half-hour email download.

Figure 11-1:
The Mail Photo dialog box not only lets you choose the size of photo attachments, it also keeps track of how many photos you've selected and estimates how large your attachments are going to be, based on your selection.

FREQUENTLY ASKED QUESTION

Using iPhoto with PowerMail, QuickMail Pro, MailSmith...

Hey, I don't use Entourage, Eudora, AOL, or Apple Mail! How can I get iPhoto to send my photos via QuickMail? It's not listed as an option in the iPhoto's Mail Preferences.

You're right. Even if you have a different email program selected in the Internet panel of System Preferences, iPhoto won't fire up anything but Entourage, Eudora, or Mail when you click the Compose button.

There's a great workaround, though, thanks to the programming efforts of Simon Jacquier. Using his free utility, iPhoto Mailer Patcher, you can make iPhoto work obediently with MailSmith, PowerMail, QuickMail Pro, or even the aging Claris Emailer. It replaces the Mail button on iPhoto's bottom-edge panel with the icon of your preferred email program. You can download iPhoto Mailer Patcher from *http://homepage.mac.com/jacksim/software.*

The Mail Photo Command

iPhoto doesn't have any emailing features of its own. All it can do is get your pictures ready and hand them off to your existing email program. iPhoto's Mail Photo command works with four of the most popular Mac email programs—Microsoft Entourage, America Online, Qualcomm's Eudora, and Apple's own Mail (the free email program that came with your copy of Mac OS X).

If you currently use Apple's Mail program to handle your email, you're ready to start mailing your photos immediately. But if you want iPhoto to hand off to AOL, Entourage, or Eudora, you have to tell it so. Choose iPhoto→Preferences (or press ⌘-comma), and then choose the email program you want from the Mail pop-up menu.

When you select some photos and then click the Email button (at the bottom of the iPhoto window,) iPhoto offers to send a scaled-down version of each photo. The Size pop-up menu in the Mail Photo dialog box, shown in Figure 11-1, offers four choices.

- Choose **Small (240x320)** to keep your email attachments super small—and if you don't expect the recipient of your email to print the photo. (A photo this size can't produce a quality print any larger than a postage stamp.) On the other hand, your photos will consume less than 100 K apiece, making downloads quick and easy for those with dial-up connections.

- Choosing **Medium (640x480)** yields a file that will fill a nice chunk of your recipient's screen, with plenty of detail. It's even enough data to produce a slightly larger print—about 2 x 3 inches. Even so, the file size (and download time) remains reasonable; this setting can trim a 2 MB, 4-megapixel image down to an attachment of less than 150 K.

- The **Large (1280x960)** setting downsizes even your large photos to about 450 K, preserving enough pixels to make good 4 x 6 prints and completely fill the typical recipient's screen. In general, send these sparingly. Even if your recipients have a cable modem or DSL, these big files may still overflow their email boxes.

- Despite all the cautions above, there may be times when a photo is worth sending at **Full Size (full quality)**, like when you're submitting a photo for printing or publication. This works best when both you and the recipient have high-speed Internet connections and unlimited-capacity mail systems.

Note: iPhoto retains each picture's proportions when it resizes them. But if a picture doesn't have 4:3 proportions (maybe you cropped it, or maybe it came from a camera that wasn't set to create 4:3 photos), it may wind up *smaller* than the indicated dimensions. In other words, think of the choices in the Size pop-up menu as meaning, "this size or smaller."

Turn on the Titles and Comments checkboxes if you want iPhoto to copy the title of the photo and any text stored in the Comments field into the body of the email.

When Titles is turned on, iPhoto also inserts the photo's title into the Subject line of the email message.

When you click Compose, iPhoto processes your photos—converting them to JPEG format and, if you requested it, resizing them. It then launches your email program, creates a new message, and attaches your photos to it. (Behind the scenes, iPhoto uses AppleScript to accomplish these tasks.) Type your recipient's email address into the "To:" box, and then click Send. Your photos are on their merry way.

Tip: iPhoto always converts photos into JPEG format when emailing them. If you to want preserve a file's original format when emailing a Photoshop file or a PDF, *don't* use the Mail Photo feature. Instead, create a new email message manually, and then drag the thumbnails from iPhoto directly into the message window to attach them. (If you want to resize the photos, export them first using the File→Export command, which offers you a choice of scaling options.)

Publishing Photos on the Web

Putting your photos on the Web is the ultimate way to share them with the world. If the idea of enabling the vast throngs of the Internet-using public to browse, view, download, save, and print *your* photos sounds appealing, read on; it's amazingly easy to get your photos from iPhoto to the Internet.

Before you can post your photos online—and on your network using iPhoto's built-in Web tools—you need a *.Mac* account. That's Apple's suite of Internet services: email accounts, secure file-backup, Web-site hosting, and a few other extras. If you don't already have a .Mac account, see the "Getting a .Mac Account" box on the next page. Follow the directions, and you'll have one in less than five minutes. (A .Mac membership costs $100 per year; a two-month trial account is free.)

Three Roads to Webdom

iPhoto actually provides three different Web-publishing routes (two of which require a .Mac account), offering varying degrees of sophistication and complexity.

- **The easiest, most hands-off approach:** Use the HomePage feature within iPhoto. With only a couple of mouse clicks, this feature lets you construct Web pages, transfer them to the Internet, and make them available to the public. (A .Mac account is required.)

  What's especially nice about the resulting Web page is that it presents a tidy collection of thumbnail images—a gallery that downloads relatively quickly into your audience's browsers. Then, when visitors click one of the thumbnails, a new window opens up to display the picture at full size (see Figure 11-2).

- **More effort, more design and layout options:** Copy photos from iPhoto to the Pictures folder of your iDisk (a 100 MB Internet-based "virtual hard drive" that comes with a .Mac account). Then use the HomePage features at Apple's Web site (instead of the layout tools in iPhoto) to set up your pages.

• **For the experienced Web page designer:** If you already have a Web site, you can use iPhoto's Export command to generate Web pages (HTML documents) that already contain your photos. You can upload these files, with the accompanying graphics, to your Web site, whether that's a .Mac account or any other Web-hosting service. (Most Internet accounts, including those provided by America Online, Earthlink, and other service providers, come with free space for Web pages uploaded in this way.)

This is the most labor-intensive route, but it offers much more flexibility if you know how to work with HTML to create more sophisticated pages. It's also the route you should take if you hope to incorporate the resulting photo gallery into an existing Web site (that is, one in which the photos aren't the only attraction).

All three of these methods are detailed in the following pages.

Figure 11-2:
You'd be nuts to stuff your full-size pictures onto the Web; the 70 percent of the population that uses dial-up modems would come after you with a lynch mob.

Fortunately, iPhoto adopts a respectful approach: It uploads only a gallery of smallish thumbnails (top). When visitors click one of them, a larger version of it opens (bottom right). This way, they wait only for the pictures they really want to see at full size. At this point, the left and right arrow buttons conduct a tour of the larger photos.

Method 1: Use HomePage in iPhoto

Web publishing doesn't get any easier than it is with iPhoto's built-in HomePage feature. Your photos end up on a handsome-looking Web page in just a few quick steps—and you don't have to know the first thing about HTML.

1. **In iPhoto, select the photos you want to put on the Web, or click the album that contains them.**

   Make sure you've got iPhoto in Organize mode. The album can be one you've dragged pictures into, a smart album, the Last Roll(s) album, a year album, and so on. Use the selection techniques described on page 106 to isolate a bunch of photos within an album.

Note: The HomePage feature in iPhoto can't handle more than 48 photos per Web page. If you want to "publish" more than that, you'll have to create a series of separate pages.

---

2. **Click the HomePage button.**

   After it connects to the Internet, iPhoto opens its Publish HomePage window, which offers a visual menu of predesigned frame styles for your photos (Figure 11-3).

Figure 11-3:
Before you even open a Web browser, iPhoto shows you what your yet-to-be-created Web page is going to look like in the Publish HomePage window. In iPhoto 4, you can choose from among 14 canned Web designs, complete with frame styles, background colors, font schemes, and so on. Better yet, you're not looking at a page of HTML code.

3. **Click a frame style.**

   The Publish HomePage window immediately displays a mock-up of your finished Web page (Figure 11-3), displaying the thumbnails in whatever order they appear in iPhoto. You can choose from 14 different frame and text styles by clicking the photo thumbnails in the drawer alongside the window.

4. **Edit the page title, subtitle, and individual photo titles.**

   If you don't bother changing the photo names, iPhoto will simply use whatever titles the photos have in the program itself. (On the other hand, be careful: Any changes you make to the photo titles here are reflected in iPhoto.)

5. **Select the layout options you want.**

   Use the Layout radio button in the lower-left corner of the window to switch between a two-column or three-column layout.

   The "Send Me a Message" option lets you include a link on your Web pages that lets your fans send their gushing admiration via email to your .Mac address. Turning on the Counter option adds an odometer-style counter to your page, so you can marvel (or despair) at the number of visitors who hit your pages once you publish them. You can see how both of these options look in Figure 11-4.

6. **Click Publish.**

   iPhoto connects to the .Mac Web site, scales down your photos to a reasonable size, and then transfers them to the server (Figure 11-4, top). When the process is complete, as indicated by the alert dialog box (Figure 11-4, bottom), you can go to the page and see your results.

Note: If you include larger photos in your Web page, iPhoto automatically scales them down to 800 x 600 pixel JPEG files, so that they can be more easily loaded and displayed in a Web browser. If you want your Web pages to include *exact* copies of your original photos—regardless of size or file format—you must copy them to your iDisk yourself and then use the online HomePage tools to create your Web pages, as described later in this chapter. Or use the Export to the Web option described on page 208.

In any case, beware: Your iDisk holds only 100 MB of data—a limit that's easy to hit once you're addicted to self-publishing. (If you're *really* addicted, Apple is happy to raise the ceiling to 200 MB or even a gigabyte—for an additional annual fee.)

What you get when you're done

When you see what you've created with iPhoto, you'll be impressed: It's a professional-looking, stylishly titled Web page with thumbnails neatly arranged in a two- or three-column grid. Clicking a thumbnail opens an enlarged version of the picture, complete with Previous and Next buttons (Figure 11-2). You can return to your main index page at any time, or use the buttons in the slideshow window to navigate through the larger versions of your pictures.

Tip: In the URLs for your .Mac-hosted Web sites (such as *http://hompage.mac.com/yackell/PhotoAlbum2.html*), capitalization counts—a point not to be forgotten when you share the site's address with friends. If you type one of these addresses into a Web browser with incorrect capitalization, you'll get only a "missing page" message.

Then again, maybe it's better to send your friends a much shorter, easier to remember address. You can convert long URLs into shorter ones using a free URL redirection service. At *www.kickme.to,* for example, you can sign up to turn *http://hompage.mac.com/gladys/PhotoAlbum22.html* into *www.gladys.kickme.to.* (And if the kickme.to service isn't working as you read this, do your own shopping for free redirection services by searching Google for *free URL redirection*.)

Figure 11-4:
Top: When you've got your titles and captions looking good, click Publish to upload the photos to your .Mac account. Depending on the size and number of the photos you've selected, and the speed of your connection, this can take some time.

Bottom: Once iPhoto has copied the photos to your .Mac account, you see this message, indicating that your new Web page has been born. You can see your finished page on the Web by clicking the Visit Page Now button, but pay heed to the URL listed above the buttons; that's the Web address you need to give out if you want others to visit the page. (You can either click this address to visit the page, or drag across it to copy it.)

Editing the text of the Web page

To touch up the picture names or page title, visit *www.mac.com*, click the HomePage icon, click the name of the page you want to edit, and then click the Edit button beneath it. You wind up right back in the page-editing mode shown in Figure 11-3, where you're free to change the text in any of the title or caption boxes.

Editing the pictures on a Web page

Remember that your photo gallery Web page depicts *all* of the photos in a specific folder in your iDisk's Pictures folder. Adding, rearranging, or deleting photos from your Web page is therefore something of a hassle.

On the other hand, why bother? Publishing Web pages like this is easy and relatively quick. In many cases, the simplest way to make changes to a page is simply to republish it from within iPhoto. When you then publish the page again, iPhoto thoughtfully offers to replace the original page with your modified one.

Method 2: Use .Mac

Although using iPhoto's HomePage feature is incredibly simple, there's another way to go about creating, editing, and managing your photo galleries online: visit your .Mac Web site. Here, you're offered a few more templates, a quick way to edit your titles and captions, and the freedom to drag your photos into a new sequence without having to fiddle around in iPhoto. As a bonus, you can use your photos in Web pages that aren't necessarily photo-gallery designs—baby announcement pages, for example.

To get started with HomePage, you first must copy the photos you want to publish from iPhoto to the Pictures folder of your iDisk—in fact, into a *new folder* in the Pictures folder, one folder per Web page. (If your iDisk isn't already onscreen, just choose Go→iDisk or Go→iDisk→My iDisk in the Finder, so that its icon appears on your desktop.) You can drag thumbnails directly out of iPhoto and into the Pictures folder on the iDisk.

Once your photos are in the iDisk's Pictures folder, you're ready to create your Web pages. Go to *www.mac.com*, sign in, click the HomePage icon, then click one of the "Create a page" tabs on the HomePage screen to view the styles of pages you can create. Some of the formatting options available are shown in Figure 11-5.

The first tab, Photo Album, offers much the same photo-gallery layouts that you find in iPhoto itself (except that you get a few bonus layout designs). But you're free to use your photos in the other Web page designs here, too, like the baby announcements, writing samples, invitations, and so on.

If you choose Photo Album, click the miniature image of the design you want. HomePage next asks which photos folder in your Pictures folder you want to place on your new Web page, as shown in Figure 11-6. Select a folder of pictures, and then click Choose. After a few moments, your new photo album page appears with photos already inserted in the appropriate spots.

(If you choose any other Web page design, like Baby, the routine is pretty much the same, except that you have to click Edit at the top of the page in order to choose the photo you want.)

Figure 11-5:
Your Web-publishing options multiply considerably once you hit HomePage. In addition to the photo album themes shown here, you can also create resumés, personal newsletters, baby announcements, and party invitations. You can find these other options by clicking the "Create a page" tabs along the left side of the screen in the main HomePage screen.

To finish the project, click Edit at the top of the page to change the chunks of dummy text on the page. (Make an effort to avoid misspellings and typos, unless you want an audience of 400 million to think you slept through fourth-grade English.)

Finally, click Preview to see how the Web page will look. When everything is just the way you want it, click Publish. The page goes live, as indicated by the confirmation dialog box shown at the bottom of Figure 11-4.

Tip: You can create as many Web pages as your iDisk will hold, by the way. When you return to the main HomePage screen, a list of your existing Web pages appears, complete with New Page, Edit Page, and Delete Page buttons.

Corporations and professional Web designers may sniff at the simplicity of the result, but it takes *them* a lot longer than two minutes to do their thing.

Method 3: Export Web Pages

If you already have your own Web site, you don't need .Mac or HomePage to create an online photo album. Instead, you can use iPhoto's Export command to generate

HTML pages that you can upload to any Web server. You're still saving a lot of time and effort—and you still get a handy, thumbnail gallery page like that shown in Figure 11-2.

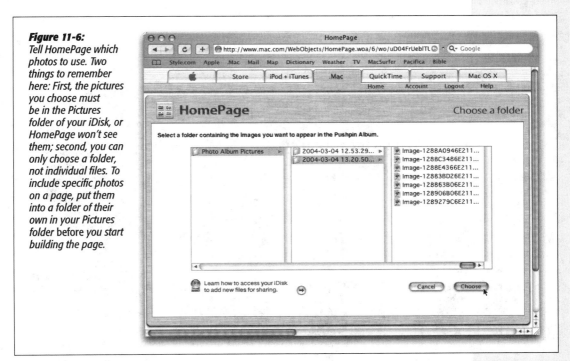

Figure 11-6:
Tell HomePage which photos to use. Two things to remember here: First, the pictures you choose must be in the Pictures folder of your iDisk, or HomePage won't see them; second, you can only choose a folder, not individual files. To include specific photos on a page, put them into a folder of their own in your Pictures folder before you start building the page.

The Web pages you export directly from iPhoto don't include any fancy designs or themed graphics. In fact, they're kind of stark; just take a look at Figure 11-7. But they offer more flexibility than the pages made with HomePage. For example, you can select the background color (or image) that appears on each page, specify the dimensions of thumbnails and images, and choose exactly how many thumbnails you want included on each page.

This is the best method if you plan to post the pages you create to a Web site of your own—especially if you plan on tinkering with the resulting HTML pages yourself.

Preparing the export

Here are the basic Web exporting steps:

1. **In iPhoto, select the photos you want to include on the Web pages.**

   Unlike the HomePage feature, the Export command puts no limit on the number of photos you can export to Web pages in one burst. Select as many photos as you want; iPhoto will generate as many pages as needed to accommodate all the pictures into your specified grid.

Tip: If you don't select any photos, iPhoto assumes you want to export all the photos in the current album (including the Photo Library or Last Roll(s) album).

2. Choose File→Export, or press Shift-⌘-E.

The Export Photos dialog box now appears.

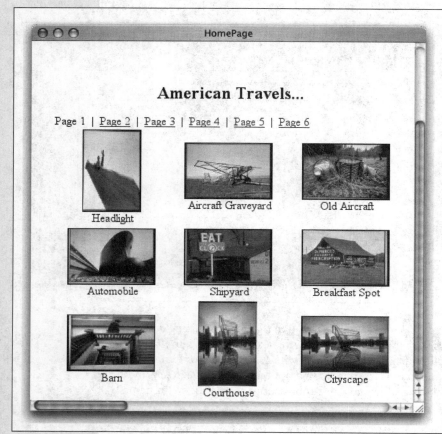

Figure 11-7:
Here's what a Web page exported straight from iPhoto to your hard drive looks like. The no-frills design is functional, but not particularly elegant. The links that let you navigate from page to page are always anchored to the top of the page, and you have no control over fonts or sizes. On the other hand, the HTML code behind this page is 100 percent editable.

3. Click the Web Page tab.

You see the dialog box shown in Figure 11-8.

4. Set the Page attributes, including the title, grid size, and background.

The title you set here will appear in the title bar of each exported Web page, and as a header in the page itself.

Tip: For maximum compatibility with the world's computers and operating systems, use all lowercase letters and no spaces.

Use the Columns and Rows boxes to specify how many thumbnails you want to appear across and down your "index" page. (The little "1 page" indicator tells you how many pages this particular index gallery requires.)

Figure 11-8:
As you change the size of the thumbnail grid or the size of the thumbnails, the number of pages generated to handle the images changes. The page count, based on your current settings, appears just to the right of the Rows field. The total count of the photos you're about to export appears in the lower-left corner of the window.

If you'd like a background page color other than white, click the rectangular swatch next to the word Color, and use the Color Picker dialog box described on page 5. You can also pick a color for the text that appears on each page by clicking the Text Color swatch.

You can even choose a background *picture* instead of a solid background color. To make it so, click the Image button, and then the Set button to select the graphics file on your hard drive. Be considerate of your audience, however. A background graphic will make your pages take longer to load, and a busy background pattern can be very distracting.

5. **Specify how big you want the thumbnail images to be, and also specify a size for the expanded images that appear when you click them.**

   The sizes iPhoto proposes are fine *if* all of your photos are horizontal (that is, in landscape orientation). If some are wide and some are tall, however, you're better off specifying *square* dimensions for both the thumbnails and the enlarged photos—240 x 240 for the thumbnails and 640 x 640 for the biggies, for example.

6. **Turn on "Show title" and "Show comment," if desired.**

Even though "Show title" may sound like your Web pages will sprout *show titles* ("Phantom of the Opera," "Oklahoma!," "Mame"), this option actually draws upon the *photo* titles you've assigned in iPhoto, centering each picture's name underneath its thumbnail. The larger version of each picture will also bear this name when it opens into its own window.

"Show comment" displays any text you've typed into the Comments field for each picture in iPhoto. Depending on which checkboxes you turn on, you can have the comments appear under each thumbnail, under each larger-size image, or both.

7. **Click Export.**

The Save dialog box appears.

8. **Choose (or, by clicking New Folder, create) a folder to hold the export files and then click OK.**

The export process gets under way.

Examining the results

When iPhoto is done with the export, you end up with a series of HTML documents and JPEG images—the building blocks of your Web-site-to-be. A number of these icons automatically inherit the name of the *folder* into which you've saved them. If you export the files into a folder named Tahiti, for example, here's what you'll find (see Figure 11-9):

- **Tahiti.html.** This is the main HTML page, containing the first thumbnails in the series that you exported. It's the home page, the index page, and the starting point for the exported pages.

- **Page1.html, Page2.html...** You see these only if you exported enough photos to require more than one page of thumbnails—that is, if iPhoto required *multiple* "home" pages.

- **Tahiti-Thumbnails.** This folder holds the actual thumbnail graphics that appear on each of the index pages.

- **Tahiti-Pages.** This folder contains the HTML documents (named Image1.html, Image2.html, Image3.html, and so on) that open when you click the thumbnails on the index pages.

- **Tahiti-Images.** This folder houses the larger JPEG versions of your photos. Yes, these are the *graphics* that appear on the Image HTML pages.

Tip: Some Web servers require that the default home page of your site be called *index.html.* To force your exported Web site to use this name for the main HTML page, save your exported pages into a *folder* called *index.* Now the home page will have the correct name (index.html) and all the other image and page files will be properly linked to it. (After exporting, feel free to rename the folder. Naming it *index* was only necessary during the exporting process.)

Once you've created these pages, it's up to you to figure out how to *post* them on the Internet where the world can see them. To do that, you'll have to upload all the exported files to a Web server, using an *FTP* program like the free RBrowser (available from the "Missing CD" page of *www.missingmanuals.com*). Only then do they look like real Web pages, as shown in Figure 11-7.

Figure 11-9:
This is what a Web site looks like before it's on the Internet. All the pieces are here, filed exactly where the home page (called, in this example, Tahiti.html) can find them.

Enhancing iPhoto's HTML

If you know how to work with HTML code, you don't have to accept the unremarkable Web pages exported by iPhoto. You're free to tear into them with a full-blown Web authoring program like Adobe GoLive, Macromedia Dreamweaver, or the free Netscape Composer (*www.netscape.com*) to add your own formatting, headers, footers, and other graphics. (Heck, even Microsoft Word lets you open and edit HTML Web pages—plenty of power for changing iPhoto's layout, reformatting the text, or adding your own page elements.)

If you're a hard-core HTML coder, you can also open the files in a text editor like BBEdit or even TextEdit to tweak the code directly. With a few quick changes, you can make your iPhoto-generated Web pages look more sophisticated and less generic.

Note: You can add a number of elegant features to your photo site using an excellent piece of add-on software that requires no hand coding—or special editing software—at all.

It's the fittingly named BetterHTMLExport, an inexpensive iPhoto 4 plug-in that extends the features of iPhoto's own HTML Exporter. You can download a copy of BetterHTMLExport from the "Missing CD" page of *www.missingmanuals.com,* among other places. BetterHTMLExport lets you add comments (not just titles) on index and image pages; create links to your *original* images instead of just JPEG versions of them; choose where on the page you want to include navigation hyperlinks; and more.

The .Mac Slideshow

iPhoto 4 also gives you perhaps the weirdest and wildest way to share your photos online—and on your network: publish them as a *.Mac slideshow*.

When you send your photos out into the world as .Mac slides, other Mac OS X users can *subscribe* to your show, displaying *your* pictures as *their* screen saver—without having to manually download any files or launch a Web browser. (They do, of course, need an Internet connection.) In a minute or so, your latest photos can appear as full-screen slides on the Macintosh of a friend, family member, co-worker, or anyone else who knows your .Mac membership name.

Note: Creating and viewing a .Mac slideshow requires Mac OS X 10.2 or later.

Note, too, that if your aim is to turn your photos into a screen saver only on *your* Mac (and not make them available to the world at large), you don't need a .Mac account, and you don't need to follow the steps below. Instead, use the Desktop button (page 226). It's quicker and cheaper, and it doesn't require an Internet connection.

Creating a .Mac slideshow

Before any other Mac users can connect to your slideshow pictures, you have to make them available via your .Mac account. (If you don't have a .Mac account, you'll be prompted to sign up for one when you attempt to use the .Mac feature. See page 57.) Here are the steps for publishing your slideshow:

1. **In iPhoto, select the photos you want to make available as screen saver slides.**

   If you don't select any specific photos, iPhoto creates your .Mac slideshow from whatever pictures are currently displayed in the iPhoto window—either the whole Photo Library, a specific album, or a combination of albums.

2. **With iPhoto in Organize mode, click the .Mac Slides button in the lower pane of the window.**

   A dialog box opens, asking if you're sure you really want to publish your personal photos to the Internet. It's a question that deserves some consideration. Once you create .Mac slides, your pictures will be freely available to hundreds of thousands of Internet-connected Mac OS X fans around the world. (They do, however, need to know—or guess—your .Mac membership name.) If you have any reservations about making these glimpses of your life available to the world at large, now's the time to click Cancel.

   Otherwise, read on:

3. **Click Publish to begin uploading your photos.**

   One by one, iPhoto grabs your photos and copies them to your iDisk, dropping them into a special location in the Pictures→Slideshows→Public folder.

When all the photos are safely online, a confirmation dialog box appears, letting you know that your slideshow is now available. (If you look at the uploaded files on your iDisk, you'll notice that iPhoto has renamed your pictures according to its own private naming scheme. It's only the uploaded copies that have been renamed, however, not the photos on your Mac.)

Note: You can publish any number of Web sites on your .Mac account, but only *one* set of .Mac slides. Each time you upload photos for a .Mac slideshow, you *replace* any earlier slideshow photos you've uploaded.

4. **Click Announce Slideshow, if you like.**

If you'd rather not email your friends to let them know about your slides, click Quit instead. Then use your Mac's screen saver feature, as outlined in the next section, to see the fruits of your labor.

Subscribing to a .Mac slideshow

After you've uploaded your photos as .Mac slides, you, or anyone else with Mac OS X 10.2 (or later) and an Internet connection, can subscribe to the show and make it into a screen saver. Here's how:

Figure 11-10:
You can connect to screen savers created by other Mac users around the world by using the .Mac Screen Effects option. Don't forget to visit the other two tabs in the Screen Effects panel—Activation and Hot Corners. On the Activation tab, you can tell your Mac how long it must sit idle before your custom screen saver kicks in. The options in the Hot Corners tab let you flip screen effects on or off by moving your mouse into a designated corner of the screen.

1. **Choose ⬥→System Preferences. Click the Screen Effects (Mac OS X 10.2) or Desktop & Screen Saver icon (Mac OS X 10.3) to open the panel.**

   Switch to the Screen Effects (Mac OS X 10.2) or Screen Saver (Mac OS X 10.3) tab of the window, if it's not already displayed. This is where you choose the particular effect that your Mac will use as a screen saver.

2. **Click .Mac in the Screen Effects list.**

   A message appears on the little black Preview screen, as shown in Figure 11-10, prompting you to click the Configure (Mac OS X 10.2) or Options (Mac OS X 10.3) button so that you can select a slideshow and set up the playback options.

3. **Click the Configure (or Options) button.**

   The Subscriptions window appears. The controls here determine which slideshows you can see on your Mac and how they're displayed.

4. **In the .Mac Membership Name box, enter the name of the .Mac member whose slideshow you want to see.**

   There's no way to *get* this name. Unless you find the creator's name at the *www. dotmac.info* Web page, you just have to know it.

Tip: You can subscribe to as many different .Mac slideshows as you want. As you do, their names accumulate in the Subscriptions window.

---

5. **Choose your Display Options.**

   Adjust the checkboxes in the lower portion of the window to change the way the slides are to be presented on your screen. You can control zooming, crossfades, and other options, as shown in Figure 11-11.

6. **Click OK to return to the main Screen Effects window.**

   This is the big moment: The Mac hooks up to the .Mac site(s) you've specified and finds the shared slideshow. Seconds later, you see the results of your tinkering: The slides you've subscribed to appear on the little Preview screen in a miniature version of the slideshow, complete with zooming effects and crossfades.

Note: If the slideshow you've subscribed to is very large, the Preview screen may remain black for a minute or two as the images get downloaded to your Mac.

---

7. **Click the Test button to preview the slideshow at full size.**

   Your screen goes black, and then the first of the slides you've subscribed to fills the screen. Depending on the options you've selected, the slideshow progresses with photos slowly zooming and cross-fading into each other. To end the test, just click your mouse.

You've now got a remote slideshow that will play back on your screen according to the rules you've set up in the Activation and Hot Corners tabs of the Screen Effects panel. Of course, at any time, you can go back into Screen Effects and reconfigure the .Mac slide settings: add additional slideshows to your subscriptions, rearrange their playback order, or (when the kid in your cousin's new-baby slideshow turns 21, perhaps) delete .Mac slideshows from the list.

Figure 11-11:
Your Mac remembers each show you've subscribed to—though you can have it use or ignore any combination of shows by turning the Selected checkbox next to each title on or off. You can also change the order in which the shows are presented by dragging them into a different order in this list.

Photo Sharing on the Network

One of the coolest features of iTunes is the way you can "publish" certain playlists on your home or office network, so that other people in the same building can listen to your tunes. Why couldn't iPhoto do the same thing with pictures?

In iPhoto 4, it can.

For this example, suppose that you're the master shutterbug who has all the cool shots. On your Mac, choose iPhoto→Preferences and click Sharing. Turn on "Share my photos" (Figure 11-12).

You might be tempted to turn on "Share entire library," so that no crumb of your artistry will go unappreciated—but don't. Even the fastest Macs on the fastest networks will grind to a halt if you try to share even a medium-sized photo library. You are, after all, attempting to ram gigabytes of data through your network to the other Macs.

It's far more practical to turn on the checkboxes for the individual albums you want to share, as shown in Figure 11-12. Finally, close the Sharing window.

At this point, other people on your network will see *your* albums show up in *their* Source lists, above the list of their own albums; see Figure 11-13. (Or at least they

Figure 11-12:
If you turn on "Share entire library," you make all of your pictures available to others on the network—and you doom your fans to a lifetime of waiting while gray empty boxes fill their iPhoto screens.

Alternatively, click "Share selected albums" and turn on the individual albums that you want to make public.

Unless you also turn on "Require password" (and make up a password), everyone on the network will see your shared pictures.

FREQUENTLY ASKED QUESTION

Trolling for .Mac Slides

The idea of sharing .Mac slides with friends sounds great, and I would do it in a heartbeat—if I had more friends. As it turns out, I don't know another soul running Mac OS X. Am I destined to watch my same boring photos cross-fade into each other, day after day, in utter solitude?

Fortunately, no. Thousands of .Mac members have already made their slideshows available to the world, and they're just waiting for you to subscribe to them.

The trick is to visit *www.dotmac. info/index.html*, where you'll find a listing of movies, photo

albums, calendars, Web sites, and—yes—.Mac slideshows, all contributed by other .Mac members. You can search for specific items or just browse the listings, then subscribe to any number of slideshows. Thanks to the miracle of modern technology, you can now fill your screen with the photos of total strangers.

Want to give the world access to *your* slideshow, too? Click the Add a Page button on the *dotmac.info* home page. Add a description of your slides along with your membership name, so that anyone who wants to can subscribe to your slides from their Mac.

will if they have "Look for shared photos" turned on in their iPhoto Preferences, also shown in Figure 11-12.)

As you may know, when you share iTunes music over a network, other people can only *listen* to your songs—they can't actually *have* them. (The large, well-built lawyers of the American record companies have made sure of that.)

But iPhoto is another story. Nobody is going to issue you a summons for freely distributing your own photos. So once you've jacked into somebody else's iPhoto pictures via the network, feel free to drag them into your own iPhoto albums, thereby copying them onto your own Mac. Now you can edit them, print them, and otherwise treat them like your very own photos.

Figure 11-13:
You can't delete or edit the photos you've summoned from some other Mac. But you can drag them into your own albums (or your own Photo Library) to copy them.

When you've had enough, click the Eject button. The flippy triangle, the list of albums, and the Eject button disappear. The name of the shared collection ("Upstairs Photos" in this example) remains on the screen, though, in case you want to bring them back for another look later.

The QuickTime Slideshow

As Chapter 9 makes clear, once you select your images and choose the music to go with them, iPhoto orchestrates the production and presents it live on your Mac's screen as a slideshow.

Which is great, as long as everyone in your social circle lives within six feet of your screen.

The day will come when you want friends and family who live a little farther away to be able to see your slideshows. Sure, you could pack up your Mac and fly across the country, but wouldn't it be easier to simply send the slideshow as a file attachment that people can play on their own computers?

That's the beauty of QuickTime, a portable multimedia container built into every Mac. Even if the recipient uses a Windows PC (every family has its black sheep), your photos will meet their public; QuickTime movies play just as well on HPs and Dells as they do on iMacs and PowerBooks.

The trick is to convert your well-composed iPhoto slideshow into a standalone Quick-Time movie—a file on your hard drive that you can email to other people, post on your Web page for downloading, burn onto a CD, and so on.

Fortunately, iPhoto makes creating the movie as simple as creating the original show itself. You just have to know which buttons to click.

Step 1: Perfect the Slideshow

Before you pack up your slideshow for release to the public, review it to make sure it plays the way you want it to. You'll probably find it easiest to create a new album just for your QuickTime slideshow (Chapter 7), so that you can fool around with the sequence and photo selection without messing up the album designed for such purposes as photo books and *onscreen* slideshows.

Now, if you're used to the slideshow feature described in Chapter 9, the method for specifying which photos are exported to your QuickTime movie might throw you.

- If *one* thumbnail is selected, that's all you'll get in the finished QuickTime movie—the world's shortest slideshow. (This is the part that might throw you: An iPhoto slideshow would begin with that one selected photo and then move on from there, showing you all the rest of the photos in the album.)

- If *several* thumbnails are selected, only they make it into the QuickTime slideshow movie.

- If *no* thumbnails are selected, the entire album's worth of photos wind up in the show.

When you're ready to convert your presentation to a QuickTime movie, choose File→ Export. The Export Photos dialog box appears, as shown in Figure 11-14. Click the QuickTime tab, where you have some important decisions to make.

Step 2: Choose the Movie Dimensions

Specifying the width and height for your movie affects not only how big it is on the screen during playback, but also its file size, which may become an issue if you plan to email the movie to other people. iPhoto generally proposes 640 x 480 pixels. That's an ideal size: big enough for people to see some detail in the photo, but not so big that the resulting movie won't play from, say, a CD. (CDs are much slower than hard drives.)

You're free to change these dimensions, however. If the movie will be played back from a hard drive, you may want to crank up the dimensions close to the size of the screen itself: 800 x 600 is a safe bet if you're not sure. Remember, though, you have to leave some room for the QuickTime Player controls, so that your viewers can start and stop the movie.

Proportion considerations

All of these suggestions assume, by the way, that your photos' dimensions are in a 4:3 ratio, the way they come from most cameras. That way, they'll fit nicely into the standard QuickTime playback window.

But there's nothing to stop you from typing other numbers into the Width and Height boxes. If most of the shots are vertical, for example, you'll want to reverse the proposed dimensions so that they're 480 x 640, resulting in a taller, thinner playback window.

Figure 11-14:
Here's the Export dialog box with the QuickTime tab selected. This is the airlock, the womb, the last time you'll be able to affect your movie before it's born.

Size considerations

As you choose dimensions, bear in mind that they also determine the *file size* of the resulting QuickTime movie. That's not such an issue if you plan to play the movie from a CD, DVD, or hard drive. But if you plan to send the movie by email or post it on a Web page, watch out.

At 640 x 480 pixels, a 24-photo movie with sound would take up 3 MB on your hard drive—and at least that much in your recipients' email inboxes. Scaling it down to a quarter of that size (320 x 240) would shave off about a third of that, resulting in a 2.1 MB file.

But even 2.1 MB is a very big file to send as an email attachment to anyone who connects with a dial-up modem. You could, of course, reduce the dimensions even further.

At some point, though, you'd reach a point of diminishing returns. The pictures would be so microscopic that the project wouldn't be worth doing.

Managing Music

In the Music section of the QuickTime export dialog box, you have the option of including the soundtrack you originally selected for your movie by turning on the box labeled, "Add currently selected music to movie."

To save file size, you could turn off this box. That 320 x 240 movie would shrink to a mere 440 K—less than one-fourth the size of the presentation with the original soundtrack—but, of course, you'd wind up with a silent movie.

Fortunately, there is a middle road: You could use iTunes to turn the music into an MP3 file with a low-ish bit rate that's much smaller than the full-blown original. Page 49 has the details.

Step 3: Seconds per Photo

How many seconds do you want each picture to remain on the screen before the next one appears? You specify this number using the "Display image for ___ seconds" box in the QuickTime Export dialog box.

When you first open the dialog box, iPhoto proposes whatever frame rate you used in your original slideshow. You're free to change it to other timings. (Although you can *type* a frame rate shorter than one second, iPhoto won't actually create the show with a rate any faster than one image per second. So much for artistic license.)

Step 4: Background Colors

The color or image you choose in the Background section of the dialog box will appear as the first and last frames of the export. It will also fill in the margins of the frame when a vertically oriented or oddly proportioned picture appears. Generally speaking, white, light gray, or black makes the best background.

If you click the Image button and then the Set button next to it, though, you can navigate your hard drive in search of a *graphics* file to use as the slideshow background.

Step 5: Export the Movie

Having specified the dimensions, frame rate, music, and background for your movie, there's nothing left but to click the Export button in the dialog box. You'll be asked to specify a name and folder location for the movie (leaving the proposed suffix *.mov* at the end of the name), and then click Save. After a moment of computing, iPhoto returns to its main screen.

Press ⌘-H to hide iPhoto, then navigate to the folder you specified and double-click the movie to play it in QuickTime Player (a program that comes with every Mac). When the movie opens, click the Play triangle or press the Space bar to enjoy your newly packaged slideshow (Figure 11-15).

Whenever playback is stopped, you can even "walk" through the slides manually by pressing the right-arrow key twice (for the next photo) or the left-arrow key once (for the previous one).

Tip: Even Windows PC users can enjoy your QuickTime movies—if they visit *www.apple.com/quicktime/ download* to download the free QuickTime Player program for Windows.

Figure 11-15:
Once you're in QuickTime Player, you can control the playback of the slideshow in a number of ways. If you don't feel like clicking and dragging onscreen controls, the arrow keys adjust the volume (up and down) or step through the photos one at a time (right and left).

Building a Custom Screen Saver

Mac OS X's screen saver feature is so good, it's been the deciding factor responsible for pushing more than one Mac fan over the edge into making the upgrade to Mac OS X. When this screen saver kicks in (after several minutes of inactivity on your part), your Mac's screen becomes a personal movie theater. The effect is something like a slideshow, except that the pictures don't simply appear one after another and sit there on the screen. Instead, they're much more animated. They slide gently across the screen, zooming in or zooming out, smoothly dissolving from one to the next.

Mac OS X comes equipped with a few photo collections that look great with this treatment: forests, space shots, and so on. But let the rabble use those canned screen savers. You, a digital master, can use your own photos as screen saver material.

Meet the Screen Saver

When you're ready to turn one of your own photo collections into a screen saver, collect the photos in an album (Chapter 7). Or, if you're using Mac OS X 10.3 or later, simply highlight the photos you want to use as screen saver fodder, whether they're in an album or not.

Then, in Organize mode, click the album to highlight it, and then click the Desktop icon on the bottom panel.

- If you're using Mac OS X 10.2 (Jaguar), the dialog box shown at top in Figure 11-16 appears. Click OK.

- If you're using Mac OS X 10.3 (Panther), you go straight to the Desktop & Screen Saver panel of System Preferences (shown at bottom in Figure 11-16).

Screen Saver Basics

You don't technically need a screen saver to protect your monitor from burn-in. Today's energy-efficient CRT monitors wouldn't burn an image into the screen unless you left them on continuously for two years, and flat-panel screens *never* burn in.

No, screen savers are about entertainment, pure and simple.

In Mac OS X, when you click a module's name in the screen saver list, you see a mini version of it playing back in the Preview screen.

You can control when your screen saver takes over your monitor. For example, the "Start screen saver" slider lets you specify when the screen saver kicks in (after what period of keyboard or mouse inactivity).

When you click the Hot Corners button, you're presented with a pane than lets you turn each corner of your monitor into a *hot spot*. Whenever you roll your cursor into that corner, the screen saver either turns on instantly (great when you happen to be shopping on eBay at the moment your boss walks by) or stays off permanently (for when

you're reading onscreen or watching a movie). If you use Mac OS X 10.3, you can use two corners for controlling the screen saver and the other two to activate Exposé (Panther's window-hiding feature).

In any case, pressing any key or clicking the mouse always removes the screen saver from your screen and takes you back to whatever you were doing.

The Options button reveals the additional settings illustrated here, some of which are very useful. Turn off "Crop slides to fit on screen," for example, if you want the Mac to show each photo, edge to edge (even if it has to use black bars to fill the rest of your monitor); otherwise, it enlarges each photo to fill the screen, often lopping off body parts in the process. (If "Crop slides" is on, you can also turn on "Keep slides centered" to prevent the Mac from panning across each photo.)

And turning off "Zoom back and forth," of course, eliminates the majestic, cinematic zooming in and out of successive photos that makes the screen saver look so darned cool.

Tip: Horizontal shots fill your monitor better than vertical ones–the verticals have fat black bars on either side to fill the empty space.

If you have an oddball camera (one whose photos have a 3:2 width-to-height ratio instead of 4:3) or an oddball screen (like the extra-wide titanium PowerBook G4 screen or the 17-inch iMac screen), there's one more step. You might want to crop the photos, or copies of them, accordingly to maximize their impact.

Ready to view the splendor of your very own homemade screen saver? If you have the patience of a Zen master, you can now sit there, motionless, staring at your Mac for the next half an hour or so—or as long as it takes for Mac OS X to conclude that you're no longer working and finally begin displaying your images on the screen.

Figure 11-16:
Top: In Mac OS X 10.2, you get to choose which album to use for your Mac's screen saver. Or, click Screen Effects Preferences to open the proper pane of System Preferences, where you can specify when the screen saver should kick in.

Bottom: In Mac OS X 10.3, all of your custom albums within iPhoto are listed in the Screen Saver panel of the Desktop & Screen Saver preferences window. Just pick the one you want to use as a screen saver, or click iPhoto Selection (in the upper part of the list) to "play" whatever pictures you've selected in iPhoto, even if they weren't in an album.

Either way, Mac OS X turns your photos into a smoothly flowing, full-screen slideshow.

If, however, you feel that life is too short as it is, click the Test button shown in Figure 11-16. See the box on page 226 for details on setting up and triggering the screen saver function.

One-Click Desktop Backdrop

iPhoto's desktop-image feature is the best way to drive home the point that photos of your children (or dog, or mother, or self) are the most beautiful in the world. You pick one spectacular shot to replace the standard Mac OS X swirling blue desktop pattern. It's like refrigerator art on steroids (Figure 11-17).

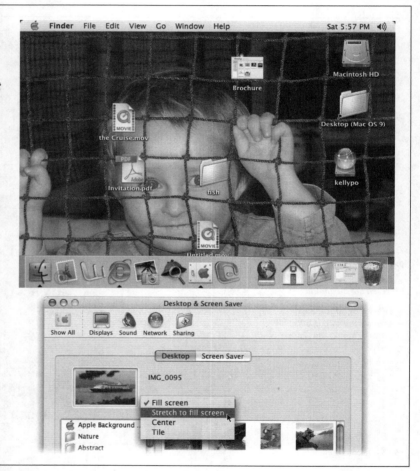

Figure 11-17:
Top: Folder and icons may occasionally mar a desktop photo's full-screen magnificence, but look at the bright side: The fact that you're getting documents in your children's eyes will be all the more incentive for you to become a better housekeeper.

Bottom: In System Prefer-ences, use this pop-up menu to tell the Mac how you want to handle desktop pictures that don't precisely match the dimensions of your screen.

Creating wallpaper in iPhoto is so easy that you could change the picture every day—and you may well want to. In Organize mode, click a thumbnail. (In Mac OS X 10.3 and later, you can even select several, or a whole album.)

Then click the Desktop button on the bottom panel. Even though the iPhoto window is probably filling your screen, the change happens instantly behind it. Your desktop is now filled with the picture you chose.

Mac OS X 10.3 even drives home the point by switching to the proper panel of System Preferences automatically. Whatever pictures or albums you selected show up in the iPhoto Selection category; click the one you want to plaster on the desktop first.

Just three words of advice. First, choose a picture that's at least as big as your screen (1024 x 768 pixels, for example). Otherwise, Mac OS X will stretch it to fit, distorting the photo in the process.

Tip: If you're really fussy, you can even crop the photo first to the exact measurements of the screen; in fact, the first command in iPhoto's Constrain pop-up menu (page 142) lists the exact dimensions of your screen, so you can crop the designated photo (or a copy of it) to fit precisely.

Second, horizontal shots work much better than vertical ones; iPhoto blows up vertical shots to fit the width of the screen, potentially chopping off the heads and feet of your loved ones.

Finally, if a photo doesn't precisely match the screen's proportions, note the pop-up menu shown at bottom in Figure 11-17. It lets you specify how you want the discrepancy handled. Your choices include:

- **Fill screen.** This option enlarges or reduces the image so that it fills every inch of the desktop. If the image is small, the low-resolution stretching can look awful. Conversely, if the image is large and its dimensions don't precisely match your screen's, parts get chopped off. At least this option never distorts the picture, as the "Stretch" option does (below).

- **Stretch to fill screen.** Use this option at your peril, since it makes your picture fit the screen exactly, come hell or high water. Unfortunately, larger pictures may be squished vertically or horizontally as necessary, and small pictures are drastically blown up and squished, usually with grisly-looking results.

- **Center.** This command centers the photo neatly on the screen. If the picture is larger than the screen, you see only the middle; the edges of the picture are chopped off as they extend beyond your screen.

  But if the picture is smaller than the screen, it won't fill the entire background; instead it just sits right smack in the center of the monitor at actual size. Of course, this leaves a swath of empty border all the way around your screen. As a remedy, Apple provides a color-swatch button next to the pop-up menu. When you click it, the Color Picker appears (page 5), so that you can specify the color in which to frame your little picture.

- **Tile.** This option makes your picture repeat over and over until the multiple images fill the entire monitor. (If your picture is larger than the screen, no such tiling takes place. You see only the top center chunk of the image.)

And one last thing: If public outcry demands that you return your desktop to one of the standard system backdrops, open System Preferences, click the Desktop & Screen Saver (or Screen Effects) icon, click the Desktop button if necessary, choose Apple Backgrounds in the list box at the left of the window, then take your pick.

Tip: Want to really blow onlookers' minds? Then turn on the Mac feature that automatically *changes* your desktop picture every 5, 15, or 30 minutes, rotating from one iPhoto photo to the next within its album. It's the wallpaper for the easily bored.

To pull this off, open System Preferences; click Desktop & Screen Saver (10.3) or Screen Effects (10.2). Turn on the Change Picture checkbox and specify the timing for the picture-changing, using the pop-up menu next to it. Stand by for applause.

While you're in the Desktop & Screen Saver or Screen Effects preferences pane, you might notice that all of your iPhoto albums are listed below the collection of images that came with your Mac. You can navigate through those albums to find a new desktop image. This approach isn't as fast (or fun) as picking pictures in iPhoto, but if for some reason iPhoto isn't open on your Mac (heaven forbid!), you can take care of business right there in System Preferences.

iPhoto File Management

When you don't have to buy film or pay for processing, photos have a way of piling up very quickly. Apple says iPhoto can hold an unlimited number of photos and, technically, that's true (as long as you have enough memory and hard drive space). But in fact, once you go much above 25,000 pictures, iPhoto winds up gasping for RAM and acts as if you've slathered it with a thick coat of molasses.

For some photo fans, this comes as a distressing bit of news. You downloaded the software, entrusted your best work to it, even bought a book about it—and now you learn it's going to cop out on you in another couple of years.

Fortunately, a little knowledge—and a handful of blank, recordable CDs or DVDs—can keep you happily in iPhoto at reasonable speeds. The trick is learning how to manage iPhoto's library files—wisdom that will also serve you when you want to transfer photos to another Mac or when it comes time to *backing up* your photo collection.

This chapter covers both iPhoto's behind-the-scenes filing system and what's involved in backing it up: swapping photo libraries, burning them to CD, transferring them to other machines, and merging them together.

About iPhoto Discs

iPhoto CDs are discs (either CDs or DVDs, actually) that you can create directly from within iPhoto to archive your entire Photo Library—or any selected portion of it—with just a few mouse clicks.

The beauty of iPhoto's Burn command is that it exports much more than just the photos themselves to a disc; it also copies the thumbnails, titles, keywords, comments, ratings, and all the other important data about your Photo Library. Once you've burned all of this valuable information to disc, you can do all sorts of useful things:

- Make a backup of your whole Photo Library for safekeeping.

- Transfer specific photos, albums or a whole Photo Library to another Mac without losing all your keywords, descriptions, ratings, and titles.

- Share discs with other iPhoto fans so that your friends or family can view your photo albums in their own copies of iPhoto.

- Offload photos to CD or DVD as your photo collection grows, to keep your current Photo Library at a trim, manageable size.

- Merge separate Photo Libraries (such as the one on your iBook and the one on your iMac) into a single master Photo Library.

Note: One thing an iPhoto CD is *not* good for is sharing your photos with somebody who doesn't have iPhoto! An iPhoto CD is designed *exclusively* for transferring pictures into another copy of iPhoto. See the details on page 232.

Burning an iPhoto CD or DVD

All you need to create an iPhoto CD is a Mac with a CD burner or DVD burner and a blank disc.

1. **In iPhoto's Organize mode, select the albums or photos that you want to include on the disc.**

   Click the Photo Library icon if you want to burn your whole photo collection. Make sure that no individual photos are selected. If you do, iPhoto assumes you want to burn *only* those selected photos to disc.

   To burn only a specific album or group of albums, select them in the Source list. Either way, the photo-viewing area should now be showing the photos you want to save onto a disc.

2. **Click the Burn icon at the bottom of the iPhoto window (Figure 12-1).**

   A dialog box appears, prompting you to insert a blank disc. Pop in the disc; the dialog box vanishes after a few moments.

3. **Check the size of your selection to make sure it will fit.**

   Take a look at the Info panel just below with Source list, as shown in Figure 12-2. If the set of photos you want to burn is smaller than 650 or 700 megabytes (for a CD) or about 4.3 gigabytes (for a DVD), you're good to go. You can burn the whole thing to a single disc.

   If your photo collection is larger than that, however, it's not going to fit. You'll have to split your backup operation across multiple discs. Select whatever number of photo albums or individual pictures you can that *will* fit on a single disc, using the indicator icons shown in Figure 12-2 as your guide. (Also shown in the figure: The Disc Name box, where you can name the disc you're about to burn.)

For example, you might decide to copy the 2001 folder onto one disk, the 2002 folder onto another, and so on, using the built-in year "collections" in the Source list as your source material.

Figure 12-1:
The Burn button, which makes it possible to create CDs or DVDs directly from within iPhoto, has two faces. The "closed shutter" icon (top) is the usual state. When you click the button to set up the disc-burning process, the shutter opens to reveal the pulsating "burn" icon (bottom).

Figure 12-2:
Top left: Once you've clicked Burn and inserted a blank disc, the Info panel lets you know how close you are to filling the disc. The indicator icon updates itself as you select or deselect photos and albums to show you how much free space is available on the disc.

Top right: If your photos take up more space than is available on the disc, the little disc icon turns red and you see the Disc Full message shown here.

Bottom: Disregarding this warning won't get you very far; if you attempt to burn the disc anyway, iPhoto will stop you with yet another message.

After burning one disc, select the next set of photos, and burn another CD or DVD. Burn as many discs as needed to contain your entire collection of photos. If and when you ever need to restore your photos from the multiple discs, you'll be able to merge them back together into a single Photo Library using the technique described in "Merging Photo Libraries" later in this chapter.

4. Click the Burn icon again.

Before iPhoto fires up your Mac's disc-burning laser, it presents a confirmation dialog box, telling you exactly how many photos it's going to burn to disc. (If you've chosen specific photo albums for backup, the total number of albums is listed, too.) If you want to back out of the operation, click Cancel.

5. Click the Burn button.

First, iPhoto makes a disk image—a sort of pretend disk that serves as a temporary holding area for the photos that will be burned. (You may even see the icon for this imaginary disk pop up on your desktop during the process.) Next, iPhoto copies the photos from your iPhoto Library folder to the disk image.

Finally, the real burning begins. When the process is done, your Mac spits out the finished CD or DVD, ready to use, bearing whatever name you gave it.

Tip: You can safely bail out of the CD-creating process at any time by clicking the Cancel button in the Progress dialog box.

But don't click the Stop button once the Burning dialog box appears. At that point, your CD or DVD drive is already busy etching data onto the disc itself. Clicking Stop will indeed bring the burning to a screeching halt—but you'll end up with a partially burned, nonfunctioning disc.

What you get

The finished iPhoto disc contains not just your photos, but a clone of your iPhoto Library folder as well. In other words, all the thumbnails, keywords, comments, ratings, photo album information—even the unedited original versions of your photos that iPhoto keeps secretly tucked away—are all included on the disk.

If you want to view the contents of your finished CD in iPhoto, pop the disc back into the drive. (If iPhoto isn't running, your Mac opens it automatically.)

Moments later, the icon for the CD appears in the Source list of the iPhoto window. If you click the disc's icon, the photos it contains appear in the photo-viewing area, just as if they were stored in your Photo Library.

You can't make changes to them, of course—that's the thing about CDs and DVDs. But you can copy them into your own albums, and make changes to the copies.

When Not to Burn

The Burn command is convenient for creating quick backups, archiving portions of your Photo Library, or transferring photos to another Mac. But it's definitely not the best way to share your photos with Windows users, or even other Mac fans running Mac OS 9.

Think about it: Burning an iPhoto CD automatically organizes your photos into a series of numerically named subfolders inside an iPhoto Library folder, surrounded by scads of special data files like *.attr* files, *Library.cache,* and *Dir.data*. All of this makes perfect sense to iPhoto, but is essentially meaningless to anyone who doesn't use iPhoto. A Windows user, for example, would have to dig through folder after folder on your iPhoto CD to find and open your photos.

So if the destination of your CD or DVD *isn't* another iPhoto user, *don't* use the Burn command. Instead, export the photos using the File Export or Web Page options described in Chapter 10. The pictures won't have any ratings, comments, keywords, and so on, but they'll be organized in a way that will be much easier for non-iPhoto folk to navigate.

iPhoto Backups

Bad things can happen to digital photos. They can be accidentally deleted with a slip of your pinkie. They can become mysteriously corrupted and subsequently unopenable. They can get mangled by a crashed hard disk and be lost forever. Losing one-of-a-kind family photos can be extremely painful, and in some documented cases, even marriage threatening. So if you value your digital photos, you should back them up regularly, perhaps after each major batch of new photos joins your collection.

Backing Up to CD or DVD

The quickest and most convenient way to back up your Photo Library is to archive it onto a blank CD or DVD using iPhoto's Burn command, as described on the previous pages. (If you don't have a disc-burning drive, don't worry; the next section explains how to perform a complete iPhoto backup *without* burning a disc.)

If anything bad ever happens to your photo collection, you'll be able to restore your Photo Library from the backup discs, with all your thumbnails, keywords, comments, and other tidbits intact (Figure 12-3).

Figure 12-3:
Pop an iPhoto CD into your Mac and it appears right along with your albums in iPhoto. Click on the disc icon itself or one of the disc's album icons (as shown here) to display the photos it contains. In essence, iPhoto is giving you access to two different libraries at once—the active Photo Library on your Mac's hard drive and a second library on the CD.

To restore your photo collection from such a backup, see "Merging Photo Libraries" later in this chapter.

Backing Up (No CD Burner)

Fortunately, even if you don't have a CD burner (and therefore can't use iPhoto's Burn command), backing up thousands of photos is a simple task for the iPhoto maven. After all, one of iPhoto's main jobs is to keep all your photos together in *one* place, one folder that's easy to copy to a backup disk of any kind.

That all-important folder is the *iPhoto Library* folder, which resides inside the Pictures folder of the Home folder that bears your name. If your user name (the short name you use to log into Mac OS X) is *corky,* the full path to your iPhoto Library folder from your main hard drive window drive is: Users→corky→Pictures→iPhoto Library.

As described in Chapter 7, the iPhoto Library folder contains not just your photos, but also a huge assortment of additional files, including:

- All the thumbnail images in the iPhoto window.
- The original, safety copies of photos you've edited in iPhoto.
- Various data files that keep track of keywords, comments, ratings, and photo albums you've created within iPhoto.

To prepare for a disaster, you should back up *all* of these components.

To perform a complete backup, copy the entire iPhoto Library folder to another location. Copying it to a different disk—to an iPod, say, or to the hard drive of another Mac via network—is the best solution. (Copying it to another folder on the *same* disk means you'll lose both the original iPhoto Library folder and its backup if, say, your hard drive crashes or your computer is hit by an asteroid.)

Note: Of course, you can also back up your photos by dragging their thumbnails out of the iPhoto window and into a folder or disk on your desktop, once you've dragged the iPhoto window to one side.

Unfortunately, this method doesn't preserve your keywords, comments, album organization, or any other information you've created in iPhoto. If something bad happens to your Photo Library, you'll have to import the raw photos again and reorganize them from scratch.

Managing Photo Libraries

iPhoto 4's best new feature may be its speed. It's enjoyable to work with as many as 25,000 photos in a single collection, give or take a few thousand, depending on your Mac model and how much memory it has.

But for some people, 25,000 pictures isn't a very distant threshold. As your collection of digital photos grows into the tens of thousands (and if you have a digital camera, this will happen sooner than you think), iPhoto eventually starts slowing down as it sifts through more and more data to find and display your pictures. At that point, scrolling the photos in the main Photo Library becomes an exercise in patience that would drive a Zen master crazy.

When your Photo Library becomes too large to manage comfortably, you can always do what people used to do in iPhoto 2, when the limit was only *2,000* pictures: Archive some of the photos to CD or DVD using the Burn command described earlier—and then *delete* the archived photos from your library to shrink it down in size. You might choose to archive older photos, or albums you rarely use.

Note: Remember, archiving photos to CD using the Burn command doesn't automatically remove them from iPhoto; you have to do that part yourself. If you don't, your Photo Library won't get any smaller. Just make sure that the CD you've burned works properly before deleting your original photos from iPhoto.

Multiple iPhoto Libraries

Here's a great way to keep your Photo Library from becoming impossibly bloated without transferring part of it to a CD: Start a new one, right there on your hard drive.

Here's what splitting your photo collection into smaller libraries gains you:

- iPhoto itself is *much* faster, especially during scrolling, because there are fewer photos in it.
- You can keep different types of collections or projects separate. You might want to maintain a Home library for personal use, for example, and a Work library for images that pertain to your business.

Creating new libraries

Unfortunately, iPhoto provides no built-in tools for retiring one Photo Library and starting a fresh one. You must fool it into creating a new one by using the following trick:

1. **Quit iPhoto.**

   Return to the Finder.

2. **Move the whole iPhoto Library folder out of your Home→Pictures folder to a different location, or just give it a new name.**

   The idea is simply to *hide* this folder from iPhoto. You can drag it to a new folder on your hard drive, rename it something like Old iPhoto Library, or even stash it in a new folder called Old Libraries *inside* your Pictures folder.

   The point is to move the *whole* iPhoto Library folder. Messing around with the files and folders inside the iPhoto Library folder can cause problems.

3. Open iPhoto again.

When iPhoto starts up, it notices that its library is missing, and tells you so, in no uncertain terms (Figure 12-4).

Figure 12-4:
If you hide the iPhoto Library from iPhoto, the program invites you either to find it or to create a new one. If your goal is to begin a fresh, smaller library for the new year, for example, click Create Library.

4. Click Create Library. In the following dialog box, type a name for the new library (like *New iPhoto Library*) and click Save.

This is a new twist in iPhoto 4, an acknowledgment by Apple that people actually use this iPhoto Library-switching routine. You're offered not only the chance to create a new library, but even the opportunities to name it anything you like and choose a location for it that's not your regularly scheduled Pictures folder.

Figure 12-5:
One way to manage your various photo libraries is to keep them in a common folder, anywhere on your hard drive (top left).

When you want to swap one in, just change its name. Add "OFF" to the name, for example, to indicate that you've deactivated it (bottom right).

The next time you open iPhoto, it will display the dialog box shown in Figure 12-4. That's your opportunity to select a different library from among those in your master folder.

When iPhoto finishes opening, all remnants of your old Photo Library are gone. You're left with a blank window, ready to import fresh photos.

Using this technique, you can spawn as many new Photo Libraries as you need. You can archive the old libraries on CD or DVD, move them to another Mac, or just keep them somewhere on your hard drive so that you can swap any one of them back in whenever you need it, as shown in Figure 12-5.

As for *how* you swap them back in, read on.

Swapping libraries

iPhoto Library Manager is a free program that can swap iPhoto libraries for you on the fly, even while iPhoto is already open. Waste no time in downloading it from the "Missing CD" page at *www.missingmanuals.com* or Brian's own site at *http://homepage. mac.com/bwebster.*

Once you have multiple iPhoto Library folders (as described earlier), you can turn any one of them on or off with just a click, as shown in Figure 12-6. You don't have to move or rename your library folders.

Tip: You can also switch libraries using the pop-up menu from iPhoto Library Manager's Dock icon.

Figure 12-6:
iPhoto Library Manager is a program that lets you switch between as many different iPhoto Library folders as you want. Just select a library folder from the list on the left by turning on the corresponding checkbox, then relaunch iPhoto to view photos from the selected library. Double-click a library name in the list on the left to edit it. The names that you give your libraries within iPhoto Library Manager are independent of names of the corresponding library folders on disk.

Merging Photo Libraries

You've just arrived home from your photo safari of deepest Kenya. You're jet-lagged and dusty, but your iBook is bursting at the seams with fresh photo meat. You can't wait to transfer the new pictures into your main Photo Library—you know, the one on your Power Macintosh G5 with 2 gigs of RAM and a 35-inch Apple Imax Display.

Or, less dramatically, suppose you've just upgraded to iPhoto 4. You're thrilled that you can now fit 25,000 pictures into a single library—but under iPhoto 2, you had to create six different iPhoto Library folders containing about 2,000 pictures each.

In both cases, you have the same problem: How are you supposed to merge the libraries into a single, unified one?

How Not to Do It

You certainly can combine the *photos* of two Macs' Photo Libraries—just export them from one (File→Export) and then import them into the other (File→Import). As a result, however, you lose all of your album organization, comments, and keywords.

Your next instinct might be: "Hey, I know! I'll just drag the iPhoto Library folder from computer #1 into the iPhoto window of computer #2!"

Big mistake. You'll end up importing not only the photos, but also the tiny thumbnail versions of each photo (which are stored separately in the iPhoto Library folder) *and* the original versions of any photos that you edited. You'll wind up with duplicates or triplicates of every photo in the viewing area, in one enormous, unmanageable, uncategorized, sloshing library.

No, merging iPhoto libraries is slightly more complicated than that.

Method 1: Use iPhoto CDs as Intermediaries

One way to merge two Photo Libraries is to burn the second one onto an iPhoto CD or DVD, as described earlier in this chapter.

Begin with the smaller library. (In the Kenya safari example, you'd begin with the laptop.)

1. **Open iPhoto and burn a CD or DVD containing all the photos you want to merge into the larger Photo Library.**

   Follow exactly the same disc-creation steps outlined in the steps beginning on page 229. If you want to preserve any albums you've created, select the albums, not just the photos themselves, when you burn the discs.

2. **Quit iPhoto. Swap iPhoto Library folders.**

If you're trying to merge the libraries of two different Macs, skip this instruction. Instead, move to the second Mac at this point—the one that will serve as the final resting place for the photos you exported.

If you're merging two libraries on the same Mac, swap the iPhoto Library folders either manually or using iPhoto Library Manager, as described earlier in this chapter. In any case, the master, larger photo collection should now be before you in iPhoto.

3. **Insert the iPhoto CD you just created.**

iPhoto opens (if it's not already running) and the iPhoto CD icon appears in the Source list of the iPhoto window, as shown in Figure 12-7. Albums on the disc appear underneath the CD icon.

Figure 12-7:
To merge photo libraries, drag and drop albums from an iPhoto CD onto a blank spot in the Source list, or onto the Photo Library icon at the very top.

In this example, the contents of photo albums named Disney World and NYC, which are stored on the iPhoto CD, are being merged into the main Photo Library.

4. **Select one album, or several, on the iPhoto CD.**

You can select multiple albums just as you would lists of files in the Finder: Shift-click to select several consecutive albums, ⌘-click to select nonconsecutive albums, and so on.

When you select the albums, the thumbnails of the corresponding photos stored on the CD appear in the photo-viewing area.

5. **Drag the selected albums (using any one of them as a handle) to a blank spot at the bottom of the Source list, below all the other albums (see Figure 12-7)—or onto the Photo Library icon at the very top.**

   You can't drag them onto an existing album, and you can't drag the entire disc icon.

   In any case, this is the big moment when the "merge" actually happens. iPhoto switches into Import mode and copies the selected albums from the iPhoto CD into your main Photo Library. Any keywords, comments, ratings, and titles that were applied to the photos on the CD are imported too.

   When it's all over, you won't find any new albums. You will, however, find that your Photo Library now contains the merged pictures. (Click the Last Roll icon to see them.)

Using this technique, you can combine the photos stored on any number of CDs into a single library, without losing a single comment, keyword, album, or original photo.

Method 2: Share the Library with Yourself

Burning iPhoto CDs is a great way to merge two or more iPhoto Libraries, because it leaves you with backup discs. And in its way, it's a lot simpler than what you're about to read.

Still, you use up a lot of blanks this way, and you spend a lot of time waiting for discs to burn.

If the photo libraries you want to merge are all on the same Mac—in separate accounts, for example, or just in different places—there's another method that doesn't involve burning iPhoto CDs. Instead, it involves using the photo sharing feature described on page 217. (It also works only in Panther, Mac OS X 10.3.)

If one of the photo libraries is already in some other account holder's copy of iPhoto, great; share the appropriate albums, exactly as described on page 217. Then in your account, just drag the shared albums onto your Photo Library or a blank spot in the album list to copy them in, essentially as shown in Figure 12-7.

If all of the library folders belong to you, however, merging through sharing is slightly hairier. You'll need two free pieces of software: ShareAlike and iPhoto Library Manager, both available on the "Missing CD" page of *www.missingmanuals.com.*

Here are the broad steps of this very sneaky, somewhat advanced procedure. For clarity, let's say that you want to merge a library called Small Batch into a bigger one called Big Library, both of which are currently in your Pictures folder.

1. **On the Accounts panel of System Preferences, click Login Options. Turn on "Enable fast user switching." Click OK in the confirmation box.**

   This operation also requires at least one account in addition to your own. Take this opportunity to create one, if necessary. Let's call that other account Casey.

2. **Using iPhoto Library Manager, make Small Batch your working iPhoto library folder, and then quit iPhoto.**

   See page 237 for details on choosing a different library folder.

3. **Open ShareAlike. Begin sharing the Small Batch library.**

   Now both you and Casey can work with the same library.

4. **Switch into Casey's account. Using iPhoto Library Manager, choose Small Batch as Casey's library folder (it's probably in your hard drive's Users→[Your Name]→ Pictures folder), and open it in iPhoto.**

   You should now see the photos from Small Batch in Casey's copy of iPhoto.

5. **In Casey's copy of iPhoto, the albums you'll want to merge.**

   See page 217 for details on photo sharing.

6. **Switch back to your own account. Using iPhoto Library Manager, open up the Big Library in iPhoto.**

   Now you're looking at the main photo collection—but there, in the Source list, you'll see an icon for Casey's shared photos. (If not, choose iPhoto→Preferences, click Sharing, and turn on "Look for shared photos." Close the Preferences window.)

   Click the flippy triangle to reveal Casey's albums.

7. **Drag Casey's albums into a blank spot in your own Source list.**

   You've just copied the albums from the Small Batch library into your own Big Library. Put another way, you've just merged two iPhoto libraries without having to burn any discs!

   (And they said it couldn't be done…)

8. **Switch back into Casey's account and quit iPhoto. If you like, use iPhoto Library Manager to re-choose Casey's original library folder. Return to your account; in ShareAlike, click Stop Sharing, click Fix Permissions, and quit the program.**

   Once you've confirmed that the photos have safely arrived in your main library, you can throw away the Small Batch folder.

Beyond iPhoto

Depending on how massive your collection of digital photos grows and how you use it, you may find yourself wanting more file-management power than iPhoto can offer. Maybe you wish you could organize 50,000 or 100,000 photos in a single catalog, without having to swap photo libraries or load archive CDs. Maybe you'd like to search for photos based on something other than just titles, keywords, and comments—perhaps by file type, creation date, or the camera model used to shoot them. Maybe you have a small network, and you'd like a system that lets a whole workgroup share a library of photos simultaneously.

To enjoy such features, you'll have to move beyond iPhoto into the world of *digital asset management,* which means spending a little money. Programs like Extensis Portfolio ($200, *www.extensis.com*), Canto Cumulus ($100, *www.canto.com*), and iView MediaPro ($160, *www.iview-multimedia.com*) are terrific programs for someone who wants to take the next step up (Figure 12-8). (All three companies offer free trial versions on their Web sites.)

Figure 12-8:
iView Media, shown here, is one of several programs that do most of what iPhoto does—and a lot more besides.

For example, it can "watch" certain folders on your Mac, so that when new graphics arrive, iView catalogs them automatically.

And its photo limit is 128,000 pictures.

Here are a few of the stunts these more advanced programs can do that iPhoto can't:

- Create custom fields to store any other kind of information you want about your files—dates, prices, Web addresses, and so on.

- Track graphics files stored in any location on a network, not just in a specific folder.

- Catalog not just photos, but other file types, too: QuarkXPress and InDesign documents, QuickTime movies, sound files, PowerPoint slides, and so on.

- Perform complex searches using multiple criteria, like "Find all JPEGs over 2 MB that contain the keyword 'yak' and have file names that start with the letter R."

- Share a catalog of images with dozens of other people simultaneously over a network.

- Rename an entire group of images en masse.

- Customize the fonts, colors, and borders of the thumbnail view.

- Create catalogs that can be read on both Mac and Windows.

- Display previews of "offline" photo files that aren't actually on the Mac at the moment (they're on CDs or DVDs on your shelf, for example).

- Handle tens of thousands of photos in a single catalog.

Some of the features in this list were obviously developed with professional users in mind, like graphic designers and studio photographers. But this kind of program is worth considering if your photo collection—and your passion for digital photography—one day outgrows iPhoto.

Exporting and Converting Pictures

The whole point of iPhoto is to provide a centralized location for every photo in your world. That doesn't mean that they're locked there, however; it's as easy to take pictures out of iPhoto as it is to put them in. Spinning out a photo from iPhoto can be useful in situations like these:

- You're creating a Web page outside of iPhoto and you need a photo in a certain size and format.

- You shot a bunch of 6-megapixel photos, you're running out of disk space, and you wish they were all 4-megapixel shots instead. They'd still have plenty of resolution, but not so much wasted space.

- You're going to submit some photos to a newspaper or magazine, and the publication requires TIFF-format photos, not iPhoto's standard JPEG format.

- Somebody else on your network loves one of your pictures and would like to use it as a desktop background on *that* machine.

- You want to set free a few of the photos so that you can copy them *back* onto the camera's memory card. (Some people use their digicams as much for *showing* pictures to their friends as for *taking* them.)

- You want to send a batch of pictures on a CD to someone.

Exporting by Dragging

It's amazingly easy to export photos from iPhoto: Just drag their thumbnails out of the photo viewing area and onto the desktop (or onto a folder, or into a window on the desktop), as shown in Figure 12-9. After a moment, you'll see their icons appear.

The drag-and-drop method has enormous virtue in its simplicity and speed. It does not, however, grant you much flexibility. It produces JPEG files only, at the original camera resolution, with the camera's own cryptic naming scheme.

Exporting by Dialog Box

To gain control over the dimensions, names, and file formats of the exported graphics, use the Export command. After selecting one picture, a group of pictures, or an album, you can invoke this command by choosing File→Export (Shift-⌘-E).

The Export Photos dialog box appears, as shown in Figure 12-10. Click the File Export tab, if necessary, and then make the following decisions:

Figure 12-9:
This technique produces full-size JPEG graphics, exactly as they appear in iPhoto. Their names, however, are not particularly user-friendly. Instead of "Persimmon Close Up," as you named it in iPhoto, a picture might wind up on the desktop named 200205040035140.JPG or IMG_5197.JPG.

Figure 12-10:
The Export dialog box gives you control over the file format, names, and dimensions of the pictures you're about to send off from iPhoto. The number of photos you're about to export appears in the lower-left corner of the box.

You can even tell iPhoto to use whatever names you gave your pictures, instead of the original, incomprehensible file names bestowed by your camera. To do so, click "Use title."

File format

You can use the Format pop-up menu to specify the file format of the graphics that you're about to export. Here are your options:

- **Original.** iPhoto exports the images in whatever format they were in when you imported them. If the picture came from a digital camera, for example, it's probably JPEG.

- **JPG.** This abbreviation is shorthand for JPEG, which stands for Joint Photographic Experts Group (that's the group of geeks who came up with this format). The JPEG format is, of course, the most popular format for photos on the Internet (and in iPhoto), thanks to its high image quality and small file size.

- **TIFF.** These files (whose abbreviation is short for Tagged Image File Format) are something like JPEG without the "lossy" compression. That is, they maintain every bit of quality available in the original photograph, but usually take up much more disk space (or memory-card space) as a result. TIFF is a good choice if quality is more important than portability.

- **PNG.** This relatively new format (Portable Network Graphics) was designed to replace the GIF format on the Web. (The company that came up with the algorithms behind the GIF format exercised its legal muscle...long story.)

  Whereas GIF graphics generally don't make good photos because they're limited to 256 colors, PNG is a good choice for photos (except the variation called *PNG-8,* which is just as limited as GIF). The resulting files are smaller than TIFF images, yet exhibit even less compression-related quality loss than JPEGs. Not all graphics programs and Web browsers recognize this relatively new format, but the big ones—including iPhoto, GraphicConverter, Photoshop, and most recent browser versions—all do.

Named option

iPhoto maintains two names for each photo: its *original file name,* as it appears in the Finder, and its *iPhoto title,* the one you may have typed in while working in the program. Click either "Use filenames" or "Use titles" to specify what names iPhoto gives the icons of the graphics you're about to export. (When you export just *one* photo, you're offered the chance to name it whatever you like.)

Your third option is "Use album name." It tells iPhoto to name your exported photos according to their album name—and sequence within that album. If an exported photo is the fourth picture in the first row of an album titled Dry Creek, iPhoto will call the exported file "Dry Creek – 04.jpg." Because *you* determine the order within an album (by dragging), this is the only option that lets you control the numbering of the exported result.

Size options

Remember that although digital camera graphics files may not always have enough resolution for prints, they generally have far *too much* resolution for displaying on the screen.

---

iPhoto offers to scale them down automatically whenever you email them or transfer them to the Web. If you turn on "Scale images no larger than," and then fill in some pixel dimensions in the boxes, you can oversee the same kind of shrinkage for your exported graphics. Points of reference: 1024 x 768 is exactly the right size to completely fill a standard 15-inch monitor, and 640 x 480 is a good size for emailing (it fills up about a quarter of the screen).

Tip: You can also use this option to de-megapixelize a bunch of photos. Suppose they're all 6-megapixel photos—more than you'll ever need. Export them at, say, 2272 x 1704 pixels (about four megapixels) to a folder on your desktop called "4 Megas" (or something). Delete the originals from your Photo Library, if you like, and then re-import the scaled-down versions by dragging that 4 Megas folder off the desktop and into the album list.

Part Three:
iMovie

3

Camcorder Meets Mac

Y ou've captured some raw footage on your camcorder, you've assembled the
ingredients you need, and you're ready to enter the kitchen. Now it's time for
the heart of the matter: editing your footage on the Mac using iMovie.

This chapter introduces you to both iMovie and *FireWire* (the high-speed cable system
that transfers footage from the camcorder to the Mac), gives you a tour of the iMovie
window, and walks you through your first transfer.

Meet Digital Video

Technically speaking, you don't need a camcorder to use iMovie. You can work
with QuickTime movies you find on the Web, or use it to turn still photos into
slideshows.

But to shoot your own video—and that is the real fun of iMovie—you need a *digital*
camcorder. This is a relatively new camcorder format, one that's utterly incompatible
with the tapes you may have filled using earlier camcorder types like VHS, 8mm, and
Hi-8. At this writing, MiniDV camcorders cost about $400 for a basic model—and
prices continue to sink, month by month.

The size of a *MiniDV cassette* (tape cartridge) is tiny, so the camcorders are also tiny.
Yet the quality is amazing; as you can see by this table, DV quality blows every previous tape format out of the water. (All camcorders, TVs, and VCRs have the same

vertical resolution; this table measures lines of *horizontal* resolution, the number of tiny horizontal stripes of color the playback uses to fill your TV screen):

Tape Format	Maximum Lines of Resolution
VHS, VHS-C	240
8mm	280
Live TV broadcast	300
S-VHS, Hi-8	400
Digital satellite broadcast	400
MiniDV	500
HDTV	720 or 1080

DV's 16-bit sound quality is dramatically better than previous formats, too. In fact, it's better than CD-quality sound, since DV camcorders record sound at 48 kHz instead of 44.1 kHz. (Higher means better.)

Tip: Most DV camcorders offer you a choice of sound-quality modes: 12-bit or 16-bit. The lower quality setting is designed to leave "room" on the tape for adding music after you've recorded your video. But avoid it like the plague! If you shoot your video in 12-bit video, your picture will gradually drift out of sync with your audio track—if you plan to save your movie to a DVD. Consult your manual to find out how to switch the camcorder into 16-bit audio mode.Do it *before* you shoot anything important.

Digital video has another advantage, too: You can copy it from DV camcorder to DV camcorder, or from DV camcorder to Mac, dozens of times, making copies of copies of copies. The last generation of digital video will be utterly indistinguishable from the original footage—which is to say, both will look fantastic.

FREQUENTLY ASKED QUESTION

Three Camcorders Not to Buy

In their never-ending quest to come up with smaller and cooler camcorder designs, electronics manufacturers have already gone well beyond the MiniDV format. Unfortunately, these alternative formats either are incompatible with iMovie or lack the necessary FireWire jack entirely. (You need a FireWire cable to connect the camcorder to the Mac.)

Here, then, is a quick list of camcorders not to buy:

• **Sony MicroMV.** These camcorders are tiny, all right: they store their footage on a tape the size of a matchbox. Too bad they record in a format that popular editing programs like iMovie don't recognize.

• **Memory-card micro-cams.** Panasonic, Fisher, and others make "camcorders" that are the size of half a sandwich and store video on a memory card. Alas, there's no FireWire jack.

• **DVD camcorders.** Sony, Panasonic, and Hitachi offer camcorders that use miniature DVD discs instead of tapes. Neat, but no FireWire jack.

• iMovie can't edit high-definition footage from **HDTV camcorders** like JVC's GR-HD1, either.

Stick to MiniDV camcorders. They're inexpensive, their quality is spectacular, and you won't be left behind when the next camcorder-format fad passes.

For that reason, although DV tapes may deteriorate over a decade or two, just as traditional tapes do, you won't care. Long before the tape has crumbled, you'll have transferred the most important material to a new hard drive or a new DV tape or to a DVD. Because quality never degrades when you do so, you'll glow with the knowledge that your grandchildren and *their* grandchildren will be able to see your movies with every speck of clarity you see today—even if they have to dig up one of those antique "Macintosh" computers or gigantic, soap-sized "DV camcorders" in order to play it.

Connecting to FireWire

The FireWire jack on the side or back of your computer is marked by a radioactive-looking Y symbol.

If you intend to edit your own camcorder footage, you'll also need a FireWire *cable,* like the one shown in Figure 13-1. One end is a plug that perfectly fits a into FireWire jack on your computer. (Apple calls it the six-pin connector.)

Figure 13-1:
Plug the larger end of the FireWire cable into the corresponding jack on the Mac. The tiny end goes into your camcorder. The FireWire connectors are convenient, but fragile, especially the small end. Take care to insert and remove these connectors straight into or out of the jacks.

On the other end is a much smaller, squarish plug (the four-pin connector). Plug this tiny end into the FireWire connector on your camcorder, which, depending on the brand, may be labeled "FireWire," "i.Link," or "IEEE 1394." This tiny end may look almost square, but it only fits in one particular way, thanks to a little indentation on one side. If you can't seem to insert it, rotate the plug and try again—gently, because this end is fragile.

That's all the setup your Mac needs. The single FireWire cable communicates both sound and video, in both directions, between the Mac and the camcorder.

Now, if you plan to transfer video to your Mac from a *tape* in the camcorder, turn the camcorder to its *VCR* or *VTR* mode. (This is what most people do most of the time.) But if you want to capture *live* video into iMovie—to pass whatever your camcorder lens is seeing directly to the Mac, without ever recording it on tape—put the camcorder into *Camera* mode instead.

For best results, plug your camcorder's adapter into the wall instead of running it from battery power. At last you're ready to begin editing video!

Getting into iMovie

After you've connected and turned on your camcorder, open iMovie by double-clicking its icon. But before you're treated to the main iMovie screen (shown in Figure 13-3), iMovie may ask you to take care of a few housekeeping details.

Monitor Resolution

All modern Mac monitors let you adjust the *resolution,* which is a measurement of how much it can show as measured in *pixels* (the tiny dots that make up the screen picture). If you choose →System Preferences→Displays, you'll see the choices awaiting you.

Why is it important to understand monitor resolution when you're about to edit video? Because iMovie likes a very big screen—a *high*-resolution monitor. If your monitor is set to one of the lower resolution settings when you launch iMovie, you'll get an error message.

The bottom line: Choose a setting that's 1024 x 768 or larger. Poor iMovie can't even run at any lower setting.

Caution: If you switch your resolution to a resolution lower than 1024 x 768 *while* iMovie is open, the program has no choice but to quit. (At least it does you the courtesy of offering to save the changes to the project file you've been working on.)

The program is more graceful when you switch between two *higher* resolutions; it instantly adjusts its various windows and controls to fit the resized screen. In other words, whenever you switch resolutions while the program is open, be extra careful not to choose, for example, 800 x 600 by mistake.

The Create/Open Dialog Box

If everything has gone well, and iMovie approves of your monitor setting, your next stop is the Create Project/Open Existing Project dialog box (Figure 13-2).

You've reached a decision point: You must now tell the program whether you want to begin a new movie (called a *project* in iMovie lingo), or open one you've already started, or quit the program.

The first time you run iMovie is probably the only time you'll ever see the dialog box shown in Figure 13-2. After that, each time you launch iMovie, it automatically

Figure 13-2:
Click Create Project to begin working on a new movie, Open Existing Project to open an existing movie, or Quit to back out of the whole thing.

opens up the movie you were most recently working on. If you ever want to see the Create Project/Open Existing Project dialog box again, you'll have to do one of the following:

- Discard the last movie you were working on (by trashing it from your hard drive), or move it to a different folder.

- Throw away the iMovie Preferences file. It bears the uncatchy name com.apple. iMovie3.plist (even though you have iMovie 4), and it's inside your Home→ Library→Preferences folder.

Saving a New Project File

If you click Create Project (Figure 13-2), you're now asked to select a name and location for the movie you're about to make—or, as iMovie would say, the *project* you're about to make.

This is a critical moment. Starting a new iMovie project isn't as casual an affair as starting a new word processing file. For one thing, iMovie requires that you save and name your file *before* you've actually done any work. For another, you can't transfer footage from your camcorder without *first* naming and saving a project file.

Above all, the *location* of your saved project file—your choice of hard drive to save it on—is extremely important. Digital video files are enormous. Your footage consumes about 3.6 MB of your hard drive *per second*. Therefore:

This much video	Needs about this much disk space
1 minute	228 MB
15 minutes	3.5 GB
30 minutes	7 GB
60 minutes	13 GB
2 hours	28 GB
4 hours	53 GB

When you save and name your project, you also tell iMovie *where* to put these enormous, disk-guzzling files. If, like most people, you have only one hard drive—the one built into your Mac—fine. Make as much empty room as you can, and proceed with your video-editing career.

But many iMovie fans have more than one hard drive. They may have decided to invest in a larger hard drive, as described in the box below, so that they can make longer movies. If you're among them, you must save your new project *onto* the larger hard drive if you want to take advantage of its extra space.

Tip: People who have used other space-intensive software, such as Photoshop and Premiere, are frequently confused by iMovie. They expect the program to have a Scratch Disk command that lets them specify where (on which hard drive) they want their work files stored while they're working.

As you now know, iMovie has no such command. You choose your scratch disk (the hard drive onto which you save your project) on a movie-by-movie basis.

Note, by the way, that digital video requires a fast hard drive. Therefore, make no attempt to save your project file onto a floppy disk, Zip disk, Jaz disk, SuperDisk, iDisk, CD-R, DVD-R, or another disk on the network. It simply won't be fast enough, and you'll get nothing but error messages.

iMovie Controls

Once you've saved your file, you finally arrive at the main iMovie window. Figure 13-3 is a cheat sheet for what all of iMovie's various screen elements do. Spend no time memorizing their functions now; the rest of this book covers each of these tools in context and in depth.

- **Monitor.** You watch your footage in this window.

- **Clips pane.** These little cubbyholes store the *clips*—pieces of footage, individual shots—that you can rearrange into a masterpiece of modern storytelling. (iMovie veterans may recognize this area as what used to be called the *Shelf.*)

  This pane won't always be the Clips pane, incidentally. It becomes the Photos pane, the Audio pane, and so on, when you click one of the buttons beneath it. The one thing all of these incarnations have in common is that they offer you lists of materials you can incorporate into your movie.

- **Project Trash.** You can drag any clip onto this icon to get rid of it. When you trim your footage, meanwhile, the trimmed portions go into this "can," too.

- **Pane buttons.** These buttons—Clips, Photos, Audio, Titles, Trans (Transitions), Effects, iDVD—each fill the Clips pane area with special tools that let you add professional touches to your movie, such as controls for crossfade styles, credit sequences, footage effects (such as brightness and color shifting), still photos, sound effects, and music. (Chapters 15, 16, 17, and 21 cover these video flourishes in detail.)

FREQUENTLY ASKED QUESTION

Saving to External FireWire Drives

I need more hard drive space. What should I do? Can I save a project onto an external FireWire drive?

It's a natural question; most Macs have two FireWire jacks. What better way to capitalize on them than by hooking up the camcorder and an external FireWire hard drive simultaneously?

Apple used to warn that you shouldn't try saving iMovie projects onto an external FireWire hard drive. These days, though, that piece of advice has been quietly retired. Modern external FireWire drives are plenty fast enough to store incoming video.

For example, an 80 GB FireWire hard drive costs, at this writing, under $160 (from *www.promax.com,* for example)—enough to hold over six hours of footage—and the prices are falling rapidly.

Like most FireWire gear, these hard drives have several advantages over hard drives you may have known in the past. They're smaller and faster, can be plugged and unplugged from the computer without turning anything off, and don't require power cords of their own.

- **Clip Viewer/Timeline Viewer.** You'll spend most of your editing time down here. Each of these tools offers a master map that shows which scenes will play in which order, but there's a crucial difference in the way they do it.

When you click the Clip Viewer button (marked by a piece of filmstrip), you see your movie represented as *slides*. Each clip appears to be the same size, even if some are very long and some are very short. The Clip Viewer offers no clue as to what's going on with the audio, but it's a supremely efficient overview of your clips' sequence.

When you click the Timeline Viewer button (marked by the clock), on the other hand, you can see the relative lengths of your clips, because each shows up as a colored band of the appropriate length. Parallel bands (complete with visual "sound waves," if you like), underneath indicate blocks of sound that play simultaneously.

- **Camera Mode/Edit Mode switch.** In Camera Mode, the playback controls operate your camcorder, rather than the iMovie film you're editing. In Camera Mode, the Monitor window shows you what's on the tape, not what's in iMovie, so that you can choose which shots you want to transfer to iMovie for editing.

In Edit Mode, however, iMovie ignores your camcorder. Now the playback controls govern your captured clips instead of the camcorder. Edit Mode is where you start piecing your movie together.

Tip: You can drag the blue dot between the Camera Mode and Edit Mode positions, if you like, but doing so requires sharp hand-eye coordination and an unnecessary mouse drag. It's much faster to click *on* one of the icons, ignoring the little switch entirely. Click directly on the little camera symbol for Camera Mode, for example, or on the scissors for Edit Mode.

- **Home.** Means "rewind to the beginning." *Keyboard equivalent:* the Home key on your keyboard. (On laptops, you must hold down both the Fn key and the left-arrow key to trigger the Home function.)

Note: In Camera Mode, the Home, Play/Stop, and Full Screen buttons described here are replaced by the Rewind, Stop, Play, Pause, and Fast Forward buttons, as described later in this chapter.

- **Play/Stop.** Plays the tape, movie, or clip. When the playback is going on, the button turns blue; that's your cue that clicking it again stops the playback.

- **Play Full Screen.** Clicking this button makes the movie you're editing fill the entire Mac screen as it plays back, instead of playing just in the small Monitor window. (It still doesn't look nearly as good as it will on your TV, however, as described on page 381.)

Tip: The Full Screen button doesn't play your movie back from the beginning. Instead, it plays back from the location of the Playhead.

If you *do* want it to play in full-screen mode from the beginning, press the Home key (or click the Home button just to the left of the Play button) before clicking the Play Full Screen button.

- **Scrubber bar.** This special scroll bar lets you jump anywhere within one piece of footage, or in the entire movie.

- **Playhead.** The Playhead is like the little box handle, or *thumb,* of a normal scroll bar. It shows exactly where you are in the footage.

- **Volume slider.** To adjust your speaker volume as you work, click anywhere in the slider's "track" to make the knob jump there. (Keep in mind that you can also boost the Mac's *overall* speaker volume by pressing the volume keys on the keyboard, using the volume slider in your menu bar, or using the Sound panel in System Preferences.)

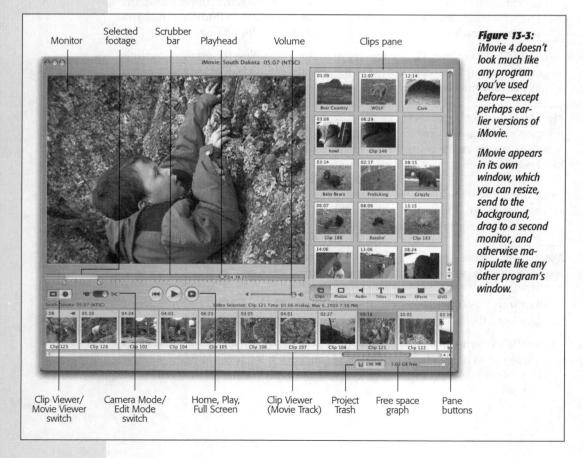

Figure 13-3:
iMovie 4 doesn't look much like any program you've used before—except perhaps earlier versions of iMovie.

iMovie appears in its own window, which you can resize, send to the background, drag to a second monitor, and otherwise manipulate like any other program's window.

- **Project Trash.** Tells you how much material you've cut out of your footage; see page 276 for details.

- **Free space.** This indicator lets you know how full your hard drive is. In the world of video editing, that's a very important statistic.

Importing Camcorder Footage

Suppose you've opened iMovie and clicked the Create Project button. At this moment, then, you're looking at an empty version of the screen shown in Figure 13-3. Connect your camcorder to the FireWire cable and turn it on. This is where the fun begins.

Click the little movie-camera symbol on the iMovie screen, if necessary, to switch into Camera Mode, as shown in Figure 13-4.

Tip: If you turn on your camcorder after iMovie is already running, the program conveniently switches into Camera Mode. (iMovie only does so the *first time* you power up the camcorder during a work session, however, to avoid annoying people who turn the camcorder on and off repeatedly during the editing process to save battery power.)

The Monitor window becomes big and blue, filled with the words "Camera Connected."

Figure 13-4:
While you're importing footage, the time code in the upper-left corner of the clip on the Clips pane steadily ticks away to show you that the clip is getting longer. Meanwhile, the Free Space indicator updates itself, second by second, as your hard drive space is eaten up by the incoming footage. The square Stop button does exactly the same thing as clicking the Play button a second time. The Pause button also halts playback, but it freezes the frame instead of going to a blank screen.

Camera mode   Playback controls   Import button   Clip length so far   Free space graph

This is only the first of many messages the Monitor window will be showing you. At other times, it may say, "Camera No Tape," "Camera Fast Forward," "Camera Rewinding," and so on.

Now you can click the Play, Rewind, Fast Forward, and other buttons on the screen to control the camcorder (see Figure 13-4).

You'll probably find that you have even more precise control by using the mouse to control the camcorder than you would by pressing the actual camcorder buttons. (Unfortunately, no keyboard shortcuts control these buttons.)

Tip: The Rewind and Fast Forward buttons work a little strangely. If you *double-click* a button, playback stops and the rewinding or fast-forwarding begins at full speed. If you click and *hold* your mouse button down on a Rewind or Fast Forward button, then playback continues with the tape moving at only twice its usual speed.

What you're doing now, of course, is scanning your tape to find the sections that you want to include in your edited movie.

The Monitor Window's Video Quality

After reading all the gushing prose about the high quality of digital-video footage, when you first inspect your footage in the Monitor window, you might wonder if you got ripped off. The picture may look grainy and far from DVD quality.

This video quality is *temporary* and visible only on the Mac screen. The instant you send your finished movie back to the camcorder, or when you export it as a QuickTime movie, you get the stunning DV quality that was temporarily hidden on the Mac screen. You'll spend much of your moviemaking time watching clips play back, so it's well worth investigating the different ways iMovie can improve the picture.

If you have a fast Mac, a great way is to choose iMovie→Preferences and then choose both "High quality" and "Enhanced video playback." (In complicated movies on slowish Macs—400-megahertz G3 iMacs, for example—these options may introduce hiccups during playback.)

An even better solution is to choose iMovie→Preferences and turn on "Play video through to camera." You've just told iMovie to play the video *through your camcorder*. In other words, if you're willing to watch your camcorder's LCD screen as you work instead of the onscreen Monitor window, what you see is what you shot: all gorgeous, all the time. (You hear the audio only through the camcorder, too.)

Best of all: If you hook up a TV to your camcorder's analog outputs, you get to edit your footage not just at full quality, but also at full size. The camcorder, still connected to the Mac via its FireWire cable, passes whatever you'd see in the Monitor window straight through to the TV set, at full digital-video quality. This is exactly the way professionals edit digital video—on TV monitors on their desks. The only difference is that you paid about $99,000 less for your setup.

Capturing Footage

When you're in Camera Mode, an Import button appears just below the Monitor window. When you click this button (or press the Space bar), iMovie imports the footage you're watching, storing it as digital-video movie files on the Mac's hard drive.

During this process, you'll notice a number of changes to your iMovie environment (Figure 13-4):

- The Import button lights up, as though illuminated by a blue spotlight.

- As soon as you click Import, what looks like a slide appears in the first square of the Clips pane, as shown in Figure 13-4. That's a *clip*—a single piece of footage that makes up one of the building blocks of an iMovie movie. Its icon is a picture of the first frame.

- Superimposed on the clip, in its upper-left corner, is the length of the clip expressed as "seconds:frames" or (if it's a longer clip) "minutes:seconds:frames." You can see this little timer ticking upward as the clip grows longer. For example, if it says *1:23:10*, then the clip is 1 minute, 23 seconds, and 10 frames long.

Getting used to this kind of frame counter takes some practice for two reasons. First, computers start counting from 0, not from 1, so the very first frame of a clip is called 00:00. Second, remember that there are 30 frames per second in NTSC digital video; 25 in PAL digital video. So the far-right number in the time code (the frame counter) counts up to 29 before flipping over to 00 again—not to 59 or 99, which might feel more familiar. In other words, iMovie counts like this: 00:28...00:29...1:00...1:01.

GEM IN THE ROUGH

iSight: The $150 Tapeless Camcorder

Thanks to a subtle new feature of iMovie 4, you don't actually need a camcorder to import live video—a relief to super-budget filmmakers all over the world. Instead, you can use the Apple iSight, a video and audio camera the size and shape of a Hostess Ho-Ho.

The beauty of this camera is that it plugs directly into the Mac's FireWire jack. Video, audio, and power all flow through its single white cable.

Especially if you already own one, the iSight represents a significant savings over buying a DV camcorder. It's not quite the same thing, however.

For one thing, using the iSight tethers you to the Mac during filming (you can't put a tape into it, and it can't store any video). For another, you can't zoom in or out, adjust focus, mount the iSight on a tripod, or use any of the other tricks of the camcorder trade.

In general, recording live video from a connected iSight is just like recording from a tape. Click the Record With iSight button to begin capturing what the iSight "sees and hears" onto the hard drive; click the

---

Tip: DV camcorders record life by capturing 30 frames per second. (All right, 29.97 frames per second; see page 390.)

That, for your trivia pleasure, is the standard frame rate for *television*. Real movies, on the other hand—that is, footage shot on film—rolls by at only 24 frames per second. The European PAL format runs at 25 frames per second.

- iMovie 4 is a Mac OS X–only program. On one hand, this feature shuts out millions of Mac OS 9 fans.

  On the other hand, you gain a huge perk: Your Mac no longer devotes every atom of its energy to capturing incoming video. While the importing is going on, you're free to open other programs, surf the Web, crunch some numbers, organize your pictures in iPhoto, or whatever you like.

  The Mac continues to give processor priority to capturing video, so your other programs may act a little drugged. But this impressive multitasking feat still means that you can get meaningful work or reading done while you're dumping your footage into iMovie in the background.

If you click Import (or press the Space bar) a second time, the tape continues to roll, but iMovie stops gulping down footage to your hard drive. Your camcorder continues to play. You've just captured your first clip(s).

Automatic scene detection

If you let the tape continue to roll, you'll notice a handy iMovie feature at work. Each time a new scene begins, a new clip icon appears in the Clips pane. The Clips pane scrolls as much as necessary to hold the imported clips.

What iMovie is actually doing is studying the *date and time stamp* that DV camcorders record into every frame of video. When iMovie detects a break in time, it assumes that you stopped recording, if only for a moment—and therefore that the next piece of footage should be considered a new shot. It turns each new shot into a new clip—a feature not found even in some of the $1,000 professional editing programs.

This behavior lets you just roll the camera, unattended, as iMovie automatically downloads the footage. As it does so, it turns each scene into a clip in successive Clips-pane cubbyholes, while you sit there leafing through a magazine. Then, later, at your leisure, you can survey the footage you've caught and set about the business of cutting out the deadwood.

(This feature relies on the use of the DV camera's internal clock. Therefore, it doesn't work if you haven't set your camcorder's clock. It also doesn't work if you're playing from a non-DV tape using one of the techniques described on page 268.)

Tip: If you prefer, you can ask iMovie to dump incoming clips into the Clip Viewer at the bottom of the screen instead of the Clips pane. You might want to do that when, for example, you filmed your shots roughly in sequence. That way, you'll have to do much less dragging to the Clip Viewer when it comes time to edit.

To bring this about, choose iMovie→Preferences. Where you see "New clips go to," click Movie Timeline. Click OK. Now when you begin importing clips, iMovie stacks them end-to-end in the Timeline instead of on the Clips pane.

If you would prefer to have manual control over when each clip begins and ends, iMovie is happy to comply. Choose iMovie→Preferences, and proceed as shown in Figure 13-5.

Once you've turned off the automatic clip-creation feature, iMovie logs clips only when you click Import (or press Space) once at the beginning of the clip, and again at the end of the clip.

Figure 13-5:
The iMovie→Preferences dialog box gives you control over the automatic clip-logging feature. You can turn off this feature entirely by un-checking the "Automatically start new clip at scene break" option (third from top).

iMovie 4's expanded Preferences dialog box contains a slew of useful options, which are cited so frequently in this book, that it's probably worth memorizing its keyboard shortcut: ⌘-comma.

As a bonus, that same keystroke works to open the Preferences dialog box in all of the other iLife programs, too.

Tip: Tapping the Space bar is the same as clicking the Import button. In fact, if you tap Space when the camcorder is stopped, it begins to play *and* iMovie begins to capture the footage.

The maximum clip length

The largest movie clip iMovie can capture is one that takes 2 GB of disk space, which translates to 9 minutes, 28 seconds, and 17 frames. At the end of that time, if the camcorder is still running (or if the iSight camera is still recording), iMovie smoothly and automatically begins a second clip, placing another icon into your Clips pane.

This limitation is no cause for panic, however. After the importing, you can place the two clips side-by-side on the Clip Viewer. iMovie will play the first one, then the next, seamlessly. No pop, blink, or dropped frame will give away the program's little secret: that during the importing, it had to split your very long clip into multiple parts.

If you follow this thought to its logical conclusion, you can see that as far as iMovie is concerned, there's really no maximum clip length. You can import an entire 60-minute DV cassette's worth of tape—if you've got 13 GB of free hard drive space, of course—and iMovie will smoothly import all of it, even if it shows up on your Clips pane in the form of seven different clip icons.

The Free Space graph

As noted earlier, the Free Space graph (Figure 13-4) updates itself as you capture your clips. It keeps track of how much space your hard drive has left—the one onto which you saved your project.

This graph includes a color-keyed early-warning system that lets you prepare for that awkward moment when your hard drive's full. At that moment, you won't be able to capture any more video. Look at the colored bar that grows out of the left side of the graph:

- If it's **green,** you're in good shape. Your hard drive has over 400 MB of free space—room for at least 90 seconds of additional footage.

- If the graph becomes **yellow,** your hard drive has between 200 and 400 MB of free space left. In about 90 more seconds of capturing, you'll be completely out of space.

GEM IN THE ROUGH

A Wrinkle in Timecode

If a clip is shorter than one minute—as most clips are—iMovie drops the "00:" minutes display from the beginning of the clip-length time code shown on every clip. You see a two-colon number (such as "1:22:03") if the clip is longer than a minute.

If you'd prefer to see the full three-segment time-code display ("minutes:seconds:frames") all the time, an iMovie preference can accommodate you. Choose iMovie→ Preferences; turn off "Display short time codes."

When you click OK, you'll find that *all* time codes appear in the full form.

- When the graph turns **red,** the situation is dire. Your hard drive has less than 200 MB of free space left. About one minute of capturing remains.

- When the Free Space graph shows that you've got less than 50 MB of free space left, iMovie stops importing and refuses to capture any more video. At this point, you must make more free space on your hard drive, either by emptying your Project Trash or by throwing away some non-iMovie files from your hard drive. (You don't have to quit iMovie while you houseclean; just hide it.)

How iMovie Organizes Its Files

Few computer programs are as compulsive about housekeeping as iMovie. Every time you save a project file, iMovie doesn't just create a document on your hard drive, as AppleWorks or Word would. Instead, it creates an entire *folder* bearing your project's name.

Inside this folder are a few important files and folders that are worth getting to know (see Figure 13-6).

Figure 13-6:
Every iMovie project gets its own folder (top left). Inside (lower left) is a document bearing the same name; a .mov "reference movie" bearing the same name; and a Media folder that contains all the clips, titles, and transitions (right). The clips are always called Clip 01, Clip 02, and so on, even if you've renamed them in iMovie.

The Project File

The actual iMovie project file—called South Dakota at lower left in Figure 13-6—occupies only a few kilobytes of space on the disk, even if it's a very long movie. Behind the scenes, this document contains nothing more than a list of internal *references* to the QuickTime clips in the Media folder. Even if you copy, chop, split, rearrange, rename, and otherwise spindle the clips *in iMovie,* the names and quantity of clips in the Media folder don't change. Instead, all of your iMovie editing, technically speaking, simply shuffles around your project file's internal *pointers* to different moments on the clips you originally captured from the camcorder.

The bottom line: If you burn the project document to a CD disc and take it home to show the relatives for the holidays, you're in for a rude surprise, because it's nothing without its accompanying Media folder. (And that's why iMovie insists upon creating a folder that keeps the document and its media files together.)

The Media Folder

Inside the Media folder are several, or dozens, or hundreds of individual QuickTime movies. Essentially, these are digital movie files, one for each clip, sound, picture, or special effect you used in your movie.

Caution: Never rename, move, or delete the files in the Media folder. iMovie will become cranky, display error messages, and forget how you had your movie the last time you opened it.

Do your deleting, renaming, and rearranging in *iMovie,* not in the Media folder. And above all, don't take the Media folder out of the folder the project document is in (or vice versa). Doing so will render your movie uneditable, at least until you put the Media folder and project document together again in the same folder.

(It's OK to rename the project folder or the project file, however.)

The Reference Movie

If your movie is called South Dakota, for example, your iMovie project folder also contains a file called South Dakota.mov.

Technically, this icon is called the *reference movie*—not because you're supposed to refer to it, but because it *contains* references (pointers) to all of the individual movie and sound clips in the Media folder, just as the project file does. That's why the reference movie is so tiny, occupying only a few kilobytes of space.

The reference movie's primary purpose is to accommodate the direct-to-iDVD movie-burning feature described in Chapter 20. You may occasionally find the reference movie handy for your own purposes, though, as it offers an effective way to make a quick playback of a movie you've been working on.

When you double-click this icon, your iMovie movie appears in QuickTime Player, where a simple tap of the Space bar starts it playing. (Feel free to make the playback window larger—full screen, even.) This method is quicker and less memory-hogging than opening it in iMovie. It's safer, too, because you don't risk accidentally nudging some clip or sound file out of alignment; in QuickTime Player, you can't do anything but *watch* the movie.

The Audio Waveforms Folder

One of the nicest enhancements in iMovie 4 is the audio *waveforms*—visual "sound waves"—that appear on audio clips. These visible peaks and valleys make it a lot easier to cue up certain video moments with the audio.

These graphic representations of your sound files don't appear by magic, though. First, you have to turn this feature on in the iMovie→Preferences dialog box. Then, iMovie has to compute the waveforms' shapes, based on the sonic information in each clip.

Because that computation takes time, iMovie stores a copy of these visuals in the Audio Waveforms folder, which it creates on the fly. Thereafter, each time you open your iMovie project, you won't have to wait for the waveforms to appear. iMovie will retrieve the information about their shapes from the files in this folder and blast them to the screen in a matter of moments. (The .wvf files are the waveform graphics; .snp files store "snap to" information for Timeline snapping, as described on page 345.)

The Shared Movies Folder

The File→Share command is the final step in almost every iMovie project. It's the last stop on your journey, where you export your masterpiece to another software or medium so it can reach an audience.

The Share command often hands off your work to some entity beyond itself. For example, when you tell iMovie that you want to burn a DVD, the program hands your work off to iDVD. When you say you want to send the movie to a Bluetooth device (like a cellphone), iMovie hands off to that wireless gadget. When you export your film to a .Mac Web page, you pass it on to that particular server.

In each case, iMovie stores the appropriately compressed version of your movie in a temporary folder inside the Shared Movies folder. Here, you'll find a folder called, for example, iDVD, Bluetooth, or HomePage.

The idea is that if you want to send the same movie out again later, you'll have a ready-to-transmit copy. You won't have to wait for iMovie to compress the movie all over again.

The Phantom "Save As" Command

Knowing how iMovie stores its files also solves what some people consider an iMovie limitation: the fact that it has no Save As command. If iMovie did have a Save As command, you could save your project under a different name halfway through working on it. You could create midproject backups, for example. Or you could create multiple versions of the same movie—like short and long versions. That way, you could spin out an intermediate version just before making some radical editing decision that you might regret later, so you'll have a safe version to return to.

You would also use up your hard drive's space fairly quickly, because each Save As process would duplicate all of the massive clip files in your project folder. But if you want to perform a Save As procedure, you can still do it—just not from within iMovie. Instead, follow the steps shown in Figure 13-7.

Sharing Clips Among Projects

It's also worth noting that, if you want to use a certain clip in more than one project, you don't have to go to the trouble of downloading it again from your camcorder. Instead, just proceed like this:

Figure 13-7:
iMovie has no traditional Save As command, but you can achieve the same effect manually. Suppose that, having finished half of your movie, you want to save it under a different name. Quit iMovie and duplicate the project folder on your hard drive (top). Give the duplicated project folder a different name; then, to help you keep your versions straight, also rename the actual project file inside it (bottom).

1. **Find out the number of the clip you want, as it appears in the Finder.**

   In other words, open the iMovie document that contains the clip you'd like to reuse. (Suppose it's in a project called Texas.) In the Clip Viewer (see Figure 13-3), double-click the clip. A dialog box appears, as shown in Figure 13-8, that identifies the clip's true name in the Finder, in the Texas→Media folder. Remember this number (such as Clip 11) and click OK.

Tip: Ordinarily, emptying the iMovie Trash before the project is complete carries a certain amount of risk (page 598). On the other hand, cropping, splitting, or trimming clips doesn't actually eliminate any video footage from your hard drive; it simply makes your iMovie project *play* a shorter chunk of the full-length video clip that's still on your hard drive.

Only by emptying the Trash can you ensure that the clip doesn't carry its trimmed-away baggage with it when you import it into another project.

---

2. **Open the iMovie project which you want to bring the clip into.**

   See "Switching Files," below.

3. **Choose File→Import (or press Shift-⌘-I).**

   The standard Open File dialog box appears.

4. **Navigate to the Media folder inside the project folder that contains the clip you want to borrow.**

   In this example, you'd locate the Texas→Media folder. There you'll see all the clips that belong to that project.

5. **Double-click the clip you want.**

   Having cleverly noted its number in step 1, you know exactly which of the clips is the scene you want. iMovie places the imported clip in your Clips pane.

Figure 13-8:
When you double-click a clip, this dialog box appears. It identifies the clip's number as it appears in the Finder—a useful piece of information, because you may have renamed it in iMovie. Doing so never renames the clip in the Finder, however. (You can rename one of your clips, but only after you've copied it out of the original Media folder—never after you've used it in a movie.)

Clip Info

Name: Fishin'
Media file: Still 02
Size: 117 KB
Capture date: Unknown
Duration: 02:04

Cancel   Set

Switching Files

To open a different iMovie Project, choose File→Open Project (or File→Open Recent, whose submenu lists the last few movies you've worked on). If you've worked on the current movie but haven't saved the changes yet, iMovie asks you whether you'd like to save them or not. Click Save or Don't Save, as appropriate.

Tip: If you're a keyboard-shortcut fan, you can press ⌘-D instead of clicking Don't Save.

Now you're shown the contents of your hard drive. Navigate to the project folder that contains the next movie you want to edit. Double-click that project folder to open it, and then double-click the identically named iMovie *document* inside it. After a moment, the new movie's clips appear onscreen, and you're ready to go.

The Phantom "Revert to Saved" Command

iMovie has a terrific memory; it can remember, and even undo, the last 30 editing steps you've taken.

But many Mac programs also offer a Revert command. Choosing File→Revert discards all the changes you've made to the file *since the last time you saved it.*

The iMovie File menu has no Revert command—at least, not in the File menu. You can achieve exactly the same effect, however, by choosing File→Open Project. When iMovie asks if you want to save changes to your project, click Don't Save. iMovie now shows the list of folders on your hard drive; all you have to do is open the *same* file you just had open a moment ago.

When it opens, you'll find it exactly as it was when you last used the Save command. (You don't recover footage you've emptied from the Trash, however.)

Starting a New Project

Starting a new project after you've been editing an older one works much the same way: Choose File→New Project; indicate whether or not you want to save the changes to your outgoing movie (if you haven't already saved them); and wait as iMovie opens a new, empty Clips pane and Clip Viewer.

Importing Footage from Non-DV Tapes

We live in a transitional period. The huge majority of the world's existing camcorders and VCRs require VHS, VHS-C, or 8mm cassettes.

DV camcorders are rapidly catching up. But for now, potential video editors face a very real problem: how to transfer into iMovie the footage they shot before the DV era. Fortunately, this is fairly easy to do if you have the right equipment. You can take any of these three approaches:

Approach 1: Use a Digital8 Camcorder

Most Sony Digital8 camcorders accommodate 8mm, Hi-8, *and* Digital8 tapes, which are 8mm cassettes recorded digitally. (Low-end models may not offer this feature, however, so ask before you buy.) Just insert your 8mm or Hi-8 cassettes into the camcorder and proceed as described in this chapter. iMovie never needs to know that the camcorder doesn't contain a DV cassette.

Actually, a Digital8 camcorder grants you even more flexibility than that. Most Digital8 camcorders also have *analog inputs,* which let you import footage from your VCR or other tape formats. Read on:

Approach 2: Record onto Your DV Camcorder

Even if you don't have a Digital8 camcorder, the digital camcorder you bought may have analog inputs anyway. If so, your problem is solved.

1. **Unplug the FireWire cable from the DV camcorder.**

    Most camcorders' analog inputs switch off when a FireWire cable is hooked up.

2. **Connect RCA cables from the Audio Output and Video Output jacks on the side of your older camcorder or VCR. Connect the opposite ends to the analog inputs of your DV camcorder.**

Tip: If both your old camcorder and your DV camcorder have *S-video* connectors (a round, dime-sized jack), use them instead. S-video connections offer higher quality than RCA connections. (Note that an S-video cable doesn't conduct sound, however. You still have to connect the red and white RCA cables to carry the left and right stereo sound channels.)

3. **Switch both camcorders into VTR or VCR mode.**

   Make sure there's a blank DV tape in your DV camcorder. You're about to make a copy of the older tape by playing it into the camcorder.

   If every fiber of your being is screaming, "But analog copies make the quality deteriorate!"—relax. You're only making a single-generation copy. Actually, you're only making *half* an analog copy; it's being recorded digitally, so you lose only half as much quality as you would with a normal VCR-to-VCR duplicate. In other words, you probably won't be able to spot any picture deterioration. And you'll have the footage in digital format forever, ready to make as many copies as you want with no further quality degradation.

4. **Press the Record button on the DV camcorder, and Play on the older camcorder or VCR.**

   You can monitor your progress by watching the LCD screen of your camcorder. Remember that the DV cassette generally holds only 60 minutes of video, compared with two hours on many previous-format tapes. You may have to change DV cassettes halfway through the process.

When the transfer is finished, you can use the newly recorded DV cassette in the DV camcorder, exactly as described in this chapter and in the rest of the book.

Tip: Not all camcorders with analog inputs require you to dump the footage onto a DV *tape* as an intermediary. As described below, modern Sony camcorders can pour the analog signal into the Mac *as it plays,* eliminating several steps (and one hour of waiting per tape).

Approach 3: Use a Media Converter

If your DV camcorder doesn't have analog inputs, you can buy an *analog-to-digital converter*—a box that sits between your Mac and your VCR or older camcorder. It's an unassuming half-pound gray box, about 3 by 5 inches. Its primary features include analog audio and video (and S-video) inputs, which accommodate your older video gear, and a FireWire jack, whose cable you can plug into your Mac.

Sony, the pioneer in the analog-to-digital adapter category, no longer makes its DVMC-DA1 or -DA2 boxes. Still, other companies have taken up the slack, including the Hollywood-DV Bridge (*www.dazzle.com*; about $200 online), the Canopus ADVC-50 (*www.canopus.com*, $200), and the Director's Cut Take 2 box (*www.miglia.com/products/index.html*; about $450).

In either case, you'll be very pleased with the video quality. And when it comes to converting older footage, the media-converter approach has a dramatic advantage over DV camcorders with analog inputs: You have to sit through the footage only once. As your old VCR or camcorder plays the tape through the converter, the Mac records it simultaneously. (Contrast with Approaches 1 and 2, which require you to play the footage *twice*—once to the DV camcorder, and then from there to the Mac.)

Unfortunately, you can't control these devices using iMovie's playback controls, as described in this chapter. Instead, you must transfer your footage manually by pressing Play on your VCR or old camcorder and then clicking Import on the iMovie screen. In that way, these converters aren't as convenient as an actual DV or Digital8 camcorder.

Approach 4: Use a Recent Sony Camcorder

Most of Sony's current DV and Digital8 camcorders offer a great solution to the "old tapes" problem: analog-to-digital *passthrough* conversion. In other words, the camcorder itself acts as one of the media converters described above. The footage never hits a DV tape. Instead, it simply plays from your older VCR or camcorder directly into the Macintosh. (Not all Sony camcorders have this feature, so ask before you buy. And on some models, you must use the camcorder's on-board menu system to enable the live passthrough.)

If you've got a drawerful of older tapes, such a camcorder is by far the most elegant and economical route, especially if you're shopping for a new camcorder anyway.

Building the Movie Track

Whether on your Mac or in a multimillion-dollar Hollywood professional studio, film editing boils down to three tiny tasks: selecting, trimming, and rearranging *clips*.

Of course, that's like saying that there's nothing more to painting than mixing various amounts of red, yellow, and blue. The art of video editing lies in your decisions about *which* clips you select, *how* you trim them, and *what* order you put them in.

At its simplest, iMovie editing works like this:

1. Trim your clips until they contain exactly the footage you want.

2. Drag your clips from the Clips pane to the Clip Viewer, where iMovie plays them in one seamless pass, from left to right.

3. Rearrange the scenes by dragging them around on the Clip Viewer (or its alter ego, the Timeline).

4. Add crossfades, titles (credits), effects, music, and sound effects.

This chapter is dedicated to showing you the mechanics of the first three tasks. The following chapters cover the fourth step, and Chapter 10 offers tips for adding taste and artistry to these proceedings.

Navigating Your Clips

As you're building your movie, you can store your clips in either of two places: the Clips pane or the strip at the bottom of the window. You put clips on the Clips pane before deciding what to do with them, and drag them down to the storyboard area once you've decided where they fit into your movie.

This clip-assembly area at the bottom of the iMovie screen can appear in either of two ways:

- **Clip Viewer.** In this view, each clip appears as an icon, as though it's a slide on a slide viewer. Each is sized identically, even if one is eight minutes long and the next is only two seconds.

- **Timeline Viewer.** This view also shows a linear map of your movie. But in this case, each clip is represented by a horizontal bar that's as wide as the clip is long. Short clips have short bars; long clips stretch across your screen. Parallel bars below the clips indicate the soundtracks playing simultaneously.

Grizzled iMovie veterans are used to switching between these two viewers by clicking the corresponding icon just above them: either the film strip or the clock. But in this crazy, hectic world, using the mouse to aim at a tiny icon is just too much trouble. Learn to use iMovie 4's new viewer-switching keystroke: ⌘-E. (That's the keyboard shortcut for the Switch Viewer command in the new View menu.)

Note: You can read much more about these two views of your work at the end of this chapter. It's important now, however, to note that Apple hasn't given a name to this bottom-of-your-screen area as a *whole*. To prevent you from having to read about the "Clip Viewer/Timeline Viewer area" 47 times per chapter, this book uses the made-up term *Movie Track* to refer to this editing track, regardless of which view it's showing.

You can do several things to a clip, whether it's in the Clips pane or the Movie Track.

Select a Clip

When you click a clip—the picture, not the name—iMovie highlights it by making its border (the "cardboard" portion of the "slide") or its bar (in the Timeline) blue. The first frame of the selected clip appears in the Monitor window. (If you're in Camera Mode at the time, busily controlling your camcorder by clicking the playback controls, iMovie immediately switches back into Edit Mode. The camcorder stops automatically.)

Once you've highlighted a clip (whether in the Clips pane or the Movie Track), you get to see some very useful statistics about it, such as its name, duration, and, surprisingly enough, the date and time you originally filmed it. To see this information, study the top edge of the Movie Track, as shown in Figure 14-1.

To *de*select a clip (all clips, in fact), choose Edit→Select None, or press Shift-⌘-A, or Control-click any clip and choose Select None from the shortcut menu. If you're menu-phobic, just click anywhere *except* on a clip (on the metallic-looking iMovie background, say), or Shift-click the first or last in a series of highlighted clips.

Knowing these five ways to deselect your clips will save you the following frustration: When several clips are highlighted in the Clips pane, the entire *movie* plays back when you press the Space bar, which isn't always what you want.

Figure 14-1:
Thanks to the automatic date-stamping feature built into every DV camcorder, you even see the date and time a highlighted clip was originally recorded.

Select Several Clips

In iMovie 4, you can highlight several clips simultaneously using more techniques than ever before. For example:

- In the Movie Track, click one clip, and then Shift-click the last one. All consecutive clips between them get selected.

- iMovie 4 also gives you a new Movie Track feature: the ability to select several clips that aren't next to each other using the same techniques you'd use to select nonadjacent icons in a Finder list view. To do so, click the first clip, then ⌘-click each additional clip. You can also ⌘-click a selected clip to deselect it.

- In the Clips pane, you can either Shift-click or ⌘-click several clips, one at a time. (You may as well learn to ⌘-click, so you can use the same shortcut in both the Clips pane and the Movie Track.)

  You can also choose a bunch of Clips pane clips by *drag-selecting* them. This technique involves positioning the cursor in the gray area between clips and dragging diagonally over the clips you want to select. As you drag, you create a yellow selection rectangle. Any clips touched by, or inside, this rectangle become highlighted.

FREQUENTLY ASKED QUESTION

The Little Ruler Lines

When I click a clip, I see little tick marks under the Scrubber bar. But I'll be darned if I can figure out what they represent. Not frames, not seconds...what are they?

They're cosmetics.

The number of tick marks has nothing to do with the length of the selected clip; in fact, it has more to do with the size of

your iMovie window (when you drag the lower-right corner to make the window smaller, fewer tick marks fit).

Even when you're working with a very short clip, the tick marks don't represent individual frames, individual seconds, or anything else—except the graphic design tastes of some programmer at Apple.

- In either the Clips pane or the Movie Track, you can select all of the clips choosing Edit→Select All (⌘-A) or by Control-clicking any clip and choosing Select All from the shortcut menu.

So why would you want to select several clips in this way? Let us count the tricks:

- Delete them all by pressing the Delete key, or drag them all to the project Trash.

- Use the Cut, Copy, or Clear commands in the Edit menu to affect all of them at once. (Why not just choose these commands from the shortcut menu that appears when you Control-click a clip? Because Control-clicking simultaneously *deselects* all other selected clips, which sort of defeats the purpose.)

- Move them around the Movie Track or the Clips pane—or drag them from one of those locations to the other—by dragging any one of them. The remaining clips slide leftward to close the gaps.

- Apply the same transition, special effect, or Ken Burns photo setting to all of them using the Apply button on the Trans, Effects, and Photo panes. Similarly, you can update them all using the Update button. (Details in Chapters 15 through 17.)

- Consolidate a batch of nonadjacent clips. That is, extract the selected clips from their current positions in the movie (Edit→Cut). Click a different clip in the movie to pinpoint a landing site, and then choose Edit→Paste. The clips that you cut, which were once scattered, now appear adjacent to each other and in sequence.

Tip: Whenever you've selected more than one clip (either in the Clips pane or the Movie Track), iMovie adds up their running times and displays the total at the top edge of the Movie Track in the seconds:frames format. It says, for example, "<Multiple> Time: 12:01."

Play a Clip

You can play a highlighted clip in the Monitor window by pressing the Space bar (or clicking the Play button underneath the Monitor window).

You can stop the playback very easily: Press the Space bar a second time, or click anywhere else on the screen—on another clip, another control, the Monitor window, the metallic iMovie background, and so on.

Jump Around in a Clip

Whether the clip is playing or not, you can jump instantly to any other part of the clip in one of two ways:

- Drag the Playhead handle to any other part of the Scrubber bar (see Figure 14-2).

- Click directly in the Scrubber bar to jump to a particular spot in the footage. Doing so while the movie is playing saves you the difficulty of trying to grab the tiny Playhead as it moves across the screen.

Tip: To play back a section repeatedly for analysis, just keep clicking at the same spot in the Scrubber bar while the clip plays.

Figure 14-2:
While a clip plays, the Playhead (the down-pointing triangle) slides across the Scrubber bar. If you can catch it, you can drag the Playhead using the mouse, thus jumping around in the movie. Or you can simply click anywhere in the Scrubber bar. Either way, the playback continues at the new spot in the clip.

Step Through a Clip

By pressing the right and left arrow keys, you can view your clip one frame at a time, as though you're watching the world's least interesting slide show. Hold down these arrow keys steadily to make the frame-by-frame parade go by faster.

Adding the Shift key to your arrow-key presses is often more useful—it lets you jump *ten* frames at a time. In time, you can get extremely good at finding an exact frame in a particular piece of footage just by mastering the arrow-key and Shift-arrow-key shortcuts. (These shortcuts work only when the clip isn't playing.)

Scan Through a Clip

The Rewind and Fast Forward keystrokes (⌘-left bracket and ⌘-right bracket; that is, the [and] keys) let you zoom through your footage faster. Press once to start, a second time to stop playback.

You don't have to click Play first. The Rewind and Fast Forward keystrokes start your clip playing at double speed even from a dead stop.

Rename a Clip

When iMovie imports your clips, it gives them such creative names as *Clip 01, Clip 02,* and so on. Fortunately, renaming a clip on the Clips pane or Clip Viewer is very easy: Just click directly on its name ("Clip 11") to open the renaming rectangle, drag through the existing name, and then type the new name. All the usual Macintosh editing techniques work inside this little highlighted renaming rectangle, including the Delete key and the Cut, Copy, Paste, and Select All commands in the Edit menu.

You can also rename a clip in its Clip Info dialog box (see Figure 14-9), which is the *only* way to change a clip's name in the Timeline Viewer. To open this box, just double-click the clip. (Or, if you're billing by the hour, Control-click the clip and, from the shortcut menu, choose Show Info.)

An iMovie clip's name can be 127 letters and spaces long. Be aware, however, that only about the first 11 letters of it actually appear under the clip icon. (The easiest way to see the whole clip name is to double-click the clip icon and then drag your cursor through the Name field in the resulting dialog box.)

The clip renaming you do in iMovie doesn't affect the names of the files in your project's Media folder on the hard drive (see page 264). Files there remain forever with their original names: Clip 01, Clip 02, and so on. That's why, in times of troubleshooting or file administration, the Clip Info box that appears when you double-click a clip can be especially useful. It's the only way to find out how a clip that you've renamed in iMovie corresponds to a matching clip on your hard drive.

Tip: Because you can only see the first few letters of a clip's name when it's on the Clips pane, adopt clever naming conventions to help you remember what's in each clip. Use prefix codes like CU (for "closeup"), ES ("establishing shot"), MS ("medium shot"), WS ("wide shot"), and so on, followed by useful keywords ("wild laughter," "sad melon," and so on). If the clip contains recorded speech, clue yourself in by including a quotation as part of the clip's name.

Reorganize Your Clips

You can drag clips from cubbyhole to cubbyhole on the Clips pane. In fact, you can even drag a clip (or even a mass of highlighted clips) onto an *occupied* cubbyhole. iMovie automatically creates enough new cubbyholes to hold them all, and shuffles existing clips out of the way if necessary.

The freedom to drag clips around in the Clips pane offers you a miniature storyboard feature. That is, you can construct a *sequence* by arranging several clips in the Clips pane. When they seem to be in a good order for your finished scene, drag the whole batch to the Movie Track at once.

Trash a Clip

You can get rid of a clip either by selecting it and then pressing the Delete key or by dragging it directly onto the project Trash icon (shown back in Figure 13-3).

At first glance, you might assume that this Trash works like the standard Mac Trash. After all, the icon looks similar, and there's an Empty Trash command in the File menu.

In fact, the project Trash is different in a number of ways. It doesn't bulge when something's in it, and you can't double-click it to open a window revealing its contents. Instead, the megabyte counter underneath tells you exactly how much footage is inside.

You're entitled to wonder, however: If you can't open the project Trash window, and therefore can't retrieve the footage inside, what good is it?

The answer is that the Trash can is primarily intended to let you delay committing to your editing decisions. For example, iMovie reaches into its own Trash whenever you quit iMovie without saving changes, paste something you've cut, or use the Advanced→Restore Clip command.

The Trash is also the secret of iMovie's ten-level Undo command. Whenever you delete some footage (either by dragging a clip to the Trash can or by using one of the trimming commands described later in this chapter), iMovie stores it in this Trash can. Then, if you decide to use the Undo command, even ten times in a row, iMovie will be able to restore the footage you had cut—by quietly pulling it out of the project Trash.

That's why, whenever you choose File→Empty Trash (or double-click the Trash can), you *lose* your ability to undo the last ten steps you took.

And when would you ever choose File→Empty Trash? The short answer is, never. Emptying the trash erases your Undo trail, dims the Restore Clip command, makes your clip trimming permanent, takes a long time, and (in very rare but upsetting circumstances) has actually been known to corrupt an iMovie project (page 298).

Once you're completely done editing a movie, and it's safely backed up onto your camcorder, then OK—empty the project Trash. Otherwise, though, empty it only when you need to reclaim the hard-drive space it's taking up. (Remember that each iMovie project continues to occupy that disk space even when the program's not running.)

Tip: As you work in iMovie, remember to choose File→Save (or press ⌘-S) frequently, just as you would with any kind of document. Fortunately, saving in iMovie is instantaneous; it doesn't require the long, disk-intensive wait that you might expect from a video-editing program. You're saving only your Project file, not making any changes to the large, underlying DV files in your Media folder.

Shortening Clips by Dragging

Almost nobody hits the camcorder's Record button at the precise instant when the action begins, and then hits the Stop button the instant the action stops. Life is just too unpredictable. That's why the first thing most people do when they get their clips into a movie is to *trim* them—to chop the boring parts off the beginning and ending of each clip before dragging them onto the timeline.

In previous versions of iMovie, you trimmed your clips by splitting them apart, by chopping off their ends, or lopping chunks out of the middle. That was OK, but things got messy if you later changed your mind; if, for example, you cut ten seconds off the end and later decided you wanted five of them back.

Those time-honored techniques—and all of their related problems—still work in iMovie 4. They're described in the following sections.

Most of the time, though, you'll want to adopt one of iMovie 4's sweetest new features instead: *nondestructive* clip trimming. Instead of chopping off the ends of your clips, you can just *hide* the ends by dragging them inward, as shown in Figure 14-3. (This kind of nondestructive edge-dragging also works with audio clips. It's a common technique in GarageBand, for instance.)

Tip: Here's a great way to use this technique. First, play back the sequence. Using the arrow keys, position the Playhead so that it pinpoints the precise frame where you want the clip to end. In other words, you're using the Playhead to mark the target for the drag-cropping you're about to perform.

Now grab the *end* of the clip and drag it up against the Playhead. Conveniently enough, the end you're dragging snaps against the ghosted Playhead line, as though it's a bookmark. As a result, you get individual-frame accuracy without having to remember precisely how far to drag. (This trick works only if "Enable timeline snapping" is turned on in iMovie→Preferences.)

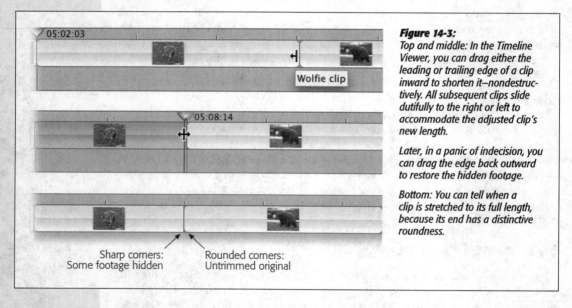

Figure 14-3:
Top and middle: In the Timeline Viewer, you can drag either the leading or trailing edge of a clip inward to shorten it—nondestructively. All subsequent clips slide dutifully to the right or left to accommodate the adjusted clip's new length.

Later, in a panic of indecision, you can drag the edge back outward to restore the hidden footage.

Bottom: You can tell when a clip is stretched to its full length, because its end has a distinctive roundness.

Sharp corners:
Some footage hidden

Rounded corners:
Untrimmed original

The beauty of this approach, of course, is its flexibility. After you crop a clip this way, you can play it back to gauge its impact on the flow of scenes. If you feel that you trimmed a little too much, simply grab the end of the clip and drag it outward a little more. If you don't think you cropped enough, drag it inward.

Tip: If you ⌘-drag a clip in the Timeline Viewer, you can move it right on top of an adjacent clip, in effect trimming the part that the dragged clip is now covering up.

There's only one limitation to this technique: It works only in the Timeline Viewer.

You can't use it to pre-shorten clips while they're still in the Clips pane, or after you've dragged them into the Clips viewer. For those purposes, read on.

Three Ways to Trim a Clip

Trimming out the deadwood from your clips, so that you're left with only the very best shots from the very best scenes, is the heart of iMovie—and video editing.

POWER USERS' CLINIC

Beyond Undo: The Restore Clip Command

As programs go, iMovie is a forgiving one. Not only does it have an Undo command—it's a *ten-step* Undo command, meaning that you can undo the last ten editing steps you took. (You can even unimport a clip from your camcorder.)

Still, a ten-level Undo isn't always ideal. If you made a mistake eight steps ago, you can undo that step, but only by undoing the seven successful editing steps you took thereafter.

The Advanced→Restore Clip command can be perfect in such situations. Remember that every time you cut or crop a clip, iMovie doesn't actually disturb the clip itself—the file on your hard drive. Instead, it simply shifts around its own internal *pointers* to the portion of the clip that you want to use. As a result, it's a piece of cake for iMovie to say, "Oh, you want me to throw away those pointers and give you back the original clip as it came from the camcorder? No problem."

In short, the Restore Clip command gives you a convenient safety net, a chance to start with a clean slate on a clip-by-clip basis.

When you use the command, iMovie displays a dialog box that lets you know what's about to happen, as shown here. If you click Restore, iMovie returns the clip to its original, pre-cut, precrop condition, even if you've already placed it into the Movie Track. In that case, the clip's bar in the Timeline

Viewer grows correspondingly wider, shoving other clips to the right to make room.

Note that if you've emptied the project Trash, as described on page 257, forget it—both the ten-level Undo and the Restore Clip command are unavailable. Emptying the project Trash empties iMovie's Undo and Restore Clip memory.

That's why some iMovie veterans are in the habit of duplicating clips before trimming and splitting them. After clicking a clip in either the Clips pane or the Movie Track, choose Edit→ Copy, followed immediately by Edit→Paste. You'll see a perfect duplicate of the clip appear.

When you do so, you're not actually duplicating any files on your hard drive, so copying and pasting clips doesn't eat away at your remaining free space. Even if you whittle away at one of these copies by trimming it or splitting it, your original is safe in its full-length, freshly imported condition. If it turns out that you trimmed too much of your clip, you can return to the copy—your backup—without sacrificing the other editing work you've done since you made the copy.

If you decide to adopt this technique, be prepared for one other twist: As you cut or crop footage, your project Trash will always remain empty. That's because any frames you're cutting from one clip are still required by the other clip, so iMovie can't afford to put anything into the Trash in readiness for permanent deletion.

Tip: Unlike the edge-dragging technique described above, all of the techniques described in this section are what digital video editors call *destructive* ones, since they chop up pieces of footage. But iMovie is fairly forgiving. If, just after performing one of these trimming techniques, you tap the Space bar and discover, during the playback, that you trimmed the wrong thing, choose Edit→Undo to restore the clip as it was before your trim.

And if even the Undo command (or ten Undo commands) can't restore the clip to its original condition, you can always rescue the chopped-up clip using the Restore Clip command described on the next page.

Highlighting Footage

iMovie works just like other Mac programs: You highlight some footage, then use the Cut, Copy, or Paste commands to move it around. All three of the following footage-trimming techniques, for example, begin with *highlighting,* or selecting, a portion of your footage. Here's how you go about it:

1. **Click a clip to select it.**

   The clip can be either in the Clips pane or the Movie Track.

2. **Position your cursor within the tick marks of the Scrubber bar.**

   See Figure 14-4.

3. **Drag horizontally until the triangle handles surround the footage you want to keep.**

   As soon as you push the mouse button down, the selection triangles jump to the position of your cursor. One remains where you clicked; the other follows your cursor as you drag. (In other words, don't waste time by dragging them painstakingly from the left edge of the Scrubber bar.)

   The Monitor window behaves as though you're scrolling the movie, so that you can see where you are as you drag the movable triangle. Also as you drag, the portion of the Scrubber bar between your handles turns yellow to show that it's highlighted. Whatever Edit menu command you use now (such as Cut, Copy, Clear, or Crop) affects only the yellow portion.

Tip: Here's a quick trick for highlighting only the first portion of a selected clip: Shift-click within the Scrubber bar at the point where you'd like the selection to *end.* Instantly, iMovie highlights everything from the left end of the clip to the position of your click.

After you've just dragged or clicked a handle, the arrow-key skills you picked up on page 274 come in handy. You can let go of the mouse and, just by pressing the left and right arrow keys, fine-tune the position of the triangle handle on a frame-by-frame basis. (You can easily tell which triangle handle you'll be moving: It's darker, and it's marked by the Playhead, as shown in Figure 14-4. To move the *other* triangle handle, click it first.) Continue tapping the left and right arrow keys until the monitor shows the precise frame you want—the first or last frame you'll want to keep in the clip.

Remember, too, that if you press *Shift*-right or -left arrow, you move the triangle handle ten frames at a time. Between the ten-frame and one-frame keystrokes, you should find it fairly easy to home in on the exact frame where you want to trim the clip.

Tip: After you've highlighted a stretch of the Scrubber bar, you can adjust the selected portion—make it bigger or smaller—by clicking or dragging again beneath any unhighlighted portion of the Scrubber bar (to the right or left of the selected region). Either way, the end of the yellow bar jumps to your cursor as though attracted by a magnet. And either way, you avoid having to redo the entire selection, since one of your two endpoints remains in place.

Figure 14-4:
Carefully drag horizontally until the triangles enclose only the scene you want to keep. Finally, when you choose the Edit→Crop command, everything outside of these handles is trimmed away and put into the project Trash.

As you drag the triangle handles, keep your eye on two readouts. First, your precise position within the clip or assembled movie appears just above your cursor, in seconds:frames format.

Second, a notation appears on the top edge of the Movie Track that identifies the amount of footage between the handles. It might say, for example, "**Video Selection: Time: 04:02**" (which means four seconds, two frames).

Being able to see exactly how much footage you're about to cut (or preserve) can be extremely useful when the timing of your movie is important, as when editing it to accompany a music track or when creating a movie that must be, for example, exactly 30 seconds long.

Tip: If you've really made a mess of your selection, click just *above* the Scrubber bar, on the brushed aluminum iMovie background. The program deselects your footage so that you can try again.

Snipping Off One End of a Clip

Having mastered the art of selecting a portion of a clip, as described in the previous section, you're ready to put it to work. Suppose, for example, that you want to shave off some footage from only one end of your clip. In that case, highlight the footage you want to delete (at the beginning or end of the Scrubber bar), and then choose Edit→Cut (or Edit→Clear), or press the Delete key.

iMovie promptly trims away whatever was highlighted between the triangles.

Cropping Out the Ends of a Clip

If you want to trim some footage off of *both* ends of a clip, it's quicker to highlight the part in the middle that you want to *keep*. Just select the footage you want to preserve and then choose Edit→Crop (or press ⌘-K).

When you use this command, all of your signposts disappear, including the two triangle handles and the yellow part of the Scrubber bar. What used to be the yellow part of the Scrubber bar has now, in effect, expanded to fill the *entire* Scrubber bar. Your clip is shorter now, as a tap on the Space bar will prove.

Figure 14-5:
To trim footage from one end of the clip, just highlight that much, using the triangle handles. The Monitor window shows you where you are in the footage as you drag the triangles. And once again, you can use the arrow keys to fine-tune the position of the triangle you've most recently clicked.

Chopping Out the Middle of a Clip

In this technique, you *eliminate* the middle part of a clip, leaving only the ends of it in your project. Select the footage you want to delete, and then choose Edit→Cut (or Edit→Clear), or press the Delete key.

If you're not prepared for it, the results of this technique can be startling—and yet it's perfectly logical. If you cut a chunk out of the middle of the clip, iMovie has no choice but to throw back at you the *two end pieces*—as two separate clips, side-by-side on the Clips pane or the Movie Track.

Either way, the name of the newly created clip will help you identify it. If the original clip was called "Cut Me Out," the new, split-off clip is called "Cut Me Out/1."

Splitting a Clip

The techniques described in the previous section work well when you want to remove some footage from a clip. Sometimes, however, it can be useful to split a clip into two separate clips *without* deleting footage in the process. For example, suppose you want the title of your movie to appear five seconds into a certain piece of footage. In iMovie, the only way to accomplish this feat is to split the clip into three pieces—the first one being five seconds long—and superimpose the title credit on the middle piece. (More on titles in Chapter 16.)

The Split Video Clip at Playhead command is exactly what you need in that case. Just click inside, or drag along, the Scrubber bar until you find the spot where you want to split the clip. (Remember that you can press the right or left arrow keys to nudge the Playhead one frame at a time to the right or left.) Then choose Edit→Split Video Clip at Playhead (or press ⌘-T).

As shown in Figure 14-6, you wind up with two different clips, both highlighted. If the original was called "Split Me Up," iMovie calls the resultant clips "Split Me Up" and "Split Me Up/1." (To remove the highlighting, click anywhere else on the screen, or choose Edit→Select None.)

Figure 14-6:
After you split a clip, iMovie cuts your clip in two and highlights both of the resulting clip icons (Clip Viewer, bottom). If the clip started out in the Movie Track, the Monitor window still lets you scroll all the way through the original clip. Only the telltale slashed number ("/1") on the second part of the clip lets you know that you're actually looking at two different clips side-by-side.

The Movie Track: Your Storyboard

When you're not trimming or splitting your clips, most of your iMovie time will be spent in the Movie Track—the horizontal strip at the bottom of the screen. The idea is that you'll drag the edited clips out of the Clips pane and into the correct order on the Movie Track, exactly as though you're building a storyboard or timeline.

As noted at the beginning of this chapter, the Movie Track offers two different views: the Clip Viewer and the Timeline Viewer. Both are illustrated in Figure 14-7.

In the Clip Viewer, you can freely rearrange clips by dragging them horizontally.

Tip: As you drag over them, the existing clips scoot out of the way, which can drive you crazy. In that case, hold down the ⌘ key until you're ready to let go of the clip you're dragging. They'll stay still.

Figure 14-7:
Top: When you click the film strip icon (indicated here by the cursor), you see your camcorder footage.

Bottom: Click the clock icon to see the Timeline Viewer, which reveals your audio tracks (Chapter 17) and shows you the relative lengths of your clips.

You can also use the View menu to switch between these views.

Moreover, you can freely drag clips back and forth between the Clips pane and the Clip Viewer. (You can drag clips into the Timeline Viewer, too—just not out again.)

Remember, by the way, that you can switch the Movie Track between its two viewers by pressing the new iMovie 4 keystroke ⌘-E. It corresponds to the second command in the new View menu, which says either "Switch to Clip Viewer" or "Switch to Timeline Viewer," whichever one you're *not* in.

Readouts in the Movie Track

iMovie identifies the name of your movie at the upper-left edge of the Movie Track (see Figure 14-7). There you'll also find a Time display that shows the total running time of the video (and its format—either NTSC, the North American standard, or PAL, the European standard).

Farther to the right, but still just above the Movie Track, the program identifies whatever is currently *selected*, if anything: the clip's name, duration, and even when it was filmed.

Dragging to the Movie Track

There's not much to using the Movie Track—just drag a clip from the Clips pane directly onto it. For your visual pleasure, iMovie shows you a ghosted, translucent image of the clip's first frame as you drag.

Here are a few tips for making the most of this Clips-pane-to-Movie-Track procedure:

- If you want a clip placed at the *end* of the clips in the Movie Track, drop it in the slice of gray, empty space at the right end.

Tip: It can be difficult to drag a clip to the end of the Timeline Viewer, because no gray gap appears there. Depending on the mood of the technology gods, a gap may appear when your cursor actually approaches the right end of the display, making the existing clips scoot leftward to make room. But sometimes that doesn't happen, and you must switch to the Clip Viewer view to tack a clip onto the end.

- If you want to put it *between* two clips on the Movie Track, drag your cursor between those clips, and watch as iMovie makes room by shoving existing clips to the right.
- You can also drag clips from the Clip Viewer *back* onto the Clips pane. You can take advantage of this feature whenever you decide that a sequence of clips isn't quite working, and you're going to postpone placing them into the movie.

Tip: Even though you can't drag clips from the Timeline Viewer to the Clips pane, you can achieve the same effect by cutting and pasting them.

- In the Clip Viewer, you can rearrange clips by dragging their icons horizontally. Once again, iMovie makes room between existing clips when your cursor passes between them.
- In the Timeline Viewer, you can drag a clip only one way: to the right. When you do so, iMovie creates a pure black "clip," as described on page 288.

Dragging Several Clips Simultaneously

You don't have to drag one clip at a time; it's often more efficient to drag several clips simultaneously. For example, you might arrange several clips on your Clips pane into a mini-sequence that you then drop into your Clip Viewer as a unit.

To highlight several clips in your Clips pane, press Shift as you click them in sequence, or ⌘-click to select nonadjacent ones, or drag-select them, as described earlier in this chapter. Each clip turns blue to indicate that it's selected. Now drag any *one* of them and watch the others go along for the ride.

Tip: As you're building your film on the Movie Track, think in terms of *sequences* of shots. By Shift-clicking, you can select, say, six or seven clips that constitute one finished sequence, and drag it (or cut and paste it) into a new location in the Movie Track to suit your artistic intentions.

That's an especially terrific tactic since the *sequence of your Shift-clicking* determines the order of the clips when they get dumped onto the Movie Track. You now have a convenient way to pluck the best clips out of your video toolbox, no matter where they sit at the moment, and then plunk them onto the Movie Track, already in the proper sequence.

You can drag multiple clips simultaneously from the Clip Viewer back up to the Clips pane, too, with even more flexibility. If you click the first one in the chain, and then Shift-click the last one, the two you clicked, and all the clips between them, are now all highlighted. (This works exactly as it does in a Finder list-view window.)

Tip: At this point, you can ⌘-click a clip to remove it from the selection, if you like. And also like the corresponding trick in the Finder, you ⌘-click a stray clip to add it to a Shift-clicked group.

Finally, drag any one of the selected icons up to the Clips pane.

Copying and Pasting Clips

Dragging isn't the only way to move footage around in iMovie; the Copy, Cut, and Paste commands can be more convenient, if only because you don't need the mouse.

For example, you can move a clip from the Clips pane to the Clip Viewer by clicking it, pressing ⌘-X, clicking the Clip Viewer, and then pressing ⌘-V. (You can also *copy* the clip by beginning that sequence with ⌘-C instead.) You can move clips around within the Movie Track in the same way.

Now, in a word processor, pasting can be dangerous: If you're not careful, pasting may *replace* some text that's already in the document. In iMovie, you have no such worries. The Paste command never pastes over anything; it only inserts new clips.

Tip: You can't use Cut, Copy, and Paste to move clips between project files—only within a project. Be especially careful with Cut: If you cut a clip out of a project, thinking that you'll paste it into another one, saving and closing the first file means that you lose the clip forever.

You may wonder how you're supposed to know where your cut or copied footage will appear when pasted. After all, there's no blinking insertion point to tell you.

The scheme is actually fairly simple:

- If there's a highlighted clip in the Clips pane or the Movie Track, the pasted clips appear immediately to the *right* of the selected clip. iMovie 4 shoves all other clips to the right to make room for the new arrival. The point is that it's always a good idea to click a clip before pasting to show iMovie *where* to paste.

- If no clip is highlighted anywhere, iMovie pastes the cut or copied clips in the Movie Track just to the right of whichever clip contains the Playhead.

Playing Clips Backward

When you hear that iMovie can play clips backward, you might assume that this feature is a gimmick that's primarily useful for applying to footage of people jumping into swimming pools or jumping off of walls. To be sure, iMovie does a fine job of creating these comic effects, even if their novelty does wear off quickly.

But reverse motion can be useful in much less obvious situations—cases where your original footage needs some help. For example, you can use this feature to create a zoom out when all you filmed was a zoom in, or a pan to the right when you shot a pan to the left. You can make your star's head turn away from the camera instead of toward it. Even reversing the playback of a slow-motion eye blink can make all the difference in the emotional impact of a certain shot.

To make a clip play backwards, select it anywhere—in the Clips pane, Clip Viewer, or Timeline Viewer. Choose Advanced→Reverse Clip Direction (⌘-R), or Control-click the clip, and from the shortcut menu, choose Reverse Clip Direction.

The video in a reverse-motion clip plays back beautifully; even the audio gets reversed, offering hours of fun to the kind of people who look for secret messages in Beatles albums. (Of course, you can always turn off the clip's sound, if that backward-audio effect isn't what you want; see page 352.)

Note: You can apply the Reverse Clip Direction command to only one clip at a time.

To help you remember that you've reversed a clip, iMovie stamps it with a left-pointing arrow, as shown in Figure 14-8.

Figure 14-8:
The tiny black symbols at the upper-right corner of a clip remind you that you've messed with its playback speed or direction, as indicated by these clips' names. (Anyone else think it's strange that the fast- and slow-motion symbols aren't perfect mirror images?)

Tricks of the Timeline Viewer

Everything you've read in the preceding pages has to do with the Movie Track in general. Most of the features described so far are available in either of the Movie Track's incarnations—the Clip Viewer or the Timeline Viewer.

But the Timeline Viewer is more than just another pretty interface. It's far more useful (and complex) than the Clip Viewer.

Many of the Timeline's super powers have to do with audio. Soundtracks, narration, music tracks, and sound effects all appear here as horizontal colored bars that play simultaneously with your video. You can read about these features in Chapter 17.

Some of the Timeline's features, however, are useful for everyday video editing—that is, if you consider playing footage in slow or fast motion everyday effects.

Zooming

The Timeline Viewer has a scroll bar, whose handle appears to be made of blue tooth gel, that lets you bring different parts of your movie into view. But depending on the length and complexity of your movie, you may wish you could zoom in for a more detailed view, or zoom out for a bird's-eye view of the whole project.

That's the purpose of the slider shown at lower left in Figure 14-7. It adjusts the relative sizes of the bars that represent your clips.

If you drag the slider handle all the way to the left, iMovie shows the entire movie in a single screen, without your having to scroll. The clip bars may be almost microscopic—if it's a long movie with short scenes, you may not even be able to see the thumbnail picture on each—but at least you get a sense of the whole.

As you drag the slider handle to the right, your clip bars expand in real time, widening to show you more detail. Finally, if the handle is all the way at the right side of the slider, a single second of video fills about two inches of the Timeline Viewer. You've zoomed in 50 times!

There's no one best setting for the zoom level. You should adjust it constantly as you work, pulling back when you need to figure out why some sound effects are firing at the wrong moment, zooming in when you want to make fine adjustments to the sound volume in mid-clip, and so on.

Sliding for Blackness

You can drag a clip in the Timeline Viewer only to the right. When you do so, you introduce a gap between the clip and the one to its left; iMovie automatically fills the gap with blackness and silence.

Tip: For greater precision, hold down the Control key and tap the arrow keys to move a clip right or left, making a wider or narrower black clip.

WORKAROUND WORKSHOP

Fast, Slow, Reverse Motion—and Transitions

If you change a clip's speed or direction, as described on these pages, iMovie doesn't bat an eye. In fact, it creates these effects instantaneously, without making you wait for any kind of rendering or processing.

If you've already placed the clip into the Movie Track and added transitions (see Chapter 15), however, the dialog box shown here pops up every time you change a clip's speed or direction. The point is clear: The crossfade into the next (or previous) clip will have to be updated, too. Otherwise, it won't match the clip's new speed or direction.

Unfortunately, this dialog box doesn't give you much of a

choice. If you click OK, iMovie proceeds to re-render the transition. If you click Cancel, iMovie ignores your request to change the clip's speed or direction. If you turn on Don't Ask Again, then iMovie will, henceforth, *always* re-render affected transitions—without showing the dialog box pictured here—when you adjust a clip's speed or direction.

None of these options, in other words, means "Please change the clip's speed or direction, but don't worry about the transition; just get rid of it." If that's what you want, do it manually by clicking Cancel, clicking the transition icon, deleting it, and then adjusting the clip's speed or direction all over again.

You can turn this gap into a bona fide, clickable black clip in either of two ways:

- Flip back to the Clip Viewer. You'll see that iMovie has actually created a new clip, represented by its own icon in the Clip Viewer, called Black.

- Position the Playhead anywhere inside the empty space (in the Timeline Viewer) and choose Advanced→Create Color Clip.

Either way, you wind up with a new clip that's black and silent.

What you do with this gap is your business. You can leave it black, creating an effective "bookend" between scenes. You can switch to the Clip Viewer and drag the black clip up onto your Clips pane for future reuse. You can precisely fill it with video from elsewhere in your project. Or you can change its color, as described next.

Note: If there's a transition to the left of a clip (Chapter 15), you can't drag the clip to the right.

Colorizing a Black Clip

It's hard to imagine that there was a groundswell of video editors clamoring for Apple to enhance its black-clip feature by letting them change its color. Yet there it is, a new command in iMovie 4's Advanced menu: Create Color Clip. (The same command appears in the shortcut menu when you Control-click a black clip.)

Turning a black clip into a colored clip is a handy way to create a colored background for some titles or credits, for example. See Figure 14-9 for the secret.

Figure 14-9:
When you double-click a black clip in the Movie Track, this dialog box appears. (Other ways to get here: Control-click a clip and choose Show Info from the shortcut menu, or click a clip and choose File→Show Info.)

Click Color to open the Color Picker dialog box, where you can choose the color you want (page 177). Note, too, that the Duration box here also lets you adjust the length of your color clip with frame-by-frame precision.

Slow Motion, Fast Motion

Slow motion is extremely effective when you're going for an emotional, nostalgic, warm feeling, especially when you delete the original soundtrack and replace it with music (see Chapter 17). On the more pragmatic side, it's also useful when analyzing your tennis swing, golf stroke, or sleight-of-hand technique.

Fast motion is generally useful only for comic effects—kids wrasslin' on the living-room floor is a sure winner—but can also help with time-lapse effects, as described on the facing page.

When you click a clip in the Timeline Viewer, the Rabbit/Turtle slider at the bottom edge of the Timeline Viewer lights up (shown at the bottom edge in Figure 14-7). You can drag this slider to the left or right to make the clip play faster or slower.

The four Faster notches on the slider (toward the rabbit icon) make your clip play two, three, four, or five times its original speed. The four Slower notches make it take two, three, four, or five times as long to play. Unfortunately, you can't make a clip play just *slightly* faster; you can park the little blue handle only on the slider notches, not anywhere between.

When you adjust this slider, a few things happen:

- The clip's blue bar grows or shrinks in the Timeline to indicate its new duration.

- A special icon appears in the corner of the clip in the Clips pane or Clip Viewer, indicating that you've toyed with its speed (see Figure 14-7). This symbol remains on the clip even if you drag it back to the Clips pane.

- iMovie speeds up and slows down the sound to match the video. Sped-up clips take on an "Alvin and the Chipmunks" quality, as though you're fast-forwarding through a tape; slowed-down clips sound like the dying computer HAL in *2001: A Space Odyssey.*

Tip: If the distortion of slow- or fast-motion audio bothers you, you may find it wise to split the audio from the video *before* applying a slow- or fast-motion effect, so that the sound will be unaffected (see page 606). Of course, the sound will no longer match the length of the video clip, but you may be able to solve this by cropping some of the audio or video.

Bookmarks

Navigating complex movies—or even simple ones—is a lot easier in iMovie 4, thanks to the new Bookmarks feature.

WORKAROUND WORKSHOP

The Time-Lapse Trick

I want to speed up my banana-slug footage beyond the scope of the speed slider—really fast. How can I do it?

The following technique involves a bit more effort than most iMovie projects. But as long as the camcorder was on a tripod during the initial filming, here's a great way to create true time-lapse movies:

Crank up the clip speed to its highest setting, and then export the clip to tape on your camera (see Chapter 19).

Then reimport the same clip into iMovie, which considers the reimported clip to be at "normal" speed. Use the speed slider again—and repeat the whole procedure as necessary—until you get the extreme speed changes you want.

It works like this: Position the Playhead at an important spot in the movie, and then choose Bookmarks→Add Bookmark (or just press ⌘-B, which is a lot quicker). iMovie responds by placing a tiny green diamond at that spot on the ruler (you can see a couple of them in Figure 14-10). Bookmarks are visible only in Timeline Viewer mode.

Figure 14-10:
Bookmarks clamp onto specific spots on the Timeline, not to specific spots in a clip. When you drag a clip, therefore, the bookmark remains right where it was. As a result, you can bookmark a certain "hit" in the soundtrack and then fiddle with the video, dragging clips into alignment with the bookmark until you find the perfect visual jolt to go with the audio burst.

Bookmarks

You'll see the real value of these markers once you've added a few of them to your movie. Now you can:

- Leap from one marker to the next using the Previous Bookmark and Bookmark commands (⌘-[and ⌘-], respectively).

- Align the Playhead with a bookmark by dragging it. You'll feel it—and even hear it—snap against the bookmark, assuming you've turned on Timeline Snapping (in iMovie→Preferences).

- Remove an individual bookmark by clicking it and then choosing Bookmarks→ Delete Bookmark. Banish all of them at once by choosing Bookmarks→Delete All Bookmarks.

Note: You can't move a bookmark once you've placed it. If you try to click its diamond, the Playhead jumps to the spot and covers up the bookmark, preventing you from dragging. Deleting the bookmark and installing a new one is your only alternative.

Playing the Movie Track

The Monitor window isn't limited to playing clips; it can also play the Movie Track. That's handy, because one of iMovie's best features is its ability to show your movie-in-progress whenever you like, without having to *compile* or *render* anything, as you sometimes do in more expensive editing programs.

Playing the Whole Movie

To play back your *entire* Movie Track, make sure that no clip is selected in the Clips pane. You can accomplish this feat in any of several ways:

- Click anywhere on the iMovie window except on a clip.

- Choose Edit→Select None, or press Shift-⌘-A.

- Press the Home key, which in iMovie means "Rewind to beginning." As a timesaving bonus, the Home key *also* deselects all clips, as though it knows that you want to play back the entire Clip Viewer now.

Tip: On recent desktop Macs, the Home key is above the number keypad. On recent laptop Macs, you simulate the Home key by holding down the Fn key (in the lower-left corner of the keyboard) and tapping the left-arrow key.

- Click the Home *button,* which is beneath the Monitor window just to the left of the Play button. Once again, iMovie deselects all clips in the process of rewinding.

You can tell at a glance when you've succeeded in preparing the Movie Track for playback by the appearance of subdivisions in the Scrubber bar (see Figure 14-11). When you tap the Space bar, iMovie plays your movie starting from the location indicated by the Playhead in the Scrubber bar. (If you press Home, you play the movie from the beginning.) iMovie plays one clip after another, seamlessly, from left to right as they appear in the Clip Viewer.

Playing your movie back is the best way to get a feeling for how your clips are working together. You may discover that, in the context of the whole movie, some are too long, too short, in the wrong order, and so on.

Figure 14-11:
When the Movie Track is ready to play, the Scrubber bar shows many different segments, one for each clip. (The segments' relative lengths indicate the lengths of the clips.) Feel free to use all of the navigating and editing tricks described in this chapter: pressing the arrow keys, splitting or trimming clips, and so on.

Playing a Segment of the Movie

You don't have to play the entire Movie Track. You can play only a chunk of it by first selecting only the clips you want (and transition icons, as described in Chapter 15). To do that, click the first clip you want to play, and then Shift-click the final one.

Now click the Play button or press the Space bar; iMovie plays only the clips you highlighted.

While the Movie's Playing

As the Movie Track plays, three simultaneous indicators show your position in the film. First, of course, the Playhead slides along the subdivided-looking Scrubber bar.

If the Timeline Viewer is visible, a duplicate Playhead slides along *it*. If the Clip Viewer is visible, on the other hand, a bright red, inverted T cursor slides along the faces of the clips themselves, which lets you know at a glance which clip you're seeing in the Monitor window—and *how much* of it you've seen (see Figure 14-12). You can't drag this cursor like a true scroll bar handle; it's purely an indicator.

Figure 14-12:
Because every clip icon is the same size, but not every clip is the same length, the T indicator speeds up or slows down as it arrives at the left edge of each clip. (You can see it in the center clip here, approaching the right side of the frame.)

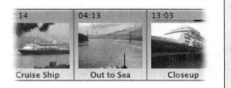

While the movie is playing, you can take control in several ways:

- Use the playback controls beneath the Monitor window (or their keystroke equivalents) to pause, stop, rewind, and so on.
- Navigate the whole movie by clicking in the Scrubber bar or dragging the Playhead, exactly as when navigating a clip.
- Adjust the volume by pressing the up-arrow or down-arrow key.
- Jump into Play Full Screen mode by clicking the Play Full Screen button.
- Add a bookmark by pressing ⌘-B.
- Stop the playback by pressing the Space bar.
- Stop the playback *and* rewind to the beginning by pressing the Home key.

Editing Clips in the Movie Track

Fortunately, all of the editing tricks for trimming and splitting clips described in this chapter also work in the Movie Track. In other words, just because you see the segmented Scrubber bar (Figure 14-4) doesn't mean you can't click below it to produce the triangle handles, or click above it in readiness to use the Split Clip at Playhead command.

You can also perform many of the same clip-editing operations that you read about in their Clips pane context, earlier in this chapter. For example, you can rename a clip, delete it from the project, or use the Edit menu commands on it, exactly as you operate on Clips pane clips.

Full-Screen Playback Mode

Whenever you're tempted to play your movie-in-progress, consider clicking the Play Full Screen button (the darkened triangle to the right of the round Play button). It makes the playback—even if it's already underway—fill the entire computer screen.

Tip: Remember that iMovie 4 lets you select nonconsecutive clips in the Timeline Viewer. You could, for example, select only clips 1, 4, 8, and 11 (by ⌘-clicking them).

In full-screen playback, iMovie even *plays* only the selected clips, even if that means skipping over some of the clips in your Movie Track. That's a huge advantage when you're experimenting with different sequences of clips—for example, when you want to show people a certain sequence with and without an intervening shot in hopes of asking their opinion.

To interrupt the movie showing, click the mouse or press any key on the keyboard. (The usual Macintosh "cancel" keystroke, ⌘-period, ironically, *doesn't* work in this context.)

Note: The quality of the full-screen playback still isn't the same pristine, crystal clear playback you'll get when you transfer your finished movie back to your camcorder for TV playback. In fact, it's little more than a blown-up version of what you see in the Monitor window while editing your movie. If it's grainy there, it's enlarged-grainy in full-screen playback.

Transitions and Special Effects

This chapter is about two iMovie tools—Transitions and Effects—that can make your raw footage look even better than it is. Both of these tools are represented by buttons on the Clips/Effects/Sound panel that occupies the right side of your screen. This chapter covers both of these powerful moviemaking techniques.

About Transitions

What happens when one clip ends and the next one begins? In about 99.99 percent of all movies, music videos, and commercials—and in 100 percent of camcorder movies before the Macintosh era—you get a *cut*. That's the technical term for "nothing special happens at all." One scene ends, and the next one begins immediately.

Professional film and video editors, however, have at their disposal a wide range of *transitions*—special effects that smooth the juncture between one clip and the next. For example, the world's most popular transition is the *crossfade* or *dissolve,* in which the end of one clip gradually fades away as the next one fades in (see Figure 15-1). The crossfade is so popular because it's so effective. It gives a feeling of softness and

Figure 15-1:
The world's most popular and effective transition effect: a cross dissolve.

grace to the transition, and yet it's so subtle that the viewer might not even be conscious of its presence.

Like all DV editing programs, iMovie offers a long list of transitions, of which crossfades are only the beginning. But unlike other DV editing software, iMovie makes adding such effects incredibly easy, and the results look awesomely assured and professional.

When to Use Transitions

When you begin to polish your movie by adding transitions, consider these questions:

- **Does it really need a transition?** Sometimes a simple cut is the most effective transition from one shot to the next. Remember, the crossfade lends a feeling of softness and smoothness to the movie, but is that really what you want? If it's a sweet video of your kids growing up over time, absolutely yes. But if it's a hard-hitting issue documentary, then probably not, as those soft edges would dull the impact of your footage.

  Remember, too, that transitions often suggest the *passage of time*. In movies and commercials, consecutive shots in the same scene never include such effects. Plain old cuts tell the viewer that one shot is following the next in real time. But suppose one scene ends with the beleaguered hero saying, "Well, at least I still have my job at the law firm!"...and the next shot shows him operating a lemonade stand. (Now *that's* comedy!) In this case, a transition would be especially effective, because it would tell the audience that we've just jumped a couple of days.

  In other words, learning to have taste in transitions is a lot like learning to have taste in using your camcorder's zoom controls. Use transitions *for a reason*.

- **Is it consistent?** Once you've chosen a transition-effect style for your movie, stick to that transition style for the entire film (unless, as always, you have an artistic reason to do otherwise). Using one consistent style of effect lends unity to your work.

- **Which effect is most appropriate?** As noted earlier, the crossfade is almost always the least intrusive, most effective, and best-looking transition. But each of the other iMovie transitions can be appropriate in certain situations. For example, the Radial wipe, which looks like the hand of a clock wiping around the screen, replacing the old scene with the new one as it goes, can be a useful passage-of-time or meanwhile-back-at-the-ranch effect.

Tip: The Fade In and Fade Out "transitions" in iMovie are exempt from the stern advice above. Use a Fade In at the beginning of *every* movie, if you like, and a Fade Out at the end. Doing so adds a professional feeling to your film, but it's so subtle, your audience will notice it subconsciously, if at all.

Creating a Transition

To see the list of transitions iMovie offers, click the Trans button, as shown in Figure 15-2. The Clips pane disappears, only to be replaced, in the blink of an eye, by a completely different set of controls.

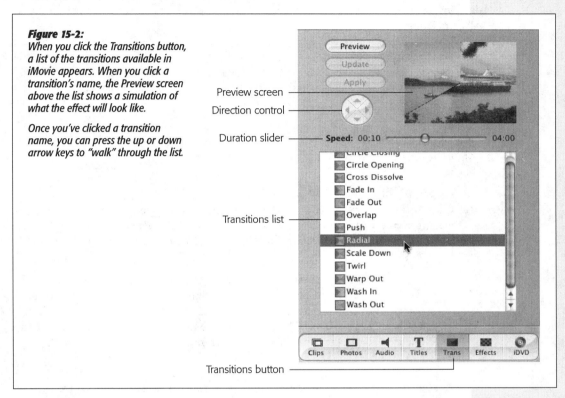

Figure 15-2:
When you click the Transitions button, a list of the transitions available in iMovie appears. When you click a transition's name, the Preview screen above the list shows a simulation of what the effect will look like.

Once you've clicked a transition name, you can press the up or down arrow keys to "walk" through the list.

Preview screen

Direction control

Duration slider

Transitions list

Transitions button

Previewing the Effect

Like most video editing software, iMovie has to do a lot of computation to produce transitions, so it can't show you an instantaneous, full-speed, full-smoothness preview. Therefore, iMovie offers a choice of lower-quality (but instantaneous) previews:

- **The Preview window.** For a very small preview, shown in the tiny screen above the Transitions list, just click the name of a transition.

   This preview plays in real time, endeavoring to make transition preview last exactly as long as the finished transition will. On slower Macs, you don't see all the frames in this little Preview window, making the transition appear jerky, but rest assured that the finished transition will be extremely smooth.

- **The Monitor window.** To see a preview in a much larger format—big enough to fill the Monitor window—click the Preview button.

Either way, you can drag the Speed slider just above the list to experiment with the length of each transition as you're previewing it. The numbers on this slider—*00:10* (ten frames) at the left side, *04:00* (four seconds) at the right side—let you know the least and greatest amount of time that a transition can last. When you release the slider, you see another quick preview in the screen above it, and you also see, in the lower-right corner of the Preview screen, the actual length of the transition you've specified.

Tip: The program doesn't yet know which clips you'll want to "transish." Therefore, iMovie uses, for the purposes of this preview, whichever clip is currently highlighted in the Movie Track, into which it crossfades from the previous clip. If the very first clip is highlighted, iMovie demonstrates by transitioning that clip into the second clip.

If no clip is highlighted, iMovie is smart enough to seek out the "clip boundary" that's closest to the Playhead's current position. It uses the clips on both sides of that boundary for the preview—if it's a two-clip transition. If it's a one-clip transition, iMovie uses the clip to the right or left.

Applying the Effect and Rendering

Once you've selected an effect and dragged the slider to specify how much time you want it to take, you can place it into the Movie Track (Clip Viewer or Timeline Viewer) by dragging the *name or icon* of the effect out of the transitions list and down onto the Movie Track.

Either way, drag until your cursor is between the two clips that you want joined by this transition; iMovie pushes the right-hand clips out of the way to make room. (Most transitions must go *between* two clips, and so they can't go at the beginning or end of your Movie Track. The exceptions are the Fade and Wash effects.) Then a slide-like icon (or, in the Timeline, triangle-branded bar) appears between the clips, as shown in Figure 15-3.

Tip: The tiny triangles on a transition icon or bar let you know what kind of transition it is. A pair of inward-facing triangles is a standard transition that melds the end of one clip with the beginning of the next. A single, right-facing triangle indicates a transition that applies to the *beginning* of a clip, such as a fade-in from black (or wash-in from white). A single, left-facing triangle indicates a transition that applies to the *end* of a clip (such as a fade or wash *out*).

Almost immediately, a tiny red line begins to crawl, progress-bar-like, along the lower edge of this icon (see Figure 15-3). In the terminology of DV editors everywhere, the Mac has begun to *render* this transition—to perform the thousands of individual calculations necessary to blend the outgoing clip into the incoming, pixel by pixel, frame by frame.

Fortunately, iMovie lets you *continue working* as this rendering takes place. You can work on the other pieces of your movie, import new footage from your camcorder, or even *play* your movie while transitions are still rendering. (If the transitions haven't finished rendering, iMovie shows you its preview version.)

In fact, you can even switch out of iMovie to work in other Mac programs. (This last trick makes the rendering even slower, but at least it's in the background. You can check your email or work on your screenplay in the meantime.)

You can even make iMovie render several transition effects simultaneously. (Experiment to find out how many. Beyond a handful, the program may slow down considerably.)

Figure 15-3:

Top: In the Clip Viewer, a transition shows up as a slide-like icon.

Bottom: In the Timeline Viewer, you get a bar whose width indicates its duration. Each transition has its own red progress bar that creeps along the bottom edge of the icon. After the clip has been fully rendered, this added strip beneath the icon disappears, and the transition is ready to play. (The Movie Track's top edge identifies the transition type and its duration when the transition icon is highlighted.)

Transition type and duration ⌐ Transition icon

Video Selection: Cross Dissolve Time: 01:20

Red progress bar (Clip Viewer)

Red progress bar (Timeline Viewer)

When rendering is complete

When the rendering is complete, you can look over the result very easily.

- To watch just the transition, click the transition's icon or bar in the Movie Track (it sprouts a pale aqua outline to show that it's highlighted) and then press the Space bar.

- To watch the transition *and* the clips that it joins together, Shift-click the two clips in question. Doing so also highlights the transition between them. Press the Space bar to play the three clips you've highlighted.

- It's a good idea to watch your transition by "rewinding" a few seconds into the preceding footage, so that you get a sense of how the effect fits in the context of the existing footage. To give yourself some of this "preroll," choose Edit→Select None (or just click anywhere but on a clip) to deselect all the clips. Then click a spot on the Scrubber bar somewhere in the clip before the transition, and press the Space bar to play the movie from that point.

- If you don't care for what you've done, choose Edit→Undo.

• If it's too late for the Undo command, you can return to the transition at any time, highlight its icon, and press the Delete key. Your original clips return instantly, exactly as they were before you added the transition.

How Transitions Affect the Length of Your Movie

As you can see by the example in Figure 15-4, most transitions make your movie shorter. To superimpose the ends of two adjacent clips, iMovie is forced to slide the right-hand clip leftward, making the overall movie end sooner.

Under most circumstances, there's nothing wrong with that. After all, that's why you wisely avoided trimming off *all* of the excess "leader" and "trailer" footage (known as *trim handles*) from the ends of your clips. By leaving trim handles on each clip—which will be sacrificed to the transition—you'll have some fade-in or fade-out footage to play with.

Sometimes, however, having your overall project shortened is a serious problem, especially when you've been "cutting to sound," or synchronizing your footage to an existing music track, as described in Chapter 17. Suppose you've spent hours putting your clips into the Movie Track, carefully trimming them so that they perfectly match the soundtrack. And now, as a final touch, you decide to put in transitions. Clearly, having these transitions slide all of your clips to the left would result in chaos, throwing off the synchronization work you had done.

Now you can appreciate the importance of iMovie's Advanced→Lock Audio Clip at Playhead command, which marries a piece of music or sound to a particular spot in the video. If all of your added music and sound elements are attached in this way, adding transitions won't disturb their synchronization. See page 356 for details on locking audio into position.

Tip: Certain transitions, including Overlap, Fade In, Fade Out, Wash In, and Wash Out, don't shorten the movie. As described at the end of this chapter, each of these four special transitions affects only *one* clip, not two. They're meant to begin or end your movie, fading in or out from black or white.

How Transitions Chop Up Clips

After your transition has been rendered, you'll notice something peculiar about your Scrubber bar: The transition has now become, in effect, a clip of its own. (If you switch to the Finder and look in your project folder's Media folder, you'll even see the newly created clip file represented there, bearing the name of the transition you applied.)

If you click the first clip and play it, you'll find that the playback now stops sooner than it once did—just where the transition takes over. Likewise, the clip that follows the transition has also had frames shaven away at the front end. Both clips, in other words, have sacrificed a second or two to the newly created transition/clip between them. Figure 15-4 illustrates this phenomenon.

Tip: You can rename a transition icon, if it helps you remember what you were thinking when you created it. To do so, double-click its icon or bar. The Clip Info dialog box appears, in which you can change the name the transition icon displays in your Movie Track.

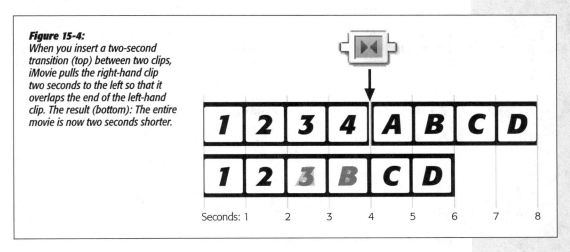

Figure 15-4:
When you insert a two-second transition (top) between two clips, iMovie pulls the right-hand clip two seconds to the left so that it overlaps the end of the left-hand clip. The result (bottom): The entire movie is now two seconds shorter.

Editing the Transition

You can edit the transition in several ways: You can change its length, its type, its direction (certain effects only), or all three. To do so, click the transition icon, and then click the Trans button (if the Transitions pane isn't already open). You can now adjust the Speed slider, click another transition in the list, or both. (You may also be able to change the direction of the effect, depending on the transition; at this writing, the Push effect is the only one that offers this option.)

When you click Update—a button that's available *only* when a transition icon is highlighted in the Movie Track—iMovie automatically re-renders the transition.

Deleting a Transition

If you decide that you don't need a transition effect between two clips after all, you can delete it just as you would delete any Movie Track clip: by clicking it once and then pressing the Delete key on your keyboard (or by choosing Edit→Clear). Deleting a transition clip does more than eliminate the icon—it also restores the clips on either side to their original conditions. (If you change your mind, Edit→Undo Clear brings back the transition.)

Transition Error Messages

Transitions can be fussy. They like plenty of clip footage to chew on, and once they've begun rendering, they like to be left alone. Here are some of the error messages you may encounter when working with transitions.

When you delete a clip

For example, if, in the process of editing your movie, you delete a clip from the Movie Track that's part of a transition, a message appears that says: "This action will invalidate at least one transition in the project. Invalid transitions will be deleted from the project. Do you want to proceed?"

iMovie is simply telling you that if you delete the clip, you'll also delete the transition attached to it (which is probably just what you'd expect). Click OK. If you first click "Don't Ask Me Again," iMovie will henceforth delete such clips without asking your permission.

When the transition is longer than the clip

If you try to add a five-second crossfade between two three-second clips, iMovie throws up its hands with various similarly worded error messages. In all cases, the point is clear: The two clips on either side of a transition must *each* be longer than the transition itself.

Put another way, iMovie can't make your transition stretch across more than two clips (or more than one clip, in the case of the Fade and Wash effects).

When you quit while rendering

Creating transitions requires a great deal of iMovie's concentration. If you try to save your project, close it, or empty its Trash, you'll be advised to wait until the rendering is over.

When you rejigger the clip

If you change a clip's playback speed after you've attached a transition to it—for example, if you try to make the clip play faster, slower, in reverse, or with an iMovie special effect applied—iMovie has to recompute the transition to match, as yet another message will tell you.

Transitions: The iMovie Catalog

Here, for your reference, is a quick list of the built-in transitions, and what editing circumstances might call for it. In each example, "first clip" refers to the clip that comes before the transition, and "second clip" is the clip that follows.

Circle Closing

This effect, called *iris close* or *iris in* in professional editing programs, is a holdover from the silent film days, when, in the days before zoom lenses, directors used the effect to highlight a detail in a scene.

It creates an ever-closing circle with the first clip inside and the second clip outside. It's useful at the end of the movie, when the second clip is solid black and the subject of the first clip is centered in the frame. In that setup, the movie ends with an ever-shrinking picture that fades away to a little dot. (If the subject in the center waves goodbye just before being blinked out of view, this trick is especially effective.)

Circle Opening

This effect is much like Circle Closing, except it's been turned inside out. Now the circle grows from the center of the first clip, with the second clip playing inside it, and expands until it fills the frame. (This effect is also called *iris open* or *iris out.*)

Cross Dissolve

The crossfade, or dissolve, is the world's most popular and effective transition. The first clip gradually disappears, superimposed on the beginning of the second clip, which fades in. If you must use a transition at all, you can't go wrong with this one.

Tip: You can use a very short cross dissolve to create what editors call a "soft cut." When the footage would jump too abruptly if you made a regular cut, put in a ten-frame cross dissolve, which makes the junction of clips *slightly* smoother than just cutting. Soft cuts are very common in interviews where the editors have deleted sections from a continuous shot of a person talking.

Fade In

Use this effect at the beginning of your movie, or the beginning of a scene that begins in a new place or time. Unlike most transition effects, this one makes no attempt to smooth the transition between two clips. The fade-in overlaps only the clip *to its right*, creating a fade-in from complete blackness.

This transition affects only the clip that follows it, so it doesn't shorten your movie or throw subsequent clips out of alignment, like genuine crossfade-style transitions.

Tip: In general, iMovie doesn't let you place one transition effect next to another. In other words, you can't transition into a transition.

The exceptions are the Fade (In and Out) and Wash (In and Out) transitions. Each of these affects only one clip, not two. By placing an In immediately after an Out, you create an elegant fade out, then in to the next shot—a very popular effect in movies and commercials.

Placing an Out just after an In isn't quite as useful, because it reveals only a fleeting glance of the footage in between. But when you're trying to represent somebody's life flashing before his eyes, this trick may be just the ticket.

Fade Out

This effect, conversely, is best used at the *end* of a movie, or at the end of a scene that requires a feeling of finality. Like its sister, the Fade In, this one doesn't involve two clips at all; it affects only the end of the clip to its left. As a result, it doesn't affect the length or synchronization of your movie.

It's worth noting, by the way, that a fade-out is almost always followed by a fade-*in*, or by the closing credits. You'll blast your audience's eyeballs if you fade out, sweetly and gracefully—and then cut directly into a bright new clip.

Both Fade In and Fade Out are very useful, and frequently used, effects. But iMovie offers you an elegant, graceful, smooth fade to blackness, and then, unfortunately, the movie ends abruptly, instead of *holding* on the black screen for a moment.

That behavior is easy to fix, however: Just add a few seconds of blackness after the fade. To do so, switch to the Timeline Viewer and create a pure black clip, as described on page 288. Switch to the Clip Viewer, cut the black clip to the Clipboard, and paste it at the end of the movie. Now iMovie will fade out to black—and hold on to that blackness.

Overlap

Overlap is almost exactly the same as the Cross Dissolve, described earlier. The sole difference: The outgoing clip freezes on its last frame as the new clip fades in. (In a Cross Dissolve, the action continues during the simultaneous fades.) As a result, the Overlap transition doesn't change the duration of your movie, which makes it a good choice for movies where you've spent a lot of time synchronizing audio and video. In those cases, a Cross Dissolve might knock things out of sync.

Push

In this transition, the first clip is shoved off the frame by the aggressive first frame of the second clip. This offbeat transition effect draws a lot of attention to itself, so use it extremely sparingly. For example, you could use it to simulate an old-style projector changing slides, or when filming a clever, self-aware documentary in which the host (who first appears in the second clip) "pushes" his way onto the screen.

When you select this transition in the list, the four directional arrows—which are dimmed for most transition types—become available. Click one to indicate how you want the incoming clip to push onscreen: up, down, to the left, or to the right.

Radial

You probably saw this one in a few movies of the 1970s. What looks like the sweep-second hand on a watch rotates around the screen, wiping away the first clip and revealing the second clip underneath. This transition suggests the passage of time even more than most transitions, clueing the audience in that the scene about to begin takes place in a new location or on a different day.

Scale Down

Scale Down, known to pro editors as the *picture zoom* effect, is a peculiar effect, whereby the end of the first clip simply shrinks away. Its rectangle gets smaller and smaller until it disappears, falling endlessly away into the beginning of the second clip, which lies beneath it. The rectangle seems to fly away into the upper-left corner of the second clip, not into dead center.

This kind of effect occasionally shows up on TV news, in documentaries, and so on, after you've been watching a closeup of some important document or photograph. By showing the closeup flying away from the camera, the film editor seems to say, "Enough of that. Meanwhile, back in real life..."

Warp In

This effect is very similar to Scale Down, except that as the first clip flies away, it seems to fold in on itself instead of remaining rectangular. That characteristic, combined with the fact that it flies away into dead center of the second clip's frame, makes it look as though the first clip is getting sucked out of the center of the picture by a giant video vacuum cleaner.

It's hard to think of *any* circumstance where this effect would feel natural, except when you're deliberately trying to be weird.

Warp Out

You might think that this effect would be the flip side of the Warp In effect, but it's quite different. This time, the second clip intrudes on the first by pushing its way, as an ever-growing sphere, into the frame. What's left of the first clip gets smashed outward, bizarrely distorting, until it's shoved off the outer edges of the picture.

Wash In, Wash Out

These two effects work exactly like Fade In and Fade Out, described earlier, with one big difference: They fade in from, and out to, *white* instead of black.

Tip: If you begin to feel hemmed in by Apple's selection of transitions, you can buy and download more from, for example, *www.geethree.com* and *www.virtix.com*. (Free samples are available at *www.apple. com/imovie*.)

Most of these products come with installers that put the plug-in files where they belong: in your Home→Library→iMovie→Plug-ins folder. Knowing where they live also makes it easy to remove them—which may come in handy in times of troubleshooting. Some people find that iMovie is more stable with fewer non-Apple plug-ins.

The Effects Pane

As noted in Chapter 14, iMovie makes it easy to play clips in slow motion, fast motion, or backward. But that's just the beginning; the Effects button summons a panel full of additional visual effects that you can apply directly to your footage. And if these don't satisfy your hunger for effects, other software companies have had a field day dreaming up new special effects that you can buy and install as plug-ins.

Some are designed to adjust the brightness, contrast, or color tints in less-than-perfect footage. Most, though, are designed to create actual special effects that simulate fog, rain, earthquakes, lightning, flashbulbs, and bleary-eyed bad LSD.

As with transitions, most of these are so out-there and distracting, you should use these only on special occasions.

Selecting the Footage

Before you apply an effect, specify which lucky region of footage you want to be affected:

- **One clip.** Click a clip in the Movie Track or Clips pane; the effect will apply to the entire clip.

- **Multiple clips.** If you highlight several clips in the Movie Track, your selected effect will apply to all of them, treating them as one giant clip. When you click the Apply button, you'll see multiple progress bars marching across the faces of the affected clips in the Movie Track. (Unfortunately, some effects, like the rocketing sparkler of Fairy Dust, aren't smart enough to continue across more than one clip. If you select several clips, the effect starts over at the beginning of each one.)

Tip: Don't forget that in iMovie 4, you can select several nonadjacent clips. At that point, you can apply an effect to all of them at once.

- **Part of a clip.** If you use the Scrubber bar's selection handles to highlight only a portion of a clip, iMovie will split the clips at the endpoints of the selection, and then apply the effect to the central clip. (iMovie can apply effects only to *entire* clips, which is why this automatic splitting takes place.)

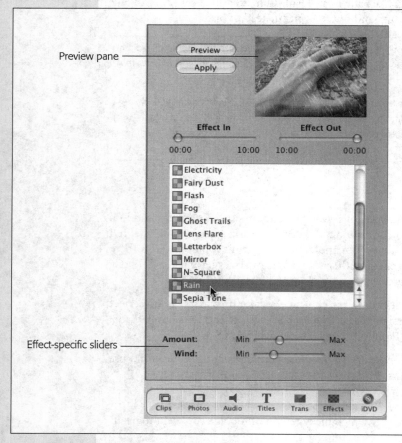

Figure 15-5:
Several of the effects in the Effects panel offer additional controls, which take the form of sliders beneath the list. You can drag the small blue handle of such sliders, or simply click anywhere in their track.

When it's not showing footage, the Preview pane shows numbers in the corners. They reflect the timings you've selected by dragging the Effect In and Out sliders.

The Effects Pane

- **Parts of multiple clips.** If you choose Edit→Select None, you can use the Scrubber bar's selection handles to enclose any stretch of clips (or portions of clips) you like. If necessary, iMovie will again split the end clips at the locations of your handles.

Surveying Your Options

Now click the Effects button. Portions of this panel (Figure 15-5) should look familiar. The list of effects, the Preview button, and the Preview pane all work exactly as they do for transitions. (For example, when you click an effect name, the small Preview pane shows a crude, jerky representation of what it will look like; if you click the Preview *button*, you see the same preview in the Monitor window.)

But you'll also find other controls that don't exist anywhere else in iMovie:

- **Effect In, Effect Out.** If you want the chosen effect to start and end exactly at the boundaries of your selection, leave these sliders at their zero points (the far left for Effect In, the far right for Effect Out).

  If you like, however, you can make these effects kick in (and kick out) gradually, after the clip has already begun (and before it has ended). That's the purpose of these two sliders: to give you control over when they begin or end.

  For example, if you drag the Effect In slider for a Black & White effect to 5:00, the clip will begin playing in full color. After playing for five seconds, however, the color will begin to leach out, leaving the rest of the clip to play in black-and-white (a useful effect if you're trying to depict someone slowly going color-blind). You can set the Effect In and Out points no more than ten seconds from the beginning or ending of a clip.

Tip: Here's how to make a knockout, professional-looking effect to open your film: Create a still clip from the first frame of a movie, as described on page 376. Split it in half. Convert the first half to black and white, then create a Cross Dissolve between it and the second half. The result: What appears to be a black-and-white photograph "coming to life" as it fades into color and then begins to play normally.

- **Effect-specific controls.** As you click the name of each effect in the list, additional sliders may appear above the Effects panel. They're described in the effect-by-effect descriptions that begin on page 309.

- **Apply.** When you click Apply, iMovie begins to render the selected clip—to perform the massive numbers of calculations necessary to bring each pixel into compliance with the effect you've specified. As with transitions, effect rendering telegraphs its progress with a subtle red line, a miniature progress bar that crawls from left to right beneath the selected clip (see Figure 15-6).

  Rendering effects works exactly like rendering transitions: You can continue working on other parts of your movie, but things can bog down if you've got several effects rendering at once. Actually, rendering effects takes much longer than rendering transitions, in part because you apply each effect to an entire clip instead of just the last couple of seconds. Press ⌘-period to cancel the rendering.

CHAPTER 15: TRANSITIONS AND SPECIAL EFFECTS

307

It's important to note, by the way, that iMovie actually applies the selected effect to a *duplicate* copy of the clip's DV file on your hard drive. iMovie creates the behind-the-scenes duplicate as a safety net for you. It gives you the option of removing or adjusting the effect at any time. (If you're curious, switch to the Finder; open your project folder, then its Media folder. Inside, you'll find a new clip called, for example, Earthquake 01, which represents the modified clip.)

So what happens to the original clip? iMovie puts it into your Project Trash. As long as you don't empty your trash, you can recover the original clip (and remove the effect) at any time.

Number of effects

Effect indicator

Progress bar

Figure 15-6:
The thin red progress bar lets you know how much longer you have to wait. You can tell at a glance that a clip has had an effect applied, thanks to the checkerboard brand in the upper right. And if there's a digit beside the checkerboard, you've applied more than one effect to the same clip.

Removing an Effect

If you click a clip and then press the Delete key, you're saying: "Throw away the effect. Bring back my original, unmodified clip." Much though it may feel like you're instructing iMovie to delete the *clip itself*, you're not. (You would have to press Delete a *second time* to achieve that purpose.)

In any case, when you delete an effect in this way, iMovie pulls your original footage out of the project Trash and reinstates it. That is, it does so *if* you haven't *emptied* the Trash (page 257). Remember that once you empty your Project Trash, you throw away your opportunity to adjust or remove effects forever.

Note: If you do empty the Trash, you'll notice something weird: The little Effect indicator shown in Figure 15-6 *vanishes* from all of your effects clips! That's because as far as iMovie is concerned, those effects *are* part of the original clips, married to them forever.

Adjusting an Effect

Despite what the iMovie online help says, there's no Update button on the Effects pane. To adjust the start time, stop time, or other parameters of a special effect, you must first delete the effect altogether, as described earlier, and then reapply it using new settings.

Superimposing Effects

It's perfectly possible to combine effects by applying first one, and then another. For example, after using the Black & White effect, you may want to use Brightness & Contrast control to adjust its gray tones. You can even apply a single effect repeatedly, intensifying its effect; for instance, you could apply Fairy Dust several times to make it appear as though multiple fireworks are going off. Or you could apply Rain twice at different intensities to add depth to your simulated deluge.

Once you've applied more than one effect to a certain clip, iMovie thoughtfully adds a "number-of-effects" number next to the effects symbol, as shown in Figure 15-6. When it comes time to *remove* some of your layered effects, you'll appreciate that indicator. It will keep you sane as you peel away one effect after another.

For example, suppose you're making a disaster movie. To one climactic clip, you've applied two Rains, three Earthquakes, an Electricity, and a pair of Fogs.

If you decide that perhaps you've laid it on a bit thick, you can click the clip and then start tapping the Delete key. With each tap, you remove one effect, in reverse chronological order, until only the original clip remains. (Be careful not to press Delete that last time; you'll remove the clip itself!)

Effects: The iMovie Catalog

iMovie comes with 18 built-in effects. The following list describes them all.

Adjust Colors

This powerful effect adjusts the actual color palette used in your clip footage. If your footage has an unfortunate greenish tint, you can color-correct it; if you're hoping for a sunset look, you can bring out the oranges and reds; if it's a sci-fi flick taking place on Uranus, you can make it look blue and spooky.

The special sliders for this effect affect the hue, saturation, and brightness of your footage. Hue, saturation, and brightness are cornerstones of color theory; you can read much more about them on the Web, or in books and articles about photo editing. In the meantime, here's a brief summary:

- **Hue Shift (Left—Right).** Adjusts the overall color tint of the clip. What iMovie is actually doing is rotating the hue around the hue circle, either to the left or the right. In practice, this effect doesn't do anything predictable to an image; you're meant to play with it until you find something you like.

- **Color (B&W—Vivid).** This slider lets you control the intensity of a color, or its *saturation*. If it's blue, you control *how* blue it is: increasing toward Vivid makes the blue more intense.

- **Lightness (Dark—Bright).** Use this slider to adjust the overall brightness or darkness of the *colors* in your clip. There's only a subtle difference between these effects and the Brightness/Contrast effect described below; this slider adjusts the brightness of the colors, rather than the overall brightness.

Aged Film

Here you've just spent $600 on a camcorder and a couple thou on a Macintosh, all in the name of attaining perfect purity of video—and then this effect comes along. It's designed to make a clip look like an old, flickering, dusty film, complete with horrible scratches along the celluloid.

Using the Exposure, Jitter, and Scratches sliders, you can control just how faded, shaky-in-the-projector, and scratched up the footage looks (Figure 15-7, top).

Combine this one with Black & White, described next, and you've got yourself something that looks authentically like a horribly preserved reel you dug up from somebody's attic.

Before

After

Figure 15-7:
Top: Modern cruise ship? No—thanks to the Aged Film effect, it's some doomed ocean liner from 1938.

Middle: Earthquake! (For a better simulation of what iMovie really does, shake this book rapidly in front of your face.) This effect looks really great when you adjust the Effect In and Effect Out sliders so that the shaking begins gradually and intensifies. (Better yet, apply the effect several times, to make the intensity of the shaking appear to fluctuate.)

Bottom: Four-year-old girl? No, it's She-Ra, mistress of the Electricity effect.

Black & White

This effect does one thing very well: It turns your clip into a black-and-white piece of footage, suitable for simulating security-camera footage or TV from the 1950s.

Brightness & Contrast

Footage that's too dark is one of the most common hallmarks of amateur camcorder work. If you're filming indoors without extra lights, you may as well accept the fact that your clip will be too dark.

The Brightness & Contrast controls can help, but they're no substitute for good lighting in the original footage. When you drag the Brightness and Contrast sliders in very small amounts, you may be able to rescue footage that's slightly murky or washed out. Dragging the sliders a lot, however, may make the too-dark footage grainy and weird-looking.

Tip: Using the Effect In and Out sliders, you can control which *parts* of the clip are affected by the Adjust Colors and Brightness & Contrast effects. If you need the colors or brightness to shift several times over the course of a clip, consider chopping up the clip into several smaller clips, each of which is an opportunity to reset the effect settings and timings.

Earthquake

Talk about an effect you'll use only rarely!

This one (Figure 15-7, middle) is designed to simulate *camera shake,* the jittery, shuddering, handheld, no-tripod, stabilizer-off look that you'd get if you felt the earth move under your feet, and felt the sky come tumblin' down. You can use the two sliders to specify *how* the earthquake is tossing your camera around: sideways or vertically, and to what degrees.

Electricity

Unlike most of the other effects, which apply equally everywhere in the video frame, this one (Figure 15-7, bottom) actually superimposes an image—in this case, a purplish, flickering bolt of lightning—onto any spot of the footage you want. You can use this one to great comic effect; when attached to the end of somebody's wand or walking stick, the electricity looks like it's shooting out. When attached to somebody's head or rear end, the electricity looks like it's zapping that hapless person.

You can probably figure out that the Rotate slider lets you change the lightning bolt's angle (CW = Clockwise, CCW = Counter-Clockwise). But what you may not realize is that you can *click* inside the Preview window to specify the landing (or starting) point of the sparkler. By using the rotation and position controls in combination, you have complete freedom in designing the placement of the zap within the frame. (Alas, you can't make the bolt move *during* a clip. It stays put, crackling away right in place, so it's primarily useful for adding to a tripod shot that you filmed expressly for the purpose of doctoring later in iMovie.)

Fairy Dust

Like Electricity, this effect is designed to superimpose a professional-looking sparkler effect on your footage. In this case, you get a shooting firework that follows a specified arc across the frame; the net effect is something like a burning fuse, except that the path, although visible in the Preview window for your reference, doesn't actually appear once you apply the effect.

Here again, you can click within the preview frame to position the arc, thereby adjusting the sparkler's trajectory. Use the Direction slider to specify whether the fire flies left to right across the frame, or right to left. (It really has no business being a slider. It has only two positions: left or right. Dragging the handle to an intermediate point does nothing.)

The Trail slider, meanwhile, governs the size of the sparkler.

Flash

This effect simulates flash bulbs going off. You won't have much call for this effect in everyday filmmaking; but when that day arrives that you're trying to depict a movie star arriving at opening night—or somebody getting electrocuted—iMovie stands ready.

- **Count (One—Max).** This slider controls how many flashes will go off in the scene. (The maximum number depends on your Speed slider setting and the length of the clip, but the most you'll get is about one every seven frames, or about four per second.)

- **Brightness (Min—Max).** Controls the intensity of each flash. For true flashbulb effects, you'll want the slider at, or close to, its Max. For storm lightning or nuclear-bomb-watching effects, use lower settings.

- **Speed (Fast—Slow).** Governs how far apart the flashes appear.

Tip: You can use this effect to create a convincing newsreel (or school science film) look. First, turn your clip into black-and-white using the Black & White effect. Now apply the Flash effect with the sliders set to Max, Min, and Fast, respectively.

Fog

You already knew that by letting you edit and add music to your movies, iMovie lets you fiddle with the emotional overtones of your own memories. What you may not have realized is that it also lets you retroactively change the weather.

The Fog effect creates a mist that seems to float in front of the camera lens. It's suitable for atmospheric effects, simulated fire or crash footage, comical hangover clips, and so on.

The Amount slider controls the opacity of the fog, the Wind slider governs how quickly it drifts, and the Color slider lets you specify the color.

Ghost Trails

This effect makes moving portions of the video leave behind "visual echoes." In addition to blurry-vision effects, it can also be handy when you're trying to depict a runner as a superhero with blinding speed.

On clips without much motion, this effect does nothing at all.

The sliders let you control the intensity of the effect:

- **Trail (Short—Long).** Governs the length of the ghost images that follow a rapidly moving object in your scene.

- **Steps (Small—Large).** Controls how closely the ghost image follows the moving object.

- **Opacity (Clear—Opaque).** Lets you specify the transparency of the ghost image.

Lens Flare

When you aim the camera toward the sun, sunshine can strike the anti-reflective coating on the inside of each lens, resulting in a reflection—a bright spot, or (on complex lens systems) a trail of bright spots—called lens flare.

Ordinarily, photographers try to avoid lens flare. But hey, as long as Apple is on a quest to let you deliberately make your footage look damaged (see Aged Film and Earthquake), why not?

Click within the Preview window to set the rotation point for the lens flare. Then use the Sweep slider to control how broadly the flare line sweeps across the frame, as happens when the camera moved during the shot. (If it did not, in fact, move, do your best to position the Sweep slider handle squarely in the middle of the slider to prevent the flare from moving at all.)

The Intensity slider adjusts the size of the primary sunshine blob. (You'll get it as soon as you try it.) Figure 15-8, top, shows the result.

Letterbox

This filter (Figure 15-8, middle) adds black letterbox bars above and below the frame, creating the look of movies (which have 16:9 proportions) as they sometimes appear when presented on a TV (which has 4:3 proportions). You may have seen this look on the Bravo channel, on a Woody Allen video, on some DVDs, or in artsy TV commercials.

The paradox, of course, is that your footage was *already* correctly shaped for a 4:3 TV screen. So to make it look as though the original was movie-shaped, iMovie has no choice but to *chop off* the top and bottom slices of your movie. It works, therefore, only when the subject matter is already vertically centered.

Of course, you can also use the Shift slider to nudge the original footage upward or downward in the gap between the black bars, or use the Size slider to make the bars themselves more or less intrusive (thinner or fatter).

Mirror

This completely freaky effect makes iMovie split the video picture down the middle—horizontally, vertically, or both (in quadrants). It then fills the left half of the screen with a mirror image of the right half, or the top half with a mirror of the bottom. As shown in Figure 15-8 (bottom), there's no seam to indicate what's going on; the result is an Alice-in-Wonderland hybrid.

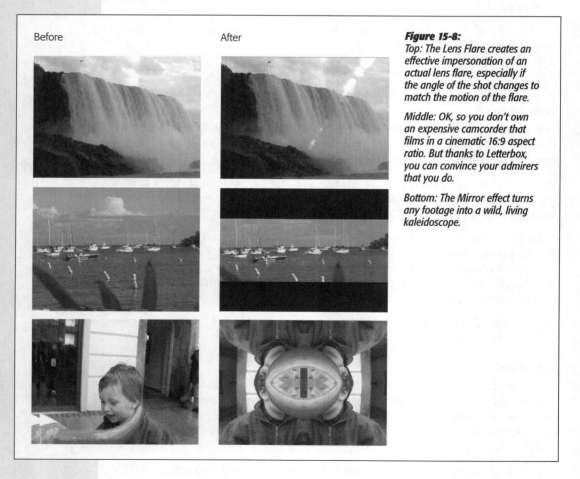

Before

After

Figure 15-8:
Top: The Lens Flare creates an effective impersonation of an actual lens flare, especially if the angle of the shot changes to match the motion of the flare.

Middle: OK, so you don't own an expensive camcorder that films in a cinematic 16:9 aspect ratio. But thanks to Letterbox, you can convince your admirers that you do.

Bottom: The Mirror effect turns any footage into a wild, living kaleidoscope.

- **Vertical (Top—Bottom).** This slider moves a horizontal "mirror" up and down the frame. At the Top setting, the footage doesn't look any different. At far right, you've flipped the entire frame upside-down.

Tip: If you drag the Vertical slider all the way to Bottom, and the Horizontal slider to Left, you neatly flip your clip upside-down—an iMovie first.

- **Horizontal (Left—Right).** This slider moves a vertical "mirror" left and right across the frame. Pushing this slider all the way to Left removes the horizontal reflections altogether. At far right, you've flipped the entire frame right-for-left. (While the Mirror effect in general doesn't seem to be very practical for most filmmaking, the ability to flip the frame horizontally can be terrifically useful. It can make the actor look left instead of right, make the fire engine drive west instead of east, and otherwise fix continuity problems.)

If you drag both sliders to their center positions, all four quadrants of the picture are, in fact, upside-down and/or horizontally flipped copies of the lower-right quadrant of the original footage. (Figure 15-7 may make this clear, or maybe not.)

The Effect In and Effect Out sliders make the mirrors fly in from the top and side of the frame as the clip plays. (Memo to music-video makers: The effect can be truly creepy.)

Tip: Be careful of *signs* (such as road signs) in footage you've mirrored. Their reverse-image type is a dead giveaway that you've rewritten history.

N-Square

If you've been secretly burning to remake *The Fly* from the insect's point of view, this is your effect. It "echoes" the video frame over and over again in miniature, like tiles of a mosaic.

The **Squares (Min—Max)** controls how many panes the frame contains, each showing the same image. At the Min position, you get four copies; at Max, you get literally hundreds. (Talk about "The Matrix!")

Tip: If you use the Effect In and Effect Out sliders, you get an interesting variation on the N-Square effect. The clip starts out looking normal; as it plays, the grid of duplicates flies in from the lower right, sliding into its final matrix.

Rain

Here's one of iMovie 4's most realistic efforts. It makes your clip look as though it was filmed in a driving rainstorm.

How driving? You determine that by adjusting the Amount slider (which controls the lengths of the raindrop slashes) or the Wind slider (which specifies how much the drop directions change over time).

Tip: You can create a better depth simulation by stacking this effect onto a clip twice: once with small droplets (farther) and once with long ones (closer). Try throwing in a little Fog, too.

Sepia Tone

You might think of this effect as a more nostalgic version of the Black & White effect. Once again, the color drains out of your clip, but instead of black-and-white, you get brown-and-white, which conveys the feeling of memory (thanks to its resemblance to the look of antique photographs). Don't forget to follow up with the Brightness/Contrast effect, if necessary, to fine-tune the effect.

Sharpen

You might guess that this effect could help repair out-of-focus scenes. In practice, however, the Sharpen effect isn't very effective in that role. Instead, it adds a fine grain to your footage, often creating a "solarized" color-banding effect, to the degree you specify using the Amount slider.

Soft Focus

Soft-focus lenses are often used when filming TV commercials that feature aging movie stars, because the fine netting or Vaseline coating on such lenses blurs fine wrinkles. (Soft-focus lenses also give everything a faintly blurry, fuzzy-edged look, but that's the price the stars pay for wrinkle obfuscation.)

Now you, too, can hide your subjects' wrinkles, by applying this soft-focus effect after the filming is complete. This effect is also good for suggesting dreams, memory, summertime nostalgia, or other hazy situations. At the sliders' extreme positions, the whole frame looks like the nuclear-holocaust scene in *Terminator 2* (especially if you use the Effect In slider to make the glow creep in over time).

Use the Softness slider to adjust the amount of Vaseline on the lens, Amount to specify what percentage of the frame is smeared, and Glow to govern just how radioactive the bright spots look.

Installing More Effects

The effects that come with iMovie 4 certainly aren't the only ones available. $25 or $30 can buy you dozens of additional effects like Mosaic, Emboss, X-ray, and so on. At this writing, you can download some free samples from *www.apple.com/imovie;* they come from the collections of companies like EZedia (*www.ezmedia.com*), GeeThree (*www.geethree.com*), and Virtix (*www.virtix.com*).

Among these collections, you'll find plug-ins that let you create picture-in-picture effects, add thought bubbles to the characters in your footage, simulate rain, smoke, or snow; tweak colors in various ways; and so on.

Titles, Captions, and Credits

Text superimposed over footage is incredibly common in the film and video worlds. You'd be hard-pressed to find a single movie, TV show, or commercial that doesn't have titles, captions, or credits. In fact, it's the *absence* of superimposed text that helps identify most camcorder videos as amateur efforts.

In iMovie, the term *title* refers to any kind of text: credits, titles, subtitles, copyright notices, and so on. You use them almost exactly the way you use the transitions or effects described in Chapter 15: by choosing a text-animation style from a list, adjusting its duration using a slider, dragging it into your Movie Track, and waiting while iMovie renders the effect.

Most of iMovie's text effects are far more focused in purpose than its transition and effect selections, so you'll have little trouble choosing the optimum text effect for a particular editing situation. For example, the Scrolling Credits effect rolls a list of names slowly up the screen—an obvious candidate for the close of your movie. Another puts several consecutive lines of text in a little block at the lower-left corner of the screen—exactly the way the text in MTV music videos appears.

Tip: Using a graphics program like AppleWorks or Photoshop Elements, you can create text "slides" with far more flexibility than you can in the Titles feature. For example, using a "title card" that you import as a graphic, you're free to use any text color and any font size. You can even dress up such titles with clip art, 3-D effects, and whatever other features your graphics software offers.

Credits that you import as still graphics in this way can't do much more than fade in and fade out. When you bypass iMovie's built-in titles feature, you give up the ability to use the fancy animations. Still, the flexibility you gain in the look, color, and size of your type may be worth the sacrifice. For details on this technique, see Chapter 18.

Setting Up a Title

Adding some text to your movie requires several setup steps:

1. Choose a title effect.

2. Type the text.

3. Specify the duration and timing.

4. Choose a font.

5. Specify the size of the lettering.

6. Choose an animation direction.

7. Turn on the Over Black checkbox, if desired.

8. Choose a color for the lettering.

9. Add a backdrop.

Here are these same steps in more detail:

Choose a Title Effect

Start by clicking the Titles button. The effects list and the other elements of the Titles palette appear, as shown in Figure 16-1.

Tip: If your mouse has a built-in scroll wheel, you can turn it to scroll the list of title effects, even without clicking the clicker, whenever the cursor is in the list area.

When you click an effect's name, you see a short preview in the Preview screen. (Use the catalog at the end of this chapter to guide you in choosing a text effect.) To see the same preview on the full-size Monitor, click the Preview button.

Incidentally, the items in the list with flippy gray triangles next to their names aren't actually titles. They're title *categories*. Click a category name to expand the triangle and see what's inside, as shown in Figure 16-1.

Tip: When showing you the preview, iMovie superimposes the text over whatever Movie Track clip is currently showing in the Monitor window. Drag the Playhead anywhere you like to specify which footage you'd like to see behind this preview. (If you haven't put any clips into the Movie Track, your preview shows only a black background, as though you'd turned on the Over Black checkbox.)

Type the Text

Beneath the list of text effects, you'll find a place to type the actual text you want to appear in this credit, caption, or title. Just click the box once to highlight the proposed text and then begin typing. (You don't have to backspace over the factory-installed dummy text first.)

The way this text box looks and acts depends on the kind of title you've selected in the list. They fall into three categories (see Figure 16-2): text blocks, title/subtitle pairs, and pair sequences.

Figure 16-1:
There are so many new title effects in iMovie 4 that Apple rejiggered the list by clumping related effects into categories. To expand a title category, you don't have to click the little triangle; you can click the category name, like Bounce Cross, instead, which gives you a broader target. Click the name a second time to collapse the list of titles.

Each time you start a new iMovie project, the proposed title and sub-title aren't very stimulating. The first title is "My Great Movie," and its subtitle is your name (or whatever you've typed into the Sharing pane of System Preferences). The second title is "Starring," and its subtitle is "Me." You get the idea.

Fortunately, these are quick enough to change: Click in the text box, press ⌘-A to select all of the dummy text, and then type right over it.

Text blocks

When you choose the Music Video or Scrolling Block text effects, you get a simple text box, into which you can type any text you want. At the end of each line, you can press Return to create a new line or press Return twice to create a blank line, exactly as you would in a word processor. (You can use the Cut, Copy, and Paste commands in the Edit menu to edit this text, too.)

The maximum amount of text you can type or paste here is just under 256 characters—one short paragraph. (See "Music Video" and "Scrolling Block" in the catalog section at the end of this chapter for more details.)

Title/Subtitle pairs

When you click the names of most effects, you're shown only two narrow boxes into which you can type text, as shown in Figure 16-2 at center. Whatever you type into the top box often appears in larger typeface than the one in the bottom box.

Such effects as Bounce In To Center, Centered Title, Flying Letters, Flying Words, Scroll with Pause, Stripe Subtitle, Subtitle, Typewriter, and Zoom fall into this category.

Tip: You don't have to type text into both of these boxes. In fact, *most* of the time you'll probably type into only the top box. The subtitle box underneath is there solely for your convenience, for those occasions when you need a second, usually smaller, line of type underneath the larger credit.

Figure 16-2:
The area into which you can type your text depends on the kind of text effect you've selected. You'll be offered either two lines for a title and subtitle (top left), one big text box (middle), or a virtually unlimited number of two-line pairs (bottom right), suitable for credit sequences at the end of your movie.

Pair sequences

When you're creating the credits for the end of a movie, you usually want two columns of text: on the left, the list of roles; on the right, the actors who portrayed them. In these situations, you need iMovie to offer *pairs* of slots—enough to accommodate the names of everybody who worked on your movie. It's easy to spot the text effects that offer these two-line pairs; they're the ones with the words "Multiple" or "Rolling" in their names.

After clicking one of these title effects, you see not one but two different text-box pairs. The window offers a scroll bar, plus a + button, so that you can add more pairs and scroll through them (Figure 16-3).

Start by clicking the top box. Drag across the dummy text ("My Great Movie"), or press a quick ⌘-A to highlight it, and then type the first character's name (*Raymond,* for example). Press Tab to highlight the lower box, and then type the actor's name (*Dustin Hoffman,* for example). If there's another empty pair of boxes beneath the one you've just filled, press Tab again, and fill in those boxes, too.

You'll know when you've filled up all the available boxes: You'll discover that either you can't scroll down any more, or that when you press Tab, you'll circle around and wind up in the *first* box you filled in. At that point, click the + button beside the text boxes to add another pair of boxes. Keep going this way—clicking +, typing a pair of names, clicking + again—until you've typed in the names of everybody you want in the list of credits.

Figure 16-3:
You can rearrange the credits in your sequence by dragging the left edge of a credit pair up or down in the list, and waiting patiently as iMovie scrolls the list (arrow). You can also remove a credit by clicking the − button.

Specify the Timing

You have a lot of control over the timing of your titles' animation. Most of the title styles offer two sliders just below the Preview screen:

- The **Speed** slider has different results with different titles; setting a faster Speed setting makes the Centered Title fade in/out faster, Flying Words fly faster, Typewriter types faster, and so on. For title styles involving motion, it controls the text speed; for title styles that remain still (such as Centered Title), it controls the total amount of time the text spends on the screen. The catalog of title styles at the end of this chapter identifies the Speed slider's effect for each style.

- The **Pause** effect depends on the style, too. For titles that fade in and out, it controls the amount of time the text will be fully manifested on the screen, readable and at full size and brightness, between its fade in and fade out segments. For titles whose text flies or rolls into place (such as Typewriter or Flying Words), Pause controls how long the finished title hangs around after it's complete.

As you adjust these sliders, the readout at the bottom of the preview screen shows you, in seconds:frames format, the time settings you've specified. (You have to wait until the preview is finished playing before these numbers appear.) For example, if it says "05:20 + 01:08 = 6:28," iMovie is trying to tell you, in its way:

"You've set the Speed slider to 5:20—that is, you've allotted 170 frames for fading in and out. So I'll make the text fade in over half of that time: 2 seconds, 15 frames. Then you've set the Pause slider to 1:08, so I'll make the text sit there on the screen for 1 second, 8 frames. Finally, I'll take another 2 seconds, 15 frames to fade out."

Take into account your viewers' reading speed. Many video editors use this guideline: Leave the words on the screen long enough for somebody to read them aloud twice.

Preview the effect

As with the transitions described in the previous chapter, iMovie offers two kinds of preview for titles:

- **Preview box.** If you click a title style's name, you see a real-time preview of your title animation in the small Preview box above the list of titles. It's very tiny, but it lasts as long as the finished title will last, giving you a good idea of your title's readability. (The Speed and Pause sliders affect these previews.)

- **Monitor window.** If you click the Preview *button,* iMovie shows another kind of preview in the Monitor window. This time, you get to see every single frame of the animation, no matter how long it takes your Mac to spew out these images. On slow Macs, you may not see the animation play at real-world speed; you're getting, in essence, a slow-motion version of the full effect.

Choose a Font

Using the pop-up menu just below the list of effects, you can choose a typeface for your text. Consider these guidelines:

- **Be consistent.** Using the same typeface for all of the titles in your movie lends consistency and professionalism to the project.

- **Remember the QuickTime effect.** If you plan to distribute your finished movie as a QuickTime file—an electronic movie file that you can distribute by email, network, CD, disk, or Web page—use the biggest, boldest, cleanest fonts you have. Avoid spindly delicate fonts or script fonts. When your movie is compressed down to a 3-inch square, what looks terrific in your Monitor window will be so small it may become completely illegible.

  Come to think of it, you might want to choose big, bold, clean fonts even if you're going to play the finished movie on a TV, whose resolution is far lower than that of your computer screen. Be especially careful when using one of the text effects that includes a subtitle; iMovie subtitles often use an even smaller typeface than the primary title font, and may lose legibility if the font has too much filigree.

  Finally, favor *sans serif* fonts—typefaces that don't have the tiny *serifs,* or "hats and feet," at the end of the character strokes. The typeface you're reading now is a serif font, one that's less likely to remain legible in a QuickTime movie. The typeface used in the next paragraph (Tip) is a sans serif font.

  Some of the standard Mac fonts that look especially good as iMovie fonts are Arial Black, Capitals, Charcoal, Chicago, Gadget, Helvetica, Impact, Sand, Techno, and Textile. Some of the fonts whose delicate nature may be harder to read are Monaco, Courier, Old English, Swing, Trebuchet, Times, Palatino, and Verdana.

Note: The beauty of iMovie's titling feature is that the fonts you choose become embedded into the actual digital picture. In other words, when you distribute your movie as a QuickTime file, you don't have to worry that your recipients might not have the same fonts you used to create the file. They'll see on their screens exactly what you see on yours.

Specify the Size of the Lettering

iMovie is fairly conservative with its font-size choices. Even with the Size slider (just to the right of the Font pop-up menu) all the way to the right, and even with "QT Margins" turned on, iMovie doesn't let you make titles that fill the screen. (Keeping your text short may help. If the phrase is very long, iMovie further reduces the point size enough to fit the entire line on the screen, even if the type-size slider is at its maximum. In other words, you can make the font for the credit *PIGGY* much larger than you can *ONE HAM'S ADVENTURES IN MANHATTAN*.)

Choose an Animation Direction

Most of iMovie's text effects are animated. They feature words flying across the screen, sliding from one edge of the frame to the other, and so on. Some feature directional arrows (seen in Figure 16-1, for example) that let you control which direction the text flies or slides in. By clicking the appropriate arrow, you can specify which direction the text should fly.

Note: In the case of the Music Video effect, the arrow specifies which *corner* the text block should sit in, motionless.

The "Over Black" Checkbox

Under normal circumstances, the text you've specified gets superimposed over the video picture. Particularly when you're creating opening or closing credits, however, you may want the lettering to appear on a black screen—a striking and professional-looking effect. In those cases, turn on the Over Black checkbox.

It's important to note that when you do so, you *add* to the total length of your movie. Adding the Over Black title is like inserting a new clip, in that you force the clips to the right of your text effect to slide further rightward to accommodate the credit you just inserted. (When the Over Black checkbox *isn't* turned on, by contrast, adding a text effect doesn't change the overall length of your movie.)

The Over Black option is attractive for three reasons. First, it looks extremely professional; it's something people who don't have an editing program like iMovie can't even do. Second, the high contrast of white against black makes the text very legible. Third, the audience will *read* it, instead of being distracted by the video behind it.

Tip: You don't have to limit yourself to adding text Over Black; you can just as easily superimpose your titles Over Blue, Over Red, or Over Fuschia. The trick is to create a colored clip as described on page 288, and add your titles to *it*. In that case, do *not* turn on Over Black; you want your lettering to float on top of the existing video, which happens to be a solid, unchanging color.

Choose a Color for the Lettering

By clicking the tiny square beside the word Color, you get a little dialog box known as the Mac OS X Color Picker. (The notes on page 5 describe it in detail.) For now, the important thing is to choose a color that *contrasts* with the footage behind the lettering. Use white against black, black against white, yellow against blue, and so on.

Note: iMovie doesn't limit you to TV-safe colors. If colors are too bright (saturated), the edges of the letters can smear and tear when played back on a TV.

Add a Backdrop

If you left your education to the Apple online help, you might assume that there are only two kinds of images that can underlie your titles: video footage or a solid black frame. Fortunately, there's a third option that greatly expands your creative possi-

The TV-Safe Area, Overscanning, and You

Millions of TV viewers every day are blissfully unaware that they're missing the big picture.

In its early days, the little cathode-ray guns inside the TV worked by painting one line of the TV picture, then turning around and heading back the opposite direction. To make sure that the screen was painted edge to edge, these early TVs were programmed to overshoot the edges of the screen—or, to use the technical term, to *overscan* the screen.

TV technology is much better now, but even modern TVs exhibit overscanning. The amount varies, but you may be missing as much as 10 percent of the picture beyond the left and right edges (and often the top and bottom, too).

TV producers are careful to keep the action and titles in the part of the frame that's least likely to be lost in overscan. But as a film editor, the *TV-safe area* is suddenly your concern, too. The overscanning effect means that when you show

your iMovie productions on a TV, you'll lose anything that's very close to the edges of the frame.

Most of the time, that's no problem; only when you're adding titles does the overscanning effect become a worry.

Fortunately, avoiding text-chopping problems is supremely easy: Just turn *off* the QT Margins checkbox. Doing so makes iMovie shrink the text enough so that it won't get chopped off on a TV—guaranteed.

This business of the TV-safe area *isn't an issue* if you plan to convert your iMovie work into QuickTime movies, which have no such complications. That's why this checkbox is worded as it is; "QT Margins" means "Assume that this movie will be shown as a QuickTime movie, and therefore won't have chopped-off margins." When the QT Margins checkbox is turned *on,* the text-size slider lets you crank your font sizes a few notches higher.

bilities: superimposing your text on a still image, such as a photo or some gradient fill you've created in, say, Photoshop Elements (Figure 16-4).

To use one of these backdrops, import it into your project as you would any graphics file, as described on page 367. That discussion also shows you how to control how long a still image should last when it appears in your movie. From there, you should have little difficulty superimposing titles as described in this chapter.

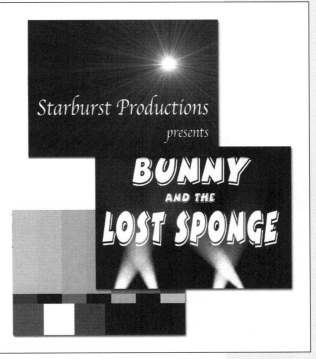

Figure 16-4:
Feeling hemmed in by the typographical limita-tions of iMovie's built-in text effects? Keep in mind that you can always hand-build a title using a graphics program like Photoshop Elements or AppleWorks. (Just create a graphic that measures 640 by 480 pixels for the North American video standard.)

Of course, you lose the ability to animate the words and letters. The results can be much more interesting than plain white text on a black background, yet less distracting than text superim-posed over footage.

Or just add color bars (lower left) to make people think you really work in television.

Inserting and Rendering a Title

When you've taken into consideration all the options described so far in this chapter, you probably have a good feel for how this title is going to look once it's inserted into your movie. Now it's time to commit it to digital film.

Dragging the Title into the Movie Track

To place the title you've selected into Movie Track, proceed as follows:

1. **Decide where you want the title to begin.**

   Consider the location of your title carefully. If you're superimposing it on a solid-colored background or a still image, no problem. But if you're planning to superimpose it on moving video, choose a scene that's relatively still, so that the video doesn't distract the audience from the words on screen. (The exception: If you're using one of iMovie 4's new "see-through" lettering styles, you may want to choose active video deliberately to call attention to the "cutouts.")

Sometimes, such as when you've selected a title style that fades in from nothing, it's OK to put the title squarely at the beginning of a clip. At other times, you'll want to position the title a few seconds into the clip.

2. **If you've selected a starting point for a title that's in the middle of the clip, position the Playhead there and then choose Edit→Split Video Clip at Playhead.**

It's a fact of iMovie life: A title can begin only at the *beginning* of a clip, never the middle. To make the title seem as though it's starting partway through a clip, therefore, you must *turn* that spot into the beginning of a new clip by chopping the clip in half.

This is not the only time the title feature will be chopping your clips into smaller clips, as Figure 16-6 makes clear.

3. **Drag the name or icon of your chosen title style from the list of titles directly onto the Movie Track, as shown in Figure 16-5.**

Drag it just to the left of the clip you'll want to play underneath the title text. All clips to the right scoot rightward to make room for your cursor.

Figure 16-5:
Drag the name of the title you want out of the Titles list directly into the Movie Track.

The clips in the Clip Viewer or Timeline Viewer scoot to the right to make room for the title you're inserting.

Rendering Begins

Now iMovie begins to *render* the title effect: to create a new clip that incorporates both the original footage and the text you're superimposing.

The longer the title is to remain on the screen, the longer the rendering process takes. But exactly as when rendering transitions, you can continue to do other work in iMovie (or even in other programs) while the title is rendering. In fact, you can play titles before they're fully baked, to see what they'll look like in your final movie —another handy preview feature that doesn't require you to wait until the rendering is finished. You can even have several titles rendering simultaneously, although iMovie slows down quite a bit if you have more than, say, three titles rendering at once.

The bright red progress bar creeps along the bottom of the clip, as shown in Figure 16-6. In other words, a title in the Movie Track doesn't have its own icon, as a transition does. Instead, you get to see a miniature illustration of what it's going to look like. (Tiny lettering appears directly *on* the superimposed clip icon to help you identify it as a title clip.)

Figure 16-6:
If you want a title to begin partway into a clip (top) instead of at the very beginning, you must first chop the clip into two pieces (middle). During rendering, a progress bar keeps track of the rendering progress (bottom).

After the title has finished rendering, you'll find that iMovie has automatically made yet another clip split—at the end of the title (bottom). The result: After you're done inserting a title, that portion of your movie occupied by the title has become a clip unto itself.

Inverted "T" shows where clip will be split

Progress bar ⌐   ⌐ Title text replaces clip's name

As soon as you've finished dragging a title into the Movie Track, the affected clip's name instantly changes. It takes on the words of your actual title (or as much as will fit; if the name is wider than the clip icon, you see an ellipsis "like … this"). If the clip was called, for example, "Chris closeup," iMovie renames it "Shoestring Productions presents," or whatever your title says. (You can see this effect, too, in Figure 16-6.) As a bonus, a tiny letter T appears in the upper-right corner of the "slide" in the Clip Viewer, a friendly reminder that you've applied a title to it.

How Titles Chop Up Your Clips

As Figure 16-6 illustrates, it's not enough that you split your clip if you want the title to begin partway into the footage. iMovie may chop up your clips on its own, according to this scheme:

- If the title you've specified is shorter than the clip, iMovie splits the clip in two. The first portion gets the title text embedded into it; the second portion is left alone.

- If the title is *longer* than the clip, iMovie *steals footage* from the next clip to the right (see Figure 16-7). In fact, it continues to eat up as many additional clips as necessary to fulfill the duration you've specified for it. This powerful feature means that you can make a single title sequence extend across series of short clips, still images, transitions, and so on. (Contrast with the transitions and effects described in Chapter 15, which limit their appetites to single clips.)

Figure 16-7:
If your title is longer than its clip, iMovie steals however many seconds of footage it needs from the next clip and incorporates it into the first clip. If you look carefully at the durations of these two clips before (top) and after the title has been applied, you'll see that the second clip has been shortened by one second, and the first clip lengthened, when the stealing process is over (middle).

If you try to apply your title to a too-short clip when there's no subsequent clip from which iMovie can steal frames, on the other hand, you get the error message shown at bottom.

The title is too long for that part of the movie; please place it at least 04:29 from the end of the movie.

OK

iMovie may still chop up the final clip in the sequence, however, to accommodate the tail end of the title sequence.

Tip: If the title is long enough, it can gobble down a number of individual clips—and turn them into a *single* title clip in your Movie Track. This can be a sneaky way to organize your movie, freezing clip sequences into easily dragged uni-clips.

Checking the Result

When the rendering process is complete—or even before it's complete—check out the effect. Click the title clip in the Movie Track and press the Space bar to view the title clip, or Shift-click the clips before and after the title clip (and then press the Space bar) to see how the title looks in the context of the clips around it. Or just drag the Playhead back and forth across the title to see how it looks.

If the title isn't quite what you wanted—if it's the wrong length, style, or font, or if there's a typo, for example—you can change its settings as described in the next section. If the title wasn't *at all* what you wanted—if it's in the wrong place, for example—you can undo the entire insertion-and-rendering process by highlighting the title clip and pressing the Delete key (or choosing Edit→Undo, if you added the title recently). The original footage returns, textless and intact.

Editing a Title

Editing a title is easy. Click the title clip's icon in the Movie Track. Click the Titles button, if the list of titles isn't already open.

Now you can adjust the title style, the text of the title itself, the title's timing, the direction of motion, or any other parameters described in the first part of the chapter. When you're finished, click the Update button just below the Preview button. iMovie begins the rendering process again, putting in place a brand-new title, and splitting the superimposed footage in a different place, if necessary.

Note: The good news is that your ability to edit the title isn't subject to the 10-level Undo limitation. In other words, you can revise the settings for a title at any time, even if it's too late to use Undo.

But if you've applied *multiple* superimposed titles, as described in the box below, you can revise only the most recent title you've applied to a particular clip.

Deleting a Title

As noted previously, a title clip is just a clip. You might wonder, therefore, how you can remove a title without also deleting the footage it affects.

Yet sure enough, iMovie remembers what your clips looked like before you overlaid a title. You can click a title clip at any time, press the Delete key, and see iMovie restore the original footage. True, pressing Delete on a conventional clip deletes it; but pressing Delete on a title clip simply deletes its "titleness." The clip to its right merges back into its formerly text-overlaid portion, leaving only one clip instead of two.

Now, if you've *moved* the clip that follows the title clip, and you *then* delete the title clip, iMovie will still put back the underlying footage that it consumed, but it may no longer be where you expect it to be. The program can't "splice" the footage back onto the beginning of a clip from which it was split, because iMovie doesn't know where that clip is (you might even have deleted it). If you move the clips back into their original sequence after deleting the title, the footage will still be continuous, but there might now be a cut or break where the title ended, as if you had split the clip at that point.

The iMovie Titles Catalog

This discussion describes each of the title effects available in iMovie. Along the way, you'll find out several useful pieces of information about each title:

- How the Speed slider affects the effect.
- Which directions you can make the text move, if any.
- When you might find each effect useful.

3D Spin

Speed slider: *Controls duration*
Direction control: *None*

This twisty title effect, new in iMovie 4, sends your title text spinning crazily in all three dimensions, as though it were typeset on a piece of transparent confetti that's tumbling down from the sky. It's not especially easy to read, since for most of the time onscreen, you're reading it in mirror-image, upside-down, or squished. (It never does come to a stop.) Its transparency also fluctuates, permitting more or less of the background video (or background black) to show through the letters.

Bounce Across

Speed slider: *Controls flying-on speed*
Direction control: *Left, right*

Don't use this effect for anything serious or hard-hitting. It's a light-hearted, almost comical animation in which your title and subtitle come rolling in on invisible roller-

---

POWER USERS' CLINIC

Behind-the-Scenes Undo Magic

iMovie can restore an original clip when you delete a title that you've superimposed on it, even weeks later.

Yet as noted in this chapter, iMovie creates titles by *modifying* the original clips—by changing the actual pixels that compose the image. So where is iMovie storing a copy of the original, for use when you decide to delete the title?

In the project's Media folder (see page 264). There you'll find the original clip from the camcorder (called "Clip 1," for example), untouched. There you'll *also* find a new clip (called "Typewriter 1," for example), bearing the name of the title style you used. *This* clip contains the modified portion of your original clip.

---

coaster tracks, bouncing up and down as they come to rest in the center of the screen. You get an additional control—a Wave slider that controls how high the bounces are, and therefore how dramatic the effect.

The Bounce Across Multiple variation (which appears when you open the Bounce Across category name) brings on a second and then a third title or title pair, each coming to rest in the center of the screen and then disappearing to make way for the next wave.

Bounce In to Center

Speed slider: *Controls flying-on speed*
Direction control: *Up, down, left, right*

In this animated effect, the title slides down from the top of the frame and comes to rest, with a little springy bounce, in the center. If you've specified a subtitle, it floats upward simultaneously from the bottom of the frame. Use it for quirky or comic opening credits—it's not very subtle.

Cartwheel

Speed slider: *Controls flying-on speed*
Direction control: *Left, right*

iMovie includes several text effects that involve spinning or tumbling words or letters. You'll probably want to avoid most of them except in special situations. Here's the first of this family.

In this version, all of the letters of your title and subtitle fly onto the screen from one side, each spinning as though pierced on its own axle. You can't actually read the titles until they're finished with their spinning and land in the center.

Read quickly, however, because the letters stand still only for a moment (the moment you specify with the Pause slider), and then spin away again, cartwheeling their way off the screen. If you chose the Cartwheel Multiple version, the next pair of credits now cartwheels on.

Centered

Speed slider: *Controls fade in/fade out speed*
Direction control: *None*

The Centered Title is one of the most useful of all the iMovie text effects. iMovie shows a single line of text (or two lines, if you take advantage of the subtitle option), fading in, staying on the screen for a moment, then fading out, making this effect ideal for displaying the title of your movie.

The Centered Multiple variation is ideal for opening credits, because each name (along with an optional subtitle) fades professionally onto the screen, remains there for a moment, and then fades away again. The next name fades in to repeat the cycle.

(If you haven't seen this particular opening-credit style used at the beginning of a million TV shows and movies, you haven't watched enough TV.)

This is a tasteful, professional, powerful effect.

Tip: By using several consecutive Centered Titles, you achieve exactly the same effect as the Centered Multiple sequence, except with individual control over the timing of each text pair.

Clip to Characters

Speed slider: *Controls fade in/fade out speed*
Direction control: *None*

Over and over again in Apple's history, its designers have noticed the masses flocking to a certain piece of shareware that fills a gaping feature hole in Apple's own software. In this case, the iMovie team observed how many people were buying add-on title effects from other companies, and decided to spare them that expense by introducing this powerful new title category. All four new text effects described here were once available only as shareware add-ons. (They're called Clip to Characters because the actual letter outlines serve as cookie cutters that clip out video or pictures behind them. You'll get the idea in a moment.)

Animated Gradient

Man, if you're into making mystery movies, you've got your opening credits right here. In this two-toned extravaganza, a moving searchlight seems to be shining out at you from behind the screen, turning the insides of the letters bright yellow as it passes from left to right. It's particularly striking when you turn on the "Over black" checkbox.

Clip Image

Here's a wild new effect with infinite possibilities. In this variation, iMovie fills the hollow outlines of your lettering with a still image—a graphic or photo. You specify which graphic you want to use by clicking the little File button that magically appears below the Size slider, and then using the Open File dialog box to peruse the contents of your hard drive.

If you're just looking for some quick graphic interest, you can choose a photo with an interesting texture—a close-up of sandpaper, clouds, or diamonds, for example. If

Clip Image

you're aiming for Sundance, you could conceivably spend a few hours in Photoshop creating a more elaborate graphic whose elements are strategically placed to peek out from inside the letters of your title: little silhouetted spy characters, mischievous monkeys, or even tiny words that will appear *inside* the larger letters.

Clip Video

This titling effect wins the award for Most Likely to Save You $30 on Shareware Title Styles. Once again, it makes your letters see-through—but instead of permitting a background still photo to peek through, it actually permits your own video to play inside the lettering. The rest of the screen is black (which is why the "Over black" checkbox is automatically turned on and dimmed when you choose this effect). The Color checkbox has no effect in this case, either.

You can use this title style to create some truly brilliant visuals, video puns, or double meanings. Maybe the title of your short film is "Energy Drink," but we see what appears to be dripping blood inside the lettering. Maybe you've made a movie about a Fourth of July picnic, and you've got some waving-flag video that fills in the hollow letters. Or maybe you're editing a home movie called "Off to Topeka," and a jet plane takes off behind the words, unforgettably appearing and disappearing through and between the letters of the words.

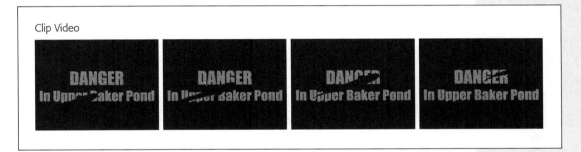

Starburst

Like Clip Image, this effect fills in your lettering with a single image that stretches across the entire title. In this case, though, you don't get to choose what image you get; it's a sunburst, bright yellow in the middle and fading out, with visible radiating lines, toward the outer edges.

The Color box is very important in this case; it specifies what color the yellow central sunball becomes as its rays reach the outer edges of your words.

Converge

Speed slider: *Controls letter-movement speed*
Direction control: *Left, right (Converge and Converge Multiple only)*

As seen on TV—or in any number of artsy serial-killer movies. The title appears with its letter spacing far too wide—and as you watch, the letters slowly glide inward until they're correctly spaced.

You get four variations. In Converge (for one line) and Converge Multiple (several pairs), the letters on the right or left side remain essentially stationary during the animation, leaving the letters on the opposite side to do all the movement. In the Multiple version, each completed title blinks out of sight to make way for the next title pair.

In Converge to Center and its Multiple variation, the text appears instantly on the screen—but spaced so widely, the right and left parts of it may even be chopped off by the borders of the frame. They immediately float inward to the center until they're readable. Once again, this form of credits has been used now and again during the openings of scary thrillers.

In all four cases, the effect is vaguely menacing and very slick.

Cross Through

Speed slider: *Controls letter-movement speed*
Direction control: *None*

The Cross Through Center title (and its Multiple variant) appears perfectly normal: centered, nicely spaced. There's only one thing wrong with it: every word is spelled backwards, sihT ekiL hcuM ytterP.

As you watch, iMovie straightens things out for you. The letters fly through the center point of the frame and out the other side, until they're in the proper order. (This one is best suited for movies about spelling bees or mirror manufacturers.)

Cross Through Center

Drifting

Speed slider: *Controls total time on screen*
Direction control: *Up, down, left right*

This effect duplicates the opening credits of many a recent Hollywood movie, not to mention TV commercials for the *New York Times* and various over-the-counter drugs. Your text appears at center screen and gracefully floats in opposite directions. The effect is eye-catching, although it can be annoying to try to read lines of text that are slipping apart. (The Pause slider is dimmed—because the text never pauses!)

Far, Far Away

Speed slider: *Controls flying-on speed*
Direction control: *None*

Star Wars geeks, rejoice! Now you, too, can simulate the legendary prologue text of the Star Wars movies. Your text appears in a block, huge at the bottom of the screen, and then scrolls up and away, in severe perspective, fading out to blackness in the distance as it approaches the top of the screen.

You can't really get away with using this effect for anything but spoofs of the Star Wars movies and tributes to them, because it's so instantly recognizable to just about everyone who's ever been to the movies. But in the right context, and when filled with just the right text, it can be truly hilarious. ("Long, long ago, in a dead-end job far, far away, Larry first saw Charlene, bent over the Xerox machine as she changed the toner cartridge. Thus began the story of their courtship…")

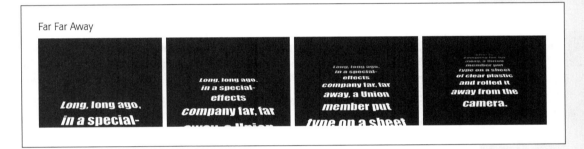

Far Far Away

Flying

Speed slider: *Controls flying-on speed*
Direction control: *Up, down*

In the Flying Letters effect, the letters of your title (and subtitle, if you've specified one) fly onto the screen one at a time from the upper-right or lower-right corner of the frame (depending on the directional arrow you click), gradually assembling the phrase you've specified. If nothing else, this effect is certainly offbeat, but it can quickly get boring if you use it more than once.

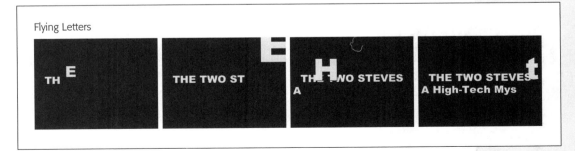

Flying Letters

The Speed slider's maximum time grows according to the length of your title. At its maximum, you and your audience could be sitting there for nearly a full minute while your letters plod onto the screen.

The Flying Words effect is similar, except that entire words fly onto the screen instead of letters. It may be less tedious for your audience to watch, but you should still use it sparingly.

Gravity, Gravity Multiple

Speed slider: *Controls overall title timing*
Direction control: *Up, down, left, right*

This time, the letters of your title and subtitle begin at the top of the screen, fading into a horizontal jumble of mixed-up letters. Then, as you watch, they slide down the screen into position, much like snowflakes or melted ice on a windowpane. It's too bizarre to be generally useful, but looks pretty cool when superimposed over snow-flurry footage.

Using the direction arrows, you can specify that your jumbled letters begin at the bottom of the screen and slide upward instead (something to remember if you ever get involved with producing grass-growing videos). You can also click the left or right direction arrows, although these don't produce any visible difference from the down and up versions.

Music Video

Speed slider: *Controls total time on screen*
Direction control: *Left, right*

If you've ever seen a music video on MTV or VH1, you'll recognize this effect instantly. It places the block of text you've typed—a short paragraph of it, anyway—into the lower-left or lower-right corner of the screen, depending on which directional arrow you select.

The authenticity of this effect is unassailable. It looks *exactly* like the credits that appear at the beginning of actual music videos. Be careful not to make the type too small, especially for videos you intend to distribute by email or on the Web.

Music Video

THE TWO
STEVES
A High-Tech
Mystery

Tip: The Music Video title is one of the most useful text styles, as it's the only iMovie text style that gives you complete freedom over placement of your text. You can make your title appear off-center, in any corner of the frame, and so on.

The trick is to use "white space" to position the text. By pressing the Space bar before typing each line, you can push your text to the middle or right side of the frame; by pressing Return after the text, you can force the text upward to the middle or top of the frame. Combine these techniques with the left/right directional buttons for various wacky placement effects.

Scrolling

Here they are: four variations of the closing-credits effect that wraps up every Hollywood movie you've ever seen. It creates what the pros call a *roll*—text that slides up the screen from the bottom, as though on an endless roll of clear plastic, showing the names of the characters and the actors who played them.

Rolling Credits, Rolling Centered Credits

These effects give you text pairs, like Director/Steven Speilberg and Writer/Robert Towne, or character name/actor name. (The Rolling Credits effect is identical to the Rolling Centered Credits except for the formatting: instead of straddling an invisible "gutter" of empty space, the two columns are separated by a dotted line.)

You can opt to have the text scroll down from the top instead (by clicking the directional arrow), although it looks very weird. (A *crawl*, on the other hand, slides onto the screen from side to side, like the tornado-warning notices that sometimes appear during a TV show. At this writing, iMovie offers no method for creating crawls, much to the disappointment of TV stations in Iowa.)

Be careful when using this effect for two reasons: First, remember that 45 seconds is the longest scroll you can create, and iMovie automatically adjusts the speed of scrolling to fit all the names you've typed into the duration you've specified. You couldn't fit even 10 percent of the closing credits of *Titanic* into 45 seconds, at least not without scrolling them too fast to read. (On the other hand, you can always use multiple *sets* of Rolling Credits titles, superimposed if necessary [page 340].)

Second, the type is very small, which could be a problem if you intend to save your movie as a QuickTime file.

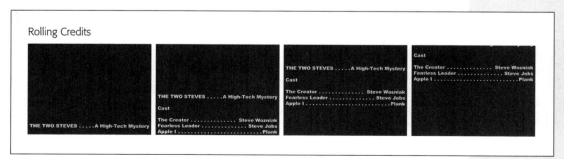

Rolling Credits

Scroll with Pause

Speed slider: *Controls scroll-in/scroll-off speed*
Direction control: *Up, down, left, right*

The title and subtitle (if you've specified one) slide, as a pair, from the edge of the screen you've specified (by clicking the directional arrows), pause at the center of the screen for the audience to read, and then continue sliding on their merry way off the screen.

This isn't an effect you're likely to use often. But it can look quirky and charming if the speed and the typeface are right. For example, when your credits slide from left to right, you suggest an old-time slide projector changing slides.

Scrolling Block

Speed slider: *Controls total time on screen*
Direction control: *Up or down*

This text style is a lot like Far, Far Away, in that a long block of introductory text scrolls slowly upward from the bottom of the screen. In this case, however, it doesn't shrink as it rolls up the screen.

This roll effect is extremely common in commercial theatrical movies. You can use it at the beginning of your movie to explain the plot setup. At the end of the movie, you can use it to provide a postscript or update to the events the audience has just witnessed (like the postscripts at the end of *October Sky* or *A Beautiful Mind*).

You can also tack one of these scrolling text blocks onto the end of another—which is fortunate because a Scrolling Block can contain no more than 254 characters. You can also tack a Scrolling Block onto one of the other iMovie scrolling-text effects (it can follow the Rolling Credits effect, for example) to provide a neatly centered copyright, an "in memoriam," or some disclaimer information. As far as the audience is concerned, it will be just one more part of the same smooth scroll.

Nor do you have to begin this follow-up block after the regular credits (or the preceding Scrolling Blocks) have completely disappeared off the top of the screen. You can make the additional Scrolling Block appear at any moment, even while the previous crawl is still finishing up its movement, using the tip in the box on page 340.

The directional arrows let you control whether this roll proceeds downward from the top or upward from the bottom. You're welcome to make your text block scroll downward, but do so with the knowledge that you're doing something unconventional, even unheard of, in the world of filmmaking.

Spinner

Speed slider: *Controls spinning-on/spinning-off time*
Direction control: *None*

It's taken four versions of iMovie, but at last you can simulate the spinning-newspaper-headline effect made popular by many an old black-and-white movie, not to mention the old *Batman* TV show of the 1960s. Each line of your credits comes spinning out of a dot at the center of the screen, finally stopping at full size at center so that you can read it. (The Spins slider even lets you control how many times it spins before coming to rest.) At that point, it retreats, spinning right back into the distance again.

Tip: The Spinner effect might be more familiar-looking if it would come to a stop and then *stay there* until the next line spun onto the screen, rather than spinning away again. Of course, if that's what you want, go ahead and render the effect—and then just chop out the spinning-away-again section of the resulting title clip.

Spinner

Spread

Speed slider: *Controls total time on screen*
Direction control: *None*

The Spread from Center effect was clearly written by the same programmer who created Converge. Once again, it's all about letter spacing—but this time, all of the letters on each line of your title begin in the center of the frame, superimposed in a chaotic, unreadable jumble. As the title rolls on, the letters drift outward and into their rightful places.

If you choose the Multiple version, they hold in place for a moment and then vanish just in time for the next set of titles to appear and blossom.

Stripe Subtitle

Speed slider: *Controls total time on screen*
Direction control: *None*

This effect creates what the pros call a *lower third*—a stripe across the bottom of the picture where the text identifies, for example, the name and affiliation of the person being interviewed. The tinted background is an unusual touch.

Oddly enough, clicking the Color swatch here *doesn't* let you change the color of the text, as it usually does. (Stripe Subtitle text is always white.) Instead, it specifies the background color of the stripe itself.

Odder still, the stripe always stops just shy of the screen's right edge.

Subtitle

Speed slider: *Controls total time on screen*
Direction control: *None*

This effect, newly restored to iMovie 4 after being strangely absent from iMovie 3, gives you the more traditional look for a "lower third" title, one that identifies the person or place being shown in the footage. The text quietly fades in, centered at the bottom of the screen, and then fades out again. (If you choose the Multiple variation, the next pair of lines now fades on.)

As the name implies, you can also use this effect to provide captions that translate, say, an opera performance, although that may be a less frequent requirement in your moviemaking career.

Twirl

Speed slider: *Controls time for text to complete rotation*
Direction control: *Left, right*

You'll really have to scratch your head to figure out the point of this one. The letters of your title appear at full size, dead center, and then begin to spin in place (either clockwise or counterclockwise, depending on your selection on the Direction control).

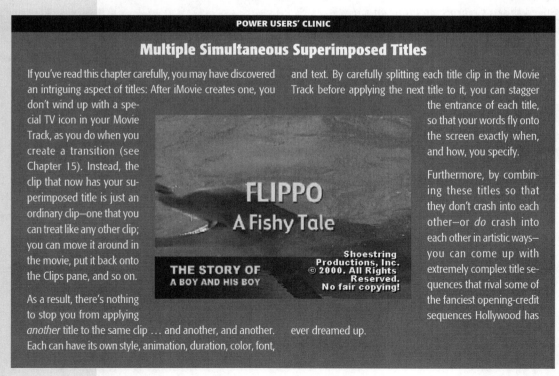

POWER USERS' CLINIC

Multiple Simultaneous Superimposed Titles

If you've read this chapter carefully, you may have discovered an intriguing aspect of titles: After iMovie creates one, you don't wind up with a special TV icon in your Movie Track, as you do when you create a transition (see Chapter 15). Instead, the clip that now has your superimposed title is just an ordinary clip—one that you can treat like any other clip; you can move it around in the movie, put it back onto the Clips pane, and so on.

As a result, there's nothing to stop you from applying *another* title to the same clip … and another, and another. Each can have its own style, animation, duration, color, font, and text. By carefully splitting each title clip in the Movie Track before applying the next title to it, you can stagger the entrance of each title, so that your words fly onto the screen exactly when, and how, you specify.

Furthermore, by combining these titles so that they don't crash into each other—or *do* crash into each other in artistic ways—you can come up with extremely complex title sequences that rival some of the fanciest opening-credit sequences Hollywood has ever dreamed up.

When they complete one rotation, they stop so you can read them. Overall, the effect looks a little bit like each letter has been fastened to a hotel-room door with only one nail—at the bottom—and they're swinging freely.

Typing

Speed slider: *Controls time for text to fully appear*
Direction control: *None*

You occasionally see the Typewriter effect in the credits of TV police dramas (especially *JAG* and *Homicide*). The letters spill across the screen from left to right, as though being rapidly typed in a word processor.

Tip: When this title style was under development at Apple, it was called *X-Files*—a reference to the animated titles in *The X-Files* that established the time and date of each new scene. Before iMovie was officially unveiled, the name was changed to Typewriter for obvious reasons (obvious to lawyers, anyway).

Video Terminal, new in iMovie 4, is only slightly different. It adds a blinking insertion-point cursor that gets pushed along as you type—not the vertical one that's familiar to millions of Mac and PC fans, but instead a horizontal underline character like the one on ancient, pre-mouse video terminals. (For some inexplicable reason, Hollywood movies generally depict text appearing on *any* computer screen using this effect, even if it's popping up in a dialog box or error message. The accompanying teletype sound makes Hollywood computers seem even less like the real-world kind.)

The Video Terminal effect is especially useful when you want to recreate the "I'm summing up my day in sentimental, bittersweet prose on my word processor" effect that concluded every episode of *Doogie Howser, M.D.*

Unscramble

Speed slider: *Controls speed of unscrambling*
Direction control: *Left, right*

Here's yet another relative of Cartwheel, Gravity, and Twirl. This time, all the letters begin both out of place and upside down, scattered on an invisible horizontal line like the pieces of a jigsaw puzzle that have been dumped out of the box. They seemed to wake up, shake it off, right themselves, and dance into proper position.

The only difference between the left and right directional arrows is which way the letters spin: clockwise or counterclockwise. (Not one audience member in one million would be able to tell the difference.)

Wipe

Speed slider: *Controls speed of reveal*
Direction control: *Left, right, up, down*

New in iMovie 4, the Wipe effect is among the most practical. Your text is revealed by a soft-edged "spotlight" that, unlike the Animated Gradient effect, reveals the entire width or height of the text at once. (You can direct the wiper to reveal your text from any direction: left, right, up, or down.) The effect is smooth, intriguing, and yet not overbearing.

During the pause while the audience reads the title, a hint of the shadow is still there, slightly obscuring one edge of the words. Then the wiper moves on, its trailing edge concealing the text that the forward edge revealed a moment earlier.

Zoom

Speed slider: *Controls zoom-in speed*
Direction control: *None*

When you select this effect, your text begins as a dot in the center of the screen, growing larger as it approaches, eventually becoming large, bold type (if the typed phrase is short). It holds for a moment, then fades out gracefully.

This effect is dramatic and punchy. Use it to get attention when the name of your movie finally appears on the screen, and to differentiate it from the opening credits that may have preceded it.

Use the Zoom Multiple variation for opening credits, especially those accompanied by rock music and exciting footage shot through the windshield of a fast-moving car. (If you know what's good for you, don't use either Zoom effect to introduce soft, sweet, or nostalgic flicks.)

Narration, Music, and Sound

I f you're lucky, you may someday get a chance to watch a movie whose soundtrack isn't finished yet. You'll be scanning channels and stumble across a special about how movies are made, or you'll see a tribute to a film composer, or you'll rent a DVD of some movie that includes a "making of" documentary. Such TV shows or DVDs sometimes include a couple of minutes from the finished movie as it looked *before* the musical soundtrack and sound effects were added.

At that moment, your understanding of the film medium will take an enormous leap forward. "Jeez," you'll say, "without music and sound effects, this $100 million Hollywood film has no more emotional impact than…my home movies!"

And you'll be right. It's true that in our society, the *visual* component of film is the most, well, visible. The household names are the directors and movie stars, not the sound editors, composers, *foley* (sound effects) artists, and others who devote their careers to the audio experience of film.

But without music, sound effects (called SFX for short), and sound editing, even the best Hollywood movie will leave you cold and unimpressed.

The Two iMovie Soundtracks

The top horizontal band of the Timeline Viewer displays the *video* component of your movie. It shows tiny thumbnails that help you identify which clips you've placed in which order. For the most part, you won't do much with this strip when you're editing audio; its primary purpose is to show where you are in the movie.

The two skinnier horizontal strips underneath it are your playground for audio clips (Figure 17-1). Both audio tracks are equivalent and each of them can hold sound from any of these sources, which you're free to drag between the two tracks: iTunes tracks, narration, sound effects, sound files like MP3 and AC, music from a CD, and the original audio from your camcorder. This chapter covers all of these sound varieties.

Tip: Ordinarily, when playing your movie, iMovie plays the sound in both audio tracks. But you can use the three checkboxes at the right end of these tracks to control which ones play back. When you want to isolate only one track, turn off the other two checkboxes (Figure 17-2). (These checkboxes also govern which soundtracks are exported when you send your finished iMovie production back to tape or to a QuickTime movie.)

Figure 17-1:
*The full Timeline Viewer is wider than this book—so here's what it would look like if you split it in half.
In this view, you see three horizontal bands, which represent the three soundtracks. The colored stripes (with triangle handles) represent pieces of audio: narration, tracks from a CD, music from your iTunes collection, sound effects, and so on.*

Note that the audio "sound waves" don't appear on the audio clips in this illustration; that feature has been turned off in iMovie→Preferences. Working with waveforms hidden reduces visual clutter and reveals each clip's name right on the clip. But turning them on, as shown in Figure 17-2, gives you a great advantage when you're trying to line up a certain audio moment with a corresponding video "hit."

Labels in figure: Video clips | Sound tracks | Pop song | Selected clip's name | Length | Selected clip

Audio Clips

In many regards, working with sound files is much like working with video clips. For example, each piece of sound appears as a horizontal colored bar in the Timeline Viewer. You can move a clip around in the movie by dragging horizontally; cut, copy, and paste it; delete by selecting it and then pressing the Delete key; and so on.

As you work, remember to use the Zoom slider (at the lower-left corner of the Timeline Viewer) to magnify or shrink your audio clips as necessary.

Renaming Sound Clips (or Not)

When you click an audio clip, iMovie intensifies its color to show that it's highlighted. The top edge of the Timeline Viewer shows the audio clip's name and duration.

To rename an audio clip, double-click it. The Clip Info box appears, where you can type a new name into the Name box.

Listening to a Sound Clip

To isolate and listen to a particular audio clip, proceed as shown in Figure 17-2.

Tip: Once your movie is playing, you can *loop* a section of audio (play it repeatedly as you study the effect) by clicking repeatedly in the same spot on the Scrubber bar, keeping the mouse very still. With each click, the Playhead snaps back to replay the segment from the position of your cursor.

Figure 17-2:
A view of the right end of the Timeline Viewer. Drag the Playhead so that the vertical line beneath it strikes the piece of sound you want to listen to. Then turn off the track checkboxes to isolate the track you want. Press the Space bar to begin listening.

Hint: If you've turned on "Enable Timeline snapping" in iMovie→Preferences, the Playhead snaps neatly and conveniently against the beginnings and ends of audio clips (and bookmarks, chapter markers, and video clips) when you drag it. In fact, it even snaps against bursts of sound within an audio clip, which helps you find the start or end of silent bits. (Shift-drag to override the snapping setting.)

1. Position the Playhead.

2. Isolate the track.

3. Press the Space bar.

Recording Narration

If anyone ever belittles iMovie for being underpowered, point out an iMovie feature that isn't even available in most of the expensive video editing programs: the ability to record narration while you watch your movie play. If your Mac has a microphone, you can easily create effects like reminiscences ("It was the year 2004. It was a time of innocence"), scene identification ("It's Halloween 2003, and little Chrissie is going out for her very first trick-or-treating. Mommy made the costume out of some fishnet stockings and a melon"), additional information ("Built in 1869, this house was extensively renovated in 1880..."), and so on.

If your Mac doesn't have a built-in microphone, you can plug in an external USB microphone (the Apple Products Guide at *www.guide.apple.com* offers a list) or an adapter (such as the iMic, *www.griffintechnology.com*) that accommodates a standard microphone.

Making the Recording

Here's how you record narration:

1. **Click the clock icon so that you're looking at the Timeline Viewer.**

   You'll do all your audio editing in Timeline view.

2. Drag the Playhead to a spot just before you want the narration to begin.

Also open the Audio panel, if it's not already open. You do so by clicking the Audio button, shown in Figure 17-3.

3. Click the round, red Record Voice button and begin to speak.

You can watch the video play as you narrate.

Note: If the level meter isn't dancing as you speak, the problem may be that your Mac is paying attention to the wrong audio input. Choose →System Preferences, and click the Sound icon. Click the Input tab, then click the microphone input that you want to use. When you're done, quit System Preferences.

Figure 17-3:
To summon the narration controls, click the Audio button. If your microphone is hooked up correctly, the round, red Record Voice button is available. (Otherwise, it's dimmed.) Just beside the Record button is a live "VU" level meter. Test your setup by speaking into the microphone; if this meter twitches in response, you're ready to record.

If the level meter bars are dancing, but not farther than halfway across the graph (see Figure 17-3), then your narration isn't loud enough. On playback, it will probably be drowned out by the camcorder audio track.

First, open System Preferences; click Sound; and click the Input tab to make sure that your input volume slider is at maximum. If that's not the problem, your only options are to lean closer to the microphone, speak louder, or use an external microphone. (There are tricks for boosting the volume of an audio track, as described later in this chapter, but it's much better to get the level right the first time.)

4. Click Stop to complete the recording.

Now a new stripe appears in the upper soundtrack, already highlighted, bearing the name Voice 01, like the one shown in Figure 17-1. Drag the Playhead to the left—to the beginning of the new recording—and then press the Space bar to listen to your voice-over work.

If the narration wasn't everything you hoped for, it's easy enough to record another "take." Just click the stripe representing your new recording and then press Delete to get rid of it. Then repeat the process.

You can edit and adjust the resulting sound clip just as you can other sounds in iMovie. See "Editing Audio Clips" later in this chapter for details.

Importing iTunes Music

Nothing adds emotional impact to a piece of video like music. Slow, romantic music makes the difference between a sad story and one that actually makes viewers cry. Fast, driving music makes viewers' hearts beat faster—scientists have proven it. Music is so integral to movies these days that, as you walk out of the theater, you may not even be aware that a movie *had* music, but virtually every movie does, and you were emotionally manipulated by it.

Home movies are no exception. Music adds a new dimension to your movie, so much so that some iMovie fans *edit to music.* They choose a song, lay it down in the audio track, and then cut the video footage to fit the beats, words, or sections of the music.

Tip: Even if you don't synchronize your video to the music in this way, you might still want to experiment with a music-only soundtrack. That is, *turn off* the camcorder sound, so that your movie is silent except for the music. The effect is haunting, powerful, and often used in Hollywood movies during montage sequences.

If you've been using iTunes to manage your music collection, you're in for a real treat. iMovie is well integrated with the other programs in its iLife software suite—including iTunes. (If you've created homemade songs in GarageBand, this feature is your ticket to importing them into iMovie, too. They show up in the iTunes playlist named after you.)

Here's how you go about choosing an iTunes track for your movie:

1. Click the Audio button, if necessary (Figure 17-3).

The Effects and Sounds panel changes to reveal your entire iTunes music collection. (If you don't see your list of songs, choose iTunes Library from the pop-up menu above the palette.)

2. Find just the right song.

The panel is filled with useful controls to help you find the right music, as described on page 3.

Tip: The playback controls in the Audio palette are independent of the playback controls in the Monitor window. You may find it useful, therefore, to play your movie in progress *as* you listen to the different songs, so that you can preview how the music might sound when played simultaneously with the video.

The easiest way to experiment in this way is to click the Play button in the Audio panel at precisely the same instant that you press the Space bar to begin the movie playback.

3. **Place the music into one of your audio tracks.**

You can go about this in either of two ways. If the Playhead is already parked where you want the music to begin, just click the song name and then click the Place at Playhead button beneath the song list. iMovie takes a moment to deposit the entire song, beginning at the point you've indicated.

You can also drag the song name directly out of the list and down into the Timeline Viewer. As long as you don't release the mouse button, and as long as the cursor is in one of the two audio tracks, you'll see that you can simultaneously move the Playhead and position the beginning of the song at just the right spot. Release the mouse when the song looks like it's in the right place.

(On the other hand, you can always adjust the starting point of the music after you've placed it, by dragging its audio-clip stripe horizontally.)

Depending on the length of the song you've selected, the importing process can take 30 seconds or more. That's how long it takes for iMovie to copy the iTunes track into a new audio file (in your project's Media folder). When it's complete, a new colored bar appears in the audio track, labeled with the song name.

Try dragging the Playhead back to the beginning of the music bar and pressing the Space bar to play it. If it doesn't have quite the effect you thought it would, click the new orange or purple stripe and then press the Delete key, to make room for your next experiment.

CD Music

If you don't use iTunes to organize your music, you can also snag a track or two directly from an audio CD. You just insert your favorite music CD (Carly Simon, Rolling Stones, the Cleveland Orchestra, or whatever), choose the track you want to swipe, and the deed is done.

Here's the procedure:

1. **Open the Audio panel, if it isn't already open.**

Do so by clicking the Audio button shown in Figure 17-3.

2. **Insert the music CD into your Mac.**

After a moment, a list of songs on the CD shows up in the list (Figure 17-4).

At first, they're probably called Track 1, Track 2, and so on. Unfortunately, audio CDs were invented before the advent of computers that could read them, and so the text of their track names isn't stored on the disc. Clearly, it would be a lot easier to find the music you want if you could see the *actual names* of the songs on the CD.

That's why, after a moment, iMovie automatically begins to download the list of songs on your CD, assuming that you're online. (iTunes may also open automatically, depending on how you've set up the CDs & DVDs panel in System Preferences.) Behind the scenes, it's consulting the Gracenote Internet CD database—a worldwide repository of track and album information. After a few moments, switch back into iMovie. You'll see that both the track names and the name of the album have now been typed in for you.

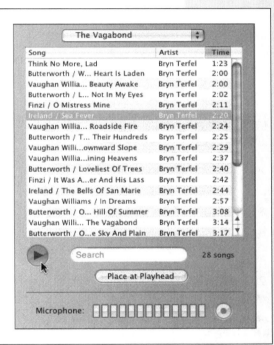

Figure 17-4:
The list in the Audio palette identifies the different songs (tracks) on your CD, along with the play length of each one. You can sort the list, audition different songs, or search the list just as you do your iTunes library (Figure 17-3). Drag an entire song into your movie, or click Place at Playhead.

You'll also notice that the pop-up menu above the Audio palette has changed to identify the name of the album.

3. **Find the song you want.**

   To do so, double-click one of the songs in the scrolling list (or click a song and then click the Play triangle button below the list). Click the Play triangle again to stop the music. Unfortunately, there's no way to fast-forward.

4. Insert the song into one of your audio tracks.

Either click the Place at Playhead button beneath the song list, or drag the song name out of the list and into position on one of your audio tracks.

When you're finished importing music, you're free to eject the CD (by holding down the Eject button on your keyboard, for example), insert another one, and nab another selection of music. iMovie no longer requires the first CD.

Sound Effects

iMovie also comes with a juicy collection of sound effects, suitable for dropping into your movies. If you choose iMovie Sound Effects from the pop-up menu at the top of the Audio palette, you'll find two flippy triangles, each denoting a collection of professional sound effects. (You don't have to click the triangle to see its contents; you can click directly on the collection's name.)

One, called Skywalker Sound Effects, is named for the Hollywood sound studio from which Apple licensed the effects (Birds, Cold Wind, Creek, and so on). The other, Standard Sound Effects, are the sounds that iMovie 4 inherited from iMovie 3 (Alarm, Bark, Crickets, and so on).

FREQUENTLY ASKED QUESTION

Fun with Copyright Law

Don't I break some kind of law when I copy music from a commercial CD, or use iTunes Music Store music in one of my movies?

Exactly what constitutes stealing music is a hot-button issue that has tied millions of people (and recording executives) in knots. That's why some iMovie fans hesitate to distribute their iMovie films in places where lawyers might see them—like the Internet.

But frankly, record company lawyers have bigger fish to fry than small-time amateur operators like you. You're perfectly safe showing your movies to family and friends, your user group, and other limited circles of viewers. In fact, Apple encourages you to use iTunes Music Store purchases in your movies; after all, Apple is the one who made them available right in iMovie.

You'll risk trouble only if you go commercial, making money from movies that incorporate copyrighted music.

Still, if your conscience nags you, you could always use one of your GarageBand compositions. And even if you're not especially musical, the world is filled with *royalty-free* music—music that has been composed and recorded expressly for the purpose of letting filmmakers add music to their work without having to pay a licensing fee every time they do so.

Some of it's even free. For example, check out *www.freeplaymusic.com,* a Web site filled with prerecorded music, in every conceivable style, that you're welcome to use in your movies at no charge. (If you've signed up for a .Mac account—see *www.mac.com*—you'll find a huge assortment of Freeplay Music tracks already on your iDisk, in the Software→Extras folder.)

If that's not enough for you, visit a search page like *www.google.com,* search for *music library* or *royalty-free music,* and start clicking your way to the hundreds of Web sites that offer information about (and listenable samples of) music that you can buy and thereafter use freely. (Many of these sites require the RealAudio plug-in, an add-on for your Web browser that you can download and install from *www.real.com.*)

Across from each sound's name, you see its length, expressed in minutes:seconds format.

You add a sound to your audio tracks exactly the way you add an iTunes tune—either by clicking the Place at Playhead button or by dragging the effect's name into either of the audio tracks in the Timeline Viewer. As your cursor moves over a track, the Playhead—accompanied by a cool, fading-out purple stripe—helps you see precisely where the sound will begin. Once placed there, the sound effect appears as a horizontal purple bar, just like any other sound clip. (If the sound effect is very short, you may have to zoom in to see it as a bar, using the Zoom slider at the left edge of the screen.)

A sound-effect clip behaves like any other sound clip. You can edit its volume in any of the ways described in "Editing Audio Clips," later in this chapter. You can slide it from side to side in the track to adjust where it begins, and even shorten, crop, or split it.

Adding or Removing Sound Effects

The list of sound effects in the Sounds palette isn't magical. It's simply a listing of the sound files that came with iMovie. If you know the secret, you can open a special folder and delete, move out, or rename your sound effects—or even install new ones.

1. **Quit iMovie. In the Finder, open your Applications folder. Control-click the iMovie icon; from the contextual menu, choose Show Package Contents.**

   The iMovie *package window* appears. You've just discovered, if you didn't already know, that many Mac OS X program icons are, in fact, thinly disguised folders (called *packages*) that contain dozens or hundreds of individual support files. You've just opened up iMovie for inspection.

2. **Open the Contents→Resources folder.**

   Welcome to the belly of the beast. Before you sit hundreds of individual files, most of them the little graphics that make up the various iMovie buttons, controls, and so on. (If you're really feeling ambitious, you can actually open up these graphics and edit them, completely changing the look of iMovie.)

   The icon you want is the folder called Sound Effects. It's a folder full of individual sound files—in MP3 and AIFF formats—that make up the list you see in the Audio palette (Figure 17-5).

   Feel free to reorganize these files. For example, you can throw away the ones you never use. You can also create new folders in the Sound Effects window to create new categories of sound effects in the Audio palette.

Tip: Looking for even more sound effects? Once again, the Internet is filled with them. You might start your search at *www.google.com.* Perform a search for *free AIFF sound effects,* for example. Happy hunting!

---

3. **Open iMovie. Click the Audio button. Choose iMovie Sound Effects from the pop-up menu above the list.**

Each folder in the Sound Effects folder forms its own subcategory of effects here.

Figure 17-5:
Left: Deep within the iMovie program itself lies a folder called Sound Effects. Any audio file that you download from the Internet, copy from a sound effects CD, create using a shareware sound-editing program, or save out of a QuickTime movie can become an iMovie "sound effect." Just drop it into this folder and relaunch iMovie.

Right: Whatever audio files you put into the Sound Effects folder and whatever you call them, determine the list of sound effects you see within iMovie.

Editing Audio Clips

Fortunately, you can do more with your audio clips than just insert them into the Timeline Viewer. You can lengthen them or shorten them, make them fade in or out, shift them to play earlier or later in time, and even superimpose them. Best of all—and here's one of the most useful features in iMovie—you can make their volume rise and fall over the length of the clip.

Making Whole-Clip Volume Adjustments

To make a particular clip louder or quieter relative to the other tracks, click its representation in the Timeline Viewer to select it. The clip darkens to show that it's highlighted.

Having selected an audio (or video) clip in this way, you can affect its overall volume level by dragging the volume slider shown in Figure 17-6. You can make it so quiet that it's absolutely silent, or you can actually make it 50 percent louder than the original.

Here are some pointers in this regard:

- You can also type a percentage number into the text box to the right of the slider. This isn't a feature only for the obsessively precise; it's a useful way to make sure that each of several audio clips are boosted to the same degree.

- iMovie stores your Fade checkbox and Volume slider settings independently for every audio clip. That's why the position of the Volume slider, for example, may jump around as you click different audio clips.

- If even 150 percent isn't enough of a volume boost, you can always open the audio clip in GarageBand for a quick boost. Drag the clip from the Finder into a waiting Real Instrument (blue) track, bump up the track's volume, export the result to iTunes, and then reimport the newly amplified file into iMovie.

Figure 17-6:
If you drag the volume slider all the way to the left, you mute the sound completely—for this clip only. If you drag it all the way to the right, you actually boost the volume up to 150%—a terrific way to compensate for weak camcorder microphones.

Volume Adjustments Within a Clip

Being able to make the volume of a clip rise and fall along its length, as you can in iMovie 4, comes in handy in a multitude of ways:

- It's a rare documentary or news show that doesn't begin a story with a full-volume, attention-getting shot (protesters shouting, band playing, airplane landing, and so on), whose audio fades to half volume after a few seconds, just in time for the reporter to begin speaking.

- Similarly, you can "pull back" the musical soundtrack whenever somebody on camera is speaking, and then bring it back to full volume in between speeches. This technique is incredibly common in movies, TV shows, commercials, and just about every other form of professional video.

- If you're a parent filming small children, your footage often winds up peppered with parental instructions recorded at a very high volume level, because you're right next to the microphone. ("Honey, stand over there by your brother," or

"Watch out for the car!") These parental voice-overs often ruin a clip—but you can rescue them by adjusting the original audio from the camcorder, which you can edit just as easily as imported audio.

- You can create smooth fade-ins or fade-outs of your music (or the sound from the original video).

Volume "Rubber Bands"

The key to turning on this feature is the Edit Volume checkbox at the bottom edge of the Timeline Viewer. When you turn it on, a horizontal line appears on every audio clip, stretching from edge to edge (and your video clips, too). This line is a graph of the clip's volume—and hallelujah, you're free to manipulate it like a rubber band. Here's how it works (consider zooming in for greater control):

- Click directly on the line and drag upward or downward (Figure 17-7, top). The original click produces a small spherical handle, and the drag produces a curve in the line from its original volume level. (Actually, you can simultaneously drag left or right to adjust the timing of this volume change.) Each "knot" in the line (the round handle) represents a new volume level that sticks until the end of the clip or the next volume level, whichever comes first.

- After you create such a curve, the point where the audio deviated from its original volume is denoted by a tiny square handle (Figure 17-7, third from top). To make the volume increase or decrease more or less gradual, drag that tiny square handle left or right, closer to your round adjustment handle or farther from it.

- To make the volume take another dip or swoop, click elsewhere on the volume line and drag again. You've just created a second round orange handle, which you can position independently (Figure 17-7, bottom).

- To remove a volume change, click the orange "knot" to select it, and then press the Delete key. (Or just drag it to the original volume level.) The knot disappears, and the "rubber band" line snaps back to the previous knot, stretched tight.

- To make a volume change extremely sudden, click a knot to highlight it, and then drag the tiny square just to its left. You'll find that you can drag this little square until it's directly above or below the knot: an instantaneous volume change.

- Consider making your volume adjustments *while* the movie plays back. Each time you make an adjustment, the Playhead jumps to that spot. As you keep clicking and adjusting, clicking and adjusting, the Playhead keeps jumping back to that spot, saving you the trouble of having to rewind and play, rewind and play, as you fine-tune the fluctuation.

- To restore the original, straight-line condition of a clip's volume, click each of the orange knots and press Delete until none of them remains.

Tip: When you've finished editing volume fluctuations, you can turn off the Edit Volume checkbox again. iMovie will remember all of the changes that you've made—you'll still hear the volume changes on playback. But iMovie hides all of the handles and rubber-band graph lines, so that you won't wind up dragging something out of alignment by accident.

Figure 17-7:
Top: The horizontal line represents the audio clip's standard, 100% volume level—too loud for the spoken dialogue.

Second from top: As you drag the little "knot" vertically, you have three sources of feedback about how much you've increased or decreased the volume at that spot: the height of the line segment itself (in which the orange or purple clip itself is the piece of graph paper, from 0% to 150%); the position of the Edit Volume slider; and the number in the percentage box to its right.

Third from top: Drag the tiny square (indicated by the cursor) to smooth out the line.

Bottom: Bring the music back up to 100% after the dialog portion is over.

Adjusting Many Clips at Once

You can adjust the volume levels of more than one clip simultaneously—a technique that comes in handy more often than you might think. For example, you may decide that *all* of the music excerpts you've grabbed from a CD are too loud compared to the camcorder audio. In one fell swoop, you can make them all softer.

Start by selecting the clips you want to affect:

- To select several clips, Shift-click them in any order. It's not like the equivalent maneuver in the Clip Viewer, where Shift-clicking selects only *consecutive* clips. When editing audio, you can Shift-click clip 1, clip 3, and so on. (On the other hand, ⌘-clicking works, too.)

- To select *all* of the clips in both audio tracks, highlight *one* clip there. Then choose Edit→Select All.

- To unhighlight a selected clip, Shift-click it.

Now when you drag the Volume slider, you're affecting all of the highlighted clips at once. (If you've fiddled around with the clips' rubber-band volume lines, adjusting the volume slider scales the volume of the whole thing up or down proportionally, maintaining the relative sizes of the fluctuations.)

Note: When several audio clips are highlighted, the Volume slider reflects whichever clip has the *highest* volume level.

Locking Audio Clips to Video

Figure 17-8 illustrates a serious problem that results from trying to line up certain video moments (like Bill-Gates-getting-hit-with-a-pie footage) with particular audio moments (like a "Splat!" sound effect). In short, when you insert or delete some video footage *after* lining up audio clips with specific video moments, you shove everything out of alignment, sometimes without even realizing it. This syndrome can rear its ugly head in many video-editing programs.

You may wind up playing a frustrating game of find-the-frame, over and over again, all the way through the movie, as you try to redo all of your careful audio/visual alignments.

In iMovie, the solution is especially elegant. Whenever you place an audio clip that you'd like to keep aligned with a video moment, get it into position and then *lock* it by choosing Advanced→Lock Audio Clip at Playhead (or press ⌘-L). What happens next depends on how you've set things up:

- If you've dragged or nudged the Playhead to the frame you care about most, iMovie locks the audio to the video at that frame, as indicated by the little pushpin (see Figure 17-8). Even if you later trim away some footage from the beginning part of the video clip, the sync moment remains intact.

- If the Playhead isn't anywhere near the highlighted audio clip, iMovie simply locks the beginning of the highlighted audio clip to whatever video frame it's currently aligned with.

- If you've highlighted several audio clips, once again, iMovie "pushpins" the beginning of each clip at its present video location.

Figure 17-8:
Top: You've carefully lined up a barking sound effect with the beginning of the dog clip.

Second from top: Uh-oh. You've selected a clip right before the dog, in preparation for deleting it.

Third from top: Now you've done it. You've deleted the clip that was just to the left of the dog. The dog clip slides leftward to close at the gap—and leaves the barking sound behind, now hopelessly out of alignment with the video above it.

Bottom: If you had remembered to lock the barking to the video above it, as indicated by the tiny pushpin, the sound effect would have slid to the left along with the dog clip, remaining perfectly in sync.

Once you've locked an audio clip to its video, you no longer have to worry that it might lose sync with its video when you edit your video clips. Nothing you do to the video clips to its left in the Timeline Viewer—add, delete, insert, or trim them—will affect its synchronization.

It's important to understand, however, that locking an audio clip freezes its position only relative to the video clip above it. The audio clip isn't locked into a particular *time* in the movie (such as 5:23:12). Put another way, "Lock Audio" actually means "*Don't Lock Audio (to one spot in the Movie Track); Let It Slide Around as Necessary.*"

Nor does locking an audio clip prevent *you* from shifting it. Dragging the audio clip will *not* drag the "attached" video clip along with it. You're still welcome to slide the audio clip left or right in its track, independent of any other clips. Doing so simply makes iMovie realign the clip with a new video frame, lining up the pushpin accordingly. (If you *cut* the audio clip and then paste it into a new location, it forgets both its original video-clip spouse and the fact that it was ever "married" to begin with. After pasting, it's pushpin-free.)

To unlock an audio clip, highlight it and then choose Advanced→Unlock Audio Clip (or press ⌘-L again).

Cropping an Audio Clip

As you may remember from Chapter 14, the ability to *crop*, or chop off the ends of, a video clip is one of the key tools in video editing. As it turns out, you can adjust the beginning or ending points of any audio clip even more conveniently.

Tip: If you use the Extract Audio command described on page 364, you can even crop the original camcorder audio in this way, without cropping the video clip in the process. Doing so is a great way to trim out an audio glitch that appears at the beginning or end of a shot without having to crop the video clip.

Figure 17-9:
You can shorten an audio clip (top) without actually deleting any of it, just by dragging the triangles inward (bottom). (Does this sound familiar? You can do the same thing with video clips.) At any time, you can restore the original length, or part of it, by dragging the triangle outward again.

You can shorten one of your music or narration clips from either the beginning or the end, just by dragging the corresponding end inward, as shown in Figure 17-9.

For finer adjustments, click one of the clip ends, so that the Playhead snaps to your cursor. Then press the right or left arrow key to move the handle in one-frame increments, or—if you press Shift as you do so—in *10*-frame increments. You might want to zoom in, using the Zoom slider at the left side of the window, if you're finding it hard to see the effects of your cropping maneuvers.

Note: As you drag the audio-clip crop handles inward or outward, any volume fluctuations you've added remain exactly where they were—which means that they might just wind up in nowhere-land. You might drag the end point of a clip so far to the left that you'll never hear the fluctuations you had programmed for the very end of the clip. If your volume fluctuations seem to be missing, turn on the Edit Volume checkbox to make your volume graph reappear. You'll see the problem right away.

Splitting an Audio Clip

When you drag an audio clip's ends inward, you're not actually trimming the clip. You're simply shortening the *audible portion* of the full-length clip. At any time in your project's lifetime, if you decide that you've overshot, you can slide the clip ends back outward again.

However, dragging the ends of clips inward doesn't reduce the amount of disk space that your audio file uses, since iMovie hangs onto the full original in case you decide to un-crop it.

There is an alternative, however. On page 282, you can read about the power of the Edit→Split Clip at Playhead command, which uses the current Playhead location as a razor blade that chops a video clip in two. In the Timeline Viewer, the equivalent command is called Split Selected *Audio* Clip at Playhead. As you'd expect, it breaks the audio clip beneath the Playhead into two independent clips.

Tip: If your Edit menu doesn't list a command called Split Selected Audio Clip at Playhead, it's because your Playhead isn't in the middle part of a *highlighted* audio clip. If no audio clip is selected, or if the Playhead's vertical insertion point isn't running through it, the command says Split Video Clip instead (and has a very different effect).

Being able to split an audio clip is useful in a number of ways. For example, suppose that you've got a voice recording of a guy recounting his days at the beginning of Apple Computer. One line goes, "We lived in a rundown tenement on the Lower East Side of Cupertino, but nobody cared. We loved what we were doing."

Now suppose you've also got a couple of terrific still photos of the original Apple building, plus a photo of the original Apple team, grinning like fools in their grungy T-shirts and beards. After using the Split Audio Clip command, you can place the first part of the recording ("We lived in a rundown tenement on the Lower East Side of

Cupertino") beneath the campus photos, and then *delay* the second utterance ("But nobody cared. We loved what we were doing.") until you're ready to introduce the group photo.

Tip: You can't split a clip and then immediately move one of the halves. After the Split command, both clips remain in position, side-by-side, both highlighted. Whatever you do will affect both pieces, as though you'd never split them at all. Shift-click the piece you *don't* want before trying to drag or cut anything.

Moving an Audio Clip

You can drag audio clips around in their tracks just as you would video clips, or even back and forth between the two audio tracks. In fact, because precision is often so important in positioning audio relative to the video, iMovie harbors a few useful shortcuts.

For example, whenever you drag an audio clip, the Playhead magnetically attaches itself to the beginning of the clip. As you drag, therefore, you get to watch the video in the Monitor window, corresponding to the precise moment when the sound begins.

Once the clip is highlighted, don't forget that you can press the left and right arrow keys to move it one frame at a time, or Shift-arrow keys to slide it 10 frames at a time. Even then, you'll see your exact position in the video by watching the Monitor window.

As a matter of fact, you can combine these two tricks. Once the Playhead is aligned with either end of a clip, you can press the arrow keys, or Shift-arrow, to move the Playhead *and* drag the audio clip along with it. You'll feel like the audio is somehow Velcro'ed to the Playhead.

Superimposing Audio Clips

iMovie may seem to offer only two parallel audio tracks, but that doesn't mean you can't have more layers of simultaneous sound. There may be only two horizontal strips on the screen, but there's nothing to stop you from putting audio clips *on top of each other*. By all means, drag a sound effect onto your already-recorded narra-

---

GEM IN THE ROUGH

The Invisible Audio "Shelf"

When you're editing video, the Clips pane provides a handy temporary working space where you can set aside clips that you haven't yet placed into the movie. If you've ever worked with a page-layout program like InDesign, you're already familiar with this "pasteboard" effect.

But iMovie doesn't come with any pane or pasteboard where you can temporarily park *audio* clips.

If you think it might be handy to have such a workspace as you manipulate your audio clips, the solution is simple: Drag them, or paste them, far off to the right of the Timeline Viewer, beyond the right edge of your video. Drag them back into place when you're ready for them. (Just don't leave any stray audio clips there by accident. You'll look pretty silly when your movie premieres at Cannes.)

---

tion clip, or superimpose two or more different CD music recordings, if that's the cacophonous effect you want. When playing back your project, iMovie plays all of the sound simultaneously, mixing them automatically (Figure 17-10).

Figure 17-10:
The first time you drag or paste a new audio clip onto an existing one, the situation is fairly clear, thanks to iMovie's tendency to put shorter clips on top of longer ones. It's impossible for a clip to become covered up entirely.

Long sound clip

Audio Selection: One Week Time: 14:22

One Week   Elephant

Short sound

If you're having trouble sorting out several overlapping sound clips, consider selecting one and then choosing Edit→Cut. Often, just getting one clip out of the way is enough for you to understand what's going on in its original location. Once you've got your bearings, you can choose Edit→Undo to put it right back where it was.

Another tactic: when you click a clip, iMovie always selects the shortest one in the stack. If you have two overlapping audio clips, therefore, and you intend to select the longer one, click one of its visible ends.

Remember, too, to glance at the top of the Timeline Viewer as you click each audio clip. You'll see its name (if you've turned off the sound waves, that is), which is another helpful clue when clips collide.

Scrubbing Audio Clips

Scrubbing once meant rotating reel-to-reel tapes back and forth manually in an effort to find a precise spot in the audio (to make a clean splice, for example). In iMovie 4, for the first time, you can scrub by Option-dragging your mouse back and forth across an audio clip. iMovie plays the sound under your cursor.

(This technique is extremely useful, but it works best when you're zoomed in and dragging very slowly. Note that Option is called Alt on some non-U.S. keyboards.)

Overlaying Video over Sound

One of the most popular editing techniques—both with editors and audiences—is the *video overlay.* (On the Internet, you may hear this technique called an *insert edit,* which actually has nothing to do with pasting video over audio.)

As shown in Figure 17-11, a video overlay is where the video cuts away to a new picture, but you continue to hear the audio from the original clip.

Suppose, for example, that you've got footage of an old man describing his first love. As he gets to the part where he describes meeting her, you want to cut to a closeup of her portrait on his mantelpiece.

Figure 17-11: When you over-lay video over sound, you can illustrate what the speaker is saying without losing her train of voice.

"What did I love about Edenville? Well, not the odor, that's for sure. And not the plant. No, what I loved most was the old canoe lake. Oh, sure, it was all foamed up with nitrates, and you didn't dare touch the water. But without a doubt, those were some of the happiest days of my life. I'd give almost anything to take one more look at that old lake."

The "Extract Audio in Paste Over" Checkbox

In iMovie 4, it's a piece of cake to paste a piece of video without disturbing the original audio track. You just have to check the status of a single checkbox in the iMovie→Preferences dialog box. Make sure "Extract audio in paste over" is selected.

If this checkbox is *on*, you'll paste only the video, preserving whatever audio is already on your audio tracks. If the checkbox is *off*, you'll wipe out both the audio and the video in the spot where you paste.

Performing the Overlay

To perform the video overlay, follow these steps:

1. **Select the footage you want to paste.**

   If it's a complete clip, just highlight its icon on the Clips pane or in the Movie Track. If it's a portion of a clip, use the crop markers to specify the part you want.

2. **Cut or copy the selected footage.**

   Use the Edit→Cut or Edit→Copy commands.

   Now you have to make an important decision. You're about to paste some copied video *over* some existing video. But how much of it do you want to paste? You can either "paste to fit" so that the pasted video begins and ends at precise frames, filling a hole in the existing footage of a particular length; or you can paste it all, without worrying about where the end of the pasted material falls. In this second scenario, you don't want to have to specify a cutoff point (where the existing video cuts in again).

   These two cases are illustrated in Figure 17-12.

3. If you want to paste the entire copied chunk, position the Playhead in the Timeline Viewer exactly where you want the insert to appear. Then choose Advanced→ Paste Over at Playhead (or press Shift-⌘-V).

The video you've pasted wipes out whatever was already there, even if it replaces multiple clips (or parts of clips). If the Extract Audio in Paste Over checkbox is turned on, as described above, your edit is complete. You've got a cutaway to new video as the original audio track continues.

Figure 17-12:
Suppose you've just copied an eight-second chunk of video.

Top: You might want to paste the entire clip, letting it overwrite the existing Timeline Viewer video for eight seconds, as shown here before and after.

Bottom: Other times, you want the pasted video to pour into the Timeline Viewer only to the extent that it fills a particular gap, like the four-second selection shown here. The trick is to highlight the portion of the Scrubber bar you want to fill before you paste.

4. If you want to paste to fit, highlight the portion of the movie that you want the pasted video to replace. Then choose Advanced→Paste Over at Playhead.

To select the region that your paste will replace, you can use any of the techniques described in Chapter 14. If you want to knock out only a portion of a single clip, for example, click the clip in the Movie Track and then use the Scrubber bar crop handles to isolate the section that will be replaced (Figure 17-12, bottom). If you want to paste into a segment that spans multiple clips (or parts of clips), choose Edit→Select None, and then use the cropping handles on the entire Scrubber bar map of your movie.

When you paste, one of three things may happen. If the pasted material is *precisely* the same length as the region you've highlighted, great; the pasted chunk drops perfectly into the hole. If the pasted material is longer than the highlighted region, however, iMovie chops off the pasted portion, using as much of the first portion as possible to fit the area you've designated. And if the pasted material is too *short* to fill the reserved space, iMovie creates a "black" clip (page 288) to fill the remaining highlighted area.

Extracting Audio from Video

iMovie is perfectly capable of stripping the audio portion of your footage apart from the video. All you have to do is click the video clip in question and then choose Advanced→Extract Audio.

As shown in Figure 17-13, the recorded audio suddenly shows up in your first audio track as an independent audio clip; its pushpins indicate that it's been locked to the original video.

Figure 17-13:
Top: Highlight some camcorder video and choose Advanced→Extract Audio.

Middle: The camcorder audio appears as an independent clip, which you can manipulate exactly as though it's any ordinary audio clip.

Bottom: You can create a reverb or echo effect by overlaying the same extracted audio several times.

This command unleashes all kinds of useful new tricks that weren't possible in the first version of iMovie:

- **Make an echo.** This is a great one. Copy the extracted clip and paste it right back into the audio track—and then position it a few frames to the right of the original. Use the slider at the bottom of the Timeline Viewer to make it slightly quieter than the original. Repeat a couple more times, until you've got a realistic echo or reverb sound.

- **Boost the audio.** The Volume slider at the bottom of the Timeline Viewer is a terrific help in boosting feeble camcorder audio. It does, however, have its limit: it can't crank the volume more than 50 percent above the original level.

Sometimes, even that's not enough to rescue a line of mumbled dialog, or the distant utterances of eighth-graders on the school stage 100 yards away.

But try this crazy technique: Copy the extracted clip and paste it *right back on top of itself.* iMovie now plays both audio tracks simultaneously, giving an enormous boost to the volume. In fact, you can stack two, three, four, or even more copies of the same clip on top of each other, all in the same spot, for even more volume boosting.

Now, there's a pretty good reason the Volume slider doesn't go higher than 150%. As you magnify the sound, you also magnify the hiss, the crackle, and whatever other underlying sonic noise there may have been in the audio. When you try this pasting-on-top trick, you may run into that problem, too. Even so, for insiders who know this technique, many an important line of dialog has been saved from oblivion.

- **Reuse the sound.** You can copy and paste the extracted audio elsewhere in the movie. (You've probably seen this technique used in dozens of Hollywood movies: About 15 minutes before the end of the movie, the main character, lying beaten and defeated in an alley, suddenly pieces together the solution to the central plot mystery, as snippets of dialogue we've already heard in the movie float through his brain, finally adding up.)

- **Crop the scene's audio.** Trim out an unfortunate cough, belch, or background car honk by cropping the audio. Now the video can begin (or end) in silence, with the audio kicking in (or out) only when required. (Of course, *silence* isn't generally what you actually want, as described next.)

- **Grab some ambient sound.** In real movie editing suites, it happens all the time: A perfect take is ruined by the sound of a passing bus just during the tender kiss moment—and you don't discover it until you're in the editing room, long after the actors and crew have moved on to other projects.

You can eliminate the final seconds of sound from the scene by cropping or splitting the clip, of course. But that won't result in a satisfying solution; now you'll have three seconds of *silence* during the kiss. The real world isn't truly silent, even when there's no talking; the air is always filled with *ambient sound,* such as breezes, distant traffic, the hum of fluorescent lights, and so on. Even inside in a perfectly still room, there's *room tone.* When you want to replace a portion of the audio track with "silence," you usually want, in fact, to replace it with ambient sound.

Professionals always record about 30 seconds of room tone or ambient sound just so that they'll have material to use in case of emergency. You may not need to go to that extreme; you may well be able to grab some sound from a different part of the same shot. The point is that by importing that few seconds of scene into iMovie, extracting the audio, and then *deleting* the leftover video clip, you've got yourself a useful piece of ambient-sound "footage" that you can use to patch over unwanted portions of the originally recorded audio.

It's important to note that iMovie never actually *removes* the audio from a video clip. You'll never be placed into the frantic situation of wishing that you'd never done the extraction at all, unable to sync the audio and video together again (which sometimes happens in "more powerful" video-editing programs).

Instead, iMovie places a *copy* of the audio into the audio track. The original video clip actually retains its original audio—but iMovie sets its volume slider to zero, thereby muting it. As a result, you can extract audio from the same clip over and over again, if you like. iMovie simply spins out another copy of the audio each time. (When you extract audio, the video clip, too, sprouts a pushpin, but don't let that fool you. It's perfectly legal to extract the audio again.)

If you intend to use the extracted audio elsewhere in the movie *without* silencing the original clip, no problem. Just click the video clip and then drag the volume slider at the bottom of the Timeline Viewer fully to the right once again.

Still Pictures and QuickTime Movies

T he DV camcorder is the source of iMovie material you'll probably use the most often, but it's not the only source. You can also bring in still images and existing QuickTime movies from your hard drive. You can also *export* still frames from your movie, a much more direct method of producing still images than using your camcorder's built-in "digital camera" feature.

Importing Still Images

You might want to import a graphics file into iMovie for any number of reasons:

- You can use a graphic, digital photo, or other still image as a backdrop for iMovie's titling feature. A still image behind your text is less distracting than video.

- You can use a graphics file *instead* of using the iMovie titling feature. Preparing your own title "slides" in, say, Photoshop Elements or AppleWorks gives you a lot more flexibility than the iMovie titling feature. You get complete control over type size, color, and placement, for starters. You can also add graphic touches to your text or to the slide on which it appears.

- One of the most compelling new uses of video is the *video photo album:* a smoothly integrated succession of photos (from your scanner or digital camera), joined by crossfades, enhanced by titles, and accompanied by music. Thanks to iMovie's ability to import photos directly from your hard drive or iPhoto collection, creating this kind of video show is a piece of cake.

Note: Of course, iPhoto can create video photo albums, too. But building them in a movie has several advantages. First of all, you're not limited to a single musical soundtrack. If your slideshow is five minutes long, you can string together two or three songs. Second, with the "Ken Burns" effect described later in this chapter, iMovie gives you complete control over how your virtual camera slowly zooms into each picture, pans across it, or both. Third, you have complete control over the timing and transition for each slide.

In iMovie 4, you have a choice of two methods for bringing still photos into a project. The first and most convenient method is to choose the photo from among those you've organized using iPhoto, using iMovie's window into your picture collection. If you're not using iPhoto to organize your digital photos, you can also use the older method of importing pictures from the hard drive.

Snagging Pictures from iPhoto

The more you work with iMovie and iDVD, the more you appreciate the convenience of the way Apple has linked them to the other i-programs, like iTunes and iPhoto. Here's a classic case:

When you click the Photos button (Figure 18-1), you're shown what amounts to iPhoto Lite: a scrolling panel of thumbnail images reflecting the contents of your entire iPhoto Library. Once you've pinpointed the picture you want, install it in your movie like this:

Photos palette

Ken Burns controls

Album list

Thumbnails

Figure 18-1:
The mini iPhoto area shows all pictures in your Photo Library or your currently selected album. (The digits above the scroll bar tell you how many pictures are in the library or album.)

Using the pop-up menu just above the thumbnails, you can even limit your view to the contents of one iPhoto album or another

Phase 1: Specify the duration

Because you're importing a still image, it doesn't have a *duration*, as a movie clip might. (Asking "How many seconds long is a photograph?" is like asking, "What is the sound of one hand clapping?")

Still, it's a clip, so iMovie has to assign it *some* duration. You can make your graphic appear on the screen for as little as three frames (a favorite of subliminal advertisers) all the way up to 60 seconds (a favorite of all other advertisers).

There's a fast way to change this number—and a more precise way. The fast way is to drag the rabbit/turtle slider shown in Figure 18-2.

Tip: When you get right down to it, 30 seconds is plenty of time for looking at one particular photo, no matter how good it is. Still, if you need it to last longer–perhaps because you're using it as a background for a series of opening credits–you can always overcome the 30-second limit by placing the same photo into the Movie Track over and over again, side by side, for 30 seconds each time.

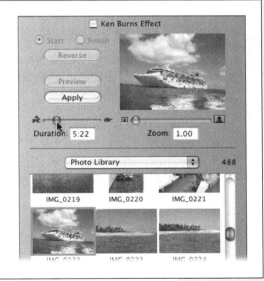

Figure 18-2:
To edit the duration of a still image, click the clip to make this Duration box appear. It illustrates the amount of time the picture will appear or on the screen, in seconds:frames format. Edit the clip's duration by changing these numbers.

When more precision is required, you can also type the number of seconds and frames into the Duration box above the thumbnail list.

Phase 2: Specify the Ken Burns effect

If you turn on the Ken Burns Effect checkbox at the top of the Photos panel, you unleash a wild and arresting feature: the ability to pan and zoom smoothly across photos, in essence animating them and directing the viewer's attention.

If you'd rather have your photo just pop onto the screen and remain stationary, make sure that the Ken Burns checkbox is turned off.

Phase 3: Insert the photo

At last you're ready to put the picture into the movie (a phrase that would hopelessly confuse Hollywood executives who already refer to movies *as* pictures). You can do so in either of two ways:

- Drag a photo out of the thumbnail palette and into the Movie Track. The other clips scoot out of the way to make room, and the photo becomes, in effect, a new silent video clip with the duration you specified.

- If you want the photo to drop into the end of the movie—as you might when assembling a slideshow one photo at a time—click the Apply button.

Tip: Speaking of slideshows: You can also drop a whole bunch of photos into the Movie Track at once. Select them in the Photos palette just as you would clips, then drag them en masse down to the Movie Track. Or click Apply to drop them all together at the end of the Movie Track.

You may notice, by the way, that black bars appear above and below (or both sides of) certain photos, creating the traditional letterbox effect. That happens when a photo doesn't have standard TV-format proportions (4:3). Use the Constrain cropping menu described on page 142 for the fix.

Importing Photos from the Hard Drive

If you want to incorporate graphics that aren't in iPhoto, begin by making sure that no thumbnails are selected in the Photos palette. (If one thumbnail remains highlighted, ⌘-click it.) Then specify the duration for the incoming photo, as described on page 369. If you don't intend to animate or crop your photo, make sure the Zoom slider is set to 1.0, and that the Ken Burns checkbox is turned off (Figure 18-4).

Finally, choose File→Import File (or just press Shift-⌘-I). When the standard Open File dialog box opens, navigate your way to the desktop (or wherever you put your graphics file), and double-click the file. Actually, because you're using Mac OS X, you can select a whole batch of photos to import simultaneously, using the Shift-clicking and ⌘-clicking techniques described on page 106.

The new photo shows up instantly in the Clips pane or the Movie Track, depending on where you've directed incoming clips to go in iMovie's Preferences box.

Tip: iMovie can import graphics in any format that QuickTime understands, which includes PICT, JPEG, GIF, Photoshop, and even PDF files (for when an IRS form is exactly what you want to illustrate in your movie). Avoid the GIF format for photos, since it limits the number of colors available to the image. But otherwise, just about any format is good still-image material.

After you've imported a graphics file into your project, it's OK to delete, rename, or move the original file. iMovie doesn't need it anymore.

And if you've been lying awake at night, wondering *how* iMovie can display your graphic after the original file is long gone, look no further than the Media folder in your movie's project folder. There you'll find copies of your imported graphics files, with their original names and at full resolution (so that the Ken Burns effect, if you turn it on now or anytime in the future, will have enough margin to animate your photo). You'll also find clip icons called Still 01, Still 02, Still 03, and so on; these are the rendered video clips, at 640 x 480 resolution, that iMovie made.

Working with Photos

Once you've installed them in the Movie Track, photos behave a lot like standard movie clips. You can rename them, drag them around, click them to view them in the Monitor window, drag them back and forth from the Clip Viewer and Clips pane, delete them, incorporate them into titles or transitions, and so on.

You can also adjust the timing of an imported picture. Just highlight its icon, adjust the Duration slider (or type new numbers into the Duration box), and then click the Update button just above those controls. (The Update button appears only when a single photo is selected. You can't change the timings of multiple photos at once.)

Tip: If you haven't applied the Ken Burns effect described later in this chapter, you can also change a photo's duration by double-clicking it and then typing a new duration into the Clip Info box. Using this method, you save yourself a click on the Photos button.

The Dimensions of an iMovie Graphic

If you want an imported graphic to completely fill the screen when it's part of your movie (and you don't plan to use the Ken Burns effect), its dimensions should be *640 pixels wide, 480 high.* (If you live in Europe or another region that uses PAL systems, substitute 768 x 576 everywhere in this chapter where dimensions are provided.)

FREQUENTLY ASKED QUESTION

The Case of the Rectangular Pixels

Why should I save my graphic at 640 x 480? I read on the Internet that each DV frame is actually 720 x 480. For best resolution, therefore, shouldn't I make my still pictures that size?

All right, Mr. Does-His-Homework. You want the technical explanation, and you shall have it.

It's true that each frame of digital video is actually 720 pixels wide, not 640. The explanation lies in an uncomfortable fact that iMovie carefully hides from you: The pixels that compose a digital video frame *aren't square*—they're actually rectangular. They're skinny, upright little rectangles.

When you see the image in iMovie or on TV, it's compressed so that it *appears* to be 640 x 480. Technically speaking, in

other words, an iMovie image is stretched by 12.5 percent from what you're seeing on the screen. With certain add-on graphics programs, you might even be able to see the picture the way iMovie really thinks of it. (When those skinny rectangles are made square again, your subjects would all appear short and fat.)

As an additional favor to you, iMovie automatically converts these stretched pixels into square ones whenever you import or export graphics or QuickTime movies. The program thinks, "Well, whenever this final movie is viewed on TV or in a QuickTime movie, its dimensions will look like they're in a 4:3 ratio anyway, so I may as well request 640 x 480 still images and do the conversion in my head, where no one can see."

If you do plan to use the Ken Burns effect, you'll get the best quality if your graphic's original resolution factors in the zooming you plan to do. If you want the photo to zoom in to twice its original size, your starting image should be 1280 x 960 pixels (that's twice 640 x 480).

If your graphic starts out with too much resolution, iMovie will automatically chop it down to 640 x 480. If it starts out *smaller* than 640 x 480, iMovie will add a black frame around it when you install it into your movie.

Now, most digital photos pop out of the camera at the proportions that iMovie expects: 4:3 (a multiple of 640 x 480 pixels). If your camera uses 3:2 proportions, or if your graphics file is anything but 4:3, you'll get black bars along either the top and bottom or the sides. For example, if your image is wider than it is tall, you'll get black bands above and below it when it's inserted into iMovie (unless it's in precisely 4:3 proportions). Either way, the result is the *letterboxed* look of some big-screen movies that are adapted to the smaller screen of a TV (see Figure 18-3).

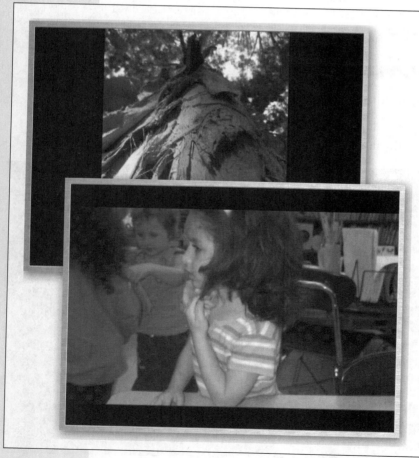

Figure 18-3:
If the dimensions of your graphic aren't in a 4:3 ratio, you'll get letterboxed bars like these.

Top: A portrait-orientation photo.

Bottom: A landscape-orientation photo that's not quite 4:3.

Fortunately, when it comes to digital photos, solving all of these proportion problems is very easy; see the box on page 375.

Creating a Graphic from Scratch

But what if you intend to design a graphic from scratch, using a program like Photoshop or GraphicConverter? The key is to create a graphic exactly 640 pixels wide and 480 pixels tall (assuming you don't intend to zoom or pan with Ken Burns).

When you're finished, see "Importing Photos from the Hard Drive," earlier in this chapter.

The Ken Burns Effect

The only problem with using still photos in a movie is that they're *still*. They just sit there without motion or sound, wasting much of the dynamic potential of video.

For years, professional videographers have addressed the problem using special sliding camera rigs that produce gradual zooming, panning, or both, to bring photographs to life.

But this smooth motion isn't just about adding animation to photos for its own sake. It also serves an editorial purpose, because it lets you draw the viewer's attention where you want it, when you want it. For example: "Little Harry graduated from junior high school in 1963"—slow pan to someone else in the school photo, a little girl with a ribbon in her hair—"little suspecting that the woman who would one day become his tormentor was standing only a few feet away."

Among the most famous practitioners of this art is Ken Burns, the creator of PBS documentaries like *The Civil War* and *Baseball*—which is why Apple, with his permission, named the feature after him.

You can endow any still graphics file with this kind of motion, either at the moment when you place it into the Movie Track, when you import it from your hard drive, or anytime thereafter.

Applying the Ken Burns Effect

In this example, you'll animate a photo that's in the iPhoto palette.

1. Select the photo.

   Actually, you can select more than one, if you intend to process all of them in the same way.

2. Turn on the Ken Burns Effect checkbox at the top of the window. Specify how long you want the picture to remain on the screen.

   Use the Duration controls, just as described on page 369.

3. Click Start. Use the Zoom controls until the photo is as big as you want it at the *beginning* of its time on screen. Drag inside the Preview screen to adjust the photo's position (Figure 18-4).

In other words, you're setting up the photo the way it appears at the beginning of the shot. Often, you won't want to do anything to it at all. You want it to start on the screen at its original size—and then zoom in from there.

But if you hope to create a zooming *out* effect, you'd begin by dragging the Zoom slider to the right, magnifying the photo in the Preview screen, and dragging the picture itself to center it properly.

Tip: It's actually possible to drag the photo partially or completely *out of the frame,* leaving an empty black void in its place. If you've done this accidentally, just nudge the Zoom slider slightly. The photo smartly snaps back into centered position.

On the other hand, there are certain creative possibilities here. You can make a photo begin offscreen and then slowly slide into place, for example—or even exit the screen by sliding off the opposite side.

Zoom out   Pan and zoom in   Horizontal pan

Figure 18-4:
Top: To set up the Ken Burns effect, establish the position and zoom level of the Start and Finish points separately. (At top right, you can see the little grabby-hand cursor that lets you shift the photo within the frame.)

Bottom: Here are three possibilities. The zoom-out pictured at left results from the Ken Burns setting shown above. The center example makes the camera appear to zoom in on the tower, as the photo shifts position to keep the tower centered. At right, the Zoom setting was the same (2.0) for both the Start and Finish points. The only thing that changes over time is the left-to-right position of the photo in the frame.

4. **Click Finish. Use the Zoom controls to set up the picture's final degree of magnification. Drag inside the Preview screen to specify the photo's final position. (Shift-drag to constrain your dragging to perfect vertical or horizontal adjustments.)**

In short, you've set up the starting and ending conditions for the photo.

Take a moment now to click the Preview button. The animated photo goes through its scheduled motion within the Preview box, so that you can check the overall effect. Repeat steps 3 and 4 till you're satisfied.

Tip: At any time, you can click the Reverse button to swap the settings of the Start and Finish positions. What was once a slow zoom in, left to right, becomes a slow zoom out, right to left.

That's handy, because zoom-out clips often look better than zoom-in clips. Use the Reverse button to see if that's true for your movie (it varies by photo). If the clip's smoothness does indeed improve, you can later use iMovie's Advanced→Reverse Clip Direction command to restore the original, intended playback direction.

---

5. **Drag the thumbnail image out of the Photos palette and into the Movie Track.**

Alternatively, you can click the Apply button to have iMovie plunk the image at the very end of the movie so far.

Either way, iMovie now begins rendering your photo effect. You specified the beginning and ending positions of the photo; now iMovie is *interpolating* (calculating each intermediate frame between the starting and ending points you've specified). The red progress bar crawls across the face of the clip, showing you how much longer you have to wait. (Of course, you're free to work on other aspects of your movie in the meantime, although you may notice a slowdown.)

GEM IN THE ROUGH

The Ken Burns Cropping Effect

You already know that the Ken Burns effect can animate a photo over time, slowly (or quickly) zooming, panning, or both, depending on where the picture is when you click the Start and Finish buttons.

But you can also zoom *before the clip even starts*—and then leave the photo that way for the duration of the clip. That is, you can use the Ken Burns tools to crop a photo as you place it into your Movie Track. It's a great way to eliminate, for example, the black letterbox bars that appear if your photo's dimensions aren't 4:3.

To try this out, click a photo, turn on the Ken Burns effect, specify the duration, and then click Start. Zoom in the way you like it—and then Option-click the Finish button.

Option-clicking the button copies the Start position and zoom level into the Finish position. The result is a clip that doesn't move or pan at all, but instead maintains whatever zoom level and position you specified for the very beginning.

(You can Option-click the Start button, too, if the Finish position and zoom level are what you want to use for the entire clip.)

This is a great trick for dealing with a vertical photo that you want to use in the horizontal orientation of a standard television. By zooming in until the black bars disappear, you've chopped off some of the top and bottom of the picture.

After the rendering is complete, click the photo clip in the Movie Track and press the Space bar to play your Ken Burns-ized "photo movie" in the Monitor window.

Tip: Option-click the Finish button to copy the Start button's pan and zoom settings (or vice versa). You wind up with a motionless photo that's frozen at the position and magnification of the copied settings.

Editing a Ken Burns Effect

If a photo clip requires adjustment, touching it up is easy. Select it in the movie track (or wherever it is). Click the Photos button (if the Photos pane isn't already open). Click Start or Finish, and reprogram the Ken Burns effect just as you did the first time around. (Feel free to edit the duration, too.) When you're finished, click Update. iMovie dutifully rerenders the clip with its new settings.

Turning Off the Ken Burns Effect

If you decide that a certain still photo really should be still, you can often remove the Ken Burns effect just by clicking the clip in the Movie Track, turning off the Ken Burns Effect checkbox, and then clicking Update.

What's neat is that you're not actually *deleting* the Ken Burns effect; instead, you're freezing the photo on the first frame of the animation. That powerful distinction means that you can use the Ken Burns control to enlarge, crop, or shift a still photo *without* animating it. Just turn on the Ken Burns effect, apply it, and then turn it off again.

But what if you really want the photo to return to its original, virginal condition? In that case, turn on the Ken Burns checkbox, and then click the Start button. Drag the Zoom slider all the way to the left, which both re-centers the photo and restores it to its original size. Only then should you click the Update button.

Tip: If you've used still images in your movie, don't even *think* about turning your project into a DVD until you've read the troubleshooting steps on page 603. Otherwise, you'll wind up with jagged, awful-looking photos.

Creating Still Images from Footage

iMovie doesn't just take still photos, it can also dish them out. It can grab selected frames from your footage, either for use as frozen frames in your movie or for exporting as graphics files. You might want a still frame to end a Ken Burns zoom, for example, so that the camera seems to hold still for a moment after the zoom.

Creating a Still Frame

The Edit→Create Still Frame command creates a still image (in the Clips pane), of the frame currently indicated by the Playhead. You can use the resulting still clip just as you would any still clip: Drag it into your Movie Track, apply effects or transitions to it, change its name or duration, and so on.

One of the most obvious uses of this feature is the *freeze-frame* effect, in which the movie holds on the final frame of a shot. It's a terrifically effective way to end a movie, particularly if the final shot depicts the shy, unpopular hero in a moment of triumph, arms in the air, hoisted onto the shoulders of the crowd. (Fade to black…bring up the music…roll credits.)

Here's how you do it. (These steps assume that you're creating a still frame from a clip that you've already placed in the Movie Track. It's possible, however, to create a still frame from a clip that's still in the Clips pane.)

1. **Position the Playhead on the frame you want frozen.**

   If it's the last shot of a clip, use the right and left arrow keys to make sure you're seeing the final frame.

2. **Choose Edit→Create Still Frame (Shift-⌘-S).**

   iMovie places a new clip either in your Clips pane or at the end of the Movie Track, depending on how you've set up the iMovie→Preferences dialog box.

   It's a still image, set to play for five seconds—but it's not the same kind of still photo you're used to. None of the controls in the Photos palette, for example, have any effect on a *still*, as iMovie calls it. (You can't apply the Ken Burns effect to it, for example.)

   If you created this still clip from the *final frame* of a clip, proceed to the next step. If you created this clip from the *middle* of a clip, however, you should now choose Edit→Split Clip at Playhead. You've just chopped the clip at the precise source of the still clip, resulting in two side-by-side clips in your Movie Track. Delete the right-hand clip.

3. **Drag the still clip just to the right of the original clip (Figure 18-5).**

   If you play back the result, you'll be impressed at how smoothly and professionally iMovie joins the frozen frame onto the moving footage; there's not even a hint of a seam as the Playhead slides from clip to still.

Figure 18-5:
*A great way to end a movie:
Chop up the final clip and
slow down each piece, finally
coming to rest on your still
image.*

4. **Adjust the still's playback duration, if necessary.**

   Remember, iMovie doesn't treat a still frame the same way it treats photos. You can't, for example, change its duration using the Duration slider in the Photos pane.

Instead, double-click the new still frame. In the Clip Info dialog box, change the number of seconds and frames in the Duration box, and then click OK.

Figuring out how to handle the *audio* in such situations is up to you, since a still frame has no sound. That's a good argument for starting your closing-credits music *during* the final clip and making it build to a crescendo for the final freeze-frame.

Exporting a Still Frame

While it's convenient to be able to grab a frame from your footage for use in the same movie (as a freeze-frame, for example), you may sometimes find it useful to be able to export a frame to your hard drive as a graphics file—for emailing to friends, installing on your desktop as a background picture, posting on a Web page, and so on. An exported frame also makes a good piece of "album art" that you can print out and slip into the plastic case of a homemade DVD.

Alas, the maximum *resolution* for a digital video frame (the number of dots that compose the image) is 640 across, 480 down. (By this time in the chapter, these numbers have probably become engraved into your cerebrum.) As digital photos go, that's pretty pathetic—on a par with the photos taken by camera phones these days.

Now that your expectations have been duly lowered, here's how you capture a frame in iMovie:

Open the project from which you want to grab a still photo. Press the Home key to make sure that no individual clips are selected, and then locate the frame you want to capture. Drag the Playhead along the Scrubber bar, for example. Remember that you can press the left and right arrow keys to step through the movie one frame at a time, or Shift-arrow keys to jump ten frames at a time, in your quest for the precise moment you want to preserve as a still image.

When the image you want appears in the Monitor window, choose File→Save Frame As (or press ⌘-F). The Save As dialog box (sheet) slides down from the top of the iMovie window (Figure 18-6).

Figure 18-6:
The Save Frame dialog box (or sheet, as it's called in Mac OS X) lets you choose a graphics-file format: JPEG or PICT. When the process is over, the saved frame appears with its own icon on your desktop (or wherever you saved it).

Use the Format pop-up menu to specify the file format you want for your exported graphic: PICT or JPEG (the better choice if you intend to email it to someone or use it on a Web page). Navigate to the folder into which you want this graphic saved (or press ⌘-D to save it onto the desktop). Click Save.

Importing QuickTime Movies

iMovie can import more than still images. It can also import existing QuickTime movies, which you can then incorporate into your footage.

Maybe you've created such QuickTime movies yourself, using other Macs or other software. Maybe you've grabbed a QuickTime movie from a CD-ROM or Web site. (You *can't* grab video from commercial DVDs, which are programmed to block such potential legal violations.)

In any case, once you've got the QuickTime movie on your hard drive, choose File→ Import (Shift-⌘-I). In the Open File dialog box, navigate to and open the QuickTime movie you want to import.

It may take iMovie some time to process the incoming movie. Behind the scenes, it's converting the QuickTime movie into DV format, just like the clips that come from your camcorder. A progress bar keeps you posted.

When it's complete, a new clip appears in your Clips pane, which you can manipulate just as you would any movie clip.

Using the Imported QuickTime Clip

It's worth noting that most of the world's QuickTime movies aren't big enough, in terms of frame size, to fill your entire monitor. In fact, most of the world's QuickTime movies play in a window only a couple of inches square.

Therefore, when you play back an imported QuickTime movie, iMovie does what it hopes is the right thing: It blows up the QuickTime movie until the footage fills the entire iMovie playback screen (640 x 480 pixels).

As you probably know by now, however, enlarging *any* graphic on the computer usually winds up degrading its quality, because each pixel that composes the image must be enlarged. Bottom line: QuickTime movies you import into iMovie usually look coarse and blotchy unless they were at least 640 x 480 to begin with.

Fortunately, the era of small-size QuickTime movies is, for you, over. In the future, you can keep all your video on DV cassettes, always at full-screen size, and always at fantastic quality.

Grabbing Clips from Other Projects

One way to reuse clips among iMovie projects is to Option-drag their clip files among the projects' Media folders, thereby making copies. But if you'd rather not switch to the Finder and muck around in folder windows, you can use the File→Import File command to simplify the process.

When you choose it, the Import File dialog box appears. Navigate to the folder that contains the project whose footage you'd like to steal, and open it. Then open the Media folder inside, and double-click the Clip file you want to import into the project that's open onscreen. After a moment—a *long* moment, as iMovie copies this enormous file into the current project's own Media folder—the imported clip appears on the Clips pane.

Of course, these cheerful instructions overlook one massive roadblock: figuring out which of the dozens of clips in the raided project's Media folder is the one you want to import. After all, they don't have descriptive names and you can't preview them.

That's why the importing-a-clip-from-another-project routine generally involves a detour: opening the *other* project, finding the clip (in the Clips pane or Movie Track) that you're trying to reuse, double-clicking it, and then reading its clip number in the Clip info dialog box. Then you can return to your newer project and import the clip as directed above.

Finding Your Audience

It's conceivable that, like the perpetual student who's never quite ready for the real world, you enjoy editing your movies so much, you don't ever want to finish up. Most people, however, use iMovie with a single goal: finishing and exhibiting the completed video before a live audience.

Fortunately, iMovie's powerful Share command offers a huge number of exporting possibilities. You can send your movie back to your camcorder, where it appears in all its original, high-resolution glory. You can dub it down to a VHS tape. You can burn it as a DVD. Or you can leave it in the realm of computers by posting it on a Web page, sending it by e-mail, or exporting it as a QuickTime movie. This chapter covers all of these possibilities.

Exporting to Tape

You might want to send your finished product back to the camcorder for any number of reasons. For example:

To Watch It on TV

Once your iMovie creations are back on the camcorder's DV tape, you can then pass them along to a television. To pull this off, you must connect the camcorder to your TV, using an S-video cable (if possible) or regular RCA phono cables (if not).

Tip: If your TV is very old, it may not have auxiliary input jacks of either type. In that case, plug your camcorder into the *VCR's* auxiliary inputs instead. It will patch the signal through to the TV.

To Transfer It to Your VCR

The glorious thing about DV tape, of course, is that its picture quality and sound quality are sensational. Unfortunately, most of the world's citizens don't *have* DV camcorders or DV decks. They have standard VHS VCRs, or they have DVD players.

Chapters 20 through 22 guide you through turning iMovie masterpieces into DVDs—but that's a stunt you can pull off only if your Mac has a built-in DVD burner. For everyone else, the best way to get your movies to the TV screens of your adoring fans is to transfer them (the movies, not the fans) to VHS cassettes.

You lose a lot of picture and sound quality when you transfer footage to a VHS cassette, whose lines-of-resolution capacity is lower than any other kind of tape reproduction. Still, your viewers will most likely remark how *good* your movies look, not how bad. That's because most people are used to playing back VHS recordings they've made from television, which (unless it's a satellite system) has its own low-resolution problems. The transfers you make from your Mac, even when played back on VHS, look terrific in comparison.

To Offload Footage from Your Mac

Another great reason to transfer your iMovie work back to the camcorder is simply to get it off your hard drive. As you know, video files occupy an enormous amount of disk space. After you've made a couple of movies, your hard drive might be so full that you can't make any more iMovies.

Offloading the movie to your DV camcorder is the perfect solution, thanks to a key advantage of digital video: the ability to transfer footage back and forth between the camcorder and your Mac as many times as you like with *no deterioration in quality*. You can safely unlearn the years of experience you've had with VHS and 8mm video and feel free to transfer video between your Macintosh and DV camcorder whenever and however you like.

Note: When you transfer an iMovie back to your camcorder–to a fresh tape, if you're wise–the footage remains in perfect, pristine condition. Remember, however, that there's a downside to doing so: Once you've thrown away the digital video files from your Mac, you've lost the ability to adjust titles, effects, transitions, and soundtracks. For best results, therefore, transfer footage back to the camcorder either when you're finished editing the movie, or haven't edited it much at all.

After transferring the movie to a DV cassette in your camcorder, you can throw away the corresponding files on your hard drive, which frees up an enormous amount of disk space. The space-consuming digital-video clips themselves sit in the Media folder that lurks within the folder you've named for your project. In other words, the Media folder is the one taking up all the disk space. Still, you may as well throw away the *entire* project folder (after "backing it up" onto the camcorder), because without the Media files, the actual iMovie document file, and the accompanying *.mov* reference-movie file, are useless.

Making the Transfer

The actual steps of transferring the project from iMovie back to the camcorder are fairly simple. The results are almost always satisfying, especially if you've had to look at your footage in its relatively coarse Mac rendition for hours or days. Finally, you get to see your masterpiece at full digital quality. Most people are particularly thrilled by the professional look of iMovie's transitions and titles when they see it on the actual TV (or camcorder LCD panel).

Before you begin, connect your camcorder to the Mac with a FireWire cable. Then:

1. **Insert a blank cassette into your camcorder.**

   Confirm that the tape is unlocked and—*this is important*—that it's cued up to a part of the tape you're willing to record over.

2. **Put the camcorder into its VTR or VCR mode.**

   Confirm that its FireWire cable is plugged into your Mac. Unless you're willing to risk running out of battery power in midtransfer, plug your camcorder into a power outlet, too.

   Open your iMovie project on the Mac, if it isn't already open.

3. **Choose File→Share (Shift-⌘-E, which is a holdover from iMovie 3 when this command was called Export).**

   The Share dialog box appears, as shown in Figure 19-1.

Figure 19-1:
The Share dialog box lets you specify whether you're sending your finished movie to a tape, a QuickTime movie, a DVD, a Bluetooth phone or Palm organizer, and so on.

4. **At the top of the dialog box, click Videocamera. Change the "seconds of black" and "seconds for camera to get ready" numbers in the dialog box, if necessary.**

The "seconds of black" numbers specify how many seconds of blackness you want to appear on the tape before the movie begins or after it ends; three or four seconds is about right. Without a black "preroll," the movie would begin instantly. Your audience would be deprived of the customary "settle down and start paying attention" moment that precedes every TV show, movie, and commercial throughout the world. And without a moment of blackness at the end, the mood created by your movie might be shattered too soon.

The other number in this box, "seconds for camera to get ready," is designed to account for the fact that no camcorder goes into Record mode instantly. Inside the camera, small wheels must first open the door of the cassette, extract the tape, and load it around the recording heads, all of which takes a moment or two. The number you enter in this box doesn't change what's recorded. In other words, your *viewers* won't have to wait this number of seconds; it's just a precaution to make sure that your camcorder is rolling to record when iMovie is playing.

Tip: As it turns out, iMovie needs a few seconds to get *itself* ready to send your movie back to the camcorder (during which a message says "Initializing"). Therefore, experiment with the "seconds for camera to get ready." A setting of 1 or even 0 may work for your camcorder model.

iMovie will remember these settings for the next time you export a movie.

You can also take this opportunity to turn on "Share selected clips only," if you like. This new iMovie 4 feature lets you split up a long movie into smaller chunks by preselecting only the clips you want before you invoke the Share command. (See page 272 for tips on selecting clips.)

Figure 19-2:
While iMovie sends your finished production back to the camcorder from whence it came, a progress bar shows how much longer you have to wait. Also, you see the playhead ride along your Movie Track to show where you are in the transfer.

You can interrupt the transfer process at any time by clicking Stop. The camcorder stops automatically, having recorded your movie up to the part where you stopped.

5. **Click Share.**

   If your project contains certain special effects, iMovie takes this opportunity to say: "Your movie contains still, slow motion, and/or reverse clips which need to be rendered for export to iDVD or tape." In that case, click "Render and Proceed." You're instructing iMovie to generate smoother, more professional looking versions of these scenes—not the quick-and-dirty, temporary ones it's been showing you during editing.

   Either way, after a moment, iMovie commands the camcorder to begin recording, and then begins pumping your finished video over the FireWire cable to the tape, from the very beginning of the movie (Figure 19-2).

   When the transfer is complete, the camcorder automatically stops recording. Your finished production is now safely on DV tape.

Figure 19-3:
Top: Connect your camcorder's RCA jacks, shown here, to those of your VCR or TV. If your TV accepts only one sound cable (and not stereo inputs), plug the camcorder's left-channel connector (usually the red one) into the sole TV audio jack.

Bottom: Some camcorders, including most Canon and Sony models, come with a special, proprietary cable. The miniplug end goes into a special output jack on the camcorder; the far ends are RCA cables for your TV or VCR.

Tip: After the transfer is complete, drag the Camera/Edit switch on your iMovie screen (at the left edge of the screen, just below the Monitor) to its Camera position. Doing so puts iMovie into "I'm controlling your camcorder now" mode. Click Rewind, then Play to watch your newly transferred production.

At this point, you can connect your camcorder to a VCR for transfer to a standard VHS cassette (or any other non-DV format). See Figure 19-3 for connection details.

Make sure that the VHS tape is blank and not protected by its erase tab. If you're smart, you'll label it, too—*now,* before you even record it, so that you won't forget. Put it into the VCR and cue it up to the right spot. Cue up the camcorder, too.

Finally, put your camcorder into VCR or VTR mode, start the VCR recording, and then press Play on the camcorder. If your TV is on, you can watch the footage as it plays into your VCR. Press Stop on both the camcorder and VCR when the transfer is complete.

Exporting to a QuickTime Movie

For the best and most cinematic viewing experience, play your finished iMovie productions on TV, via VHS tape or DVD. That way, your public gets to see the full-sized picture that your camcorder captured.

But when you want to distribute your movies electronically, convert them into QuickTime files instead. Both Mac and Windows machines can play these files right on the screen with little more than a double-click.

Your distribution options for QuickTime files are far greater than for videocassette or DVD, too. You can email a QuickTime file to somebody or post it on the Web for all the world to see. You can put bigger QuickTime files onto a disk, like a recordable CD, a Zip disk, or an Apple iPod, to transport them.

Here's how you do it:

1. **Choose File→Share.**

   The Share dialog box appears.

2. **Click the QuickTime icon at the top.**

   Now the dialog box looks like Figure 19-4.

3. **Using the Formats pop-up menu, choose one of the preset export formats such as Email, Web, CD-ROM, or Expert Settings.**

   This decision dramatically affects the picture quality, motion smoothness, file size, and window size of the finished QuickTime movie.

   Making a smart choice in this step requires some comprehension of the QuickTime technology itself, so although "Understanding QuickTime" in the next section is many pages long, it's well worth absorbing. It's critical to your grasp of QuickTime movies, what they are, and what they can do.

That section also describes the choices in this pop-up menu one by one.

4. **Click Share.**

Now the standard Save File dialog box appears, sprouting from the title bar of the iMovie window.

Figure 19-4:
Using the pop-up menu in this dialog box, you can indirectly specify how much compression you want applied to your movie, and what the dimensions of the finished movie frame will be. The small print below the pop-up menu warns you that many of these settings will reduce the size and quality of the finished product.

5. **Type a name for your movie.**

(Unless, of course, you really do want to call your movie "My Great Movie," as iMovie suggests.)

Don't remove the letters *.mov* from the end of the file's name, especially if it might be played on Windows computers. That suffix is a requirement for machines that aren't savvy enough to know a movie file when they see one.

6. **Navigate to the folder where you'll want to store the resulting QuickTime file.**

You can just press ⌘-D if you want your QuickTime Movie saved onto the desktop, where it'll be easy to find.

7. **Click Save.**

Now the time-consuming exporting and *compression* process begins. As you can read in the next section, compression can take a long time to complete—from a minute or two to an hour or more, depending on the settings you selected in step 2, the length of your movie, and the speed of your Mac. Feel free to switch into other programs—check your email or surf the Web, for example—while iMovie crunches away in the background.

When the exporting is complete, the progress bar disappears. Switch to the Finder, where you'll find a new QuickTime movie icon (see Figure 19-5). Double-click it to see the results.

Tip: You can click Stop anytime during the export process, but you'll wind up with no exported movie at all.

Figure 19-5:
When you double-click the resulting QuickTime movie on your hard drive (left), it opens into your copy of QuickTime Player, the movie-playing application included with every Mac. Press the Space bar to make the movie play back (right).

Understanding QuickTime

A computer displays video by flashing many still images in rapid succession. But if you've ever worked with graphics, you know that color graphics files are data hogs. A full-screen photograph file might occupy 5 or 10 MB of space on your hard drive and take several seconds to open up.

Unfortunately, most computers are far too slow to open up 30 full-screen, photographic-quality pictures per second. Even if they could, full-screen, full-quality QuickTime movies would still be mostly useless. Each would consume hundreds of gigabytes of disk space, requiring days or weeks to download from the Web or by email—a guaranteed way to annoy citizens of the Internet and doom your movie-making career to obscurity.

That's why most QuickTime movies *aren't* full-screen, photographic-quality films by any stretch of the imagination. In fact, most QuickTime movies are much smaller—in three different dimensions:

- **The window is much smaller.** It's rare to see a QuickTime movie that, when played back, fills the computer screen. Instead, most QuickTime movies today play in a much smaller window (see Figure 19-6), therefore requiring far less data and resulting in far smaller files.

- **The frame rate is lower.** Instead of showing 30 frames per second, most Quick-Time movies have far lower frame rates; even fifteen frames per second produces smooth motion. On the Web, especially during live QuickTime "broadcasts," still lower frame rates are common, such as two or five frames per second. This kind of movie is noticeably jerky, but sends so little data that people using telephone-line modems can watch live events in this format.

Figure 19-6:
Here's the same movie in three standard playback sizes (on a laptop screen so you can gauge its size). Movies designed for playback from the hard drive are often 640 pixels wide, 480 tall (640 x 480). Movies intended for the Web email are smaller—often 320 x 240—and movies sent by email are often as tiny as 160 x 120. The common denominator: Almost all QuickTime movies have the same relative dimensions—a 4:3 width-to-height ratio, which is exactly the same ratio as the picture produced by your TV and your camcorder.

- **The video is *compressed*.** This is the big one—the technical aspect of QuickTime movies that gives you the most control over the resulting quality of your movie. In short, when iMovie uses QuickTime to compress your video, it discards information that describes each frame. True, the picture deteriorates as a consequence, but the resulting QuickTime movie file is a tiny fraction of its original size. The following section describes this compression business in much greater detail.

The bottom line is that by combining these three techniques, iMovie can turn your 10 GB DV movie into a *3 MB* file that's small enough to email or post on your Web page. The resulting movie won't play as smoothly, fill as much of the screen, or look as good as the original DV footage. But your viewers won't care. They'll be delighted to be able to watch your movie at all, and grateful that the file didn't take hours to download. (And besides, having already been exposed to QuickTime movies, most know what to expect.)

About Codecs

At the moment you save your QuickTime movie, iMovie asks you which of several schemes you want to use for compressing your footage. To use the technical terminology, it asks you to choose a *codec* from a long list. That term is short for compressor/

decompressor, the software module that translates the pixel-by-pixel description of your DV footage into the more compact QuickTime format—and then *un*translates it during playback.

Each QuickTime codec works differently. Some are ideal for animations, and others for live action. Some work well on slower computers, others on faster ones. Some try to maintain excellent picture quality, but produce very large QuickTime files on the disk, and others make the opposite tradeoff.

In the meantime, all of this background information should help explain a few phenomena pertaining to converting DV movies into QuickTime files:

- **Saving a QuickTime movie takes a long time.** It's nothing like saving, say, a word processing document. Comparing every pixel on every frame with every pixel on the next frame involves massive amounts of number crunching, which takes time. (Some codecs take longer than others, however.)

- **QuickTime movies don't look as good as the original DV.** Now you know why: In the act of shrinking your movie down to the file size that's reasonable for emailing, copying to a CD-ROM, and so on, a codec's job is to *throw away* some of the data that makes a movie look vivid and clear.

- **QuickTime is an exercise in compromise.** By choosing the appropriate codec and changing its settings appropriately, you can create a QuickTime movie with excellent picture and sound. Unfortunately, it will consume a lot of disk space. If you want a small file on the hard drive *and* excellent picture and sound, you can make the QuickTime movie play in a smaller window—160 x 120 pixels, for example, instead of 320 x 240 or something larger—or at a slower frame rate. The guide in this chapter, some experimentation, and the nature of the movie you're making all contribute to helping you make a codec decision.

RARELY ASKED QUESTION

30 fps Drop-Frame

OK, I'll bite. Why on earth did the USA, which is supposed to be so technically advanced, settle on a TV standard that plays at such an oddball frame rate? Why is it 29.97—why couldn't it be rounded off to 30?

The 29.97 frame rate, known in the TV business as *30 fps drop-frame*, dates back to the dawn of color TV. As they prepared to launch color TV broadcasts in January 1954, network engineers wanted to make sure that the expensive black-and-white TV sets of the day could receive the color

shows, too. (Talk about backward-compatible software!)

Trouble was, when they tried to broadcast a color signal at the then-standard 30 frames per second, the extra color information wound up distorting the audio signal. Eventually, they hit upon a discovery: If they slowed down the frame rate just a hair, the distortion disappeared. The video, meanwhile, looked just as good at 29.97 frames per second as it did at 30.

A standard was born.

The Share Presets: What They Mean

iMovie offers several ready-to-use QuickTime compression settings that govern the quality, file size, and playback-window size of the movie you're exporting. Here's a guide to these presets to help you choose the one that's appropriate for your movie-distribution plans.

Each of the descriptions below includes the information about each preset's codec, size (see Figure 19-6), and frame rate. (The frame rate indicates how many individual pictures you'll see per second when the QuickTime Movie plays back. Thirty frames per second is standard NTSC television quality. Ten to fifteen frames per second begins to look less smooth, and anything under ten yields a flickering, old-time movie effect.)

Trivia: Old-time silent movies actually played at *eighteen* frames per second.

- **Audio codec.** This statistic is the sonic equivalent of the frame rate, in that it tells you what kind of sound quality you'll get. At 44.1 kHz, the quality is exactly the same as that of a commercial music CD. At 22 kHz, it's half as good, but you won't hear any difference except when you listen through headphones or stereo speakers. When the sound plays through the *built-in* speaker on the standard Macintosh, most people can't tell the difference between 44.1 and 22 kHz.

- **Time to compress one minute of video.** The "Time to Compress" statistic provided below indicates how long it took a PowerBook G4 to compress a standard sample movie that's exactly one minute long. (Compressing a 10-minute movie, of course, would take about ten times as long.) Of course, the time it will take your movie to get compressed and saved depends on the codec you've chosen, the length of the movie, how much motion is visible on the screen, and your Mac's speed, but the next section offers a rough guide.

- **File size.** The final statistic provided for each option shows you how big the resulting QuickTime file might be (in megabytes). These numbers, too, refer to the sample one-minute DV movie described in the preceding paragraph.

Email

Video codec: *H.263*
Size: *160 x 120*
Frame rate: *10 per second*
Audio codec: *QDesign Music 2, mono, 22 kHz*
Time to compress one minute of video: *1 minute*
File size: *1.2 MB*
The movie you export with these settings is fairly blurry, and the size of the QuickTime screen is closer in size to a Wheat Thin than a Cineplex.

Still, the H.263 video codec has two important benefits. First, it makes the exporting much faster than if you used, say, the Sorenson 3 codec (which takes nearly twice as long). Second, the resulting QuickTime file is relatively tiny; at just over 1 MB for a minute-long movie, it's actually within the realm of possibility that you could email this thing to somebody without incurring their wrath. (The Sorenson 3 codec produces a better-looking movie. But its movies are 3.3 MB per minute—far too large for casual emailing.)

Web

Video codec: *H.263*
Size: *240 x 180*
Frame rate: *12 per second*
Audio codec: *QDesign Music 2, stereo, 22 kHz*
Time to compress one minute of video: *1 minute, 35 seconds*
File size: *2.4 MB*
This kind of movie is much more satisfying to watch than the Email type. The image is over twice as big, and the higher frame rate produces smoother motion.

Once again, the Sorenson Video codec could provide far better image quality; but at 2.4 MB per minute, the product of the H.263 codec is small enough to download from a Web page without a high-speed Internet connection.

Web Streaming

In quality and size, this preset is identical to the Web preset described above. The only difference is that this kind of movie comes set up for *streaming* delivery from the Web, meaning it's played on your audience's screens *as* it's being sent from the Web. In other words, your viewers don't have to download the entire movie before playing it.

Streaming means that your movies can be extremely long, even if they're therefore extremely large files. Only a tiny bit at a time is sent to your spectators' computers.

For details on putting your QuickTime movies on the Web, see page 398.

CD-ROM

Video codec: *H.263*
Size: *320 x 240*
Frame rate: *15 per second*
Audio codec: *IMA 4:1, Stereo, 44.1 kHz*
Time to compress one minute of video: *1 minute, 30 seconds*
File size: *6 MB*
As you can see by the specs above, a movie with the CD-ROM setup generally contains too much data to be suitable for live Web delivery. But saving your QuickTime productions into this kind of QuickTime file is ideal if you plan to play it from a hard drive or a CD-ROM that you record yourself, as described later this chapter. The high frame rate means that motion will seem smooth, and the 320 x 240 dimensions of the window mean that the movie will fill a decent fraction of the computer screen. That's big enough to see a good amount of detail.

Tip: If you're willing to endure more compressing time and a larger resulting file, you can give your CD-ROM movies a dramatic picture-quality upgrade by substituting the Sorenson Video 3 codec for the H.263 codec. (Use the Expert settings described on the next page to do so; duplicate the settings described here, but choose the Sorenson Video 3 codec instead of H.263.)

The only downside is that the resulting QuickTime movie contains too much data for older, slower CD-ROM drives, such as those rated below 12X, to deliver to the computer's brain. The movie will *play* on slower CD-ROM drives, but it will skip a lot.

Full Quality DV

Video codec: *DV*
Size: *720 x 480*
Frame rate: *29.97 per second (for NTSC; 25 for PAL)*
Audio codec: *No compression; stereo, 32 kHz*
Time to compress one minute of video: *1 minute*
File size: *411 MB*
As the numbers (and the example in Figure 19-6) show you, this is the QuickTime format for people whose equipment doesn't mess around. The file size is massive—much too large for playback from a CD-ROM drive.

That's because this setting isn't intended for playback; it's intended to offer you a means of *storing* your iMovie production without sacrificing any video quality. The Full Quality DV setting applies *no compression at all* to your audio or video.

Yet preserving your iMovie work as a giant, single DV clip on the hard drive is still a useful exercise. It can save hard drive space, for one thing, since the resulting Quick-Time file is still far smaller than the collection of DV clips in your project's Media folder from which it was made. After creating a Full Quality DV movie, you could delete the project folder to free up some disk space, confident that you've got your entire movie safely preserved with 100 percent of its original DV quality intact.

The Expert Settings

The canned presets aren't the only ways you can turn your iMovie project into a QuickTime movie. By choosing Expert Settings from the pop-up menu shown in Figure 19-5, and then clicking the Share button, you embark on a tour of crazy nested dialog boxes. Along the way, you'll be offered control of every aspect of the compression process, including which codec it uses, the degree of sound compression, how many frames per second you want, and so on.

The first dialog box to appear is the "Save exported file as" box, where you can type a name and choose a folder location for the file you're about to save (Figure 19-87, top). Resist the temptation, for now.

The real power lies in the buttons and pop-up menus elsewhere in this little box. For starters, the Export pop-up menu (shown at top in Figure 19-7) offers a wealth of conversion options. This is your opportunity to save your film as:

- An AVI file to give to your Windows PC-using friends. (Choose **Movie to AVI.**)

- A huge folder full of still images, one per frame of your movie. (Choose **Movie to Image Sequence.** Click Options to specify the file format—like JPEG or Photoshop—and how many stills per second you want.)

- A soundtrack. Here's a great opportunity to convert the audio tracks of your movie into standalone sound files. (Choose **Sound to AIFF, Sound to Wave,** or whatever format you want.)

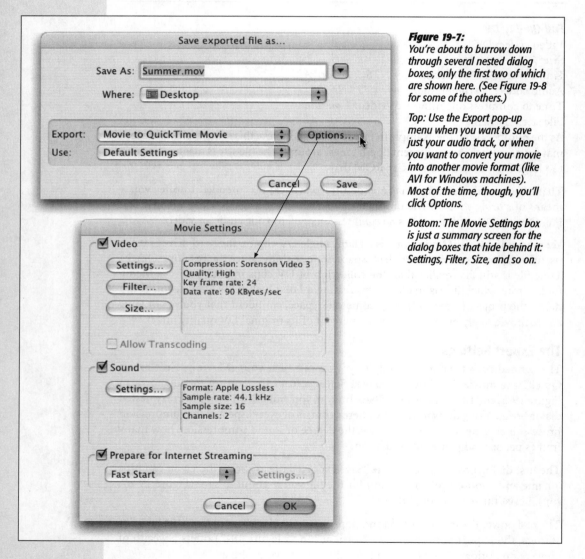

Figure 19-7:
You're about to burrow down through several nested dialog boxes, only the first two of which are shown here. (See Figure 19-8 for some of the others.)

Top: Use the Export pop-up menu when you want to save just your audio track, or when you want to convert your movie into another movie format (like AVI for Windows machines). Most of the time, though, you'll click Options.

Bottom: The Movie Settings box is just a summary screen for the dialog boxes that hide behind it: Settings, Filter, Size, and so on.

But most of the time, you'll ignore this Export pop-up menu. Most of the time, you'll want to leave it set to "Movie to QuickTime Movie," and then click the Options button to make some settings changes.

As illustrated in Figure 19-7, that Options button opens a very important dialog box: the Movie Settings box. Here's where you can export your finished product with *exactly* the size-smoothness-speed compromise you want.

You'll notice that this box offers three buttons for video: Settings, Filter, and Size. Below that, you get one Settings button for Sound; and at the bottom of the box, you get options for *Internet streaming*. All of these settings are covered in the next few pages.

The Settings button

The Settings button takes you to the powerful Compression Settings dialog box (Figure 19-8), the heart of the entire Expert software suite. Here's where you'll find options like the unlabeled Compressor pop-up menu, which lists at least 27 codecs—or None, which means that iMovie won't compress your project at all.

Figure 19-8 :
Top: This dialog box gives you point-by-point control over the look, size, and quality of the QuickTime movie you're exporting. Not all of these controls are available for all codecs. That is, depending on what you choose using the top pop-up menu, some of the controls here may be dimmed and unavailable. Furthermore, only some of the codecs offer an Options button in the middle of the dialog box.

In the Sorenson 3 codec controls, shown here, the "Limit data rate to ___" option is useful when you're trying to produce a movie that will stream from the Web. Note, however, that this setting overrides the Quality slider setting. (Many people have been baffled by a crummy-looking Sorenson movie that they'd set to Best quality. Now you know why.)

Bottom: Here's where you can specify the dimensions of the movie you're saving, in pixels. (This box appears when you click the Size button shown at bottom in Figure 19-7.)

As it turns out, few of these codecs are very useful for everyday use. Many of them are designed for saving still frames (not movies), for storing your movies (not playing them), or for compatibility with very old versions of the QuickTime software. Most of the time, the Sorenson Video 3 compressor (for CD or hard drive playback) or Apple H.263 (for Internet playback) are the ones that will make you and your audience the happiest.

Here, however, are some of the most useful.

Note: Your codecs reflect the version of QuickTime that you have installed, which may be older or newer than the 6.5 version described here.

- **Animation.** This codec is significant because, at its Best quality setting, it maintains *all* of the original DV picture quality, while still managing to convert files so that they're smaller than files with no compression at all. (As the name implies, this codec was originally designed to process video composed of large blocks of solid colors—that is, cartoons.) The resulting file is therefore huge when compared with the other codecs described here, but not as huge as it would be if you used the None choice in this pop-up menu.

  As a result, the Animation codec is a popular format for storing or transferring QuickTime footage from one piece of video-editing software to another. Because the files are so huge, however, it's not so great as a finished movie file format.

- **Apple H.263, Apple VC H.263, H.261.** These codecs were designed for video teleconferencing (VC), in which a tiny, jerky image of you is transmitted over a telephone line to somebody who's also equipped with a video telephone. Apple's version, however, does a very good job at maintaining a good picture, while keeping the file size very small. In fact, Apple H.263 should be one of your first choices if you plan to send your video by email or post it on a Web page.

Tip: These codecs work best in footage where very little is going on—like a person sitting in front of a video telephone. The more that the frame remains the same, the better the picture quality, which is yet another argument for using a tripod whenever you can.

- **DV-PAL, DVCPRO-PAL.** These options are here so that you can export your iMovie masterpiece in the European video format (PAL), while retaining full DV size and frame rate. (DVCPRO is a slight variant of the DV format, intended for use with super-expensive professional broadcast TV video gear.)

  Unfortunately, the quality of the video suffers when you make this kind of conversion, especially in action scenes.

- **DV/DVCPRO - NTSC.** Suppose you've just completed a masterful movie, and the thought of compressing it to some much smaller, image-degraded QuickTime movie breaks your heart. You can use this codec to turn your finished, effect-enhanced, fully edited iMovie production into a new, raw DV clip, exactly like the DV clips in the Media folder in your project folder. You might do so if, for example, you wanted to import your entire movie into another DV-editing program, such as Final Cut Express or Final Cut Pro, or if you wanted to turn it into a Video CD or DVD, as described at the end of this chapter. (*DV*, of course, means digital video; NTSC is the format used in the Western Hemisphere and Japan.)

- **Sorenson Video, Sorenson Video 3.** Here it is—the codec that gives you very high quality with very good compression, and files so small that you can play them from a CD-ROM or even over the Internet. Sorenson-compressed movies play back on either Macs or Windows computers, too. (Use Sorenson Video 3 if possible. Use the older Sorenson Video—without a number—only if your audience might still be using some ancient version of QuickTime to play back your opus.)

Here, too, is the Quality slider (another tradeoff between the size of the resulting QuickTime file and the quality of its picture) and the Frames per Second control. Anything under 12 looks jerky; 15 is typical for today's QuickTime movies; 24 to 29.97 are roughly TV quality.

The Filter button

The Filter button opens up a rabbit hole into a world of QuickTime video controls. By opening the various flippy triangles, you'll find a lot of effects you've seen before in iMovie (color balance, brightness and contrast, lens flare, fake old-film grain)—and a few you haven't (blur or sharpen, emboss, edge detection). You can apply any of these to the movie you're about to export.

The Size button

The Size button summons the dialog box shown at bottom in Figure 19-9, where—after clicking "Use custom size"—you can specify the dimensions for the playback window of your QuickTime movie. See Figure 19-6 for some examples of these different sizes.

Of course, the larger the window you specify, the longer the movie will take to save, the slower it will be transmitted over the Internet, and the larger the resulting file will be.

The huge majority of QuickTime movies play in at one of several standard sizes, such as 160 x 120, 240 x 180, or 320 x 240. All of them maintain the 4:3 aspect ratio. Still, there are dozens of other possible sizes that maintain the correct proportions.

Audio Settings

At the bottom of the dialog box shown in Figure 19-7 is a second button called Settings. It opens a dialog box that lets you specify how—and how much—your soundtrack is compressed in the exported QuickTime movie (Figure 19-8).

For example, you can specify these parameters:

- **Compressor.** When most people think of codecs—those who've even *heard* of codecs, that is—they think of *video* compression. But iMovie offers a choice of audio codecs, too. This pop-up menu lets you specify which one you want to use.

Many of them aren't, in fact, appropriate for movie soundtracks. Remember that these codecs are provided by QuickTime, not by iMovie, and that QuickTime is designed to be an all-purpose multimedia format. It's supposed to be just as good at creating pictureless sound files as it is at creating movies. For best results in most movies, use the QDesign or IMA setting. (Apple Lossless can also be useful. "Lossless" means that although this codec cuts the audio track's file size in half, it doesn't lose *any* of the sound quality in the process. The resulting files are too big for the Web or emailing, but Apple Lossless is a great alternative to "None" when you're saving a movie for best-quality playback from a hard drive.)

Figure 19-9:
It probably goes without saying that the better the audio quality you specify, the larger your QuickTime movie will be. In any case, this is the dialog box where you make such decisions. Audio isn't nearly as data-greedy as video, so compressing it isn't nearly as urgent an issue (unless you want your movie to play over the Internet).

- **Rate, Size.** A computer captures and plays back sound by capturing thousands of individual slices, or snapshots, of sound per second. As though describing somebody at a wine tasting, computer nerds call this process *sampling* the sound.

   The two controls here let you specify how *many samples* you want the Mac to take per second (the sampling Rate) and how *much data* it's allowed to use to describe each sample (the sampling Size). For example, **11 kHz, 8 bits** sounds like you're hearing the audio track over a bad telephone connection. Tinny. Use it only for speech. 662 K per minute. **22 kHz, 16 bits** is fine for playing on a computer equipped with external speakers. 2.6 MB per minute. And **44.1 kHz, 16 bits** is CD-quality audio, suitable for listening to with headphones.

- **Use: Mono/Stereo.** Exporting your QuickTime movie with a stereo format is often a waste of data. Most computers that might play back your movie, including tower Power Macs and iBooks, don't *have* stereo speakers. Therefore, consider using the Mono setting when you're trying to minimize the amount of data required to play back the soundtrack.

Posting Movies on the Web

After editing your iMovie to perfection, you'll want to show it to the world. Sure, you can preserve your work on videotape, or save it as a DVD; that's fine if you want to make a handful of copies for a few friends.

But the big time is the Internet. This 400-million-seat megaplex is where the action is, where unknown independent filmmakers get noticed, and where it doesn't cost you a penny to distribute your work to a vast worldwide audience.

All of the techniques described in this section assume that you've exported your iMovie production as a QuickTime movie.

Now, you *could* post your 24-frames-per-second, 640 x 480, stereo-CD-quality sound motion picture on your Web page. But you'd have to include instructions that say, "Please download my movie! It's only 2 GB—about five days of continuous downloading with a 56 K modem. But trust me, it's worth the wait!"

A vast audience still connects to the Internet using an ordinary telephone-line modem, such as a 28.8 K or 56 K model. These modems receive data very slowly, so they're not very well equipped for receiving video from the Internet.

If you expect anyone to actually watch your movies, therefore, you, like thousands of Internet moviemakers before you, will have to make your Web-based movies *tiny*. To make your movie watchable by people with telephone-line modems, use the Web setting described on page 392.

If the need to downsize your movie like this doesn't crush your artistic pride, the worst is over. Here, then, is how you can make your videos available to the universe.

Posting to Your .Mac Account

By far the easiest way to post your movies on the Internet is to use one of Apple's $100-per-year .Mac accounts (visit *www.mac.com* for details, or open System Preferences, click .Mac, and click Sign Up). A .Mac account gives you a whole raft of Internet-based services and conveniences: electronic greeting cards, synchronizing of calendars and Web bookmarks among the different Macs in your life, a backup program, an antivirus program, the ability to check your email online—and HomePage, which lets you generate your own Web page and occupy it with an iMovie movie.

In iMovie 4, you can post your finished masterpiece on a .Mac Web page with little more than a couple of clicks:

1. **In iMovie, choose File→Share; in the resulting dialog box, click HomePage.**

   The dialog box tells you how jerky your movie will be online (Figure 19-10).

2. **Type a name for your movie and then click Share.**

   iMovie springs into action, compressing your movie to Web proportions and uploading it to the .Mac Web site. (This is not, ahem, a particularly quick process.)

   When the uploading is complete, your Web browser opens automatically and takes you to the .Mac sign-in page.

3. **Type your name and password. (Capitalization counts.) Click Enter.**

The HomePage screen appears (Figure 19-11). A miniature version of the movie appears at the top left, and begins playing automatically for your approval and enjoyment. Farther down the page, you're offered about a dozen standard iMovie Web-page templates, such as Invite, Baby, and so on.

Figure 19-10:
The message here tells you just how small and jerky your movie will be on the Web—12 frames per second, 240 by 180 pixels—and how many megabytes it will occupy. (All of your Web-based movies together can't exceed your 100-megabyte iDisk account limit, unless you pay more money to Apple for more storage.)

New in iMovie 4: You don't have to post the entire movie online. If you select only specific clips in iMovie before choosing the Share command, you're now offered the "Share selected clips only" checkbox, which posts only the selected stretch of your movie online.

Figure 19-11:
The "Publish your iMovie" page is a summary of the three page-preparation steps you're about to take. At this point, the most urgent task is step 2, choosing a "frame" for the movie as it will appear on the finished Web page.

Remember that your movie will occupy only a small rectangle in the center of your visitors' screens; the rest is graphic fluff to fill up the window.

4. **Click the "theater" style you prefer.**

   Next you arrive at the "Edit your page" page (Figure 19-12, top).

5. **Fill in the movie title, description underneath the movie, and so on.**

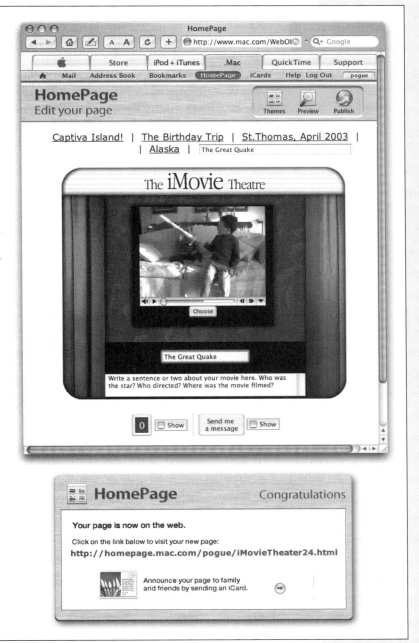

Figure 19-12:
Top: Here's what your selected movie design looks like. If you don't want the caption to appear beneath it—especially one that says, "Write a sentence or two about your movie here"—delete this dummy text.

Bottom: When it's all over, HomePage tells you the Web address for your new page. Copy this address and publicize it to spread the word about your new masterpiece.

If you click the little arrow button beneath the address, you can send an iCard (electronic greeting card sent by email) to announce it.

If you'd like to omit one of the proposed pieces of information (if you don't have any particular directorial notes, for example), edit it anyway, if only to delete the dummy text that appears there (see Figure 19-12).

6. Click Preview to see how the Web page will look.

Click the triangular Play button, shown in Figure 19-12, to try playing your movie over the Internet.

7. If everything looks good, click Publish.

When you click the Publish button at the top of the screen, the URL (Web address) for your Web page appears on your screen, which you can copy and then email to anyone who'd be interested (Figure 19-12, bottom). Finally, your Web page is now available for everyone on the Internet to see.

You can create as many Web pages as you want (within the space constraints of your iDisk). When you return to the HomePage screen, a list of your existing Web pages appears (complete with Edit and Delete buttons). So does the Add button, which you can click to start the process of building another Web page.

Behind the scenes, iMovie builds your movie Web site by placing new Web page (HTML) documents in the Sites folder of your iDisk (Figure 19-13). If you know how to use a Web-page creation program like Dreamweaver or even Microsoft Word, you can make changes to your Web page by editing these documents.

Figure 19-13:
Top left: To summon your iDisk icon to the screen, choose its name from the Go menu in the Finder. Now wait: Even with a high-speed Internet connection, it can take awhile for your iDisk icon to appear on your desktop.

Top right: At last, however, it does, bearing your member name (top right). Double-click it—and wait—to see its contents (bottom).

The HTML documents for your movie site are in the Sites folder; the movies themselves are in Movies.

Posting a Movie on Your Own Web Site

Posting movies on other people's Web pages is one thing. In many cases, however, you might prefer the control and the freedom of putting movies onto your *own* Web page, designed the way you like it.

If you have a Web page, you're probably already familiar with the notion of *FTP* (file transfer protocol), the method you use to deposit new Web pages, graphics, and other elements onto your Web site. You do this using a program like Captain FTP or RBrowser, both of which are available for download from the "Missing CD" page at *www.missingmanuals.com*.

Setting up streaming playback

QuickTime provides a feature called Fast Start, which means that when a Web page visitor clicks your movie, he can begin to watch it before it's downloaded in its entirety. His copy of QuickTime estimates when enough movie data has been downloaded so that the whole movie can play without having to pause for additional data. The effect is a lot like the *streaming video* feature described earlier, except that there's a considerable pause as the first portion of the movie is downloaded. (On the other hand, you save thousands of dollars on the cost of specialized hardware and software that's required for a true streaming-video system.)

To take advantage of this feature, use the Expert Settings dialog box when you're creating your QuickTime movie from the iMovie project. As shown in Figure 19-7, iMovie offers a checkbox called "Prepare for Internet Streaming." If you turn on this checkbox and choose Fast Start from the pop-up menu, iMovie automatically encodes some extra instructions into the resulting QuickTime file that permit your movie to do this "fast starting" when played back from your Web page.

Playing your movie

Once you've uploaded your iMovie, you—and everyone else on the Internet—can watch it just by typing in the correct address. If your Web site's usual address is *www.imovienut.com,* and the name of your movie file is *mymovie.mov,* then the URL (address) for your new movie is *www.imovienut.com/mymovie.mov.* (If you placed it into a folder within your Web site listing—called *flicks,* for example—then the address is *www.imovienut.com/flicks/mymovie.mov.*)

Tip: Mac and Windows computers consider capital and lowercase letters equivalent in Web addresses like these. The Unix machines that dish out Web pages by the millions, however, don't. Therefore, using only lowercase letters is a good precaution to avoid subjecting your visitors to "Web page not found" messages.

If one of your fans types this address into the Web browser or clicks a link that goes to this address, one of three things happens:

- If your visitor's computer has the *QuickTime plug-in* software installed (almost all modern Macs do), a new little movie window opens automatically. (See Figure 19-14.) A few seconds later, it begins to play automatically.

• If your visitor doesn't have this QuickTime plug-in installed, which is possible if she's using a Windows computer, a message appears onscreen. It offers three choices: Track down the necessary plug-in, download the QuickTime movie to the hard drive, or choose another program to play the movie.

Tip: To make it easier for your Windows friends to download the plug-in necessary to watch QuickTime movies, create a link on your Web page that says something like: "To watch this movie, please download the free QuickTime plug-in at *http://www.apple.com/quicktime.*"

• Some browsers have been configured to hand off all downloadable files whose names end with *.mov* to a *helper application,* such as QuickTime Player. In such cases, QuickTime Player now opens (independently from the browser), and the movie appears in its window.

Figure 19-14:
The easiest way to put a movie on your Web page is simply upload it there. Then create a link to it. When clicked, the link makes the movie pop up in its own, separate window. Your viewers can use the Play, Stop, and scroll controls as they see fit.

POWER USERS' CLINIC

QuickTime Streaming Server

The Fast Start feature of QuickTime is a great feature. Without it, your movie wouldn't begin to play until its entire multimegabyte mass had been downloaded to your visitor's browser.

That's a good beginning. But in the professional world of Web video, the next step is *QuickTime streaming.* This relatively young technology lets many viewers simultaneously watch your movie in real time, live, as it's played from the host hard drive—without waiting for *anything* to download.

QuickTime streaming makes possible live *Webcasts,* such as the occasional Steve Jobs keynote speech and other historic events.

Serving up QuickTime streaming isn't something that the average Mac can do. It requires a Power Mac equipped with special streaming QuickTime software, a full-time, high-speed Internet connection, and a copy of the Mac OS X Server operating system. Apple's QuickTime Streaming Web site has the details at *www.apple.com/quicktime/servers.*

HTML coding

If you know how to write HTML code (the language of Web pages), you can make
the presentation of your movie a little bit more elegant. For example, you can use the
<embed> tag to make the movie play right on the Web page, instead of in a separate
window. You can also use the <autoplay> tag to make the movie begin playing the
instant the browser has received enough data from the server. If you set the tag to
false, your visitor must click the Play button.

Movies on Your Phone

When most people hear the word movie, they think "big screen." But high-tech has
marched on, small is beautiful, and suddenly we've entered an era when people are
content to watch video on *very small* screens. Thanks to a new feature in iMovie 4,
you can now send movies directly to the screens of certain cellphones, like the Nokia
6600, 3650, 6230, and 6630. No longer must you show people lame wallet photos of
your family; you can play them *movies* of your family, right there on the street.

Unfortunately, you can't send your movies to any old cellphone—only those with
Bluetooth that are *3GPP-compliant.* Here's what that means:

- **Bluetooth** is a radio technology with a maximum range of 30 feet. The whole idea
  isn't so much networking as eliminating cables from our lives, which is an idea
  most people wholeheartedly support.

  Already you can get Bluetooth—either built-in or as a plug-in USB device—for
  computers, printers, cellphones, cellphone headsets, Palm and PocketPC organiz-
  ers, Sony camcorders, and so on. Apple's wireless keyboard and mouse both rely
  on Bluetooth.

  All iMovie cares about, though, is whether or not your Mac has Bluetooth—many
  models do, including all PowerBooks—and whether your cellphone does. (Technically, iMovie can send movies to more than just phones and Macs; it can send to
  palmtops, too. At the moment, though, there aren't any 3GPP palmtops.)

- **3GPP** is a video standard for cellphones. (It stands for Third Generation Partner-
  ship Program, since you asked.) If your Bluetooth phone is fairly recent, it may be
  3GPP-compliant, but check with your cell company.

  The phone has to have a movie-playing program on board, too; all 3GPP video-
  phones do.

If you're suitably equipped, here's how the transfer goes:

1. **When your movie is fully edited, save it. Choose File→Share.**

   The Share sheet appears, as shown at top in Figure 19-15.

2. **Click the Bluetooth icon on the toolbar.**

As usual when you export a movie, you can turn on "Share selected clips only" if you want to send only a piece of your movie (and you highlighted the appropriate clips before choosing File→Share).

3. Click Share.

iMovie takes quite awhile to compress your movie. Of course, ordinarily iMovie strives to maintain the best quality possible, with high resolution, full TV-screen size, CD-quality stereo sound, and so on. But for a phone, you want super-compressed, ultra-tiny, monophonic movies, and converting from the high-res format to the low-res one takes some time.

When the compression is complete, the Select Bluetooth Device dialog box appears (Figure 19-15, bottom). Make sure your phone is turned on. Make sure, too, that in its Bluetooth settings, Bluetooth is turned on and *discoverable*, meaning that your Mac can "see" it.

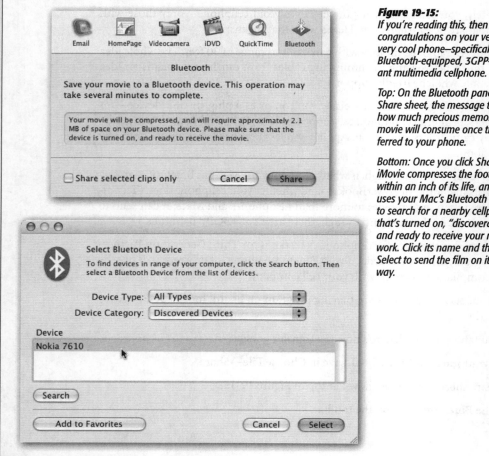

Figure 19-15:
If you're reading this, then congratulations on your very new, very cool phone—specifically, your Bluetooth-equipped, 3GPP-compliant multimedia cellphone.

Top: On the Bluetooth pane of the Share sheet, the message tells you how much precious memory this movie will consume once transferred to your phone.

Bottom: Once you click Share, iMovie compresses the footage to within an inch of its life, and then uses your Mac's Bluetooth antenna to search for a nearby cellphone that's turned on, "discoverable," and ready to receive your masterwork. Click its name and then click Select to send the film on its merry way.

4. Click Search.

After a moment, your phone's name appears in the list.

5. Click the phone's name, and then click Select.

That's all there is to it. On the phone's screen, you'll probably see a message to the effect that it's receiving a file. After a while, the movie's transmission will be complete. Open the phone's media-playing program and play away.

Tip: iMovie stores a copy of the super-compressed movie in your project folder→Shared→Bluetooth folder. Its file name ends with .3gp.

If you're ever inclined to send that movie again—to one of your many other friends who have 3GPP-compliant, Bluetooth phones—you can shoot it right over without having to wait for iMovie to crunch the thing down to pocket size, thus eliminating step 3 above. Use the Bluetooth File Exchange program in your Applications →Utilities folder to do it.

Part Four: iDVD

4

From iMovie to iDVD

I DVD lets you turn your iMovie movies and iPhoto slideshows into Holly-
wood-style DVDs that play on most standard DVD players. As you'll see in the
following chapters, iDVD 4 is loaded with enhancements that can make your
DVDs look breathtakingly close to the commercial Hollywood discs on the shelves
at Blockbuster.

The software requirement is iDVD. The hardware requirement is a DVD recording
drive, preferably an Apple SuperDrive built into your Mac.

Note: The word is *preferably* a built-in SuperDrive, because there are two circumstances in which you
don't need one.

One is that although you need a SuperDrive to *burn* a DVD, you can do the design work on another machine.
That's a great feature in, for example, school computer labs that have 12 Macs, but only two that can burn
DVDs. (For step-by-step instructions, see page 504.)

The other is that a sneaky secret feature in iDVD 4 lets you use an *external* DVD burner, or even a non-Apple
DVD burner, to create DVDs. See page 467.

Why iDVD?

You already know from Chapter 19 that you can export your finished iMovie project
back to a good old VHS cassette, one of the world's most sure-fire distribution methods. Anyone who doesn't have a VCR in this day and age probably wouldn't appreciate
your cinematic genius anyway.

But preserving your work on a DVD gives you a boatload of benefits. DVDs are cheap, compact, long-lived, easy to mail—and they never need rewinding.

Still, there are reasons to pause before committing your work to DVD. For one thing, homemade DVDs don't work in as many DVD players as commercial discs do. Stick an iDVD production into an older DVD player, and you may see the dreaded "No Disc" message on the TV screen. (In this regard, DVD-RW discs—the ones that you can erase and rerecord over and over—are worse than DVD-Rs, which you can record on only once.)

DVD players sold since 2002 are generally a safe bet, but check the master player compatibility list at *www.dvdrhelp.com* if you're ever in doubt. (Some players are fussy about which DVD-R brand discs they'll play, too.)

Remember, furthermore, that when it comes to your home movies, a DVD's picture quality isn't as good as the original tape's. That fact comes as a shock to many people, who assume that a DVD offers the best reproduction quality on earth. But in fact, video on every DVD is stored in a compressed format, and therefore doesn't have quite the same quality as the original footage. When it comes to very important movies, save a copy on a DV tape to serve as the master.

What You're in For

In Chapter 21, you can read about using iDVD *manually,* in which you can integrate movies, still pictures, and sound in very flexible ways. But especially at first, most people take the simplest approach: create the movie in iMovie, and then hand it off to iDVD.

That's what this chapter is all about. It will guide you through the five broad steps of using iMovie and iDVD together:

1. **Prepare your audio, video, and pictures.**

    In addition to movies, iDVD can incorporate all kinds of other files—like audio and graphics files—into your shows. iDVD doesn't, however, offer any way to create or edit these files. You must prepare them in other programs first.

2. **Insert chapter markers.**

    In a commercial Hollywood DVD, you can jump around the movie without rewinding or fast-forwarding, thanks to the movie's *scene menu* or *chapter menu.* It's basically a screenful of bookmarks for certain scenes in the movie. You can create one of these useful menus right in iMovie by indicating which spots you want to turn into scene markers.

3. **Hand off to iDVD.**

    The beauty of iMovie 4 and iDVD 4 is that they're tied together behind the scenes. The former can hand off movies to the latter, automatically creating menu buttons in the process.

4. Design the menu screen.

A DVD menu is a menu *screen,* usually containing buttons that you click with the remote control. One button, called Play, starts playing the movie. Another, called Scene Selection, might take you to a second menu screen full of individual "chapter" buttons, so your audience doesn't have to start watching from the beginning.

DVD menu design is at the heart of iDVD. The program allows you to specify where and how each button appears on the screen, and you can customize the overall look with backgrounds and titles.

5. Burn your DVD.

To create a DVD, iDVD compresses your movie into the universal file format of DVD movies, called *MPEG-2,* and then copies the results to a blank DVD-R disc. This process, called *burning,* lets you produce a DVD that plays back either in a computer or in most recent set-top DVD players.

Phase 1: Insert Chapter Markers

If you've ever rented or bought a movie on DVD, you're already familiar with *chapters,* better known as scenes (Figure 20-1).

DVD chapters let viewers skip to predefined starting points within a movie, or pick up where they last left off watching, by either using the scene menu or pressing the Next Chapter or Previous Chapter buttons on the remote control. Thanks to the partner-

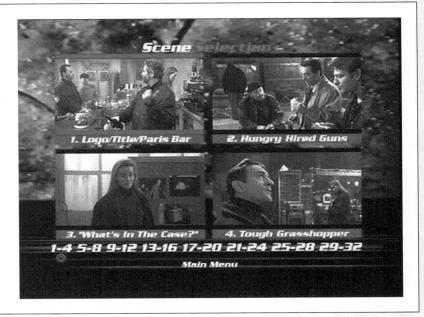

Figure 20-1:
Most DVDs offer some-thing called a scene menu like this one (from the movie Ronin*), which lets viewers jump directly to their favorite scenes in the movie. Your DVD scene menus probably won't be quite this elaborate, but you get the idea.*

ship of iMovie and iDVD, you can add markers to your own movies that perfectly replicate this feature. Here's how to go about it.

1. In iMovie, click the iDVD button.

You'll find it among the other palette buttons, just to the right of the Effects button, as shown in Figure 20-2. In any case, the iDVD palette now opens.

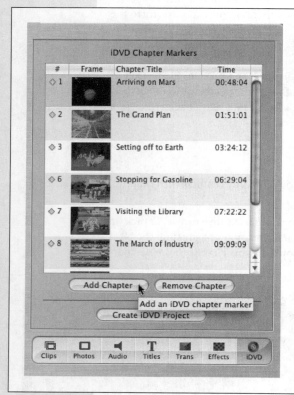

Figure 20-2:
The iDVD palette lets you add, remove, and name chapters—and then publish your iMovies to iDVD. New iMovie chapters are numbered sequentially, as they appear in your movie from left to right. Chapter references appear in your timeline as small yellow diamonds, just above the video track. iMovie can add up to 99 chapters per movie with the iDVD palette.

2. In the iMovie monitor, drag the playhead along the scrubber bar to locate the position for your new chapter.

You may want to choose Edit→Select None (Shift-⌘-A) first, which makes sure that no individual clip is selected. Now you can move the Playhead anywhere in your movie.

Tip: Use the arrow keys for precise Playhead positioning, or press Shift-arrow to jump 10 frames at a time.

---

3. Click Add Chapter.

You'll find this button near the bottom of the iDVD palette. iMovie adds the chapter to your list, as shown in Figure 20-2.

---

4. **Type a chapter title into the Chapter Title box.**

   Whatever you type here will wind up as the chapter name in the finished DVD menu. Select a short but meaningful name. (You don't have to delete the proposed name first; just type right over it.)

5. **Repeat steps 2–4.**

   Repeat until you've added all the chapters for your movie.

6. **Save your project.**

   Choose File→Save to save your iMovie project, including the chapter marks you just defined.

Removing Chapters

If you've added a chapter in error, you can remove it by clicking its name in iMovie's iDVD palette and then clicking the Remove Chapter button.

Tip: You can also select a bunch of chapters at once, using the usual list-keyboard shortcuts—⌘-click individual markers to select them, or select a consecutive batch by clicking the first and Shift-clicking the last. Now clicking Remove Chapter nukes all of them at once.

Changing Chapter Names

To change the name of any chapter that appears in the iDVD Chapter Markers list, just double-click it to open the editing box, and then edit away.

When you press Return or Enter, iMovie accepts the new chapter name and automatically moves to the next chapter. When you're at the last chapter of your project, iMovie cycles back to the first—in short, you can edit a bunch of chapter names in sequence with a minimum of mouse clicks. To finish editing chapter names, click the mouse outside the iDVD palette.

Chapter Marker Pointers

Here are a few key points to keep in mind about chapters:

- **Chapter markers appear in the Timeline Viewer.** They appear as small, yellow diamond shapes. (Chapter markers don't appear in the Clip Viewer.)

- **You can't adjust the starting frame.** If you've used the wrong start frame when creating your chapter, iMovie doesn't let you adjust the frame in the iDVD palette. To fix it, you have no choice but to delete the chapter marker entirely and create a new one with the correct starting point.

- **You can't reorder chapter markers in the iDVD palettes.** Chapter order depends on the associated starting times, which appear chronologically in the palette.

- **When you move (and erase) clips, chapter markers go along for the ride.** iMovie associates chapters with individual clips. If you reorder your clips, the chapter markers move with them. If you delete a clip, iMovie removes the included chapters.

- **When you copy a clip, you copy chapter markers.** When you duplicate a clip, iMovie copies all of its chapters at their original positions. (That's a change from iMovie 3, which didn't copy chapter markers with a clip.)

- **Frames matter, not timing.** When you slow down or speed up a clip, the included chapter marks slide accordingly, retaining their relative positions within the clip.

- **There's a "secret" unlisted chapter.** iMovie and iDVD always create one more chapter than you see on the iDVD Chapters list. This extra chapter corresponds to the very beginning of your movie (00:00:00), and starts out with the label "Beginning." (You won't see it until you arrive in iDVD.)

- **Your finished iDVD screens can fit up to 12 buttons per screen.** The actual number used depends on the *theme* you pick. (Themes are prebuilt designs with coordinating backgrounds, buttons, fonts, and, if you like, background audio.) When you include more chapters per screen than the theme allows (including "Beginning"), your scene-selection menus will extend to more than one screen, as shown in Figure 20-3.

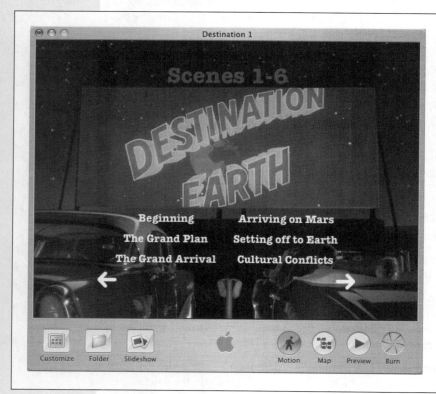

Figure 20-3:
Many iDVD themed menus can accommodate only six or seven buttons per screen. If you've got more than that, left and right arrows appear, so that your audience can navigate to additional screens full of buttons. iDVD automatically adds the scene numbers to your menu title for easier navigation.

Phase 2: Hand Off to iDVD

Once you've added your chapter markers in iMovie, you're ready to hand off the whole thing to iDVD, where you can do your menu design and DVD burning.

Start by saving your iMovie project—a necessary step before handing off to iDVD. Then click the Create iDVD Project button at the bottom of the chapter list. If your movie contains slow motion, fast motion, or reverse-motion clips, you'll be asked whether you want them to be *rendered* for better quality. Click Render and Proceed (unless you're using still photos in your movie; see page 603).

Your hard drive whirs, thunder rolls somewhere, and after a few minutes, you wind up in iDVD itself. If this is your first time using iDVD, the white curtains on the gold themed background will start to blow in the background, confirming your arrival in iDVD land. (If you've run iDVD before, you see whatever theme you used last.)

Tip: To turn off the Apple logo that appears in the lower-right corner of every iDVD Project, choose iDVD→ Preferences and turn off "Show Apple logo watermark."

Phase 3: Design the Menu Screens

On the main menu screen now before you, you'll find two buttons:

- **Play.** On the finished DVD, this button means, "Play the movie from the beginning."

- **Scene Selection.** On the finished DVD, this button will take your audience to a second screen, which is filled with individual buttons for the chapters you created. (In fact, this second screen may well have arrows that lead to third and fourth screens, because iDVD menus vary in the number of buttons that fit per screen. Wedding Bronze One holds six buttons per scene selection menu.)

  If you'd like to have a look at this scene-selection screen, double-click the words "Scene Selection." To get back to the main menu, click the left-pointing arrow on the scene-selection screen.

Tip: If iDVD seems very sluggish when you change screens, it's because the program is busily processing video in the background. To make it work faster, choose iDVD→Preferences, click the General icon, and turn off "Enable background encoding." (Then close the General window.)

Creating your DVD at the end of the process will take longer now, because the video hasn't been preprocessed. But at least you'll be able to work in the program without feeling like you're walking through quicksand.

(If things are still slow, your Mac may need more memory. iDVD consumes RAM.)

All about Themes

The blowing curtains, any music that's playing, and the font for your buttons are all part of a *theme:* a unified design scheme that governs how the menus look and behave, complete with attractive backgrounds, coordinated typography, and background music.

In iDVD 4, Apple added 20 new themes. Special events inspire some themes, like the wedding and childbirth themes. Others key into special interests, including sports and travel.

Themes also vary in complexity. Some offer completely realized presentations. Others provide little more than colors and fonts, leaving it up to you to mold them. Either way, the built-in themes, both old and new, provide an excellent jumping-off point for your DVDs.

It takes a lot of individual design decisions to make a theme. For example:

- **Background Image or Video.** A theme specifies the art that appears in the background, which could be either still images or video clips. The movement of the white curtain is one example of video in action.

Tip: If the repetitive looping of a theme's motion drives you crazy, click the round Motion button below the menu-design screen. The Motion button turns the looping motion on and off while you're working on a DVD. (It also affects the finished DVD, so check its status before you burn the disc.)

- **Button Type.** The buttons in iDVD Project can be either little graphics or just text phrases that your audience will "click" with the remote control.

- **Button Look.** The look of your buttons can vary. Text buttons may have simple backgrounds; graphic buttons may have a range of frame borders.

- **Button Positions.** Each menu can hold up to 12 buttons, depending on your theme. Themes are preset to place their buttons in certain favored positions.

- **Drop Zones.** Drop zones are areas into which you can drag a favorite video clip (sometimes more than one) that plays continuously as a background for the main menu screen. (If you've ever seen a commercial Hollywood DVD movie, you've seen this effect. One key scene from the movie plays over and over, looping until you choose one of the buttons on the menu screen—or go quietly insane.)

- **Text Boxes.** In iDVD 4, you can freely add text blocks to your menu screens. You could use this sort of text to provide instructions to your viewers, for example, to add copyright notices, or to provide details about what they're about to see.

- **Font selections.** Themes also specify the color, font size, and typeface for menu titles and buttons.

Figure 20-4 shows two very different looks for the same project. The difference lies only in the chosen theme (and that one project was retitled).

Choosing a Theme

Goodness knows, you don't have to be satisfied with the blowing-curtain Wedding theme. A wide range of canned themes awaits your inspection:

1. **Click Customize to open the Customize drawer, if it isn't already open.**

   The Customize button shows or hides the *drawer* shown in Figure 20-5. (You can also close the drawer by dragging its outside edge inward.)

2. **From the pop-up menu at the top of the drawer, choose a theme set.**

   iDVD offers two built-in theme sets: 4.0 Themes (new to iDVD 4, 20 themes in all) and 3.0 Themes (left over from iDVD 3, offering 24 additional themes). You can use this pop-up menu to switch between them (Figure 20-6), or just choose All to see all installed themes in a single scrolling list.

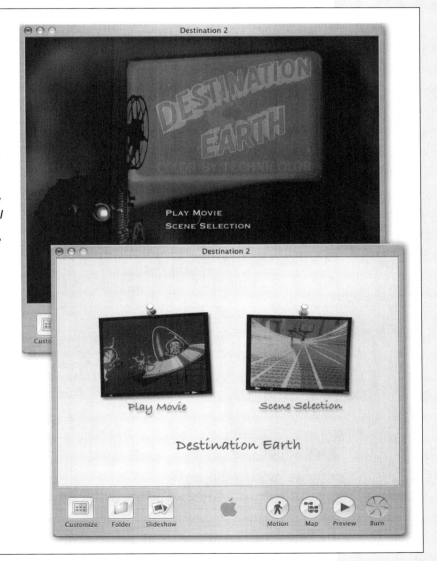

Figure 20-4:
iDVD Themes can create strikingly different interfaces for similar projects.

Top: The Projector theme uses a drop zone (the movie screen, which would be showing flickering video if this weren't a frozen picture on a book page) and all-capital text buttons in a formal font.

Bottom: The Portfolio theme uses mixed upper/lower case, a more casual font, no drop zones (that is, no moving video in the background), and image buttons that preview the video scenes they link to.

You'll notice that some of the new themes seem to appear twice: "Wedding Theme Bronze One" and "Wedding Theme Bronze Two," for example. That's a harbinger of another iDVD new feature: predesigned screens for *submenu* screens, like the

Figure 20-5:
The Customize button reveals iDVD's Customize drawer. You'll be spending a lot of your time here, so mastering its layout is important. For example, when you click one of the buttons at the top, the pane changes to show its contents. For example, Themes lets you choose a design scheme. Settings lets you choose motion menu duration, background video and audio, title fonts, and the look and placement of buttons. The Media pans link directly to iTunes and iPhoto.

Figure 20-6:
You can buy additional themes, or download free samples, from other companies (such as iDVDThemePAK.com or iDVD-themetastic.com). You install them by creating a folder called Favorites in your Library→iDVD folder (the Library folder in the main hard drive window, not in your Home folder)—and putting them inside.

Scene Selection screens you'd find on a commercial DVD. The "Two" designs are intended for these second-level screens full of buttons.

Scroll through the list of themes, clicking each one to see what it looks like in the main work area, or just rely on the little thumbnail icons to get a sense of the theme's overall flavor.

You'll discover that, in both quality and usability, iDVD themes range from the elegant to the absurd. Some, like Kids Theater and Drive-In, are busy and nerve-jangling. Others, like Wedding and (in the 3.0 set) Book, are elegant and clean. Explore each one with the round Motion button turned on, and ask yourself: How would my parents/spouse/audience react if this display were left on the TV for a minute or two?

Tip: You'll find an excellent interactive overview of iDVD's built-in themes at *www.apple.com/idvd/theater/themes.html*.

---

3. **Select a theme by clicking its thumbnail.**

   If your DVD menu system consists of only a single screen—the main menu you've been looking at the whole time—it takes on your chosen theme instantly.

   A movie you've exported from iMovie, however, probably has chapter markers in it, and therefore your movie probably has at least one additional menu screen: your scene-selection screen.

   It turns out that clicking a theme choice in the Customize drawer affects the *current* menu screen only. If you click, say, the Brushed Metal theme on the main menu, your scene-selection screen remains unaffected—it still shows the red-curtained Theater theme. Therefore, follow up like this:

4. **Choose Advanced→Apply Theme to Project.**

   This is an important step, because this command applies the same theme to every screen. Now all of your menu screens look alike.

Tip: If you want all of your menu screens to have the same look *except* the main menu, *first* use the Apply Theme to Project command described here. Then return to the main menu screen and click the theme thumbnail you want for just it.

For example, you might apply Kid's Theater Two to your entire project, and then choose Kid's Theater One for your main screen.

When you're happy with the way the new theme looks, you're ready to proceed with your iDVD design work. Fortunately, you don't have to commit to a theme at this moment; you can swap in a different theme at any time until you actually burn the DVD.

Editing Menus

If you like the way everything looks when you click a desired theme, great. You're good to go. Skip ahead to "Phase 4: Burn Your DVD."

Note, however, that a great deal of flexibility and control await in the meantime. You don't have to accept every element of the theme as it appears when you first select it. You can move your buttons around, change the labels on them, and so on.

Chapter 21 offers the full scoop on these procedures, but here are a few of the most common redesign tasks.

Editing Titles and Buttons

iDVD usually adds a title to your menu screens, usually near the top of the page, and usually in a larger font than any other text. You can edit it just as you would a Finder icon name: Click inside it to open up an editing box, type your changes, and then press Enter or Return.

Editing button names works almost the same way, except that you single-click the button first, and then click the text itself to open the editing box.

Keep these points in mind when working with iDVD text:

- **Be succinct.** DVD screens are small. There's not much room for long text blobs.

- **Be contained.** Don't let one text box overlap another.

- **Spell check.** Nothing speaks worse of your attention to detail than a lovingly crafted masterpiece called "For Mouther's Day."

Tip: If your buttons' text labels are crashing into one another, try making the text wrap into a narrow column, so that it's several lines long. Simply press Return to start a new line; unlike previous versions of iDVD, pressing Return doesn't close the editing box.

Moving Buttons Around

Each theme comes with predetermined locations for your buttons. In fact, internally, each theme stores separate layout maps: one that specifies the button positions if you have three buttons, another for four buttons, another if you have five, and so on.

iDVD lets you move your buttons around into new positions, but it's not as easy as just dragging them with your mouse. There's no grid to guide you, so the new button positions might not look especially professional. For example, when you play your iDVD disc on a standard DVD player, your menu buttons will sprout glowing rectangles to indicate which button is highlighted. If you've positioned the buttons too closely together, this highlighting might overlap other buttons—with ugly results.

If you're absolutely, positively sure that you want the freedom to drag buttons around into new positions, open the Customize drawer. Click the Settings button at the top, and then in the lower third of the pane, turn on Free Position. Now the buttons are liberated from their grid. (You may want to choose Advanced→Show TV Safe Area so that you don't wind up dragging the buttons off the TV screen.)

Apple disavows all responsibility for the cosmetic quality of the results.

Tip: At any time, you can make your buttons snap back to their original positions by choosing Snap to Grid from the Settings pane.

Reordering Buttons

Apple may not want you to drag buttons randomly around the screen, but reordering them is a different story. See Figure 20-7.

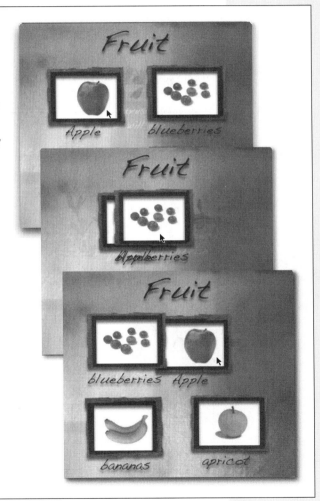

Figure 20-7:
In this example, dragging one button on top of another swaps the two positions, but iDVD doesn't always work this way. If you drag the first button into the fourth position, the sequence becomes #2, #3, #4, #1 (instead of just swapping #1 and #4).

iDVD attempts to maintain as much of the original sequence as possible, so that when your audience uses the remote control's arrow button on the resulting DVDs, the highlighting won't jump around confusingly.

Removing Buttons

To remove a button from a menu screen, click it and then press the Delete key.

Tip: You can also click the first button, and then Shift-click another button, to highlight all of the buttons in between. Or ⌘-click individual buttons to highlight only those.

Of course, if your purpose in removing a button is to move it to a different menu screen, you can use the Cut and Paste commands in the Edit menu.

Setting Button Images

Except for text buttons, every button displays an icon, picture, or tiny movie clip to give viewers a hint as to what lies in store if they click it. Here's how you specify what that image is.

Moving previews

Suppose you have a button that, when clicked, plays a movie you've created. Here's where you can make iDVD display up to 30 seconds of that movie right there on the button.

Tip: A button can display video on a button only if that button actually *links* to a video—not to a folder or a slideshow, as described in the next chapter.

---

1. **Select the button.**

   When you click a button, a slider and a Movie checkbox appear above it, as shown in Figure 20-8.

Figure 20-8:
Turn on Movie to create a video button. Use the slider to specify where you want the tiny button movie to begin looping.

2. **Turn on Motion, if necessary.**

   If motion isn't already turned on, click the round Motion button at the bottom of the iDVD window. The button turns green when it's on, gray when it's not.

Note: If your movie clips don't start playing, don't worry. Some menus, including Kids Theater Two, come with their button loop times set to *zero*.

To make your video buttons come alive, you have to adjust their timing manually, as described below.

3. **Make sure the Movie checkbox is turned on. Drag the slider to the spot where you want playback to begin.**

   The slider is a map of your entire movie, from start to end. Pinpoint where you want the button's video playback to begin. You've just set what Apple calls the *poster frame* for the linked movie.

   So how do you specify where you want the button's looping video to end?

4. **Make sure the Customize drawer is open. Click the Settings icon at the top, and then drag the Motion Duration slider to specify how many seconds of video you want your button to loop.**

   The maximum loop time varies by theme and project. For some themes, you can specify a loop of up to 30 seconds. That should be plenty of time for your audience member to make a selection from the menu screen.

   Note, however, that changing this duration also affects the looping time of the background video—not just video buttons (see "Drop Zones" on page 426).

5. **Click anywhere on the background to hide the slider and the Movie checkbox.**

   You'll see the video begin playing on the button immediately.

Tip: If your video buttons don't seem to be moving, remember to set their loop lengths to more than 0 seconds, as described in the previous note. Also make sure that you've turned on the Motion button at the bottom of the screen, so that it's green.

A still frame from the movie

Instead of a looping video, your button's face can display a still image that comes from a particular frame of the movie. This is the style in Hollywood DVD movies, where a still image represents the scene that lies behind each button.

The steps are exactly the same as described in the previous section—except that you turn *off* the Movie checkbox shown in Figure 20-8.

Drop a Picture or Movie

The picture on a button doesn't have to be a scene from the movie. It can be any graphic you want. Just drag any graphics file right onto the button itself; you'll see the button image change instantly.

This graphic can come from just about anywhere. For example:

- **The Finder.** Drag any graphics file out of a folder window or from the desktop.

• **iPhoto.** In the Customize drawer, click the Photos button. You now see a list of all of the albums in your Mac's iPhoto collection. You can drag any photo onto a button to install it as the new button face.

Drop Zones

Drop zones let you use video, slideshows, and graphics as the backgrounds of your menu screens. Not every theme offers drop zones, but many do: Wedding Silver One, Kids Theater One, Transparent Green, and so on. Look for the words "Drag a photo or movie here," as shown in Figure 20-9, indicating the presence of a drop zone.

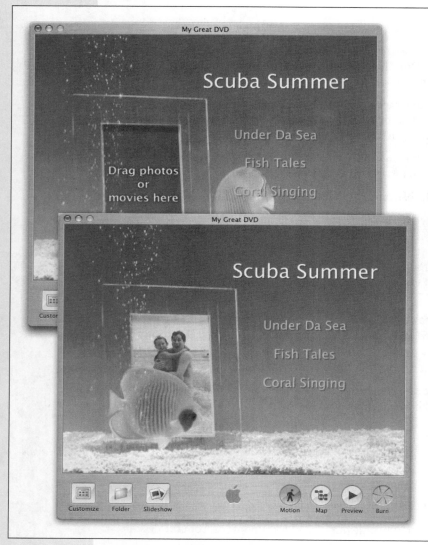

Figure 20-9:
Top: The words "Drag a photo or movie here" show you where the drop zones are. Note, by the way, that drop zones aren't always perfect rectangles or squares, so your video may get clipped around the edges.

Bottom: On the other hand, you can drag the picture or movie within the drop zone outline so that the most important part shows up. In this theme, the animated fish actually swims around in front of whatever's in the drop zone!

Tip: If you don't see the telltale phrase, "Drag a photo or movie here," choose iDVD→Preferences. Click the General icon, and then turn on Show Drop Zones.

(Note, furthermore, that the Theater theme, which is part of the 3.0 Themes collection, hides its drop zone behind closed curtains if you've turned off the Motion button at the bottom of the window.)

Here's how drop zones work:

- **Adding to a drop zone.** Drag any video, photo album, image, or collection of images right into a drop zone outline to install it there. You can drag icons out of the Finder, or directly out of the Media pane in the Customize drawer.

Tip: Albums added to drop zones can contain 30 images at most. What you'll get is a mini slideshow, right there within the drop zone. (More on dragging out of the Photos pane in Chapter 21.)

- **Replacing items in a drop zone.** To replace what you've installed in a drop zone, just drag something new into it.

- **Removing items from a drop zone. To get rid of an item in the drop zone,** drag it out, just as you'd drag something off the Mac OS X Dock or the Sidebar. You get a cute little puff of smoke to indicate the movie's or picture's disappearance. (If you drag it onto a menu button in the process of removing it from the drop zone, it becomes a video menu button.)

- **Editing a drop zone slideshow.** If you've decided to create a mini-slideshow within the drop zone, you may wonder how you're supposed to adjust the order of the photos. Figure 20-10 tells all.

Tip: Instead of clicking the drop zone and then clicking Edit Order, you can just double-click the drop zone. You go straight to the Drop Zone Editor window.

- **Adding sounds.** Drop zones have no sounds; they play in the background of your menus. To add sound to your drop zones, you must import audio into the menu screen that *contains* the drop zone. See page 455.

- **Turning on Motion.** If you've installed video into a drop zone and it doesn't seem to be playing, click the round Motion button at the bottom of the iDVD window. (When it's turned on, the button is green; when it's turned off, it's gray.) If it still doesn't seem to be playing, the menu duration may be set to 0 (page 425).

  Turning off Motion also turns off any background audio track and brings motion menus and motion buttons to a standstill. (Caution: The status of this button affects both your onscreen project and the final DVD.)

- **Changing the duration.** Use the Settings pane in the Customize drawer to adjust the loop duration for your menus (how long a movie clip plays before starting over). Whatever time you specify here controls the loop length of movies in both menu backgrounds and drop zones.

Note: If you drag a movie into a drop zone, you can't control where the movie begins, as you can with button movies. In a drop zone, a movie always begins at the beginning.

Redesigning the Theme

If you have the time, patience, and artistic vision, you can change every tiny aspect of your theme: the music, the background, the colors, the fonts, and so on. Turn to Chapter 22 for a full discussion of theme creation.

Figure 20-10:
Top: When you click the drop zone itself, a transparent control panel appears just above it. Use the slider to specify which photo appears on the button, or click the Edit Order button to open the Drop Zone editor.

Bottom: In the Drop Zone editor window, a thumbnail display lets you drag the photos around. Reorder the slides until your aesthetic sensibilities are satisfied, and then click Return to go back to the menu editor screen.

Phase 4: Burning Your DVD

Once your scene-selection screen is looking pretty good, you're almost ready to burn the DVD. Before you go using up a blank disc, however, you should test it, using the virtual DVD player known as the Macintosh screen.

Previewing Your Project

iDVD's Preview button lets you test your menu system to avoid unpleasant surprises. When you click it, iDVD enters Preview mode, which simulates how your DVD works on a standalone set-top DVD player. You even get a simulated remote control to help you navigate, as shown in Figure 20-11. To return to iDVD's edit mode, click Exit, Stop (the filled square) or reclick Preview.

> *Tip:* Instead of using the arrow buttons on the remote to highlight and "click" screen buttons, you can just use your mouse. You'll find it not only less clumsy, but also a good indication of how your DVD will play back on Macs or PCs that can play DVDs.

Figure 20-11:
Use iDVD's simulated remote control to navigate through your DVD's menus, movies, and so on. To "click" your buttons, for example, use the arrow buttons on the remote to highlight the one you want, and then click the Enter button in the middle.

Maximum DVD Playback Time

In iDVD 4, you no longer have to make the Hobson's choice between 60 minutes of video at best quality and 90 minutes at lower quality. Apple has thoughtfully raided its own professional DVD creation software (DVD Studio Pro) to bless iDVD with one of its best features: now any DVD you burn can contain 120 minutes of footage at best quality.

To see the on/off switch for this feature, choose iDVD→Preferences. On the General panel (Figure 20-12), you'll see two options under Encoding Settings. Both produce superior video quality to what you got from iDVD 3:

- **Best Quality.** This option gives you 120 minutes of video at best quality. The tradeoff: It takes a lot longer to burn your DVD, because the program performs quite a bit of analysis before burning.

- **Best Performance.** Video will look fantastic, and your Mac will burn the disc relatively quickly—but the DVD you burn this way can contain a maximum of 60 minutes of video.

Figure 20-12:
iDVD 4 offers two ways to compress the video on your masterpiece. Choose Best Performance for up to 60 minutes of excellent looking footage or Best Quality for up to 120 minutes of video.

When iDVD's work is over, the DVD that pops out of your Mac will come delightfully close to looking and working like a professionally mastered, commercial DVD from Blockbuster. There will, however, be one giveaway: it won't be over two hours long.

In fact, iDVD prefers to burn 60-minute DVDs, because they have the best quality. The instant you try to add the 61st minute of footage to your project, you see the message shown in Figure 20-13. You can change your settings as suggested, or delete some video from the project to make it fit within 60 minutes again.

Figure 20-13:
iDVD is telling you that you've put more than 60 minutes of footage onto this DVD. To fit all this video onto your disc, you'll need to use the General Preferences (⌘-comma) window to switch from Best Performance (60 minutes max) to Best Quality.

A disc that exceeds 60 minutes uses a lower *bit rate*—that is, it uses less data to describe the video, which allows iDVD to fit more information on the same size disc.

(For example, 60-minute iDVD projects depict video using 8 megabits (Mbps) per second; 90-minute projects use 5 Mbps; 120-minute discs use 4 Mbps.)

The tradeoff, of course, is video quality. Higher bit rates generally provide clearer and more accurate picture reproduction than lower bit rates do, especially in action scenes.

If the bit rate of a DVD is *very* low, you get blocky-looking, unclear video. But iDVD's "lowest-quality" mode—4 Mbps—is still above the minimum bit rate needed for clear video for home movies. Don't constrain yourself needlessly to the 60-minute format until you've given the Best Quality format a try.

Burning Your Project

When you've finished editing your disc and testing it thoroughly, it's time to proceed with your burn. This is the moment you've been working for.

Note: The following steps walk you through the process for burning with an internal Apple SuperDrive (or equivalent). If you want to burn your discs to an external drive, see page 467.

1. **Make sure iDVD is ready to burn.**

   Part of iDVD's job is to encode your movies, music, and pictures into the MPEG-2 format required by standard DVDs.

   Therefore, it's a good idea to open the Customize Drawer, click the Status button at the top, and make sure that the word "Done" appears next to each *asset*. (Apple uses the term "asset" as shorthand for "picture, movie, soundtrack, or what have you.") See Figure 20-14.

Figure 20-14:
Look for the word "Done" to the right of each asset. If a status bar appears instead, let iDVD 4 continue encoding until "Done" appears. There's no further action you must take. iDVD encodes in the background without any intervention.

Tip: If iDVD doesn't say "Done" for all assets in the list, and yet it doesn't seem to be processing them automatically, make sure you've turned on background compression. Choose iDVD→Preferences, click the General button, and turn on "Enable background encoding."

The only time you'd want to turn off background encoding is when you discover that it's slowing down your Mac as you work.

2. **Check your Motion setting.**

   As noted earlier in this chapter, the Motion button at the bottom of the window determines whether your finished DVD will have animated menus, buttons, and backgrounds, and whether music will play. If the Motion button is green, you'll get all this stuff. If you click it so that it turns gray, motion and audio features won't appear on the final disc. (This button has no effect on regular movies and slideshows—only the ones on menu screens.)

3. **Choose File→Save Project.**

   Or press ⌘-S.

4. **Check your disk space.**

   As iDVD works, it needs some extra working space on your hard drive. Make sure there's plenty of free space—at least the amount indicated by the "Project size" statistic on the Status pane of the Customize drawer. If your hard drive doesn't have enough space, do some cleanup.

5. **Click the Burn button twice.**

   See Figure 20-15.

POWER USERS' CLINIC

Best Quality/Best Performance: How It Works

When a DVD-burning program goes to work, it faces an important decision. Given that a blank DVD contains a limited amount of space (4.7 GB or so), how much picture-quality data can it afford to devote to each frame of video?

The Best Performance option in iDVD 4 makes that decision like this: "I'll allot a fixed, predetermined amount of data to each frame of video—enough to make it look great—no matter how many minutes of video my human master has included. A lot of the DVD might wind up being empty—if, for example, the project contains less than an hour of video. But at least the burning process will go quickly, and the video will look really great."

The Best Quality option takes a different approach. It says:

"I'm going to use every micron of space on this blank DVD. I'm going to analyze the amount of video my human has included, and divide it into the amount of space available on the DVD. The amount of information used to describe an individual frame of video will vary from project to project, and it will take me a lot longer to burn the DVD because I'm going to have to do so much analysis. But at least my human will get two hours of great-looking video per disc."

Incidentally, if you'd like some insight into how iDVD is thinking of the project you're working on at the moment, open the Customize drawer and click the Status button. This new panel shows you how close you are to filling up the DVD with your movies, menus, and other elements.

---

6. Insert a blank DVD-R disc when the Mac asks for it.

Be sure you're using the correct kind of blank DVD for the speed of your DVD burner. For example, don't attempt to burn 1x or 2x blanks at 4x speed. Don't use DVD+R discs, either—they must be DVD-R (note the + and – difference).

Figure 20-15:
The first click on the gray, closed Burn button "opens" it, revealing a throbbing yellow-and-black button. The second click begins the burning process.

FREQUENTLY ASKED QUESTION

Hollywood, DVD Length, and You

The Hollywood DVDs I rent from Blockbuster are at least two hours long. How come I'm limited to 120 minutes in iDVD?

Most Hollywood DVDs use dual-layer technology—discs that are recorded in two layers of video data. The extra layer increases the DVD's capacity from 4.7 GB to nearly 8 GB.

When you watch one of these movies, you may even be able to spot the moment when the DVD player's laser jumps from one layer to the other: the movie pauses for a moment during playback, always at the same place in the movie.

Unfortunately, dual-layer technology is very expensive, and only now becoming available for recordable DVDs. The special dual-layer blanks required by these recorders are hard to find, even for professional DVD authors. Even worse, the early prototype discs don't play back in normal DVD players—only in the DVD recorders that made them. It will take several years for the price to come down and the technology to hit the consumer marketplace.

Hollywood uses another trick, too: variable bit-rate (VBR) encoding. When creating a DVD movie for commercial distribution, professional DVD authors use advanced software to analyze each piece of the movie, using more or less data to describe each frame depending on how much action is visible. The disc stores the same amount of data as a constant bit-rate recording like the ones iDVD makes, but conserves data for when the video needs it the most.

The trouble is, VBR encoding takes a very long time. The software often requires several passes through the whole movie to analyze it and optimize the data. Apple figures that iDVD fans would just as soon not wait all night to see their finished productions.

If you feel that iDVD's 120-minute limitation is standing between you and a glorious career in filmmaking, you could always upgrade to a program like Apple's DVD Studio Pro. It can squeeze up to six hours of video onto a single 4.37 GB disc (at marginal quality, of course). It can also export files for those 8 GB DVDs that can be produced at a professional replication plant.

---

7. **Wait.**

It takes iDVD quite awhile to process all of your audio, video, and photos, encoding them into the proper format for a DVD. Your wait time depends on how complex your project is and how fast your Mac is.

Apple says that you should allow two or three minutes of processing per minute of video in your movie, but burning times vary significantly. After a while, or a bit more than a while, a freshly burned DVD automatically ejects from your SuperDrive.

Note: After your new DVD pops out, a message says: "Your disc has been created. If you want to create another DVD, insert another disc now." Sure enough, if you want to spin out multiple copies of your project, you can insert another blank DVD right then, so that iDVD can record it while it's on a roll.

Otherwise, click Done.

---

iDVD Slideshows

Let's face it. Most of the methods iPhoto gives you to show off your prize photos are geek techniques like sending them by email, posting them on a Web page, turning them into a desktop picture, and so on. All of these methods involve making your audience sit, hunched and uncomfortable, around a computer screen.

Now imagine seating them instead in front of the big-screen TV in the family room, turning down the lights, cranking up the surround sound, and grabbing the DVD remote to show off the latest family photos.

You can do it—if you have a DVD-burning drive and iDVD, Apple's DVD-creation software. (iDVD 4 came with your iLife package, if indeed it wasn't already aboard your Mac when you bought it.) With iDVD, you can create DVD-based slideshows from your photo collection, complete with soundtracks and navigational menus and screens just like the DVDs you rent from Blockbuster.

This chapter covers the basics of how to bring your photos from iPhoto to iDVD and how to customize, preview, and burn your slideshows once you've exported them to iDVD.

The iDVD Slideshow

You don't actually need iPhoto to create a slideshow in iDVD. By itself, iDVD has all the tools you need to create interactive DVDs that include movies and soundtracks as well as slideshows.

But using iPhoto can save you a lot of time and trouble. You can use iPhoto to preview, edit, and organize all your photos into albums. Then, once your photos are arranged into neatly organized albums, one click hands them off to iDVD, which converts them into a DVD-readable format. iDVD also hooks up all the navigational links and menus needed to present the show.

Creating an iDVD Slideshow

Creating a DVD of your own photos entails choosing the photos that you've organized in iPhoto, selecting a theme, building menus, and configuring the settings that determine how your slideshow will look and operate. Finally, you can preview the entire DVD without actually burning a disc to test navigation, pacing, and other settings. When the whole thing looks right, you burn the final disc.

You can begin in either of two ways: from inside iPhoto or from inside iDVD. The following pages walk you through both methods.

Starting in iPhoto

You can save a few steps by beginning your odyssey in iPhoto.

1. **If you want a musical soundtrack, select one for each selected album (or for the whole Photo Library).**

   Music is optional, of course. See Chapter 9 for complete instructions on how to add a soundtrack to a slideshow. Whatever music you've assigned to your slideshows in iPhoto will automatically carry over into iDVD.

2. **In Organize mode, select the photo album(s) you want to turn into a slideshow.**

   You can select either a single photo album or multiple albums in the Source list. If you want to include your *entire* Photo Library in the slideshow, click the Photo Library icon (although you can't have more than 99 photos in a slideshow).

Tip: Remember that any photos that aren't in a 4:3 aspect ratio will wind up flanked by black bars when displayed on a standard TV set.

Figure 21-1:
If you don't see an iDVD button in your copy of iPhoto (bottom right, next to the Burn button), it's probably because you don't have a copy of iDVD 3 installed on your Mac. The iDVD icon doesn't appear in iPhoto's Organize pane unless you've got iDVD 3 installed.

3. **Click the iDVD icon in the lower pane of the iPhoto window (Figure 21-1).**

   This is the big hand-off. iDVD opens up a default presentation window (see Figure 21-2). See how the names of your selected albums are already listed as menu items that can be "clicked" with the DVD's remote control?

   If you included your whole photo collection when exporting to iDVD, the sole menu item is called Photo Library.

   Technically, at this point, your slideshow is ready to meet its public. If you're looking for some instant gratification, click Preview on the bottom of the window to flip iDVD into presentation mode. Then click the name of your album as it appears on the DVD menu page to make the show begin. Use the iDVD remote control shown in Figure 21-7 to stop, pause, or rewind the show in progress.

   To really make the finished show your own, though, you'll want to spend a few minutes adding some custom touches. See "Customizing the show" on page 439.

Starting in iDVD

You can also begin building the show right in iDVD. To see how, click the Customize button (shown in lower left of Figure 21-2). The slide-out Customize "drawer"

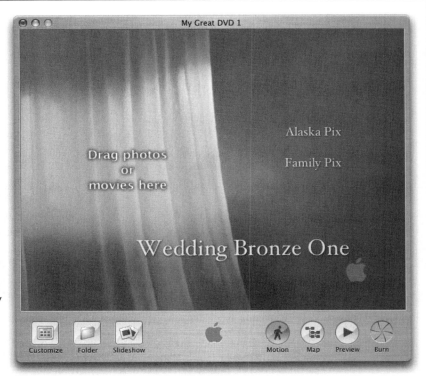

Figure 21-2:
Here's what you see when iDVD first opens. The name of each iPhoto album you exported appears on the main menu page of the DVD. Click a name once to select it, and (after a pause) click again to edit and change it. Double-click a menu title quickly to open a window where you can view thumbnails of the included pictures and change their order (Figure 21-6).

Oh—and if your DVD is not, by chance, going to be about a wedding, read on to find out how to change this starter design.

opens. Click the Media tab, and from the pop-up menu, choose Photos (see Figure 21-3); if you don't see this drawer, click the Customize button. You now see a little tiny iPhoto window, right there in iDVD, complete with thumbnails, your Source list, and even a Search box.

Figure 21-3:
All the hard work you've done in iPhoto titling your photos and organizing them into albums pays off when it's time to use those pictures in iDVD. Clicking the Photos tab gives you instant access to your whole Photo Library. You can even use the Search box to find photos by name or comments.

Each album you drag out of the list and onto the main iDVD stage area becomes another menu name that your audience will be able to click with their remotes. (If the album won't "stick" and bounces back to the Source list, it's because that album is too full. iDVD doesn't like albums that hold more than 99 photos.)

Tip: You can also drag photos, or folders full of them, right off of your Finder desktop and onto the main menu screen to install them there as slideshows.

If you'd selected a piece of music to accompany the slideshow of that album in iPhoto, then iDVD remembers, and plays it automatically when you play the DVD slideshow. As of iDVD 4.0.1, however, iDVD doesn't remember the playlist you've chosen.

To fix that, or to assign different music altogether, choose Audio from the pop-up menu at the top of the Customize drawer and survey your iTunes collection. When you find a song or playlist that seems right, double-click the name of your slideshow to reveal the Slideshow Editor window shown in Figure 21-4. Drag the playlist or song onto the little square Audio "well," also shown in Figure 21-4. (Click the Return button to return to the menu-design page.)

Figure 21-4:
In the Media panel of the Customize drawer, choose Audio. You see your entire list of iTunes music—in fact, you even see your playlists here. To avoid the music-ending-too-soon syndrome, drag an entire playlist into the little Audio well beneath the slide display. Your DVD will play one song after another according to the playlist.

Customizing the Show

iDVD provides an impressive number of options for customizing the look, feel, and sound of the slideshows you create, including its overall design scheme. That's merciful, because otherwise, every DVD you create would look like a bronze Wedding album.

1. **Choose a Theme.**

   With the Customize drawer open as shown in Figure 21-4, click the Themes button at the top to reveal the list of ready-to-use visual themes that you can apply to your slideshow. (Several are shown in Figure 21-4.) Click a theme to select it and apply it to your DVD's main-menu screen.

2. **Add your own background graphics, if you like.**

   All themes let you drop in a background photo. (Click Settings in the Customize drawer, and drag the picture into the Background "well.") Some let you drop a photo into more interesting, animated *regions* of the background called *drop zones*, as described in Figure 21-5.

3. Add, remove, and reorder your pictures.

When you bring albums into iDVD directly from iPhoto, your photos arrive in the same sequence as they appeared within their iPhoto albums. Once you're in iDVD, however, you can change the order of these photos, remove them from the show, or add others.

To edit a slideshow in this way, double-click its title on the DVD menu page; the editing window shown in Figure 21-6 appears.

Figure 21-5:
In this animated main-menu screen (the theme called Fish One), the fish actually swims around the screen. As for the photo in the frame: That's a "drop zone," an area that you can fill with a photo or movie of your choosing. (Click the Media button at top, choose Photos or Movies, and drag the picture or movie you want directly into the drop zone.)

In this window, you can also set up other options, like switching between automatic and manual advancing of photos, selecting a different soundtrack, and adding navigation buttons to a slideshow.

You can rearrange the slides by dragging them (the other slides scoot aside to make room), delete selected slides by pressing the Delete key, or add more pictures to them by dragging new photos out of the Customize drawer or from the Finder.

Then, of course, there are the controls at the bottom of the window. They offer a great deal of control over the show. For example:

Loop slideshow makes the slideshow repeat endlessly.

Display < > during slideshow adds navigation arrows to the screen as your slideshow plays. Your audience can click these buttons with their remote controls to move back and forth within your slideshow.

They're not technically necessary, of course. If you set your slides to advance automatically (read on), you won't need navigation arrows. And even if you set up the slideshow for manual advance, your audience can always press the arrow buttons on their DVD remote to advance the slides. But if you think they need a visual crutch, this option is here.

Add original photos on DVD-ROM is an interesting one. When iDVD creates a slideshow, it scales all of your photos to 640 by 480 pixels. That's ideal for a standard television screen, which, in fact, can't display any resolution higher than that.

Figure 21-6:
Changing the sequence of slides involves little more than dragging them up or down in the list. As in iPhoto, you can select multiple slides at once and then drag them en masse.

Don't miss the tiny icon at the top-right corner of the window. It switches to a list view that reveals the names of the photos—and still lets you drag them up or down to rearrange them.

Click Return to go back to your main-menu design screen.

But if you intend to distribute your DVD to somebody who's computer savvy, you may want to give them the original, full-resolution photos. They won't see these photos when they insert the disc into a DVD player. But when they insert your DVD into their computers, they'll see a folder filled with the original, high-res photos, suitable for printing, using as Desktop wallpaper, paying you for, and so on. (In other words, you've created a disc that's both a DVD-video disc and a DVD-ROM.)

Slide Duration, of course, lets you specify how much time each slide spends on the screen before the next one appears: 1, 3, 5, 10 seconds, or Manual. Manual means that your audience will have to press the Next button on the remote control to change pictures.

Then there's the **Fit to Audio** option, which appears in the pop-up menu only after you've added a sound file to your slideshow (Figure 21-4). In this case, iDVD will determine the timing of your slides automatically—by dividing the length of the soundtrack by the number of slides in your show. If the song is 60 seconds long, and you've got 20 slides in the show, each slide will sit on the screen for three seconds.

Transition lets you specify any of several graceful transition effects—Dissolve, Cube, and so on—to govern how one slide morphs into the next. Whatever transition you specify here affects all slides in the show.

4. **Add more menu pages and slideshows, if you like.**

The "home page" (main menu) for your DVD can show no more than 12 buttons. If you have more than 11 slideshows to store, you can create a secondary menu page to hold the overflow. It will be represented on the main menu by a "More Shows…" button, for example.

If you're making a "Family Photos 2004" DVD, for instance, you might want to create a separate menu page called Holidays with its own theme. On that page, you can add slideshows like Halloween, Labor Day Weekend, and so on.

To add a new menu page in iDVD, click the Folder button in the main iDVD window; a corresponding menu button called My Folder appears on the main "home page." Double-click "My Folder" to open your secondary, empty menu page. Then add slideshows to it by dragging albums onto it from the mini-iPhoto browser shown in Figure 21-3.

At any time, you can return to the main menu by clicking the Back button (a left-pointing arrow). Once you're there, don't forget to rename the My Folder menu button to say, for example, "More Shows."

6. **Click the Return button to go back to the menu-design screen.**

FREQUENTLY ASKED QUESTION

Crazy-Fast Slideshows

I turned a photo album into a slideshow in iDVD and it came out perfect—except that when I preview the slideshow, iDVD acts like it's on amphetamines and races frantically through the photos, flashing each one so briefly that you can hardly see it. What's going on?

What's going on is the Fit to Audio feature. You turn it on or off in the editing window, shown in Figure 21-6.

This option is designed to assist you with making your photos and your music end tidily together. It essentially divides the song length by the number of photos you've

selected. If you've selected a one-minute soundtrack and have 99 photos in your album, iDVD will try to flash one photo every six-tenths of a second to make the pictures "fit" the soundtrack!

You'll have the same problem if you've chosen a more reasonable number of slides but a very short soundtrack.

You can solve the problem when editing a slideshow in iDVD by changing the Slide Duration setting from Fit to Audio to a specific interval, like 3 Seconds or 5 Seconds.

Previewing the DVD

Your last step is to test your DVD presentation (without burning a disc) to check navigation, timing, photo sequences, and so on.

1. **Click the Preview button.**

   iDVD switches into Preview mode, which simulates how your disc will behave when inserted into a DVD player. This is a great chance to put your DVD-in-waiting through its paces before wasting an expensive blank disc.

2. **Use the iDVD remote control to click your menu buttons, stop, pause, or rewind the show in progress.**

   See Figure 21-7.

Figure 21-7
When you put iDVD in Preview mode (by clicking the Preview button) a small remote control panel appears next to the main window. It works just like your real DVD player's remote control. You can pause, rewind, or fast-forward slideshows. Clicking the Menu button takes you out of a slideshow and back to the main menu page of the DVD, where you can select other slideshows or movies to view.

3. **From the View menu, choose Show TV Safe Area. Click through your slides looking for decapitations.**

   In its early days, the little cathode-ray guns inside the TV worked by "painting" one line of the TV picture, then turning around and heading back in the opposite direction. To make sure that the screen was painted edge to edge, these early TVs were programmed to overshoot the edges of the screen—or, to use the technical term, to *overscan* the screen.

   TV technology is much better now, but even modern TVs exhibit some overscanning. The amount varies, but you may be missing as much as 10 percent of the picture beyond the edges of the glass.

   The overscanning effect means that when you show your slides on a TV, you'll lose anything that's very close to the edges of the frame. Avoiding this problem, fortunately, is supremely easy, thanks to the Show TV Safe Area command. Using a dimmed, gray frame, it shows you exactly how much of your photos might get lopped off by overscanning. See Figure 21-8 for instructions on how to proceed.

4. **Click the Exit button on the "remote" when you're finished.**

When everything in the DVD looks good, you're ready to master your disc. Insert a blank disc in your SuperDrive and click the Burn button.

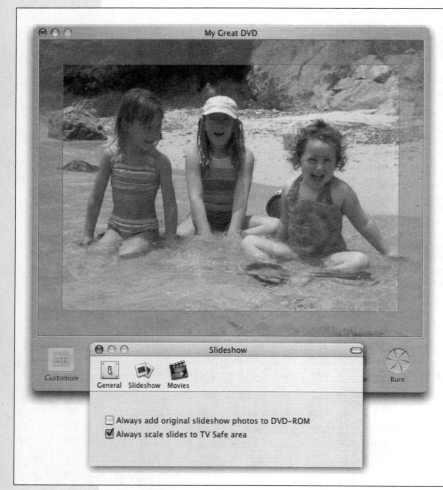

Figure 21-8:
When checking for decapitations, you may discover that nothing important is lost (top), that in fact the cropping of the average TV helps focus attention on your photos' subjects. If you discover too many scalps missing, on the other hand, choose iDVD→Preferences, click the Slideshow icon, and turn on "Always scale slides to TV Safe area" (bottom). Doing so makes iDVD shrink the pictures enough so that they won't get chopped off on a TV–guaranteed.

Extra Credit: Self-Playing Slideshows

As you work on your DVD menu structure, behind the scenes, iDVD builds a handy map. You can't add to it, or drag or delete any elements you see there, but you can double-click one of the icons to open the corresponding menu, movie, or slideshow.

To view the map, just click the Map button at the bottom of the main iDVD window (see Figure 21-9). The element you were working on appears with colored highlighting. (Click the Map button again to return to the menu screen you were working on.)

But the map is more than just a pretty navigational aid. It also makes possible a self-playing slideshow, one that plays automatically when the DVD is inserted, before your viewers even touch their remote controls.

Figure 21-9:
The Map view is most useful when you're creating a complex DVD with nested menu screens, like one you might rent from Blockbuster.

But for slideshow purposes, its most useful feature is the AutoPlay icon. Any pictures or albums you drag onto this tile begin to play automatically when you insert the DVD into a DVD player—no remote control fussing required.

AutoPlay icon   Map button

Once you've got the Photos list open in the Customize drawer, you can also drag an entire iPhoto album onto the Autoplay icon. Alternatively, you can click and ⌘-click just the photos you want in the Customize panel, and then drag them en masse onto the Autoplay icon. In fact, you can even drag photos—as a group or in a folder—right out of the Finder and onto this icon.

To control how long your still image remains on the screen, or how quickly your Autoplay slideshow plays, double-click the AutoPlay tile. You arrive at the slideshow editor shown in Figure 21-6, where you can adjust the timing, transition, and even the audio that plays behind the picture(s).

If you decide to replace your Autoplay material, just drag new stuff right onto it. Or, to eliminate the Autoplay segment, drag it right off the Autoplay tile. It disappears in a little puff of Mac OS X cartoon smoke.

You can design a project that way for the benefit of, for example, technophobic DVD novices whose pupils dilate just contemplating using a remote control. They can just insert your Autoplay-only DVD and sit back on the couch as the pictures flash by automatically.

It's even possible to create a DVD that never even gets to the menu screen—a DVD consisting only of Autoplay material, a slideshow that repeats endlessly during, say, your cocktail reception. Just highlight the Autoplay tile and then choose Advanced→

Loop Slideshow. You've got yourself a self-running, self-repeating slideshow of digital photos that plays on a TV at a party or wedding reception. The DVD will loop endlessly—or at least until it occurs to someone in your audience to press the Menu or Title button on the remote, which displays your main menu at last. The Menu button redisplays the previous menu screen; the Title button causes a return to the main menu.

CHAPTER

22

Advanced iDVD

Although iDVD appears simple, straightforward, and direct, there's more power lurking inside than you might expect. You can see, change, and control things you never knew you could—if you're willing to try new and unusual approaches. Some of these approaches require add-on software programs. Others demand nerves of steel and a willingness to dive into hidden iDVD files. And a few even require some familiarity with programming.

In this advanced chapter, you'll discover how some of these sideways (and backwards and upside down) methods can expand your iDVD repertoire.

Designing Your Own Themes

Apple's iDVD themes can be hit or miss. Some themes offer great backgrounds but weak audio. Others provide terrific sounds but terrible text. Some create a nearly perfect package, while others seem broken beyond repair. Fortunately, in the end it doesn't matter, because iDVD lets you adapt themes to your taste and save them as new *Favorites*.

With iDVD customization, you can move buttons around and change their styles, change the fonts and colors for button and menu titles, move text around the screen, substitute new background art or background patterns, replace or remove the audio loop that plays when the main menu is onscreen, and much more. Let the following pages be your guide.

The Themes Pane

To view your list of starter Themes, click Customize to open the Customize drawer, then click the Themes button at the top of the pane.

As you study the scrolling list of themes, you'll notice that:

- **Favorites appear together.** When you choose Favorites from the Theme Set pop-up menu at the top of the pane, all Favorites (themes that you've created) appear together in the same list. This list is empty when you first start out with iDVD.

- **Most non-Apple themes appear separately.** Themes you've bought from other companies (like *www.idvdthemetastic.com* or *www.idvdthemepak.com*) are listed separately in the pane's pop-up menu.

- **View several sets at once.** iDVD 4 lets you view a single set of themes, or all themes at once. To view just one set, select its name from the Theme Set pop-up menu. To view all themes, choose All from that menu.

- **The walking-man icon means sound or audio.** When you see a small, round, walking-man logo in the lower-right corner of the theme thumbnail, that's your signal that the theme uses a motion background or audio loop.

- **The ribbon means favorite.** A gray prize ribbon appears in the lower-left corner of certain themes. This icon lets you know that the theme is a Favorite—a theme that you created yourself. You'll find out how to create Favorites later in this chapter.

Tip: If your mouse has a scroll wheel, you can scroll the list of theme thumbnails without having to use the scroll bar. Just turn the wheel whenever the cursor is hovering over the list.

Button Styles

iDVD's various button designs range from hearts to stamps to film frames—but you don't have to be content with the proposed button style for the theme you're using. To change the look of your buttons, do this:

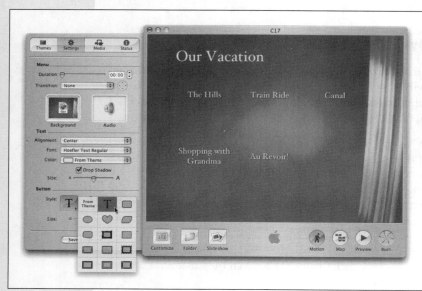

Figure 22-1:
Text buttons offer a stylistic alternative to the picture buttons used by many iDVD themes. To use them, select the letter T from the list of button styles in the Settings pane. iDVD removes the picture component, leaving only the button titles.

1. **Open the Settings pane, if it's not already open.**

   That is, open the Customize drawer (click the Customize button if necessary) and click the Settings button at the top.

2. **Click From Theme.**

   From Theme appears near the bottom of the pane, in the Button section. When you click it, you get a pop-up menu of button shapes (Figure 22-1).

3. **Click the button style you want.**

   Choose T to use a text button, for example. To revert to whatever button style the theme originally came with, choose From Theme.

Text Buttons

Text buttons offer a stylish alternative to iDVD's framed, picture-based buttons. See Figure 22-1 for details.

Editing and Positioning Text

Although most people focus primarily on iDVD's video buttons, drop zones, and so on, text also plays a critical role. It's a dependable, instantly recognizable part of a DVD menu system.

The text that you can fiddle with falls into three categories:

- **Menu titles** help viewers figure out where they are in the DVD menu system by providing clues to the current context: "Our Vacation," "Pictures (Week 1)," and "Scene Selection Menu," for example. Title text usually appears at the top of the screen, although you can put it anywhere you like.

- **Button text** can appear either as labels above, below, beside, or on top of graphic buttons—or all by itself.

- **Text boxes** can appear anywhere on your screen. Thanks to this new iDVD 4 feature, you can create text boxes on your menu screens and fill them with whatever explanatory text you think is appropriate—instructions, introductions, a description of the project, and so on.

   To do this, choose Project→Add Text. Double-click the placeholder text and type away. Use the Settings panel of the Customize drawer to specify the font, color, and size of the text.

It's a lot easier to edit text in iDVD 4 than in version 3, and a lot more consistent. Just select the text you want to modify and use the Text adjustments in the Settings pane.

Here, for example, is a boatload of techniques to help customize your text. Each method changes the selected text on only the *currently displayed* DVD menu screen.

Tip: Style changes (font, size, color) affect a title *or* a text box *or* the buttons on a screen, whichever is currently selected. Changes to one of these items do not affect other items although all buttons change as a group; you can have only one button style per screen.

Many New (Old) Themes—Yours Free!

If there's still a copy of iDVD 3 on your Mac—and you didn't just let iDVD 4 overwrite it during installation—you can recover a whole bunch of themes for use in iDVD 4. You get a handy collection of themes left over from iDVD 1 and 2, with titles like Claim Check, Burlap, Global, Happy Days, Leather, and Lavender.

If you'd like to press them back into service in the name of variety, it's easy enough.

In the Finder, open your old Applications→iDVD 3 folder (or wherever you've put your old copy of iDVD 3). Control-click the iDVD icon; from the contextual menu, choose Show Package Contents.

The first set of extra files appears in the Contents→ Resources folder you'll find inside. Their names begin with numbers in the 200s and 900s, as shown here at top left. Select the ones you want to recover and Option-drag them to the desktop to make copies. (They occupy just under 1 GB of data in all.)

Open TextEdit, the simple word processor in your Applications folder. Choose TextEdit→Preferences. In the upper-left corner of the Preferences dialog box, click "Plain text," and close the window. (You're about to edit some iDVD text files, and you want TextEdit to leave them in plain-text format—not convert them to Rich Text format.)

Now repeat that whole Control-clicking business, this time

on each theme you'd like to resurrect (914 Surfs Up.theme, for example). Select a theme, Control-click (right-click), and choose Show Package Contents. This time, open the Contents→Resources→English.lproj folder. (If you don't run iDVD in English, click another language folder.)

See the file called Description.plist? That's the preference file you need to edit. Drag it onto the TextEdit icon on the Dock, so that it opens up into a long list of computery gibberish.

Scroll down to the very bottom. In the third line from the bottom, where it says <integer>1</integer> or <integer>2</integer>, change the 1 (or 2) to a 3 (shown here at lower left). Save the file. You've just convinced that theme that it's an iDVD 3 theme, not an iDVD 1 or iDVD 2 theme.

Repeat this process with any other themes that look promising.

Quit TextEdit, close all the windows, and use the Control-click trick with iDVD 4. Select the iDVD icon in your Applications folder, Control-click (right-click) it and navigate to Contents/Resources. Drag your updated themes into this folder. Now, re-open iDVD. In the Themes pane, choose Default (listing the iDVD 1 themes) or Old Themes (the iDVD 2 themes) from the pop-up menu at the top. You'll see your newly resurrected themes, back from the dead (shown here at right) and ready for service.

- **Change the text.** To highlight a piece of text, click anywhere inside it. (If the text is the title of a picture or video button, you must first click the button and then single-click the associated text.)

  You'll note that iDVD automatically highlights the entire phrase, meaning that you can just begin to type, replacing the entire text blob, without first dragging across it. (Of course, if you want to edit only part of the existing text, drag with the mouse first.) Press Return or Enter when you're finished.

- **Change the text color.** In the Settings pane, choose a new color from the Text→ Color pop-up menu). iDVD offers 18 colors and shades to choose from. Titles, buttons, and text boxes can each use different colors.

- **Choose a font.** To select a new typeface, choose from the Text→Font menu on the Settings pane. You're not allowed to mix and match fonts *within* a text box, but each *kind* of text box (button labels, title, and text boxes) can have a different font.

- **Change the font size.** Adjust the Text→Size slider in the Settings pane to choose a new font size for your selected text. As with fonts, you can pick only one font size per text category.

- **Remove the Title.** Highlight the text in the menu, and then press the Delete key. The empty title text box remains, but it's invisible. Later, if you like, you can click inside the title box to reopen it and type new text.

- **Remove button text.** To remove the labels from your buttons, choose No Text from the Button→Position pop-up menu in the Settings pane.

- **Remove text boxes.** Select the text box you want to remove and press Delete.

- **Reposition (icon) button text.** iDVD lets you place button text on any side of the button, or even directly in its center. Locate the Button→Position pop-up menu in the Settings pane. Choose a button-label position relative to the button graphic: Top, Center, Bottom, Left, and Right.

- **Align text.** To change the alignment of text (titles, text boxes, or text buttons), use the Text→Alignment pop-up menu. Choose from Left, Centered, and Right.

- **Position the Title or a Text Box.** You can drag titles and text boxes anywhere on the screen you like. (Be careful not to park one somewhere that the *overscanning* effect of older TVs [page 324] might chop off some of your letters. To avoid that problem, choose Advanced→Show TV Safe Area before you drag, taking care to keep the text inside the superimposed guideline rectangle that iDVD now puts on the screen.)

Changing Backgrounds

More than any other menu component, your background sets the tone. It provides the look and atmosphere that defines the entire menu screen, and choosing a new background can add a unique twist to an existing theme.

Background Still Images

Using a graphics file as a backdrop is a lot easier than using a video as a backdrop. You don't have to think about timing and loops, and you don't have to worry about how the motion will interact with your buttons and drop zones.

Adding a background image 1: Preserving drop zones

It's incredibly easy to change the backdrop for a particular menu screen: Just drag any graphics file directly onto the existing background. (Avoid dropping it onto a button or a drop zone.) You can drag a JPEG file, for example, right out of the Finder, out of iPhoto if it's open, or out of the Photos pane of the Customize drawer.

iDVD instantly sets the image as your new menu background.

Adding a background image 2: Overwriting drop zones

If you'd rather cover up any existing drop zones, replacing the background with a single image, drag a graphics file into the Background *well,* identified in Figure 22-2.

Tip: Both of the preceding techniques change only the currently displayed menu screen. To apply the change to *all* menu screens, choose Advanced→Apply Theme To Project.

Image/Movie well
(Drag a movie or
graphics file here)

Audio well
(Drag a sound file
here)

Figure 22-2:
In the Customize drawer, click the Settings button. Drag a graphics file into the Background well (from the Finder or from iPhoto, for example). iDVD installs the graphic as the new background, covering up any drop zones in the process.

Replacing background images

If you want to try out a different picture in the background, just repeat the steps above. You can drop new graphics as many times as you want: iDVD displays only the most recent one.

Removing background images

If you decide that the original theme's background was superior to your own graphics after all, it's easy enough to restore the original image. On the Settings pane of the Customize drawer, just drag the graphic icon out of the Background well. iDVD deletes it, displaying the increasingly familiar puff-of-smoke animation. The original theme's background returns.

Adding and Changing Background Video

iDVD makes it easy enough to fill your menu screens with moving, animated, *video backgrounds,* just like the ones you find on many commercial movie DVDs.

Note: In all, iDVD provides three different places to install movies onto your menu screens. The following instructions pertain to only full-screen *background videos.* Don't confuse video backgrounds with *drop zone videos* or *button videos.*

Before you delve into this exciting new career, keep these points in mind:

- **Your video will loop.** Your background video file will play, then restart and play again as long as your audience leaves the menu on the TV screen. There's no way to make a video play just once.

- **iDVD adds both video and sound.** When your imported background video contains a soundtrack, that sound becomes the new soundtrack for the menu screen. It wipes out whatever music came with the theme.

- **iDVD handles timing.** iDVD automatically adjusts the Duration slider (at the top of the Settings pane) to match the length of your movie.

Tip: If you try to drag the Duration slider longer than the length of your movie, weird things happen. Suppose, for example, that you have a 15-second movie, a 20-second bit of audio, and you set the slider to 20 seconds. iDVD plays your movie once, plays 5 seconds more of the start of your movie, and then loops to start your movie again. It's an effect worth avoiding.

Background video selection

Choosing background video can be harder than selecting a still image, for two important reasons:

- **Video moves.** Make sure that the video doesn't hide or overwhelm your titles, buttons, and drop zones. "Audition" your videos and make sure they work with your menus before you burn. In particular, watch for moving objects and scenes that are too bright or too dark.

• **Motion menus loop.** Unless you take special care when creating your video, menu looping will create sudden, sharp, sometimes distracting transitions between the end and start of your video.

Adding background video 1: Preserving drop zones

iDVD offers two ways to add background video to a menu screen. (Once again, remember that each of them changes only the currently displayed menu screen. To apply the change to *all* menu screens, choose Advanced→Apply Theme To Project after following the steps provided here.)

This first method ensures that you won't wind up covering up any drop zones that are part of your chosen theme.

1. **Bring up the menu screen you want to change.**

   Make sure that the Customize drawer is open.

2. **Switch to the Finder and locate the movie file you want to use as a background.**

   It can be a finished QuickTime movie, or it can be the *.mov* reference movie in one of your iMovie project folders (page 264).

3. **While pressing the Option key, drag the video file onto the menu screen.**

   Avoid all drop zones and buttons. Make sure that a colored rectangle appears around the edges of the entire menu screen before you drop the video.

   Let go of the Option key when the new video appears in the menu background.

POWER USERS' CLINIC

Designing Video Loops in iMovie

Background videos don't have to jump between the end of one play-through and the beginning of the next. If you're willing to take a little time in iMovie, you can get rid of sudden visual changes that create unpleasant jumps. Consider these techniques:

Fade or Wash In and Out: Create a smooth fade-out at the end of the movie clip, and a smooth fade-in at the beginning, using the Fade In and Fade Out transition styles described on page 302 (or, if you're partial to white, Wash In and Wash Out).

Use Cross Dissolve: If you prefer, you can design your movie so that the end cross-dissolves into the beginning each time it loops.

Move the playhead to 4:02 seconds before the end of your movie. Choose Edit→Split Video at Playhead to break off

that 4-second segment into a clip of its own.

Now drag this 4:02-second clip to the front of your movie, add a 4-second cross-dissolve between the transposed clip and the start of your movie, and save your work.

You can choose a different length for the crossfade; just make sure that the transposed clip lasts at least two frames longer than the desired transition time. This method works particularly well on stock footage, such as windswept grass, fish in an aquarium, and so forth.

You may discover a couple of drawbacks to this method. First, the start and end audio and video will overlap, and you may not like the results. Second, the background video will, unfortunately, start with the crossfade. There's no way to make it start playing from an un-crossfaded spot.

Adding background video 2: Overriding drop zones

To replace the background with a single, full-width video, just drag a movie file out of the Finder and onto the Background well (see Figure 22-2). iDVD installs the video (and its audio) as the new background, covering up any drop zones in the process.

Removing background video

If you decide to restore the original background video and audio to your theme, drag the icons out of both the Background well and the Audio well. You'll get an animated puff of smoke with each drag, confirming that you've successfully removed both the audio and video that you had previously installed onto this menu screen.

Choosing Menu Audio

Some of Apple's canned themes come with a preinstalled musical soundtrack, and some don't. If you'd like some music to play during, for example, the Wedding Bronze theme, you'll have to install it yourself.

You can also *replace* the music that comes with any of Apple's themes with a song you like better. In the case of musically challenged themes like Kids Theater One, this ability is a true blessing, possibly saving lives and sanity.

- **iTunes Method.** If you've got a decent music collection already in Apple's free iTunes jukebox software, adding background music is really easy. In the Customize

Figure 22-3:
Here's your mini iTunes, right in the Customize drawer. Use the playlists list at the top, or the Search box at the bottom, to find an appropriate song for your menu screen. Use the Play button (or double-click a song name) to listen to a song before placing it. Finally, drag the song you want directly onto the menu screen to install it there.

drawer, click the Audio button. You'll see a complete list of all your iTunes songs and playlists. Proceed as shown in Figure 22-3.

Tip: Keep in mind that some of the most satisfying and appropriate soundtracks of all are the ones that you create yourself, using GarageBand. Any finished compositions that you've exported from GarageBand show up in this iTunes list, too.

- **Drag-from-the-Finder Method.** If you're not a big iTunes user, you can also drag in almost any kind of audio file straight from the desktop. Make sure that you've clicked the Settings button at the top of the Customize drawer, and then drag the audio file directly into the Audio well (shown in Figure 22-2) or onto the menu background.

Incidentally, iDVD doesn't do anything to compensate for background video and background audio that aren't the same length. If the music is too short, it will repeat until the video is finished playing, cutting off the music if necessary to start in sync with the video track. If the music is too long, the video will repeat until the music ends, cutting off the video mid-repeat. Use the Duration slider in the Settings pane to set the loop time; this duration applies to both sound and video.

Or, if you're really a perfectionist, you could always use a sound-editing program (like GarageBand) to match the soundtrack length to the video. Create a nice fade-out at the end of the audio, and a fade-in at the beginning, so that the looping won't be quite so jarring.

Tip: Just another reminder: This technique affects the background music of only the currently displayed menu screen. To apply the change to *all* menu screens, wrap up by choosing Advanced→Apply Theme To Project.

Replacing Menu Audio

To replace a custom audio file with another, simply repeat the steps you used to install the music to begin with. iDVD replaces the current track with the new one.

Removing Menu Audio

To remove audio, drag it out of the Audio well, which is pictured in Figure 22-3. (When the audio well is empty, it shows a 3-D picture of a speaker.)

If you want to remove *all* audio from your menu screen, you may have to drag twice: Your first drag removes custom sounds. The second removes the theme sound, if one exists.

Muting Menu Audio

To mute your audio, click the small speaker icon in the corner of the Audio well (Figure 22-3). iDVD disables menu sound and hides the two tiny sound waves. Click the icon again to restore menu audio. Don't forget to check your audio before burning. Muting the audio in the Settings pane affects the final DVD!

Saving Favorites

After applying all the techniques described so far in this chapter, you may end up creating masterpieces of adapted iDVD themes. Fortunately, iDVD allows you to save and reuse these modified themes after you adjust them to your liking:

1. **Open the Settings pane in the Customize drawer. Click Save as Favorite (at the bottom of the pane).**

   The Save sheet (dialog box) appears at the top of the window.

2. **Type the name for your new theme. Turn on "Shared for all users," if you like.**

   If you're the only person who uses your Mac, then never mind. But if you share a Mac with other students, workers, or family members, each of whom has a Mac OS X *account,* the "Shared for all users" option makes your new theme available to other people who use the machine. (Otherwise, your masterpiece will appear in the list only when *you* use iDVD.)

3. **Turn off "Replace existing" if you want to create a new entry in the theme list.**

   If you turn *on* "Replace existing," iDVD will treat your adapted theme as a replacement for the one you based it on, rather than creating a new entry in the list.

4. **Click OK.**

Figure 22-4:
In general, you'll call up your stored Favorite themes by choosing Favorites from the pop-up menu of the Themes pane (left). Behind the scenes, your Favorites are actual icons hidden on your hard drive (right). That's good to know in case someday you want to throw one away.

iDVD saves your theme as a new Favorite. You'll be able to apply it to other DVDs in the future by choosing its name from the Themes pane. (Choose Favorites from the pop-up menu to see its listing, shown in Figure 22-4.)

If you tire of a saved Favorite, see the box below.

Buying Sound and Vision

Let's face it. iDVD has a lot of nice themes—but they're not always the *right* themes. Life isn't limited to theaters, road trips, and weddings. There are other holidays, other life events, other styles. If you're celebrating Christmas or Valentine's Day, a graduation, or a new home, or if you're just looking for a *different* look, then you might want to think about going commercial. With some money to spend, you can expand the way your iDVD projects look and sound.

Store-Bought Themes

If you want new themes that just *work*, the way that built-in iDVD themes do, then buying pre-built themes can be the way to go. Once installed, third-party themes appear in your iDVD themes list; just click to use. Theme prices start at about $6 for a single theme or about $30 for a pack of six or more. Price, quality, and availability vary. Figure 22-5 showcases a couple of third-party offerings.

Motion Backgrounds

If you're looking for another way to kick up your DVD productions a notch, then consider buying some commercial video loops for your menu backgrounds. Dozens of companies sell royalty-free video clips for use in movies and television. The price varies from barely affordable to "they've-got-to-be-kidding." Page 451 describes how to add a motion background to your iDVD project for a professional flair.

POWER USERS' CLINIC

Secrets of the Theme Files

Whenever you save a new Favorite theme, iDVD does a good bit of administrative work. Behind the scenes, iDVD creates a new theme file on your hard drive. If you decided to share your theme with other account holders, this file appears in the Library→iDVD→Favorites folder. If not, it winds up in your Home→Library→iDVD→Favorites folder. Unlike regular themes, whose names end with the suffix .theme, Favorites use a .favorite file name extension.

Why is this good to know? Because it tells you how to remove a saved favorite: Just drag the .favorite file out of the secret folder and into the Trash. The next time you open iDVD, that favorite will no longer appear in the Themes pane pop-up menu.

It's also worth noting that when you create a favorite, iDVD copies all relevant materials, including background audio and video, to the newly created theme. (Don't believe it? To view these materials, navigate to the saved .favorite file. Control-click its icon; from the contextual menu, choose Show Package Contents. Then open the Contents→Resources folder.)

Because iDVD has made copies of your movies, pictures, and soundtrack files, you no longer need to keep the originals, as far as iDVD is concerned. Feel free to discard, rename, or move these components from their original locations on your hard drive.

Among the least expensive are Ulead's Pick-a-Video and Pick-a-Video Pro lines (*www.ulead.com/pav_pro*), which, at $60 per disc, cost a fraction of what you'd pay through a normal royalty-free video clearinghouse like FotoSearch (*www.fotosearch. com*). A typical Ulead disc contains about eight motion backgrounds with coordinating still images (good for submenus) and video overlays (great for iMovie and Final Cut, not so great for iDVD). The CG Festivities disc (volume 20), for example, has ringing bells, floating balloons, flying stars, streaming ribbons, rotating hearts, and gift boxes, among others.

Stock Art

Don't overlook commercial graphics when customizing your themes. *Stock art* (professional photos and illustrations that you can buy) can add a professional look to

Figure 22-5:
You can buy new themes from, for example, www. idvdthemetastic.com or www.idvdthemepak.com. (Virtix, which used to sell iDVD themes, recently dropped its offerings to focus its business on iMovie and Final Cut plug-ins.) iDVD Themetastic (top) sells themes á la carte, specializing in holiday items. iDVD ThemePak (bottom) sells themes in groups, offering great-looking motion and still graphics. Check their Web sites for some free downloadable samples.

your menus without costing a lot of money. The right stock image may look better than the snaps you took with your digital camera.

Third-Party Buttons

In the crazy, blossoming world of homemade DVDs, there's now such a thing as commercially available *buttons*. They let you add stylish new buttons to your menu screens without having to buy full themes. Stylized buttons can give a personalized twist to even fairly plain backgrounds, as shown in Figure 22-6.

Figure 22-6:
Why buy an entire custom theme when button styles do so much to create an individual feel for your iDVD menus? Mix and match buttons with background art to create a unique look on a budget. These samples are from iDVDThemePak ($40 for 21 custom buttons).

Audio

When you buy songs at the iTunes Music Store, you also buy the right to use them in any of your personal-use iLife creations. Why settle for the mayhem of the Kid's Theater audio track when you can throw a buck at Apple and pick the music you really want?

iDVD—The DVD-ROM Maker

iDVD's ability to add data files to the DVD-ROM portion of your disc may be its least-known feature. When it creates a DVD-ROM, iDVD sets aside a portion of your DVD for normal computer files. This area of the disc won't show up on a DVD player—only on a computer.

With iDVD, you can store any variety of data on your DVD. Here are just a few ways you can use this feature to enhance your disc:

• **Store documents that relate to your DVD contents.** The DVD-ROM area provides a perfect place to store copies of documents related to the DVD, like the movie script, different versions of an invitation, extended family narratives, copies of email and other correspondence, and so on. Remember: TV sets aren't much good for displaying text, but a DVD-ROM and a computer can come to the rescue.

Or store the full-resolution versions of the digital photos featured in your DVD slideshow (one of the most common uses for this feature.)

• **Store Web pages.** Web pages are perfect additions to the DVD-ROM disc area. Create a Web site that relates to your DVD and add your source files to the disc. When distributed, your viewers can open these files with an ordinary Web browser. For example, a DVD with a training video can contain supplementary lessons in HTML (Web page) format.

• **Store "email quality" versions of your video.** Use the DVD-ROM area of your disc to store small, compressed versions of your video, or "wallet size" pictures from a slideshow, suitable for email. Now your audience can share your movie experience with other people.

Adding Files to DVD-ROM

iDVD's DVD-ROM file management couldn't be simpler. Just drag icons out of the Finder and into the DVD-ROM Contents list (Advanced→Edit DVD-ROM Contents), as shown in Figure 22-7.

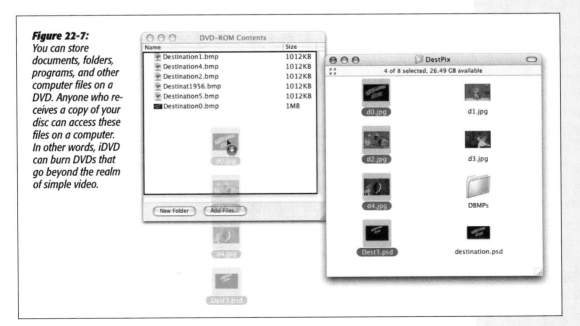

Figure 22-7:
You can store documents, folders, programs, and other computer files on a DVD. Anyone who receives a copy of your disc can access these files on a computer. In other words, iDVD can burn DVDs that go beyond the realm of simple video.

Organizing DVD-ROM Contents

The DVD-ROM Contents pane lets you organize your files in several ways:

- **Add folders.** Click New Folder to add a folder to your list.

- **Remove things.** Either drag files or folders right out of the list, or select them and then press the Delete key. (Dragging out of the list gives you the cool puff-of-smoke animation.)

- **Move items into or out of folders.** You can drag icons into one of the little folder icons to file them there—or drag them out again to remove them.

- **Reorder the list.** Drag icons up or down the list into new positions.

- **Create subfolders.** Drag one folder into another to create subfolders.

- **Rename a Folder.** Double-click the name of a folder to select and edit it. Press Return or Enter when you're finished typing.

- **List/hide folder contents.** You can click a folder's flippy triangle to expand it and see what's inside, exactly as in Finder list views.

Archiving Your Project

Ordinarily, iDVD doesn't store any videos, photos, or sounds in your iDVD project file. It remains a tiny, compact file that stores only *references* that *point* to those files elsewhere on your hard drive.

That's why, if you delete or move one of those media files, iDVD will mildly freak out. (See page 613 in that case.)

In previous versions of iDVD, you couldn't transfer a project from one Mac to another for this very reason. And that meant that you couldn't *design* a DVD on one Mac (one that lacked a DVD burner), and then *burn* it on another. You also couldn't back up your project file, content that you'd included all of its pieces.

Fortunately, the geniuses at Apple have packed a solution into iDVD 4. The new Archive Project command lets you completely "de-reference" your project, so that the project file *contains* every file that you've incorporated into your project: movies, photos, sounds, theme components, and DVD-ROM files. Your project file is now completely self-contained, ready for backup or transfer to another computer. It's also now really, really huge.

Follow these steps to produce your archive.

1. **Save your project.**

   If you forget this step, iDVD will remind you.

2. **Choose File→Archive Project.**

   The Save As panel shown in Figure 22-8 appears.

3. **Turn the checkboxes on or off, if you like.**

"Include themes" copies your theme files into the project—something that's unnecessary if you're using standard iDVD 4 themes. This checkbox is important only if the themes you've used come from other companies, were designed by you, or are modified versions of Apple's originals.

"Include encoded files" is the more important option, because it's very unlikely that all of your sounds, photos, and movies are also on the destination Mac.

Turn the boxes on and off to see how much space you'll recover.

Figure 22-8:
The Archive Project save-as panel lets you specify whether you want to include themes and encoded files in your archived project. You can save quite a bit of disk space by leaving these options unchecked–the Size indicator to the right of "Include themes" tells you how much space your project will occupy.

4. **Name the archive file, choose a folder location for it, and then click Save.**

Wait as iDVD builds the new archive. This can take a few minutes, so be patient. You may be working with *very* large files.

Archived projects look like any other project—they use the same .dvdproj extension—but inside, they're very different. You can prove this to yourself by opening the archive file as a package (page 485). Inside its Contents→Resources folder, new folders called Assets and Themes store the extra archived elements (Figure 22-9).

Tip: To turn your photos and videos into DVD material, iDVD must *encode* (convert) them into a format called MPEG. Depending on your Preferences settings, iDVD may be working constantly on this time-consuming task, or it may do the job only when you burn the DVD.

Either way, an archived project also stores any MPEG files iDVD has created so far. They'll save you time when you burn the DVD, but they'll make the archive's file size balloon up like a blimp.

If you'd rather keep the file smaller, choose Advanced→Delete Encoded Assets before saving the archive. iDVD removes the encoded MPEG files–but you'll pay for this gesture in re-encoding time when you're ready to burn your discs.

Copying the archive to a different Mac

Suppose that, using a Mac that lacks a DVD burner, you've designed a DVD. Now, as Apple intended, you've used the Archive command to prepare it for transfer to a Mac that *does* have a burner.

Transfer the archive project using any convenient method: copy it across a network, burn it to a CD or a DVD-ROM, copy it onto an iPod, or whatever. (It's too big for email, of course, but you could also post it on a Web site for downloading directly.)

The project opens normally on the other machine, with all of its pieces intact and ready to touch up and burn.

Figure 22-9:
When archiving a project, iDVD creates additional folders within the new project bundle. The Assets folder stores original copies of your audio and video files (in the "av" subfolder), DVD-ROM content (in "data") and images (in "stills"). If you've chosen to save themes, they show up in the Themes folder.

Duplicating a DVD

Unfortunately, iDVD takes nearly as long to burn a second DVD as it does to build and burn the first. When you need to burn multiple copies of your work, you'll wish you had a faster way.

You do. Using the Mac OS X program called Disk Utility, you can convert the first DVD into a *disk image:* a file on your hard drive that perfectly replicates the contents of a disk. Whenever you need a copy of the original, you can use either Disk Utility or the disc-burning program known as Roxio Toast to burn a new DVD based on the disk image you made.

Here's how to go about it.

Phase 1: Create a Disk Image

The following steps use the Disk Utility program to copy your new DVD to a disk image. Insert the master DVD into your Mac, and then proceed like this:

1. **Insert your DVD. Then open Disk Utility.**

   Disk Utility sits at this moment in your Applications→Utilities folder. (In versions of Mac OS X before Panther 10.3, it was called Disk Copy. The steps generally follow the outline presented here.)

   The window shown at top in Figure 22-10 appears, listing all of your drives. (For most people, that means one hard drive and one DVD burner.)

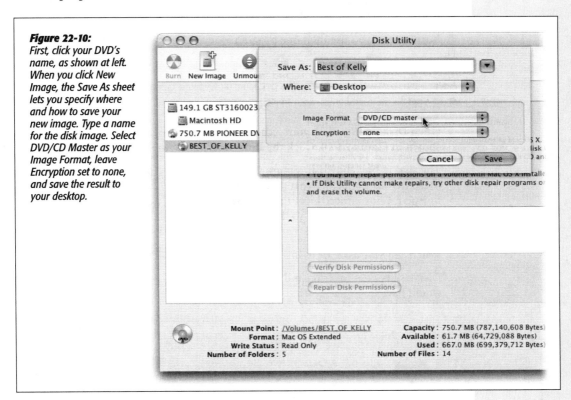

Figure 22-10:
First, click your DVD's name, as shown at left. When you click New Image, the Save As sheet lets you specify where and how to save your new image. Type a name for the disk image. Select DVD/CD Master as your Image Format, leave Encryption set to none, and save the result to your desktop.

2. **Click the DVD's name. On the toolbar, click New Image.**

   Disk Utility prepares to convert the DVD into a disk image by presenting the dialog box "sheet" that's also shown in Figure 22-10.

3. **Set up the dialog box as shown in Figure 22-10. Save the result to your desktop.**

   If Disk Utility asks for your Administrator account password, type it in and then click OK.

   It can take mucho minutes for Disk Utility to create the image. Patience.

4. **Quit Disk Utility and eject the DVD.**

When Disk Utility finishes, you'll have a disk image file on your desktop (whose file name ends with *.cdr*) that duplicates the contents of your DVD.

You're halfway home.

Phase 2: Burn a DVD from a Disk Image

You've got a disk image, made from your original DVD, that you can now use as a master to burn additional copies without having to wait for iDVD to perform its laborious compression ritual again with each new copy.

To burn a copy, you use the same program you used to create the disk image—Disk Utility.

Note: It should go without saying that this procedure can duplicate only *homemade* DVDs. It doesn't work on commercial Hollywood ones, which are copy-protected.

---

1. **Open Disk Utility. Click your .cdr disk image's name in the list at the left side, as shown in Figure 22-10. Click the Burn icon on the toolbar.**

   The dialog box shown in Figure 22-11 appears. The only decision you have to make here is to decide what you want to happen when the copy of the DVD is finished: Click either "Eject this" or "Mount on Desktop" (which leaves the new DVD's icon on the screen, so that you can try playing it in Mac OS X's DVD Player program).

2. **When the Mac asks for it, insert a blank DVD and click Burn.**

   Disk Utility goes to work, and it can take quite a while—just not as long as iDVD would have.

Figure 22-11:
There's not much for you to do in this dialog box. You should, however, check the Speed setting. Always match the burning speed to the maximum rating for your blank DVDs and the capability of your DVD-R drive.

When the process is complete, you've got yourself a copy of the original DVD. To make yet another copy, repeat these two steps.

Tip: Once you've created the disk image, you can use Toast Titanium (*www.roxio.com*) to burn your DVD copies, too. You gain a few additional options and controls.

For example, if your video is less than 10 minutes long, you can insert a CD-R or CD-RW disc rather than a DVD blank. Toast will burn you a handy little hybrid known as a *miniDVD* (also called a *compact DVD* or *cDVD*). Most modern DVD players—especially those made in China—can play miniDVDs, which have all the quality of DVD but cost a lot less for blanks. Check *www.dvdrhelp.com* to find out if your DVD player recognizes miniDVD discs.

Professional Duplicating

Maybe you've organized a school play, and you want to sell copies of the performance to parents as a fundraiser. Maybe you want to send out "new baby" videos to your family circle. Or maybe you've used iDVD to create a video brochure of your small business's products and services.

In each of these cases, burning the DVDs one at a time on your own Mac looks more and more like a time-consuming, expensive hassle.

When you want to make more than a handful of copies of your DVD, you might want to consider enlisting the aid of a *DVD service bureau.*

Technically, these companies offer two different services:

POWER USERS' CLINIC

Burning the Unburnable

Apple says that iDVD requires an Apple SuperDrive to work with iDVD, but that's not quite true. In fact, iDVD fans have had good luck with many Pioneer internal DVD-burning drives, including models 103, 104, and 105. (And no wonder: an Apple SuperDrive is, in fact, a Pioneer drive.)

But what about external drives? iDVD has been around for years; isn't it time that Apple fix whatever glitch is limiting iDVD to internal Pioneer burners?

As with so many of life's mysteries, the explanation has to do with money. Some of the technology in iDVD comes from the Motion Picture Engineering Group (MPEG), and when Apple licensed this technology, it agreed to limit iDVD to Superdrives. (The price of the royalties to MPEG is included in the price of the drive.) Needless to say, this policy is an annoying hassle if you have an external or non-SuperDrive burner.

Fortunately, you can now get around this limitation. It's undocumented. It's sneaky. And it bypasses Apple's royalty system. You may want to consult with a clergyperson on hand before proceeding.

The step-by-step instructions are waiting for you on the "Missing CD" page at *www.missingmanuals.com.*

Why aren't they here? First, because it's a long procedure of value to a relatively small number of people. Second, because it's subject to change as Apple gets wind of it. Third, because it involves some special command files that, instead of painstakingly typing out without errors yourself, you can just download with one quick click.

- **Duplicated** discs are copies of your original DVD. Service bureaus use banks of DVD burners, five or ten at a time, that churn out copy after copy on DVD-Rs—the same kinds of blanks you used.

  You pay for materials and labor, usually by the hour. (Discs with less data burn quicker, producing more discs per hour.) This is the way to go if you need fewer than 200 copies of your disc.

- **Replication** is designed for huge numbers of copies: 200 and up. In this process, the company actually presses the DVDs just the way Hollywood movie studios do it—and the results play back in virtually every DVD player.

  Replicated discs are produced in factories. (DVD service bureaus are middlemen between you and the large replication plants, which don't deal directly with the public.) When replicated, the data from your master DVD-R is placed on a pressed 4.7 GB "DVD-5" disc—a standard DVD, not a DVD-R.

  Expect to pay about a dollar per disc for a run of 1,000 discs. Smaller runs will cost more per disc, larger runs less, but $1,000 is about the least you'll pay for a replication job.

UP TO SPEED

Making DVDs Last

Your homemade DVDs (which are "burned" using dyes) probably won't last the 100 years expected of commercial DVDs (which are etched with lasers). But don't get too depressed by the occasional article about homemade DVDs "going bad" in a matter of months. Most cases of "DVD rot" come down to one of two things: problems created during manufacturing or poor handling by their owners.

There's not much you can do about manufacturing errors, apart from buying name-brand blank DVDs.

As for handling, these tips should ensure that your recordable DVDs will last for years:

Store your discs in a cool, dry place. DVD-Rs are sensitive to both temperature and humidity. In an ideal world, DVDs would love to live in a cupboard that's 68 degrees Fahrenheit with 30 to 50 percent humidity. In the real world, room temperature is fine as long as temperature *swings* aren't a fact of life. Recordable DVDs hate large changes in humidity, too.

Keep your discs out of the light. Prolonged exposure to ultraviolet light degrades the organic dyes in the recordable

layer, possibly making the data on your discs unreadable. Regular light may also hurt your discs, primarily through heat.

Don't flex your discs. With their laminated polycarbonate layers, recordable DVDs are very sensitive to bending or flexing. In fact, the quickest way to destroy your disc is to bend it.

So don't. Store your discs in soft envelopes or in cases where you pinch a center hub to release the DVD. Don't store them in CD jewel boxes that have a snap-on hub.

Hold discs by the edges. Fingerprints, scratches, and dust on the disc surface interfere with a laser's ability to read data. DVDs are much more sensitive than CDs in this regard, because the data is crammed together so much more tightly.

Don't stick on labels. Adhesive labels throw off the disc's balance—and might even ruin your drive when the heat makes the glue melt. Instead, use a CD-safe marker to write on your DVD-Rs.

Part Five: GarageBand

5

Setting Up the Garage

G arageBand is an extremely powerful, easy-to-use program that lets anyone create professional sounding musical recordings. But as you can imagine, not everybody was thrilled when Apple released it.

"They're putting too much power in the hands of amateurs," complained certain professional musicians. "This is like when Apple came out with desktop publishing. Everybody used all 22 fonts in every document, and every flyer and newsletter looked like a ransom note for the next two years."

And sure enough, on the Web sites where people post their GarageBand compositions, you can find a lot of polished, professional sounding, handsomely processed...dreck.

But Apple has a long history of taking elite creative tools, simplifying them, and making them available to the masses. Yes, iMovie lets amateurs make absolutely terrible films, but it has also open the gates to talented filmmakers who otherwise would have lived in obscurity. One iMovie movie actually won a prize at Sundance last year!

In this regard, GarageBand's cultural effects maybe even more profound. Until recently, the record companies were the gatekeepers to America's pop-music marketplace, and therefore the dictators of musical taste to the masses. After all, the record companies had sole possession of the two things talented musicians needed to build an audience:

- **Production facilities,** like recording studios, equipment, and engineers.

- **Distribution channels**—namely, record stores.

As you're already aware, the Internet turned out to be a killer replacement, or at least companion, to traditional distribution systems. A song, photo, or movie can become popular on the Internet without any help from a record company, publisher, or Hollywood studio—in fact, it can be all over the world in a matter of days. So much for the iron grip the record companies once had on the distribution channels.

With GarageBand, the other shoe has now dropped. Suddenly, no-name singers and undiscovered players can produce recordings that sound like they were made at a $1,000-an-hour recording studio. No longer must great talent remain untapped, or recorded on a tape recorder with an accompaniment by the local church organist. In the *American Idol* era, new artists can grow from the grass roots—and inevitably will.

The Two GarageBand Challenges

Before you fill out your Grammy award application, however, two cautions are in order.

First, GarageBand is much more demanding of your Mac than its little i-cousins (iPhoto, iTunes, and so on). Its underlying technology was spun out from a $1,000 professional recording program called Logic, which Apple acquired in 2002 when it bought a company called Emagic.

As one result, GarageBand contains some of the world's most sophisticated musical-instrument and studio-effect simulators. As another result, however, GarageBand craves more memory and processor than almost any other program you'll ever use. Your first challenge in using GarageBand, therefore, will be making it comfortable on your Mac.

At first, you may find that job about as exciting as feeding a team of sumo wrestlers who've taken up residence in your guest room. But these pages, especially Chapters 26 and 27, will ease the way.

The second challenge you'll face is understanding the two different kinds of musical information that GarageBand can record, edit, and play back (which, not too long ago, required two different pieces of music software): digital audio and MIDI data. Each looks different and behaves differently in GarageBand.

The point is that if you can overcome these two challenges—the one in your Mac, the other in your brain—GarageBand offers an incredible musical experience. It will let you into a world of music production that was once restricted to people with several thousand, or hundreds of thousands, of dollars to invest.

Either that, or buy a new Mac.

Opening GarageBand

For this guided tour, you need a GarageBand file that's already been completed. You can get yourself one by downloading the GarageBand Examples CD, a "virtual disc" available for free at *www.missingmanuals.com*. (In fact, the rest of this book assumes that you've already done so. For details, see the box on page 474.)

Once you've downloaded the GarageBand Examples disk, open the file called "01—Garage Door." After a moment, GarageBand opens and presents you with the simulated studio shown in Figure 23-1.

Figure 23-1:
GarageBand isn't just the only iLife program that doesn't start with i; it's also the only program made of "wood." (You can move the window around by dragging any of the wood or "brushed aluminum" surfaces.) At first, the program tends to cower in a smallish window. Click the Zoom button to make it fill your screen. There—much better!

Zoom button · Playhead · Beat ruler · Timeline (track display)

Track headers · New Track · Play · Tempo · Master volume

Playback

You'll probably spend most of your time in GarageBand *playing back* music. That, after all, is the only way to fine-tune and perfect your work.

There's a Play button at your disposal—the big triangle indicated in Figure 23-1—but that's for suckers. Instead, press the Space bar. That's a much bigger target, and a very convenient start/stop control. (You may recognize it as the start/stop control for iTunes and iMovie, too.)

Once you've got the 01—Garage Door file open, press the Space bar to listen to this fonky, fonky piece. It's about a minute long.

Tip: If you hear nothing, it's probably because your Mac's speakers are turned down. You can adjust your Mac's overall volume by pressing the volume keys on the top row of your keyboard.

If you have a very old keyboard (or a very non-Apple one), and you therefore lack these keys, you can also adjust the volume by clicking the speaker *menulet* (the black, right-facing speaker icon in your menu bar).

(If the speaker control doesn't appear on your menu bar, open System Preferences, click the Sound icon, and then turn on "Show volume in menu bar.")

Whenever music is playing back, you can manipulate it using keystrokes, some of which should be familiar from iTunes. For example:

- **Stop the music.** Press the Space bar again.

- **Slow it down (or speed it up).** Use the Tempo control, as shown in Figure 23-2.

- **Adjust the volume.** You can drag the master volume slider shown in Figure 23-1, or you can press ⌘-up arrow (louder) or ⌘-down arrow (softer).

- **Jump around in the song.** See the next section for navigation techniques. They work equally well whether the music is playing or not.

Figure 23-2:
Left: To adjust the tempo (speed) of your piece, position the arrow cursor on the number shown here (which shows how many beats per minute you're getting).

Right: Hold down the mouse button to produce a slider. You're setting the tempo for the entire piece; you can't program in a change in tempo (at least not in GarageBand 1.1).

GarageBand Examples CD

Examples make any learning process easier and more fun—and this book is no exception. Throughout this book, you'll find references to GarageBand project files, some finished and some intended for you to complete, on something called the GarageBand Examples CD.

You can download these files right now. First, visit *www.missingmanuals. com.* At the top of the page, click the "Missing CD" button.

You arrive at a page listing the downloadable files for the entire Missing Manual series. Under the GarageBand heading, click to download the "GarageBand Examples CD" disk image. It contains all of the sample music you'll work with in this book.

When the download is complete, you'll find on your desktop a file called GarageBand Examples.dmg. That's a disk image file, shown here at lower left.

When you double-click it, you'll find a second icon on your desktop, resembling a hard drive icon, shown here at lower right. (If Safari is your Web browser, just relax and wait as the icon opens automatically.) This is the actual "CD" icon. If you open it up, you'll find all the files for this book. Copy them to a folder on your hard drive, if you like.

If you're in a hurry or using a slow connection, you can also download the various tutorial pieces one at a time. You'll find them listed under the appropriate chapter numbers.

Cycling (Looping)

Looping means playing a certain section of the music over and over again continuously. (That's what musicians call it. Apple calls it *cycling*, because in GarageBand, the word *loop* has a very different meaning. You can read about loops in the next chapter.) Cycling can be very handy in a number of different situations:

- **Recording.** When you're laying down new music from a MIDI keyboard, Garage-Band merges *everything* you play during all repetitions of the loop. So if your keyboard skills aren't especially dazzling, you can play one hand's part, or even one finger's part, on each "pass" through the loop. GarageBand adds all your passes together.

- **Editing.** In Chapter 26, you'll see that you can edit the notes in Software Instruments sections—adding or deleting notes, rewriting musical lines, and so on. By cycling the section you're editing, you can hear the effects of your edits even while you're making them, in the context of all the other playing instruments.

- **Playing.** Sometimes, it's useful to loop a section just for the sake of listening and analyzing—when a clashing note, for example, is driving you, well, loopy.

To loop a certain section of your piece, start by clicking the Cycle button (identified in Figure 23-3). Or just press the letter C key on your Mac's keyboard.

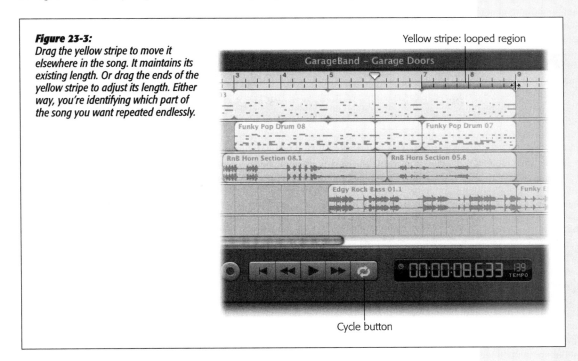

Figure 23-3:
Drag the yellow stripe to move it elsewhere in the song. It maintains its existing length. Or drag the ends of the yellow stripe to adjust its length. Either way, you're identifying which part of the song you want repeated endlessly.

Yellow stripe: looped region

Cycle button

Either way, the Cycle button lights up, and a yellow stripe appears on the beat ruler (the numbered "ruler" strip at the top of the screen). That stripe—the *cycle region*—tells you which part of the song GarageBand intends to repeat.

In a new song, the yellow stripe appears across measures 1 through 4. You can adjust its length and position, though, as shown in Figure 23-3.

If you tap the Space bar now, GarageBand plays *only* the music enclosed by that yellow stripe.

To end the cycling, click the Cycle button again to turn it off, or tap the letter C key again. (You can do so even while the music is playing.)

Navigating the Music

Your current position in the song—that is, the spot from which you'll start recording or playing—is always indicated by the *Playhead* (Figure 23-1) and the moving vertical line beneath it.

You can drag the Playhead around manually, of course; you can also click anywhere in the beat ruler to make the Playhead snap to that spot. You can even jump to a spot in your piece by typing in its time or measures-and-beats position into the digital time display (page 513).

But you'll feel much more efficient if you take the time to learn GarageBand's navigational keyboard shortcuts:

- **Jump back to the beginning.** Pressing either the letter Z key or the Home key rewinds the piece to the beginning without missing a beat.

Tip: On Mac laptops, the Z key is easier to press than the Home key, because triggering the Home function requires first pressing the Fn key in the lower-left corner. Too much trouble.

- **Jump to the end.** Press Option-Z or the End key. That's a great technique for people who like to build up their songs section by section. After you've finished the first part, you can jump to the end of it, ready to begin recording the second.

Note: As far as GarageBand's playback is concerned, the *end* of your piece isn't necessarily where the music stops. It's the point indicated by the small left-pointing triangle on the ruler.

Sometimes you'll trim a piece to make it shorter—and wind up stranding the End marker way off to the right, so that GarageBand "plays" a minute of silence after the actual music ends. In that case, you can fix the problem by dragging the End marker inward until it lines up with the end of the colored musical regions. (You can never drag it inward past the end of the music, though.)

- **Jump back, or ahead, a measure at a time.** As you may recall from your childhood music lessons, a *measure* is the natural building block of musical time. It's usually two, three, or four beats long. (Think of a *beat* as one foot-tap, if you were tapping along with the music.)

In GarageBand, the measures are indicated on a numbered *beat ruler* (identified in Figure 23-1) that helps you figure out where you are in the music. You can jump forward or back a measure at a time by pressing the left and right arrow keys. (Clicking the Rewind and Fast-forward buttons serves the same purpose.)

Tip: You can also *hold down* the arrow keys, or the onscreen Rewind and Fast-forward buttons, to zoom faster through the piece. Both of these techniques work even when the music is playing.

- **Jump right or left one screenful at a time.** Press the Page Up or Page Down key. (It may feel a little odd to press *up/down* keys to scroll *right/left,* but you'll get used to it.)

- **Zoom in or out.** Once you begin editing your own music, you'll occasionally want a God's-eye view of your whole piece for a visual overview of its structure. Or you'll want to zoom in to see the individual soundwaves or notes of a certain musical passage.

  That's what the Control-right arrow and Control-left arrow keystrokes are for. They stretch and collapse the ruler, respectively, making the onscreen representation of your music take up more or less space. (You can also drag the Zoom slider beneath the instrument names, but that's more effort.)

Two Kinds of Music

If you've been reading along with half your brain on the book and half on the TV, turn off the TV for a minute. The following discussion may be one of the most important you'll encounter in your entire GarageBand experience.

Understanding how GarageBand produces music—or, rather, the *two* ways it can create music—is critically important. It'll save you hours of frustration and confusion, and make you sound *really* smart at user-group meetings.

GarageBand is a sort of hybrid piece of music software. It can record and play back music in two different ways, which, once upon a time, required two different music-recording programs. They are:

Digital Recordings

GarageBand can record, edit, and play back digital audio—sound from a microphone, for example, or sound files you've dragged in from your hard drive (AIFF files, MP3 files, unprotected AAC files, or WAV files, for example).

If you've spent much time on computers before, you've already worked with digital recordings. They're the error beeps on every Mac, the soundtrack in iMovie, and whatever sounds you record using programs like SimpleSound, Amadeus, and ProTools. The files on a standard music CD are also digital audio files, and so are the ones you can buy at iTunes.com.

Digital recordings occupy a lot of room on your hard drive: 10 MB per minute, to be exact (stereo, CD quality).

Digital recordings are also more or less permanent. GarageBand offers a few rudimentary editing features: you can copy and paste digital audio, chop pieces out, or slide a recording around in time. But in general, you can't *transpose* these recordings (make them play back at a different pitch), and you can't change their tempo (make them play back faster or slower).

Now then: To avoid terrifying novices with terminology like "digital recordings," Apple calls this kind of musical material *Real Instruments*.

On the GarageBand screen, Real Instrument recordings appear in blue or purple blocks, filled with what look like soundwaves (Figure 23-4).

Software Instruments (MIDI notes)
Green; individual notes visible inside

Figure 23-4:
GarageBand can process two very different kinds of musical material, which Apple calls Real Instruments and Software Instruments. Each offers advantages and drawbacks—but learning the difference is a key part of learning to love GarageBand.

Real Instruments (digital audio)
Blue or purple; sound waveforms inside

MIDI Recordings

You know what a text file is, right? It's a universal exchange format for typed text.

In the early 1980s, musicians could only look on longingly as their lyricists happily shot text files back and forth, word processor to word processor, operating system to operating system. Why, they wondered, couldn't there be a universal exchange format for *music,* so that Robin in Roanoke, with a Roland digital piano, could play back a song recorded by Susan on her DX-7 synthesizer in Salt Lake City?

Soon enough, there was a way: the *MIDI file.* MIDI stands for "musical instrument digital interface," otherwise known as "the musical version of the text file." To turn your Mac into a little recording studio, a musician only had to rack up three charges on the Visa bill:

- **A MIDI keyboard,** such as a synthesizer.

- **A MIDI interface,** a little $40 box that connects the keyboard to the computer.

- **A MIDI sequencer,** which is software capable of recording, editing, and playing back what you play on the MIDI keyboard.

Although Apple would go bald in horror at using such intimidating language, Garage-Band is, in fact, a MIDI sequencer. It can record your keyboard performances; display your performance as bars on a grid, piano-roll style; allow you to edit those notes and correct your mistakes; and then play the whole thing back.

Behind the scenes, GarageBand memorizes each note you play as little more than a bunch of computer data. When it's playing back MIDI music, *you* might hear "Three Blind Mice," but your Mac is thinking like this:

```
01|01|000  E3 00|01|000     60
01|02|000  D3 00|01|000     72
01|03|002  C3 00|02|240    102
```

From left to right, these four columns tell the software when the note is played, which note is played, how long it's held down, and how hard the key was struck. That's everything a computer needs to perfectly recreate your original performance.

Musical information that's stored this way has some pretty huge advantages over digital recordings like AIFF files. For example, you can *change the notes*—drag certain notes higher or lower, make them last longer or shorter, or delete the bad ones entirely—whenever you like. You can also *transpose* a MIDI performance (change its key, so it plays higher or lower) with the click of a button. You can even speed up or slow down the playback as freely as you like. When you make such an adjustment, the Mac just thinks to itself, "Add 3 to each pitch," or "Play this list of notes slower."

The downside of MIDI recordings is, of course, that you can't *capture* sound with them. You can't represent singing, or rapping, or sound effects this way. A MIDI file is just a list of notes. It needs a synthesizer to give it a voice—like the synthesizer built into GarageBand.

Apple refers to the sounds of GarageBand's built-in synthesizer as *Software Instruments.* They show up in GarageBand as green blocks, filled with little horizontal bars representing the MIDI notes that will be triggered. Figure 23-4 makes this distinction clear.

Why It Matters

Why is it important to learn the difference between Real Instruments (sound recordings) and Software Instruments (MIDI data)? Because if you confuse the two, you can paint yourself into some very ugly corners.

For example, suppose you "lay down" (record) the background music for a new song you've written. But when you try to sing the vocals, you discover that the key is way too high for you.

If most of your accompaniment is constructed of MIDI (green) musical material, no big deal. You can transpose the entire band down into a more comfortable range.

But if you recorded, say, a string quartet as part of the backup group, you're out of luck. Those are Real Instruments (digital recordings), and you can't change their pitch.

The bottom line: If you began your work by constructing a backup band out of green Software Instruments, you should always finalize your song's key and tempo *before* you record live audio.

GarageBand lets you another perform a neat trick with Software Instruments. After recording a part using, for example, a MIDI keyboard, you can reassign the whole thing to a different instrument whenever you like, freely fiddling with the orchestration. You can drag a blob of notes from, say, the Electric Piano track into the Country Guitar track. The Mac doesn't care which sound you use; its job is simply to trigger the notes for "Three Blind Mice" (or whatever).

But although you can drag a blue or purple Real Instrument region into a different Real Instrument track, its instrument sound won't change (see Figure 23-5). In fact, you can *never* change the instrument sound of a Real Instrument.

Figure 23-5:
You can drag a Software Instrument recording into a different Software Instrument track, thereby changing which sound plays those notes. However, GarageBand won't let you drag a Real Instrument snippet into a Software Instrument track.

Tracks

When you work in GarageBand, the *timeline* is your primary canvas. It's something like the timeline view in iMovie: a scrolling map of the overall project, marked at the top by a *beat ruler* that helps you figure out where you are in the song.

Tracks are the horizontal, parallel stripes that represent instruments playing simultaneously. Which is lucky, because if this software could play only one instrument at a time, it would have to be renamed GarageSolo.

You'll learn how to *fill* these gray stripes in the following chapters. For the moment, though, it's useful to learn your way around the tracks themselves. After all, like the musicians in a real garage band, they're paid very little, but respond well if you treat them with a little respect.

As you read the following instructions, you might want to follow along by working with the Garage Door song you opened in the previous section.

Creating a Track

You can add a track in any of three ways.

- **Click the + button below the track names.** It's shown in Figure 23-1.

- **Choose Track→New Track.** Or press Option-⌘-N.

  Both of these methods open the New Track dialog box shown in Figure 23-6. Click the appropriate tab—Real Instrument or Software Instrument—and then, on the right side of the dialog box, click the name of the kind of instrument you plan to add.

  (If you intend to record sound—that is, if what you need is a Real Instrument track—you can bypass the dialog box by simply choosing Track→New Basic Track. Details in Chapter 27.)

Tip: A track's *header* is the dark area at the left edge of the track, where you see its name and icon. To find out which kind of track you're dealing with—Real Instrument or Software Instrument—click the track header. If it turns greenish, you're dealing with a Software Instrument (MIDI) track. If it's purplish, you've clicked a Real Instrument (live recording) track.

You can select one track after another, "walking" through the list of them, by pressing the up or down arrow keys on your keyboard.

Figure 23-6:
A certain track can handle either a Real Instrument (sound file) or a Software Instrument (MIDI notes), so you have to tell GarageBand which sort of instrument you intend to add. If you're going to record a Real Instrument, also specify which effects you want GarageBand to add to the track, like reverb or EQ (equalization). Details in Chapter 28.

- Drag a loop into an empty gray spot in the *timeline* (the track display area). Chapter 24 covers this method in delicious detail.

In any case, a new track appears *below* all the existing tracks.

The number of simultaneous tracks that GarageBand can play depends on the horse-power of your Mac and which *kind* of tracks they are; Software Instruments make the Mac work a lot harder than Real Instrument recordings. On slower Macs, four or five tracks is about the limit; ten or twelve tracks is typical on a Power Mac G4. If you have a fully tricked-out, top-of-the-line Power Mac G5 loaded with RAM, then you can build tracks into the dozens.

Fortunately, there's a whole chapter's worth of tips and tricks for helping GarageBand overcome the strain of track-intensive compositions awaiting in Chapter 33.

Tip: As you add and work with tracks, keep your eye on the Playhead handle. As described in Figure 23-7, it's an early-warning system that lets you know when you're overwhelming your Mac.

Figure 23-7:
As you play and record music, the Playhead triangle darkens—from white, to yellow, to orange, and finally red—to indicate how much trouble your Mac is having. If it spends a lot of time in the red, you're approaching your maximum track limit.

Rearranging Tracks

You can rearrange your tracks' top-to-bottom order just by dragging them vertically. You might, for example, like to keep the track you're working on up at the top where it's easy to find. Or maybe you like to keep your tracks in traditional "score order" (that is, as the instruments would appear in standard full-orchestra sheet music).

Deleting a Track

Before you nuke one of your tracks, scroll through the whole thing to make sure you're not about to vaporize some important musical material. (Consider zooming out—tap Control-left arrow repeatedly—until the entire track fits on your screen.)

Then click the track header to select it. Choose Track→Delete Track, or press ⌘-Delete, to send the track into the great sheet music stack in the sky. (Of course, GarageBand's amazing Undo command can resurrect it if necessary; see the box on page 483.)

Renaming a Track

Click a track's header to select it, and then click carefully, once, on its name. It's now a simple matter to edit the track's name, as shown in Figure 23-8.

Figure 23-8:
If a track header is already selected, click once on the track's name to open its "renaming rectangle." If not, click inside the track header's colored area first, then click the track name. (Just don't double-click the track name; you'll open up a dialog box by accident.) Hold your breath and remain very still. At last, the name-editing box appears.

Edit the name by typing. Then press Return or Enter, or click somewhere else in GarageBand, to make the new name stick.

Track Characteristics

The importance of the New Track dialog box shown in Figure 23-6 depends on what kind of musical material you intend to record (that is, which of the two tabs you click):

• **Real Instrument.** This tab lists instruments, all right, but they actually refer to *effects presets* that contain canned settings for reverb, echo, and other processing

---

GEM IN THE ROUGH

There's Undo, and Then There's Undo

GarageBand offers a multiple-level Undo command. That is, you can take back more than one editing step, backing up in time. GarageBand can, in fact, take back the last 30 steps! By choosing the Edit→Undo command (or pressing ⌘-Z), you can rewind your file closer and closer to its condition when you last saved it. (Or if you haven't saved the file, Undo takes you closer and closer to the moment you opened it.)

That fine print may startle people who are used to, say, Microsoft Word, which lets you keep undoing even past the point of saving a document. It's also a strong argument for saving a GarageBand file less frequently, because once you

save the document, you lose the ability to undo changes up to that point.

Of course, if you really do want to rewind your work all the way back to the instant when you last saved the piece, you can bypass all of those Edit→Undos and instead choose File→Revert to Saved. GarageBand tosses out all the work you've done since the last save.

And one last thing: If you rewind too far, and you inadvertently Undo your way past a good edit you made, you also have a multiple Edit→Redo command at your disposal. In effect, it undoes the Undos.

---

effects that have been optimized for each instrument type. The actual instrument sound is determined by your microphone or whatever electronic instrument you hook up to your Mac. Chapter 27 has details.

- **Software Instrument.** This tab also lists instruments, but here, you're choosing an instrument *sound* that will play when you press the keys of your MIDI keyboard. Details in Chapter 26.

Tip: Either way you can also choose an icon for the track, using the pop-up menu at the lower-left corner. Apple gives you 68 little graphics to choose from—every instrument in GarageBand, plus silhouettes of singers. (These are purely graphic ornaments; they don't affect the sound in any way.)

To open this palette of icons, by the way, you don't have to click the tiny, down-pointing triangle, as you might expect. Instead, click squarely on the icon itself. The broader target means quicker access.

The appearance of the New Track dialog box is not, fortunately, the only chance you get to adjust these parameters.

You can summon the same box at any time, even after recording into the track, by double-clicking the track header or, if a track is already selected, by choosing Track→ Track Info (⌘-I). The resulting dialog box is now called Track Info, but it looks overwhelmingly familiar.

Note: In fact, when you open the Track Info dialog box, you get a Details button at the bottom that you *don't* get in its New Track dialog box. For more on effects, see Chapter 28.

You also get a Master Track tab at the top of the dialog box; it's described in Chapter 29.

Muting and Soloing Tracks

Most of the time, GarageBand plays all of your tracks simultaneously—and most of the time, that's what you want.

Figure 23-9:
You can tackle the on/off status of your tracks in two ways: either by specifying which ones don't play (by turning on their Mute buttons), or by specifying which tracks are the only ones that play (by turning on their Solo buttons).

Sometimes, though, it's useful to ask one track to drop out for a minute. You might want to mute a track when:

• You've recorded two different versions of a part, and you want to see which one sounds better.

• You're trying to isolate a wrong note, and you want to use the process of elimination to figure out which track it's in.

• The Playhead is bright red, indicating that the Mac is gasping under its load of tracks. So you'd like to lighten its burden by shutting off a couple of tracks without deleting them forever.

Silencing a track is easy: Just click the little speaker icon below the track's name (see Figure 23-9). Or, if the track header is selected, just tap the letter M key on your keyboard.

The speaker, officially called the Mute button, lights up in blue, which means: "I'm shutting up until you change your mind." The regions of notes in that track grow

The Weirdness of the Files

Veteran Mac fans know that some programs, like Word and TextEdit, create documents—that is, individual file icons on the hard drive.

Other programs, like iMovie, create project folders filled with supporting elements like sound and movie clips.

GarageBand falls into a third category unto itself.

When you save a new GarageBand song, it appears to be a standard, self-contained document file. You'll soon discover, though, that it doesn't act like a document file. For example, you can't attach it to an outgoing email message in Entourage unless you first compress it as a .zip or .sit file.

Turns out GarageBand creates a sort of hybrid, a cross between a folder and a file, known as a package. A Mac OS X package looks like an icon, but acts like a folder, in that it contains other files and folders.

In times of troubleshooting—for example, when you're trying to figure out why a certain GarageBand "document" is

so big—you can actually open up one of these packages to see what's inside.

To do so, Control-click the GarageBand song icon and, from the shortcut menu, choose Show Package Contents, as shown here. Lo and behold, a new window opens, exactly as though you'd opened a folder.

Inside you'll find two important elements. First, there's the projectData file, which is the actual "edit list" that tells GarageBand what to play when. (If you're familiar with iMovie, the projectData file is the equivalent of the iMovie project document.)

Second, there's the Media folder (again, exactly as in an iMovie project folder). Here, GarageBand stashes several kinds of song component: any digital audio files you've recorded (singing tracks, for example); copies of sound files you added to a composition by dragging them into the program from the Finder; and in some cases (page 504), copies of any loops you've used in your masterpiece.

pale to drive home the point. (You can turn the Mute button on or off *while* the music is playing—a clever way to compare your mix with and without a certain instrument.)

There's nothing to stop you from muting *more* than one track, either. If you need the entire percussion section to sit out for a minute, so be it.

Of course, if you find yourself muting more than half of your tracks, you should be using the *Solo* button instead. That's the tiny pair of headphones right next to the Mute button.

Here again, the point is to control which tracks play, but the logic is now reversed. When you click the headphones (or, if the track header is selected, press the letter S key on your Mac's keyboard), that's the *only* track you hear. The note regions in all other tracks grow pale.

Oxymoronic though it may sound, you can actually Solo as many tracks as you like. All other tracks are silent.

To turn a track's Mute or Solo button off again, click it again (or press the M or S key a second time).

Loops

Apple claims that GarageBand can be a blast even if your mastery of music never even progressed to the "Chopsticks" stage. And it's true: GarageBand lets you create authentic-sounding, studio-quality music even if you can't carry a tune, let alone a tuba. This chapter, dear nonmusicians, is sure to be one of your favorites.

That's because GarageBand comes with over 1,100 *loops*—short, prerecorded snippets performed in recording studios by professionals who most certainly do know their instruments. According to Apple, some of GarageBand's Motown drum loops, in fact, were played by the original studio musicians who recorded classic Motown hits like "My Girl" and "I Heard It Through the Grapevine."

Loops are only a few seconds long, but they're designed to repeat seamlessly for as long as you specify. That's a serious help when you want to create a drum part, for example.

Using some extremely advanced technological mojo, GarageBand manages to make every loop sound good with almost any other. So all you have to do is choose the drum beat, bass line, and guitar noodling you like (for example), and trust GarageBand to make them all sound like they were recorded in perfect sync. As you'll see, it's all about dragging and dropping.

Starting a New GarageBand Project

The first time you open GarageBand—or whenever you choose File→New—you get the dialog box shown in Figure 24-1.

If you *do* know a little bit about music or the Mac, you can use this dialog box to specify details like this:

- **What to call your new piece.** You'll almost certainly want to type a new title into the Save As box—"My Song" gets old fast.

- **Where to file it.** The program always hopes that you'll keep all your compositions in your Home→Music→GarageBand folder, which the iLife installer created. You can, of course, choose to file it anywhere else (press ⌘-D, for example, to save it onto your desktop). But you'll have to redirect GarageBand in this way each time you create a new piece.

Figure 24-1:
The overwhelming majority of Garage-Band masterpieces that people have posted online are built with these settings: 120 beats per minute, 4/4, key of C. Clearly, most people do not, in fact, ever get around to changing these parameters.

Incidentally, if you're interested in learning about time signatures, keys, tempo, and so on, see Appendix A for a crash course.

- **The song's tempo.** That is, how fast or slow it is, expressed in beats per minute. You can either drag the Tempo slider or type a new number into the "bpm" box just below it.

You don't really have to know what you're doing at this stage. You can adjust a song's tempo at any time, even after you've recorded it.

- **The song's time signature (meter).** Now you're getting into musician territory; this setting specifies how many *beats* (foot-taps, you might say) there are in a measure. Put another way, the first number in a time signature—like the upper digit in the time signature 4/4—is what you'd count off to your garage band to get it off to a synchronized start. ("And-a one! Two! Three! Four!")

This is a rather important decision. You *can* change your mind later, but not without introducing a good bit of chaos into whatever music you've already recorded. (You can't change the time signature midway through a piece, either.)

Note: GarageBand offers a choice of some less common time signatures like 9/8 (think "Jesu, Joy of Man's Desiring"), 2/4 (every march you've ever heard), and 12/8 ("Everybody Wants to Rule the World"). GarageBand's loops, however, are designed to work only in 4/4. For most of the other time signatures, no loops are available at all. A couple show up for 2/4 and 6/8, but they're actually mislabeled and don't fit into the beats.

In short, GarageBand is prepared to handle time signatures other than 4/4—but only if you intend to record your *own* music performances, as described in the following chapters. So, if you want to work with loops, you're stuck with 4/4.

- **What key your piece is in.** The *key* of a piece specifies how high or low it is—where it falls on the piano keyboard, for example.

  If you have enough musical knowledge to understand keys, now is the time to choose the one you want. You can *transpose* GarageBand's loops and your MIDI-instrument performances at any time—that is, move them into a different key. But some of GarageBand's loops start to distort if you shift them too far from their starting points. Furthermore, anything you record into a Real Instrument track, using a microphone or electronic instrument, remains locked in pitch forever.

Note: The key you choose also affects which loops are available to you, since GarageBand ordinarily hides the loops that are far from the key you choose. More on this topic on page 501.

Once you've made your choices, click OK. After a moment, you see a screen that looks something like Figure 23-1. GarageBand is now a blank canvas—ready to receive input, captain! It starts you off with a $50,000 Yamaha C7 grand piano sound and (if no external keyboard is attached) a 29¢ onscreen keyboard to "play" it.

For the moment, close the little keyboard by clicking the tiny, round Close button at its top-left corner. When you get time, you can read all about it on page 516.

The Loop Browser

If you're following along with this chapter, leave the one empty Grand Piano track on the screen. Close the onscreen keyboard for the moment. (If you've been fooling around on your own, start a fresh project by choosing File→New.)

Now, if the plan is to build a piece of music out of 1,100 musical spare parts, you'd better have a *very* organized toolbox. Sure enough, GarageBand offers an extremely clever loop-finding system called the Loop browser. To open it, use one of these three methods:

- Click the eyeball icon below the list of tracks, as shown in Figure 24-2.
- Choose Control→Show Loop Browser.
- Press ⌘-L.

Later, you can hide the Loop browser by repeating the same step (except that the menu command will say Hide Loop Browser).

Tip: When you first open the Loop browser, you're seeing only a sampling of the musical smorgasbord Apple has prepared for you. Only about half of the Loop browser buttons—35 of them—are visible.

To view the rest of the buttons, drag the dark gray brushed metal divider bar upward into the Track area, as shown in Figure 24-2.

Figure 24-2:
You can sort the loop list by name, by originally recorded tempo or key, and so on, just by clicking the corresponding column heading. Click the heading a second time to reverse the sort order. You can also drag the heading divider lines to adjust column widths, or drag the heading names horizontally to rearrange them.

At this point, GarageBand offers three different ways to search its massive database of juicy sonic tidbits to locate the one you're seeking: Button View, Column View, and the Search box.

Loop Quest 1: Button View

Here's how to use the grid of oval Loop browser buttons:

1. **Click the oval button named for the instrument you want.**

   Eventually, you'll cultivate your own work routine. But in the recording biz, it's common to lay down the *rhythm tracks* first—the bass, guitar, and drums, for example—and then, later, record the melodic lines, like the vocals or instrumental solos, on top of that background.

   Suppose, then, that you're hunting for just the right drum pattern for a new song you're writing. Click Drums.

At this point, the Drums button remains lit in blue, and the other instrument buttons fade out. The right side of the Loop browser displays a long, scrolling list of drum riffs. These are your loops.

The light gray readout next to the volume slider at the bottom of the window displays how many of GarageBand's 1,100 loops are in the category you're now browsing ("282 items," for example).

Tip: You can reorganize the buttons of the Loop browser, either by dragging one button onto another, or by Control-clicking a button and choosing from the shortcut menu. The point, of course, is to arrange the buttons so they're easy to find. For example, you might want to install the most useful buttons into the cluster of the top 35, making them visible when you initially open the Loop browser. That way, you needn't expand the Loop browser manually every time you open GarageBand.

2. **To listen to a loop, click its name.**

   Immediately, GarageBand begins playing that prerecorded snippet—cleverly adjusting the loop's speed to match the current tempo of your piece—and then repeating it endlessly. (Now you know why it's called a loop.) A little speaker icon, as well as some colored highlighting, lets you see at a glance which loop is playing.

   Drag the slider at the bottom edge of the window to adjust the loop volume.

   To stop the playback, click the name again, or click a different loop name.

POWER USERS' CLINIC

Auditioning: The Loop's Big Break

Once your GarageBand skills grow beyond staying up into the wee hours just clicking loop names and giggling with power-mad glee, you may begin to hunt down the little efficiencies that mark the skilled software master. And when it comes to choosing just the right loop for the piece you're building, that means learning to use loops with cycling.

Cycling is when GarageBand repeats a certain section of the music endlessly. Cycling is a great feature when you're experimenting to find just the right loop to add, or as you practice what you're going to record on top of it.

To loop a certain section of your piece, click the Cycle button (identified on page 475), or press the letter C key. The Cycle button lights up, and a yellow stripe appears on the beat ruler to identify which part of the song GarageBand will repeat. Adjust its length and position, as shown in Figure 23-3.

If you tap the Space bar now, GarageBand plays only the music indicated by that yellow stripe.

Now here's the cool part: If you click a loop's name in the Loop browser, you'll hear the loop begin playing in perfect sync with the music you've already installed in the piece. It may even wait a moment to start playing the loop, to ensure that the loop will play together with the rest of the "band."

Now, previewing loops by selecting them as the music plays works whether cycling is on or off. But with cycling on, it's easier to audition (listen to) one loop after another, just by clicking each one's name, without having to keep rewinding and starting the playback over. Better yet, just press the up- or down-arrow key to walk through the list of loops, listening to each in turn.

To stop playback, press the Space bar; to turn off cycling, click the Cycle button again, or tap the letter C key again.

Tip: Whenever you find a loop that you especially like, or think you'll use again, turn on its Fav checkbox, usually located in the rightmost column. (Make your GarageBand window wider if you don't see this column of checkboxes.) You've just added it to your list of Favorite loops.

At any time, you can recall these favorite loops by clicking the Favorites button at the left edge of the Loop browser. You've just saved yourself the effort of crawling through the 1,100 choices to find that awesome Nordic Fiddle again.

Now, you can have hours of fun just scrolling through this vast list of drum loops, muttering, "Hey! That's the one from 'Brick House'!" But since over 275 drum loops come with GarageBand, by the time you find just the right hip-hop beat, hip-hop won't be hip anymore!

That's why GarageBand comes equipped with features that help narrow the loops to just the one that suits the piece you're building.

3. **Click a category or adjective button: Country, Jazz, Relaxed, Acoustic, and so on. In fact, click as many as you like.**

MUSIC CLASS

Scale: Any

The pop-up menu on the bottom edge of the Loop browser, called Scale, offers another way to filter GarageBand's list of loops. It lets you view only the loops that, musically speaking, "go" with certain kinds of scales.

A scale is the series of notes—you know, "Do, re, mi," and so on—that fits a particular key. Most simple melodies are constructed of only the seven notes in a particular scale.

Most GarageBand loops sound good when played simultaneously with other loops—but not all of them. For instance, a guitar loop playing in a major key and a piano loop in a minor key will clash horribly. That's why the Scale pop-up menu exists: so you can match your loops, major with major or minor with minor.

Your options are:

Any: You're seeing all loops. None are hidden.

Minor: A minor key, and its associated scale, is one that sounds sad or angry. (To hear a melody played using a minor scale, set the Scale pop-up menu to Minor. Then, in the Loop browser, click Reset and then Guitars. Click the

loop called Acoustic Noodling 03.)

Minor keys are fairly rare in pop music, but when you're feeling a little depressed, GarageBand can accommodate you. Choose this option to display only loops played on minor scales.

Major: A major key, and its associated scale, sounds happy. Most pop music uses this kind of scale. To hear the idea, set the Scale pop-up menu to Major. Then click Reset, Guitars, and Acoustic Picking 02.

Neither, Good For Both: Many loops don't have any particular key, pitch, or scale. Drums, for example, have no pitch, so they "go" with music in any key without clashing. Certain bass, guitar, and string loops are more or less scale-less, too—meaning they could go with either major or minor music. (Musicians' Note: Octaves, unisons, and open-fifth "power chords" are some examples. The common thread: you don't hear the third of the chord.)

In any case, after fiddling with this pop-up menu, be sure to set it back to Any, so you won't later wonder what happened to your huge master list of loops.

Each time you click one of these buttons, GarageBand filters its list of loops to show you only the ones that match your description—and dims another set of oval buttons. For example, if you click Drums, and then Electronic, and then Distorted, you wind up with a list of only five loops.

This method isn't utterly foolproof, as you might disagree with the categorization of some of the loops. It's not crystal clear how GarageBand is doing its filtering, either. For example, once you've clicked Drums and then Jazz, turning on the Part and Clean buttons doesn't produce any changes in the list.

Still, most of the time, you can find your way to your desired loop in just a few clicks.

Tip: Most people start drilling down by clicking the instrument button (like Piano) first, followed by the category buttons (Clean, Cheerful, and so on). But in fact, you can start with *any* button and work backward: Click Cheerful first, then Piano, and so on.

---

4. **Once you've added a loop to your piece, or if you give up on your hunt and want to start over, click the Reset button to turn off all buttons and start anew.**

On the other hand, it's often less time-consuming just to *back up* in your button-clicking. Just turn *off* the most recent blue buttons that you've turned on. For example, suppose you click Drums, then Electronic, then Cheerful, only to find that there's just one loop in this category. If you decide you've barked up the wrong tree, just click Electronic (for example) to backtrack to the intersection of the Drums/Electronic categories. This way, you can begin drilling down again.

Loop Quest 2: Column View

This business of narrowing your loop quest by clicking successive descriptive buttons is a pleasure, but it isn't right for everyone. Because all 63 of the loop buttons are displayed in one big nonhierarchical pile, it's not always clear which are instrument categories, which are mood categories, and so on.

Figure 24-3:
Start by clicking the Column View button. Click a "folder" in the first pane (like By Instruments) to see its contents (like Banjo or Bongo). Click an instrument to see, in the third column, the loop categories within that instrument (Clean, Dark, and so on). Finally, choose from the far-right list.

Column view

Column view solves that problem rather quickly. It turns the Loop browser into a close cousin of the Finder column view, so that you can drill down in successive panes and never lose track of the path you took (Figure 24-3).

Because the third column shows, in parentheses, how many loops fall in each category, Column View provides a good deal of insight into how GarageBand's loops come categorized. There are 11 categories in the Flute group, for example (Cheerful, Orchestral, Acoustic, and so on), but that doesn't mean that you've got dozens and dozens of flute samples. In fact, GarageBand comes with only four flute licks, and the same set of four appears in each of the 11 Flute categories.

Loop Quest 3: The Search Box

Once you've worked with GarageBand awhile, you may not feel quite so browsy as you did when you first began fooling around with it. Eventually, you come to know which loops you have, and then wish for a more direct way to pluck them out of the haystack of music.

That's what the Search box is for (on the bottom edge of the Loop browser). You may not remember, for example, that a certain hyper-funky keyboard loop was played on something called a clavinet; you remember only that its name was something like "Cop Show."

So you type *cop* into the Search box and press Return or Enter. Instantly, GarageBand reveals all eight of its Cop Show loops, without requiring that you drill down through the categories (see Figure 24-4).

Figure 24-4:
In light gray lettering, the text just to the right of the Search box lets you know how many loop names match your search. (It's sometimes a wake-up call to let you know that you need to scroll the list in the far-right column.)

And now, three notes about the Search box:

- It searches only within the *currently selected* Loop browser category (Bass→Acoustic, for example). It you intend to search the entire GarageBand loop collection, therefore, click the Reset or All button first.

- You can use it to search either for a loop's name or for its category. That is, you can search for terms like *intense* or *strings,* even if those words don't actually appear in any loop names.

- To empty the Search box (and return to seeing all loops), click the circled X at its right end.

Placing a Loop

Suppose that you've used one of the three loop-finding techniques, and you've homed in on just the right loop. Now it's time to install it into your song.

To do that, drag the loop's name upward and into position, as shown in Figure 24-5. The leftmost edge of the loop will align with the spot where you release the mouse.

What happens when you release the mouse depends on *where* you release the mouse.

Drag into a Blank Gray Area

If you drag into an empty track area, you create a brand new track, already set to play the instrument whose name you dragged (Figure 24-5). At the beginning of your song-building session, this is the technique you'll probably use the most. (It makes no

Figure 24-5:
If you drag a loop into an empty track area (top), you create a new track and fill it with one repetition of the loop (bottom). You can save time by dragging it carefully into the horizontal position you want, using the beat ruler at the top of the window as your guide. Of course, you can always adjust the loop's position after placing it, just by dragging it from side to side.

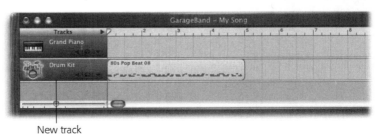

New track

difference whether you release the mouse in the light gray area beneath the existing music or the darker gray area beneath the existing track headers.)

Tip: If you *Option*-drag a green Software Instrument loop into an empty track area, GarageBand converts that green Software Instrument into a blue Real Instrument loop—and creates a Real Instrument track to hold it.

This is an important trick when your Mac is wheezing under the weight of too many tracks. See the box on the facing page for the explanation.

On the other hand, once you've added a track for Cool Upright Bass, for example, there's little point in creating a second or third Cool Upright Bass track for bass licks that occur later in the song. Simply keep all of your Cool Upright Bass in a single track. That's why you can also drag into an existing track.

Drag into an Existing Track

If you drag a loop into a track that's assigned to the same instrument sound, you get just what you'd expect. For example, if you drag the Acoustic Noodling 04 loop into an Acoustic Guitar track that you created earlier (by dragging Acoustic Noodling 01 into place, for example), you get more Acoustic Noodling, just as you'd expect.

But suppose you drag a loop into a track whose instrument *doesn't* match the loop you're dragging. For example, suppose you drag Dreamy Guitar Pattern 01 into a Grand Piano track. What now?

Here's where things can get wacky—and confusing. To understand what's going on, you must understand the distinction between Real Instruments (digital recordings—blue or purple) and Software Instruments (MIDI note data—green); see page 477 for a refresher.

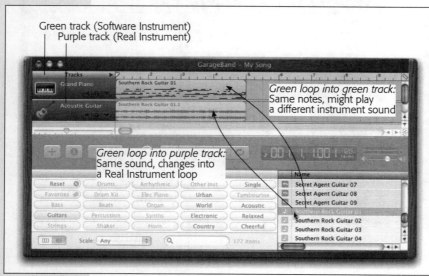

Green track (Software Instrument)
Purple track (Real Instrument)

Green loop into green track: Same notes, might play a different instrument sound

Green loop into purple track: Same sound, changes into a Real Instrument loop

Figure 24-6:
Some funky things can happen when you drag a Software Instrument (green) loop into an existing track. If you drag into a Software Instrument track, the loop takes on the instrument sound of that track. If you drag into a Real Instrument track, though, GarageBand actually converts the MIDI notes of the loop into a blue digital audio (Real Instrument) loop.

In any case, here's what happens when you drag:

- **Green loop→Green track with different sound.** Suppose you drag a Software Instrument loop into a Software Instrument track, but the instrument doesn't

---

GEM IN THE ROUGH

The Secret Lives of Green Loops

If you've managed to grasp the difference between Garage-Band's two kinds of musical building blocks, congratulations. If you've never worked with music on the Mac before, getting over this conceptual hurdle is a huge accomplishment. (To review: Software Instruments = green = MIDI data = editable notes. Real Instruments = blue or purple = digital audio = frozen as is.)

But wait—there's more.

It turns out that GarageBand's green loops have a little secret. Yes, each contains MIDI note-trigger information, represented by those horizontal bars. But behind the scenes, each one also contains a digital-audio representation of itself—a true-blue AIFF recording. (For proof, switch to the Finder, press ⌘-F, and search for the name of a green GarageBand loop, like Deep Electric Piano. You'll find out that each Software Instrument loop shows up as an .aif file—an AIFF sound file—as it sits in a folder on your hard drive. Each is also far larger than a pure MIDI file would be.)

Go ahead, ask it: What's the point?

Turns out it's actually easier for the Mac to play back digital recordings (blue or purple) than MIDI material (green), because it doesn't have to synthesize the sound itself, in real time. Therefore, if your Mac is having trouble playing back the number of tracks you need, converting green loops into blue ones makes them easier for the Mac to play back. Since blue loops require less processing power to play back, you can use more tracks and effects in a piece.

The downside is that you lose all the great features of MIDI loops, like the freedom to change its notes, transpose it into any key you like, make different notes play louder or softer, adjust its post-processing effects (like reverb), and so on. You're freezing it as it is, complete with whatever effects it came with.

Now, if your Mac isn't having trouble managing all your tracks, you can ignore this entire discussion. But if this MIDI-to-AIFF conversion still interests you, here's a summary of the three ways to pull it off.

First, you can drag a green loop into a blue (Real Instrument) track.

Second, you can Option-drag a green loop out of the Loop browser into an empty spot in the gray timeline area. GarageBand converts the loop into digital audio and creates a new Real Instrument track to hold it.

Finally, you can request that GarageBand always convert green loops into noneditable blue ones, every time you drag one into your piece. Just choose GarageBand→Preferences, click the Advanced tab, turn on "Convert to Real Instrument" (shown here), and close the dialog box.

At that point, the effect of the Option key changes. Now, Option-dragging a green loop does not make it change into a blue one; GarageBand leaves the green loop green.

To sum up, the Option key always reverses the status of the "Convert to Real Instrument" checkbox in GarageBand's preferences.

---

match. To use the example above, let's assume you drag Dreamy Guitar Pattern 01 into a Grand Piano track.

In that case, something rather cool happens: GarageBand plays the *notes* of the loop using the instrument sound of the track. Suddenly you're hearing that dreamy guitar pattern played on a piano. See Figure 24-6.

This simple twist vastly multiplies your options as you build a song. When you think about it, you can reassign any green loop to any of dozens of instrument sounds. Apple's categorization is only a starting point for your creativity.

- **Green loop→Blue track.** If you drag a Software Instrument loop into a Real Instrument track, something weird and wonderful happens: GarageBand turns the MIDI loop into a digital recording! Right before your eyes, the green loop turns blue, and its horizontal bars into soundwaves, indicating that its transformation is complete. Once again, see Figure 24-6.

  This behavior isn't exactly consistent with the blue-loop-to-green-track "no go" behavior described above, but it's rather cool nevertheless. It may just give you the speed relief you need when your Mac is straining under the load of your composition; see the box on page 619 for complete details.

- **Blue loop→Blue track with different sound.** This combo produces yet another surprising effect. Dragging a digital-audio (blue) loop into an existing digital-audio track has no effect at all on its instrument sound. Figure 24-7 illustrates this phenomenon.

Figure 24-7:
You can drag any number of different digital audio loops back-to-back into the same Real Instrument track, as shown here in the second track: Effected Drum Kit, Alternative Rock Bass, and Shaker 4, for example. They'll all play back with the proper instrument sounds, even if the track is called, for example, Acoustic Guitar.

Note: Although blue loops always play back with their original instrument sounds when added to an existing blue track, they're still altered by the effects and settings of that track—echo, reverb, stereo, and so on. See Chapter 28 for more on track effects.

- **Blue loop→Green track.** If you drag a blue loop (Real Instrument) into a green track (Software Instrument), nothing happens at all. GarageBand shakes its little software head "no" and throws the loop back where it came from. You can't park digital audio in a track that expects the horizontal bars of MIDI notes.

All Together Now

In any case, the magic of loops is that most of them sound amazing together, as you'll quickly discover.

Now, if your GarageBand window is wide enough, you'll see columns of information for your loops: Key, Tempo, and so on. And you might wonder how a bass loop that's listed as 80 beats per minute, key of D, would sound good with a piano loop that says it's 110 beats per minute, key of C.

Ah, welcome to the magic of software. The listings of tempo and key in the Loop browser indicate the originally recorded tempos and keys. When you actually install a loop into your piece, though, GarageBand automatically tweaks it, nudging into the key and tempo of *your* piece, no matter how it was originally recorded.

Tip: See Chapter 25 for details on working with loops you've placed into your tracks, like making them actually loop (repeat), moving them around, shortening them, and so on.

More Loops

GarageBand comes with 1,100 loops. That should be plenty—for the first half-hour or so!

As your lust for deeper musical expression grows, though, you might find yourself wishing you had a more comprehensive sonic palette. You might have noticed, for example, that GarageBand comes with a healthy selection of rhythm parts (bass, drums, guitars, keyboards, mallet instruments), plus some strings and brass—but no solo instruments, like trumpet, clarinet, harp, or solo violin. As noted earlier, GarageBand is also heavily slanted toward music in 4/4 time.

Fortunately, expanding the possibilities is easy enough, since you can add more loops in any of these forms.

Note: You can add almost any sound file to a GarageBand composition just by dragging it into the timeline area. That doesn't make it a loop, however.

A true GarageBand loop comes in *Apple Loop* format. That's basically a dressed-up AIFF file with built-in tags that specify its original length, key, category, and so on.

The GarageBand Jam Pack

This $100 expansion pack from Apple offers 2,000 more loops, 15 more guitar-amp simulations, 100 more audio effects, and 100 additional instrument sounds.

That's a lot of add-on fun. It's worth noting, though, that most of the new instruments are in the same categories as the original GarageBand set: guitars, vibraphones, drums, basses, and keyboard instruments. Many of the "100 new instrument sounds" are actually processed or combined versions of the sounds you already have. Only a few wholly new instrument sounds actually join your squad, including a couple of new solo saxophones, a solo flute, new guitars, and bass samples. Fortunately, they're well worth having. There's also a few sound effects, like a car starting, vinyl record scratching, and phone sounds.

Figure 24-8:
Top: Suppose you've just downloaded some loops, or maybe bought them on CD. Open your Loop browser (page 489) and drag them anywhere into the open window.

Middle: In a spirit of helpfulness, Garage-Band offers to save disk space by offering you a choice. If you click Index Only, GarageBand registers the list of new loops and adds their names to the Loop browser, but doesn't copy them. If you click Move to Library, GarageBand actually copies them into its official storage folders for loops and instruments.

Bottom: And that official storage folder is the Library→ Application Support→ GarageBand folder on your hard drive, organized by each batch of imported loops.

Soundtrack

Apple's $300 soundtrack-creation program, Soundtrack, comes with 4,000 Apple Loops of its own. You can share its musical riches with GarageBand. Just drag the Soundtrack loops from the desktop into GarageBand's Loop browser, as described in Figure 24-8.

GEM IN THE ROUGH

More Loops Than You Bargained For

When you first peruse the loops that come with GarageBand, you may be pleasantly surprised by how many you have. You may be vaguely aware that you can buy an add-on pack of loops in the form of the Apple GarageBand Jam Pack, but you may not realize that you've got a bunch more loops already on your hard drive. They're just hidden at the moment.

The problem is that GarageBand's different loops were recorded in different keys. (Inspect the Key column in the Loop browser for proof.) If you've ever heard a tone-deaf, slightly drunk karaoke singer at a party, you know how painful it is to listen to clashing keys (two different ones at once). And Apple firmly believes in the old Chinese proverb, "May all your loops sound good together."

Now, one of GarageBand's most amazing features is its ability to transpose its loops (shift them up or down in pitch). If you find a bass loop recorded in the key of D, and drag it into a piece that's in C, it will still sound great, because GarageBand will automatically process it to fit the neighboring key—yes, even if it's a blue (digital-audio) Apple Loop.

So why does GarageBand start out hiding loops that don't match your key?

Apple worries that you might get greedy with that auto-transposing feature. If you choose a blue key-of-F guitar loop, well, that key is rather distant from the key of C. GarageBand's magic software-processing elves will dutifully transpose it into C for you, but the result occasionally sounds

funny—slightly distorted, or, more often, inappropriate for the instrument. (This caveat applies only to blue Real Instrument loops. Green Software Instrument loops sound fabulous in any key.)

Therefore, to protect you against madcap transpositions, GarageBand comes set to hide all Real (blue) loops that don't match the key of your piece.

You can request that it not be such a diva, and show you all of the loops in its bag of tricks. To do that, choose GarageBand→Preferences, click the General icon, and turn off "Filter for more relevant results." Close the dialog box, return to the Loops browser, and click Reset.

Now examine the loops again. As you can see, many more loops appear in the list. For example, if your piece is in C, you now see seven loops in the Bass→Jazz→Cheerful category instead of four.

You may notice that even when "Filter for more relevant results" is turned on, by the way, the listed loops aren't all in your piece's key. For example, scrolling through the list of Bass loops reveals that many of the bass licks were indeed recorded in the key of C. Yet the list also offers you blue loops in keys like C# and D.

The "Filter" option leaves you with blue loops in your song's key and in keys within two half-steps (piano keys) of it. (It also shows you *green* loops in all different keys, because GarageBand can transpose these into any key with no loss of fidelity.)

Apple Loops from Other Companies

Apple isn't the only company getting into the loop-selling act. There are a few other sources of loops in the Apple Loop format. Some, mercifully, are free. (You'll even find a few free samples on the "Missing CD" page for this book at *www.missingmanuals. com.*) They include BandMateLoops.com, TuneupLoops.com, Samples4.com, Bit-ShiftAudio.com, and Access-music.de.

And that's just the beginning. Fire up your Web browser, visit Google.com, and search for *free Apple loops.* You'll find plenty of downloads to keep you busy.

GEM IN THE ROUGH

Insta-Samples: Canned Sound Without Loops

Now you know where to find additional loops to buy, download, and install into GarageBand.

In many cases, though, going to all that trouble and expense isn't worth it when all you need is a quick sound effect, or even a sample of a pop song already in your iTunes library. What many Garage-Band aficionados don't realize is that you can use any MP3 file, AIFF sound, AAC file (except copy-protected ones), or even Windows-format WAV file right in a GarageBand compo-sition just by dragging it there, as illustrated here.

Need a breaking-window sound to open your new love ballad, "When You Left Me, There Was Only One Way Out"? Zoom over to Google.com, con-duct a search for free AIFF sound effects, download a choice candidate, and simply drag its icon off your desktop into the GarageBand Timeline window. That sound effect now plays right along with your music.

Want to sample a killer drum hit from a pop song in your

iTunes music library? No problem. Position your iTunes and GarageBand windows so you can see them both at the same time. Drag the MP3 file's name right out of iTunes and into the GarageBand Timeline window. After the importing dialog box disappears, edit the imported file just as you would any region (see Chapter 25), chopping it up until only the choice moment remains.

Or, similarly, want to create your own version of a pop song? Your first step might be to drag the song into GarageBand from the iTunes window to use as a reference. Adjust the GarageBand tempo control, for example, until the metronome more or less clicks right along with the imported song. Try playing the bass line along with the imported song, or lay down your own singing track on top of it, even if you ultimately intend to delete the imported reference track.

(About that business of copy-protected AAC files, like the ones you buy from the Apple Music Store: If you're desperate to include one, burn a CD of the song, leaving a non-copy-protected copy on the disc. Once when you insert the CD into your Mac, just drag the appropriate song file right out of its desktop window and into GarageBand.)

How to Install New Loops

Once you've got your hands on a new set of loops, install them into GarageBand just by dragging them there, as shown in Figure 24-8.

What happens now depends on *where* the loops are coming from. In each case, Garage-Band tries to do the smartest thing:

- **From a hard drive.** Some Mac fans have enormous loop collections, which they've amassed using other software (like Apple's Soundtrack). These power users are understandably reluctant to let GarageBand *copy* their hundreds of megabytes of loops into its own private loop folder, thus duplicating the loops on the hard drive.

  That's why, when you drag a folder of loops from a hard drive (whether your own built-in one, an external one, or even a networked one), you get the dialog box shown in Figure 24-8. It's asking how you want to handle this new set of loops. You can opt to have them copied into GarageBand's own Loops folder, or you can have GarageBand *index* them (add them to its list of available loops) but leave the actual files where they are, for the sake of conserving hard drive space.

- **From a CD or DVD.** GarageBand copies the loops into your existing loops folder. It's assuming that this particular disc may not always be in your Mac when you use GarageBand, and that the loops therefore may not always be available. As a result, it copies them to your hard drive for safekeeping.

Once you've installed a loop by dragging into the Loop browser, it becomes available to every GarageBand project you ever work on, a permanent addition to your collection (until you choose to delete it, of course).

Removing Loops and Rebuilding the Index

Not everybody feels straitjacketed by the meager 1,100 loops that come with Garage-Band. Some people actually feel overwhelmed. For them, the trick is not finding new loops to add to their collections—it's deleting the loops they know they'll never need. After all, if your specialty is composing lush, romantic waltzes, it's not immediately apparent how Vinyl Scratch 09 will be useful to you.

Removing loops is a matter of finding them on your hard drive. Open your hard drive→Library→Application Support→GarageBand→Apple Loops folder to find them.

Ordinarily, fooling around with these behind-the-scenes GarageBand folders isn't such a hot idea. Moving, deleting, or renaming the wrong file could profoundly confuse GarageBand.

However, if you make your way directly to the Apple Loops folder and don't do anything but remove the loops you really don't want to see, you'll be all right. For sanity's sake, don't simply delete them. Instead, drag them into some other folder on your hard drive, so you can return them in the unlikely event that you're commissioned to write "The Record Scratching Waltz."

Now, just moving loops out of the Apple Loops folder doesn't actually delete their names from GarageBand's Loop browser. Their names will still appear the next time you fire up GarageBand, because they're still in GarageBand's master *index file* of loops.

But the moment you click the loop's name, you see the dialog box shown in Figure 24-9. Click OK, wait a moment, and then relish your newly pruned collection of loops.

Figure 24-9:
If you delete loops behind GarageBand's back—in the Finder, that is—the program complains with this dialog box. Just click OK, and all will be well.

Apple Loop not found!

This Apple Loop was not found. Your Apple Loops will be reindexed to make sure that you only see existing Apple Loops. This may take a while.

OK

"Save as Archive"

As noted in the box on page 485, a GarageBand document isn't much of a document at all. It's actually a Mac OS X *package,* a folder disguised to work like a document icon.

As long as you use *only* the built-in Apple loops in your composition, you can freely exchange your GarageBand "document" with any agents, producers, or groupies who also have GarageBand. They'll be able to open the project and hear it exactly the way you did. After all, your composition is made exclusively of:

- Built-in Apple Loops, the same ones your audience also has on their Macs.

- Vocal lines and other Real Instrument recordings that you made, which are embedded inside the GarageBand package icon. (They're stored as AIFF files there.)

But what about other loops? What about Jam Pack loops, or loops you've made yourself, or loops bought from other companies?

Your audience does *not* have these on hand. They will *not* hear your masterpiece as it exists on your Mac.

The solution is the File→Save as Archive command. It creates what *looks* like a standard GarageBand document icon—but inside, it actually stores copies of all the loops you've used in your piece.

Needless to say, the resulting file takes up a lot more disk space than a regular GarageBand document. In fact, it can be huge. But at least it's self-contained and ready for glitch-free distribution.

Regions

A *region,* in GarageBand lingo, is one of the round-ended green, blue, or purple music blocks in the timeline. These are your GarageBand building blocks. A region may contain musical material or silence. Each may last only a fraction of a second, or the entire length of a song. Just by chopping, copying, pasting, and dragging regions around, you can build an infinite number of compositions that have never been heard before.

Loops, described in Chapter 24, are one kind of region (green or blue), but they're not the only kind. In subsequent chapters, you can read about how to record material of your own. Regions containing MIDI note information are always green, Apple Loops containing digital audio recordings are blue, and audio recordings you make yourself (or audio files you drag in from the Finder) are always purple.

The following discussions tell you how to manipulate regions in general, although these techniques are especially useful for manipulating loops.

Selecting Regions

Before you cut, copy, delete, split, join, or move regions around, you must first select them. This isn't rocket science, of course—just perform the same "Select, then apply" ritual in just about every Macintosh program.

Here's the complete GarageBand region-selecting handbook:

- **Select one region** by clicking it.
- **Select an additional region** by Shift-clicking it. If you Shift-click one by accident, Shift-click it again to deselect it.

- **Select all the regions in one section of the piece** by drag-selecting (Figure 25-1).

- **Select all the regions in one track** by clicking the track header (on the left side, where the track's name and icon appear).

- **Select the entire song** by choosing Edit→Select All (or pressing ⌘-A).

You can tell when a region is selected because its color deepens and its text darkens.

To deselect everything and start over, simply click in any empty gray spot in the timeline.

Figure 25-1:
By dragging enormous chunks of your song, you can rearrange sections and experiment with musical arrangements. The trick is selecting so many regions all at once. To do so, start by zooming out. Then, drag a box around the entire area you want to select. Now you can drag any of the selected regions to move them all at once, exactly as with icons in the Finder.

Zoom slider (drag left to zoom out)

Renaming Regions

Regions usually begin life named after their tracks or instruments. But giving them more descriptive names—like "Vocal Intro," "Bridge," or "Zither Solo"—goes a long way in helping you recognize where you are in your song at any given moment.

To change a region's name, double-click it; an editing window appears. You'll read more about this Track Editor later, but for now, what you care about is the Track Name box (Figure 25-2).

Dragging Regions

You can change when a region plays by shifting its horizontal position. Just drag it by its center.

Dragging is a very handy tactic. When you drag a region *horizontally*, you make it play earlier or later in time. When you drag it *vertically*, you move it to a different track.

Figure 25-2:
When you double-click any region, the Track Editor appears at the bottom of the window. One key feature is the Track Name box, where you can type a new name for the region. Press Return or Enter to make the name stick.

(Try not to worry about the inconsistency of having to edit the region's name so far away from the region itself.)

Figure 25-3:
This pop-up menu determines how fine or how coarse the underlying drag-and-drop grid is. It lists basic musical rhythmic units, from largest to smallest (that is, slowest to quickest). In 4/4 time, a region will snap only to the beginnings of measures if you choose "1/1 Note" (that is, a whole note); it'll move much more freely if you choose "1/16 Note" (a sixteenth note).

And when you select a huge chunk of your song (Figure 25-1), you can rearrange huge chunks of your piece at once.

The Grid

You may notice that a dragged region tends to snap to positions on an underlying grid, whose vertical lines correspond to the markings on the beat ruler across the top of the window. Here are the keys to understanding this snapping motion:

- In general, the snapping is a good thing. It keeps your loops aligned with one another, so that your GarageBand players have a virtual conductor keeping them together.

- A region you're dragging snaps to the nearest measure, quarter note, and so on. One way to control the fineness of this invisible grid is to use the Grid pop-up menu at the upper-right corner of the GarageBand window, as shown in Figure 25-3.

- If you choose Automatic from the Timeline Grid pop-up menu, the grid expands or contracts according to how much you've zoomed in. As you magnify your music, you get more gridlines per measure, which offers you finer positioning options. (The onscreen gray gridlines show you where GarageBand intends to snap.)

- If you want complete dragging freedom—no snapping grid at all—choose Control→Snap to Grid, or just press ⌘-G. Now you can drag a region wherever you like. (Repeat the command to turn the grid on again.)

Looping Regions

If you install a loop, hit the Home or Z key to rewind, and then press the Space bar to play, you may wonder why you went to all the trouble. The newly installed loop plays once—and then stops.

Fortunately, they're not called loops for nothing. The first and second illustrations in Figure 25-4 show how you can make a loop repeat (or any region, for that matter).

You can make a region repeat as many times as you like. In many songs, for example, you might want the drums to play continuously for the entire song. You can even stop dragging halfway through a repetition, giving you, for example, one-and-a-half repetitions. That might be useful if, say, you want those drums to stop short halfway through a measure to create a dramatic break.

Tip: When you make a loop repeat by dragging its upper-right edge, you're *cloning* the original loop, and the copies remain genetically linked to their progenitor. If you edit the first occurrence, all attached repetitions also change.

If you'd prefer the ability to edit each repetition separately, duplicate the loop region by copying and pasting (or Option-dragging) instead. That way, you create fully independent regions that you can edit independently.

Shortening Regions I

You don't have to use Apple's canned loops in their entirety. By shortening a region from its right end, you can isolate only a favorite first portion of it.

Shortening a region is simple enough: Drag the end inward, as detailed at bottom in Figure 25-4. You'll know you've grabbed the right spot when the cursor changes to a vertical bar with a rightward arrow, as opposed to the curly cursor that appears when you make a loop repeat. This movement is exactly the same cropping motion you can use on clips in iMovie's Movie Track.

Tip: If the region is blue or purple—a Real Instrument region—you can drag *either* end inward. That is, you can shorten it either from the beginning or end. (You can't shorten a green Software Instrument loop except from its right end.)

And now some cool mix-and-match editing pointers:

- Once you've shortened a region, you can then drag its upper-right corner to make *just that shortened version* repeat over and over. This trick does amazing things for

Figure 25-4:
If you drag a region by its upper-right corner (top), you make it repeat seamlessly (bottom); the curly cursor tells you that you've grabbed the correct corner. The farther to the right you drag, the more repetitions you get.

Middle: The little notches—four of them shown here—illustrate where the region will repeat.

Bottom: If you grab the middle or bottom of a region's right side, you can shorten it by dragging it to the left. (See the difference in the cursor shape?) You can also grab the left side of a blue or purple region and drag inward, cropping out the beginning of the region.

drum and bass loops, for example, creating fresh, shorter, more repetitive loops that never existed in Apple's imagination.

- The advantage of shortening a region by dragging its end—as opposed to splitting the region and deleting the unwanted portion, as described below—is that you can always restore the region to full length by dragging its end outward again.

- If the *middle* of a blue or purple region is your favorite part, use this technique to crop out both the beginning and ending of it.

Shortening Regions II

If your goal is to shorten a certain drum loop and then place a different region right next to it, try this shorthand: Drag the second region right *on top* of the one you want to shorten, so that they overlap. When you release the mouse, you'll see that you've vaporized the overlapped portion of the stationary region.

In some cases, you'll just leave the dragged region where it is now, so that it plays side-by-side with the shortened one. But once the chopping is done, you don't *have* to leave it where you dropped it. You can drag it right back where it started from, having used it as only a temporary chopper-offer.

Lengthening Regions

You can also make a region longer by dragging its right end to the right. That's not the same thing as dragging the top right *corner,* which makes the loop *loop.* Instead, dragging the loop's right edge extends the loop's width without making it repeat.

You might wonder what the point is, since the extended area of the region is filled with silence. Well, this trick can be handy when, for example, you recorded only seven measures, but want to loop the region so that it repeats every *eight* measures. By making the region an even eight measures long, you can now drag its upper-right *corner* to make it loop evenly.

Splitting Regions

You don't have to use a region in its entirety. Drum loops, in particular, are fun to split down the middle; the resulting half-loops or quarter-loops often serve as useful *fills* (drum riffs right before a musical moment).

All you have to do is position the Playhead precisely where you want the split to occur, click the region to select it, and then choose Edit→Split (or press ⌘-T). You'll see that the region is now in two separate pieces. You can manipulate, cut, copy, drag, shorten, repeat, or otherwise process each of these two pieces independently.

As noted earlier, what's especially intriguing is that you can split off a snippet of a region, and then make *that* repeat over and over, creating a whole new effect.

And now, some important region-splitting tips:

- You can simultaneously split *stacked* regions—that is, parallel regions in several tracks at once. Just make sure that you've first selected the ones you want to split by Shift-clicking each one (Figure 25-5).

Figure 25-5:
Top: Zoom in, and then position the Playhead where you want to hack up the loop, or loops, since you can chop several simultaneously, as shown here. Just make sure they're both selected. (Here, the middle track is not selected, so it won't be split.)

Bottom: After the split, the two loop pieces still sound alike when played in succession. However, now they're independent entities that you can copy and paste, drag around, and so on.

- After you split a region, both pieces of it remain highlighted. That's great if you now want to copy, delete, or move both pieces as a unit—but if *that* were your aim, why would you have just split them?

No, most of the time, you want to handle them individually. And that's why it's important, just after a split, to click an *empty* track area to deselect them. Only then can you drag or click one of the split pieces all by itself.

You'll use this technique in the tutorial that concludes this chapter.

Joining Regions

What the Split command hath rendered asunder, the Join Selected command shall restore.

Combining two or more regions on a track into a single, unified one has a number of benefits. For example, musical riffs that you've painstakingly assembled and positioned turn into a single, easy-to-manipulate block. Copying, pasting, and dragging regions around is much simpler, too, provided you can select the music in question with one quick click, without having to select a bunch of itty-bitty individual regions one at a time. And, of course, you can loop a region that you've created by joining them.

There is, however, one condition: The Join Selected command is dimmed if you've selected *blue* regions—that is, Real Instrument Apple loops. It works only on two green regions (MIDI, aka Software Instruments) or two purple ones (those you've recorded yourself, or sound files you've dragged in from the Finder).

Tip: According to GarageBand's online help, there are other conditions, too—but don't believe it. For example, the regions you're about to join do *not* have to be adjacent. In fact, you can even Shift-click two regions that are separated by *other* regions! They'll still merge into one long region that appears to float behind the intervening ones—the only time you'll ever see superimposed regions in GarageBand. Weird!

Figure 25-6 shows the routine.

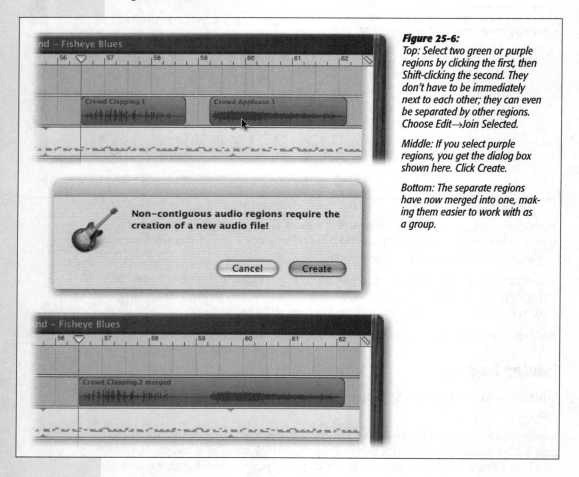

Figure 25-6:

Top: Select two green or purple regions by clicking the first, then Shift-clicking the second. They don't have to be immediately next to each other; they can even be separated by other regions. Choose Edit→Join Selected.

Middle: If you select purple regions, you get the dialog box shown here. Click Create.

Bottom: The separate regions have now merged into one, making them easier to work with as a group.

Copy and Paste

Let's face it: Copy and paste form the cornerstone of the personal-computer religion. If you couldn't copy and paste, where would word processing be? Where would Photoshop be? Where would college students be?

It works with regions just as it does with fields in FileMaker, objects in a drawing program, or icons in the Finder. Select the region or regions you want to copy, press ⌘-C (or choose Edit→Copy), click in the beat ruler to indicate where you want the Clipboard regions to reappear, and then press ⌘-V (or choose Edit→Paste). The cut or copied music appears at the position of the Playhead.

Since the regions always reappear in the tracks from which you cut or copied them, you can't paste into a different track.

Option-Drag

Copy and paste is all well and good, but it's a four-step procedure. When you want to copy a region into a nearby spot, there's a much more efficient technique: Option-dragging.

Press the Option key (called Alt on non-U.S. keyboards). While it's down, drag a region to a new position. You peel off a perfect copy of the original. (You may recognize this technique from working with icons in the Finder.)

As with copy-and-paste, this feature is very useful when you drag *horizontally*, because:

- Unlike looping, Option-dragging offers a quick and easy way to make a region repeat *periodically*, as opposed to immediately.

- As noted earlier, Option-dragging creates a separate, fully independent region. That's a handy tactic when you want to edit the copy or copies, creating slight variations from the original.

Option-dragging (or copy-and-paste, for that matter) is also useful when you drag a region vertically into a different track. For example, you can set up part *doubling* (two instruments playing the exact same notes) in a matter of seconds.

Delete

To delete a selected region or regions, press the Delete key (or, if you're in no particular hurry, choose Edit→Delete).

The Time Display

The Time Display is the blue "LED" number counter just below the timeline.

As shown in Figure 25-8 at top, this display can express the position of the Playhead in either of two ways:

• **As measure and beats.** If you're musically inclined, you'll probably prefer the standard musical notation that appears here. It's this format: 025.15.3.100, which refers to measures, beats, *sub-beats* (that is, quarters of a beat), and *ticks* (of which there are 240 per sub-beat).

That's probably *way* more precision than you'll ever need, but hey—overkill is in these days. (Just ask anyone who's bought a Hummer.)

• **As hours, minutes, and seconds.** The Time display can also display your position in pure time code—that is, how many hours, minutes, seconds, and thousandths of a second you are into the song.

This mode is especially handy when you're preparing music to accompany, say, an iMovie movie, because you can use it to make sure that the music fits the important moments in the movie exactly.

To switch between these two displays, click to the left of these digits, where you see the tiny clock (absolute time) or musical note (measures:beats).

Note: As you work, remember to save your project file every few minutes (choose File→Save, or press ⌘-S). The dark dot inside the window's red Close button (upper- eft) lets you know that your project has unsaved changes.

Measure/Beat/Sub-beat/"Tick"   Hour/Minute/Second/¹⁄₁₀₀₀ sec.

Click in this area to switch between measure display (left) and minutes

Method 1

Click, hold...   *...and carefully drag upward.*

Method 2

Double-click a number to make it blink.   *Type the new number, and then press Enter or Return.*

Figure 25-8:
Top: The Time display can show either musical time or in stopwatch time.

Middle: The Time display is also a navigation tool. Method 1: Click a number, but keep the mouse button pressed. Now drag up or down to make the number bigger or smaller.

Bottom: In Method 2, double-click a number (which now begins to blink), type new numbers, press the right or left arrow key to jump to the next number, and so on. Press Return or Enter. Either way, the Play-head jumps immediately to the point you specified.

Software Instruments (MIDI)

As you know from the previous chapters, GarageBand's loops can provide hours of fun and profit even if you don't have a lick of musical training. If you have some semblance of musical chops, though, GarageBand can quickly take you to the next level of creativity. It can record your live keyboard performances, whether you're a painstaking, one-note-at-a-time plunker or a veteran of Carnegie Hall.

To generate the notes that GarageBand records, you can play either an external musical keyboard or an onscreen one. Either way, the cool part is that you can combine your own performances with GarageBand's other tools. For example, some people use GarageBand's loops to create a rhythm section—a backup band—and then they record a new solo on top. Other people ignore the loops altogether and play all of the parts themselves, one instrument at a time, using GarageBand as a multitrack "tape recorder."

Anything you record like this shows up in *green* GarageBand regions. If you made it through Chapter 25, you now know that these regions contain MIDI information (that is, note data that you can edit). If you played a wrong note, no biggie—just drag it onto a different pitch, or delete it altogether. If your rhythm wasn't perfect, so what? No human being's rhythm is perfect (at least compared to a computer's), not even that of rock star millionaires. GarageBand can fix it for you.

How to Feed a Hungry GarageBand

To record a musical performance in this way, you need some way to feed GarageBand a stream of live musical data. You can do so in any of several ways: use the onscreen keyboard, use your Mac's keyboard as piano keys, or connect an actual electronic keyboard. The following pages take you through these three methods.

Your FREE! Onscreen Digital Piano

When you fire up a new GarageBand document (on a Mac with no physical MIDI keyboard connected), the GarageBand keyboard appears automatically in a floating window. This onscreen piano is a gift from Apple to people who would like to record notes of their own (instead of just using loops), but don't own a physical MIDI keyboard (Figure 26-1).

Scroll to lower octaves

Scroll to higher octaves

Click higher for softer "key presses," lower for "harder" playing

Drag to reveal more keys

Figure 26-1:
You can make this keyboard appear at any time by pressing ⌘-K (or, if you're charging by the hour, choosing Window→Keyboard). Hide it by clicking its tiny upper-left Close button.

Clicking the keys of this little keyboard with your mouse plays the instrument sound of whatever Software Instrument (green) track is currently selected. (The corresponding instrument name appears at the top of the keyboard.)

The onscreen keyboard is a pretty bare-bones beast. For example, it lets you play only one note at a time.

MUSIC CLASS

A Different Kind of Velocity

As you get to know GarageBand, and as you get to know the language of electronic music, you'll encounter one term with increasing frequency: velocity or key velocity.

That's a measurement of how hard you struck the keys of your MIDI controller or synthesizer. After all, GarageBand is required to notice and record that information; if it didn't, how could it play back what you recorded with perfect accuracy?

Now, if you're like most people, your first question is: "Um, why don't they just say volume? I mean, the harder you hit the key, the louder it plays, right?"

And that's where things get tricky. It's true that on a piano, hitting the keys harder makes the music louder. In fact, most

of the instrument sounds in GarageBand work like that.

But in the wacky world of computerized music, your key velocity might not affect the loudness of the note. It might change the quality of the sound instead, or even what notes are played.

For example, in most of GarageBand's acoustic-guitar sounds (Auditorium Acoustic, for one), pressing a key harder adds a little slide into the note—a grace note, a glissando up the fretboard from the next lower note. In the Fuzz Clav sound, banging harder gives the notes more of an Austin Powers-era "wah wah" sound.

In short, "velocity" means the velocity of your finger coming down on the key. It says nothing about the resulting sound, which is just the way MIDI linguists like it.

But the onscreen keyboard also harbors two secrets that you might not discover on your own. First, it actually has more keys than the 88 of a real piano—well over 10 octaves' worth of keys! To reveal the keyboard's full width, drag its lower-right ribbed resize handle. Or just scroll the keyboard by clicking the tiny gray triangles on either end.

Second, you can actually control how hard you're "playing" the keys. No, not by mashing down harder on the mouse button. Instead, you control the pressure on the keys by controlling the position of your mouse when it clicks. Click higher up on the key to play softer; click lower down to play harder.

Playing harder usually means playing louder, but not always. Depending on the Software Instrument you've picked, hitting a key harder may change the *nature* of the sound, not the volume.

For instructions on using the onscreen keyboard to record, skip ahead to page 519.

The Mac Keyboard as Piano

It's nice that Apple provided a little onscreen keyboard so that even the equipment-deprived can listen to GarageBand's amazing sound collection. But you'll never make it to the Grammy Awards using nothing but that single-note, mouse-driven display.

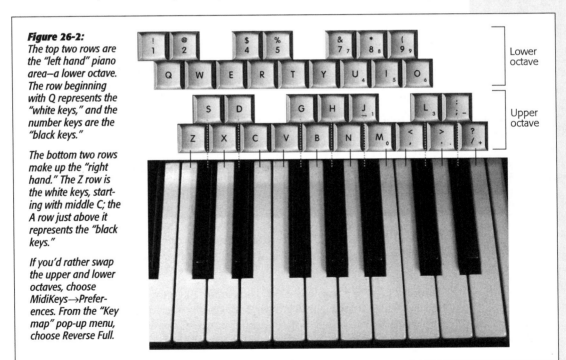

Figure 26-2:
The top two rows are the "left hand" piano area—a lower octave. The row beginning with Q represents the "white keys," and the number keys are the "black keys."

The bottom two rows make up the "right hand." The Z row is the white keys, starting with middle C; the A row just above it represents the "black keys."

If you'd rather swap the upper and lower octaves, choose MidiKeys→Preferences. From the "Key map" pop-up menu, choose Reverse Full.

Fortunately, a program called MidiKeys costs the same as the GarageBand keyboard ($0), but lets you trigger notes by playing, rather than clicking. You can download MidiKeys from the "Missing CD" page at *www.missingmanuals.com*.

MidiKeys turns your *Mac* keyboard into a *piano* keyboard, as shown in Figure 26-3.

MidiKeys takes some getting used to. Nonetheless, it's a powerful tool for scratching out GarageBand pieces—chords and all—when you're on a plane, on a bus, in bed, and anywhere else where lugging along an external keyboard would get you arrested, expelled, or divorced.

MIDI Synths and Controllers

The best way to record keyboard performances, though, is to bite the bullet, break the bank, and buy an actual, external musical instrument. It might take any of these forms:

- **A MIDI controller.** MIDI (pronounced "middy"), you may recall, stands for *musical instrument digital interface*. It's an electronic language that lets musical equipment and computers communicate over a cable.

  Because your Mac is perfectly capable of playing any of hundreds of musical-instrument sounds (like the ones built into GarageBand), you don't really need an electronic keyboard that can *produce* sounds; all you really need is one that can *trigger* them.

  That's the point of a MIDI *controller;* it looks and feels like a synthesizer keyboard, but produces no sounds of its own. It makes music only when it's plugged into, for example, a Mac running GarageBand.

  Apple sells (or, rather, resells) a MIDI controller for $100 called the M-Audio Keystation 49e. If you can live with 49 keys, it's a very nice keyboard. It draws its power directly from your USB jack, so you don't need a power adapter, and it's *velocity-sensitive,* which means that its keys are touch-sensitive. The harder you play, the louder the piano sound, for example.

- **A MIDI synthesizer.** If you already own a MIDI synth—an electronic keyboard that provides an assortment of sounds and has MIDI connectors on the back—there's no point in buying a MIDI controller. You can connect the keyboard directly to your Mac and use it the same way, and simply ignore the keyboard's own sound banks.

- **Another MIDI instrument.** Keyboards aren't the only MIDI instruments. There are also such things as MIDI guitars, MIDI drum sets, and even MIDI gloves. They, too, generate streams of note information that GarageBand can record and play back.

Once you've hooked up a MIDI instrument, create a Software Instrument track and try playing a few notes. You'll hear whatever sound you established for that track, and you'll see the little MIDI activity "light" blinking in GarageBand's time display. Now you're ready to record.

Tip: An external instrument is also great when it's time to *choose* a sound for a new track, because you can walk through the various instrument names without ever having to close the Track Info dialog box. See Figure 26-3 for more information.

Figure 26-3:
This dialog box appears when you choose Track→New Track. These instrument sounds all look delicious, but how are you supposed to know which one sounds exactly right for your piece? Simple: Press a few keys on your MIDI controller (or, if you're using MidiKeys, the bottom row of your keyboard). Use your arrow keys to "walk" through the instrument list, and "play" a few more keys to hear the next sound.

Recording a MIDI Track

Whether your keyboard is on the screen or on your desk, virtual or physical, you use it to record in GarageBand the same way. Here's the routine:

1. **Click the track you want to fill with music.**

    Remember, it must be a Software Instrument (green) track.

    If you don't already have a green track ready to record, choose Track→New Track to create one. In the New Track (Track Info) dialog box, click the Software Instrument tab, and then choose the instrument sound you want (Figure 26-3). Click OK.

2. **Turn on the metronome, if you like.**

    A *metronome* is a steady beat clicker that's familiar to generations of musicians. By clicking away "1, 2, 3, 4! 1, 2, 3, 4!" it helps to keep you and GarageBand in sync.

    Use the Control→Metronome command, or the ⌘-U keystroke, to turn the metronome clicker on or off. (See the box below.)

Tip: On the General pane of GarageBand→Preferences, you can indicate whether or not you want the metronome to play during *playback,* or only when you're recording.

3. Choose a tempo for recording.

This is a very important step. Because you're using a *sequencer* (recording software) instead of a tape recorder, it makes no difference how slowly you record the part. You can *record* at 60 beats per minute, for example, which is basically one note per second—and then *play back* the recording at a virtuosic "Flight of the Bumblebee" tempo (229 beats per minute, say). Your listeners will never be the wiser.

This isn't cheating; it's exploiting the features of your music software. It's a good bet, for example, that quite a few of the pop songs you hear on the radio were recorded using precisely this trick.

So how do you find a good tempo for recording? First, just noodle around on your keyboard. Find a speed that feels comfortable enough that the music maintains *some* momentum, but is still slow enough that you can make it through the part without a lot of mistakes.

When Not to Use the Metronome

GarageBand is perfectly capable of recording a keyboard performance without clicking away at you with its metronome. In fact, there's a very good reason you may not want the metronome turned on: If the piece you intend to play speeds up and slows down with the mood and the spirit. In those musical situations, a rigid, inflexible tempo would rob your music of all its spontaneity and feeling.

Of course, playing without the metronome means that your sense of where the beats and measures fall won't correspond with GarageBand's. Your measure 1, 2, and 3 won't line up with the beat ruler at the top of the GarageBand window.

That's not necessarily a bad thing. Listen to "03-Expressive Tempo," for example. (It's one of the songs on the Garage-Band Examples CD—see page 474.) It's a perfectly lovely piece. True, its beats and measures are all out of whack with GarageBand's sense of beats and measures. But when people listen to the music, they'll never know or care.

Playing without the metronome does mean, however, sacrificing some very useful GarageBand features. For one thing, you may find it difficult to add another track to the same piece. It's hard to play together with a free-form, flexible-tempo track that you've already recorded.

You lose much of the drag-and-drop region-editing flexibility described in Chapter 25, too. Remember how GarageBand regions' ends snap neatly against the underlying grid of beats and measures? If your more expressive grid doesn't align with GarageBand's, you're out of luck.

Finally, you won't be able to adjust the rhythm of your performance using GarageBand's Fix Timing button (page 535).

In more expensive recording programs (like Digital Performer, for example), you can actually teach the program to follow your own expressive tempo curve as you speed up and slow down; that is, you can make its conception of beats match what you play.

GarageBand, however, is a much more basic program that offers no way to automate a tempo change in the course of a piece. If you're trying to record anything that's more expressive than, say, a typical pop or rap song, you may be forced to go off the grid.

Then adjust the GarageBand tempo slider to match. Hit the Space bar to play the music you've already got in place, if any, and adjust the Tempo control (page 474) during the playback until it matches the foot-tapping in your head.

Tip: If you haven't recorded *any* music, one way to hear the tempo as you fiddle with the Tempo control is to turn the metronome on during playback, as described in the preceding tip. Then play back your empty song, using the clicks as your guide while you adjust the Tempo slider.

Once you've found a good recording speed, stop playback.

4. **Position the Playhead to the spot where you want to begin recording.**

   If that's the beginning, great; just press the letter Z key or the Home key. If it's in the middle of the piece, click in the beat ruler or use the keyboard shortcuts (page 476) to position the Playhead there. (Most often, though, you'll want to put the Playhead a couple of measures before the recording is supposed to begin, as described in the next step.)

5. **Set up your countoff.**

   It's very difficult to begin playing with the right feeling, volume, and tempo from a dead stop. That's why you always hear rock groups (and garage bands) start each other off with, "And a-one! And a-two!" That's also why most orchestras have a conductor, who gives one silent, preparatory beat of his baton before the players begin.

   GarageBand can "count you in" using either of two methods. First, it can play one measure full of beats, clicking "one, two, three, go!" at the proper tempo so you'll know when to come in. That's the purpose of the Control→Count In command. When this command has a checkmark, GarageBand will count you in with those clicks.

   If you intend to begin playing in the middle of existing music, though, you may prefer to have the music itself guide you to your entrance. This is the second method. For example, you might decide to plant the Playhead a couple of measures *before* the spot where you want to record. As long as doing so won't record over something that's already in your track, this is a convenient way to briefly experience the "feel" or "groove" of the music before you begin playing.

6. **Get ready to play—hands on the keyboard—and then click the red, round Record button.**

   Or just press the letter R key on your Mac keyboard.

   Either way, you hear the countoff measure, if you've requested one, and then the "tape" begins to roll. Give it your best, and try to stay in sync with the metronome, if you've turned it on.

7. **When you come to the end of the section you hoped to record—it might be the entire piece, or maybe just a part of it—tap the Space bar (or click the Play button) to stop recording.**

On the screen, you'll see the new green region you recorded.

8. Play back your recording to see how you did.

Rewind to the spot where you started recording. If you recorded *under tempo* (that is, slower than you intend the playback to be), boost the tempo slider to a better setting. (Because you recorded a stream of MIDI note information and did not record actual digital audio, you can adjust the playback tempo at any time without changing the pitch of the notes. You couldn't get an "Alvin and the Chipmunks" effect if you tried.)

Tap the Space bar to hear your performance played back just as you recorded it.

Tip: Do what the pros do: Record a section at a time. The odds of a good take are much greater when the segment is short. Remember, too, that if your song contains repeating sections, you can reuse one perfect take by copying and pasting it to a different spot in the song.

Retakes

The beauty of a MIDI sequencer like GarageBand is that you can keep your take, redo it, or trash it, instantly and guilt-free, having used up no tape or studio time.

Here's how to proceed after recording a MIDI performance:

• **Trash the whole thing.** If the whole thing stank, press ⌘-Z to trigger the Edit→ Undo command. The new green region disappears. Adjust the tempo, if necessary, and try recording again.

Note: Before you go nuts deleting "bad" performances, remember that it's sometimes more efficient just to manually fix what was wrong with it, using the GarageBand track editor. See page 529.

Figure 26-4:
Top: You've recorded this take twice, with mixed results each time.

Middle: Suppose the middle section of the second take was the best performance. Chop off both ends.

Bottom: Drag the remaining middle section upward onto the first take; this obliterates the corresponding moments of the first take. The result: A hybrid final track containing the best portions of each recording.

- **Trash part of it.** Use the Edit→Split command to cut the region into pieces, so that you can preserve the good parts but rerecord the bad ones.

- **Keep it.** If the whole thing was great, or mostly great, save your file (⌘-S) and move on to the next track.

- **Mark it "best so far."** Press the letter M key to mute the track you just recorded. Then create a new track and repeat the entire process, hoping to do better this time. After this second attempt—or your third, fourth, or fifth—you can compare your various takes by muting and un-muting them as they play back. You can also chop up these various regions and use only the best parts of each attempt, yet another extremely common practice in professional recording studios (Figure 26-4).

Tip: One great way to create a new track for the next attempt is to duplicate the first one (choose Track Duplicate→Track). GarageBand creates a new, empty track just below the first one—with the same instrument sound and effects (reverb and so on) already selected.

Spot Recording (Punch In/Punch Out)

If you're able to record an entire song perfectly the first time, with no mistakes—well, congratulations. Sony Records is standing by.

Most people, though, wind up wishing they could redo at least part of the recording. Usually, you played most of it fine, but botched a few parts here and there.

In the professional recording business, patching over the muffed parts is so commonplace, it's a standard part of the studio ritual. Clever studio software tools can play back the track right up until the problem section, seamlessly slip into Record mode while the player replays it, and then turn off Record mode when it reaches the end of the problem part, all without missing a beat. Recording engineers call this *punching in and out.*

Believe it or not, even humble GarageBand lets you punch in and punch out. Once you master this technique, you'll be very grateful.

Here's how it goes:

1. **Turn on cycling.**

   Page 475 describes *cycling* in the context of playing a section of music over and over again. For recording, the steps are much the same (see Figure 26-5). In this case, though, the beginning and end of the yellow Cycle bar designate your punch-in and punch-out points—the part you're going to rerecord.

2. **Set up your metronome and tempo. Turn on the Count In command (in the Control menu).**

   In this case, Count In is very important; it makes GarageBand play the one measure of music that precedes your punch-in point. (You don't have to position the Playhead for this exercise. Whenever Cycling is turned on, the Playhead always snaps to the beginning of the yellow stripe when playing or recording begins.)

3. Begin recording (by pressing the letter R key, for example).

During the countoff measure, you don't just hear metronome clicks—you also hear the *existing* music in that preceding measure. GarageBand begins recording after the countoff, as the Playhead reaches the yellow cycle area.

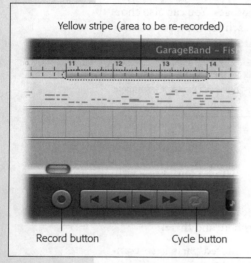

Yellow stripe (area to be re-recorded)

Record button

Cycle button

Figure 26-5:
Click the Cycle button—or press the letter C key—to make the yellow "repeat this much" bar appear at the top of the screen. Drag the ends of the yellow bar to identify the musical section you'll be loop-recording. (If you don't see the yellow bar, or if you want it to appear in a totally different section of the piece, drag through the lower section of the beat ruler.)

As you record, you'll also hear the *old* material—the part you're trying to rerecord. Don't worry, though; it will disappear after you replace it. (If it bothers you, delete it manually before punching in.)

GarageBand doesn't play past the end of the yellow bar. Instead, it loops back to the beginning of the yellow bar and keeps right on recording. (This loop-record feature is the key to *cumulative recording,* described next.) If you nailed it on the first take, just stop playing.

4. Press the Space bar (or click the Play button) to stop recording.

When you play back the piece, GarageBand flows seamlessly from your original take to the newly recorded "patch" section.

Tip: This punch-in/punch-out routine is the only way to go if your goal is to rerecord precisely measured sections.

When the parts you want to rerecord have nicely sized "bookends" of silence before and after, though, there's a more casual method available. Just play the piece from the beginning—and "ride" the letter R key on your keyboard. With each tap, you jump into and out of Record mode as the piece plays. This *manual* punch-in/punch-out method offers another way to record over the bad sections and preserve the good ones.

Cumulative Recording

GarageBand's tricks for people with less-than-stellar musical ability don't stop with the slow-tempo-recording trick and the ability to rerecord certain sections. The Cycle button described earlier is also the key to cumulative recording, in which you record *one note* at a time, or just a few, building up more complexity to the passage as GarageBand loop-records the same section over and over (Figure 26-6).

Figure 26-6:
Using GarageBand's Cycle feature, you can record the same section of music over and over, adding more notes on each pass. Here, you see the music from three successive loops through the same three-measure section; with each repetition, you add more notes to what you've already recorded.

First pass (bass drum)

Second pass (add snare)

Third pass (add hi-hat)

This trick is especially useful for laying down drum parts. In real life, drummers are surrounded by different kinds of drums; they're constantly reaching out and twisting to hit the different instruments at different times.

When you want to perform your *own* drum parts, you'll probably be using a MIDI keyboard. It turns out that GarageBand's various drum sounds—bass drum, snare drum, tom-toms, and so on—are "mapped" to the various keys of the keyboard (see Figure 26-7). Unless you have an extraordinarily unusual limb structure, you'll probably find it very difficult to play all the drums you want in a single pass, since they're scattered all over the keyboard.

It's much easier to record drum parts in successive passes, as GarageBand continues to record: the bass drum the first time, the snare on the next pass, and so on.

Here's how to set up loop recording:

1. **Turn on cycling.**

   See step 1 of the preceding instructions. Figure 26-5 explains how to adjust the yellow Cycle bar. The point here is to "highlight" the portion of music you want to record.

2. **Set up the recording.**

   Adjust the metronome, the Count In option, and the tempo, just as described in the previous pages. If you plan to record in the middle of a piece, place the Playhead to the left of the cycled region to give yourself a running start. (GarageBand will be in playback-only mode until it reaches the yellow Cycle bar.)

Click a track header to indicate which track you want to record. If you intend to lay down a drum track, fool around with your keyboard to identify which key plays which drum sounds. (The basic setup for GarageBand's drum kit is shown in Figure 26-7.)

Figure 26-7:
Cumulative recording is especially useful for drum parts, because it lets you focus on only one drum sound at a time. This diagram illustrates how GarageBand's drums are mapped to the keys of your keyboard. (The different drum kits are all mapped identically, although what constitutes a snare or a low tom in the Jazz kit may not sound anything like the one in the Techno kit.)

The bass drum (kick drum), snare, and ride cymbals are the foundation of most drum parts, so these may be the keys you want to "ride" with three fingers as you record.

3. **Click the Record button (or press the letter R).**

Each time GarageBand plays through the yellow-striped section, it will record any notes you play. Remember, GarageBand accumulates *all* the notes you play, adding them to the piece even if you play them on different repetitions of the looped passage.

Tip: It's OK to let a pass or two go by without playing anything. You just haven't added anything to the recording in progress, so no harm done. In fact, you might want to consider routinely sitting out a couple of repetitions between recording bursts.

Each time GarageBand loops back to the beginning of the section, you'll notice that it's already playing back what you laid down on previous passes. And when you finally stop (tap the Space bar) and play back the new passage, you'll discover that every note you played during the various repetitions plays back together.

Tip: Believe it or not, you can stop the playback, listen, do other work on your piece, and return much later to add yet another layer of cumulative-recording notes—as long as you haven't disturbed the yellow cycling bar in the beat ruler. Once you move that yellow stripe or turn off cycling, GarageBand ends your chance to record additional material in that region. The next recording you make there will wipe out whatever's there.

Mod Wheels and Other MIDI Fun

Many of GarageBand's built-in sounds are *samples*—brief recordings of actual instruments. That's why the grand piano sounds so realistic: because it *is* a grand piano (a $50,000 Yamaha, to be exact).

But behind the scenes, GarageBand's sounds have been programmed to respond to various impulses beyond just pressing the keys. They can change their sounds depending on what other MIDI information GarageBand receives from your keyboard.

For example:

- **Sustain pedal.** If you have a sustain or damper pedal, you can ride it with your foot just as you would on a piano. (It's designed to hold a note or a chord even after your hands have released the keys.) Almost any MIDI keyboard—including the $100 M-Audio Keystation—has a jack on the back for a sustain pedal, which costs about $15 from online music stores like *www.samash.com.*

- **Key velocity.** As noted earlier in this chapter, a number of GarageBand sounds respond to key velocity (that is, how hard you strike the keys). Most of the instrument sounds just play louder as you hit the keys harder, but some actually change in character. Acoustic guitars feature a little fingerboard slide; clavichords get more of a "wah" sound; Wah Horns also "wah" more; and many of the synthesizer keyboard sounds sound "rounder" as you hit the keys harder.

  Using the correct technical language, you would say that these instruments are velocity-sensitive.

- **Pitch and mod wheels.** Some keyboards, including that $100 M-Audio controller that Apple sells, have one or two *control wheels* that also affect GarageBand's sounds (Figure 26-8).

  For example, a *pitch bend* wheel makes a note's pitch slide up or down while you're still pressing the key. It's an essential tool for anyone who wants to make brass or wind instruments sound more realistic, since those instruments are capable of sliding seamlessly from pitch to pitch—something a keyboard, with its series of fixed-pitch keys, can't ordinarily do.

You can use the pitch wheel in either of two ways. First, turn the wheel downward, for example, and hold it (it's spring-loaded). Then, play the key you want—and simultaneously release the key. What you hear is a slide *up* to the desired note.

Figure 26-8:
On the M-Audio MIDI controller keyboards that Apple sells, two control wheels liven up the MIDI proceedings. The pitch-bend wheel actually bends the note's pitch. Just turn the wheel either before or after striking the note, depending on the effect you want. The modulation wheel, meanwhile, produces sound-changing effects, or does nothing, depending on the GarageBand sound you've selected.

Second, you can strike the key first and *then* turn the wheel, or even wiggle the wheel up and down. The sound winds up wiggling or bending away from the original note, which is a common technique when you're trying to simulate, for example, the bending notes of a blues harmonica.

Tip: You can hear these effects in the sample file called 04-Control Wheels. It's on the GarageBand Examples CD described on page 474.

The pitch wheel affects *all* GarageBand sounds.

• Your keyboard may also have a *mod wheel*, short for modulation wheel. It's an all-purpose control wheel that produces different effects in different sounds. For example, the mod wheel brightens the bass instruments, produces a vibrato (pretty wavering) in choir, horn, and string sounds, and "sweeps" the phase of synthesizer sounds.

Learning to use your mod wheel can add a great deal of beauty, realism, and grace to your GarageBand recordings. Note, in particular, that you don't have to turn it all the way up; you can turn the wheel only part way for a more subtle effect. Remember, too, that the mod wheel is usually most effective when you turn it *after* the note has begun sounding. It's the contrast of the mod wheel (versus the unaffected note) that produces the best effect.

Editing Software Instrument Parts

Recording MIDI data, as described above, has a huge advantage over recording with a microphone: The results are almost infinitely *editable*. For example, you can delete wrong notes or drag them onto the right ones. If you played a section too loud, you can lighten it up after the fact. You can change the tempo or key of the music, making it faster, slower, higher, or lower, without distortion. If you discover a more appropriate instrument sound for a certain part, you can reassign the whole part.

In fact, GarageBand even lets you edit the invisible data generated by the foot pedal and control wheels.

The key to all of this freedom is the nature of the recordings you make with a MIDI keyboard: GarageBand stores your performance as a series of scheduled note triggers. When you play back your piece, GarageBand plays its own built-in synthesizer in real time. It's not playing back a sound recording.

The Track Editor

The doorway to all of this editing magic is the Track Editor, shown in Figure 26-9.

You can open this window in any of several ways:

- **Double-click a green region in the timeline.** This is the best way to open the Track Editor, because it appears prescrolled to the notes in the region you clicked.

- **Click the scissors icon (✂) beneath the track headers.** The Track Editor opens to the beginning of the first region on the track.

- **Choose Control→Show Editor, or press ⌘-E.** Once again, the Track Editor opens to the beginning of the track.

Figure 26-9:
The Track Editor reveals a close-up of your MIDI performance. Like an old-time piano roll, it resembles a grid. Time goes by horizontally, while the bars indicate the recorded notes on a vertical grid representing pitch. (The little piano-keys "ruler" at left should help you gain your bearings.)

Open/close Advanced panel

Beat ruler

Drag upward here to enlarge Editor

Playhead Lock

Zoom slider

Note bars

Grid ruler pop-up menu

Tip: When the Editor window first appears, it shows only about an octave's worth of vertical space. Fortunately, you can drag upward on GarageBand's dark gray "brushed metal" divider strip–see Figure 26-9–to double the Editor's height. (You might remember having to do this when using the Loop browser, too. Unfortunately, you'll have to do it again each time you open GarageBand.)

Once you know your way around the Editor window, the editing itself is very easy. You can tug on the little note bars with your mouse to move, stretch, or shrink them. More about this in a moment.

For now, gain your bearings by noticing these controls:

- **Note bars.** These are the notes in the green MIDI region. (MIDI regions can be either GarageBand loops or music you've recorded yourself, as described in this chapter.) Longer bars represent longer notes.

  Darker bars represent notes with greater *key velocity*—that is, keys that were hit harder. The lighter the shade of gray, the lighter that note was played.

- **Beat ruler.** These are the same measures of your piece that are represented by the beat ruler at the top of the GarageBand window.

  But in designing the Track Editor, Apple's programmers faced a quandary. Should this Track Editor window be matched to the timeline area above it, so that when you scroll the top window, the Track Editor scrolls too? Or should you be able to scroll the top and bottom parts of the GarageBand window independently?

  As it turns out, Apple gives you a choice (read on).

- **Playhead Lock button.** When this little icon looks like this ⚏, you can scroll the Track Editor independently of the main GarageBand window. In fact, during playback, the Playhead in the Track Editor screen may chug merrily right off the screen. In this situation, GarageBand scrolls automatically only when the *upper* Playhead hits the edge of your window.

  But when you click the icon so that it looks like this ⚏, both parts of the window scroll together. The Playhead line moves across (and autoscrolls) both parts of the window.

- **Zoom slider.** You can see more of the song at once in the Time Editor by dragging this slider to the left, which causes the beat ruler (and all the notes) to get smaller. To zoom in for finer editing, drag the slider handle to the right, which makes the ruler and the note bars grow.

Tip: You don't have to drag the little slider's handle. It's often faster simply to click *in* the slider. The handle jumps to the spot of your click. (In fact, this tip applies to *all* GarageBand sliders.)

- **Scroll bars.** These scroll bars work like any Macintosh scroll bars, but they're especially important in the Track Editor. If you open the Editor using either the scissors icon or the Show Editor command, the Track Editor window often appears to be completely *blank*. It opens to some portion of the track that has no notes in it.

You're left to wonder whether the notes are higher or lower than what's currently on display, or sooner or later. In both of those situations, you'll wind up doing a lot of scrolling.

This sense of Editor disorientation is a good argument for opening it using the first method described above: by double-clicking a region in the timeline.

Tip: You can also scroll the Track Editor by dragging your cursor through it in the direction you want to go. (Avoid beginning your drag directly on a note bar, though.)

- **Advanced panel.** You can read about the editing controls of this panel in the following pages. For now, just note the tiny triangle that opens and—when you need more space—closes it, as identified in Figure 26-9.

- **Grid ruler pop-up menu.** This little + menu works just as it does in the Timeline window. It's a list of basic rhythmic values (1/4 Note, 1/2 Note, and so on) that adjusts the fine vertical grid lines in the Track Editor.

This rhythmic grid comes into play in several situations. First, the beginnings and endings of your note bars automatically snap against these gridlines when you drag, as described below. Second, GarageBand makes *all* selected notes snap to the nearest gridline when you use the Fix Timing command (page 535). Third, this setting determines the value of any new notes you create by ⌘-clicking, as described in the next section.

The Encyclopedia of MIDI Editing

Now that you know how to navigate the Track Editor, you can get down to the business of using it to rewrite history: changing the recorded music.

Note: Any edits you make to a MIDI region that you've *looped* (by dragging its upper-right corner) appear in *all repetitions* of that loop, which may take you by surprise.

If you'd like to edit only *one* repetition, create it by copying and pasting the original region, so that it's no longer related to the original.

- **Hear a note** by clicking it. (Clicking a note bar also turns it bright green to show that it's selected.)

- **Delete a selected note** by pressing the Delete key.

- **Change a note's pitch** by dragging its note bar up or down, using the center of the note bar as a handle. (If the note won't seem to budge, try zooming in. GarageBand probably considered the note bar too small to make a decent handle.)

- **Shorten or lengthen a note** by dragging the right end of its bar. You'll discover that GarageBand forces the note's end to align with the current note grid, described above. (Once again, try zooming in if you're having trouble.)

Note: You can't shorten a note from its left side. If your intention is to lop off the "front" of a note, drag the entire note, as described next, and then shorten the *right* side.

- **Make a note play sooner or later** by dragging its center horizontally.

  You'll notice that as you drag a note, it snaps to the next rhythmic grid line (quarter note, eighth note, or whatever value you've selected from the Grid Ruler pop-up menu shown in Figure 26-9). That's GarageBand's attempt to help keep your music in sync.

  If you'd like to be able to drag freely, choose Control→Snap to Grid (⌘-G), so that the checkmark no longer appears.

- **Duplicate a note** by Option-dragging its bar. This trick works whether you drag vertically or horizontally.

- **Insert a new note** by ⌘-clicking at the appropriate spot. (As soon as you press the ⌘ key, the cursor turns into a little pencil to let you know what's about to happen.)

  Use the vertical, left-side piano keyboard ruler as a guide to pitch, and the beat ruler to help you figure out where you are in the song.

  You'll soon discover, by the way, that you can't ⌘-*drag* to determine the length of the note you insert. Every new note you create has the same duration. That value (eighth note, for example) is determined by the setting in the Grid Ruler pop-up menu shown in Figure 26-9.

  You can always adjust a note's length once it appears in the Track Editor, of course, by dragging its right end. But when you intend to insert a bunch of notes of similar value, it's worth taking the time to select that duration from the Grid Ruler pop-up menu first.

Tip: Very often, the fastest way to create a new note is not to use the ⌘-click trick at all. Instead, Option-drag an existing note bar to duplicate it; then, before you release the mouse, move it to the proper pitch and time. The first advantage here is that you can duplicate a note that already has the duration and velocity you want; the second is that you can duplicate a *batch* of selected notes at once.

- **Select a few notes** by clicking one, then Shift-clicking each additional note. (Shift-click a second time to remove a note bar from the selected group.)

- **Select a lot of notes** by dragging a selection box around them (Figure 26-10).

  Either way, once you've selected notes, you can perform several editing maneuvers to all of them at once. For example, you can cut or copy them (described next), delete them, Option-drag to duplicate them, stretch or shorten them (drag the right end of any *one* selected note bar), drag them up or down in pitch, drag them left or right in time, and so on. They retain their original timings and relationships.

- **Cut/copy and paste notes to a different spot** by selecting them, choosing Edit→ Copy (⌘-C) or Edit→Cut (⌘-X), clicking in the Editor's beat ruler to place the Playhead, and then choosing Edit→Paste (⌘-V). The notes you copied or cut appear at the Playhead position.

GarageBand *adds* pasted notes to whatever already occupies the paste position, rather than wiping out what's there.

Figure 26-10:
To select a batch of notes, begin dragging diagonally from a blank spot of the Track Editor. Your selection will include any note bar that's even partly enclosed by the resulting box.

When you drag them, they remain in perfect formation.

Transposing Notes or Regions

To *transpose* music means to shift it up or down into a different key, raising or lowering its pitch. The ability to transpose recordings and loops is a key advantage that Software Instruments (green) have over digital recordings from a microphone. You can also transpose Apple's own digital recordings (blue loops), although they sound funny if you move them too far from their originally recorded pitches.

Transposing is a very useful feature. For example, it lets you adapt a song that was in the perfect singing key for somebody else into the perfect singing key for *you*, without rerecording it. It also lets you reuse Apple's canned loops in other keys, greatly expanding your palette of chords and harmonies (see Figure 26-11).

Now, if you want to transpose only *some* of the notes in a green Software Instrument region, open the Track editor and use any of the selection techniques described in the previous section. Then drag them up or down, using any one of them as a handle.

The official GarageBand Transpose slider, though, works only on *entire regions*. It goes like this:

1. **Select the region you want to transpose.**

   If you've opened a region for editing in the Track Editor, GarageBand will transpose all of it, regardless of which notes are selected.

You can click a region in the timeline, select a number of regions simultaneously (Shift-click them in the timeline), select all the regions in a track (click the track header), or select the entire piece at once (click in the timeline area and then choose Edit→Select All, or press ⌘-A).

Advanced panel   C chord   C chord   F chord   C chord
                                      (transposed)

Figure 26-11:
The loop called Latin Lounge Piano 01 is a great little lick. The only problem is that it's a C major chord, now and forever. By transposing copies of this loop, though, you can turn it into any other major chord—F and G, for example—and thereby make it fit the harmonies of many harmonically simple compositions.

2. Open the Advanced panel, if necessary.

You open it by clicking the little triangle identified back in Figure 26-9.

3. Specify how far you want to transpose the region(s).

Use the Transpose slider—drag right to transpose the notes higher, left to make them play lower—or type a number into the box just above the slider.

Both of these controls display the number of *half steps* by which you're about to transpose the selected notes. (A half-step is one piano key to the right or left.)

For example, typing *1* here would transpose a middle C up to C sharp, which is the black key just to its right. If you type *2* here, you'd transpose a middle C up to D, the *white* key just to its right.

If you know a little bit about music, you may find the following equivalents handy: To transpose up a major third, enter *4*. Up a fourth, enter *5*. Up a perfect fifth, type *7*. Up an octave, enter *12*.

And to transpose the selection *down*, either drag the slider handle to the left, or type a *negative* number into the box (*-12* for an octave down, for example).

You can transpose green Software Instrument regions up to 36 half-steps in either direction (that is, three octaves up or down). You can transpose blue Real Instrument loops 12 half-steps up or down (one octave).

Tip: If you transpose a Real Instrument loop upward and it sounds a little funny—because you've shifted it out of its natural range—try transposing it down a whole octave, so that it lands on the same pitch but in a lower register.

For example, suppose you transpose a bass lick down 4 half-steps, from C to A flat, and it winds up sounding muddy. Think to yourself: *I transposed it by -4; what would be the equivalent pitch 12 half-steps higher? Well, -4 plus 12 = 8.* Drag the slider to 8, and sure enough, you get the same notes, but in a more natural-sounding range.

---

4. Remain calm.

What's slightly alarming about transposing in GarageBand is that there's *no visible change,* which is especially puzzling when it comes to green Software Instruments. You might expect to see the note bars move higher on the Editor grid when you transpose them upward, or lower when you transpose them downward. But instead, the note bars remain exactly where they are (Figure 26-10 proves the point). Blue loops don't look any different, either.

Even though they don't *look* different, they do *sound* different. Play back a section that you transposed, and you'll hear the difference immediately.

You'll just have to get used to the audio-visual disconnect.

Tip: If, much later in the editing process, you can't figure out why some notes don't seem to be playing on the proper pitches, click one of them. The Transpose slider reveals whether or not you've transposed the region.

If you ever want to restore a region to its original recorded pitch, select it and set the Transpose slider to its center position (or type *0* into the box above it).

Quantizing (Fix Timing)

When Apple representatives demonstrate GarageBand in public, the feature that often gets the most oohs and aahs from the audience is the Fix Timing button. With one quick click, it magically cleans up any recording that has less-than-perfect rhythm. What sounds at first a little ragged, a bit stumbling, suddenly plays back with clean, perfect timing.

Among computer-based musicians, the term for this cleanup is called *quantizing* or *quantization.* In GarageBand, you quantize your music using a button in the Track Editor called Fix Timing.

When you click this button, GarageBand automatically moves all of the notes in a region into perfect alignment with the underlying rhythm grid. In effect, it "rounds off" each note's attack to the nearest eighth note, sixteenth note, or whatever rhythmic value you've specified in the Grid Ruler pop-up menu.

When Not to Quantize

This all sounds wonderful, of course—who wouldn't want a magic button that makes you sound like a better player?—but quantizing is a delicate art. It *can* make your music sound better and cleaner. But it can also create a cacophonous mess.

Figure 26-12:
Top: These notes were supposed to be running sixteenth notes (four fast notes per beat), but they're not quite precise.

Bottom: One click on "Fix Timing" later, they're precise, all right, but they don't sound anything like the original music. They've turned into ugly, clomping chords.

(Part of the problem was the quarter-note grid—selected for comic purposes to make this point.)

Many musicians regard quantizing with a certain degree of skepticism. For one thing, if Fix Timing nudges some notes into alignment with the *wrong* gridlines, your recording may turn into a horrible sounding, clashing crash (Figure 26-12).

Furthermore, quantizing drains a lot of the humanity out of a performance. After all, the tiny quirks and inconsistencies are what give a performance its personality; they make a performance *yours*. When you make every note snap against a fixed-rhythm grid, the music can wind up sounding machine-generated and robotic.

Finally, quantizing flattens out musical effects like grace notes (a lightly played, very quick note right before the main note), glissandos (sliding down the keyboard with a finger), and rolled chords (rolling the hand through a chord rather than striking all notes of it at once). All of the notes in these musical figures get pushed to the nearest eighth-note or sixteenth-note gridline, thereby changing them from delicate special effects into clashing, wrong-note chords.

Tip: On the GarageBand Examples CD (page 474), listen to the file called 05-Quantizing. Double-click the piano region, set the Grid Ruler pop-up menu to "1/8 Note," and then click Fix Timing.

Let this sample file be a lesson about when *not* to use quantization.

How to Quantize

These downsides notwithstanding, quantizing can still be a very useful cleanup maneuver, especially in the kinds of rock, rap, and hip-hop music for which GarageBand is so well suited. Subtlety and nuance are not necessarily the most prized qualities in those styles.

Here's how to go about fixing the timing of your performance:

1. **Select the music you want to quantize.**

   To quantize an entire region, click its green, rounded rectangle in the timeline (and don't click inside the Track Editor). You can even select more than one region for quantizing just by Shift-clicking them, or an entire track by clicking its header. (You can't quantize more than one track at a time.)

   To quantize only some of the notes in a region, open the Track Editor and select the bars as described on page 531.

2. **Using the Grid Ruler pop-up menu (the tiny ruler icon just above the Editor window's vertical scroll bar), choose the kind of grid you want.**

   If you choose too large a value, like "1/4 Note," all of the faster notes in the region will wind up clumped around the quarter-note gridlines in big, ugly, clashing chords. But if you choose too fine a value, like "1/32 Note," then GarageBand may nudge some of your notes into alignment with the *wrong* gridline—for example, moving certain notes forward instead of backward where you meant them to go—resulting in a stuttering, halting disaster.

   The "correct" setting depends on the tempo of your piece, what kind of notes are in it, and the effect you're looking for. Experimentation is the only way to find a setting that works.

   Fortunately, if the Fix Timing button makes a mess of things, you can always choose Edit→Undo (⌘-Z) and try a different setting—or just drag the offending note bars into grid alignment by hand.

Velocity, Pedaling, and Other MIDI Data

As you've probably started to gather by now, there's more to a musical performance than deciding which notes to play when. A keyboard player, for example, adds nuance and interest to a performance using a number of other tools. The *velocity* of the playing (how hard each key is struck), the pedaling (using a sustain pedal connected to the keyboard), and the control wheels (pitch and modulation) can all affect the way the music sounds.

GarageBand records all of this information as you play and lets you edit it later. The key to viewing and editing these kinds of MIDI information is the Advanced panel of the Track Editor (Figure 26-13).

Figure 26-13:
To edit key velocity, first select the note or notes you want to affect, as shown here. Then, change their velocity using either the Velocity number box—type in a new number from 0 to 127—or the slider beneath it.

Open/close Advanced panel

Velocity number box and slider

Darker bars = struck harder

Editing Key Velocity

Key velocity is a digital record of how hard you pressed each key when you recorded a MIDI region. On some instruments, greater key velocity just means "louder," as it does on a piano. But in others, greater velocity means "more vibrato," "crunchier sound," and so on.

Key velocity is measured on a scale of 0 to 127, which may not seem like an especially logical scale to *you,* but (because it's a power of 2) it's very convenient for the Mac to understand. In any case, a velocity of 1 indicates a key pressed with all the force of a falling pigeon feather; a velocity of 127 reflects the force of, say, a second piano falling onto the first. (GarageBand doesn't actually let you change a note's velocity to 0, because that would be a nonsensical value for most musical purposes.)

In the Track Editor, a note bar's *color* indicates its key velocity, as you can see here:

Note color	Key velocity
Light gray	0–31
Medium gray	32–63
Dark gray	64–95
Black	96–127

To edit your notes' key velocities, see Figure 26-13.

Note: Things can get tricky when you've selected multiple notes with different velocities. In that case, the slider and the number box show the *highest* key velocity among the selected notes. But as you make the adjustment, you're adding or subtracting the *same* amount from all other notes.

If you select three notes, therefore, that have velocity settings of 20, 30, and 40, the Velocity box will say 40. If you drag the slider to shave 10 off the heaviest note, the first two notes will also have decreased by 10. The three notes will now have velocity settings of 10, 20, and 30.

By adjusting key velocities in this way, you can perform a number of different musical-surgical procedures:

• Make an entire *lick* (short musical passage) play with more emphasis. Or less.

• Change the "color" of a chord by lightening up on some notes, and bringing out others.

• Add vibrato to the *money note* (the highest, longest, most important note) of a flute solo.

• Edit an acoustic guitar part so that the sliding grace notes play only where you want them to. (When struck with a key velocity of 124 or higher, most GarageBand acoustic-guitar samples add a little sliding grace note upward from the next lower note.)

Editing Pedaling

If your MIDI keyboard has a sustain pedal—the electronic equivalent of the rightmost pedal on a regular piano—then GarageBand records your foot-presses right along with the key-presses. In the Track Editor, it draws a map of the ups and downs of the

Figure 26-14:
Don't be fooled: When the line is up, the sustain pedal is down, and vice versa. In the world of MIDI software, this particular graph is upside-down from the physical control—the foot pedal—that generates its data. That is, up is "on," and down is "off."

Pedal pressed

Pedal released

pedal, as shown in Figure 26-14. Each little ball represents one change in the sustain pedal's status.

You can use the Track Editor to edit pedaling you recorded during a performance, of course. But you can also use it to add pedaling to a performance that didn't have any to begin with—a performance you created using MidiKeys, for example.

Pedaling step by step

Either way, the steps are the same. (If you'd like to follow along, create a new document and insert the loop called Upbeat Electric Piano 03. Its notes are short and sharp, so you'll hear a clear difference when you start adding the sustain pedal.)

1. **Open the Advanced panel of the Track Editor.**

   You can see the little triangle to click for the Advanced panel in Figure 26-13.

2. **From the Display pop-up menu, choose Sustain.**

   You've just told GarageBand which invisible MIDI data you want to change.

3. **While pressing the ⌘ key, click a spot along the light gray, top line (labeled 1 in Figure 26-14).**

   GarageBand creates a round handle at the point you clicked. You've just created a "sustain pedal down" event where none existed. (Technically, you can click anywhere in the upper half of the Track Editor window, since GarageBand "rounds off" your click to the top line to indicate a full press of the foot pedal.)

   If you play back your region at this point, you'll hear all the notes get "stuck on" at the point where you created the pedal-down event. Unless you enjoy the cumulative, mushy, clashing sound of every note in the piece being held down forever, find a spot to *release* the sustain pedal:

4. **Move the cursor to the right, and then ⌘-click a spot on the bottom gray line.**

   Another round handle appears, this time indicating where your virtual player should take his foot off the pedal. A quick playback will prove the point.

Editing existing pedaling

If you've ever edited volume levels of an iMovie video soundtrack, these round handles should seem familiar. They're audio control points, which you can slide around to fine-tune where they appear.

For example, you can move or delete pedaling points exactly as you would the control points in an iMovie audio track. You can also ⌘-click **the top or bottom line** to introduce a new control point.

Control Wheel Data

As noted on page 527, many MIDI keyboards—including the $100 M-Audio keyboard that Apple sells as a companion for GarageBand—have one or two *control wheels* at the left side.

The Track Editor also lets you edit any pitch wheel or mod wheel information you generated while recording. It even lets you "turn" one of those wheels after the fact, even if you don't even have a keyboard with control wheels.

To inspect your control wheel data, open the region in the Track Editor, open the Advanced panel (Figure 26-13), and from the Display pop-up menu, choose either Pitchbend or Modulation. If pitch wheel or mod wheel information is already a part of the recording, you'll see something like Figure 26-15.

Note: As shown in Figure 26-15, pitch wheel effects usually involve turning the wheel *in between* notes, getting into ready position, and then releasing it, so that it returns to its spring-loaded "at rest" position *during* a note. Or you can do the opposite: Press a key, turn the pitch wheel up or down, and then release both together. Either way, don't be fooled by the up-down and down-up "hills" graphed in Figure 26-15; half of each "hill" actually takes place during the silence between notes.

Most people turn the mod wheel, the other hand, both up and down during a single note (to make the vibrato gradually begin and end, for example).

Figure 26-15:
When you're viewing pitch wheel information, as shown here, the ruler scale goes both upward and downward from 0, because a pitch wheel's "at rest" position is in the middle. You can turn it either up or down. A mod wheel's "at rest" position, though, is turned all the way down, and you turn it only upward, so its scale goes from 0 (at rest) to 127 (all the way up).

Pitch wheel is turned between notes, then released during the following note

Pitch wheel data is represented on a scale of 0 (when you're not touching the wheel) to positive or negative 63 (when you've turned the wheel as far as it will go); the mod wheel's scale goes from 0 (at rest) to 127 (turned all the way).

In the case of the pitch wheel, each notch (from 0 to 1, for example) represents one half-step, which is one adjacent key on a piano keyboard. That's useful to remember if you're inclined to add pitch wheel data to a recording manually (because your keyboard doesn't have wheels, for example).

Once you've got that fact in mind, the techniques for adjusting or creating wheel control points are very similar to the methods for working with sustain pedal data:

- ⌘-click in the Track Editor to create a new round control handle. This is how you'd start "turning" the wheel during a note even if you don't actually have a keyboard with wheels.

- Drag a control handle horizontally to change its timing, or vertically to adjust the intensity of its effect; see Figure 26-16. (Again, 0 means "wheel is at rest.")

Figure 26-16:
Most instruments' vibratos sound most realistic with the mod wheel turned up only part way—about 50 or so. For added realism, make the vibrato begin and end gradually, and don't begin the wheel turn until a moment after the note has been struck.

- Select a group of control handles to move them all at once; drag any *one* of them as a handle.

This tactic is especially useful when you want to edit pitch bend or mod wheel data in a track that you recorded live. As shown in Figure 26-15, using a control wheel during a live performance generates a *torrent* of control handles. Turning the wheel smoothly and gradually, as you would in a live performance, spits out dozens of control points (0-3-5-11-22-24, and so on). By dragging a whole batch of points at once, you can adjust the timing or intensity of a wheel turn with a single drag. The selected points retain their spatial relationship as you drag them.

- Delete a turn of the wheel by selecting all of the representative control points and then pressing the Delete key.

Real Instruments (Live Audio)

GarageBand is actually three programs in one. It's a loop-building program that lets anyone build great-sounding compositions, even with no musical training. It's a MIDI sequencing program that records whatever you play on a MIDI-compatible keyboard, guitar, or drum set. And now, as you're about to find out, it's also a digital multitrack tape recorder that can record live sound.

The beauty of GarageBand is that lets you layer these recordings *on top of* tracks that you've built using its other tools (like loops and MIDI performances), and play all of it back together at once. The creative possibilities that result are mind-blowing—and make possible a world where Joe Nobody, a guy with a great voice but no money, can produce a studio-caliber demo CD in his living room.

The Setup

GarageBand can record live audio from two kinds of sound inputs: microphones and direct line inputs (from electronic instruments like guitars and keyboards, audio interface boxes, and mixers).

The Microphone

To record singing, acoustic instruments, or the world around you, you'll need a microphone.

Note: Some acoustic guitars have built-in pickups. If yours does, you don't need a microphone; you can plug the guitar straight into an audio interface, as described next.

This mike can take any of several forms:

- **The built-in microphone on Mac laptops, iMacs, and eMacs.** The drawback of this approach is that you might also pick up the Mac's own fan sounds, and the quality isn't quite studio caliber. But it's cheap, it's built-in, and it works fine for everyday recordings.

- **A cheapo USB microphone.** At Amazon.com or Buy.com, you can pick up a microphone that plugs directly into your Mac's USB port for under $20. They come in two forms: Headset mikes, designed for use with speech-recognition software, and desktop mikes, which stick up, stalk-like, from a little stand on your desk. Both work great for recording vocals and—if you position them close to the sound source—acoustic instruments.

- **A regular microphone.** If you have access to a more professional microphone, then by all means, use it. You might run into two problems, though.

First, there's the little matter of fitting the microphone's cable into the Mac's tiny, 1/8-inch, Walkman-headphones miniplug microphone input (see Figure 27-1). If your microphone's cable ends in a 1/4-inch phono plug instead, or even a professional, nickel-sized XLR connector, the cheerful staff at your local Radio Shack will be happy to sell you an adapter. (At Apple's Web site and others, you can buy this adapter in the form of the $20 Monster iStudioLink.)

Adapter (XLR-to-1/4-inch phone plug)

Figure 27-1:
Adapting your microphone to the Mac may require more than one adapter. Here, a professional microphone (with an XLR connector on the end) connects to a plug adapter, which goes into a Griffin iMic for signal boosting. The iMic then plugs into the Mac's USB jack.

Adapter (1/4-inch phone plug to miniplug)

iMic (preamp and USB adapter)

Second, many microphones (and other sound sources, like record players and tape decks) don't put out enough signal for the Mac's microphone jack. You'll probably need a *preamp* to boost the signal to audible levels.

The most inexpensive option is the $40 Griffin iMic (*www.griffintechnology.com*), which offers not only a built-in preamp but also cleaner sound circuitry than what's built into the Mac. (It, too, is shown in Figure 27-1.)

For even more flexibility, you can use an *audio interface* box like the M-Audio MobilePre USB, which you can also find on the Apple Web site ($150). This more professional box offers three different kinds of input jacks for various microphones and instruments, including both microphone preamp inputs and high-impedance instrument inputs for guitars and basses.

Both the iMic and the MobilePre draw their power from the USB jack, so you don't even have to carry along a power adapter.

Line Inputs

If you have an electric guitar, electric violin, or synthesizer keyboard whose built-in sounds you want to capture, don't bother with the microphone. Instead, connect the instrument's line output cable (which would otherwise go into an amplifier) into an audio interface, like the iMic or M-Audio MobilePre described above. The audio interface then plugs into your Mac's USB port.

In more elaborate setups, you can even connect the outputs from a standalone mixing console. You'd do that if, for example, you wanted to record the playing from several live instruments at once into a single GarageBand track. (Of course, using a very basic program like GarageBand to record from thousands of dollars' worth of recording equipment in this way is a little like using iMovie to edit *Lord of the Rings,* but hey—whatever floats your boat.)

Because this cable is coming directly from a sound source and not from a microphone, it's called a *line input*.

Introducing the Mac

As you're starting to realize, the Mac is capable of recording sound from a number of different sources: its own built-in mike, an external mike, a line input, and so on. When the moment comes to click the Record button in GarageBand, how will the Mac know what to listen to?

You'll tell it ahead of time, that's how. Figure 27-2 shows the two-step procedure.

Recording a Live Audio Track

Once you're hooked up, recording a voice or electronic instrument is a lot like recording from a MIDI instrument as described in Chapter 26. In general, though, you'll spend a lot more time in the New Track (or Track Info) dialog box, telling GarageBand about the nature of the sound you're about to record.

Phase 1: Create the Track

What you want is a track that turns bluish when you click it. That's a *Real Instrument* track, as opposed to the green Software tracks described so far in this book.

Note: When you record digital audio, you create *purple* regions in the timeline. They're the same digital audio as GarageBand's blue, digital audio *loops,* and you work with them the same way; a single track can contain both blue and purple regions.

Still, the color-coding is a handy means of helping you tell *your* creations apart from Apple's canned ones. (Yours can't be transposed, sped up, or slowed down, for example.)

Figure 27-2:
Top: From the menu, choose System Preferences. Click the Sound icon; then click the Input tab. Specify which sound source you want to record (in this case, a microphone connected to the iMic adapter). Before you close this window, drag the slider to adjust the general volume level for your singing or playing. Ideally, the loudest notes should illuminate the rightmost dancing bars briefly. (The highest level bar "sticks on" for about a second to make it easier for you to spot your volume peaks, as shown here.)

Bottom: Now return to Garage-Band. Choose GarageBand→ Preferences, and click the Audio/MIDI tab. Using the Audio Input pop-up menu, check to make sure that the correct input is selected—that, in effect, GarageBand is prepared to listen using the correct "ear."

If you don't already have a digital audio track ready to record, there's a short way and a long way to go about creating one.

The short way is to choose Track→New Basic Track. You get a new, empty Real Instrument track that comes with no effects, monitoring off, and stereo recording on. (You can read about these settings in the following paragraphs.) *Basic* is right.

If you'd like more control over your new track, though, choose Track→New Track instead. This way, the New Track/Track Info dialog box appears (Figure 27-3).

Click the Real Instrument tab, and then work through the options as follows:

- **Bass, Drums, Guitars, etc.** It's important to realize that the names listed here don't represent instrument *sounds;* you're going to supply the sound yourself.

  Instead, these are canned sets of *effects,* like reverb and echo, that, in the opinions of GarageBand's creators, are especially well suited to these instrument types. If you plan to sing, for example, you'll find that Live Vocals (in the Vocals category at left) gives your singing sound just a gentle touch of pro-sounding reverb; Ambiente Vox sounds like you're at the bottom of the Grand Canyon; and so on.

  Technically, though, there's nothing to stop you from selecting the "wrong" instrument type, choosing one of the Horns effects to apply to your guitar playing, for example. You might even come up with a strange, spooky sound that's just right for the effect you seek.

Tip: It's a great idea to "walk" through these various effect presets with the up and down arrow keys on your Mac keyboard, listening to each as you play or sing a few notes. Eventually, you'll begin to associate the specific sounds of each preset with its name, and you'll identify your favorites for use in subsequent hit singles.

Figure 27-3:
The instruments listed here aren't instrument sounds. They're effect presets that audio engineers consider ideal for the listed instrument types. To use it, click an instrument name in the left column, then an individual effect preset in the right-side list.

You can read much more about GarageBand's effects in Chapter 28. For now, though, note that you don't have to make a decision before you record: you can change the effects applied to your live-audio track at any time, before or after the recording session.

To sing without any help from GarageBand's studio-engineer elves, for example, just click the Vocals category, and then click Unprocessed. (On the other hand, a little reverb tends to smooth out the rough edges of the voice, making it sound more professional. As a result, you may feel more comfortable and confident in your singing or playing. That's a psychological by-product technically called the Singing in the Shower Effect.)

- **Mono or Stereo.** GarageBand can record both the left and right channels of sound from a stereo signal—a stereo microphone, for example, or the left and right outputs from a mixing board. If your sound source does, indeed, produce both left- and right-channel sound, turning on Stereo here tells GarageBand to record them simultaneously. Later, you can use GarageBand's mixing tools to emphasize or de-emphasize one channel or the other, if you like.

  Plenty of instruments, however, produce only a single stream of sound. These are *monophonic,* or mono, sound sources: an electric guitar, for example, or a cheap USB desktop microphone. If that's what you're using, click Mono instead. You'll save a lot of disk space. (Stereo recordings, of course, use up twice as much disk space as mono.)

- **Input.** Even though this pop-up menu appears *above* the Mono/Stereo switch, you'll generally use it *after* making your Mono/Stereo choice. If you've selected Stereo, this pop-up menu is irrelevant: it always says Channel 1/2 (meaning that it will record from both left and right channels).

  This pop-up menu is useful when, for example, you've indicated that you want to record a Mono track, but you've connected a stereo sound source. In that case, this pop-up menu lets you specify *which* channel you want to record: the left (Channel 1) or the right (Channel 2).

  The Input pop-up menu is also important when you've connected an audio interface that has enough input jacks for several mikes or instruments at once. Suppose you have an eight-channel box connected, with different microphones or instruments connected to each pair of inputs. In that case, with the Stereo button turned on, you would use the Input pop-up menu to specify which channels you want to record: "Channel 1/2 ," "Channel 3/4," "Channel 5/6," or "Channel 7/8."

- **Monitor: Off/On.** "Monitor," in this case, means "play what I'm playing through the speaker, so that I can hear it."

  Now, your first reaction to this option might well be, "Well, DUH! Of *course* I want to hear myself. It's called an electric guitar, hello! It doesn't make any sound at all unless it's hooked up to an amp or some speakers!"

And sure enough, if you're playing an electronic instrument like a synthesizer or electric guitar, you'll want Monitor to be On. That way, you'll be able to hear your own playing in the context of any other tracks you've already recorded. (You'll also be able to hear yourself when you're *not* recording, so you can rehearse parts before recording them.)

But if you're recording from a microphone, you can already hear what you're playing or singing. Furthermore, if Monitor is turned on during the recording, your microphone will also pick up *that* sound, coming out of the Mac's speakers.

Unfortunately, that kind of setup produces the ear-splitting, high-pitched whine known as *feedback* (a staple of the standard teen-movie scene in which the doofus principal first steps up to the microphone at the school assembly).

So how do you avoid feedback? Your first instinct might be to turn *off* the Monitor feature. Now you'll hear only the *existing* GarageBand tracks playing as you sing or play—no feedback. Trouble is, GarageBand may then wind up recording both your voice *and* any previously recorded tracks as they play along with you—an ugly situation, because their sound will become a permanent part of your vocal track.

Fortunately, there's a simple solution to both problems: If you're recording from a microphone, *listen through headphones.* Leave the Monitor feature On, so you can hear yourself as you play or sing.

Tip: Turn Monitor to Off when you're finished recording. That way, you won't reopen this GarageBand project next week without headphones connected—and get a blast of feedback in your ears.

- **Icon pop-up menu.** Use this pop-up menu, if you like, to choose a little picture to represent the recording you're about to make. (It's purely cosmetic, and has no audible link to the instrument sound.) Apple gives you 68 little graphics to choose from—every instrument in GarageBand, plus silhouettes of singers.

Tip: To open this palette of icons, you don't have to click the tiny, down-pointing triangle, as you might expect. Instead, click squarely on the icon itself. That broader target means quicker access.

When you're finished setting up your new Real Instrument track, click OK. You return to the main GarageBand window, where your new, blue track appears, ready for recording.

Phase 2: Prepare the Studio

From here, recording live audio is much like the MIDI-recording procedure described on page 519. Turn on the metronome and countoff, if you like, and choose a tempo.

Note: It's very important to set the final, finished tempo *before* you record. That's because when you change the tempo of a piece, audio regions that you've recorded yourself don't expand or contract to stay aligned with the rest of the music, as GarageBand loops do. Every track in your piece will therefore change tempo *except* what you've recorded, which will remain locked in its own independent tempo track, sounding clueless, clashy, and out of step when you play it back with the other tracks.

Then proceed like this:

1. Choose a key.

Go through the piece a couple of times to make sure it's not too high or too low for your singing voice, or—if you're playing an instrument—to make sure it's in a comfortable key for playing. Once you've recorded a digital audio track, you're stuck. If you sing in the key of D, the vocal track will have to stay in the key of D forevermore; you can't transpose digital audio.

Note: Yes, OK, fine, you *can* if they're GarageBand's blue-tinted audio loops. But they've been blessed by some kind of secret Apple audio-transposing mojo—and *your* digital audio regions don't have it.

2. Put the Playhead where you want recording to begin.

Of course, you may find it best to put the Playhead a few measures to the *left* of the part where you want to begin singing or playing, so you'll be able to get into the groove of the music before you begin.

3. Put on your headphones, if you're using them. Get ready to play or sing, and then click the red, round Record button.

Or just press the letter R key on your Mac keyboard. Either way, you hear the count-off measure, if you've requested one, and then GarageBand begins to record.

4. When you come to the end of the section you hoped to record, tap the Space bar (or click the Play button) to stop recording.

On the screen, you'll see the new purple region you recorded.

Tip: Instead of stopping altogether, you can also tap the R key on your keyboard to stop recording but *keep playing.* You can then listen for a while, and then tap R again to record a later section.

In fact, you can tap R as often as you like during recording. Each time, GarageBand seamlessly kicks into, or out of, Record mode as it plays.

8. Play back your recording to hear how you did.

Rewind to the spot where you started recording. Tap the Space bar to hear your performance played back.

Multiple Takes

As long as you've got yourself a high-quality software studio, you may as well avail yourself of the various cheats that professional recording artists use—and that means mixing and matching the best parts of each "take."

One strategy involves recording your live audio part for the entire song, start to finish. If you mess up, just keep going.

Then prepare for a second attempt like this:

1. **Mute the first track.**

   That is, click it and press the letter M key on your keyboard, or click the little speaker icon in its track header.

2. **Create a second Real Instrument track with the same settings.**

   As it turns out, GarageBand offers a handy shortcut for this step: Choose Track→ Duplicate Track (⌘-D). GarageBand gives you a perfect duplicate of the track— empty of notes or regions, but with its settings and effects intact.

Figure 27-4:
Top: In this example, you've recorded two different attempts at the same vocal track. The first take was superior in almost every way—except for the middle part.

Middle: Click the first track and Shift-click the second, so that they're both selected. Position the Playhead just before the messed-up portion and press ⌘-T (the Split command). Then position the Playhead just after that section and press ⌘-T again. You've just chopped up both takes.

Bottom: Drag the middle segment of the bottom track (the good one) upward so that it replaces the bad portion of the first take. Now you have a single, unified track containing the best of both attempts. Delete the second-take track.

3. Rerecord.

Repeat these three steps until you've got yourself a number of alternate takes to choose from.

Now it's a simple—and, frankly, enjoyable—matter to chop up these various takes, deleting the bad portions and leaving only the good ones, as shown in Figure 27-4. (Of course, you can also copy and paste successful parts—the chorus, for example—without having to redo them.) For a discussion of splitting, recombining, and otherwise editing Real Instrument regions, see page 505.

Punching In and Out

If *most* of the first take was good, but you flubbed a shorter section somewhere in the middle, you may want to record right over the bad spot. That's where *punching in* comes in.

Punching in and out is when the software switches from Play mode to Record mode automatically during a segment of the music that you've bracketed in advance (in GarageBand's case, using the yellow Cycle stripe at the top of the window).

Yellow stripe (cycle region)

Figure 27-5:
When you're set up to punch in (rerecord a specified section), GarageBand plays one measure of music before you come in, and then begins to record whatever you play or sing. When you reach the end of the cycle region (identified by the yellow stripe), GarageBand continues to loop the playback of the cycle region until you click the Play button (or press the Space bar).

Using punch in/punch out for a Real Instrument track is *almost* exactly the same as for a Software Instrument track. Once again, the idea is to turn on cycling (press the letter C key on your keyboard), adjust the yellow Cycle stripe so that it highlights the music you want to rerecord, turn on the Control→Count In command, and then press the letter R key (or click the round, red Record button) and get ready to play. (See Figure 27-5 for the rest of the story.)

There is, however, one big difference between punching into Real Instrument and punching into a Software Instrument. With a Real track, GarageBand records only what you sing or play the *first time through* the cycle region. Then, when the Playhead reaches the end of the yellow cycle stripe, GarageBand instantly stops recording and switches to playback-only mode. (In other words, you can't keep playing or singing to build up a cumulative take, one pass at a time, as you can when playing a MIDI instrument.)

The nice part is that if even your punched-in recording wasn't quite right, taking another stab at it is supremely easy. Just tap the letter R key again. GarageBand automatically plays the measure before the yellow stripe, and once again auto-records whatever you play when the Playhead reaches the punch-in region. You can repeat this exercise as many times as you need to get the passage perfect.

Editing Real Instrument Regions

When it comes to editing, Real Instrument regions don't offer nearly as much flexibility as Software Instruments. Real Instrument regions are digital recordings of live performances; you can't very well correct a wrong note, boost the emphasis of a sung word, shift the performance in pitch, draw in new notes, or have any of the kind of fun described in Chapter 26.

Still, as Chapter 25 makes clear, you can massage *any* kind of region—Real or not—in a number of useful ways. You can chop them up, rejoin them, drag them around in time, copy and paste them, and so on.

Playhead sync button

Figure 27-6:
By zooming in, you gain incredible precision in selecting portions that you intend to cut or copy.

Note, however, that if you can't use this zoomed-in view for the purpose of positioning the Playhead to split a region unless you've turned on Playhead synchronization. To do that, make sure that the button circled here shows two aligned Playheads; if not, click there!

Area where dragging moves the region
instead of making a selection

If you double-click a blue or purple region, in fact, you behold the sight in Figure 27-6: actual audio waveforms that make it very easy to isolate certain notes or syllables. You've just opened the Track Editor for a Real Instrument region. (If you've clicked a blue track to select it, you can open the corresponding Track Editor in any of three other ways: Choose Control→Show Editor, press ⌘-E, or click the ▓ button below the track headers.)

The "mountains" on display in the Track Editor for a Real Instrument region show the bursts of volume in the track—individual notes of an instrument, for example, or words in a vocal track. (A flat, straight line means silence.)

There are a few tricks worth noting here:

- The top edge of a region in the Track Editor—maybe about the top eighth of it (Figure 27-6)—is a special zone. Inside it, the cursor changes to this ◁▷ shape. You can now *move* the region by dragging it from side to side.

Tip: When your cursor has that shape, you can also select an *entire* region with a single click. (Yes, that's easy to do in the *timeline,* but it wouldn't otherwise seem possible in the *Track Editor.*)

  If you click any lower, your cursor becomes a simple cross ✛, and you actually wind up dragging across waveforms and highlighting them. Learning to know how high to position your cursor for these two different purposes is just part of the game.

- If you drag the upper-right corner of a Real Instrument region *in the Track Editor,* your cursor takes on the curly Loop shape, and you wind up *looping* the region—that is, making it repeat. In other words, it behaves exactly as though you're dragging the upper-right corner of the *un*magnified region up in the timeline, as described in Chapter 25.

- If you drag leftward on the *lower*-right corner of a region in the Track Editor, the cursor changes to this ┣ shape, and you wind up *trimming* the region—essentially hiding the outer notes. It's just like dragging the trailing edge of a region in the timeline (except that you must use only the lower-right corner as a handle—not the entire right edge, as in the timeline).

- If you paste Real region B on top of Real region A, the pasted region wipes out whatever was underneath, just as you'd expect. But suppose you change your mind.

  If you then move or cut away the pasted region, you can tug outward on the end of original region A. The wiped-out soundwaves *grow right back,* revealing that GarageBand was only hiding them, not forgetting them.

  Which gives you a great trivia question for your next bar bet: How is a GarageBand region like the leg of a starfish?

Effects, Guitar Amps, and Instrument Modules

arageBand is more than a MIDI sequencer, more than a loop-based music construction set, even more than a multitrack tape recorder. It's also the equivalent of a six-foot-tall, $100,000 rack of studio processing equipment and a room full of guitar amplifiers.

The point is to give you exactly the same professional edge that recording artists have. If your singing sounds a little dry, you can "sweeten" the track with a little reverb. If you're looking for a distinctive keyboard sound for the indie post-grunge trash music you're trying to record, you can bleach out all of the low frequencies and add some stereo tremolo. And if you're a guitarist, GarageBand is pleased to offer you a music store's worth of amplifiers from every decade since 1960.

You can apply these effects to both Real and Software Instruments. You can also apply them on a track-by-track basis (when you're trying to fine-tune one instrument's sound) or to the entire mix at once (when you want to tweak the acoustics of your "garage" space).

Instrument-Named Presets

Whenever you double-click a track's header, its Track Info dialog box appears. At the top of it, GarageBand presents a list of what appear to be instrument names (Figure 28-1).

At first glance, these instrument names may seem to have completely different functions for the two kinds of tracks in GarageBand:

- If you've opened a blue Real Instrument track, these instrument names don't refer to instrument sounds; they identify *effects presets*. Each is a carefully adjusted combination of studio processing effects—reverb, EQ (equalization), and so on—that, in the opinion of a professional recording engineer, is well suited to the instrument named in the list.

- If you've opened a green Software Instrument track, you might assume that the instrument names here—Grand Piano, Orchestral Strings, and so on—*are* instrument sounds. After all, selecting a different instrument in the list changes the sound of whatever's in the track.

But as you'll find out in this chapter, these instrument names also include custom-tailored effects. These are, in other words, instrument-and-effect presets.

For each one, you can modify not only the effect Apple has assigned, but even the sounds themselves, which GarageBand generates from 18 built-in modules—Piano, Strings, Guitar, and so on. For a given instrument named in the list, you can even substitute a different sound module altogether.

These effect presets...

Figure 28-1:
The Track Info dialog box is a lot like the New Track dialog box. But when you click Details, some important controls appear at the bottom. These are the building-block effects generators that make up the instrument-named presets in the top list. (And the two pop-up menus in the Details panel list the building blocks of those building blocks. It's possible to burrow down very deeply into GarageBand's effects-processing underworld.)

...are composed of these settings.

When you click an instrument category in the left-side list, the presets are listed in the right-side list. Apple has tried to name them helpfully, to suggest their sonic effect: for example, Edgy Drums, Punk Bass, or (in the Vocals category) Epic Diva. In the Guitar category, most of these presets incorporate the famous GarageBand *guitar-amplifier simulations*.

Whatever effect preset you choose becomes part of the track. Any sound in that track is affected the same way by those effects.

Save Instrument, Delete Instrument

For want of a better term, Apple calls the effects presets in this dialog box *Instruments*.

In the following pages, you'll learn how to operate the knobs and dials of the individual effect processors (Compressor, Reverb, and so on) that make up each Instrument.

Figure 28-2:
"Save file?" What file? Turns out GarageBand means, "Save this instrument-named effect preset?" In other words, you've made some changes to the effects associated with, in this case, Female Basic, and GarageBand wants to know if you want them permanently stored as part of the Female Basic preset.

(If you turn on "Never ask again," GarageBand won't just never ask again—it will never save your preset changes, either. If you miss seeing this warning box, choose GarageBand→Preferences, click General, and turn on "Ask before discarding unsaved changes."

The process begins by clicking the Details triangle to expand the dialog box, as shown in Figure 28-1.

It's comforting to know, though, that once you've spent some time tweaking the effects settings for a certain "instrument" (effects preset), you can save your work for use with other tracks and in other GarageBand projects. All you have to do is click the Save Instrument button at the bottom of the dialog box. GarageBand invites you to name your new effect preset. Thereafter, it will appear in the right-side list (see "Giggly Baritone" shown in Figure 28-2).

In fact, GarageBand is so concerned that you might lose hours of effects fiddling that, if you try to close the dialog box or select a different "instrument" *without* clicking Save Instrument, it shows you the warning box in Figure 28-2.

So yes, it's very easy to create *new* effect presets. Fortunately, it's also easy to prune the list, throwing away any that you've created that, in the cold light of day, you decide really aren't such masterpieces. Just highlight their names in the right-side list and then click Delete Instrument at the bottom of the dialog box.

Note: You can't use the Delete Instrument button to delete any of *Apple's* effect presets—only your own misbegotten attempts.

Effect Modules

See the flippy triangle next to Details? As noted earlier, clicking it makes the Track Info dialog box expand. You've just revealed a set of building-block effects like Gate, Compressor, Reverb, and so on (Figure 28-3). These are the components of the instrument-named presets in the lists above.

Now, if you've spent the prime years of your life hanging around recording studios, terms like *Gate, Compressor,* and *Equalizer* may already be familiar to you.

If you're anyone else, well, resign yourself to the fact that *reading* about effects is not a very good way to learn about them. The fact is, their names are little more than puny human attempts to describe sounds that are, in many cases, otherworldly and indescribable.

Still, the prose that follows may be helpful if you read it *while* performing any of these three self-guided exercises:

- Play with the tutorial file called "06—Effects" (on the GarageBand Examples CD described on page 474). It's a project whose tracks are already set up with various processing effects. To compare them, all you have to do is solo one track at a time (click it and type the letter S key) and play it back.

- As a convenient software quirk, the Track Info dialog box behaves more like a separate program than a true dialog box. That is, even when it's in front of the main GarageBand window, you have full access to GarageBand's controls. You can start and stop playback, add loops, edit notes, and so on.

Tip: You can even click a different track without first closing the Track Info dialog box. You'll see the dialog box update itself instantly to reflect the effects of the currently selected track.

If you've already recorded a live performance onto a track, therefore, one great way to experiment with effects is to turn on *cycling playback* for some of it (page 475). Now, in the Track Info dialog box, expand the Details section if necessary, and start the music playing. (You can just tap the Space bar to start and stop the music.)

The music continues to play, looping over and over again, as you tweak its sound with the GarageBand effects controls.

- You can also listen to how each effect changes the sound *while* you play—that is, before you've actually recorded anything. Just connect your microphone or instru-

Figure 28-3:
The instruments named in the top part of the dialog box refer to combinations of effects that Apple engineers set up using the Details panel. Yet even these components have components. As you can see here, the true effects aficionado can work this dialog box from the bottom up, first creating a sub-preset for each effect, then naming the collection of presets for the list at top.

To edit one of these sub-presets, click the adjacent pencil button.

ment output to the Mac. Play or sing, listening with headphones, as you fiddle with the controls in the dialog box.

In any case, here's a summary of what you'll find in the Details panel. (For a deeper analysis of what these common studio effects do, visit *www.harmony-central.com/ Effects/effects-explained.html*.)

To apply a certain effect to the track you're editing, turn on the checkbox next to its name, and then explore the pop-up menu to its right.

Note: Before you go nuts adding effects to an individual *track,* remember that you can also apply any of these effects to the *entire song,* using the Master Track feature described in the next chapter. Part of the art of mixing is knowing when to process just one instrument, and when to tweak the entire overall mix.

Generator (Software Instruments Only)

This pop-up menu appears only in the Track Info dialog box for Software Instrument tracks. Most people, most of the time, are content to let GarageBand's piano be a piano, its guitar be a guitar, and so on.

You can, however, delve into the sophisticated modeling software that GarageBand uses to produce these sounds, either to subtly tweak the built-in sounds or to radically remake them. In fact, using the Save Instrument button described earlier, you can even create an entirely new Software Instrument, named whatever you please. You also use this pop-up menu to load new sounds that you've found online; see Chapter 17.

The first step is to choose the basic instrument sound you want from the pop-up menu. Most of them are just what they sound like: Piano, Strings, Horns, Woodwind, Guitar, Bass, Drum Kits. The remaining ten modules are software versions of synthesizers, capable of generating a wild variety of sounds—and not just musical notes (see Figure 28-4).

Familiar instrument names

When you select a traditional instrument name from the Generator pop-up menu, the pop-up menu to its right comes to life. It lists subspecies of the instrument's type: Alto Sax, Tenor Sax, and so on.

If you now click the pencil button, you see a dialog box like the one shown in Figure 28-4. Here's where you can adjust several parameters of the underlying sound. For most instrument sounds, you get three sliders:

- **Volume.** You guessed it: How loud the sound is.

- **Cutoff.** This slider adjusts cutoff frequency for a *lowpass filter*, whose effect is to filter out high frequencies. If you try it on the Grand Piano, for example, dragging the Cutoff slider to the left muffles the sound, as though you're turning down the treble control on a stereo.

- **Release.** This slider governs how long a note "rings" after you've struck the key. In the real world, a piano note, for example, falls silent the instant you take your finger off the key. But by dragging this slider toward Slow, you can make the notes hang in the air longer before fading away.

Synthesizer generators

When you choose one of the synthesizer modules from the first pop-up menu, however, your options multiply considerably. Now when you click the pencil button, the manual-settings dialog box contains a full arsenal of synth controls—and learning what they all do could take you years. In the real world, synth programming is a full-time hobby, if not a full-time job.

In addition to the Volume, Cutoff, and Release parameters described above, the synth generators offer many other sliders. They vary by module, but here's a taste:

Figure 28-4:
You can adjust the quality of GarageBand's built-in instrument sound generators by clicking the little pencil button. Sometimes you're offered only a few options; sometimes, as with the synthesizers (like the one shown here), you can adjust as many as eight different sliders. In combination, they offer you a nearly infinite number of different sound possibilities.

- **Tuning.** Some synth sounds are actually composed of multiple "voices" playing simultaneously. Using this slider, you can make the secondary voices play out of tune with the primary one. At the Narrow setting, detuning the voices in this way adds only a subtle piquancy to the sound, an intriguing twang; as you drag the slider toward Wide, the secondary voices begin to sound like completely different notes, farther and farther from the one you're actually playing.

- **Attack, Decay.** A slow *attack* means that when you strike the key, the sound eases in, rather than sounding instantly. A slow *decay* means that after you release the key, the sound eases out instead of cutting off sharply.

- **Character, Harmonics, Timbre.** These controls, found primarily in the Digital synth modules, change the character of the sound in ways that are impossible to describe in words. Set your Software Instrument track a-playing (or even a-cycling) and drag these sliders to hear for yourself.

Gate (Real Instruments Only)

The *gating* function (often called a *noise gate* by recording geeks) simply eliminates all sound that's quieter than a certain level, which you specify by dragging this slider. The result: total silence in the quieter sections of a track.

In the recording industry, gating can be useful to eliminate hiss from the silent parts of, for example, an old recording. Very few of the GarageBand presets use gating, but you can apply it to your own recordings—for example, when you're trying to get rid of the hum from a microphone or other component.

Compressor

Imagine a graph of your song's volume level over time. A studio *compressor* limits this volume graph so that it doesn't vary so wildly. There's less difference between the loudest and softest parts.

Because compressors can bring out the "highlights" of a track without making the background so low as to be inaudible, they're among the most frequently used effects in today's pop music. A compressor adds punch to a solo or—if you apply it to the Master Track—the overall song. It also helps the music sound better on cheap speakers—like boombox speakers, portable iPod speakers, or your Mac's speakers.

To try out this effect, turn on its checkbox and then drag the slider. 0 means no compression; 100 means maximum compression.

Equalizer

If you've ever fiddled with the *graphic equalizer* on a stereo, or even the software one that's built into iTunes, you already know about these controls. An equalizer lets you boost or repress certain frequencies—like the bass or the treble—to suit different kinds of music. A "graph" for classical music, for example, might slightly boost the low and high frequencies for more sparkle, letting the middle ones "sag"; a pop-rock setting might boost instead the middle frequencies, to bring out the vocal parts.

When you turn on GarageBand's Equalizer checkbox, the pop-up menu to its right offers 21 canned equalizer setups bearing self-explanatory names like Bass Boost, Brighten Strings, and Reduce "S." In the unlikely event that none of these presets is quite what you want, you can click the pencil button to its right to adjust the various frequencies yourself (Figure 28-5).

Figure 28-5:
When you click GarageBand's pencil button (indicated by the cursor), you open the Equalizer dialog box (lower right). Adjust the sliders to boost or reduce the corresponding sound frequencies. If you like, you can then save your settings by choosing Make Preset from the pop-up menu (where it now says Add Brightness). You'll be asked to name the settings, which will thereafter appear in the pop-up menu along with Apple's own presets. (Figure 28-6 shows this process in more detail.)

The truth is, many of the Equalizer presets might make more sense when applied to a finished composition than just one instrument track. But now and again, they can be useful in giving a recording just the right nuance. For example, in the guitar preset called Summer Sounds, the "EQ" of the midrange has been boosted to give your guitar more of a Beach Boys sound.

"Additional Effects" Pop-Up Menus

These two unlabeled pop-up menus, near the middle of the Details panel, are complex and deep enough to merit a book of their own. These are fantastically sophisticated software controls that emulate racks full of studio equipment. You can spend hours in here, fiddling with the sliders and checkboxes, in an effort to find the perfect tweak for your vocal or instrumental line.

Note: The two pop-up menus are identical. Apple has given you two of them so that you can apply two effects simultaneously.

Actually, there are a total of *four* pop-up menus. Each time you choose an effect category from a *left-side* pop-up menu, the pop-up menu to its *right* comes to life, pre-stocked with useful presets. (As you're beginning to notice, GarageBand offers presets for the component effects that make up the *instrument-named* presets listed at the top of the dialog box.)

Presets within presets

You may find only three presets in this second pop-up menu (Soft, Medium, Hard) or as many as 20 (Birdish, Club at Next Door, Slow and Deep, and so on). You can add your own presets to this second pop-up menu, too, as shown in Figure 28-6.

Figure 28-6:

Left: Here, you've selected Chorus; the second menu offers Chorus presets.

Top right: But if you click the pencil button, this box lets you craft your own manual settings.

Middle right: If you come up with some jaw-dropping sound, save your creation by choosing Make Preset.

Lower right: Name this effect. From now on, it will show up in the presets pop-up menu (the one that's shown being opened here at left).

Now that you understand the basic ritual—choose an effect generator from the first pop-up menu, choose a preset from the second, and adjust manually if you like—here's a list of the primary effect generators as they appear in the first pop-up menu.

Treble Reduction, Bass Reduction

As you might expect, these effects crank down the high or low frequencies of this track's music, respectively. Use Treble Reduction if the source material is too hissy; use Bass Reduction if it's too boomy. (The equalizing options perform much the same function, but with more precision.)

Distortion

Most musicians go out of their way to make sure that the *input volume* of their microphone or instrument isn't up too high. (That's why you opened System Preferences and adjusted the level slider before making a live recording.) If the input is too "hot," the level meters go off the scale, resulting in the screechy, garbled sound known as *distortion* or *clipping*.

In some musical circles, however—especially heavy-metal ones—distortion is the whole point. It's the trademark sound of guitarists who turn their amplifiers "up to 11," as the cast of *This is Spinal Tap* might say.

Using this option, you can drive *any* musical material into distortion-land, even if the levels were perfectly fine in the original recording.

Overdrive

This effect, also common in electric guitar music, is related to distortion. It simulates the sound of an overdriven tube amplifier, adding the intensity of distortion without quite as much "trashiness."

Bitcrusher

The Bitcrusher effect is designed to throw away musical data *on purpose,* giving your track a retro, played-over-the-phone-line sound. Its presets include AM Radio, Classic 8-Bit (that is, like the oldest Macs), Meet Atari, and others. Some, like Other World, reduce lyrics to unintelligibility; others, like SR Crush, give vocal lines a buzzing, robotic, Vocoder quality. All of the presets do a real number on the sound quality of your track, blasting it into awfulness for use only in special circumstances. (Ever heard the beginning of the Electric Light Orchestra's "Telephone Line?" The opening verse is meant to sound as though it's sung over the phone—and now you can perform the same processing in the privacy of your own home.)

Automatic Filter

This pop-up menu unleashes a wide spectrum of truly wild and severe effects. Most introduce some form of pulsing, tremolo, or wobbling. A few highlights among the others:

- **Birdish** adds a high-frequency sweep to the sound, as though your composition were so good, aliens were trying to beam you up.

- **Club at Next Door** is truly hilarious. It removes all frequencies except the very lowest, so that only the throbbing bass remains. It's pretty much exactly what you'd hear of your next door neighbor's stereo through an apartment wall, or, as the name suggests, if a dance club were across the street.

- **Slow Shutter** sounds exactly as though an older brother is covering up your mouth with his hand, then flapping it open and closed while you try to speak or sing. It has an extreme "wah-wah" sound to it.

Chorus

Chorusing is a famous and frequently used effect in pop music (ever heard Abba?). The fundamental idea is that the computer duplicates your track and offsets the copy by just a millisecond or two, so that you sound like there's two (or more) of you singing or playing together. It also makes the two copies slightly out of tune with each other, which helps with the illusion of multiple voices singing at once.

The presets here are primarily designed to let you control how *much* chorusing you want. Among them, Spread Stereo is among the most interesting, because it attempts to place you and your clones in different spots along the left-to-right stereo "soundstage."

Flanger

Here's another classic rock processor, frequently applied to guitars and keyboards by a little foot switch-operated box on the stage floor. And now it's yours, at no extra charge.

You'll recognize it when you hear it: a sweeping, side-to-side, filtery effect. It's something like chorusing described above, but the duplicates of the sound are played back much more out of tune from the original. (Hint: It's most effective in stereo. Go dig out your iPod headphones.)

Phaser

Sometimes called a *phase shifter,* this flanger-like whooshing effect should also strike you as familiar from the pop world. It, too, sounds like somebody is cyclically rotating the dials on some selective-frequency machine, and it, too, sounds especially good on guitars, keyboards, and vocals.

Tremolo

Tremolo is a close relative of *vibrato.* On paper, you might describe it as a subtle up-and-down wobble, either in pitch or in volume—but in the real world of solo voice or solo instruments, you'd describe it as a beautiful, professional sound. It's also a characteristic sound of guitar amps from the '50s and '60s (think The Ventures).

The GarageBand Tremolo effect won't turn a tone-deaf screecher into Pavarotti, though. You can't apply it selectively just to the ends of longer notes, as musicians tend to do in live performance. Many of the presets sound just a hair machine-generated, especially because many of them create the vibrato effect not by subtle waves of *pitch* but by whipping back and forth from left to right in stereo. (Here's another effect that sounds best with headphones on.)

Still, several of these presets can lend interest and magic to a track, especially to a solo line with sustained notes. (If you're a singer and don't have a natural vibrato, try the preset called Soft and Fast, for example. Especially if you've also dialed up a little reverb, as described below.)

Auto Wah

"Wah" here refers to the *wah-wah pedal,* a staple of electric guitar players. The name, as you can probably guess, is an onomatopoeia—the name describes the sound of the effect.

Onstage, guitar players traditionally control the timing and intensity of the "wah" by riding a pedal with one foot. In GarageBand, you can't actually control either the timing or intensity, except in your selection of preset.

Even so, you have an entire music store's worth of wah-wah pedal simulators here, with names like Wow, Duck, and CryBaby. Some of them distort the music beyond recognition; others make you sound like you're playing live from outer space. All of them take the range of sounds you can make with your guitar alone (or whatever your instrument) far beyond what you can play without GarageBand's assistance.

Amp Simulation

If you're an electric guitarist, and you've slogged along this far, here's what you've been waiting for, the gem of GarageBand for guitarists: the amp simulators (Figure 28-7). These are the effects Steve Jobs and pop artist John Mayer demonstrated onstage when

Figure 28-7:
These core effects lie at the heart of the amplifier simulations for guitars. The manual options here are the most elaborate of any GarageBand effect. Beginning with the type of guitar you're playing, these controls let you specify everything about the amp, from its gain (the strength of the incoming signal) to output (the strength of the post-processed signal).

You can tweak the controls to your heart's delight— just as guitarists love to do with their real amps.

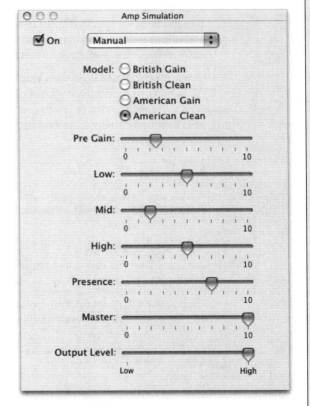

GarageBand was first unveiled at a Macworld Expo; this is the feature that gets true garage-band musicians drooling.

As it turns out, the sound an electric guitar makes is profoundly affected by the amplifier it's plugged into. Various bands of the last 40 years have put both themselves and certain amps on the map by creating trademark guitar sounds.

Unfortunately, amplifiers are expensive, heavy, and impractical to transport in big numbers. To have a single software program on, say, a laptop, that can deliver perfect impersonations of 17 classic amplifiers—with names like Grunge, Scorching Solo, British Invasion, and Seventies Rhythm—is, for guitarists, quite a treat.

(For anyone else, it may be no more than a big yawn. That's an OK reaction, too.)

As you can guess, these amp simulations work best if you have an electric guitar connected to your Mac. Listen on headphones as you experiment and noodle.

Echo, Reverb

You might suppose that *echo* and *reverb* are the same thing: the nice echoey sound of, for example, your shower.

Actually, in studio terms, they're different. *Echo,* sometimes called *delay,* is literally an echo, giving you fainter and fainter distinct repetitions of each sound, each separated by a fraction of a second (think Grand Canyon). *Reverb* is a sweet, subtle, professional-sounding reverberation that smooths the rough edges of a musical performance (think shower stall, empty alley, or concert hall).

You'll probably use Echo only rarely, for special effects. Reverb, on the other hand, is useful for practically any kind of solo. There's not a pop star alive, for example, whose recordings aren't "sweetened" with a little reverb. The audience may not be able to pinpoint why your singing or playing sounds so great, but they'll definitely hear the difference.

Each of these effects has its own on/off checkbox and slider, which goes from 0 to 100 percent.

Note: If the Echo and Reverb checkboxes are dimmed, it's because these effects are turned off in the Master Track (see Chapter 29).

The fix: In the Track Info dialog box, click the Master Track tab, and then turn on the Echo and/or Reverb checkboxes. When you return to the Software Instrument or Real Instrument tab, you'll see these checkboxes come back to life.

The explanation: As it turns out, the individual tracks' Echo and Reverb sliders simply govern how much of these effects are sent to the Echo and Reverb in the Master Track. Studio musician call these *send effects.* (The Track Echo effect in the two unnamed pop-up menus are different; it gives you a truly track-independent echo.) So if Echo and Reverb are turned off for the entire song, they're also turned off for every individual track.

Mixing and Publishing

B y this time, you may have mastered GarageBand. Perhaps you've dialed up your own effects, masterfully combined loops with live audio, honed your mastery of musical arrangements and orchestration, and even added a little mod-wheel tweak here and there. At this point, you may even have the next "Oops, I Did It Again" right there on your screen.

But it's not doing anyone much good sitting in GarageBand. For most people, the whole point of making music is sharing it with others.

This chapter describes how to wrap up your workflow in GarageBand and present it to a wider audience. It's all about fine-tuning your piece, mixing the tracks (adjusting their relative volume levels), and finally handing the whole thing off to iTunes. From there, you can convert the song to any common music file format (like MP3), burn it to a CD, load it onto an iPod, or post it online for your screaming fans to discover.

Mixing Tracks

Next time you listen to the radio, notice how each song ends. A few of them end with a dramatic climactic stopping chord, but most gradually fade out.

GarageBand not only lets you create convincing fade-outs for your songs, but even lets you adjust the volume graph for individual tracks along their lengths. For example, you can make the piano part loud during the introduction of the piece, and then pull back to a softer level when your singing begins.

This business of adjusting the relative volume levels of a song's tracks is called *mixing*. It's both an art and a science; two different people mixing the same song can create totally different psycho-musical effects. You're no longer wearing the composer's hat, or even the rock star's hat: you're now assuming the engineer's and producer's roles.

Here are the tools at your disposal, as described in the following pages:

- You can adjust the relative overall volume levels of the tracks.

- You can create volume fluctuations *within* a track.

- You can adjust the left-to-right positions of your track instruments in the stereo "soundstage."

- You can make overall volume changes—to all tracks at once—to create, for example, a fade-out at the end of the song.

Overall Track Volume

The most basic mixing skill is knowing how to adjust track volumes relative to each other. That is, you might want to make the drum track a little quieter, the vocals a little louder, and so on.

The key to this basic mixing feature is the *track mixer,* a little panel that sprouts when you click the small triangle identified by the arrow cursor in Figure 29-1.

Figure 29-1:
Top: If you point your cursor at various GarageBand screen controls and wait a moment, a tiny balloon pops up to tell you what it does—in this case, the track mixer.

Bottom: When you click the little triangle, the track mixer panel appears. Here, you can adjust the overall volume level of a track and use the knob to specify where it sits in the left-to-right stereo "soundstage" when you listen with headphones or stereo speakers.

Using the volume slider that you find here is simple enough:

- Drag the tiny, white, round handle to decrease or increase the track volume.

- Click inside the slider to make the volume handle jump to that spot, without having to drag.

- Option-click one of the tiny speaker icons, or anywhere along the slider's length, to restore the track volume to its original factory-set volume level. (Note to studio veterans: technically, you're setting the track to 0 decibels. Note to everyone else: And why is "normal" zero? It's a long story with its origins in the world of recording-studio equipment, but the bottom line is that on this kind of meter, 0 dB means "anything higher will distort." Absolute silence, incidentally, is represented on these meters as −96 dB.)

Tip: If you can't seem to adjust the slider at all, it's because you've programmed in volume changes using the Track Volume track described next. The track mixer slider is "live" only if you've never fiddled with the track's volume track.

GEM IN THE ROUGH

Check One, Check Two...

You can use the track volume slider shown in Figure 29-1 even while the song is playing back.

Why is that so useful? Because the two tiny graphs just above the volume slider illustrate the volume level of the left and right stereo channels in real time. They light up with tiny bars, as illustrated here, resembling the digital LED level meters on modern studio equipment.

When you're preparing your song for release to the masses, observe these meters while the song plays back. You want to adjust the volume so that they dance primarily in the green area, slipping into the yellow area only during the loudest passages.

What you don't want is for the graph to extend into the red bars, or, worse, for the two tiny dots at the right end—the *clipping* indicators—to illuminate. That's a sign that the volume is so loud, distortion may result. You'll be pumping out too much signal for the speakers on the

Mostly green: about right

Lingering peak indicators

In the red zone: too much

Red clipping indicators

other end, resulting in a garbled, overblown sound.

(Once the two clipping-indicator dots have turned red, they stay red to get your attention. They return to black only when you click them, telling them, in effect, "OK, OK, I get it—I've got a clipping problem. I'll fix it.")

As the music plays, you'll notice that while these volume meters are bouncing around, every so often, one graph bar will remain illuminated for a second. That's your peak volume meter. It remains illuminated for a moment to help you spot the high points of your track volume.

You can boost or reduce the volume of green Software Instrument tracks whenever you feel like it. But when it comes to Real Instrument recordings, the time to pay attention to these level meters is while you're recording. If the microphone or line input setting was too loud or too soft, adjusting the track volume slider may not rescue the recording.

Volume Adjustments Within a Track

All this time, GarageBand has been concealing a little secret from you. Each track can, at your command, sprout a real-time graph of its volume over time. By dragging this "rubber band" line up or down, you can program in gradual (or sudden) volume changes that GarageBand will incorporate into the playback.

To reveal this graph, select a track and then press the letter A key, or click the tiny triangle identified in Figure 29-2. (To hide the volume track, repeat the same procedure.)

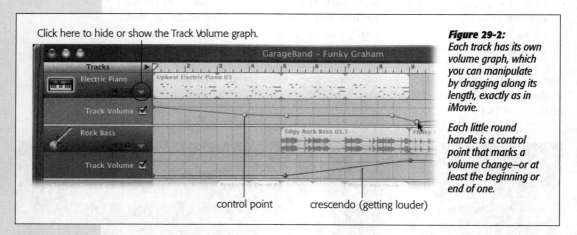

Click here to hide or show the Track Volume graph.

control point   crescendo (getting louder)

Figure 29-2:
Each track has its own volume graph, which you can manipulate by dragging along its length, exactly as in iMovie.

Each little round handle is a control point that marks a volume change—or at least the beginning or end of one.

This graph of track volume comes in handy in many ways. For example, you can begin the piece with its instrumental introduction at full volume, and then pull back the band so that you can hear the singing. You can also create professional sounding fade-ins and fade-outs at the beginnings and ends of your songs.

The key to this feature is the Track Volume checkbox. When you turn it on, a horizontal line appears in the volume track, stretching from edge to edge. This line is a graph of the track's volume, which you can manipulate like a rubber band. Here's how it works:

- If you've also opened the track mixer panel (Figure 29-1), adjusting the overall track volume makes this horizontal volume graph float up or down accordingly.

- Click directly on the line and drag upward or downward to add a small spherical handle. These handles, and the "rubber band" lines connected to them, represent volume fluctuations. You add, drag, and remove them exactly like the similar handles in iMovie (page 353).

- To make a sudden volume change, zoom way in, then drag an orange handle carefully until it's *almost* directly below the previous or next one. (Don't drag it directly underneath—if you do that, the other handle will disappear. In that case, use the Edit→Undo command to restore it.)

- Consider making your volume adjustments *while* the music plays back. GarageBand dutifully changes the mix in real time as you fiddle.

- You can drag a group of handles higher or lower—thus proportionally boosting or decreasing the volume for an entire stretch of music—by selecting them en masse first. You can also drag a group of control points sideways, making the volume fluctuation take place sooner or later. Figure 29-3 has the details.

Tip: In fact, you can use that same trick to drag the *entire* volume graph up or down for the length of the song. To select all of the handles in the entire volume track, click the volume track *header* (marked by the words "Track Volume" at the left edge of the window).

Figure 29-3:
Top: You can select a group of control points either by Shift-clicking the ones you want, or, as shown here, by dragging horizontally through them.

Bottom: Then, you can drag the group either horizontally (to change the timing) or vertically (to change the overall level of the volume change), using one of them as a handle.

- To restore the original, straight-line condition of a clip's volume, select all of the orange handles (see the previous Tip) and press Delete. (Of course, you can also delete only a subset of them by first dragging a selection, as shown in Figure 29-3, at top.)

Tip: When you're finished editing volume fluctuations, you can turn off the Track Volume checkbox again. GarageBand will remember all of the changes that you've made—you'll still hear the volume changes on playback—but it dims all of the handles and rubber-band graph lines, so you won't drag something out of alignment by accident.

Pan Position

The beauty of stereo is that there are *two* speakers or headphones, which happens to correspond very nicely with the number of ears on your head. When you listen to music in stereo, part of the realism stems from the instruments' varied placement in the stereo *sound field* or *soundstage*. In other words, some instruments seem to be coming from the left side of the room, some from the right, and some from directly in front of you, almost as though you were listening to them live.

Over the ages, record producers have become very skilled at exploiting this phenomenon. When they mix the song, they use knobs or software to specify where each track should sound like it's coming from—left, right, center, or anywhere along the scale. In short, they spend a lot of time thinking about the *pan position* of each instrument (that is, its position along the sonic *panorama* before you).

As it turns out, GarageBand provides this flexibility, too. All you have to do is to open the track mixer panel, as described in Figure 29-1.

Unless you intervene, every instrument starts out sounding like it's coming out of both speakers—left and right—with equal volume. Every instrument starts out with a *center* pan position; accordingly, every track's pan knob starts out with the little white notch pointing straight up to the center position.

Here's how to work this knob (Figure 29-4):

- Don't even bother grabbing the tiny rim of the knob and then dragging the mouse along it. This will effectively turn the knob, but it requires the precision of a neurosurgeon.

  Instead, click one of the tiny white dots around the *outside* of the knob (or, for extreme panning, click the letter L or R). Instantly, the white notch on the knob turns to face your click.

- Option-click anywhere on the knob to reset it to center, making its little white notch point straight up again.

Figure 29-4:
You can't really gauge the effects of the pan control unless you're listening with headphones, or sitting between two stereo speakers. And it probably goes without saying that you should keep the music playing while you make these adjustments.

Leaving everything set to the center is fine if people are going to be listening in mono anyway—from a Power Mac speaker, say, or over the Internet in a file that you've distilled down to a single mono track to make it a quicker download.

Most professionally recorded songs, however, feature instruments that are carefully spread out across the stereo field. In general, the most important instruments—the soloist, the drummer, bass player, and maybe the guitars—stick with center positions, but the "flavor" instruments might be spread out to the left and right sides.

You can inject some fun into the process by introducing variations on this formula. If you're singing a duet—maybe even a duet with yourself—you could put the two voices on opposite channels, so it sounds like they're really facing each other. (The more you turn the pan knob, for example, the farther to the left or right you place that instrument.)

Using volume, pan, and reverb together, in fact, you can dial up a pretty convincing sonic impression of a track's position in three-dimensional space.

The Master Track

It's nice that you can control the volume of individual tracks, and of individual sections of music along their lengths. But as a final step before unveiling your masterpiece to the world, you'll want to look over the master volume for the entire mix and set up any master effects, like reverb, that you want to apply to the entire garage band.

Tip: Perform the following adjustments *after* adjusting the mix of your individual tracks.

You apply most of these all-track changes using the *Master Track*. It's an additional track that appears at the bottom of the track list, as shown in Figure 29-5.

To make it appear, choose Track→Show Master Track, or press ⌘-B. (To hide the Master Track once again, choose Track→Hide Master Track, or press ⌘-B a second time.)

Figure 29-5:
This track is probably hidden most of the time that you're working in GarageBand. It's especially useful, however, at the end of the compositional process, just before you "publish." In this illustration, the song ends with a nice fade-out, courtesy of the Master Track volume graph.

Master level meters

Master track   Fadeout   Master mix volume

If you've learned to manipulate the effects, overall volume, and volume graphs for individual tracks, you already know how to operate them for the Master Track. The only difference is that you're now affecting all tracks simultaneously. For example:

- **Set the overall volume level for your song** using the master volume slider identified in Figure 29-5. Play back the entire song, watching the volume-level meters just above the slider to make sure that they don't cross into the red zone during the loudest portions of the music, and that the two little clipping indicators don't light up. (See the box on page 571 for more detail on using these meters.)

The point is to make sure the music will sound good when other people play it on their computers, iPods, or CD players. Volume that's too low to hear the detail, or so high that you're introducing distortion, will seriously hinder your chances of getting picked for *American Idol*.

Tip: Don't get into the habit of using this master slider to adjust GarageBand's playback volume while you're working on your compositions. For that purpose, use the speaker-volume keys on the top row of your keyboard. Or, if you don't see them on your keyboard, use the speaker-volume mini-menu in your menu bar. (And if you don't see *that*, choose →System Preferences, click Sound, and turn on "Show volume in menu bar.")

Use the master output volume slider only to determine the final volume level for your piece, as it will be when you export it to iTunes, post it online, and so on.

- **Create fade-ins, fade-outs, and other whole-song volume fluctuations** by turning on the Master Volume checkbox and then manipulating the horizontal master-volume graph, exactly the way you would adjust an individual track's graph.

- **Set up reverb, compression, and any other whole-song processing effects** by double-clicking the Master Track's header (where it says Master Volume at the left edge of the window). Doing so produces the Track Info dialog box for the Master Track, as shown in Figure 29-6.

In this dialog box, you can specify a degree of echo, reverb, equalization, or compression. You can also apply any of the GarageBand "additional effects" like Bitcrusher, Chorus, Flanger, and so on, using the pop-up menu in the middle of the Details panel. All of these effects are described at length in Chapter 28.

Tip: If you create a combination of effects that sounds particularly appropriate for your style of music, and you think you might use them for subsequent compositions, click the Save Master button shown in Figure 29-6. You're asked to type a name for this effects preset, and then click Save. From now on, you'll see your new Master Track preset listed in the right-side list of the Track Info dialog box—or at least until you use the Delete Master button to remove it.

Publishing the Song

Suppose that the music sounds great, the mix is on target, and everybody who hears the song playing in GarageBand is blown away. This is the moment you've been waiting for. You're about to liberate your tune, freeing it from GarageBand and getting it into a program that's far better at playing and distributing digital music—iTunes. From there, you can burn it to a CD; convert it to an MP3 file; use it as background music for iPhoto, iMovie, or iDVD; and so on.

Figure 29-6:
You can get to this dialog box either by double-clicking the Master Track header, or by double-clicking any other track's header and then, in the Track Info dialog box, clicking the Master Track tab. Either way, this is where you set up processing effects for the entire mix. This is also, incidentally, the only place where you can change the time signature or key signature of the piece once you've created the file.

Here's how the process works.

1. **Choose GarageBand→Preferences.**

   The GarageBand Preferences dialog box appears.

   The music you create in GarageBand will wind up in one iTunes *playlist* (a subset of your music collection that you've built for a certain purpose). Unless you specify otherwise, iTunes will name it "Casey's Playlist" (or whatever your account name is, as identified on the Accounts panel of System Preferences in Mac OS X). Here's your opportunity to assign your collected GarageBand works a more resonant title.

Publishing the Song

2. **Click the Export tab. Edit the iTunes Playlist, Composer Name, and Album Name boxes (Figure 29-7).**

Once you've filled out the last line of the dialog box, click once in another one of the text boxes to make your changes "take."

Figure 29-7:
In iTunes, almost every song displays labeling information: composer name, album name, and so on. All right, maybe you're not much of a composer, and you probably don't yet have an album out—but at least you can pretend by filling in the boxes here.

3. **Close the Preferences box.**

The only information you didn't have to fill in is the name of the song. But of course, iTunes already knows that information—it's whatever name you gave your GarageBand project when you created it.

4. **Specify which tracks you want to export.**

Most of the time, you'll want to export *all* of the tracks. In certain situations, though, you may not want some tracks to be a part of the finished mix. If you really *do* have a garage band, for example, you might want to make yourself a track that includes the backup band but omits your part, so that you can practice by playing along with it.

Maybe, too, your intention is to create a karaoke album of your own greatest hits—that is, minus the vocals.

Or maybe you just want to send a record company's talent scout a couple of different mixes, each with a different instrumentation. (Some people, for example, like to try out a couple of different drum loops for the same song. Each one lends a different flavor to the piece. So for comparison, you can export the song twice, one with each drum track playing.)

Either way, silence the tracks you want omitted by clicking each one and then pressing the letter M key (or clicking the little speaker in the track header). Doing so mutes the track. Now when you export your song to iTunes, they won't be part of the mix.

5. Specify how much of the song you want to export.

Selecting a specific part of the song can be useful now and then. Maybe you've got a shorter version that you want to keep distinct from the extended mix, for example.

Maybe, too, you want to export a region that's *longer* than the song. You might want to incorporate a few seconds of silence at the end, so that your listeners can reflect thoughtfully on the impact of what they just heard. Or, more practically, maybe you've discovered that GarageBand exports only up to the end of the last region, and is therefore chopping off a little bit of reverb that rings past that moment.

In any case, the trick to specifying how much of the song you want to export lies in the cycle region. Figure 29-8 explains.

Figure 29-8:
Press the letter C key, or click the cycle button, to make the yellow highlighting bar appear at the top of the GarageBand window. Zoom out as much as necessary, and then drag the edges of this yellow bar until it brackets the portion of the song you want to include. GarageBand will export only as much of the song as you've indicated with this cycle region.

Yellow bar: Only this much will be exported

Cycle button

6. Give the piece one last listen.

Put on headphones if possible, press the letter Z key to rewind, press the Space bar to play, and watch the output-level meters at the lower-right corner of the GarageBand window to make sure that the two little clipping dots are turning red—or that your piece isn't so quiet that the dancing meter bars never even touch the yellow region. (See the box on page 571.)

7. Choose File→Export to iTunes.

GarageBand takes a moment to create your final mix, merging all those tracks down to just two channels: left and right stereo. In a moment, the iTunes window appears automatically.

As shown in Figure 29-9, a new playlist has joined the others in the Source list at the left side of the window. This is where you'll find your exported GarageBand masterpieces.

Tip: Of course, you can always change the playlist name in the GarageBand→Preferences dialog box. Doing so will build a second playlist in iTunes, containing all your GarageBand exports henceforth.

To hear your opus now that it's been freed from the protective walls of GarageBand, click the playlist name and then double-click the name of the song displayed to its right.

Figure 29-9:
Your GarageBand creations ultimately land in iTunes, which also came on your iLife DVD. (You can find it in your Applications folder.) Many of the keyboard shortcuts are exactly the same as in GarageBand: Press the Space bar to start and stop a selected song, press ⌘-up arrow and ⌘-down arrow to adjust the volume during playback, and so on.

Your GarageBand playlist   Songs you've exported

Having your finished GarageBand pieces stored in iTunes, rather than GarageBand, is a wonderful convenience. iTunes starts up faster than GarageBand, it's easier to search and sort, you can't accidentally mess up your piece by clicking in the wrong place, and the actual music file is much smaller than your original GarageBand project.

Tip: Behind the scenes, your exported GarageBand song is saved as an AIFF file in your Home→Music→ iTunes→iTunes Music→Import folder. Back up this folder if you want to make safety copies of your finished projects.

Part Six:
Troubleshooting

6

Troubleshooting iTunes

W hen you get right down to it, iTunes is a glorified database. It's a list—a searchable, sortable list—but a very high-profile one with some stiff competition (at least in the Windows world, where iTunes is also popular). For these reasons, Apple has put a lot of effort into making iTunes rock-solid. Not a lot goes wrong in iTunes.

But when the planets don't align your way, may this chapter be your guide to iTunes wholeness.

Rule 1: Get the Latest

Upgrading to iTunes 4.6 or later is the most important step you can take. It cures a long list of glitches that were possible in 4.5 and earlier versions. For example:

- You can't listen to someone else's shared music over the network if they have a big music library. (The "Loading" message appears, but the shared library never does appear.)

- iTunes suddenly crashes when you try to listen to certain radio stations (those whose Web addresses don't begin with *http://*).

- You try to share music with a version of iTunes before 4.5 (and get a "not compatible with this version of iTunes" message).

In these cases and many others, just downloading the free update to iTunes 4.6 or later solves the problem.

Rule 2: Back Up Your Library

Having a backup of your music files is excellent insurance against all sorts of music-library corruption. It's also a safety net for all the music you've bought from the iTunes Music Store; if something goes wrong with your hard drive, and you don't have a backup, you have to buy all of it again.

Backing Up to a Hard Drive or Another Mac

If you've got an external hard drive (the hard drive in another Mac on the network counts), backing up your music collection is extremely easy. Open your Home→Music folder, and copy the iTunes folder inside it. That's it—you're backed up. (In the event of catastrophe, simply restore this backup copy to its original location.)

Backing Up to CD or DVD

You can copy about 650 megabytes of music files to a recordable CD, or (if your Mac has a DVD burner) about 4.7 gigabytes to a blank DVD.

Start by creating a playlist of your entire music library, like this:

1. **In iTunes, click Library in the Source list.**

   Make sure that the Search box is empty—that you're viewing your entire list of songs.

2. **Click a song, and then choose Edit→Select All.**

   iTunes highlights all of your songs.

3. **Choose File→New Playlist From Selection.**

   iTunes asks you to name the new playlist.

4. **Type *Full Backup* (or whatever name you like).**

   Now you're ready to create the backup disc.

5. **Choose iTunes→Preferences; in the Preferences dialog box, click Burning. Click "Data CD or DVD," and click OK.**

   You're going to burn a computer disc, that is, not one intended for playing in stereos.

6. **Select the playlist you created in step 4, and then click the Burn Disc button. Insert a blank CD or DVD (either an -R or -RW blank format), and click Burn Disc again.**

   iTunes backs up all your audio files. If you need more than one disc to hold it all, iTunes will let you know, and invite you to insert a second disc.

Tip: You don't have to back up your entire music library each time. Thanks to the magic of the Smart Playlist, you can back up only the newest arrivals on successive backups.

To do that, note the date and time of the *first* complete backup. Then just create a new Smart Playlist that includes all songs with whose Date Added is after that. When you want to back up that newest batch, just repeat the steps above—but click your Smart Playlist's name in step 6.

Each time you perform one of these so-called *incremental* backups, remember to click the Smart Playlist, choose Edit→Edit Smart Playlist, and change the date to today's date. You've just reset the Smart Playlist so that it will begin collecting *new* new songs.

Store-Bought Songs Won't Play

If you can't play songs you've bought online, the problem almost always boils down to one of these three things:

- **You don't have QuickTime 6.5.1 or later.** You need this version of Apple's QuickTime music-and-movie-playing software if you hope to use your store-bought songs in the other iLife programs, like using a song as a background in an iMovie movie.

  To find out what version you have, open System Preferences, click QuickTime, and click the About QuickTime button. If it turns out you don't have the latest version of QuickTime, stay right there in System Preferences. Click View→Software Update, click Update Software, make sure you can get online, and then click Check Now. After a moment, you'll be offered the opportunity to download the latest, greatest version of QuickTime.

- **Your permissions are scrambled.** An amazing number of mysterious glitches arise because the *permissions* of either that item or something in your System folder have become muddled—that is, Mac OS X's complex mesh of interconnected Unix permissions settings. Music-store songs not playing back is among them.

FREQUENTLY ASKED QUESTION

QuickTime Player vs. QuickTime Player Pro

OK, I tried to update my copy of QuickTime like you said. But the updater asks me for my name, company, and a "QuickTime Pro key!" What the heck is that?

QuickTime Pro is a $30 upgrade (to the free QuickTime you just downloaded). It adds the ability to edit QuickTime movies (instead of just watching them), among other goodies.

If you had paid for this upgrade, this would be your opportunity to plug in the serial number you were sent by email. But if you have no intention of upgrading to Pro, just leave the boxes blank and click Continue.

In that case, open your Applications→Utilities folder and open Disk Utility. Then proceed as shown in Figure 30-1.

Figure 30-1:
Click your hard drive's name in the left-side list; click the First Aid tab; click Repair Disk Permissions; and then read an article while the Mac checks out your disk. If the program finds anything amiss, you'll see messages like these.

- **You've authorized too many computers.** Remember, once you buy a song online, you're allowed to play it on a maximum of five computers (Macs or PCs).

  Rack your brain: Is it possible you authorized somebody's Mac so they could hear something you bought, forgot to de-authorize it, and now you're over the limit?

  Anyway, you remove a computer from your designated set by choosing Advanced→ Deauthorize Computer while you're online. In the resulting dialog box, choose "Deauthorize Computer for Apple Account" and then click OK.

- **You can't listen to store-bought songs across the network.** If you, seated at Computer A, are trying to listen to the music on Computer B using the playlist-sharing feature described on page 217, you may notice that iTunes skips over any songs that came from the iTunes Music Store. That, alas, is normal behavior. Unless you make Computer A one of the five authorized machines for your account, you won't be able to hear Computer B's store-bought tunes.

Playback Problems

Playing back music is a pretty essential and simple task: Just tap the Space bar. Troubleshooting playback is pretty simple, too:

The Music Is Too Quiet

Remember that you're now contending with two different volume levels: your Mac's own speaker volume (which you can adjust with the volume keys on your keyboard, or using the Sound panel of System Preferences) and the little volume slider at the top of the iTunes window. Adjust both of them.

If you can't hear anything at all, make sure that you don't have external speakers or headphones plugged into your Mac (which cuts off all sound to the built-in speaker).

And if you have an AirPort Express wireless networking base station, make sure that the pop-up menu at the bottom edge of the iTunes window is set correctly. If you're trying to play back the music using your Mac's built-in speakers, make sure this pop-up menu says Computer. And if you're attempting to direct playback to whatever speakers are attached to the AirPort Express, make sure they're turned on and hooked up right.

The Songs Overlap Each Other

It's a feature, not a bug. Choose iTunes→Preferences, click Audio, and turn off Crossfade Playback.

Troubleshooting iPhoto

Photo isn't just a Mac OS X program—it's a *Cocoa* Mac OS X program, meaning that it was written exclusively for Mac OS X. As a result, it should, in theory, be one of the most rock-solid programs under the sun.

Still, iPhoto does have its vulnerabilities. If trouble strikes, keep hands and feet inside the tram at all times—and consult the following collection of problems, solutions, questions, and answers.

Importing

Getting photos into iPhoto is supposed to be one of the most effortless parts of the process. Remember, Steve Jobs promised that iPhoto would forever banish the "chain of pain" from digital photography. And yet…

iPhoto doesn't recognize my camera.

iPhoto generally "sees" any recent camera model, even if it's not listed on Apple's Device Compatibility page (*www.apple.com/iphoto/compatibility*). If you click the Import mode button and see "No camera is connected" in the lower-left corner of the screen, even though the camera most assuredly *is* connected, try these steps in order:

- Turn on the camera *after* connecting its USB cable to the Mac.

- Turn the camera off, then on again, while it's plugged in.

- If iPhoto absolutely won't notice its digital companion, use a memory-card reader as described on page 89.

iPhoto crashes when I try to import.

This problem is most likely to crop up when you're bringing pictures in from your hard drive or another disk. Here are the possibilities:

• The culprit is usually a single corrupted file. Try a test: Import only half the photos in the batch. If nothing bad happens, split the remaining photos in half again and import *them*. Keep going until you've isolated the offending file.

• Consider the graphics program you're using to save the files. It's conceivable that its version of JPEG or TIFF doesn't jibe perfectly with iPhoto's. (This scenario is most likely to occur right after you've upgraded either your graphics program or iPhoto itself.)

  To test this possibility, open a handful of images in a different editing program, save them, and then try the import again. If they work, then you might have a temporary compatibility problem. Check the editing program's Web site for update and troubleshooting information.

• If you're attempting to import hundreds of photos at once, break the import into batches. You'll have fewer problems with a couple of medium-sized imports instead of a single big one.

What if I don't want iPhoto to import **all** *the pictures from my camera?*

You can't tell iPhoto not to import them all—but you can use Image Capture. A sort of grandfather to iPhoto, this Mac OS X program comes on every Mac. Although it doesn't perform even a hundredth of the feats that iPhoto can, it does offer one feature iPhoto lacks—*selective* importing.

First, however, you must tell iPhoto not to open automatically when you plug in your camera. You want Image Capture to do your importing, instead. To make this change, see Figure 31-1. From now on, Image Capture, not iPhoto, will open whenever you plug in your camera.

Once the pictures are on your hard drive, copy them into iPhoto simply by dragging them (or the folder they're in) into the photo-viewing area.

But you're not out of the woods yet. If you change the title of a photo *in iPhoto*, remember that you haven't changed the original file name of the JPEG file buried deep within your Library folder.

After you've changed your picture titles, therefore, you should export them to a folder on your desktop, delete the originals from iPhoto, and then reimport the set you exported. Doing so makes sure that iPhoto adopts their new, authorized names, both internally and externally. They should now give you no further trouble.

Printing

How many things can go wrong when you print? Let us count the ways.

Check the following:

- Have you, in fact, selected more than one photo to print?

- Choose File→Page Setup. Make sure the paper size is US Letter (or whatever paper you've loaded). Click OK.

- Choose File→Print. From the Presets pop-up menu, choose Standard; from the Style pop-up menu, choose N-Up; then choose a number from the "Photos per page" pop-up. (Make sure "One photo per page" is turned off.) You'll now see all of your selected images side by side in the preview pane. They're ready to print.

Figure 31-1:
Top: First, make sure that Image Capture, not iPhoto, intercepts and downloads the photos when you connect your digital camera. To do so, open Image Capture, then choose Image Capture→Preferences.

From the Camera Preferences pop-up menu, choose Image Capture. You could even choose another program to intervene when your camera is plugged in (by choosing Other).

Middle: This is the main Image Capture window that now appears when you plug in your camera. To download only some of the photos, click Download Some.

Bottom: This "slide sorter" window is where you can choose the individual pictures you want to download. Or, use the buttons at the top to rotate or delete selected shots from the camera. In slide sorter view, Shift-click or ⌘-click the thumbnails of the pictures you want. In list view, Shift-click or ⌘-click as though they're Finder list-view files.

Editing

There's not much that can go wrong here, but when it does, it *really* goes wrong.

iPhoto crashes when I double-click a thumbnail to edit it.
You probably changed a photo file's name in the Finder—in the iPhoto Library folder, behind the program's back. iPhoto hates this! Only grief can follow.

Sometimes, too, a corrupted picture file will also make iPhoto crash when you try to edit it. Open the file in another graphics program, use its File→Save As command to replace the corrupted picture file, and then try again in iPhoto.

iPhoto won't let me use an external graphics program when I double-click a thumbnail.
Choose File→Preferences. Make sure that the Other button is selected and that a graphics program's name appears next to it. (If not, click Other, then click Set, and then choose the program you want to use.)

Also make sure that your external editing program still *exists*. You might have upgraded to a newer version of that program, one whose file name is slightly different from the version you originally specified in iPhoto.

My picture doesn't fit right on standard photo paper.
Most digital cameras produce photos in a 4:3 width-to-height ratio. Unfortunately, those dimensions don't fit squarely into any of the standard print sizes.

The solution: Crop the photos first, using the appropriate print size in the Constrain pop-up menu (see page 142).

I've messed up a photo while editing it, and now it's ruined!
Highlight the file's thumbnail and then choose File→Revert to Original. iPhoto restores your photo to its original state, drawing on a backup it has secretly kept.

General Questions

Finally, here's a handful of general—although perfectly terrifying—troubles.

iPhoto's wigging out.
If the program "unexpectedly quits," well, that's life. It happens. This is Mac OS X, though, so you can generally open the program right back up again and pick up where you left off.

If the flakiness is becoming really severe, try logging out (choose →Log Out) and logging back in again.

Man, this program's slow!

Installing more memory is by far the best solution to this problem. iPhoto loves RAM like Madonna loves attention.

For an immediate (and less expensive) fix, keep your Photo Library a reasonable size (page 234) and collapse your film rolls (page 103).

When I try to choose a soundtrack for a slide show, my iTunes music collection doesn't show up!

First, try opening iTunes before opening iPhoto. That way, iPhoto will be sure to "see" the open iTunes library.

If that doesn't solve the problem, you might have to recreate one of your iTunes preference files, like this:

First, quit all of your iLife programs. Open your Home→Music→iTunes folder. Drag the file called iTunes Music Library.xml file to your desktop.

Now open iTunes and create a new playlist by choosing File→New Playlist. (Doing so triggers iTunes to build a new .xml file, which is what you want.) Quit iTunes.

When you return to iPhoto, your iTunes library should show up just fine.

I can't delete a photo!

You may be trying to delete a photo right out of a smart album. That's a no-no.

There's only one workaround: Find the same photo in the Photo Library, the Last Roll icon, or the Last Months icon—and delete it from there.

My QuickTime slideshows don't show the right transitions between slides.

That's normal, actually. All you get in QuickTime Player are standard cross-dissolves between photos. The fancy cube effect, wipe effect, and so on are just for use within iPhoto.

When I edit a photo, it appears blocky, and takes a minute to become sharp.

That's an iPhoto speed trick, and it's normal for high-megapixel images. When you're just paging through pictures, the low-resolution, blocky version is usually enough for you to get the visual idea without having to wait for iPhoto to display the full high-res version. When you finally pause, iPhoto will rebuild its display of that photo at the highest resolution your window will allow.

I've got the opposite problem. The photo appears sharp, and then gets blurry after a moment.

You're probably witnessing the same effect described above—but you're just describing it differently. That is, the "blurry" version of the photo is iPhoto's approximation of it; remember, your monitor simply isn't big enough to show the entire photo at full size (that is, showing every pixel). So iPhoto, in effect, averages pixels to come up with a smaller version.

Some people report being able to kick iPhoto into displaying a sharper image just by clicking inside it, or by paging to the next photo and then back again.

I get an error message when I try to share my albums on a network.

Ah, yes—the old, "Other users will not be able to access your shared photos because port 8770 is being blocked by your firewall software" message.

Evidently, you've turned on the Mac OS X firewall feature, which is designed to insulate your Mac from no-goodnicks on the Internet. Trouble is, it's also blocking innocent activity like sharing your photos.

You can turn the firewall off, if you like (open System Preferences, click Sharing, click the Firewall tab, and click Stop). That will certainly solve the problem.

If you want the firewall on in general, though, you may prefer to simply poke a hole in the firewall just big enough—and only on the proper channel—for iPhoto's photo sharing feature to work.

To try this slightly more involved workaround, see Figure 31-2.

Figure 31-2:
To allow photo sharing to pass through your firewall, open System Preferences, click Sharing, click the Firewall tab, and click New. From the Port Name pop-up menu, choose Other, as shown here; type 8770 into the middle box; and type a description, if you like. Click OK to complete the deed.

iPhoto freezes up when rebuilding thumbnails.

The iPhoto 4.0.1 updater is designed to make iPhoto convert every thumbnail image into a newer, better format that takes less time to display on the screen. Unfortunately, the thumbnail converter chokes when it encounters graphics that aren't JPEG images, even though iPhoto itself is perfectly compatible with them. The upgrader stalls when it attempts to build a new thumbnail image for, say, a Photoshop document.

Here's how you solve the problem.

1. **Start iPhoto. When the program announces that it wants to convert your thumbnails, click Upgrade Later.**

   Now, at least, you can get into your collection.

2. **Create a smart album (page 126) whose criteria read, "Title" "does not contain" ".jpg."**

   The idea is to ferret out all pictures that aren't JPEG files. Once you've confirmed that they're all rounded up in your smart album, continue:

3. **Export the smart album's photos to a new folder on your hard drive.**

   See page 243 for instructions on exporting. The point is to get these pictures out of iPhoto.

4. **Delete all of the non-JPEG images.**

   As noted earlier in this appendix, you can't delete them straight from the smart album; you have to delete them from the photo library itself. Be sure to empty the iPhoto Trash once you're done.

5. **Quit iPhoto. Reopen it and this time, permit the program to update its thumbnails.**

6. **Finally, reimport the non-JPEG photos that you had exported to a folder.**

iPhoto is doing something bizarre.

Maybe it's trying to import phantom photos. Maybe it's stuck at the "Loading photos..." screen forever. Maybe the photos just don't look right. There's a long list, in fact, of rare but mystifying glitches that can arise.

Fortunately, setting things aright is fairly easy if you know what to do. Follow these steps, in order; after each one, check to see if the problem is gone.

- **Rebuild the photo library.** Quit iPhoto. Press the Shift, Option, and ⌘ keys as you reopen it.

   iPhoto asks you if you're sure you want to "rebuild your Photo Library," and warns that you might lose some data. What it's referring to here is corrupted data—photo files that are slightly damaged, for example. Since these are probably what's causing iPhoto to misbehave, you probably don't mind losing them. Click Yes.

   In the next dialog box, iPhoto asks you to save the freshly rebuilt iPhoto Library folder somewhere. You can name it "Rescued Library" or whatever you like, and save it into your Pictures folder or wherever you like.

   Once you click Save, iPhoto works its way through each album and each photo, inspecting it for damage, repairing it if possible, and finally presenting you with your new, cleaned-up library.

- **Repair your file permissions.** An amazing number of mysterious glitches—not just in iPhoto—arise because file *permissions* have become muddled. Permissions is a complex subject, and refers to a complex mesh of interconnected Unix settings on every file in Mac OS X.

  When something just doesn't seem to be working right, therefore, open your Applications→Utilities folder and open Disk Utility. Click your hard drive's name in the left-side list; click the First Aid tab; click Repair Disk Permissions; and then read an article while the Mac checks out your disk. If the program finds anything amiss, you'll see Unix shorthand messages that tell you what it fixed.

Tip: Most Mac mavens, in fact, believe in running this Repair Permissions routine after running *any kind of installer*, just to nip nascent problems in the bud. That includes both installers of new programs and of Apple's own updates.

- **Throw away the iPhoto preferences file.** Here we are in the age of Mac OS X, and we're still throwing away preference files?

  Absolutely. A corrupted preference file can still bewilder the program that depends on it.

  Before you go on a dumpfest, however, take this simple test. Log in using a *different account* (perhaps a dummy account that you create just for testing purposes). Run iPhoto. Is the problem gone? If so, then the glitch exists only when *you* are logged in—which means it's a problem with *your* copy of the program's preferences.

  Return to your own account. Open your Home→Library→Preferences folder, where you'll find neatly labeled preference files for all of the programs you use. In this case, trash the file called com.apple.iPhoto.plist.

  The next time you run iPhoto, it will build itself a brand-new preference file that, if you're lucky, lacks whatever corruption was causing your problems.

Troubleshooting iMovie & iDVD

O n the great spectrum of software complexity, iMovie falls pretty far to the left end, closer to the Mac OS X Calculator than to Microsoft Excel. It's a fairly streamlined application that only rarely leaves you scratching your head.

But with each successive version, iMovie becomes a more complex, larger program. There are very few glaring, ticking-time-bomb bugs—but a few doozies strike a few people now and then: photos that look awful on the finished DVD, mysteriously dropping volume when you apply titles or effects, projects that corrupt themselves, and so on. This chapter covers them all.

Three Golden Rules

If there's any common wisdom at all about iMovie, here it is: a set of three golden rules that will stave off a huge number of problems down the road.

- **Use the latest version.** Each ".01" or ".02" upgrade zaps a whole host of bugs and glitches. These updates are free, so when your Software Update program advises you that one is available, jump at the chance to install it.

- **Set your camcorder to 16-bit audio.** The typical digital camcorder can record its audio track using either 12-bit or 16-bit audio. The factory setting is 12-bit, which gives non–computer owners a chance to overlay a second audio track without erasing the original camera sound. Trouble is, 12-bit audio may slowly drift out of sync with the video when you burn the finished project to a DVD.

Use your camera's menu system to switch to 16-bit audio. You, an iMovie aficionado, can easily overlay additional audio using your computer, so you give up nothing—except a lot of frustration. (Make this change *now,* before you record anything important.)

- **Hold off on emptying the Trash.** As noted in the box below, you'd be wise to avoid emptying the iMovie Trash until your project is done and safely exported. Not only does emptying the Trash eliminate your chances to use the Undo or Restore Clip commands, but in rare cases, it has corrupted iMovie projects.

General iMovie Troubleshooting

Let's start general, shall we?

Weird Inconsistent Problems

When a program's preferences file becomes scrambled, all kinds of peculiar behavior can result. Buttons and functions don't work. Visual anomalies appear. Things just don't work right.

If iMovie starts having a bad hair day, suspect its preferences file. Quit the program, open your Home→Library→Preferences folder, and throw away the file called *com .apple.iMovie3.plist.*

The next time you run iMovie, it will automatically build a new preferences file. This file will have the original factory settings (for the options in, for example, the Preferences dialog box), but at least it will be healthy and whole.

PARANOIDS' CORNER

Of Trash and Project Corruption

As you may have read in several places in this book, it's wise to put off emptying the iMovie project Trash until after you're finished editing. Most people, most of the time, empty the Trash without a hitch. But in that one-in-ten-thousand case when it causes harm to your project file, it causes *severe* harm.

The truly paranoid, therefore, adopt a rigid protocol of safety. They don't empty the Trash until the project is completely done. And even then, they follow these steps:

Quit iMovie. Reopen the project to make sure it opens OK. If so, you've escaped project corruption—so far. Quit again without saving.

In the Finder, make a backup of the entire project folder. (The duplicate will be large, because it will include the project's Media folder.)

Open the original project again. *Now* empty the iMovie project Trash, and then save the file.

Quit iMovie. Reopen the original project yet again. If it opens and plays OK, it survived emptying the Trash, and you're home free.

When you're sure everything is working, you can discard the duplicate project folder.

These steps give you both the convenience of recovering wasted space on your hard drive *and* the confidence that doing so won't corrupt your movie.

Keeping Your Hard Disk Happy

Remember the old expression "If Mama ain't happy, ain't nobody happy"? Well, if your hard disk isn't happy, iMovie won't be happy, either.

Here's a short list of maintenance suggestions. A little attention every week or so may help keep minor hard drive problems from becoming major problems.

- After installing or updating any software, use Disk Utility to Repair Permissions. (Disk Utility is in your Applications→Utilities folder. Click the First Aid tab, click your hard drive, and then click Repair Permissions.)

- Every couple of months, restart your Mac from the Mac OS X CD, choose File→ Disk Utility, click the First Aid tab, click your hard drive icon, and click Repair Disk.

- Mac OS X runs three behind-the-scenes Unix disk-checking programs at regular intervals between 3 a.m. and 5 a.m. If you don't regularly leave your Mac running overnight, take a minute, every month or so, to run MacJanitor—a free program that runs those same maintenance programs, but on your command. (You can get it from the "Missing CD" page at *www.missingmanuals.com,* among other places.)

Starting Up and Importing

Trouble getting going? Here's some advice.

"Stray Clip Files" Message

You're never supposed to move, delete, rename, or fiddle with any of the icons in your project folder's Media folder. iMovie itself is supposed to manage those clips, behind the scenes.

If you put a clip into that folder yourself, however, then the next time you open the project, you get the message shown in Figure 32-1. iMovie doesn't recognize some of the clips it found there, and it's inviting you to (a) add them to the Clips pane for use in your movie, or (b) not.

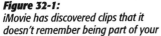
Figure 32-1:
iMovie has discovered clips that it doesn't remember being part of your project. Maybe you put them in the project folder (deliberately or not); maybe the clips were always part of the project, but iMovie somehow forgot.

That's the theory, anyway. In the real world, you'll probably get the "stray clips" message from time to time even when you haven't been anywhere near the Media folder. Sometimes iMovie just gets confused, as may be the case when the program bombs, or when you force quit it.

There's no real trouble to shoot here; click the option you prefer and get on with your life.

It is worth noting, however, that you can *deliberately* exploit iMovie's attentiveness in some useful ways. For example, later in this appendix, you can read about curing project-file corruption by manually deleting references to a certain clip (by editing your project file in TextEdit). The next time you open the edited project file, iMovie "discovers" the clips in its Media folder—clips that you've made it forget. The "stray clips" dialog box is your chance to add them back into the project.

Similarly, when you want to reuse a piece of footage from another project, one approach is to copy its icon into the new project folder's Media folder. (Of course, you could also use iMovie's Import command, but sometimes it's just quicker to copy a file like this in the Finder.)

When you next open the new project, up pops the "stray clips" message, offering to make the recycled clip part of the new project.

"Camera not connected"

If you get this message in the Monitor window when you click the Camera button, it probably means that:

- Your camcorder isn't plugged into the Mac with a FireWire cable.

- The camcorder isn't turned on.

- You're using a camcorder whose FireWire circuitry isn't completely compatible with the Macintosh. (Some older JVC camcorders—circa 1999–2000—fall into this category.)

If you get the "Camera not connected" message the very first time you try to connect a new camcorder to your Mac, and you've checked to make sure that the cable is connected properly and the camera is turned on, then you probably need to replace either the camera or the FireWire cable. (The occasional iMovie owner has become frustrated that a new camcorder doesn't work, but upon exchanging it for another of the same model, finds that it works beautifully.)

Dropouts in the Video

A *dropout* is a glitch in the picture, as shown in Figure 32-2. Fortunately, dropouts are fairly rare in digital video. If you get one, it's probably in one of these three circumstances:

- You're using a very old cassette. Remember that even DV cassettes don't last forever. You may begin to see dropouts after rerecording the tape 50 times or so.

- You're playing back a cassette that was recorded in LP (long play) mode. If the cassette was recorded on a different camcorder, dropouts are especially likely.

- It's time to clean the heads on your camcorder—the electrical components that actually make contact with the tape and, over time, can become dirty. Your local electronics store sells head-cleaning kits for just this purpose.

If you spot the glitch at the same moment on the tape every time you play it, then the problem is on the tape itself. If it's there during one playback, but gone during the next, the problem more likely lies with the heads in your camcorder.

Tip: Different DV tape manufacturers use different lubricants on their tapes. As a result, mixing tapes from different manufacturers on the same camcorder can increase the likelihood of head clogs. It's a good idea, therefore, to stick with tapes from one manufacturer (Sony, Panasonic, or Maxell, for example) when possible.

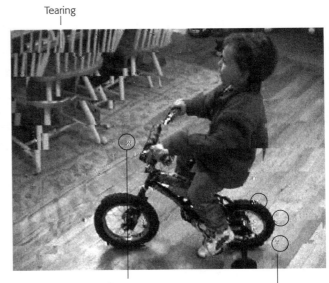

Figure 32-2:
DV dropouts are always square or rectangular. They may be a blotch of the wrong color or may be multicolored. They may appear every time you play a particular scene, or may appear at random. In severe circumstances, you may get lots of them, such as when you try to capture video to an old FireWire hard drive that's too slow. Such a configuration may also cause tearing of the video picture, shown here as well.

Tearing

Dropouts

Title Trouble

For some reason, titles and credits seem to have their own phalanx of problems and issues. For example:

Jagged, Crummy-Looking Titles

iMovie titles and credits look terrific when played on a TV. But on your screen, you may notice that the edges of your lettering look jagged and disintegrated.

One quick way to make text look smooth and nice is as simple as turning on "Enhanced Video Playback" in iMovie's Preferences, if your Mac is fast enough to handle it.

Half Volume During Titles

A bug in iMovie 4.0.1 has the peculiar effect of lowering the volume of a clip to which you've applied a title or an effect. Weirdly enough, the trouble is the main iMovie volume slider (just above the Movie Track); the title or effect somehow takes its volume setting cue from this control.

The trick, then, is to delete the title or effect (click the clip and then press Delete). Drag the iMovie volume slider all the way to the right, and then apply the title or effect again. (Or, for titles only, you can take a shortcut: drag the volume slider all the way to the right—and then just click the Update button on the Titles panel.)

Chopped-off Type on Playback from Tape

The actual dimensions of a TV picture aren't what you'd expect. To avoid the risk that some oddball TV model might display a sliver of black empty space at a corner or edge of the glass, all NTSC television signals are *overscanned*—deliberately transmitted at a size *larger* than the TV screen. Sure, that means that the outer 5 percent of the picture at each edge doesn't even show up on your TV, because it's beyond the glass borders. But TV directors are aware of this phenomenon, and carefully avoid shooting anything that might get chopped off by the overscanning.

Unfortunately, iMovie has one foot in the world of video, and the other in the QuickTime world, where no overscanning is necessary. QuickTime movies always show *everything* in the picture, perfectly and precisely—nothing is ever lost beyond the borders of a QuickTime window. That's why some footage that looks spectacular and perfect in iMovie (or in an exported QuickTime movie) gets chopped off around the edges when viewed on a TV.

(This quirk explains the "QT Margins" checkbox, described on page 324.)

Photo Problems

iMovie 4's photo features are, in general, a delight—and they let you get mileage out of iMovie even if you don't own a camcorder. But you may encounter some rough edges.

Can't Change the Duration of a Still Photo

iMovie distinguishes between still *photos* and still *frames,* of the sort that you capture using the Edit→Create Still Frame command. Moreover, it differentiates between photos that exhibit the Ken Burns effect and those that don't.

It's so complicated, you practically need a cheat sheet—and here it is.

- To change the duration of a Ken Burnsized photo (imported from iPhoto or from the hard drive), click the clip and then use the Duration slider (or Duration box) in the Photos palette. Click Update.

- To change the duration of a still frame, double-click it. Change the duration in the Clip Info box.

- To change the duration of a *non*–Ken Burnsized photo, use either method: the Duration slider in the Photos palette or the Clip Info box.

Photo Corruption

Examine Figure 32-3, and you'll recognize the syndrome instantly if it ever happens to you.

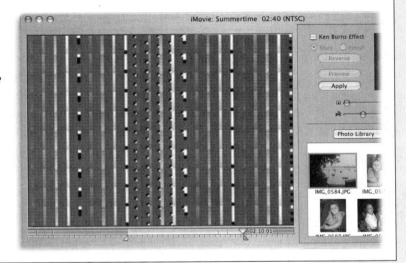

Figure 32-3:
This bizarre form of photo corruption may arise when the first clip of your movie is a still photo. It may also result from, of all things, emptying the iMovie Project Trash.

Fight back by making the first clip not be a still photo.

The solution is beyond bizarre, but it really works. First, insert any old video clip (including a Ken Burnsized still photo) at the very beginning of your project. It can be only a couple of frames long, and you'll remove it in a moment.

Now delete the corrupted still-photo clip. When you import it afresh, it won't display the grisly vertical lines of Figure 32-3. Of course, you'll have to reapply any transitions or effects that involved it, but that's a small price to pay. Finally, delete the placeholder clip you placed at the beginning of your movie.

Tip: You can avoid this problem altogether by making sure that the first clip of your movie is a DV or Ken Burns clip—not a still clip. Again, you can always delete it after you're finished editing the movie.

Photos Look Jaggy and Awful on DVD

All over the world, every single day, more Mac fans try to turn their digital photos into DVD slideshows using iMovie—and find out that the photos look *terrible*. What makes this syndrome so baffling is that the photos probably began life with super high resolution and look fantastic in Photoshop or iPhoto. But once they arrive on a DVD, the pictures look lousy.

It turns out that when you click the Create iDVD Project button in iMovie (the usual way to hand off the project to iDVD), iMovie offers to process any still photos—to *render* them, turning them into what amounts to motionless video. "Your movie contains still, slow motion, and/or reverse clips," it says. If you click "Render and Proceed," iMovie does a pretty poor job at converting them into video, resulting in jaggy blockiness. (This conversion is permanent in iMovie. Once it's done, your photos will always look bad in iMovie until you reinsert the originals.)

One way to help your stills' quality is to turn on both "High quality" and "Enhanced video playback" in iMovie's preferences.

But the more important step is to bypass iMovie's low-quality photo-rendering cycle altogether. You can do that in either of two ways.

The Ken Burns Method

If you turn your photos into digital video clips, then iMovie doesn't consider them stills any more, and won't attempt to render them. Here's how to do that:

1. **Click the still photo, whether it's already in your Movie Track or still in the Photos palette.**

   Actually, you can select as many photos as you want. Remember that you can ⌘- click to select multiple photos in the Movie Track simultaneously.

2. **Click the Photos button to reveal the Ken Burns pane. Turn on the Ken Burns checkbox.**

   Make sure there are no Ken Burns effects already in place: click Start and drag the zoom slider all the way left. Then Option-click the Finish button to copy those "no zoom" settings into the Finish position.

3. **Click the Start button. Drag the Ken Burns magnification slider to 1.02.**

   Use the slider. If you type into the box instead, iMovie will later round off to 1.0, which isn't what you want.

4. **Now click the Finish button. Drag the magnification slider to 1.00.**

   Your goal here is to produce a very tiny degree of inward zoom. You want iMovie to think that it's zooming, but you don't want your audience to notice.

5. **Drag the Duration slider until the clip will be about one second longer than you need. Click Apply to insert the photo into the timeline.**

   Don't worry—you're not going to leave the "photo clip" that long.

6. **After the bright red progress bar finishes its trip across your photo clip, shorten each photo from its right end, cutting it down to the length you want.**

   That final second is where the visible zooming animation falls.

   You're left with a very high quality "still" video clip that iMovie won't attempt to process when you hand off to iDVD.

Repeat this process for any other still photos in your movie.

At this point, your still photos are no longer still photos. Clicking the "Create iDVD Project" button is now safe. iMovie will make no attempt to render your stills, because they've already been rendered by the far superior Ken Burns feature.

The Drag-from-Finder Method

The second way to bypass iMovie's still-photo rendering feature is to avoid the "Create iDVD Project" button altogether. As you may remember, there's another way to bring an iMovie movie into iDVD: drag its icon from the desktop right into the iDVD window. See Figure 32-4 for the proper technique.

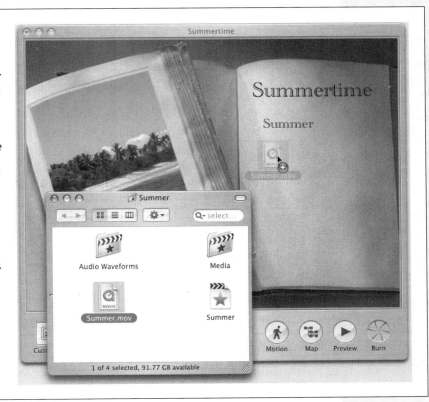

Figure 32-4:
To bypass iMovie's photo-to-video rendering routines, don't use its "Create iDVD Project" button. Instead, open up iDVD manually.

Then, at the desktop, open your iMovie project folder. Locate the reference movie (whose name ends with ".mov") and drag it manually onto your iDVD menu screen.

At disc-burning time, iDVD will perform the photo processing itself, with much better results.

If you do that, iMovie's weak photo-rendering software doesn't touch your stills—and iDVD's own, much better rendering software processes them instead. You may find that the Ken Burns technique looks slightly better on some photos, but of course it's much more work than the drag-from-Finder method. Either way, though, you'll be delighted with the results.

Exporting Troubles

Now suppose that you're able to capture the video successfully, and even edit it into a masterful work of art. The big moment arrives: You're ready to play the movie back onto the tape, or export it as a QuickTime movie, so that you can then play it for friends and venture capitalists. Here are a few things that can go wrong.

Video and Audio Aren't In Sync

On some longer movie projects (20 minutes or more), everything plays fine in iMovie—but when you turn your project into a QuickTime movie or burn it to a DVD, the audio and video grow slowly, horrifyingly out of sync. The longer the movie plays, the farther apart they drift.

To find your solution, follow this list in order:

• The most important thing to check is the audio recording settings of your camcorder. As described at the beginning of this chapter, most camcorders come set to record *12-bit audio,* which lies at the heart of the video/audio drift problem. Change it to 16-bit audio, using the camcorder's own menus. (If you use a video converter like the Formac Studio or Dazzle Hollywood Bridge, make sure it, too, is set to import 16-bit audio, not 12-bit.)

• If it's too late for that step, here's one possible fix: *Extract* the audio from the video (page 606). Separating the audio from the video makes your project very hard to edit, however, so make this the last edit of your project. (Or make a duplicate of your entire project folder and work on that.) Just extracting the audio into a separate clip solves the audio drift problem for some people.

• Here's the last resort. First, set your camcorder to 16-bit audio. Once editing is complete, export the entire movie to your camcorder.

Then start a new iMovie project file, and import the camcorder's footage right back into your Mac (Chapter 13). This time, you should be able to export the project without the drift.

Project Corruption

Most of the time, iMovie stops people's hearts only with the beauty and magnificence of its creations. Unfortunately, every now and then, it can stop your heart in a much more terrifying way. At some random moment when you least expect it, some iMovie project that you've worked on for days or weeks refuses to open. Instead, you see the error message pictured in Figure 32-5.

You've got yourself a case of project corruption.

Editing the Project File to Rescue It

Project corruption can result from errors in the project file, or even damage to the source files in the Media folder.

Now, some project corruption problems can't be fixed at all. Fortunately, two of the most common problems are simple to fix.

Believe it or not, an iMovie project file is nothing more than a simple text file containing pointers to various pieces of video in the Media folder. If you know what you're doing, you can edit it directly.

Figure 32-5
Uh-oh. Big uh-oh. iMovie can't read the project file. You can't edit your project.

It's time to sweat, but not yet time to panic. This file may be salvageable.

Your project file is not readable.

OK

The project file contains a description of each clip in your project, how each clip is used, and the name of its *source file* (the corresponding clip file in your Media folder). Each clip has a multiline description. If any line of the description gets scrambled, iMovie may be unable to open the project file.

Technically, you could open up this project file with any old text editor—even Text-Edit. Trouble is, TextEdit will turn the file into a TextEdit document when you save your changes.

Here's a far better bet: Edit the project file using a program like BBEdit ($180 from *www.barebones.com*) or, if you're on a budget and in a hurry, BBEdit Lite (discontinued, but free; you can find a link to it at *www.missingmanuals.com*). BBEdit and BBEdit Lite can edit your project file without changing its identity.

To open up a project file in BBEdit, drag the project file's icon onto the BBEdit icon. It opens up looking like Figure 32-6.

Finding a Flawed Clip Reference

The three-clip excerpt shown in Figure 32-6 is typical: Each clip in your project appears with its name on the first line, and below it, several indented descriptive lines.

The problem here is indicated by the cursor in Figure 32-6: the name of the source file is missing from the last clip. Where a file name would normally appear after the "File:" label, there's nothing now but a blank space. A missing file name guarantees that iMovie will be unable to open the file.

To remove that clip reference, remove the line "Clip: Cross Dissolve" and all the indented lines associated with it. iMovie will now forget that the clip was ever part of your project. Of course, it's still sitting in your Media folder. The next time you open this project, you'll see a dialog box offering to reimport the clip automatically.

Project Corruption

Repairing a Flawed Clip Reference

Before you can repair a clip reference, you must first diagnose its problem. The two most common diagnoses are:

- **Invalid frame numbers.** Valid frame numbers normally look like this:

```
Frames: 60 In:0 Out:60 Thumb:0
```

The line contains the number of frames in the clip (60), the beginning frame number in the source file (0), and the last frame number in the source file (60).

But a *flawed* frame reference might look like this:

```
Frames: 60 In:-90 Out:-30 Thumb:0
```

The clip length looks OK (60), but the in and out frame numbers are negative—an impossibility, and a sure sign of clip corruption.

To fix this clip, you must change the digits to positive numbers that reflect the position of the frames in the source file. A good guess would be to change the In position to 0, and the Out position to 60.

If that doesn't result in a happier project file, delete the clip reference from the text file altogether, as described on the previous page. Save the file in BBEdit. When you reopen the file in iMovie, you'll be offered the chance to reimport the clip—the right way, this time.

Figure 32-6:
In this example, each clip reference begins with the word Clip, but you may also see Shelf (referring to a clip that's still on the Clips pane), Voice (narration you've recorded), or other labels.

See the cursor? It indicates a problem with your project. The "File:" line fails to identify the name of the clip, meaning that iMovie has lost track.

- **Missing file names.** Each clip should show the name of its source file, which always resides in the Media folder. As shown in Figure 32-6, the name label normally looks like this:

```
File: Clip:01
```

(Don't be confused by colons in the file name. iMovie substitutes colons for spaces when it stores the name in the project file.)

If the file name is missing entirely, once again, you've got yourself some project corruption. Delete the clip reference—thus removing it from your project—and let iMovie offer to reimport it the next time you open this project file.

Tip: It's not unusual for a corrupted project file to have more than one problem. If you find one, keep looking through the file; it may have company.

Using the .mov File to Recover the Project

So what happens if you try to edit the project file, but have no luck finding or repairing the glitch?

There's still hope.

Each time you save an iMovie project, iMovie updates the *.mov* reference movie file in the project folder. This is a special kind of QuickTime movie that contains very little data of its own—just pointers to the files in the Media folder.

If the files in the Media folder are intact, the .mov file can usually play your project movie even when the iMovie project file itself is corrupt. In other words, the .mov file doesn't depend on the project file; it depends on the files in the Media folder.

So if your .mov file plays just fine, you can probably use it to build a new project based on your corrupted project. Not everything will be editable, but you'll be off to a good start.

To try this rescue operation, start a new iMovie project. Choose File→Import; navigate to the old project folder, open it, and double-click the .mov file to import it.

As you'll quickly discover, the .mov file arrives in iMovie as a single, giant clip, not individual editable clips. That's not ideal, but it's very useful. At least the .mov file delivers your clips in their original order.

Tip: Knowing about this safety net should affect your disaster planning. When you first realize something has gone wrong with your project, stop a moment to think about protecting your .mov file. Do whatever's necessary to preserve that file—right then—by Option-dragging it out of the project folder as a backup, for example. You don't want to save any changes to the iMovie project before you do so, for example, because you'll just replace the good .mov file with a bad one.

Project File Backups

Backing up the small project file is quick and easy, so do it often. Click the project file (in the project *folder*) and choose File→Duplicate.

Most project corruption involves just the project file, so frequent backups of the project file are a good idea. (Backups of the entire project folder are even better, but of course they require a lot of disk space.)

Using the Camera for Backups

Exporting your iMovie project to a new tape in the camera page 381 at various stages of project completion is a helpful backup, too—not as good as a backup of your whole project folder, but better than no backup at all. And backing up to tape, of course, doesn't use up any hard drive space. See the box below for details.

"Project could not be opened"

If trying to open your project results in the dreaded "Project could not be opened because folder is locked or the folder permissions are incorrect" message, then Mac

---

How to Save Your Project For Future Generations

OK, I'm done editing my iMovie. How do I back up my project folder to reclaim the hard drive space?

That's an excellent question. Considering the hours you've probably spent building your masterpiece, preserving a full-quality copy, preferably in editable form, is probably extremely important.

(As you know, exporting the movie to QuickTime, cellphones, the Web, or VHS entails a huge deterioration in video and audio quality. Surprisingly, even burning to DVD involves losing some of the original quality, because the video is stored on the disc in a compressed form.)

In the end, there are only three ways to preserve a movie at its full original quality.

First, you can store it on a big old hard drive. This method is pricey and mechanical—will there even be such a thing as a FireWire connector in 20 years?—but it means that you can store your entire project folder. Therefore, you can re-edit the project next year when iMovie 5 comes out with enhancements you can't resist.

Second, you can use a backup program like Retrospect to copy your project folder onto multiple DVDs (not video DVDs, but DVD-ROMs—like glorified blank CDs). It takes a handful of these blanks to store one hour of video. But this solution is certainly cheap. And in a pinch, you'll be able to reconstruct your entire project folder, with full editing capability.

Finally, you can send the movie back out to your DV camcorder, as described on page 381. MiniDV tapes have about a 15-year life span, but they store the original video quality, even if you rescue the footage by copying it onto a fresh tape once every ten years.

You lose the ability to edit your titles and substitute new background music, of course, but you don't lose all editing possibilities. If you ever re-import that movie back to iMovie, most of the clips will still appear as distinct, rearrangeable clips in your Movie Track (because clip boundaries are nothing more than breaks in the originally recorded time code).

(The exception: Clips that you create within iMovie, as opposed to capturing from a camcorder, don't have a time stamp, so they'll re-import as one conjoined clump of scenes.)

OS X's *permission* settings (invisible switches that specify which account holders are allowed to open which files and folders) have become profoundly confused. Permissions incorrect? Hey, whose movie is it, anyway?

The solution is to create new folders for your project—folders whose permissions are healthy and normal—and then copy your iMovie files into them. Try this:

1. **Create a new folder on your desktop. Name the new folder, for example, "Fixed Project."**

   The point is to keep it separate from the original, corrupted project folder.

2. **In the Fixed Project folder, create another new folder called Media. Open the Media folder of the iMovie project that won't open. Choose Edit→Select All. Option-drag all the selected files into the *new* Media folder.**

   Option-dragging duplicates the files instead of moving them. (If there's not enough disk space to duplicate them, just drag without the Option key. Note, too, that the Option key is labeled Alt on some non-U.S. keyboards.)

3. **Option-drag the files inside the corrupted iMovie project folder into the Fixed Project folder.**

   You now have a new project folder (Fixed Project) that contains all the files from the original project folder.

4. **Double-click the project file inside the Fixed Project folder.**

   If the project opens successfully, quit iMovie. Throw away the corrupted project folder, rename the Fixed Project folder, if you like, and celebrate. (If it doesn't open, open the Fixed Project folder and throw away the ".mov" file inside. Try opening the project file again.)

Problems with Sound

Sound problems are especially frustrating when you're working with digital video, because they bear no resemblance to sound problems with more familiar equipment. In any other situation, if sound is too low or too loud, for example, you can adjust it with a knob. But what you do about random electronic beeps and buzzes that weren't there on the original tape?

Sound Is Too Soft

If one particular clip is too soft, see page 352.

If, however, the entire movie soundtrack plays back too quietly, it's probable that iMovie has nothing to do with the problem. Instead, your overall Mac volume is probably too low. Visit the Sound panel of System Preferences and adjust the output volume of your machine, or tap the Volume Up key on the top row of your keyboard. Make sure that iMovie's own volume slider (just above the Movie Track) is up all the way, too.

Random Beeps or Pops

It's hard to imagine anything more frustrating than finding a permanent—or, worse, intermittent—buzzing, crackling, or popping in the audio tracks of your project.

This problem has been on many minds, and its victims have come up with various solutions. Fortunately, most people manage to solve it by following one of these steps:

- Just as there are video dropouts, as described in the beginning of this appendix, cheap tapes may sometimes give you *audio* dropouts. The problem is exactly the same: a tiny bit of dirt or a nonmagnetized particle on the tape. But this time, it affects the audio, not the video. Try cleaning the heads of your camcorder, and then reimport the video.

- If cleaning the heads doesn't solve the problem, consider turning off the Audio Filtering feature. To do so, choose iMovie→Preferences. Turn off "Filter audio from camera." Click OK. Again, try reimporting the video to see whether the sound-buzzing problems have disappeared.

Of course, these workarounds assume that the audio glitch began life on the camera, rather than being created within iMovie itself.

If the pop is intermittent, there's not much you can do. But if you hear the pop in the same place every time you play your movie, you may be able to repair it using a sound-editing program, like this:

1. **Export the audio of the video clip as a sound-only AIFF file.**

   That is, turn on only the relevant audio-track checkboxes (at the right end of the Timeline Viewer). Then Choose File→Share. In the Share dialog box, choose the Expert Settings option, and then click Export. In the following dialog box, use the pop-up menu to choose Sound as AIFF.

   The result: You've just exported the soundtrack of your movie as a standalone audio file.

2. **Using GarageBand, cut out the beeps.**

   GarageBand lets you highlight the specific sound waves that represent the beeps and change their volume, or replace them with pieces of sound you've copied from neighboring moments in the soundtrack.

3. **Reimport the AIFF sound file into your iMovie project.**

   For example, choose File→Export to iTunes, and then, in iMovie, use the Audio panel to import that "track" from iTunes. Once it has appeared on an audio track, you can turn off the existing camcorder audio track.

Pops or Silence Resulting from a Transition or Title

If the volume simply drops after you apply a transition or title, see page 602 for the solution to this well-known iMovie bug.

But if you're getting actual pops or audio glitches, the workaround is slightly more involved. First, remove the transition or title as described on pages 301 and 329.

Next, select the video clip that will be affected. Finally, choose Advanced→Extract Audio.

iMovie places the audio from that video clip into one of its two audio tracks. If you apply the title or transition now, iMovie will leave the audio—now an independent entity—alone.

Relinking Missing iDVD Files

When you're working with regular projects (not archived ones), iDVD is pretty helpless if you move or rename any of the photo, movie, or sound files that it expects to use in your DVD (see Figure 32-7).

Figure 32-7:
Top: If you open a project whose original movies, photos, or sounds have been moved or renamed, you see this message. Click Cancel to proceed without those files, or click Find File to show iDVD where the file is now.

Bottom: The broken link image indicates a file that iDVD can't find. Avoid this problem by keeping all your source files on the hard drive until after you've burned your project.

If you encounter the dialog box shown in Figure 32-7 at top, click Find File, navigate to a folder that contains at least one of the files, and click Open; iDVD dutifully inspects that folder for *any* missing files. Repeat until you've located all the missing files.

If you *can't* find a file—for example, you deleted one by accident—then keep showing iDVD the files you *can* find. At the end of the process, click Cancel.

Your project will open just fine, but you'll see a broken-chain/missing link icon (Figure 32-7, bottom) where the missing file ought to be. At this point, you can replace it with a file that you *do* have.

Troubleshooting GarageBand

The truth is, most of the troubleshooting you'll do in GarageBand has to do with accommodating its horsepower demands. You'll know there's a problem when you watch the Playhead turn orange or red, hear skips in the music, or get a note that "Some parts were not played." That's why most of this chapter is devoted to solving speed and horsepower problems.

Still, a few other things can go wrong, or at least can baffle you. Here, for your head-ache-relieving pleasure, are recipes for solving the most common problems.

The Speed Problem

GarageBand is a power hog. It thrives on memory and processor speed, eternally craving more, more, and more. Even a handful of tracks is enough to redline your system, turning the Playhead orange, then red, and finally summoning the dreaded dialog box shown in Figure 33-1 as playback grinds to a halt.

Figure 33-1:
When GarageBand can't keep up with everything going on in your tracks, you'll see this message, or one that says, in the smaller type, "This song has too many real instrument tracks to be played in real-time. To maximize performance, look in Garage-Band Help under Performance."

Part of the song was not played

This song has too many tracks, effects, or notes to be played in real-time.
To optimize performance, see the 'Optimizing GarageBand performance' page in GarageBand Help.

Continue

The following section presents the accumulated wisdom of thousands of online GarageBand fans sharing their workarounds, plus Apple's own suggestions. They're presented here in decreasing order of importance and urgency.

Set the Stage

You can avoid many overburdened-Mac situations just by taking the time to set up your GarageBand environment smartly. For example:

- Quit as many other programs as possible, so GarageBand can have their RAM.

- Every PowerBook, iBook, and Power Mac G5 lets you switch your computer's brain into a slower, reduced-power mode to save heat and battery charge. But for GarageBand, that's asking for trouble; it needs all the horsepower it can get.

  So choose →System Preferences, click Energy Saver, then click the Options tab. Now from the pop-up menu, choose Highest. Close the window. Your laptop battery won't last quite as long, and your G5's fan might spin up a little more, but at least you'll be able to get some meaningful work done in GarageBand.

- Turn off FileVault, if you're using it, by choosing →System Preferences, clicking Security, and clicking Turn FileVault Off. (FileVault is a Mac OS X security feature that encrypts your entire Home folder; you'd remember turning it on.) It slows down data transfer from your Home folder dramatically.

Mute Some Tracks

Any track that you silence is one more task crossed off the Mac's real-time To Do list. By selectively muting and un-muting tracks, you should be able to get your piece mostly ready. Afterward, you can either export the thing, convert some Software Instrument tracks to Real Instruments, or even bounce the whole thing into iTunes and back. Both of these radical tactics are described later in this chapter.

Combine Tracks

Playing more tracks makes GarageBand work harder. In many cases, though, you can combine the *material* from several tracks into a single one. It's especially easy to combine blue Real Instrument tracks. Figure 33-2 shows the procedure.

Combining green Software Instrument tracks is more difficult, because dragging a region into a different track usually means that its instrument sound changes. Not to worry: You can always turn a Software Instrument region into a Real Instrument region, as described on page 619, and then merge them.

Temporarily Squelch the Effects

The *effects* described in Chapter 28 (reverb, EQ, and so on) represent the state of the art in software simulators. But it's still quite a feat for the Mac to pass the sound of your various tracks into these software modules, calculate the new, post-processed sound, and then send it back out your speakers—all in real time.

One of the quickest and easiest ways to alleviate the Mac's speed burden, then, is to turn off some effects. (Double-click a track to open the Track Info dialog box, expand the Details panel, and start turning off checkboxes.) You can always turn them on again before you export the finished piece to iTunes.

Figure 33-2:
Top: These three Real Instrument tracks are making this old Power Mac's heart race. There's no good reason for them to occupy different tracks, since their regions aren't playing simultaneously.

Bottom: By dragging all of their regions into a single track, you ease your Mac's burden considerably. The only downside is that you've lost the ability to specify different effect settings for each track.

A reminder: Use this trick only on regions that don't overlap.

Enlarge Your Buffer

In GarageBand→Preferences, click the Audio/MIDI button to see the controls shown at top in Figure 33-3. Setting it to "Maximum number of simultaneous tracks" devotes more of the Mac's energies to playing back your piece.

The disadvantage of this setting is that when you record from a MIDI keyboard, you may experience *latency*—a frustrating, fraction-of-a-second delay between each keypress and the playing of its sound.

The trick, then, is knowing when to switch this setting. Leave it on "Minimum delay when playing instruments live" when you're recording, and compensate by turning off some tracks if the Mac begins gasping. After the recording, change the setting to "Maximum."

Lose Some Software Instrument Voices

Some instruments, like flutes and kazoos, can play only one note at a time—in software parlance, one *voice* at a time. A piano, meanwhile, can theoretically play 88 notes at once, although you'd need a few friends to help you press the keys if you wanted to hear more than 10 notes simultaneously.

But the more Software Instrument voices GarageBand must play, the more your Mac sweats. As shown in Figure 33-3 at bottom, a certain pop-up menu in the Garage-Band Preferences dialog box lets you limit the number of voices that get played. In a pinch, you can set a limit on these voices, thus saving GarageBand further effort and sometimes making an unplayable song playable again on your Mac.

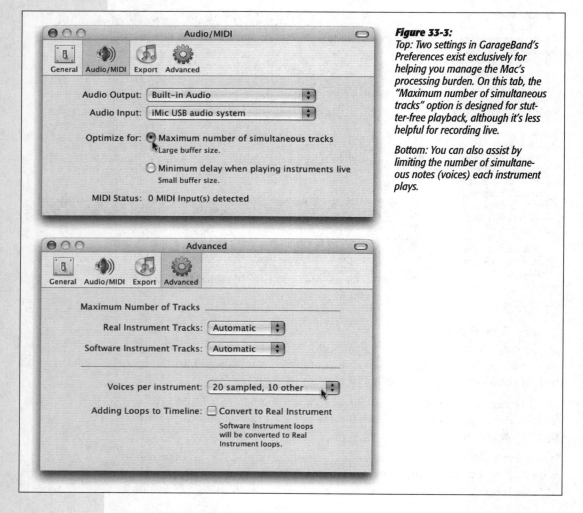

Figure 33-3:
Top: Two settings in GarageBand's Preferences exist exclusively for helping you manage the Mac's processing burden. On this tab, the "Maximum number of simultaneous tracks" option is designed for stutter-free playback, although it's less helpful for recording live.

Bottom: You can also assist by limiting the number of simultaneous notes (voices) each instrument plays.

The wording of this dialog box is a tad cryptic, in that it refers to "sampled" and "other" voices. To understand this lingo, it helps to understand the two different ways that GarageBand can create Software Instrument sounds:

- **With samples.** A *sampled* instrument sound began life as a recording of a real-world instrument playing one note in a real-world studio. Pressing a key on a MIDI keyboard triggers a playback of that short recording. In the case of woodwind instruments, the sampled sound seamlessly repeats for as long as you press the key.

  In GarageBand, all the woodwind, brass, piano, guitar, bass, strings, and drum sounds are sampled sounds.

- **With synthesis.** The rest of the Software Instrument sounds are created using software algorithms; in essence your Mac becomes a musical synthesizer. GarageBand's clavinet, organ, electric piano, and synthesizer Software Instrument sounds are all created this way.

  Synthesized sounds put a greater strain on your Mac than sampled sounds, since GarageBand must compute these sounds on the fly.

Suppose, for example, that you choose "10 sampled, 5 other." You've just specified that no Software Instrument will be allowed to play more than 5 notes simultaneously if it's an electronic keyboard sound (organ, electric piano, and so on), or more than 10 notes at once for any other Software Instrument.

You might never miss the notes that GarageBand leaves out of a busy orchestration. Meanwhile, thinning out the voices could make all the difference in a GarageBand composition that's too complex for your Mac.

Reduce the Track Overhead

Every time you create a new GarageBand project file, the program allots some memory to hold a certain number of tracks. (The exact number depends on the speed of your Mac and how much memory is installed.) But if you intend to create nothing but a single-line kazoo recording, that's a lot of memory being set aside that could be used for other purposes...like keeping up with playback.

That's why, as soon as you know how many total tracks your piece will have, you should choose GarageBand→Preferences, click the Advanced tab, and change the Maximum Number of Tracks pop-up menus (shown in Figure 33-4 at bottom).

You're telling the program: "I intend to use no more than eight Software Instrument tracks and eight Real Instrument tracks" (or whatever), "so please put whatever additional memory you were holding back into the pot. I could use it right about now."

Convert Software Instrument Loops

As it turns out, Software Instruments are much more trouble for the Mac to play back than Real Instruments.

Now, at first glance, that statement might seem to be illogical—in fact, reversed. After all, green Software Instrument regions contain very little data—only a list of note triggers ("Play middle C for one beat, then C sharp for two"). MIDI *files* take up only a few kilobytes on the hard drive. They're absolutely minuscule compared with digital recordings like Real Instrument regions, which take up 10 MB per minute. So why isn't it easier for the Mac to play the little files than the big ones?

Because it must also *generate the instrument sounds,* not to mention processing them with effects, as it plays each MIDI note. It's not the triggering that's so much work; it's the synthesizing. To play a blue or purple Real Instrument region, on the other hand, the Mac just plays back a bunch of sound data that's already fully formed on the hard drive.

In any case, exploiting this little quirk of Software and Real Instruments is an excellent way to reduce the load on your Mac's processor, because GarageBand makes it easy to *convert* the former into the latter.

For example, GarageBand offers at least three ways to convert green loops into blue ones that are easier for the Mac to play:

- If you press the Option key before dragging a green loop out of the Loop browser and into an empty spot on the timeline (and keep the key down), GarageBand creates a blue Real Instrument track and a Real Instrument region.

Software Instrument track to be converted

Figure 33-4:
Top: Isolate the Software Instrument track by turning on its Solo button, the tiny headphones button (circled). Send the track to iTunes.

Middle: You can reimport the converted music by dragging it from iTunes into an available Real Instrument track in GarageBand. Or, if screen space is very tight, you can also drag the file out of iTunes and onto the desktop, where it turns into an icon, and then drag that icon into Garage-Band.

Bottom: The resulting mix sounds exactly the same, but takes up much less processing power.

Same music—now in Real Instrument form!

- If you'd *always* like GarageBand to convert green loops, choose GarageBand→ Preferences, click the Advanced tab, and turn on "Convert to Real Instruments." From now on, every loop you drag out of the Loop browser (into a blank spot in the timeline area) creates a blue Real Instrument track and region.

Tip: Pressing the Option key simply reverses this Preferences setting. If "Convert to Real Instruments" is turned on, for example, then Option-dragging a green loop does *not* convert it to a blue one.

- You can drag a green loop that's already *in* a track into a blue Real Instrument track. GarageBand converts it to a Real Instrument region.

Remember, though, that once converted to digital-audio form, a loop loses much of the editing flexibility it once had. You can no longer change individual notes inside it, for example.

Convert Software Instrument Recordings

The three green-to-blue conversion tricks described above work only on Software Instrument *loops*. They don't work on MIDI regions that you've recorded yourself (using, for example, a MIDI keyboard controller). That's a shame, because converting your *own* Software Instrument regions into Real Instrument regions would take even more pressure off your Mac's processor.

Still, you *can* convert this kind of region—just not quite as easily. You can send the region (or its whole track, if you like) to iTunes and back, as shown in Figure 33-4.

Your piece should sound exactly the way it did before you performed this little operation. The only differences:

- The Macintosh doesn't have to work nearly as hard to play it.

- You can no longer change the tempo of the piece without leaving your converted track out of sync with the rest of the piece. Your converted track is locked forever at the original tempo. (You can't transpose it or edit its notes, either.)

Tip: Want the best of both worlds? Then keep the original, green Software Instrument tracks around, but mute them. If you ever want to make changes, you can modify the original, editable tracks and then re-convert them.

"Bounce Down" Many Tracks into One

And now, one of the most useful and powerful tools in the GarageBand musician's arsenal. It starts with the idea behind the GarageBand→iTunes→GarageBand conversion described earlier and takes it to the logical extreme: exporting *more* than one track, or even *all* of your tracks, and boiling them all down into one!

Suppose, for example, that your Mac can play only five tracks at once before bogging down. But you've got 20 tracks' worth of music in your head! Using the "bounce down" trick, no problem. You could simply proceed like this:

- Export all five tracks to iTunes. Reimport the result into GarageBand as *one* track (it would look something like Figure 33-4 at middle). Delete the original five component tracks, or just mute them. Now you're free to add another four! (Effective total now: nine tracks.)

- Export *these* five tracks (which sound like nine) to iTunes. Reimport into GarageBand as *one* track, delete the original five—and add yet another four. (Effective total: 13.) Figure 33-5 shows the basic idea.

The one big caution here is that each time you export your tracks, you're freezing them. You're giving up any ability to adjust their effects, rebalance their volume levels, change the song's tempo, and so on. Take care to finalize each semi-mix as much as possible before exporting.

Tip: You might also want to use the File→Save As command along the way, preserving each set of exported tracks before you delete them, so you can return to the original GarageBand files if necessary. (Like when you get a dual-processor Power Mac G5 with 1 gig of RAM.)

Install More Memory

After a certain point, bending over backward to accommodate all of these workarounds, settings, and cheats just isn't worth it. If you're still getting "Parts were not

Figure 33-5:
Top: Five tracks, just crackling with music. Finalized and polished to within an inch of its life. And pushing the Mac to its max. How will you gain the headroom necessary to add the four vocal tracks you have in mind?

Bottom: Easy: just export the half-finished mix to iTunes, and then bring it right back in as a single track, shown here. Delete the original five.

Now you've got a nearly empty track canvas in which to add four more tracks.

You've just created what studio musicians call a submix.

played" messages after following all, or even some, of the steps in this chapter, you should just break down and give your Mac the gift of more memory.

In particular, if your Mac has only 256 or even 512 megabytes of memory, you're living at the edge, as far as GarageBand is concerned. (To find out how much you have, choose → About This Mac.) Hie thee immediately to *www.ramseeker.com,* choose your Mac's model name from the pop-up menu, and see just how inexpensive a memory upgrade can be these days.

Trouble with Loops

Loops, as described in Chapter 24, are among the greatest joys of GarageBand. So when they don't work, they're among the biggest disappointments.

Your Loop Browser Is Empty

Adding more loops to GarageBand isn't just a matter of stuffing them into a certain folder on your hard drive. You also have to make GarageBand *aware* of them. To do that, you force GarageBand to *index* any new loops, building an internal card catalog of which loops you have and where they're stored.

If anything goes wrong with GarageBand's loop index, you may discover that all of the buttons in the Loop browser are dimmed and no loops appear in its list. Other wackiness can result, too, like loops that exist in name only or simply misbehave.

In all of these situations, the solution is to *rebuild* the GarageBand loop index. You do it like this:

1. **Quit GarageBand. In the Finder, open your hard drive window. Then open the Library→Application Support→GarageBand→Apple Loops folder (see Figure 11-1, top).**

   Inside, you'll see the actual text files that constitute your current index.

2. **Drag the index files to the Trash.**

   GarageBand will rebuild fresh, healthy ones in just a moment.

3. **Open GarageBand and click the Loop Browser (eyeball) button.**

   GarageBand suddenly realizes that it has no loops, and shows the dialog box at bottom in Figure 33-6.

4. **In the No Apple Loops Found dialog box, click OK.**

   Now return to the Finder.

5. **Open your hard drive→Library→Application Support→GarageBand folder. Drag the Apple Loops folder directly into any visible portion of GarageBand's Loop browser.**

   GarageBand dutifully recreates its loop index, based on the current location and contents of that Loops folder.

Note: If you've installed the Jam Pack, drag *its* folder (also in the Library→Application Support→GarageBand folder) into the Loop browser, too.

Figure 33-6:
Top: You've found your secret stash of index files, buried deep within the GarageBand folder. If you're having loop problems, throw them away; Garage-Band will recreate better ones.

Bottom: Garage-Band, too, knows that you've fooled with its indexes.

New Add-On Loops Don't Show Up

It's a nice perk that GarageBand can accommodate additional loops that were designed for other music-software programs. Note, however, that:

- You should install them by dragging them into GarageBand's Loop browser, *not* by dragging them into a folder in the Finder. Dragging them into the Loop browser ensures that GarageBand indexes the new loops (that is, adds them to its internal database).

- Occasionally, non-Apple loops don't show up in the Loop browser even when you've installed them correctly. In that case, you may have no choice but to drag them from the Finder directly into the GarageBand timeline area, bypassing the Loop browser entirely.

Recording and Editing Problems

What can go wrong during the main working phase? Let us count the ways.

There's a Delay When Playing Live

On slower Macs, you may experience an annoying lag between the time you press a key on your instrument and the time the sound comes out of the Mac's speakers. That's *latency,* baby, and there's one—and only one—step you can take to solve it.

See page 617 for the details.

No Sound from a Microphone or Real Instrument

If GarageBand doesn't seem to be "hearing" anything from your microphone or line input, the problem is usually that the Mac hasn't been taught to "listen" to the right audio source. Review the setup steps, including visiting System Preferences and choosing the correct input in the GarageBand→Preferences panel.

Otherwise, double-check these points:

- Make sure that you've clicked a blue Real Instrument track. If a green Software Instrument track is selected, GarageBand ignores your microphone or instrument.

- Also make sure you haven't muted this track, or soloed another one. (The speaker icon in your track's header should be lit up in blue, and no other instrument's headphones icon should be blue.) While you're at it, make sure that the track's volume slider isn't set to zero.

- It's possible that GarageBand is set up to listen to the wrong channel (mono instruments). Double-click the track header and check the Input pop-up menu and Format (mono/stereo) buttons.

- Are you getting *any* sound from GarageBand? That is, is your Mac's speaker turned up? Of course, you won't hear anything at all from your real instrument unless you've turned on Monitor in its Track Info dialog box. Check by double-clicking the track header.

- If you're using a mixer or audio interface, is its volume turned all the way down?

- Are you getting any sound from the instrument? If it's electric, do you have it turned on, with the volume turned up? Make sure all the connections are good—especially if you've incorporated plug adapters into the mix.

Tip: If you're using a Griffin iMic adapter to connect your microphone or instrument to the Mac, you have some additional checking to do. Make sure you've connected the mike or instrument to the iMic's input jack (the one with a microphone symbol). Also make sure to switch the iMic's selector toward the microphone symbol.

Finally, in GarageBand, you have to choose GarageBand→Preferences, click the Audio/MIDI button, and, from the Audio Input pop-up menu, choose "iMic USB audio system." You should be ready to roll.

No Sound from a MIDI Instrument

Are you having trouble getting GarageBand to "hear" an external MIDI instrument, like a keyboard controller or MIDI guitar? In that case, use the MIDI status light identified in Figure 33-7 as an assistant detective.

The status light doesn't flicker when you play

If that little light isn't flashing when you play your MIDI instrument, the MIDI information isn't reaching GarageBand, for some reason. Here are two things to try:

• Make sure the instrument is turned on and connected to the Mac. If a MIDI interface box is involved, pay close attention: It's very easy to get the MIDI In and MIDI Out cables confused. (You want one cable to run from the instrument's MIDI Out jack to the interface's MIDI In jack, and another cable going from In to Out.)

• Choose GarageBand→Preferences. Click the Audio/MIDI button. See the MIDI Status line? It should say "1 MIDI Input(s) detected" (or 2, or whatever number you have).

If not, it's remotely possible that you're using a MIDI interface that requires driver software of its own. Visit the manufacturer's Web site to seek out a Mac OS X–compatible driver. Without this software installed, the MIDI interface may not work at all.

Figure 33-7:
This handy little light flickers blue whenever GarageBand is receiving note data, either from its own onscreen keyboard, an external MIDI instrument, or an onscreen virtual keyboard like MidiKeys or LoudK.

Flashing MIDI indicator

The status light flickers when you play

If that little indicator *does* flicker on and off, then everything is correctly hooked up and working.

In that case, here's your checklist:

• Make sure you've selected a green Software Instrument track. Otherwise, Garage-Band won't produce sound for your MIDI instrument.

• Make sure that you haven't muted this track or soloed another one, or set your track's volume to zero.

• Choose Window→Keyboard and click a few keys on the onscreen keyboard to make sure that the selected track has a working instrument selected. (Incidentally, playing a few notes will also help you find out whether your Mac's speaker is turned down all the way.)

You might also try double-clicking the track header to open the Track Info dialog box. Make sure you've selected an instrument and effects preset in the top two lists. And in the Details panel, consider turning off some effects until you find the problem. (Believe it or not, it's technically possible to fiddle with the effects so much that no sound emerges.)

• Do you, in fact, have any Software Instruments available? (Double-click a track header to see if anything's in the list.) If you or somebody else has been doing some naughty playing in the Library→Application Support→GarageBand folder, the files may be so dismantled that you need to reinstall GarageBand to get it going again.

Transposing Created Cacophonous Chaos

You can *transpose* (shift in pitch) green Software Instrument loops and blue Real Instrument loops, which is kind of amazing.

You cannot, however, transpose these kinds of regions:

- Your own live recordings (purple Real Instrument regions).

- Non-Apple loops you installed yourself. (If they're called *Apple* Loops, though, they should be transposable.)

No Sound from External Speakers (or Audio Interface)

Ordinarily, GarageBand sends the sound of its own playback through your Mac's audio circuitry, whether that's through your Mac's built-in speakers or speakers connected to its headphone jack.

But what if you've bought fancy external USB speakers? Or what if you've connected an audio interface box that's hooked up to its own sound system?

In those cases, choose GarageBand→Preferences. Click the Audio/MIDI button. Use the Audio Input Driver pop-up menu to choose the name of your external speakers or interface box. (This assumes, of course, that it's *listed* in the pop-up menu, which often means that you've installed some driver software that came with the speakers or audio box.)

Mixing and Publishing Glitches

There's nothing more annoying than something going wrong when your masterpiece is finished. Here's what to do.

Finished Song Is Too Quiet

If your GarageBand masterpiece arrives in iTunes playing far too softly relative to your other tunes, revisit Chapter 576 for tips on setting the master volume level before exporting.

But if the master volume slider is turned all the way up and the music is *still* too soft, you can also:

- **Add the Compression effect before exporting.** (Double-click the track header, turn on Compressor, and then drag the slider to the right.) Doing so boosts the softest passages and flattens the loudest ones, so that the whole thing remains at a more consistent volume level.

- **Use the iTunes preamp after exporting.** Once the song is in iTunes, you can also boost the volume there. Figure 33-8 has the details.

Tracks Panned to One Side Still Play in Both Speakers

Here's a tricky one. Suppose you've used the Pan knob (page 573) to "place" a certain track's instrument all the way to the left side of the stereo field, or all the way to the right. Yet when you listen with headphones, you still hear the darned thing coming out of both speakers!

There are two possibilities:

• Most of the time, the culprit is the Echo or Reverb effect that you've applied to that track. When you turn on these checkboxes for one track, you're actually telling GarageBand how *much* of the *master* track's Echo and Reverb to apply. You're not really applying a *different* echo or reverb to this individual track.

What you're hearing, then, is the sound of your fully panned track reverberating through both speakers, courtesy of the master echo or reverb. And the solution is to turn *off* the track's individual echo or reverb effect. (Double-click its track header and turn off the corresponding checkboxes.)

• Turning on the Compressor effect for the master track also makes all tracks play in both left and right channels. (In this case, though, turning off Compressor for an individual track makes no difference. What matters is the Compressor effect on the *master* track.)

See Chapter 28 for much more detail on these effects, including how to turn them on or off.

Figure 33-8:
To open this graphic equalizer in iTunes, choose Window→Equalizer, or press ⌘-2, or click the tiny equalizer button in the lower-right corner of the iTunes window. Drag the Preamp slider upward to boost this song's playback level, being careful not to overdo it.

Exported Song Won't Appear in iTunes

If a dialog box or alert message is open in iTunes at the moment you export from GarageBand, the handoff won't be successful. Click OK to dismiss whatever's going on in iTunes, and then try exporting again.

Index

Index

Colophon

This book was written and edited in Microsoft Word X on various Macs.

The screenshots were captured with Ambrosia Software's Snapz Pro X *(www. ambrosiasw.com)*. Adobe Photoshop CS and Macromedia Freehand MX *(www.adobe. com)* were called in as required for touching them up.

The book was designed and laid out in Adobe InDesign 3.0 on a PowerBook G3, Power Mac G4, and Power Mac G5. The fonts used include Formata (as the sans-serif family) and Minion (as the serif body face). To provide the and ⌘ symbols, custom fonts were created using Macromedia Fontographer.

The book was then generated as an Adobe Acrobat PDF file for proofreading, indexing, and final transmission to the printing plant.

Keep in touch with O'Reilly

1. Download examples from our books

To find example files for a book, go to:

www.oreilly.com/catalog

select the book, and follow the "Examples" link.

2. Register your O'Reilly books

Register your book at *register.oreilly.com*

Why register your books?

Once you've registered your O'Reilly books you can:

- Win O'Reilly books, T-shirts or discount coupons in our monthly drawing.
- Get special offers available only to registered O'Reilly customers.
- Get catalogs announcing new books (US and UK only).
- Get email notification of new editions of the O'Reilly books you own.

3. Join our email lists

Sign up to get topic-specific email announcements of new books and conferences, special offers, and O'Reilly Network technology newsletters at:

elists.oreilly.com

It's easy to customize your free elists subscription so you'll get exactly the O'Reilly news you want.

4. Get the latest news, tips, and tools

www.oreilly.com

- "Top 100 Sites on the Web"—PC Magazine
- CIO Magazine's Web Business 50 Awards

Our web site contains a library of comprehensive product information (including book excerpts and tables of contents), downloadable software, background articles, interviews with technology leaders, links to relevant sites, book cover art, and more.

5. Work for O'Reilly

Check out our web site for current employment opportunities:

jobs.oreilly.com

6. Contact us

O'Reilly & Associates
1005 Gravenstein Hwy North
Sebastopol, CA 95472 USA

TEL: 707-827-7000 or 800-998-9938
(6am to 5pm PST)

FAX: 707-829-0104

order@oreilly.com
For answers to problems regarding your order or our products. To place a book order online, visit:

www.oreilly.com/order_new

catalog@oreilly.com
To request a copy of our latest catalog.

booktech@oreilly.com
For book content technical questions or corrections.

corporate@oreilly.com
For educational, library, government, and corporate sales.

proposals@oreilly.com
To submit new book proposals to our editors and product managers.

international@oreilly.com
For information about our international distributors or translation queries. For a list of our distributors outside of North America check out:

international.oreilly.com/distributors.html

adoption@oreilly.com
For information about academic use of O'Reilly books, visit:

academic.oreilly.com